COLONIES
TO
NATION,
1763–1789

A Documentary History of the American Revolution

COLONIES

TO

NATION,

1763–1789

A Documentary History of the American Revolution

Edited by
JACK P. GREENE

W · W · NORTON & COMPANY

New York · London

Selections 12 *D* and 17 *A* are reprinted with permission of Appleton-Century Crofts, Inc., from Leonard Woods Labaree (ed.), *Royal Instructions to British Colonial Governors, 1670–1776* (1935), volume I, pages 107, 190–193, 208–209, 218; volume II, pages 748–749.

Selection 13 *C* is reprinted with permission of the editor from D. H. Watson (ed.), "Joseph Harrison and the *Liberty* Incident," *Williams and Mary Quarterly,* third series, volume 20 (1963), pages 587–595.

Selection 15 *F* is reprinted by permission of Bruce Humphries, Publishers, from *Boston under Military Rule* by Oliver Morton Dickerson.

Selection 17 *B* is reprinted with permission of the South Carolina Archives Department from *Journals of the Commons House of Assembly,* Aug. 29, 1770, volume 38, pages 431–433; (BPRO CO5/499, pages 25–27).

Selections 25 *A* and 29 *B* are reprinted with permission of the present Lord Dartmouth from the Dartmouth Papers, William Salt Library.

Selection 27 is reprinted with permission of Yale University Press, from Clarence E. Carter (ed.), *The Correspondence of General Thomas Gage* (1931–1933), volume I, pages 396–397; volume II, pages 68–69.

Selection 31 *A* is reprinted with permission of the editor from William H. W. Sabine (ed.), Historical Memoirs of William Smith (1956–1958), volume I, pages 271–277.

Selection 31 *B* is reprinted with permission of the Virginia Historical Society from Jack P. Greene (ed.), *The Diary of Colonel London Carter of Sabine Hall, 1752–1778,* (1965), volume I, pages 116–117.

Selection 31 *C* is reprinted with permission of The Historical Society of Pennsylvania from *The Pennsylvania Magazine of History and Biography,* volume 65 (1941), pages 468–476, 478–481.

Selection 40 *B* is reprinted with permission of Columbia University Library from *A Letter from Henry Laurens to His Son John Laurens* (1964), *pages 20–21.*

Selection 45 *A* is reprinted by permission of Princeton University Press from J. Boyd (ed.), *Papers of Thomas Jefferson* (1952), volume 5, page 156. Copyrighted by Princeton University Press, Princeton, New Jersey.

Selections 57 *A, B, C, D, E, F* are reprinted with permission of Yale University Press from Max Farrand (ed.), *The Records of the Federal Convention,* volume I, pages 20–23, 48–50, 150–156, 250–252, 397–407, 411–412, 421–426, 578–581, 586–588; volume II, pages 369–375, 449–453, 641–643, 648.

W. W. Norton & Company, Inc., 500 Fifth Avenue, New York, N.Y. 10110

Library of Congress Cataloging in Publication Data
Greene, Jack P   comp.
Colonies to nation, 1763-1789.
Reprint of the 1967 ed. published by McGraw-Hill, New York, which was issued as v. 2 of A Documentary history of American life; with new pref.
Includes bibliographical references.
1. United States — History — Revolution, 1775-1783 — Sources.   2. United States — History — Confederation, 1783-1789 — Sources. I. Title II. Series: A Documentary history of American life; v. 2.
E203.G7   1975   973.3   74-34094
ISBN 0-393-09229-1

W. W. Norton & Company, Inc., 500 Fifth Avenue, New York, NY 10110
W. W. Norton & Company Ltd., 10 Coptic Street London WC1A 1PU

Printed in the United States of America

9 0

CONTENTS

PART TWO Stamp Act Crisis

PART THREE Internal Dissensions

PART **SIX**   The Tea Act Revives the Dispute

PART **SEVEN**   From Lexington to Independence

PART **EIGHT**   Reconstituting the Polity

PART **NINE** Transformation: The Revolution in Ideals

PART **TEN**   The War for Independence

PART **ELEVEN**   The Confederation Period

PART **TWELVE**   Constitutional Revolution

Between 1763 and 1789 the thirteen British colonies from New Hampshire south to Georgia challenged the authority of Britain, declared and successfully fought a war for independence, established republican governments, and united in a bold experiment in federal union that was without precedent and has survived for over 175 years. These accomplishments have never ceased to astonish and puzzle later generations of Americans, and the American Revolution has been a continuously challenging subject of inquiry. The documents included here, chosen from the wealth of available material because they seemed to indicate most clearly the dominant trends of thought and events, hopefully will aid the reader in coming to his own understanding of that remarkable happening. This volume was originally published in 1967 as the second volume in McGraw-Hill's multivolume *A Documentary History of American Life* under the general editorship of David Donald.

In preparing this volume, I was assisted by and am deeply indebted to Churchill E. Ward for helping me collect documents; the staffs of The Johns Hopkins University Library, the Library of Congress, the Newberry Library, the William L. Clements Library, the University of Michigan General Library, Houghton Library of Harvard University, Butler Library of Columbia University, the Library of the Massachusetts Historical Society, the Rutgers University Library, and the William Salt Library for supplying me with xeroxed copies of documents; Milton M. Klein, Darrett B. Rutman, Alden T. Vaughan, Robert M. Calhoon, Shaw Livermore, Jr., Thad W. Tate, and Gordon S. Wood for suggestions in choosing selections; Michael A. Burlingame and William Joseph Evitts for thoroughly checking facts and bibliographical citations; and Sue N. Greene and David Donald for valuable editorial advice.

Jack P. Greene

COLONIES
TO
NATION,
1763–1789

A Documentary History of the American Revolution

The American Revolution

*O**n the surface, prospects for the British Empire in general and the British colonies in North America in particular had never looked better than they did in early 1763. Fresh from a stunning victory over France and Spain in the French and Indian War (the Seven Years' War in Europe), the British had by the Treaty of Paris, signed on February 10, acquired control of all of North America east of the Mississippi River, outright possession of several previously disputed islands in the West Indies, and hegemony in India. Not since the halcyon days of the Roman Empire, said panegyrists on both sides of the Atlantic ignoring Spanish achievements in the late sixteenth century, had one nation gained so extensive a dominion over so much of the surface of the earth. Among the old colonies stretched along the Atlantic seaboard from Nova Scotia to Florida the inhabitants had never been happier to be a part of so vast and so thriving an institution, and British nationalism had never been greater. To have suggested that these colonies during the next quarter-century would openly revolt against Britain, weld themselves together in a loose confederation, make good a bid for independence, and embark upon a grand experiment in federalism would have seemed, except possibly to the most acute observer at the time, preposterous.*

Below the surface, however, there were disturbing indications of possible trouble. Colonial satisfaction with economic and political arrangements within the empire depended in large measure upon a considerable amount of imperial permissiveness, upon a lax enforcement of the Navigation Acts on the one hand and the continued ability of colonial lower houses to manipulate royal and proprietary governors and exercise the dominant voice in colonial government on the other. Any general change in the direction of greater imperial control would obviously encounter opposition in the colonies, and, as was abundantly clear in London, there was by 1763 strong sentiment among imperial officials for exerting stricter controls over the colonies. A tightening process had been inaugurated in a tentative and piecemeal way by the Earl of Halifax after he took over the Board of Trade in 1748. The need for colonial cooperation during the French and Indian War had required him to relax his efforts, but the war contributed to the sentiment for reform by calling attention frequently and dramatically to the extent of colonial violations of the Navigation Acts and the enormous

1

power of colonial lower houses of assembly in relation to royal and proprietary governors. The result was a growing conviction among imperial officials that corrective measures had to be undertaken with the peace. To that end Halifax resumed his efforts to strengthen imperial authority in the colonies in 1759 as soon as the French had been largely defeated on the continent.

This campaign for reform, together with the attempt to solve the immediate problems arising out of the peace, initiated a process by which the extreme British patriotism of colonial Americans was virtually extinguished in twelve short years. The most important catalyst in this process was Parliament's effort—first by the Sugar Act of 1764 and then by the Stamp Act of 1765—to tax the colonies for revenue to pay for troops to defend and police the newly acquired areas of Quebec, the Floridas, and the trans-Appalachian West. That effort touched off a debate over the extent of parliamentary authority in America that forced American leaders and Parliament into a precise formulation of directly opposing views and created an atmosphere of mutual suspicion that pervaded all subsequent developments. Although the colonists had been paying with protest various duties levied by Parliament in the Navigation Acts to regulate trade, they denied that Parliament could levy taxes on the colonies for revenue purposes without violating the most sacred right of Englishmen—the right not to be taxed without the consent of one's representatives—and declared that Americans were represented not in Parliament but in their own lower houses of assembly. This view Parliament could not accept, and at the same time it repealed the Stamp Act in 1766 it passed a Declaratory Act asserting its legislative authority over the colonies "in all cases whatsoever."

For nearly a decade, a debate, punctuated by acts of violence on both sides, raged over which of these two mutually exclusive conceptions of the constitution of the British Empire would prevail. There was never, on either side, any real possibility of compromise. Through the crisis generated by the Townshend revenue and reform program (1767–1770) and the uneasy quiet that followed the repeal of most of the Townshend duties (1770–1773) both sides clung steadfastly to the positions they had taken during the Stamp Act crisis. All the while the suspicions engendered by that episode steadily deepened. Persuaded that there was a natural tendency for men in authority to seek to destroy liberty so that they might better pursue their own cravings for riches and power, Americans saw in each new British measure mounting evidence of a sinister conspiracy among British ministers to deprive them and perhaps eventually all Englishmen of their liberties. At the same time British authorities became increasingly convinced that American resistance could only be interpreted as part of a design to shake off the restraints of the navigation system and eventually all dependence upon Great Britain.

What turned these suspicions into overt hostility were the Tea Act of 1773 and the actions that followed. Designed simply as a measure to help an ailing East India Company repair its sagging fortunes by selling tea cheaply in the colonies, it was viewed by American leaders as another link in the chain of ministerial conspiracy, a clever ruse to inveigle colonists into paying the existing tax on tea and thereby openly admitting Parliament's right to tax the colonies. Their resistance, including the daring dumping of the Massachusetts consignment of tea into Boston Harbor on the night of December 16, 1773, put imperial authorities in a fighting mood and led to Parliament's passage of the Coercive Acts, a series of punitive measures against Boston, one of which, the Massachusetts Government Act, fundamentally altered the constitution of Massachusetts Bay. In response to these measures Americans began to deny that Parliament had any authority over the colonies, that it could either tax or legislate for those portions of the empire from which it had no representatives. Meeting in the fall of 1774, the First Continental Congress, while offering to submit to parliamentary regulations of imperial trade, made this position official and adopted economic sanctions against Britain in the form of a Continental Association.

The unwillingness of British authorities to make any significant retreat and military preparations by both sides led directly to the outbreak of hostilities at Lexington and Concord on April 19, 1775. By declaring the colonies in a state of rebellion and committing the monarchy to vigorous military measures to force the colonies to yield to parliamentary authority in August, 1775, George III convinced most American leaders that he was now, if he had not been all along, at the head of the plot to deprive the colonies of their liberties. This conviction, though rejected by a minority of Americans who chose even after the fighting broke out to remain loyal to the Crown, paved the way for the total alienation from Great Britain of the vast majority of Americans and the movement for independence, which gained momentum throughout the early months of 1776 and culminated in the Declaration of Independence the following July. Convinced that there was no protection for their liberties as long as they retained their connection with a deluded nation presided over by an evil king in combination with power-hungry ministers and a corrupt Parliament, American leaders decided to seek safeguards for their liberty and property outside the British Empire.

Having thus dismembered their old polities, American leaders quickly proceeded to reconstitute them in slightly different forms, and the Declaration of Independence was accompanied not by social upheaval and chaos but by a spontaneous outbreak of constitution making in the states. Just as they had invoked the British and their own colonial constitutions to protect them from the unlimited might of British power between 1763 and 1776 so they now set about the task of constructing constitutions that would safeguard the liberty and property for which they had been contending and ensure that they would live under a government of impartial laws rather than partial men. Beginning with the adoption of the Virginia Declaration of Rights in June, 1776, most of the new state constitutions included a statement of the fundamental and inviolable rights of citizens upon which government was forbidden to encroach. The initial period of constitution making which extended into the early 1780s was a time of great political experimentation. Massachusetts leaders devised the constitutional convention, a device by which the people could exercise their constituent power to make their own government, and the extreme political ferment provoked an intensive examination of many of the traditional assumptions and institutions of American life. The result was a revolution in ideals, the first step in a process that would ultimately transform the very foundations of American society.

The security of these constitutions and the broader achievements that accompanied them depended, of course, upon American victory in the war, and that was not to prove an easy matter. It became clear early in the war that the American Army would have a difficult time in subduing a superior British force. On the other hand, it was equally clear that the Americans could not be easily defeated. As commander in chief of the Continental Army George Washington gained sufficient experience and expertise to keep his army intact and to avoid a major setback, and the destruction of one wing of the British Army at Saratoga in the fall of 1777 encouraged the French to come into the war on the side of the Americans. Ultimately, it was the French contribution and the inability of the British to control effectively any area not occupied by British troops that led to American victory. The surrender of a large portion of the British Army at Yorktown in October, 1781, finally convinced a significant number of British politicians to give up the fight, and British recognition of American independence followed with the Treaty of Paris in January, 1783.

Winning the War for Independence was not just a military undertaking. There was a host of fiscal, administrative, and diplomatic problems that had to be solved, and from 1775 to early 1781 these problems were the primary responsibility of the Second Continental Congress. Even before the Declaration of Independence, the Congress had considered the desirability of establishing a more permanent and elaborate national government, and in November, 1777, adopted the Articles of Confederation and submitted it to the states for ratification. Only after the states with Western lands had agreed to place them under the jurisdiction of the Articles would Maryland agree to ratify, however, and the Articles did not go into effect until March 1, 1781, just a little more than six months before Yorktown.

Over the next eight years—the period during which the Articles were in effect—the central government made some notable achievements. It not only brought the war to a satisfactory conclusion and negotiated an acceptable peace but also established the basic land policy for the West and worked out the arrangements by which new states could be admitted to the Union on an equal basis with the older ones. In addition, it survived a severe postwar depression and presided over the beginnings of a successful adjustment from a colonial to an independent economy. Still, its lack of energy and, more especially, its inability to raise money on its own or to coerce the states into complying with its requisitions exasperated Washington and the Army and many members of the Confederation Congress. There were repeated proposals throughout the early 1780s both in and out of Congress to strengthen the Articles. Shays's Rebellion in Massachusetts, beginning in August, 1786, raised the specter of anarchy and gave rise to the terrible fear that the principles for which Americans had fought might fall prey to their own internal dissensions. Though the state government in Massachusetts was able to put down the uprising without outside help, this fear and the obvious inability of the Confederation government to deal with internal disorder intensified the demand for a stronger central government. At the suggestion of the Annapolis Convention—an abbreviated interstate commercial conference—in September, 1786, Congress called a special convention to meet at Philadelphia in May, 1787, to amend the Articles.

The decision of the Federal Convention of 1787 to abandon the Articles and embark upon a bold new experiment in federalism resulted—after a torturous summer in Philadelphia, involving a searching debate about the nature of government and the most suitable form of polity for the United States and a series of necessary compromises—in the Federal Constitution, which after a vigorous debate was ratified by eleven states over the next year and went into effect in early 1789. The supreme achievement and a logical culmination of the American Revolution, the Constitution was intended by the Founding Fathers to protect society from the tyranny of its rulers by checking and balancing the various powers of government against one another while still giving the government sufficient power to protect the various segments of society from one another. In so doing, they sought both to create a government with energy and vitality and to secure those principles that were the ultimate concern of the Revolution.

Tightening the Reins of Empire

Blueprint for Reform: Governor Francis Bernard, "Principles of Law and Polity, Applied to the Government of the British Colonies in America" (1764)

The growing conviction in London that measures had to be undertaken at the end of the French and Indian War to shore up British authority in the colonies was revealed by the stream of proposals for imperial reform that poured from the pens of Crown officials and other interested observers during the early 1760s. One of the most perceptive and comprehensive of these proposals came from Francis Bernard (1712–1779), governor of Massachusetts Bay. Unable to support a growing family in what he considered proper style on his earnings as a county barrister in Lincolnshire, Bernard in 1758 had secured an appointment as governor of New Jersey through the influence of his wife's cousin, Lord Barrington. So successful was he in reducing the turbulent politics of that colony to some semblance of order that he quickly won the praise of his superiors in London and in 1760 secured a promotion to the governorship of the wealthier and more important colony of Massachusetts.

Persuaded by his experience in both New Jersey and Massachusetts that imperial authority in the colonies had to be somehow strengthened and aware of the general sentiment for colonial reform in London, Bernard early came to conceive of himself as the architect of imperial reform. As early as December, 1761, he began to pepper Barrington and other friends in England with suggestions for reorganizing the empire, and in the spring of 1764 he drew up a series of ninety-seven propositions entitled "Principles of Law and Polity, Applied to the Government of the British Colonies in America," a systematic and comprehensive blueprint for the total reconstruction of the British imperial system. In this document Bernard proposed a number of specific innovations to redefine the nature of the imperial-colonial relationship and to remodel the governments within the colonies in such a way as to satisfy both the imperial demand for closer control over the colonies and the colonial aspirations for an expanded role in the empire and for specific guarantees of their local self-governing rights. An ingenious scheme, Bernard's plan, if adopted, might have removed the ambiguities that lay behind the constitutional debate between Britain and the colonies and the catastrophes that accompanied it over the next decade. Circulated in manuscript, it won high praise from colonial officials in London, but the King's chief ministers, confronted with several specific colonial problems that seemed to require immediate and particular solutions, operated within a narrower focus and displayed no serious interest in such wholesale reforms. Ironically, one of Bernard's proposals, which were not published until 1774, was incorporated into the punitive legislation against Massachusetts Bay in that year and thus actively contributed to bring about the revolution it might have prevented.

Edmund S. Morgan and Helen M. Morgan, The Stamp Act Crisis: Prologue to Revolution *(1953), contains the best analysis of Bernard's career as colonial governor, his aspirations to be an imperial statesman, and his "Principles of Law and Polity," though the discussion in Richard Koebner,* Empire *(1961), may also be read with profit. The most important portions of Bernard's proposals are reprinted below from the original London edition.*

1. THE Kingdom of *Great Britain* is *imperial;* that is, Sovereign, and not subordinate to or dependent upon any earthly power.

2. In all *imperial* states there resides somewhere or other an absolute power, which we will call the *Sovereignty.*

3. The *Sovereignty* of *Great Britain* is in the *King in Parliament;* that is, in the King, acting with the advice and consent of the *Lords* and the *Commons* (by their Representatives), assembled in the *Parliament* of *Great Britain.*

4. The *King in Parliament* has the sole right of legislation, and the supreme superintendency of the government; and, in this plenitude of power, is absolute, uncontrolable, and accountable to none; and therefore, in a political sense, can do no wrong. . . .

9. The kingdom of *Great Britain* has, belonging to and depending upon it, divers external dominions and countries; all which, together with *Great Britain,* form the *British Empire.* Let, therefore, the *British Empire* signify the aggregate body of the *British* dominions, and the *Kingdom of Great Britain* the island which is the seat of the government.

10. The *King in Parliament,* is the sole and absolute Sovereign of the whole *British Empire.*

11. No members of the *British Empire,* other than the *Parliament* of *Great Britain,* can have a right to interfere in the exercise of this Sovereignty, but by being admitted into the *Parliament,* as *Wales, Chester,* and *Durham* have been, and *Ireland* may be.

12. Such an union is not necessary to the generality of the *British* external dominions; but it may be expedient with most of them.

13. The external *British* dominions, without such an union, are subordinate to and dependent upon the *Kingdom* of *Great Britain,* and must derive from thence all their powers of legislation and jurisdiction.

14. Legislation is not necessary to an external and dependent government; jurisdiction is necessary and essential to it. Therefore,

15. A separate Legislation is not an absolute right of *British* subjects residing out of the seat of Empire; it may or may not be allowed, and has or has not been granted, according to the circumstances of the community.

16. Where it is granted or allowed, it must be exercised in subordination to the Sovereign power from whom it is derived.

17. No grant of the power of Legislation to a dependent government, whether it comes from the *King* alone, or from the *Parliament,* can preclude the *Parliament* of *Great Britain* from interfering in such dependent government, at such time and in such manner as they shall think fit. . . .

29. The rule that a *British* subject shall not be bound by laws, or liable to taxes, but what he has consented to by his representatives, must be confined to the inhabitants of *Great Britain* only; and is not strictly true even there.

30. The *Parliament* of *Great Britain,* as well from its rights of *Sovereignty* as from occasional exigences, has a right to make laws for, and impose taxes upon, its subjects in its external dominions, although they are not represented in such *Parliament.* But,

31. Taxes imposed upon the external dominions ought to be applied to the use of the people, from whom they are raised. . . .

36. The Colonies ought, so far as they are able, to pay the charge of the support of their own Governments, and of their own defence.

37. The defence of the *American* Colonies, being now almost wholly a sea service, is connected with the defence of trade. Therefore,

38. Duties upon imports and exports, make the most proper funds for the expenses of such defence. And

39. It being the proper business of the *Parliament* of *Great Britain*, to establish and determine the necessary regulations and restrictions of the trade of their external dominions; and the duties upon the *American* imports and exports being interwove with the regulations and restrictions of trade; the imposition of such Duties is the proper business of the *Parliament*.

40. The port duties being most properly applicable to the defence of the Colonies, it remains that the support of the Governments be provided for by internal duties. . . .

44. Although the right of the *Parliament* of *Great Britain*, to raise taxes in any parts of the *British Empire*, is not to be disputed; yet it would be most advisable to leave to the Provincial Legislatures the raising the internal taxes.

45. If the sums required were fixed, there would be no inconvenience in letting the Provincial Legislature determine the manner in which they shall be raised.

46. It will be more agreeable to the people, that the necessary internal taxes should be raised by the Provincial Legislatures; as they will be most able to consult the particular convenience of their respective provinces. Whereas,

47. It may be difficult to form a general Parliamentary tax, so as to make it equally suitable to all Provinces.

48. It would make it more agreeable to the people, though the sum to be raised was prescribed, to leave the method of taxation to their own Legislature.

49. If the Provincial Legislatures should refuse to raise the sums required for the support of Government, or should insist upon doing it by improper means, the *Parliament* might then take the business into their own hands.

50. But it is most probable that the people would acquiesce in this measure, and would soon be reconciled to it, when they observed the good effects of a certain and adequate establishment for the support of Government. For

51. The want of such an establishment has had bad consequences in many of the Governments of the *American* colonies, and has contributed more than all other things put together, to contention in the legislature, and defect of justice in the courts of law. Therefore,

52. The establishment of a certain, sufficient, and independent Civil List, is not only expedient, but necessary to the welfare of the *American* Colonies.

53. Such an appointment will tend greatly to remove all the seeds of contention, and to promote a lasting harmony and good understanding between the government and the people. . . .

59. The subjects of the *British Empire*, residing in its external dominions, are intitled to all the rights and privileges of *British* subjects, which they are capable of enjoying.

60. There are some rights and privileges which the *British* subjects, in the external dominions, are not equally capable of enjoying with those residing in *Great Britain*.

61. The right of having a share in the Imperial Legislature, is one of these

incapacities in those external dominions, where a representation is impracticable.

62. A Representation of the *American* Colonies in the Imperial Legislature is not impracticable: and therefore,

63. The propriety of a Representation of the *American* Colonies in the Imperial Legislature, must be determined by expediency only.

64. A Representation of the *American* Colonies, in the Imperial Legislature, is not necessary to establish the authority of the *Parliament* over the Colonies. But

65. It may be expedient for quieting disputes concerning such authority, and preventing a separation in future times.

66. The expediency of *American* Legislatures, does not arise from the want of their having Representatives in the Imperial Legislature.

67. If the *American* Colonies had Representatives in *Parliament,* still there would be an occasion for provincial Legislatures, for their domestic œconomy, and the support of their Governments. But

68. All external Legislatures must be subject to, and dependent on, the Imperial Legislature: otherwise there would be an *Empire* in an *Empire.* . . .

70. The same form of Government is not equally proper to a Colony in its infant and in its mature state. . . .

72. There is but one most perfect form of Government for Provinces arrived at maturity.

73. That is the most perfect form of Government for a *dependent* province, which approaches the nearest to that of the *sovereign* state, and differs from it as little as possible.

74. There is no such form of Government among the *American Colonies.* And therefore

75. Every *American* Government is capable of having its Constitution altered for the better. . . .

85. To prevent revolts in future times (for there is no room to fear them in the present) the most effectual means would be, to make the governments large and respectable, and balance the powers of them.

86. There is no Government in *America* at present, whose powers are properly balanced; there not being in any of them a real and distinct third Legislative power mediating between the *King* and the *People,* which is the peculiar excellence of the *British* Constitution.

87. The want of such a third Legislative power, adds weight to the popular, and lightens the royal scale: so as to destroy the balance between the *royal* and *popular* powers.

88. Although *America* is not now (and probably will not be for many years to come) ripe enough for an hereditary *Nobility;* yet it is now capable of a *Nobility* for life.

89. A *Nobility* appointed by the *King* for life, and made independent, would probably give strength and stability to the *American* governments, as effectually as an hereditary *Nobility* does to that of *Great Britain.*

90. The reformation of the *American* governments should not be controlled by the present boundaries of the colonies; as they were mostly settled upon partial, occasional, and accidental considerations, without any regard to a whole.

91. To settle the *American* governments to the greatest possible advantage,

it will be necessary to reduce the number of them; in some places to unite and consolidate; in others to separate and transfer; and in general to divide by natural boundaries instead of imaginary lines. . . .

95. The *American* colonies, in general, are at this time arrived at that state, which qualifies them to receive the most perfect form of government, which their situation and relation to *Great Britain* make them capable. of.

96. The people of *North America,* at this time, expect a revisal and reformation of the *American* Governments, and are better disposed to submit to it than ever they were, or perhaps ever will be again.

97. This is therefore the proper and critical time to reform the *American* governments upon a general, constitutional, firm, and durable plan; and if it is not done now, it will probably every day grow more difficult, till at last it becomes impracticable.

SELECTION

New Measures

The failure of London officials to inaugurate the broad reconstruction program proposed by Bernard was not the result of any absence of sentiment on their part for colonial reform. Never before, in fact, had there been in British government circles such widespread concern about colonial problems and such a clear consensus that something had to be done about them as there was in the early 1760s. To stop the wholesale violations of the Navigation Acts by merchants from the middle and northern colonies; to organize, administer, and police the vast new territories acquired from France and Spain in both North America and the West Indies; to keep the Indians quiet in the new territories and provide some orderly means for westward expansion from the seaboard colonies; to render royal officials in the colonies independent of grasping colonial legislatures and pay for the army necessary to secure the new acquisitions from possible reconquest by their former possessors; and to regulate in a way acceptable to British mercantile interests the vast quantities of legal-tender paper money issued by colonial legislatures during the war—all of these problems obviously demanded immediate attention. But they seemed to call for a series of patchwork reforms rather than a total reconstruction of the colonial system.

Many such reforms were already in progress by the time Bernard put together his proposals. Acting upon orders from William Pitt, who was outraged by colonial trading with the enemy, the Treasury initiated a number of administrative reforms in the colonial customs service during the last years of the war. In a now-famous letter presented to the Privy Council in October, 1763, the Treasury described the nature of these reforms, explained the motives behind them as well as the general objectives of British commercial policy toward the colonies in the postwar years, and proposed several additional measures to secure colonial obedience to the Navigation Acts and increase the revenue from colonial customs. Put into legal effect by an Order in Council (an executive decree issued by the Crown in conjunction with the Privy Council), this report is printed below as Selection 2 A.

Three days later imperial authorities dealt with the problems of the new territories and westward expansion in the royal proclamation of October 7, 1763. By this document, most of which is included below as Selection 2 B, they provided for the creation of three new mainland colonies—Quebec, East Florida, and West Florida—and placed the West under the control of the commander in chief of British forces in North America. An earlier plan called for limited and controlled expansion and the eventual establishment of a colony in the Ohio Valley, but Pontiac's Rebellion, a major Indian uprising in the Ohio country which began in May, 1763, prompted them to prohibit all settlement to the west of the crest of the Appalachian Mountains. For the time being, at least, the West was to be left to the Indians, settlers already in the area were to be removed, private purchases of land from the Indians were outlawed, and all Indian affairs, including both trade and diplomacy, were placed under the control of the two royal superintendents of Indian affairs, originally appointed to handle such problems at the beginning of the Seven Years' War. Intended merely as a stopgap measure to serve until a permanent policy could be worked out, the proclamation of 1763 erred seriously in failing to provide any form of civil government for several thousand French settlers in the Illinois country and in substituting English for French law in Quebec.

Committed to maintain a large army in the colonies to secure the new acquisitions from any attempts by France and Spain to reconquer them and faced with a large war debt and high taxes in Great Britain, the imperial government initiated a program of taxing the colonies for revenue with the Sugar Act of 1764. This measure lowered to 3d the 6d-per-gallon duty on foreign molasses and revised most of the other duties levied by the Molasses Act of 1733. All earlier duties levied by Parliament on the colonies had been purely regulatory in nature —designed not to raise a revenue but only to channel trade in directions most beneficial to the parent state—and the molasses duty in particular had never been strictly enforced. By contrast, the new duties levied by the Sugar Act were intended to raise a revenue to help pay for the military establishment in North America and were obviously going to be rigorously enforced. Indeed, most of the provisions of the measure were concerned with further strengthening the customs service, plugging up loopholes in the enforcement system, and establishing a more elaborate system of controls over all aspects of colonial trade. Among other things, it placed the burden of proof upon the accused in all cases arising under the Navigation Acts, made it possible for customs officials to bring suits against suspected violators in a new vice-admiralty court to be established in Halifax, Nova Scotia, rather than in the local colonial courts where juries had repeatedly refused to grant convictions, and added a number of products—including iron, hides, and whale fins—to the list of enumerated articles which could not be exported outside the British Empire by colonial shippers. These and other important provisions of the act are printed below as Selection 2 C.

At the same session Parliament in response to demands from British merchants extended the Currency Act of 1751, which forbade the emission of legal-tender paper money in the New England colonies, to the rest of the continental colonies by the Currency Act of 1764. This act, included below as Selection 2 D, prohibited any further issuance of legal-tender paper after September 1, 1764, required that all such currency then in circulation be punctually retired at the time appointed by the act of issue, and threatened any governor who violated the act with a fine of £1,000 sterling, immediate dismissal, and lifetime exclusion from places of public trust.

Bernhard Knollenberg, Origin of the American Revolution: 1759–1766 *(1960), contains the most detailed discussion of the general British reform program undertaken between 1759 and 1764. The strengthening of the customs regulations is treated in Thomas C. Barrow, "Background to the Grenville Program, 1757–1763,"* William and Mary Quarterly, *third series, volume 22 (1965), pages 93–104, and the proclamation of 1763 in Jack M. Sosin,* Whitehall and the Wilderness: The Middle West in British Colonial Policy, 1760–1775 *(1961), and John Shy,* Toward Lexington: The Role of the British Army in the Coming of the American Revolution *(1965). The Shy volume also includes a full discussion of the decision to keep an army in the colonies. Edmund S. Morgan and Helen M. Morgan,* The Stamp Act Crisis: Prologue to Revolution *(1953), and Allen S. Johnson, "The Passage of the Sugar Act,"* William and Mary Quarterly, *third series, volume 16 (1959), pages 507–514, discuss the Sugar Act of 1764, while Joseph Albert Ernst, "Genesis of the Currency Act of 1764: Virginia Paper Money and the Protection of British Investments," ibid., volume 22 (1965), pages 33–74, and Jack P. Greene and Richard M. Jellison, "The Currency Act of 1764 in Imperial-Colonial Relations, 1764–1776," ibid., volume 18 (1961), pages 485–518, explore the origins of and colonial reactions to the Currency Act of 1764.*

A. REFORM OF THE CUSTOMS SERVICE: ORDER IN COUNCIL (OCT. 4, 1763)*

We the Commissioners of your Majestys Treasury beg leave humbly to represent to your Majesty, that having taken into Consideration the present state of the Duties of Customs imposed on your Majestys Subjects in America and the West Indies, We find, that the Revenue arising therefrom is very small and inconsiderable having in no degree increased with the Commerce of those Countries, and is not yet sufficient to defray a fourth Part of the Expence necessary for collecting it. We observe with concern that through Neglect, Connivance and Fraud, not only the Revenue is impaired, but the Commerce of the Colonies is diverted from its natural Course and the salutary Provisions of many wise Laws to secure it to the Mother Country are in great Measure defeated: Attention to Objects of so great Importance, we are sensible is at all times our Duty, but at this it is more indispensable when the Military Establishment necessary for maintaining these Colonies requires a large Revenue to support it, and when their vast Increase in Territory and Population makes the proper Regulation of their Trade of immediate Necessity, lest the continuance and extent of the

* Reprinted in full from W. L. Grant and James Munro (eds.), *Acts of the Privy Council of England, Colonial Series* (6 vols., 1908–1912), vol. IV (1745–1766), pp. 569–572.

dangerous Evils abovementioned may render all Attempts to remedy them hereafter infinitely more difficult, if not utterly impracticable. We have endeavoured therefore to discover, and as far as the Power of our Department will allow, remove the Causes, to which the Deficiency of this Revenue and the contraband Trade with other European Nations are owing. For this Purpose We have ordered all the Officers belonging to the Customs in America and the West Indies to be fully instructed in their Duty to repair forthwith to their respective Stations and constantly to reside there for the future; and where We find, that a sufficient number of proper Officers are not yet established, it is intended to supply the Deficiency by the appointment of others. We have directed that all the Officers of the Revenue in your Majestys Plantations should be furnished with new and ample Instructions, enforcing in the strongest manner the strictest attention to their Duty, and requiring that by regular and constant correspondence, they give an Account as well of their own Proceedings, as of the conduct of the Officers under them, and inform Us likewise of any Obstructions they may meet with in discharging the Business of their respective Offices. We have ordered them to transmit exact Accounts of the Imports and Exports in their several Districts, of the state of the Revenue, and of the illicit Commerce with other European States from time to time in consequence of these directions, with such Observations as may occurr to them in regard either to the Efficacy and Inefficacy of any subsisting regulations or to such Alterations as they may judge conducive to the farther Improvement of the Revenue to the prevention of those Frauds by which it is impaired, and to the Suppression of the contraband Trade which has been hitherto carried on with too much Impunity: and We have directed the Commissioners of your Majesty's Customs immediately to dismiss every Officer, that shall fail to pay obedience to these Instructions or be any way deficient in his Duty. But as the Restraint and Suppression of Practices which have unhappily prevailed too long will certainly be encountered with great difficulties in such distant Parts of your Majestys Dominions, We apprehend that these Our Regulations will not fully answer the end for which they are designed, unless, in consequence of your Majestys Commands, the other Departments of Your Government afford their utmost Assistance in support of them. With this View, We thought it became us thus to lay Our Proceedings before your Majesty, and further humbly to represent, that it appears to Us of the highest Importance, that strict Orders should be given to the Governors of all the Colonies, to make the Suppression of the clandestine and prohibited Trade with foreign Nations, and the Improvement of the Revenue, the constant and immediate Objects of their Care, and by a vigorous discharge of the duty required of them by several Acts of Parliament and a due exertion of their legal Authority, to give the Officers of the Revenue the necessary Protection and Support, and that they from time to time transmit such Observations as occur to them on the state of the Illicit and Contraband Trade, and on the conduct of all Persons, whose duty it is to prevent the same, in order that the necessary Directions may be given for punishing such Persons, as shall appear to be guilty of any Misbehaviour and correcting all abuses for the future.—We are further humbly of opinion that it will greatly contribute to the same salutary ends, and to the carrying of the several Laws and Regulations into execution with Success, if all Officers both Civil and Military are

strictly commanded to give their Assistance upon all proper Occasions, and
if the Commanders in Chief of Your Majestys Ships and Troops in America
and the West Indies are directed to attend to this object with the utmost
care, and to make such a Disposition of the Force under their respective
Commands as will be most serviceable in suppressing these dangerous Practices, and in protecting the Officers of the Revenue from the violence of any
desperate and lawless Persons, who shall attempt to resist the due execution
of the Laws in the same manner as is practiced in England.—The Advantages of a Sea Guard more especially in those Parts are sufficiently obvious.
We depend upon it as the likeliest means for accomplishing these great
Purposes: and the good Effects, that have already been experienced from
the Measures lately taken for that purpose at Home, make us earnestly
wish, that the same may not only be continued, but even extended and
strengthened as far as the Naval Establishment will allow.—And lastly it
appears to Us highly necessary that there should be established by Law a
new and better method of condemning Seizures made in the Colonies; The
Commissioners of the Customs have reported to Us, that they have received
various Complaints of Great Difficulties and Partialities in the Trials on
these Occasions, and the several Statutes in force from the 12th of Charles
the Second to the third of Your Majesty vary so much both as to the Mode
and Place of Trial, that the Officers of the Revenue when they have made a
Seizure cannot but be under great doubt and Uncertainty, in what manner
they should proceed to the condemnation of it. It is therefore humbly submitted to Your Majesty whether from the Importance of this Object it would
not be of the greatest Public Utility, that an Uniform Plan be prepared for
establishing the Judicature of the Courts of Admiralty in that Country
under Persons qualified for so important a Trust, in order that Justice may
hereafter in all Cases be diligently and impartially administered and that
such Regulations, as Parliament may think proper to make, may be duly
carried into Execution.

B. STOPGAP REGULATIONS FOR
THE NEW TERRITORIES:
THE PROCLAMATION OF (OCT. 7) 1763 *

WHEREAS we have taken into our royal consideration the extensive and
valuable acquisitions in America, secured to our crown by the late definitive
treaty of peace concluded at Paris the 10th day of February last; and being
desirous that all our loving subjects, as well of our kingdoms as of our
colonies in America, may avail themselves, with all convenient speed, of the
great benefits and advantages which must accrue therefrom to their commerce, manufactures, and navigation; we have thought fit, with the advice
of our privy council, to issue this our royal proclamation, hereby to publish
and declare to all our loving subjects, that we have, with the advice of our
said privy council, granted our letters patent under our great seal of Great

* These excerpts are reprinted from the *Annual Register*, vol. VI (1763), sec. 1,
pp. 208–212.

Britain, to erect within the countries and islands, ceded and confirmed to us by the said treaty, four distinct and separate governments, stiled and called by the names of Quebec, East Florida, West Florida, and Grenada. . . .

We have also, with the advice of our privy council aforesaid, annexed to our province of Georgia, all the lands lying between the rivers Attamaha and St. Mary's.

And whereas it will greatly contribute to the speedy settling our said new governments, that our loving subjects should be informed of our paternal care for the security of the liberties and properties of those who are, and shall become inhabitants thereof; we have thought fit to publish and declare, by this our proclamation, that we have, in the letters patent under our great seal of Great Britain, by which the said governments are constituted, given express power and direction to our governors of our said colonies respectively, that so soon as the state and circumstances of the said colonies will admit thereof, they shall, with the advice and consent of the members of our council, summon and call general assemblies within the said governments respectively, in such manner and form as is used and directed in those colonies and provinces in America, which are under our immediate government; and we have also given power to the said governors, with the consent of our said councils, and the representatives of the people, so to be summoned as aforesaid, to make, constitute, and ordain laws, statutes, and ordinances for the public peace, welfare, and good government of our said colonies, and of the people and inhabitants thereof, as near as may be, agreeable to the laws of England, and under such regulations and restrictions as are used in other colonies; and in the mean time, and until such assemblies can be called as aforesaid, all persons inhabiting in, or resorting to, our said colonies, may confide in our royal protection for the enjoyment of the benefit of the laws of our realm of England; for which purpose we have given power under our great seal to the governors of our said colonies respectively, to erect and constitute, with the advice of our said councils and respectively, courts of judicature and public justice within our said colonies, for the hearing and determining all causes, as well criminal as civil, according to law and equity, and, as near as may be, agreeable to the laws of England, with liberty to all persons who may think themselves aggrieved by the sentence of such courts, in all civil cases, to appeal, under the usual limitations and restrictions, to us, in our privy council. . . .

And whereas it is just and reasonable, and essential to our interest, and the security of our colonies, that the several nations or tribes of Indians, with whom we are connected, and who live under our protection, should not be molested or disturbed in the possession of such parts of our dominions and territories as, not having been ceded to, or purchased by us, are reserved to them, or any of them, as their hunting grounds; we do therefore, with the advice of our privy council, declare it to be our royal will and pleasure, that no governor, or commander in chief, in any of our colonies of Quebec, East Florida, or West Florida, do presume, upon any pretence whatever, to grant warrants of survey, or pass any patents for lands beyond the bounds of their respective governments, as described in their commissions; as also that no governor or commander in chief of our other colonies or plantations in America, do presume for the present, and until our further pleasure be known, to grant warrant of survey, or pass patents for any lands beyond the heads or sources of any of the rivers which fall into the Atlantic Ocean from the west or north west; or upon any lands whatever, which not having been ceded to, or purchased by us, as aforesaid, are reserved to the said Indians, or any of them.

And we do further declare it to be our royal will and pleasure for the present, as aforesaid, to reserve under our sovereignty, protection and dominion, for the use of the said Indians, all the land and territories not included within the limits of our said three new governments, or within the limits of the territory granted to the Hudson's Bay company; as also all the land and territories lying to the westward of the sources of the rivers which fall into the sea from the west and north-west as aforesaid; and we do hereby strictly forbid, on pain of our displeasure, all our loving subjects from making any purchases or settlements whatever, or taking possession of any of the lands above reserved, without our especial leave and licence for that purpose first obtained.

And we do further strictly enjoin and require all persons whatever, who have either wilfully or inadvertently seated themselves upon any lands within the countries above described, or upon any other lands, which not having been ceded to, or purchased by us, are still reserved to the said Indians as aforesaid, forthwith to remove themselves from such settlements.

And whereas great frauds and abuses have been committed in the purchasing lands of the Indians, to the great prejudice of our interests, and to the great dissatisfaction of the said Indians; in order therefore to prevent such iregularities for the future, and to the end that the Indians may be convinced of our justice and determined resolution to remove all reasonable cause of discontent, we do, with the advice of our privy council, strictly enjoin and require, that no private person do presume to make any purchase from the said Indians of any lands reserved to the said Indians within those parts of our colonies where we have thought proper to allow settlement; but that if at any time any of the said Indians should be inclined to dispose of the said lands, the same shall be purchased only for us, in our name, at some public meeting or assembly of the said Indians, to be held for that purpose by the governor or commander in chief of our colony respectively within which they shall lie: and in case they shall lie within the limits of any proprietaries, conformable to such directions and instructions as we or they shall think proper to give for that purpose: and we do, by the advice of our privy council, declare and enjoin, that the trade with the said Indians shall be free and open to all our subjects whatever, provided that every person who may incline to trade with the said Indians, do take out a licence for carrying on such trade, from the governor or commander in chief of any of our colonies respectively, where such person shall reside, and also give security to observe such regulations as we shall at any time think fit, by ourselves or commissaries, to be appointed for this purpose, to direct and appoint, for the benefit of the said trade: and we do hereby authorise, enjoin, and require the governors and commanders in chief of all our colonies respectively, as well as those under our immediate government, as those under the government and direction of proprietaries, to grant such licences without fee or reward, taking especial care to insert therein a condition that such licence shall be void, and the security forfeited, in case the person to whom the same is granted, shall refuse or neglect to observe such regulations as we shall think proper to prescribe as aforesaid. . . .

C. BEGINNINGS OF PARLIAMENTARY TAXATION FOR REVENUE: THE SUGAR ACT OF (APR. 5) 1764*

WHEREAS *it is expedient that new provisions and regulations should be established for improving the revenue of this kingdom, and for extending and securing the navigation and commerce between* Great Britain *and your Majesty's dominions in* America, *which, by the peace, have been so happily enlarged: and whereas it is just and necessary, that a revenue be raised, in your Majesty's said dominions in* America, *for defraying the expences of defending, protecting , and securing the same; we, your Majesty's most dutiful and loyal subjects, the commons of* Great Britain, *in parliament assembled, being desirous to make some provisions, in this present session of parliament, towards raising the said revenue in* America, *have resolved to give and grant unto your Majesty the several rates and duties herein aftermentioned. . . .*

IV. And whereas an act was made in the sixth year of the reign of his late majesty King *George* the Second, intituled, *An act for the better securing and encouraging the trade of his Majesty's sugar colonies in* America, which was to continue in force for five years . . . and which, by several subsequent acts . . . was, from time to time, continued; and, by an act made in the first year of the reign of his present Majesty, was further continued until the end of this present session of parliament; and although the said act hath been found in some degree useful, yet it is highly expedient that the same should be altered, enforced, and made more effectual; but, in consideration of the great distance of several of the said colonies and plantations from this kingdom, it will be proper further to continue the said act for a short space, before any alterations and amendments shall take effect, in order that all persons concerned may have due and proper notice thereof; be it therefore enacted by the authority aforesaid, That the said act made in the sixth year of the reign of his late majesty King *George* the Second, intituled, *An act for the better securing and encouraging the trade of his Majesty's sugar colonies in* America, shall be, and the same is hereby further continued, until the thirtieth day of *September,* one thousand seven hundred and sixty four.

V. And be it further enacted by the authority aforesaid, That from the twenty ninth day of *September,* one thousand seven hundred and sixty four, the said act, subject to such alterations and amendments as are herein after contained, shall be, and the same is hereby made perpetual.

VI. And be it further enacted by the authority aforesaid, That in lieu and instead of the rate and duty imposed by the said act upon melasses and syrups, there shall, from and after the said twenty ninth day of *September,* one thousand seven hundred and sixty four, be raised, levied, collected, and paid, unto his Majesty, his heirs and successors, for and upon every gallon of melasses or syrups, being the growth, product, or manufacture, of any colony or plantation in *America,* not under the dominion of his Majesty, his heirs or successors, which shall be imported or brought into any colony or plantation in *America,* which now is, or hereafter may be,

* These excerpts are reprinted from Danby Pickering (ed.), *Statutes at Large,* vol. XXVI, pp. 33, 35, 37, 39–45, 48–51.

under the dominion of his Majesty, his heirs or successors, the sum of three pence. . . .

XI. And it is hereby further enacted by the authority aforesaid, That all the monies which . . . shall arise by the several rates and duties herein before granted; and also by the duties which, from and after the said twenty ninth day of *September,* one thousand seven hundred and sixty four, shall be raised upon sugars and paneles, by virtue of the said act made in the sixth year of the reign of his said late majesty King *George* the Second (except the necessary charges of raising, collecting, levying, recovering, answering, paying, and accounting for the same) shall be paid into the receipt of his Majesty's Exchequer, and shall be entered separate and apart from all other monies paid or payable to his Majesty, his heirs or successors: and shall be there reserved, to be, from time to time, disposed of by parliament, towards defraying the necessary expences of defending, protecting, and securing, the *British* colonies and plantations in *America.* . . .

XVIII. And be it further enacted by the authority aforesaid, That . . . no rum or spirits of the produce or manufacture of any of the colonies or plantations in *America,* not in the possession or under the dominion of his Majesty, his heirs or successors, shall be imported or brought into any of the colonies or plantations in *America* which now are, or hereafter may be, in the possession or under the dominion of his Majesty, his heirs or successors, upon forfeiture of all such rum or spirits, together with the ship or vessel in which the same shall be imported, with the tackle, apparel, and furniture thereof, to be seized by any officer or officers of his Majesty's customs, and prosecuted in such manner and form as herein after is expressed; any law, custom, or usage, to the contrary notwithstanding. . . .

XX. And, for the better preventing frauds in the importation of foreign sugars and paneles, rum and spirits, molasses and syrups, into any of his Majesty's dominions, under pretence that the same are the growth, produce, or manufacture, of the *British* colonies or plantations, it is further enacted by the authority aforesaid, That from and after the twenty ninth day of *September,* one thousand seven hundred and sixty four, every person or persons loading on board any ship or vessel, in any of the *British* colonies or plantations in *America,* any rum or spirits, sugars or paneles, molasses or syrups, as of the growth, product, or manufacture, of any *British* colony or plantation, shall, before the clearing out of the said ship or vessel, produce and deliver to the collector or other principal officer of the customs at the loading port, an affidavit signed and sworn to before some justice of the peace in the said *British* colonies or plantations, either by the grower, maker, or shipper, of such goods, or his or their known agent or factor, expressing, in words at length and not in figures, the quality of the goods so shipped, with the number and denomination of the packages, and describing the name or names of the plantation or plantations, and the name of the colony where the same grew or were produced and manufactured; which affidavit shall be attested, under the hand of the said justice of the peace, to have been sworn to in his presence; who is hereby required to do the same without fee or reward: and the collector or other principal officer of the customs to whom such affidavit shall be delivered, shall thereupon grant to the master, or other person having the charge of the ship or vessel, a certificate under his hand and seal of office (without fee or reward) of his having received such affidavit pursuant to the directions of this act; which certificate shall express the quality of the goods shipped on board such ship or vessel, with the number and denomination of the packages: and such collector or other principal officer of the customs shall also (without fee or reward) within thirty days after the sailing of the ship or vessel, transmit an exact copy of the said affidavit to the secretary's office for the respective colony or plantation where the goods were shipped, on forfeiture of five pounds.

XXI. And it is further enacted, That upon the arrival of such ship or vessel into the port of her discharge, either in *Great Britain* or any other port of his Majesty's dominions, where such goods may be lawfully imported, the master or other person taking the charge of the ship or vessel shall, at the time he makes his report of his cargo, deliver the said certificate to the collector or other principal officer of the customs, and make oath before him, that the goods so reported are the same that are mentioned in the said certificate, on forfeiture of one hundred pounds; and if any rum or spirits, sugars or paneles, molasses or syrups, shall be imported or found on board any such ship or vessel, for which no such certificate shall be produced, or which shall not agree therewith, the same shall be deemed and taken to be foreign rum and spirits, sugar and paneles, molasses and syrups, and shall be liable to the same duties, restrictions, regulations, penalties, and forfeitures, in all respects, as rum, spirits, sugar, paneles, molasses, and syrups, of the growth, produce, or manufacture, of any foreign colony or plantation, would respectively be liable to by law. . . .

XXIII. And whereas by an act of parliament made in the twelfth year of the reign of King *Charles* the Second, intituled, *An act for encouraging and increasing of shipping and navigation,* and several subsequent acts of parliament which are now in force, it is, amongst other things, directed, that for every ship or vessel that shall load any commodities, in those acts particularly enumerated, at any *British* plantation, being the growth, product, or manufacture thereof, bonds shall be given with one surety, to the value of one thousand pounds, if the ship be of less burthen than one hundred tons, and of the sum of two thousand pounds; if the ship be of greater burthen, that the same commodities shall be brought by such ship or vessel to some other *British* plantation, or to some port in *Great Britain;* notwithstanding which, there is great reason to apprehend such goods are frequently carried to foreign parts, and landed there: and whereas great quantities of foreign molasses and syrups are clandestinely run on shore in the *British* colonies, to the prejudice of the revenue, and the great detriment of the trade of this kingdom, and it's *American* plantations: to remedy which practices for the future, be it further enacted by the authority aforesaid, That . . . bond and security, in the like penalty, shall also be given to the collector or other principal officer of the customs at any port or place in any of the *British American* colonies or plantations, with one surety besides the master of every ship or vessel that shall lade or take on board there any goods not particularly enumerated in the said acts, being the product or manufacture of any of the said colonies or plantations, with condition, that, in case any molasses or syrups, being the produce of any of the plantations, not under the dominion of his Majesty, his heirs or successors, shall be laden on board such ship or vessel, the same shall (the danger of the seas and enemies excepted) be brought, without fraud or wilful diminution, by the said ship or vessel to some of his Majesty's colonies or plantations in *America*, or to some port in *Great Britain;* and that the master or other person having the charge of such ship or vessel, shall, immediately upon his arrival at every port or place in *Great Britain*, or in the *British American* colonies and plantations, make a just and true report of all the goods laden on board such ship or vessel under their true and proper denominations; and if any such non-enumerated goods shall be laden on board any such ship or vessel before such bond shall be given, the goods so laden together with the ship or vessel and her furniture shall be forfeited, and shall and may be seized by any officer of the customs, and prosecuted in the manner herein after directed.

XXIV. And it is hereby further enacted by the authority aforesaid, That every master or person having the charge of any ship or vessel shall, before he departs from any *British* colony or plantation where he receives his lading, take a certificate under the hands and seals of the collector or other principal officer of the customs there (which certificate such officers are hereby required to grant without fee or reward) that bond hath been given, pursuant to the directions of this or any other act of parliament, as the case shall require; and the master or person having the charge of such ship or vessel, shall keep such certificate in his custody till the voyage is compleated, and shall then deliver the same up to the collector or other chief officer of the customs at the port or place where he shall discharge his lading, either in *Great Britain* or any *British American* colony or plantation, on forfeiture of one hundred pounds for each and every offence.

XXV. And it is hereby further enacted, That if any *British* ship or vessel laden, as aforesaid, with any goods of the produce or manufacture of any *British* colony or plantation in *America*, or having on board any molasses or syrups the produce of any foreign colony or plantation, shall be discovered by any officer of his Majesty's customs within two leagues of the shore of any *British* colony or plantation in *America*, and the master or person taking charge of such ship or vessel shall not produce a certificate that bond has been given, pursuant to the directions of this or any other act of parliament, as the case may require; or if he shall not produce such certificate to the collector or other chief officer of the customs where he shall arive, either in *Great Britain* or any *British American* colony or plantation, such ship or vessel, with her tackle, apparel, and furniture, and all the goods therein laden, shall be forfeited, and shall and may be seized and prosecuted. . . .

XXVII. And it is hereby further enacted by the authority aforesaid, That from and after the twenty ninth day of *September*, one thousand seven hundred and sixty four, all coffee, pimento, cocoa nuts, whale fins, raw silk, hides, and skins, pot and pearl ashes, of the growth, production, or manufacture, of any *British* colony or plantation in *America*, shall be imported directly from thence into this kingdom, or some other *British* colony or plantation, under the like securities, penalties, and forfeitures, as are particularly mentioned in two acts of parliament made in the twelfth and twenty fifth years of the reign of King *Charles* the Second, the former intituled, *An act for the encouraging and increasing of shipping and navigation,* and the latter intituled, *An act for the encouragement of the* Greenland *and eastland trades, and for the better securing the plantation trade,* or either of them, with respect to the goods in those acts particularly enumerated; any law, custom, or usage, to the contrary notwithstanding.

XXVIII. And it is hereby further enacted by the authority aforesaid, That . . . no iron, nor any sort of wood, commonly called *Lumber,* as specified in an act passed in the eighth year of the reign of King *George* the First, intituled, *An act for giving further encouragement for the importation of naval stores, and for other purposes therein mentioned,* of the growth, production, or manufacture, of any *British* colony or plantation in *America,* shall be there loaden on board any ship or vessel to be carried from thence, until sufficient bond shall be given, with one surety besides the master of the vessel, to the collector or other principal officer of the customs at the loading port, in a penalty of double the value of the goods, with condition, that the said goods shall not be landed in any part of *Europe* except *Great Britain.* . . .

XXIX. And, for the better preventing frauds in the importation or exportation of goods that are liable to the payment of duties, or are prohibited, in the *British* colonies or plantations in *America,* it is further enacted by the authority aforesaid, That . . . no goods, wares, or merchandizes, of any kind whatsoever, shall be shipped or laden on board any ship or vessel in any of the *British* colonies or plantations in *America,* to be carried from thence to any other *British* colony or plantation, without a sufferance or warrant first had and obtained from the collector or other proper officer of the customs at the port or place where such goods shall be intended to be put on board; and the master of every such ship or vessel shall, before the same be removed or carried out from the port or place where he takes in his lading, take out a cocket or cockets expressing the quantity and quality of the goods, and marks of the package, so laden, with the merchants names by whom shipped and to whom consigned . . . which cocket or cockets shall be produced by the master of such ship or vessel, to the collector or other principal officer of the customs at the port or place where such ship or vessel shall arrive in any of the *British* colonies or plantations in *America,* before any part of the goods are unladen or put on shore: and if any goods or merchandizes shall be shipped as aforesaid without such sufferance, or the vessel shall depart and proceed on her voyage without such cocket or cockets, or the goods shall be landed or put on shore before such cocket or cockets are produced at the port or place of discharge, or if the goods do not agree in all respects therewith, the goods in any or either of those cases, shall be forfeited and lost. . . .

XXX. . . . That . . . no ship or vessel shall, upon any pretence whatsoever, be cleared outwards from any port of this kingdom, for any land, island, plantation, colony, territory, or place, to his Majesty belonging, or which shall hereafter belong unto or be in the possession or under the dominion of his Majesty, his heirs, or successors, in *America,* unless the whole and entire cargo of such ship or vessel shall be *bona fide,* and without fraud, laden and shipped in this kingdom. . . .

XXXI. Provided always, That this act shall not extend, nor be construed to extend, to forfeit, for want of such cocket or clearance, any salt laden in *Europe* for the fisheries in *New England, Newfoundland, Pensylvania, New York,* and *Nova Scotia,* or any other place to which salt is or shall be allowed by law to be carried; wines laden in the *Madeiras,* of the growth thereof; and wines of the growth of the *Western Islands,* or *Azores,* and laden there; nor any horses, victuals, or linen cloth, of and from *Ireland,* which may be laden on board such ships or vessels. . . .

XXXVIII. And it is hereby further enacted by the authority aforesaid, That . . . if any officer of his Majesty's customs shall, directly or indirectly, take or receive any bribe, recompence, or reward, in any kind whatsoever; or connive at any false entry, or make any collusive seizure or agreement; or do any other act or deed whatsoever by which his Majesty, his heirs or successors, shall or may be defrauded in his or their duties, or whereby any goods prohibited shall be suffered to pass either inwards or outwards, or whereby the forfeitures and penalties inflicted by this or any other act of parliament relating to his Majesty's customs in *America* may be evaded; every such officer therein offending shall, for each and every offence, forfeit the sum of five hundred pounds, and be rendered incapable of serving his Majesty in any office or employment civil or military: and if any person or persons whatsoever shall give, offer, or promise to give, any bribe, recompense, or reward, to any officer of the customs, to do, conceal, or connive at, any act, whereby any of the provisions made by this or any other act of parliament relating to his Majesty's customs in *America* may be evaded or broken, every such person or persons shall, for each and every such offence (whether the same offer, proposal, or promise, be accepted or performed, or not) forfeit the sum of fifty pounds. . . .

XLI. . . . that all the forfeitures and penalties inflicted by this or any other act or acts of parliament relating to the trade and revenues of the said *British* colonies or plantations in *America,* which shall be incurred there, shall and may be prosecuted, sued for, and recovered in any court of record, or in any court of admiralty, in the said colonies or plantations where such offence shall be committed, or in any court of vice admiralty which may or shall be appointed over all *America* (which court of admiralty or vice admiralty are hereby respectively authorized and required to proceed, hear, and determine the same) at the election of the informer or prosecutor. . . .

XLV. And it is hereby further enacted by the authority aforesaid, That from and after the twenty ninth day of *September,* one thousand seven hundred and sixty four, if any ship or goods shall be seized for any cause of forfeiture, and any dispute shall arise whether the customs and duties for such goods have been paid, or the same have been lawfully imported or exported, or concerning the growth, product, or manufacture, of such goods, or the place from whence such goods were brought, then, and in such cases, the proof thereof shall lie upon the owner or claimer of such ship or goods, and not upon the officer who shall seize or stop the same; any law, custom, or usage, to the contrary notwithstanding.

XLVI. And be it further enacted by the authority aforesaid, That . . . in case any information shall be commenced and brought to trial in *America,* on account of any seizure of any ship or goods as forfeited by this or any other act of parliament relating to his Majesty's customs, wherein a verdict or sentence shall be given for the claimer thereof; and it shall appear to the judge or court before whom the same shall be tried, that there was a probable cause of seizure, the judge or court before whom the same shall be tried shall certify on the record or other proceedings, that there was a probable cause for the prosecutors seizing the said ship or goods; and, in such case, the defendant shall not be intitled to any costs of suit whatsoever; nor shall the persons who seized the said ship or goods, be liable to any action, or other suit or prosecution, on account of such seizure. . . .

D. PROHIBITION OF LEGAL—TENDER PAPER CURRENCY: THE CURRENCY ACT OF (APR. 19) 1764*

WHEREAS *great quantities of paper bills of credit have been created and issued in his Majesty's colonies or plantations in* America, *by virtue of acts, orders, resolutions, or votes of assembly, making and declaring such bills of credit to be legal tender in payment of money: and whereas such bills of credit have greatly depreciated in their value, by means whereof debts have been discharged with a much less value than was contracted for, to the great discouragement and prejudice of the trade and commerce of his Majesty's subjects, by occasioning confusion in dealings, and lessening credit in the said colonies or plantations:* for remedy whereof, may it please your most excellent Majesty, that it may be enacted; and be it enacted by the King's most excellent majesty, by and with the advice and consent of the lords spiritual and temporal, and commons, in this present parliament assembled, and by the authority of the same, That from and after the first day of *September,* one thousand seven hundred and sixty four, no act, order, resolution, or vote of assembly, in any of his Majesty's colonies or plantations in *America,* shall be made, for creating or issuing any paper bills, or bills of credit of any kind or denomination whatsoever, declaring such paper bills, or bills of credit, to be legal tender in payment of any bargains, contracts, debts, dues, or demands whatsoever; and every clause or provision which shall hereafter be inserted in any act, order, resolution, or vote of assembly, contrary to this act, shall be null and void.

II. And whereas the great quantities of paper bills, or bills of credit, which are now actually in circulation and currency in several colonies or plantations in *America,* emitted in pursuance of acts of assembly declaring such bills a legal tender, make it highly expedient that the conditions and terms, upon which such bills have been emitted, should not be varied or prolonged, so as to continue the legal tender thereof beyond the terms respectively fixed by such acts for calling in and discharging such bills; be it therefore enacted by the authority aforesaid, That every act, order, resolution, or vote of assembly, in any of the said colonies or plantations, which shall be made to prolong the legal tender of any paper bills, or bills of credit, which are now subsisting and current in any of the said colonies or plantations in *America,* beyond the times fixed for the calling in, sinking, and discharging of such paper bills, or bills of credit, shall be null and void.

III. And be it further enacted by the authority aforesaid, That if any governor or commander in chief for the time being, in all or any of the said colonies or plantations, shall, from and after the said first day of *September,* one thousand seven hundred and sixty four, give his assent to any act or order of assembly contrary to the true intent and meaning of this act, every such governor or commander in chief shall, for every such offence, forfeit and pay the sum of one thousand pounds, and shall be immediately dismissed from his government, and for ever after rendered incapable of any public office or place of trust.

* Reprinted in full from Pickering (ed.), *Statutes at Large,* vol. XXVI, pp. 103–105.

IV. Provided always, That nothing in this act shall extend to alter or repeal an act passed in the twenty fourth year of the reign of his late majesty King *George* the Second, intituled, *An act to regulate and restrain paper bills of credit in his Majesty's colonies or plantations of* Rhode Island *and* Providence *plantations,* Connecticut, *the* Massachuset's Bay, *and* New Hampshire, *in* America, *and to prevent the same being legal tenders in payments of money.*

V. Provided also, That nothing herein contained shall extend, or be construed to extend, to make any of the bills now subsisting in any of the said colonies a legal tender.

SELECTION

Colonial Response

All of the new measures encountered some opposition in the colonies. The restrictions upon Western settlement produced some grumbling among ambitious land speculators in Virginia, Maryland, and Pennsylvania; the decision to keep so large a contingent of British troops in the colonies alarmed many colonial leaders who, in the best English tradition, looked upon standing armies as the instruments of tyrants; and the paper-currency prohibition, although it threatened no immediate hardships because of the large quantities of paper issued in the colonies during the war, caused men in all of the colonies to which it applied to decry the long-range consequences of the money shortage that would inevitably occur with the retirement of the wartime emissions.

None of these measures, however, evoked such immediate and pronounced opposition as the new commercial regulations and, to an even greater extent, the program of parliamentary taxation of the colonies for revenue. Especially in the middle colonies and New England, where the trade regulations and revised sugar duties would have the most serious impact, the large overseas trading merchants complained bitterly about the Sugar Act, forecast total economic ruin for their respective colonies, and questioned the wisdom of a measure that would so impoverish the Americans as to limit drastically their ability to purchase English manufactures. More significantly for the future of the British Empire, the colonists also questioned the constitutionality of parliamentary taxation. In pamphlets and in official statements from their legislatures they attacked both the sugar duties and the stamp taxes proposed by First Minister George Grenville in March, 1764, when he introduced the resolutions that formed the basis for the Sugar Act.

The best known of these pamphlets was The Rights of the British Colonies Asserted and Proved, *written by James Otis (1725–1783), published in Boston in the summer of 1764, and here reprinted in part as Selection 3 A. A learned and eloquent lawyer, Otis was one of Boston's representatives to the Massachusetts*

House of Representatives. He was graduated from Harvard College in 1743, studied law with Jeremiah Gridley, the colony's leading lawyer, until 1748 when he established his own practice, and acquired a reputation as a successful lawyer by the middle of the 1750s. Disappointed by the failure of his father to obtain appointment as a judge of the superior court, young Otis became in the early 1750s the implacable and impassioned opponent of Governor Francis Bernard, the man chiefly responsible for the failure of his father's ambitions. At least partly as a result of this quarrel, Otis had already become known as a strong opponent of royal power in Massachusetts Bay, and it was entirely fitting that he should lead the attack in that colony on Parliament's authority to tax the colonies for revenue and that his pamphlet should be endorsed by a majority of the House of Representatives.

Otis built his case upon the premises that in every society absolute power resided originally in the "whole people" and that they could entrust it to whomever they wished. Because Britons had entrusted their absolute power to the King, Lords, and Commons assembled in Parliament it followed that Parliament had "supreme, sacred and uncontrollable legislative power, not only in the realm, but through the dominions." However supreme and uncontrollable its power might be, Parliament, nevertheless, could not act contrary to the laws of nature and could not violate so sacred and fundamental a maxim of that law and the British constitution as the right of every man to be taxed only by his representatives. Unless and until the colonists were represented in Parliament—a measure advocated by Otis, as well as Bernard—Parliament could not legally and constitutionally tax them. Because Parliament's authority in the colonies as well as in the realm was supreme, however, it had to be obeyed, and the only recourse of the colonists when faced with unconstitutional measures like the sugar and stamp taxes was to petition Parliament to reconsider its actions so that it could, once it had become aware of its errors, correct them.

A much more direct denial of Parliament's right to tax the colonies for revenue was contained in the petition of the New York General Assembly to the House of Commons adopted in October, 1764. Protesting the wisdom of the new trade restrictions, the expansion of the jurisdiction of the vice-admiralty courts, and the prohibition on legal-tender currency, the petition, most of which is reprinted below as Selection 3 B, was largely concerned with delimiting the boundaries of parliamentary authority in the colonies. It did not deny Parliament's jurisdiction over trade, but it emphatically asserted the right of its constituents "to an Exemption from the Burthen of all Taxes not granted by themselves" not "as a Privilege" but "as their Right," the "most essential of all the Rights to which they are intitled, as Colonists from, and connected, in the common Bond of Liberty, with the uninslaved Sons of Great-Britain." All taxes other than those required by "a necessary Regard to the particular Trade of Great-Britain" and hence purely regulatory and not revenue-producing in intent ought to be left, the petition stated unequivocally, "to the legislative Power of the Colony."

Bernhard Knollenberg, Origin of the American Revolution: 1759–1766 *(1960), contains a full discussion of the colonial reaction to the new British measures of 1763–1764, and Edmund S. Morgan and Helen M. Morgan,* The Stamp Act Crisis: Prologue to Revolution *(1953), briskly analyzes the initial colonial protest against the Sugar Act and proposed stamp duties. There is no adequate modern biography of James Otis, but Bernard Bailyn (ed.),* Pamphlets of the American Revolution, 1750–1776 *(1965), volume I (1750–1765), pages 409–417, includes an extended discussion of* The Rights of the British Colonies.

A. NO LEGISLATURE HAS A RIGHT TO MAKE ITSELF ARBITRARY: JAMES OTIS, "THE RIGHTS OF THE BRITISH COLONIES ASSERTED AND PROVED" (1764)*

Let no Man think I am about to commence advocate for *despotism,* because I affirm that government is founded on the necessity of our natures; and that an original supreme Sovereign, absolute, and uncontroulable, *earthly* power *must* exist in and preside over every society; from whose final decisions there can be no appeal but directly to Heaven. It is therefore *originally* and *ultimately* in the people. I say this supreme absolute power is *originally* and *ultimately* in the people; and they never did in fact *freely,* nor can they *rightfully* make an absolute, unlimited renunciation of this divine right. It is ever in the nature of the thing given in *trust,* and on a condition, the performance of which no mortal can dispence with; namely, that the person or persons on whom the sovereignty is confered by the people, shall *incessantly* consult *their* good. Tyranny of all kinds is to be abhored, whether it be in the hands of one, or of the few, or of the many.—And though "in the last age a generation of men sprung up that would flatter Princes with an opinion that *they* have a *divine right* to absolute power;" yet "slavery is so vile and miserable an estate of man, and so directly opposite to the generous temper and courage of our nation, that it is hard to be conceived that an *Englishman,* much less a *gentleman,* should plead for it:" Especially at a time when the finest writers of the most polite nations on the continent of *Europe,* are enraptured with the beauties of the civil constitution of *Great-Britain;* and envy her, no less for the *freedom* of her sons, than for her immense *wealth* and *military* glory.

But let the *origin* of government be placed where it may, the *end* of it is manifestly the good of *the whole. Salus populi suprema lex esto,* is of the law of nature, and part of that grand charter given the human race (though too many of them are afraid to assert it) by the only monarch in the universe, who has a clear and indisputable right to *absolute* power; because he is the *only* ONE who is *omniscient* as well as *omnipotent. . . .*

The *British* constitution in theory and in the present administration of it, in general comes nearest the idea of perfection, of any that has been reduced to practice; and if the principles of it are adhered to, it will, according to the infallible prediction of *Harrington,* always keep the *Britons* uppermost in *Europe,* 'till their *only* rival nation shall either embrace that perfect model of a commonwealth given us by that author, or come as near it as *Great-Britain* is. Then indeed, and not till then, will that rival and our nation either be eternal confederates, or contend in greater earnest than they have ever yet done, till one of them shall sink under the power of the other, and rise no more. . . .

Every British Subject born on the continent of America, or in any other of the British dominions, is by the law of God and nature, by the common law, and by act of parliament, (exclusive of all charters from the crown) entitled to all the natural, essential, inherent and inseparable rights of our fellow subjects in Great-Britain. Among those rights are the following, which it is humbly conceived no man or body of men, not excepting the parliament,

* These excerpts are reprinted from the second edition (1764), pp. 12–13, 21, 52–62, 70–72, 98–99.

justly, equitably and consistently with their own rights and the constitution, can take away.

1st. *That the supreme and subordinate powers of legislation should be free and sacred in the hands where the community have once rightfully placed them.*

2dly. *The supreme national legislative cannot be altered justly till the commonwealth is dissolved, nor a subordinate legislative taken away without forfeiture or other good cause.* Nor then can the subjects in the subordinate government be reduced to a state of slavery, and subject to the despotic rule of others. A state has no right to make slaves of the conquered. Even when the subordinate right of legislature is forfeited, and so declared, this cannot effect the natural persons either of those who were invested with it, or the inhabitants, so far as to deprive them of the rights of subjects and of men.— The colonists will have an equitable right, notwithstanding any such forfeiture of charter, to be represented in parliament, or to have some new subordinate legislature among themselves. It would be best if they had both. Deprived, however, of their common rights as subjects, they cannot lawfully be, while they remain such. A representation in Parliament from the several colonies, since they are become so large and numerous, as to be called on not only to maintain provincial government, civil and military, among themselves, for this they have chearfully done, but to contribute towards the support of a national standing army, by reason of the heavy national debt, when they themselves owe a large one, contracted in the common cause, cannot be thought an unreasonable thing, nor if asked, could it be called an immodest request. *Qui sentit commodum sentire debet et onus,* has been thought a maxim of equity. But that a man should bear a burthen for other people, as well as himself, without a return, never long found a place in any law-book or decrees, but those of the most despotic princes. Besides the equity of an American representation in parliament, a thousand advantages would result from it. It would be the most effectual means of giving those of both countries a thorough knowledge of each others interests; as well as that of the whole, which are inseparable.

Were this representation allowed; instead of the scandalous memorials and depositions that have been sometimes, in days of old, privately cooked up in an inquisitorial manner, by persons of bad minds and wicked views, and sent from America to the several boards, persons of the first reputation among their countrymen, might be on the spot, from the several colonies, truly to represent them. Future ministers need not, like some of their predecessors, have recourse for information in American affairs, to every vagabond stroller, that has run or rid post through America, from his creditors, or to people of no kind of reputation from the colonies; some of whom, at the time of administring their sage advice, have been as ignorant of the state of this country, as of the regions in Jupiter and Saturn.

No representation of the colonies in parliament alone, would, however, be equivalent to a subordinate legislative among themselves; nor so well answer the ends of increasing their prosperity and the commerce of Great-Britain. It would be impossible for the parliament to judge so well of their abilities to bear taxes, impositions on trade, and other duties and burthens, or of the local laws that might be really needful, as a legislative here.

3dly. *No legislative, supreme or subordinate, has a right to make itself arbitrary.*

It would be a most manifest contradiction, for a free legislative, like that of Great-Britain, to make itself arbitrary.

4thly. *The supreme legislative cannot justly assume a power of ruling by extempore arbitrary decrees, but is bound to dispense justice by known settled rules,* and by duly *authorized independent judges.*

5thly. *The supreme power cannot take from any man any part of his property,* without his consent in *person or by representation.*

6thly. *The legislative cannot transfer the power of making laws to any other hands.*

These are their bounds, which by God and nature are fixed, hitherto have they a right to come, and no further.

1. *To govern by stated laws.*
2. *Those laws should have no other end ultimately, but the good of the people.*
3. *Taxes are not to be laid on the people, but by their consent in person, or by deputation.*
4. *Their whole power is not transferable.*

These are the first principles of law and justice, and the great barriers of a free state, and of the British constitution in particular. I ask, I want no more—Now let it be shewn how it is reconcileable with these principles, or to many other fundamental maxims of the British constitution, as well as the natural and civil rights, which by the laws of their country, all British subjects are entitled to, as their best inheritance and birth-right, that all the northern colonies, who are without one representative in the house of Commons, should be taxed by the British parliament.

That the colonists, black and white, born here, are free born British subjects, and entitled to all the essential civil rights of such, is a truth not only manifest from the provincial charters, from the principles of the common law, and acts of parliament; but from the British constitution which was re-established at the revolution, with a professed design to secure the liberties of all the subjects to all generations.

In the 12 and 13 of Wm. cited above, the liberties of the subject are spoken of as their best birth-rights—No one ever dreamed, surely, that these liberties were confined to the realm. At that rate, no British subjects in the dominions could, without a manifest contradiction, be declared entitled to all the privileges of subjects born within the realm, to all intents and purposes, which are rightly given foreigners, by parliament, after residing seven years. These expressions of parliament, as well as of the charters, must be vain and empty sounds, unless we are allowed the essential rights of our fellow-subjects in Great-Britain.

Now can there be any liberty, where property is taken away without consent? Can it with any colour of truth, justice or equity, be affirmed, that the northern colonies are represented in parliament? Has this whole continent, of near three thousand miles in length, and in which, and his other American dominions, his Majesty has, or very soon will have, some millions of as good, loyal and useful subjects, white and black, as any in the three kingdoms, the election of one member of the house of commons?

Is there the least difference, as to the consent of the Colonists, whether taxes and impositions are laid on their trade, and other property, by the crown alone, or by the parliament? As it is agreed on all hands, the Crown alone cannot impose them, we should be justifiable in refusing to pay them, but must and ought to yield obedience to an act of parliament, though erroneous, till repealed.

I can see no reason to doubt, but that the imposition of taxes, whether on trade, or on land, or houses, or ships, on real or personal, fixed or floating property, in the colonies, is absolutely irreconcileable with the rights of the Colonists, as British subjects, and as men. I say men, for in a state of nature, no man can take my property from me, without my consent: If he does, he deprives me of my liberty, and makes me a slave. If such a proceeding is a breach of the law of nature, no law of society can make it just. —The very act of taxing, exercised over those who are not represented, appears to me to be depriving them of one of their most essential rights, as freemen; and if continued, seems to be in effect an entire disfranchisement of every civil right. For what one civil right is worth a rush, after a man's property is subject to be taken from him at pleasure, without his consent? If a man is not his *own assessor* in person, or by deputy, his liberty is gone, or lays intirely at the mercy of others.

I think I have heard it said, that when the Dutch are asked why they enslave their colonies, their answer is, that the liberty of Dutchmen is confined to Holland; and that it was never intended for Provincials in America, or any where else. A sentiment this, very worthy of modern Dutchmen; but if their brave and worthy ancestors had entertained such narrow ideas of liberty, seven poor and distressed provinces would never have asserted their rights against the whole Spanish monarchy, of which the present is but a shadow. It is to be hoped, none of our fellow subjects of Britain, great or small, have borrowed this Dutch maxim of plantation politics; if they have, they had better return it from whence it came; indeed they had. Modern Dutch or French maxims of state, never will suit with a British constitution. It is a maxim, that the King can do no wrong; and every good subject is bound to believe his King is not inclined to do any. We are blessed with a prince who has given abundant demonstrations, that in all his actions, he studies the good of his people, and the true glory of his crown, which are inseparable. It would therefore be the highest degree of impudence and disloyalty to imagine that the King, at the head of his parliament, could have any, but the most pure and perfect intentions of justice, goodness and truth, that human nature is capable of. All this I say and believe of the King and parliament, in all their acts; even in that which so nearly affects the interest of the colonists; and that a most perfect and ready obedience is to be yielded to it, while it remains in force. I will go further, and really admit, that the intention of the ministry was not only to promote the public good, by this act, but that Mr. Chancellor of the Exchequer had therein a particular view to the "ease, the quiet, and the good will of the Colonies," he having made this declaration more than once. Yet I hold that it is possible he may have erred in his kind intentions towards the Colonies, and taken away our fish, and given us a stone. With regard to the parliament, as infalibility belongs not to mortals, it is possible *they* may have been misinformed and deceived. The power of parliament is uncontroulable, but by themselves, and we must obey. They only can repeal their own acts. There would be an end of all government, if one or a number of subjects or subordinate provinces should take upon them so far to judge of the justice of an act of parliament, as to refuse obedience to it. If there was nothing else to restrain such a step, prudence ought to do it, for forcibly resisting the parliament and the King's laws, is high treason. Therefore let the parliament lay what burthens they please on us, we must, it is our duty to submit and patiently bear them, till they will be pleased to relieve us. And it is to be presumed, the wisdom and justice of that august assembly, always will afford us relief by repealing such acts, as through mistake, or other human infirmities, have been suffered to pass, if they can be convinced that their proceedings are not constitutional, or not for the common good. . . .

Every subject has a right to give his sentiments to the public, of the utility or inutility of any act whatsoever, even after it is passed, as well as while it is pending.—The equity and justice of a bill may be questioned, with perfect submission to the legislature. Reasons may be given, why an act ought to be repealed, and yet obedience must be yielded to it till that repeal takes place. If the reasons that can be given against an act, are such as plainly demonstrate that it is against *natural* equity, the executive courts will adjudge such acts void. It may be questioned by some, though I make no doubt of it, whether they are not obliged by their oaths to adjudge such acts void. If there is not a right of private judgment to be exercised, so far at least as to petition for a repeal, or to determine the expediency of risking a trial at law, the parliament might make itself arbitrary, which it is conceived it cannot by the constitution.—I think every man has a right to examine as freely into the origin, spring and foundation of every power and measure in a commonwealth, as into a piece of curious machinery, or a remarkable phenomenon in nature; and that it ought to give no more offence to say, the parliament have erred, or are mistaken, in a matter of fact, or of right, than to say it of a private man, if it is true of both. If the assertion can be proved with regard to either, it is a kindness done them to shew them the truth. With regard to the public, it is the duty of every good citizen to point out what he thinks erroneous in the commonwealth. . . .

To say the parliament is absolute and arbitrary, is a contradiction. The parliament cannot make 2 and 2, 5: Omnipotency cannot do it. The supreme power in a state, is *jus dicere* only:—*jus dare,* strictly speaking, belongs alone to God. Parliaments are in all cases to *declare* what is for the good of the whole; but it is not the *declaration* of parliament that makes it so: There must be in every instance, a higher authority, *viz.* GOD. Should an act of parliament be against any of *his* natural laws, which are *immutably* true, *their* declaration would be contrary to eternal truth, equity and justice, and consequently void: and so it would be adjudged by the parliament itself, when convinced of their mistake. Upon this great principle, parliaments repeal such act, as soon as they find they have been mistaken, in having declared them to be for the public good, when in fact they were not so. When such mistake is evident and palpable, as in the instances in the appendix, the judges of the executive courts have declared the act "of a whole parliament void." See here the grandeur of the British constitution! See the wisdom of our ancestors! The supreme *legislative,* and the supreme *executive,* are a perpetual check and balance to each other. If the supreme executive errs, it is informed by the supreme legislative in parliament: if the supreme legislative errs, it is informed by the supreme executive in the King's courts of law. Here, the King appears, as represented by his judges, in the highest lustre and majesty, as supreme executor of the commonwealth; and he never shines brighter, but on his throne, at the head of the supreme legislative. This is government! This, is a constitution! to preserve which, either from foreign or domestic foes, has cost oceans of blood and treasure in every age; and the blood and the treasure have upon the whole been well spent. British America, hath been bleeding in this cause from its settlement: we have spent all we could raise, and more; for notwithstanding the parliamentary reimbursements of part, we still remain much in debt. The province of the *Massachusetts*, I believe, has expended more men and money in war since the year 1620, when a few families first landed at Plymouth, in proportion to their ability, than the three Kingdoms together. The same, I believe, may be truly affirmed, of many of the other colonies; though the *Massachusetts* has undoubtedly had the heaviest burthen. This may be thought incredible: but materials are collecting; and though some are lost, enough may remain, to demonstrate it to the world. I have reason to hope at least, that the public will soon see such proofs exhibited, as will shew, that I do not speak quite at random. . . .

The sum of my argument is, That civil government is of God: that the administrators of it were originally the whole people: that they might have devolved it on whom they pleased: that this devolution is fiduciary, for the good of the whole: that by the British constitution, this devolution is on the King, lords and commons, the supreme, sacred and uncontroulable legislative power, not only in the realm, but through the dominions: that by the abdication, the original compact was broken to pieces: that by the revolution, it was renewed, and more firmly established, and the rights and liberties of the subject in all parts of the dominions, more fully explained and confirmed: that in consequence of this establishment and the acts of succession and union, his Majesty GEORGE III. is rightful king and sovereign, and with his parliament, the supreme legislative of Great-Britain, France and Ireland, and the dominions thereunto belonging: that this constitution is the most free one, and by far the best, now existing on earth: that by this constitution, every man in the dominions is a free man: that no parts of his Majesty's dominions can be taxed without their consent: that every part has a right to be represented in the supreme or some subordinate legislature: that the refusal of this, would seem to be a contradiction in practice to the theory of the constitution: that the colonies are subordinate dominions, and are now in such a state, as to make it best for the good of the whole, that they should not only be continued in the enjoyment of subordinate legislation, but be also represented in some proportion to their number and estates in the grand legislation of the nation: that this would firmly unite all parts of the British empire, in the greatest peace and prosperity; and render it invulnerable and perpetual.

B. EXEMPTION FROM PARLIAMENTARY TAXATION, A RIGHT, NOT A PRIVILEGE: THE NEW YORK PETITION TO THE HOUSE OF COMMONS (OCT. 18, 1764)*

THAT from the Year 1683, to this Day, there have been three Legislative Branches in this Colony; consisting of the Governor and Council appointed

* These excerpts are reprinted from *Journal of the Votes and Proceedings of the General Assembly of the Colony of New-York* (1766), vol. II, pp. 776–779.

by the Crown, and the Representatives chosen by the People, who, besides the Power of making Laws for the Colony, have enjoyed the Right of Taxing the Subject for the Support of the Government.

Under this Political Frame, the Colony was settled by Protestant Emigrants from several Parts of *Europe,* and more especially from *Great-Britain* and *Ireland:* And as it was originally modelled with the Intervention of the Crown, and not excepted to by the Realm of *England* before, nor by *Great- Britain,* since the Union, the Planters, and Settlers conceived the strongest Hopes, that the Colony had gained a civil Constitution, which, so far at least as the Rights and Privileges of the People were concerned, would remain permanent, and be transmitted to their latest Posterity.

It is therefore with equal Concern and Surprize, that they have received Intimations of certain Designs lately formed, if possible, to induce the Parliament of *Great-Britain,* to impose Taxes upon the Subjects *here,* by Laws to be passed *there;* and as we who have the Honour to represent them, conceive that this Innovation, will greatly affect the Interest of the Crown and the Nation, and reduce the Colony to absolute Ruin; it became our indispensible Duty, to trouble you with a seasonable Representation of the Claim of our Constituents, to an Exemption from the Burthen of all Taxes not granted by themselves, and their Foresight of the tragical Consequences of an Adoption of the contrary Principle, to the Crown, the Mother Country, themselves and their Posterity.

Had the Freedom from all Taxes not granted by ourselves been enjoyed as a *Privilege,* we are confident the Wisdom and Justice of the *British* Parliament, would rather establish than destroy it, unless by our abuse of it, the Forfeiture was justly incurred; but his Majesty's Colony of *New-York,* can not only defy the whole World to impeach their Fidelity, but appeal to all the Records of their past Transactions, as well for the fullest Proof of their steady Affection to the Mother Country, as for their strenuous Efforts to support the Government, and advance the general Interest of the whole *British* Empire.

It has been their particular Misfortune, to be always most exposed to the Incursions of the *Canadians,* and the more barbarous Irruptions of the Savages of the Desert, as may appear by all the Maps of this Country; and in many Wars we have suffered an immense Loss both of Blood and Treasure, to repel the Foe, and maintain a valuable Dependency upon the *British* Crown.

On no Occasion can we be justly reproached for with-holding a necessary Supply, our Taxes have been equal to our Abilities, and confessed to be so by the Crown; for Proof of which we refer to the Speeches of our Governors in all Times of War; and though we remember with great Gratitude, that in those grand and united Struggles, which were lately directed for the Conquest of *Canada,* Part of our Expenses was reimbursed, yet we cannot suppress the Remark, that our Contribution surpassed our Strength, even in the Opinion of the Parliament, who under that Conviction, thought it but just to take off Part of the Burthen, to which we had loyally and voluntarily submitted; in a Word, if there is any Merit in facilitating on all Occasions, the publick Measures in the remote Extremes of the national Dominion, and in preserving untainted Loyalty and chearful Obedience, it is ours; and (with Submission) unabused, nay more, well improved Privileges cannot, ought not, to be taken away from any People.

But an Exemption from the Burthen of ungranted, involuntary Taxes, must be the grand Principle of every free State.—Without such a Right vested in themselves, exclusive of all others, there can be no Liberty, no Happiness, no Security; it is inseparable from the very Idea of Property, for who can call that his own, which may be taken away at the Pleasure of another? And so evidently does this appear to be the natural Right of Mankind, that even conquered tributary States, though subject to the Payment of a fixed periodical Tribute, never were reduced to so abject and forlorn a Condition, as to yield to all the Burthens which their Conquerors might at any future Time think fit to impose. The Tribute paid, the Debt was discharged; and the Remainder they could call their own.

And if conquered Vassals upon the Principle even of *natural Justice,* may claim a Freedom from Assessments unbounded and unassented to, without which they would sustain the Loss of every Thing, and Life itself become intolerable, with how much Propriety and Boldness may we proceed to inform the Commons of *Great-Britain,* who, to their distinguished Honour, have in all Ages asserted the Liberties of Mankind, that the People of this Colony inspired by the Genius of their Mother Country, nobly disdain the thought of claiming that Exemption as *a Privilege.*—They found it on a Basis more honourable, solid and stable; they challenge it, and glory in it as their Right. That Right their Ancestors enjoyed in *Great-Britain* and *Ireland;* their Descendants returning to those Kingdoms, enjoy it again: And that it may be exercised by his Majesty's Subjects at Home, and justly denied to those who submitted to Poverty, Barbarian Wars, Loss of Blood, Loss of Money, personal Fatigues, and ten Thousand unutterable Hardships, to enlarge the Trade, Wealth, and Dominion of the Nation; or, to speak with the most unexceptionable Modesty, that when *as Subjects,* all have equal Merit; a Fatal, nay the most odious Discrimination should nevertheless be made between them, no Sophistry can recommend to the Sober, impartial Decision of common Sense.

Our Constituents exult in that glorious Model of Government, of which your Hon. House is so essential a Part; and earnestly pray the Almighty Governor of all, long to support the due Distribution of the Power of the Nation in the three great Legislative Branches. But the Advocates for divesting us of the Right to tax ourselves, would by the Success of their Machination; render the Devolution of all civil Power upon the *Crown alone,* a Government more favourable, and therefore more eligible to these *American* Dependences. The supreme Ruler in a Monarchy, even in a despotic Monarchy, will naturally consider his Relation to be, what it is, equal to all his good Subjects: An equal Dispensation of Favours will be the natural Consequence of those Views; and the Increase of mutual Affection must be productive of an Increase of the Felicity of *all.* But no History can furnish an Instance of a Constitution to permit one Part of a Dominion to be taxed by another, and that too in Effect, but by a Branch of that other Part; who in all Bills for public Aids, suffer not the least Alteration.—And if such an absurd and unequal Constitution should be adopted, who, that considers the natural Reluctance of Mankind to burthens, and their Inclination to cast them upon the Shoulders of others, cannot foresee, that while the People on one Side of the *Atlantic,* enjoy an Exemption from the Load, those on the other, must submit to the most unsupportable Oppression and Tyranny.

Against these Evils, the Indulgence of the present Parliament, of which we have had such large Experience, cannot provide, if the grand Right to tax ourselves is invaded. Depressed by the Prospect of an endless Train of the most distressing Mischiefs, naturally attendant upon such an Innovation, his Majesty's *American* Subjects, will think it no inconsiderable Augmentation of their Misery, that the Measure itself implies the most severe and unmerited Censure, and is urged, as far as they are acquainted, by no good Reasons of State.

They are unconscious of any Conduct, that brings the least Imputation upon their Love and Loyalty, and whoever has accused them, has abused both the Colonies and their Mother Country; more faithful Subjects his Majesty has not, in any Part of his Dominions, nor *Britain* more submissive and affectionate Sons.

And if our Contributions to the Support of the Government upon this Continent, or for the Maintenance of an Army, to awe and subdue the Savages should be thought necessary, why shall it be presumed, without a Trial, that we more than others, will refuse to hearken to a just Requisition from the Crown? To Requisitions for Aids salutary to our own Interests? Or why should a more incorrigible and unreasonable Spirit be imputed to us, than to the Parliament of *Ireland,* or any other of his Majesty's Subjects?

Left to the Enjoyment of our antient Rights, the Government will be truly informed when a Tax is necessary, and of the Abilities of the People; and there will be an equitable Partition of the Burthen. And as the publick Charges will necessarily increase with the Increase of the Country, and the Augmentation or Reduction of the Force kept up, be regulated by the Power and Temper of our barbarian Enemy, the Necessity for continuing the present Model must appear to be most strongly inforced.—At the remote Distance of the *British* Commons from the sequestered Shades of the interior Parts of this Desart, false Intelligence of the State of the *Indians* may be given; whereas the Vicinity of the Colonies will enable them, not only, to detect all false Alarms, and check all fraudulent Accounts, but urge them by the never failing Motive of Self-Preservation, to oppose any hostile Attempts upon their Borders.

Nor will the Candour of the Commons of *Great Britain,* construe our Earnestness to maintain this Plea, to arise from a Desire of Independency upon the supreme Power of the Parliament. Of so extravagant a Disregard to our own Interests we cannot be guilty.—From what other Quarter can we hope for Protection? We reject the Thought with the utmost Abhorrence; and a perfect Knowledge of this Country will afford the fullest Proof, that nothing in our Temper can give the least Ground for such a Jealousy.

The peaceable and invariable Submission of the Colonies, for a Century past, forbids the Imputation, or proves it a Calumny.—What can be more apparent, than that the State which exercises a Sovereignty in Commerce, can draw all the Wealth of its Colonies into its own Stock? And has not the whole Trade of *North-America,* that growing Magazine of Wealth, been, from the Beginning, directed, restrained ,and prohibited at the sole Pleasure of the Parliament? And whatever some may pretend, his Majesty's *American* Subjects are far from a Desire to invade the just Rights of *Great-Britain,* in all commercial Regulations. They humbly conceive, that a very manifest Distinction presents itself, which, while it leaves to the Mother Country an incontestible Power, to give Laws for the Advancement of her own Commerce, will, at the same Time, do no Violence to the Rights of the Plantations.

The Authority of the Parliament of *Great-Britain,* to model the Trade of the whole Empire, so as to subserve the Interest of her own, we are ready to recognize in the most extensive and positive Terms. Such a Preference is naturally founded upon her Superiority, and indissolubly connected with the Principle of Self-Preservation.—And therefore, to assign one Instance, instead of many, the Colonies cannot, would not ask for a Licence to import woolen Manufactures from *France;* or to go into the most lucrative Branches of Commerce, in the least Degree incompatible with the Trade and Interest of *Great-Britain.*

But a Freedom to drive all Kinds of Traffick in a Subordination to, and not inconsistent with, the *British* Trade; and an Exemption from all Duties in such a Course of Commerce, is humbly claimed by the Colonies, as the most essential of all the Rights to which they are intitled, as Colonists from, and connected, in the common Bond of Liberty, with the uninslaved Sons of *Great-Britain.*

For, with Submission, since all Impositions, whether they be internal Taxes, or Duties paid, for what we consume, equally diminish the Estates upon which they are charged; what avails it to any People, by which of them they are impoverished? Every Thing will be given up to preserve Life; and though there is a Diversity in the Means, yet, the whole Wealth of a Country may be as effectually drawn off, by the Exaction of Duties, as by any other Tax upon their Estates.

And therefore, the General Assembly of *New-York,* in Fidelity to their Constituents, cannot but express the most earnest Supplication, that the Parliament will charge our Commerce with no other Duties, than a necessary Regard to the particular Trade of *Great-Britain,* evidently demands; but leave it to the legislative Power of the Colony, to impose all other Burthens upon it's own People, which the publick Exigences may require.

Latterly, the Laws of Trade seem to have been framed without an Attention to this fundamental Claim.

Permit us, also, in Defence of our Attachment to the Mother Country, to add, what your Merchants (to whom we boldly make the Appeal) know to be an undoubted Truth; that this Continent contains some of the *most useful* of her Subjects.—Such is the Nature of our Produce, that all we acquire is less than sufficient to purchase what we want of your Manufactures; and, be the Policy of your Commerce what it will, all our Riches must flow into *Great-Britain.*—Immense have been our Contributions to the National Stock.—Our Staple, Industry, Trade and Wealth, all conduce to the particular Advantage of our fellow Subjects there.—The natural State of this Country, necessarily forms the Ballance of Trade in her Favour.— Her growing Opulence must elevate her above all Fear and Jealousy of these Dependences. How much stronger then the Reasons for leaving us free from ungranted Impositions? Whoever will give full Scope to his Meditations on this Topic, will see it the Interest of *Great-Britain,* to adopt the Maxim, that her own Happiness is most intimately connected with the Freedom, Ease and Prosperity of her Colonies: The more extensive our Traffick, the Greater her Gains; we carry all to her Hive, and consume the Returns; and we are content with any constitutional Regulation that inriches her, though it impoverishes ourselves. But a fuller Display of these Principles, being prepared by our Merchants, to be laid before the honourable House, at the last Sitting, we shall only beg Leave to add, that any Information, repugnant to this Account of the low State of our Traffick, must proceed from partial, or incompetent Witnesses; who may have formed their Estimate of the Wealth of the Colony, during the late War, when the *French* and *Spanish West-Indies,* were laid open to our Trade, and those immense Profits acquired there, for the Manufactures of *Great-Britain* and *Ireland,* flowed into the Colonies, and Luxury advanced upon us slower than our Gains.—But Trade being now confined to it's old Channels, and indeed still more restricted, and the late acquired Cash, remitted home for necessary Cloathing, other very indifferent Appearances begin to take place, and the *British* Merchants are, or will soon be convinced to their Sorrow, that our Splendor was not supported by solid Riches.

The honourable House will permit us to observe next, that the Act of the last Session of Parliament, inhibiting all Intercourse between the Continent and the foreign Sugar Colonies, will prove equally detrimental to us and *Great-Britain.—That* Trade, gave a value to a vast, but now alas unsaleable Staple, which being there converted into Cash and Merchandize, made necessary Remittances for the *British* Manufactures we consumed:—The same Law contains a Clause unfriendly to the Linen Manufactory in *Ireland,* for the Restraint upon the Exportation of Lumber to that Kingdom, prevents even our dunnaging the Flax-Seed Casks sent there with Staves.—And when we consider the Wisdom of our Ancestors in contriving Trials by Juries, we cannot stifle our Regret, that the Laws of Trade in general, change the Current of Justice from the common Law, and subject Controversies of the utmost Importance to the Decisions of the Vice-Admiralty Courts, who proceed not according the old wholesom Laws of the Land, nor are always filled with Judges of approved Knowledge and Integrity.—To this Objection, the aforementioned Statute will at first View appear to be so evidently open, that we shall content ourselves with barely suggesting, that the amazing Confidence it reposes in the Judges, gives great Grief to his Majesty's *American* Subjects; and pass on to a few Remarks on that other Law of the same Session, which renders our Paper Money no legal Tender.

The Use of this Sort of Currency in procuring a speedy Supply on Emergencies, all the Colonies have often experienced.—We have had Recourse to this Expedient in every War, since the Reign of King *William* the Third; and without it we could not have co-operated so vigorously in the Reduction of *Canada,* that grand stroke which secured to *Great-Britain,* the immense Dominion of the Continent of *North-America.* We had no other Alternative but *that,* or the taking up Money upon Loan, Lenders could not have been easily found, and if they were, the Interest upon all the Sums raised in that Way, would have exceeded our Ability now to discharge. Happy for us, therefore, that we fell upon the Project of giving a Credit to Paper, which was always supported by seasonable Taxes on our Estates; the Currency of the Bills being prolonged only till we were able to burn up the Quantity from Time to Time emitted.—Our Laws, or the Copies transmitted to the Plantation Office, will evince that of the numerous Emissions we have made since the first, which was on the 8th of *June,* 1709, all were for the urgent Service of the Crown.—One Instance is so recent, and shows the Necessity of the Continuation of such a Power in the Colonies, in so striking a Point of Light, that it deserves more particular Notice. The Operations of the

Year 1759, were nearly at a Stand for want of Money. The military Chest being exhausted, the General was alarmed, and seeing no other Method to ward of the impending Disaster, was obliged to ask the Colony for a Loan of *One Hundred and Fifty Thousand Pounds:* We immediately gratified his Request.—Such was our Concern for the publick Weal! We wish his Majesty's Service may suffer no Impediment, by this new Restraint in an Article which has been of so much Utility.—The Traffick of the Colony certainly will, for want of a competent Medium; and on that Account, and in behalf of those miserable Debtors, whose Estates, through the Scarcity of legal Cash, must be extended by Executions, and hastily sold beneath their true Value, to the Ruin of many Families, permit us to implore your tender Commiseration.

The General Assembly of this Colony have no desire to derogate from the Power of the Parliament of *Great-Britain;* but they cannot avoid deprecating the Loss of such Rights as they have hitherto enjoyed, Rights established in the first Dawn of our Constitution, founded upon the most substantial Reasons, confirmed by invariable Usage, conducive to the best Ends; never abused to bad Purposes, and with the Loss, of which Liberty, Property, and all the Benefits of Life, tumble into Insecurity and Ruin: Rights, the Deprivation of which, will dispirit the People, abate their Industry, discourage Trade, introduce Discord, Poverty and Slavery; or, by depopulating the Colonies, turn a vast, fertile, prosperous Region, into a dreary Wilderness; impoverish *Great-Britain,* and shake the Power and Independency of the most opulent and flourishing Empire in the World. . . .

PART

Stamp Act Crisis

New Revenue Measures

Parliament paid scant attention to the colonial protests against the Sugar Act and the proposed stamp duties. From the behavior of First Minister George Grenville it is clear, in fact, that he had already decided to levy the stamp duties in 1764 and had postponed them for a year only to permit his staff to gather the data necessary to prepare the bill. Although in 1764 he offered to entertain an alternative scheme for the colonies to tax themselves, he never communicated this offer to officials in the colonies or formulated it in terms precise enough to permit definite action despite repeated efforts by the agents representing the colonies in London to induce him to do so. By early 1765 the Stamp Act was ready, and on February 6 Grenville reminded the House of Commons of his proposal of the previous year. A spirited debate followed, but Grenville obtained leave by a large majority to present the bill. Refusing to hear petitions against the bill on the grounds that it was a violation of parliamentary privilege to receive petitions against money bills, Parliament approved the measure, and on March 22 it became law. The preamble and the clause stipulating how the revenue arising from the stamp duties was to be employed are printed below as Selection 4 A.

At the same session Parliament passed the Quartering Act which set down the regulations requiring the housing of British troops in America. Although the act did not directly levy a tax upon the colonies, it did so indirectly in Sections VII and VIII by requiring the colonies to furnish provisions and necessaries for troops quartered in them. The most important provisions of the act are reprinted here as Selection 4 B.

Edmund S. Morgan, "The Postponement of the Stamp Act," William and Mary Quarterly, *third series, volume 7 (1950), pages 353–392, discusses Grenville's motives in delaying the Stamp Act; Edmund S. Morgan and Helen M. Morgan,* The Stamp Act Crisis: Prologue to Revolution *(1953), treats the details surrounding the passage of the act; and John Shy,* Toward Lexington: The Role of the British Army in the Coming of the American Revolution *(1965), describes the background and workings of the Quartering Act.*

A. DIRECT TAXATION: THE STAMP ACT (MAR. 22, 1765)*

WHEREAS *by an act made in the last session of parliament, several duties were granted, continued, and appropriated, towards defraying the expences of defending, protecting, and securing, the British colonies and plantations in America: and whereas it is just and necessary, that provision be made for*

---

* These excerpts are reprinted from Danby Pickering (ed.), *Statutes at Large*, vol. XXVI, pp. 179, 201.

raising a further revenue within your Majesty's dominions in America, towards defraying the said expences . . . be it enacted . . . That from and after
the first day of *November*, one thousand seven hundred and sixty five, there
shall be raised, levied, collected, and paid unto his Majesty, his heirs, and
successors, throughout the colonies and plantations in *America* which now
are, or hereafter may be, under the dominion of his Majesty, his heirs and
successors . . . [stamp duties on legal papers, commercial papers, liquor
licences, land instruments, indentures, cards, dice, pamphlets, newspapers,
advertisements, almanacs, academic degrees, and appointments to office].

LIV. And be it further enacted by the authority aforesaid, That all the
monies which shall arise by the several rates and duties hereby granted
(except the necessary charges or raising, collecting, recovering, answering,
paying, and accounting for the same, and the necessary charges from time
to time incurred in relation to this act, and the execution thereof) shall be
paid into the receipt of his Majesty's exchequer, and shall be entered separate and apart from all other monies, and shall be there reserved to be from
time to time disposed of by parliament, towards further defraying the necessary expences of defending, protecting, and securing, the said colonies and
plantations. . . .

B. INDIRECT TAXATION:
THE QUARTERING ACT (MAY 15, 1765)*

WHEREAS *in and by an act made in the present session of parliament,
intituled,* An act for punishing mutiny and desertion, and for the better
payment of the army and their quarters; *several regulations are made and
enacted for the better government of the army, and their observing strict
discipline, and for providing quarters for the army, and carriages on marches
and other necessary occasions, and inflicting penalties on offenders against
the same act, and for many other good purposes therein mentioned; but the
same may not be sufficient for the forces that may be employed in his
Majesty's dominions in* America: *and whereas, during the continuance of the
said act, there may be occasion for marching and quartering of regiments
and companies of his Majesty's forces in several parts of his Majesty's
dominions in* America: *and whereas the publick houses and barracks, in his
Majesty's dominions in* America, *may not be sufficient to supply quarters for
such forces: and whereas it is expedient and necessary that carriages and
other conveniencies, upon the march of troops in his Majesty's dominions in*
America, *should be supplied for that purpose:* be it enacted by the King's
most excellent majesty, by and with the advice and consent of the lords
spiritual and temporal, and commons, in this present parliament assembled,
and by the authority of the same, That for and during the continuance of
this act, and no longer, it shall and may be lawful to and for the constables,

* These excerpts are reprinted from Pickering (ed.), *Statutes at Large,* vol.
XXVI, pp. 305–309.

tithingmen, magistrates, and other civil officers of villages, towns, townships, cities, districts, and other places, within his Majesty's dominions in *America* . . . to quarter and billet the officers and soldiers, in his Majesty's service, in the barracks provided by the colonies; and if there shall not be sufficient room in the said barracks for the officers and soldiers, then and in such case only, to quarter and billet the residue of such officers and soldiers, for whom there shall not be room in such barracks, in inns, livery stables, ale-houses, victualling-houses, and the houses of sellers of wine by retail to be drank in their own houses or places thereunto belonging, and all houses of persons selling of rum, brandy, strong water, cyder or metheglin, by retail, to be drank in houses; and in case there shall not be sufficient room for the officers and soldiers in such barracks, inns, victualling and other publick alehouses, that in such and no other case, and upon no other account, it shall and may be lawful for the governor and council of each respective province in his Majesty's dominions in *America,* to authorize and appoint to take, hire, and make fit for the reception of his Majesty's forces, such and so many uninhabited houses, outhouses, barns, or other buildings, as shall be necessary, to quarter therein the residue of such officers and soldiers for whom there should not be room in such barracks and publick houses as aforesaid, and to put and quarter the residue of such officers and soldiers therein. . . .

V. Provided nevertheless, and it is hereby enacted, That the officers and soldiers so quartered and billeted as aforesaid (except such as shall be quartered in the barracks, and hired uninhabited houses, or other buildings as aforesaid) shall be received and furnished with diet, and small beer, cyder, or rum mixed with water, by the owners of the inns, livery stables, alehouses, victualling-houses, and other houses in which they are allowed to be quartered and billeted by this act; paying and allowing for the same the several rates herein after mentioned to be payable, out of the subsistence-money, for diet and small beer, cyder, or rum mixed with water. . . .

VII. And whereas there are several barracks in several places in his Majesty's said dominions in *America,* or some of them, provided by the colonies, for the lodging and covering of soldiers in lieu of quarters, for the ease and conveniency as well of the inhabitants of and in such colonies, as of the soldiers; it is hereby further enacted, That all such officers and soldiers, so put and placed in such barracks, or in hired uninhabited houses, out-houses, barns, or other buildings, shall, from time to time, be furnished and supplied there by the persons to be authorized or appointed for that purpose by the governor and council of each respective province . . . with fire, candles, vinegar, and salt, bedding, utensils for dressing their victuals, and small beer or cyder, not exceeding five pints, or half a pint of rum mixed with a quart of water, to each man, without paying any thing for the same. That the respective provinces shall pay unto such person or persons all such sum or sums of money so by them paid, laid out, or expended, for the taking, hiring, and fitting up, such uninhabited houses, out-houses, barns, or other buildings, and for furnishing the officers and soldiers therein, and in the barracks, with fire, candles, vinegar, and salt, bedding, utensils for dressing victuals, and small beer, cyder, or rum, as aforesaid; and such sum or sums are hereby required to be raised, in such manner as the publick charges for the provinces respectively are raised. . . .

Debate over Parliament's Right to Tax the Colonies

Passage of the Stamp Act was the signal for a full-scale debate over the extent of parliamentary authority over the colonies. In early 1765, even before the Stamp Act had been passed, various writers rushed into print with pamphlets and newspaper essays answering American writers such as Otis, denying the validity of the constitutional claims of the American assemblies, and defending Parliament's right to tax the colonies. The most elaborate and best argued of these was The Regulations Lately Made, *written by no less a personage than Thomas Whately (d. 1772), M.P. for Ludgershall, secretary to the treasury, confidant of George Grenville, and principal author of the Stamp Act. Nearly one hundred pages of Whately's pamphlet were a defense of the Sugar Act as a regulatory measure, but in the last section, reprinted below as Selection 5 A, he sought to counter the American arguments against the constitutionality of parliamentary taxation. Agreeing that no Englishman could be taxed without the consent of his representatives, he argued that colonists, like the vast majority of residents in the home islands who did not vote for representatives to the House of Commons, were* virtually, *if not* actually, *represented in Parliament and that members of Parliament represented not just the constituency they sat for—not merely the voters who participated in their election—but the whole of the British world.*

Echoed by other English writers, the virtual-representation argument got a cool reception in the colonies, where there was a rash of newspaper essays and pamphlets seeking to refute it. The most famous and effective of these pamphlets, Considerations on the Propriety of Imposing Taxes in the British Colonies, for the Purpose of Raising a Revenue, by Act of Parliament, *was by Daniel Dulany (1722–1797), an English-educated lawyer and member of the Proprietary Council in Maryland since 1757. In this pamphlet Dulany admitted that the concept of virtual representation might be applicable to Great Britain, where the "interests . . . of the non-electors, the electors, and the representatives are individually the same." Because there was "not that intimate and inseparable relation between the electors of Great-Britain, and the Inhabitants of the colonies, which must inevitably involve both in the same taxation," however, he denied that it was valid for the colonies. Unlike Otis, Dulany did not advocate colonial representation in Parliament to put an end to this dilemma. Rather, he proposed to delineate the constitutional boundaries between the authority of Parliament and that of the colonial legislatures. In contrast to Whately, who had argued that taxation and legislation were inseparable and that Englishmen could not be bound by any laws (whether they were tax measures or not) without the consent of their representatives, Dulany distinguished sharply between legislation and taxation. Admitting the right of Parliament to exercise a general legislative power over the colonies and to bind them "by statute . . . in every other instance," he denied only its right to impose taxes on the colonies "for the single purpose of revenue." It could even levy duties as long as they were intended to regulate trade and not to produce a revenue, and the constitutionality of such duties was to be judged by their intent. Dulaney's pamphlet was first published in Annapolis in October, 1765; portions of it are reprinted here as Selection 5 B.*

Edmund S. Morgan and Helen M. Morgan, The Stamp Act Crisis: Prologue to Revolution *(1953), contains the fullest treatment of the debate over the Stamp Act as well as a perceptive discussion of Dulany and his pamphlet. The American position in the debate is analyzed in more detail in Edmund S. Morgan,* "Colonial Ideas of Parliamentary Power, 1764–1766," *William and Mary Quarterly, third series, volume 5 (1948), pages 311–341. A biographical study of Dulany and his father is Aubrey C. Land,* The Dulanys of Maryland *(1955).*

A. THE BRITISH POSITION: THOMAS WHATELY, "THE REGULATIONS LATELY MADE . . ." (1765)*

The Revenue that may be raised by the Duties which have been already, or by these [stamp dates] if they should be hereafter imposed, are all equally applied by Parliament, *towards defraying the necessary Expences of defending, protecting, and securing, the British Colonies and Plantations in America:* Not that on the one hand an *American* Revenue might not have been applied to different Purposes; or on the other, that *Great Britain* is to contribute nothing to these: The very Words of the Act of Parliament and of the Resolution of the House of Commons imply, that the whole of the Expence is not to be charged upon the Colonies: They are under no Obligation to provide for this or any other particular national Expence; neither can they claim any Exemption from general Burthens; but being a part of the *British* Dominions, are to share all necessary Services with the rest. This in *America* does indeed first claim their Attention: They are immediately, they are principally concerned in it; and the Inhabitants of their Mother-Country would justly and loudly complain, if after all their Efforts for the Benefit of the Colonies, when every Point is gained, and every wish accomplished, they, and they alone should be called upon still to answer every additional Demand, that the Preservation of these Advantages, and the Protection of the Colonies from future Dangers, may occasion: *Great Britain* has a Right at all Times, she is under a Necessity, upon this Occasion, to demand their Assistance; but still she requires it in the Manner most suitable to their Circumstances; for by appropriating this Revenue towards the Defence and Security of the Provinces where it is raised, the Produce of it is kept in the Country, the People are not deprived of the Circulation of what Cash they have amongst themselves, and thereby the severest Oppression of an *American* Tax, that of draining the Plantations of Money which they can so ill spare, is avoided. What Part they ought to bear of the national Expence, that is necessary for their Protection, must depend upon their Ability, which is not yet sufficiently known: to the whole they are certainly unequal, that would include all the military and all the naval Establishment, all Fortifications which it may be thought proper to erect, the Ordnance and Stores that must be furnished, and the Provisions which it is necessary to supply; but surely a Part of this great Disbursement, a large Proportion at least of some particular Branches of it, cannot be an intolerable Burthen upon such a Number of Subjects, upon a Territory so extensive, and upon the Wealth which they collectively possess. As to the Quota which each Individual must pay, it will be difficult to persuade the

* These excerpts are reprinted from the original London edition, pp. 101–114.

Inhabitants of this Country, where the neediest Cottager pays out of his Pittance, however scanty, and how hardly soever earned, our high Duties and Customs and Excise in the Price of all his Consumption; it will be difficult I say, to persuade those who see, who suffer, or who relieve such Oppression; that the *West Indian* out of his Opulence, and the *North American* out of his Competency, can contribute no more than it is now pretended they can afford towards the Expence of Services, the Benefit of which, as a Part of this Nation they share, and as Colonists they peculiarly enjoy. They have indeed their own civil Governments besides to support; but *Great Britain* has her civil Government too; she has also a large Peace Establishment to maintain; and the national Debt, tho' so great a Part, and that the heaviest Part of it has been incurred by a War undertaken for the Protection of the Colonies, lies solely still upon her.

The Reasonableness, and even the Necessity of requiring an *American* Revenue being admitted, the Right of the Mother Country to impose such a Duty upon her Colonies, if duly considered, cannot be questioned: they claim it is true the Privilege, which is common to all *British* Subjects, of being taxed only with their own Consent, given by their Representatives; and may they ever enjoy the Privilege in all its Extent: May this sacred Pledge of Liberty be preserved inviolate, to the utmost Verge of our Dominions, and to the latest Page of our History! but let us not limit the legislative Rights of the *British* People to Subjects of Taxation only: No new Law whatever can bind us that is made without the Concurrence of our Representatives. The Acts of Trade and Navigation, and all other Acts that relate either to ourselves or to the Colonies, are founded upon no other Authority; they are not obligatory if a Stamp Act is not, and every Argument in support of an Exemption from the Superintendance of the *British* Parliament in the one Case, is equally applicable to the others. The Constitution knows no Distinction; the Colonies have never attempted to make one; but have acquiesced under several parliamentary Taxes. The 6 *Geo.* II. c. 13. which has been already refered to, lays heavy Duties on all foreign Rum, Sugar, and Melasses, imported into the *British* Plantations: the Amount of the Impositions has been complained of; the Policy of the Laws has been objected to; but the Right of making such a Law, has never been questioned. These however, it may be said, are Duties upon Imports only, and there some imaginary Line has been supposed to be drawn; but had it ever existed, it was passed long before, for by 25 *Charles* II. c. 7. enforced by 7 and 8 *Wil.* and *Mary*, c. 22. and by 1 *Geo.* I. c. 12. the Exports of the *West Indian* Islands, not the Merchandize purchased by the Inhabitants, nor the Profits they might make by their Trade, but the Property they had at the Time, the Produce of their Lands, was taxed, by the Duties then imposed upon Sugar, Tobacco, Cotton, Indigo, Ginger, Logwood, Fustick, and Cocoa, exported from one *British* Plantation to another.

It is in vain to call these only Regulations of Trade; the Trade of *British* Subjects may not be regulated by such Means, without the Concurrence of their Representatives. Duties laid for these Purposes, as well as for the Purposes of Revenue, are still Levies of Money upon the People. The Constitution again knows no Distinction between Impost Duties and internal Taxation; and if some speculative Difference should be attempted to be made, it certainly is contradicted by Fact; for an internal Tax also was laid on the Colonies by the Establishment of a Post Office there; which, however it may be represented, will, upon a Perusal of 9 *Anne* c. 10. appear to be essentially a Tax, and that of the most authoritative Kind; for it is enforced by Provisions, more peculiarly prohibitory and compulsive, than others are usually attended with: The Conveyance of Letters thro' any other Channel is forbidden, by which Restrictions, the Advantage which might be made by public Carriers and others of this Branch of their Business is taken away; and the Passage of Ferries is declared to be free for the Post, the Ferrymen being compellable immediately on Demand to give their Labour without pay, and the Proprietors being obliged to furnish the Means of Passage to the Post without Recompence. These Provisions are indeed very proper, and even necessary; but certainly Money levied by such Methods, the Effect of which is intended to be a Monopoly of the Carriage of Letters to the Officers of this Revenue, and by Means of which the People are forced to pay the Rates imposed upon all their Correspondence, is a public Tax to which they must submit, and not meerly a Price required of them for a private Accommodation. The Act treats this and the *British* Postage upon exactly the same Footing, and expresly calls them both *a Revenue*. The Preamble of it declares, that the new Rates are fixed in the Manner therein specified with a View *to enable her Majesty in some Measure to carry on and finish the War.* The Sum of 700*l. per* Week out of all *the Duties arising from time to time by virtue of this Act is* appropriated for that Purpose, and for other necessary Occasions; the Surplus after other Deductions, was made part of the civil List Revenues; it continued to be thus applied during the Reigns of *George* I: and *George* II. and on his present Majesty's Accession to the Throne, when the Civil List was put upon a different Establishment, the Post Office Revenues were carried with the others *to the aggregate Fund, to be applied to the Uses, to which the said Fund is or shall be applicable.* If all these Circumstances do not constitute a Tax, I do not know what do: the Stamp Duties are not marked with stronger Characters, to entitle them to that Denomination; and with respect to the Application of the Revenue, the Power of the Parliament of *Great Britain* over the Colonies was then held up much higher than it has been upon the present Occasion. The Revenue arising from the Postage in *America* is blended with that of *England,* is applied in Part to the carrying on of a continental War, and other public Purposes; the Remainder of it to the Support of the Civil List; and now the whole of it to the Discharge of the National Debt by Means of the aggregate Fund; all these are Services that are either national or particular to *Great Britain;* but the Stamp Duties and the others that were laid last Year, are appropriated to such Services only as more particularly relate to the Colonies; and surely if the Right of the *British* Parliament to impose the one be acknowledged; that of laying on the other cannot be disputed. The Post-Office has indeed been called a meer Convenience; which therefore the People always chearfully pay for. After what has been said, this Observation requires very little Notice; I will not call the Protection and Security of the Colonies, to which the Duties in question are applied, by so low a Name as a Convenience.

The Instances that have been mentioned prove, that the Right of the Parliament of *Great Britain* to impose Taxes of every Kind on the Colonies, has been always admitted; but were there no Precedents to support the Claim, it would still be incontestable, being founded on the Principles of our Constitution; for the Fact is, that the Inhabitants of the Colonies are represented in Parliament: they do not indeed chuse the Members of that Assembly; neither are Nine Tenths of the People of *Britain* Electors; for the Right of Election is annexed to certain Species of Property, to peculiar Franchises, and to Inhabitancy in some particular Places; but these Descriptions comprehend only a very small Part of the Land, the Property, and the People of this Island: all Copyhold, all Leasehold Estates, under the Crown, under the Church, or under private Persons, tho' for Terms ever so long; all landed Property in short, that is not Freehold, and all monied Property whatsoever are excluded: the Possessors of these have no Votes in the Election of Members of Parliament; Women and Persons under Age be their Property ever so large, and all of it Freehold, have none. The Merchants of *London,* a numerous and respectable Body of Men, whose Opulence exceeds all that *America* could collect; the Proprietors of that vast Accumulation of Wealth, the public Funds; the Inhabitants of *Leeds,* of *Halifax,* of *Birmingham,* and of *Manchester,* Towns that are each of them larger than the Largest in the Plantations; many of less Note that are yet incorporated; and that great Corporation the *East India* Company, whose Rights over the Countries they possess, fall little short of Sovereignty, and whose Trade and whose Fleets are sufficient to constitute them a maritime Power, are all in the same Circumstances; none of them chuse their Representatives; and yet are they not represented in Parliament? Is their vast Property subject to Taxes without their Consent? Are they all arbitrarily bound by Laws to which they have not agreed? The Colonies are in exactly the same Situation: All *British* Subjects are really in the same; none are actually, all are virtually represented in Parliament; for every Member of Parliament sits in the House, not as Representative of his own Constituents, but as one of that august Assembly by which all the Commons of *Great Britain* are represented. Their Rights and their Interests, however his own Borough may be affected by general Dispositions, ought to be the great Objects of his Attention, and the only Rules for his Conduct; and to sacrifice these to a partial Advantage in favour of the Place where he was chosen, would be a Departure from his Duty: if it were otherwise, *Old Sarum* would enjoy Privileges essential to Liberty, which are denied to *Birmingham* and to *Manchester;* but as it is, they and the Colonies and all *British* Subjects whatever, have an equal Share in the general Representation of the Commons of *Great Britain,* and are bound by the Consent of the Majority of that House, whether their own particular Representatives consented to or opposed the Measures there taken, or whether they had or had not particular Representatives there.

The Inhabitants of the Colonies however have by some been supposed to be excepted, because they are represented in their respective Assemblies. So are the Citizens of *London* in their Common Council; and yet so far from excluding them from the national Representation, it does not impeach their Right to chuse Members of Parliament: it is true, that the Powers vested in the Common Council of *London,* are not equal to those which the Assemblies in the Plantations enjoy; but still they are legislative Powers, to be exercised within their District, and over their Citizens; yet not exclusively of the general Superintendance of the great Council of the Nation: The Subjects of a By-law and of an Act of Parliament may possibly be the same; yet it never was imagined that the Privileges of *London* were incompatible with the Authority of Parliament; and indeed what Contradiction, what Absurdity, does a double Representation imply? What difficulty is there in allowing both, tho' both should even be vested with equal legislative Powers, if the one is to be exercised for local, and the other for general Purposes? and where is the Necessity that the Subordinate Power must derogate from the superior Authority? It would be a singular Objection to a Man's Vote for a Member of Parliament, that being represented in a provincial, he cannot be represented in a national Assembly; and if this is not sufficient Ground for an Objection, neither is it for an Exemption, or for any Pretence of an Exclusion.

The Charter and the proprietary Governments in *America,* are in this Respect, on the same Footing with the Rest. The comprehending them also, both in a provincial and national Representation, is not necessarily attended with any Inconsistency, and nothing contained in their Grants can establish one; for all who took those Grants were *British* Subjects, inhabiting *British* Dominions, and who at the Time of taking, were indisputably under the Authority of Parliament; no other Power can abridge that Authority, or dispense with the Obedience that is due to it: those therefore, to whom the Charters were originally given, could have no Exemption granted to them: and what the Fathers never received, the Children cannot claim as an Inheritance; nor was it ever in Idea that they should; even the Charters themselves, so far from allowing guard against the Supposition.

And after all, does any Friend to the Colonies desire the Exemption? he cannot, if he will reflect but a Moment on the Consequences. We value the Right of being represented in the national Legislature as the dearest Privilege we enjoy; how justly would the Colonies complain, if they alone were deprived of it? They acknowledge Dependence upon their Mother Country; but that Dependence would be Slavery not Connection, if they bore no Part in the Government of the whole: they would then indeed be in a worse Situation than the Inhabitants of *Britain,* for these are all of them virtually, tho' few of them are actually represented in the *House of Commons;* if the Colonies were not, they could not expect that their Interests and their Privileges would be any otherwise considered there, than as subservient to those of *Great Britain;* for to deny the Authority of a Legislature, is to surrender all Claims to a Share in its Councils; and if this were the Tenor of their Charters, a Grant more insidious and more replete with Mischief, could not have been invented: a permanent Title to a Share in national Councils, would be exchanged for a precarious Representation in a provincial Assembly; and a Forfeiture of their Rights would be couched under the Appearance of Privileges; they would be reduced from Equality to Subordination, and be at the same Time deprived of the Benefits, and liable to the Inconveniences, both of Independency and of Connection. Happily for them, this is not their Condition. They are on the contrary a Part, and an important Part of the Commons of *Great Britain:* they are represented in Parliament, in the same Manner as those Inhabitants of *Britain* are, who have not Voices in Elections; and they enjoy, with the Rest of their Fellow-subjects the inestimable Privilege of not being bound by any Laws, or subject to any Taxes, to which the Majority of the Representatives of the Commons have not consented.

If there really were any Inconsistency between a national and a provincial Legislature, the Consequence would be the Abolition of the latter; for the Advantages that attend it are purely local: the District it is confined to might be governed without it, by means of the national Representatives; and it is unequal to great general Operations; whereas the other is absolutely necessary for the Benefit and Preservation of the whole: But so far are they from being incompatible, that they will be seldom found to interfere with one another: The Parliament will not often have occasion to exercise its Power over the Colonies, except for those Purposes, which the Assemblies cannot provide for. A general Tax is of this Kind; the Necessity for it, the Extent, the Application of it, are Matters which Councils limited in their Views and in their Operations cannot properly judge of; and when therefore the national Council determine these Particulars, it does not encroach on the other, it only exercises a Power which that other does not pretend to, never claimed, or wished, nor can ever be vested with: The latter remains in exactly the same State as it was before, providing for the same Services, by the same Means, and on the same Subjects; but conscious of its own Inability to answer greater Purposes than those for which it was instituted, it leaves the care of more general Concerns to that higher Legislature, in whose Province alone the Direction of them always was, is, and will be. The Exertion of that Authority which belongs to its universal Superintendance, neither lowers the Dignity, nor deprecates the Usefulness of more limited Powers: They retain all that they ever had, and are really incapable of more.

The Concurrence therefore of the provincial Representatives cannot be necessary in great public Measures to which none but the national Representatives are equal: The Parliament of *Great Britain* not only may but must tax the Colonies, when the public Occasions require a Revenue there: The present Circumstances of the Nation require one now; and a Stamp Act, of which we have had so long an Experience in this, and which is not unknown in that Country, seems an eligible Mode of Taxation. From all these Considerations, and from many others which will occur upon Reflexion and need not be suggested, it must appear *proper to charge certain Stamp Duties in the Plantations to be applied towards defraying the necessary Expences of defending, protecting, and securing the British Colonies and Plantations in America.* This Vote of the House of Commons closed the Measures taken last Year on the Subject of the Colonies: They appear to have been founded upon true Principles of Policy, of Commerce, and of Finance; to be wise with respect to the Mother-Country; just and even beneficial to the Plantations; and therefore it may reasonably be expected that either in their immediate Operations, or in their distant Effects, they will improve the Advantages we possess, confirm the Blessings we enjoy, and promote the public Welfare.

B. THE AMERICAN POSITION: DANIEL DULANY, "CONSIDERATIONS ON THE PROPRIETY OF IMPOSING TAXES IN THE BRITISH COLONIES . . . " (1765)*

IN the constitution of *England*, the three principal forms of government, monarchy, aristocracy, and democracy, are blended together in certain pro-

* These excerpts are reprinted from the original edition (1765), pp. 5–11, 13–15, 34, 47–48.

portions; but each of these orders, in the exercise of the legislative authority, hath its peculiar department, from which the others are excluded. In this division, the *granting of supplies,* or *laying taxes,* is deemed to be the province of the house of commons, as the representative of the people. . . . All supplies are supposed to flow from their gift; and the other orders are permitted only to assent, or reject generally, not to propose any modification, amendment, or partial alteration of it.

This observation being considered, it will undeniably appear, that, in framing the late *Stamp Act,* the commons acted in the character of representative of the colonies. They assumed it as the principle of that measure, and the *propriety* of it must therefore stand, or fall, as the principle is true, or false: For the preamble sets forth, that the commons of *Great-Britain* had resolved to *give and grant* the several rates and duties imposed by the act; but what right had the commons of *Great-Britain* to be thus munificent at the expence of the commons of *America?* . . . To give property not belonging to the giver, and without the consent of the owner, is such evident and flagrant injustice, in *ordinary cases,* that few are hardy enough to avow it; and therefore, when it really happens, the fact is disguised and varnished over by the most plausible pretences the ingenuity of the giver can suggest. . . . But it is alledged that there is a *virtual,* or *implied representation* of the colonies springing out of the constitution of the *British* government: And it must be confessed on all hands, that, as the representation is not actual, it is virtual, or it doth not exist at all; for no third kind of representation can be imagined. The colonies claim the privilege, which is common to all *British subjects,* of being taxed *only* with their own consent given by their representatives, and all the advocates for the *Stamp Act* admit this claim. Whether, therefore, upon the whole matter, the imposition of the *Stamp Duties* is a *proper* exercise of constitutional authority, or not, depends upon the single question, Whether the commons of *Great Britain* are *virtually* the representatives of the commons of *America,* or not.

The advocates for the Stamp Act admit, in express terms, that "the colonies do not choose members of parliament," "but they assert that the colonies are *virtually* represented in the same manner with the non-electors resident in *Great Britain."*

How have they proved this position? Where have they defined, or precisely explained what they mean by the expression, *virtual representation?* As it is the very hinge upon which the rectitude of the taxation turns, something more satisfactory than mere assertion, more solid than a form of expression, is necessary: for how can it be seriously expected, that men, who think themselves injuriously affected in their properties and privileges, will be convinced and reconciled by a fanciful phrase, the meaning of which can't be precisely ascertained by those who use it, or properly applied to the purpose for which it hath been advanced?

They argue, that "the right of election being annexed to certain species of property, to franchises, and inhabitancy in some particular places, a very small part of the land, the property, and the people of *England* are comprehended in those descriptions. All landed property, not freehold, and all monied property, are *excluded.* The merchants of *London,* the proprietors of the public funds, the inhabitants of *Leeds, Halifax, Birmingham,* and *Manchester,* and that great corporation of the *East-India* company, *none of them* choose their representatives, and yet are they all represented in parliament, and the colonies being *exactly* in *their* situation, are represented in the *same manner.*"

Now, this argument, which is all that their invention hath been able to supply, is totally defective; for, it consists of facts not true, and of conclusions inadmissible.

It is so far from being true, that all the persons enumerated under the character of *non-electors,* are in that predicament, that it is indubitably certain there is *no* species of property, landed, or monied, which is not possessed by *very many* of the *British electors.*

I shall undertake to disprove the supposed similarity of situation, whence the same kind of representation is deduced, of the inhabitants of the colonies, and of the *British* non-electors; and, if I succeed, the notion of a *virtual representation* of the colonies must fail, which, in truth, is a mere cob web, spread to catch the unwary, and intangle the weak. I would be understood: I am upon a question of *propriety,* not of power; and, though some may be inclined to think it is to little purpose to discuss the one, when the other is irresistible, yet are they different considerations; and, at the same time that I invalidate the claim upon which it is founded, I may very consistently recommend a submission to the law, whilst it endures. I shall say nothing of the use I intend by the discussion; for if it should not be perceived by the sequel, there is no use in it, and, if it should appear then, it need not be premised.

Lessees for years, copyholders, proprietors of the public funds, inhabitants of *Birmingham, Leeds, Halifax,* and *Manchester,* merchants of the city of *London,* or members of the corporation of the *East-India* company, are, *as such,* under no personal incapacity to be electors; for they may acquire the right of election, and there are *actually* not only a considerable number of electors in each of the classes of lessees for years, etc. but in many of them, if not all, even members of parliament. The interests therefore of the non-electors, the electors, and the representatives, are individually the same; to say nothing of the connection among neighbours, friends, and relations. The security of the non-electors against oppression, is, that their oppression will fall also upon the electors and the representatives. The one can't be injured, and the other indemnified.

Further, if the non-electors should not be taxed by the *British* parliament, they would not be taxed *at all;* and it would be iniquitous as well as a solecism, in the political system, that they should partake of all the benefits resulting from the imposition, and application of taxes, and derive an immunity from the circumstance of not being qualified to vote. Under this constitution then, a double or virtual representation may be reasonably supposed. The electors, who are inseparably connected in their interests with the non-electors, may be justly deemed to be the representatives of the non-electors, at the same time they exercise their personal privilege in the right of election; and the members chosen, therefore, the representatives of both. This is the only rational explanation of the expression, *virtual representation.* None has been advanced by the assertors of it, and their meaning can only be inferred from the instances, by which they endeavour to elucidate it, and no other meaning can be stated, to which the instances apply.

It is an essential principle of the *English* constitution, that the subject shall not be taxed without his consent, which hath not been introduced by any particular law, but necessarily results from the nature of that mixed government; for, without it, the order of democracy could not exist.

Parliaments were not formerly so regular in point of form as they now are. Even the number of knights for each shire were not ascertained. The first writs now extant for their choice, are 22d *Edward* I. by which, two, as at this day, were directed to be chosen for each county; but the king not being satisfied with that number, other writs were issued for choosing two more. This discretionary power being thought inconvenient, was afterwards restrained by the statutes of *Richard* II, *Henry* IV, and subsequent acts.

In earlier times there was more simplicity in the rules of government, and men were more solicitous about the essentials, than the forms of it. When the consent of those who were to perform, or pay anything extrafeudal, was fairly applied for and obtained, the manner was little regarded; but as the people had reason to be jealous of designs to impose contributions upon them without their consent, it was thought expedient to have formalities regulated, and fixed, to prevent this injury to their rights, not to destroy a principle, without which, they could not be said to have any rights at all.

Before the introduction of those formalities, which were framed with a view to restrain the excursions of power, and to secure the privileges of the subject, as the mode of proceeding was more simple, so perhaps this foundation of consent was more visible than it is at present, wherefore it may be of use to adduce some instances, which directly point out this necessary and essential principle of *British liberty*.

The lords and commons have separately given aids and subsidies to the crown. In 13th *Edward* III, the lords granted the tenth of all the corn, etc. growing upon their demesnes, the commons then granting nothing, nor concerning themselves with what the lords thought fit to grant out of their own estates. At other times, the knights of shires, separating from the rest of the commons, and joining with the lords, have granted a subsidy, and the representatives of cities and boroughs have likewise granted subsidies to the crown separately, as appears by a writ in 24th *Edward* I, which runs in these words . . . *The earls, barons, and knights, having given unto us in parliament, the eleventh part, and the citizens and burgesses the seventh part of their goods and chattels, etc.* When an affair happened, which affected only some individuals, and called for an aid to the crown, it was common for those individuals *alone* to be summoned; to which purpose several writs are extant. In 35th *Edward* III, there is a writ (which *Dugdale* has printed in his collection of writs of summons to parliament) directed to the earl of *Northampton*, which, after reciting the confusion the affairs of *Ireland* were in, and that he, and some other *English* lords had possessions in that kingdom, and were therefore more particularly obliged to the defence of it, follows in these words: . . . *We will confer with you, and others of the same kingdom (viz.* England) *possessed of lands in the said country.*

But, that the reader may perceive how strictly the principle, of no person's being taxed without his consent, hath been regarded, it is proper to take notice, that, upon the same occasion, writs were likewise directed even to women, who were proprietors of land in *Ireland,* to send their deputies to consult, and consent to what should be judged necessary, to be done on the occasion: . . . *We command you to send to* Westminster, *some person or persons, whom you may confide in, to confer with us, on the abovesaid affair, and to do and assent, in your name, to whatever shall be there decreed.*

A reflection naturally arises from the instances cited:—When, on a particular occasion, *some* individuals *only* were to be taxed, and not the *whole* community, *their* consent *only* was called for, and in the last instance it appears, that they, who upon an occasion of a general tax, would have been bound by the consent of their *virtual representatives* (for in that case they would have had no *actual representatives*) were in an affair calling for a particular aid from them, *separate* from the rest of the community, required to send their *particular deputies.* But how different would be the principle of a statute, imposing duties without *their* consent who are to pay them, upon the authority of *their* Gift, who should undertake to give, what doth not belong to them.

That great king, *Edward* I, inserted in his writs of summons, as a first principle of law, that . . . *what concerns all, must be approved by all,* which by no torture can be made to signify that *their* approbation or consent *only* is to be required in the imposition of a tax, who are to pay *no* part of it.

The situation of the non-electors in *England*—their capacity to become electors—their inseparable connection with those who are electors, and their representatives—their security against oppression resulting from this connection, and the necessity of imagining a double or virtual representation, to avoid iniquity and absurdity, have been explained—the inhabitants of the colonies are, *as such,* incapable of being electors, the privilege of election being exerciseable only in person, and therefore if *every* inhabitant of *America* had the requisite freehold, not *one* could vote, but upon the supposition of his ceasing to be an inhabitant of *America,* and becoming a resident of *Great-Britain,* a supposition which would be impertinent, because it shifts the question—should the colonies not be taxed by *Parliamentary impositions,* their respective legislatures have a regular, adequate, and constitutional authority to tax them, and therefore there would not necessarily be an iniquitous and absurd exemption, from their not being represented by *the house of commons.*

There is not that intimate and inseparable relation between the *electors of* Great-Britain, and the *Inhabitants of the colonies,* which must inevitably involve both in the same taxation; on the contrary, not a single *actual* elector in *England,* might be immediately affected by a taxation in *America,* imposed by a statute which would have a general operation and effect, upon the properties of the inhabitants of the colonies. The latter might be oppressed in a thousand shapes, without any Sympathy, or exciting any alarm in the former. Moreover, even acts, oppressive and injurious to the colonies in an extreme degree, might become popular in *England,* from the promise or expectation, that the very measures which depressed the colonies, would give ease to the Inhabitants of *Great-Britain.* It is indeed true, that the interests of *England* and the colonies are allied, and an injury to the colonies produced into all it's consequences, will eventually affect the mother country; yet these consequences being generally remote, are not at once foreseen; they do not immediately alarm the fears, and engage the passions of the *English* electors; the connection between a freeholder of *Great-Britain,* and a *British American* being deductible only thro' a train of reasoning, which few will take the trouble, or can have opportunity, if they have capacity, to investigate; wherefore the relation between the *British Americans,* and the *English electors,* is a knot too infirm to be relied on as a competent security, especially against the force of a present, counteracting expectation of relief.

If it would have been a just conclusion, that the *colonies* being exactly in the *same* situation with the *non-electors* of *England,* are *therefore* represented in the same manner; it ought to be allowed, that the reasoning is solid, which, after having evinced a total *dissimilarity* of situation, infers, that their representation is *different.*

If the commons of *Great-Britain* have no right by the constitution, to GIVE AND GRANT property *not* belonging to themselves or others, without their consent actually or virtually given; If the claim of the colonies not to be taxed *without their consent,* signified by their representatives, is well founded; if it appears that the colonies are not actually represented by the commons of *Great-Britain,* and that the notion of a double or virtual representation, doth not with any propriety apply to the people of *America;* then the principle of the *Stamp act,* must be given up as indefensible on the point of representation, and the validity of it rested upon the *power* which they who framed it, have to carry it into execution. . . .

The colonies have a complete and adequate legislative authority, and are not only represented in their assemblies, but in *no other manner.* The power of making bye-laws vested in the common council is inadequate and incomplete, being bounded by a few particular subjects; and the common council are actually represented too, by having a choice of members to serve in parliament. How then can the reason of the exemption from internal parliamentary taxations, claimed by the colonies, apply to the citizens of *London?*

The power described in the provincial charters, is to make laws, and in the exercise of that power, the colonies are bounded by no other limitations than what result from their subordination to, and dependence upon *Great Britain.* The term *bye-laws* is as novel, and improper, when applied to the *parliament* of Great Britain; and it is as absurd and insensible, to call a colony a common corporation, because not an independent kingdom, and the powers of each to make laws and bye-laws, are limited, tho' not comparable in their extent, and the variety of their objects, as it would be to call lake *Erie,* a *Duck-puddle,* because not the atlantic ocean.

Should the analogy between the *colonies* and *corporations* be even admitted for a moment, in order to see what would be the consequence of the *postulatum,* it would only amount to this, The *colonies* are vested with as complete authority to all intents and purposes to tax themselves, as any *English corporation* is to make a bye-law, in any imaginable instance for any local purpose whatever, and the *parliament* doth not make laws for *corporations* upon subjects, in every respect proper for *bye-laws.*

But I don't rest the matter upon this, or any other circumstance, however considerable, to prove the impropriety of a taxation by the *British* parliament. I rely upon the fact, that not one inhabitant in any colony is, or can be *actually* or *virtually* represented by the *British house of commons,* and therefore, that the Stamp duties are severely imposed.

But it has been alledged, that if the right to *give and grant* the property of the colonies by an internal taxation is denied by the house of commons, the subordination and dependence of the colonies, and the superintendence of the *British* parliament can't be consistently establish'd. . . . That any supposed line of distinction between the two cases, is but "a whimsical imagination, a chimerical speculation against fact and experience." . . . Now, under favour, I conceive there is more confidence, than solidity in this assertion; and it may be satisfactorily and easily proved, that the subordination and dependence of the colonies may be preserved, and the *supreme authority* of the mother country be firmly supported, and yet the principle of representation, and the right of the *British* house of commons flowing from *it*, to *give and grant* the property of the commons of *America*, be denied.

The colonies are dependent upon *Great Britain*, and the supreme authority vested in the king, lords, and commons, may justly be exercised to secure, or preserve their dependence, whenever necessary for that purpose. This authority results from, and is implied in the idea of the relation subsisting between *England* and her colonies; for, considering the nature of human affections, the inferior is not to be trusted with providing regulations to prevent his rising to an equality with his superior. But, though the right of the superior to use the proper means for preserving the subordination of his inferior is admitted, yet it does not necessarily follow, that he has a right to seize the property of his inferior when he pleases, or to command him in every thing; since, in the degrees of it, there may very well exist a *dependence* and *inferiority*, without absolute *vassalage* and *slavery*. In what the superior may *rightfully* controul, or compel, and in what the inferior ought to be at liberty to act without controul or compulsion, depends upon the nature of the dependence, and the degree of the subordination; and, these being ascertained, the measure of obedience, and submission, and the extent of the authority and superintendence will be settled. When powers, compatible with the relation between the superior and inferior, have, by express compact, been granted to, and accepted by, the latter, and have been, after that compact, repeatedly recognized by the former---. When they may be exercised effectually upon every occasion without any injury to that relation, the authority of the superior can't properly interpose; for, by the powers vested in the inferior, is the superior limited.

By their constitutions of government, the colonies are empowered to impose internal taxes. This power is compatible with their dependence, and hath been expressly recognized by *British* ministers and the *British* parliament, upon many occasions; and it may be exercised effectually without striking at, or impeaching, in any respect, the superintendence of the *British* parliament. May not then the line be distinctly and justly drawn between such acts as are necessary, or proper, for preserving or securing the dependence of the colonies, and such as are not necessary or proper for that very important purpose?

When the powers were conferred upon the colonies, they were conferred too as privileges and immunities, and accepted as such; or, to speak more properly, the privileges belonging necessarily to them as *British* subjects, were solemnly declared and confirmed by their charters, and they who settled in *America* under the encouragement and faith of these charters, understood, not only that They *might*, but that it was their *right* to exercise those powers without controul, or prevention. In some of the charters the distinction is expressed, and the strongest declarations made, and the most solemn assurances given, that the settlers should not have their property taxed without their own consent by their representatives; though their legislative authority is limited at the same time, by the subordination implied in their relation, and They are therefore restrained for making acts of assembly repugnant to the laws of *England*; and, had the distinction not been expressed, the powers given would have implied it, for, if the parliament may in any case interpose, when the authority of the colonies is adequate to the occasion, and not limited by their subordination to the mother country, it may in every *case,* which would make *another* appellation more proper to describe their condition, than the name by which their inhabitants have been usually called, and have gloried in.

Because the parliament may, when the relation between *Great Britain* and her colonies calls for an exertion of her superintendence, bind the colonies by statute, therefore a parliamentary interposition in every other instance, is justifiable, is an inference that may be denied. . . .

A right to impose an internal tax on the colonies, without their consent *for the single purpose of revenue,* is denied, a right to regulate their trade without their consent is admitted. The imposition of a duty, may, in some instances, be the proper regulation. If the claims of the mother country and the colonies should seem on such an occasion to interfere, and the point of right to be doubtful, (which I take to be otherwise) it is easy to guess that the determination will be on the side of power, and that the inferior will be constrained to submit. . . .

Any oppression of the colonies, would intimate an opinion of them I am persuaded they do not deserve, and their security as well as honour ought to engage them to confute. When contempt is mixed with injustice, and insult with violence, which is the case when an injury is done to him who hath the means of redress in his power; if the injured hath one inflammable grain of honour in his breast, his resentment will invigorate his pursuit of reparation, and animate his efforts to obtain an effectual security against a repetition of the outrage.

If the case supposed should really happen, the resentment I should recommend would be a legal, orderly, and prudent resentment, to be expressed in a zealous and vigorous industry, in an immediate use and unabating application of the advantages we derive from our situation . . . a resentment which could not fail to produce effects as beneficial to the mother country as to the colonies, and which a regard to her welfare as well as our own, ought to inspire us with on such an occasion.

The general assemblies would not, I suppose, have it in their power to encourage by laws, the prosecution of this beneficial, this necessary measure; but they might promote it almost as effectually by their example. I have in my younger days seen fine sights, and been captivated by their dazzling pomp and glittering splendor; but the sight of our representatives, all adorned in compleat dresses of their own leather, and flax, and wool, manufactured by the art and industry of the inhabitants of *Virginia,* would excite, not the gaze of admiration, the flutter of an agitated imagination, or the momentary amusement of a transient scene, but a calm, solid, heart-felt delight. Such a sight would give me more pleasure than the most splendid and magnificent spectacle the most exquisite taste ever painted, the richest fancy ever imagined, realized to the view . . . as much more pleasure as a good mind would receive from the contemplation of virtue, than of elegance; of the spirit of patriotism, than the ostentation of opulence.

Not only, "as a friend to the colonies," but as an inhabitant having my all at stake upon their welfare I desire an "exemption from taxes imposed *without my consent,* and" I have reflected longer than "a moment upon the consequences:" I value it as one of the dearest privileges I enjoy: I acknowledge dependance on *Great Britain*, but I can perceive a degree of it without slavery, and I disown all other. I do not expect that the interests of the colonies will be considered by some men, but in subserviency to other regards. The effects of luxury, and venality, and oppression, posterity may perhaps experience, and SUFFICIENT FOR THE DAY WILL BE THE EVIL THEREOF.

SELECTION

Colonial Resistance

Like Otis, Dulany had not advocated open defiance of parliamentary measures. Rather, he counselled a "legal, orderly, and prudent resentment." For other colonists, however, more drastic action seemed to be called for. One of these was Patrick Henry (1736–1799), an ambitious and impetuous young lawyer from Hanover County, Virginia, already famous in his own colony for his speech in December, 1763, during the Parson's Cause—the culmination of a long dispute between the Virginia government and the Anglican clergy—in which he denounced the Crown's right to disallow laws. Only just elected as a representative from Louisa County to the House of Burgesses, Henry persuaded the House, against the better judgment of its more sober members, to adopt on May 30, 1765, a set of five resolutions that boldly challenged Parliament's right to tax the colonies. Substantively, the resolutions simply restated the arguments contained in three formal petitions sent by the Burgesses to the King, Lords, and Commons the previous December, but in tone and form they were strikingly different. In tone they were emphatic, in form an unequivocal declaration of rights. Yet, the Burgesses would not go as far as Henry had originally intended. Two still stronger resolutions—one declaring that Virginians were not obliged to pay any tax not imposed by their assembly and the other stating that anyone upholding the power of any other agency to tax the colony would "be deemed an Enemy to his Majesty's Colony"—apparently failed to pass, if Henry actually introduced them. On May 31 the Burgesses even rescinded the narrowly carried fifth resolution that specifically asserted that it held the "only exclusive Right and Power to lay Taxes and Imposts upon the Inhabitants of this Colony" and branded "every Attempt to vest such Power in any other Person or Persons" as illegal, unconstitutional and unjust. The four remaining resolutions, reprinted below as Selection 6 A, thus asserted the right of the colonists not to be taxed without the consent of their representatives but neither denied explicitly Parliament's right to tax the colonies nor advocated any form of resistance. Nevertheless, the Virginia resolves became the rallying call for a general American uprising against the Stamp Act, inspiring similar protests from lower houses in eight of the other twelve colonies. Because almost every American printer published the resolves in his newspaper and included the fifth, sixth, and seventh as well as the four the Burgesses actually passed, the declarations passed by the other lower houses went beyond those of the Virginia body.

But American resistance was not confined to mere legislative declarations of rights. In the summer of 1765, well before November 1, when the Stamp Act was scheduled to go into effect, Sons of Liberty organizations, taking their name from a phrase used by Colonel Isaac Barré in opposing the Stamp Act in the House of Commons and directed by some of the leading political figures in the colonies, used violence where necessary to force stamp distributors to resign and to prevent enforcement of the law. Some of the riots got out of hand, resulted in the destruction of property belonging to people thought sympathetic to the Stamp Act, and served as a means for the men behind the mobs to get even with their political opponents. The most destructive of the riots occurred in Boston on the night of August 26 and led to the looting of the house of Chief Justice Thomas Hutchinson, political rival of James Otis and mistakenly thought by the mob to have been one of the projectors of the Stamp Act. The riot is described in Selection 6 B below, an extract from the diary of Josiah Quincy, Jr. (1744–1775), a young Boston lawyer and recent graduate of Harvard College.

In the meantime, on June 8, 1765, the Massachusetts House of Representatives issued a call for a general congress to meet in New York and consider the Stamp Act and other colonial grievances. Delegates from nine colonies participated in the Stamp Act Congress, which met on October 7 and adopted on October 19 a Declaration of Rights and Grievances, printed below as Selection 6 C. Written by John Dickinson (1732–1808), a Pennsylvania lawyer who would become one of the most prominent colonial leaders in the constitutional debates over the next decade, the Declaration contained fourteen resolutions and may be taken as the most deliberate and "official" statement of the colonial constitutional position during the Stamp Act crisis.

The most comprehensive discussion of colonial resistance to the Stamp Act is in Edmund S. Morgan and Helen M. Morgan, The Stamp Act Crisis: Prologue to Revolution (1953). Thad W. Tate, "The Coming of the Revolution in Virginia: Britain's Challenge to Virginia's Ruling Class, 1763–1776," William and Mary Quarterly, third series, volume 19 (1962), pages 323–343, is the best analysis of the internal political implications of the Henry resolutions. Robert Douthat Meade, Patrick Henry: Patriot in the Making (1957) is a detailed treatment of the early years of Patrick Henry, and David L. Jacobson, John Dickinson and the Revolution in Pennsylvania, 1764–1776 (1965), is the most recent study of Dickinson.

A. CALL TO RESISTANCE: THE VIRGINIA RESOLVES (MAY 30, 1765)*

Resolved, That the first Adventurers and Settlers of this his Majesty's Colony and Dominion of *Virginia* brought with them, and transmitted to their Posterity, and all other his Majesty's Subjects since inhabiting in this his Majesty's said Colony, all the Liberties, Privileges, Franchises, and Immunities, that have at any Time been held, enjoyed, and possessed, by the people of *Great Britain.*

* These excerpts are reprinted from H. R. McIlwaine and John Pendleton Kennedy (eds.), *Journals of the House of Burgesses of Virginia, 1761–1765* (11 vols., 1905–1915), p. 360.

Resolved, That by two royal Charters, granted by King *James* the First, the Colonists aforesaid are declared entitled to all Liberties, Privileges, and Immunities of Denizens and natural Subjects, to all Intents and Purposes, as if they had been abiding and born within the Realm of *England*.

Resolved, That the Taxation of the People by themselves, or by Persons chosen by themselves to represent them, who can only know what Taxes the People are able to bear, or the easiest Method of raising them, and must themselves be affected by every Tax laid on the People, is the only Security against a burthensome Taxation, and the distinguishing Characteristick of *British* Freedom, without which the ancient Constitution cannot exist.

Resolved, That his Majesty's liege People of this his most ancient and loyal Colony have without Interruption enjoyed the inestimable Right of being governed by such Laws, respecting their internal Polity and Taxation, as are derived from their own Consent, with the Approbation of their Sovereign, or his Substitute; and that the same hath never been forfeited or yielded up, but hath been constantly recognized by the Kings and People of *Great Britain*.

B. RESORT TO VIOLENCE: THE BOSTON RIOT OF AUG. 26, 1765, AS RECORDED IN THE DIARY OF JOSIAH QUINCY, JR. (AUG. 27, 1765)*

There cannot, perhaps, be found in the records of time a more flagrant instance to what a pitch of infatuation an incensed populace may arise than the last night afforded. The destructions, demolitions, and ruins caused by the rage of the Colonies in general—perhaps too justly inflamed—at that singular and ever-memorable statute called the Stamp Act, will make the present year one of the most remarkable eras in the annals of North America. And that peculiar inflammation, which fired the breasts of the people of New England in particular, will always distinguish them as the warmest lovers of liberty; though undoubtedly, in the fury of revenge against those who they thought had disclaimed the name of sons, for that of enslavers and oppressive tax-masters of their native country, they committed acts totally unjustifiable.

The populace of Boston, about a week since, had given a very notable instance of their detestation of the above unconstitutional Act, and had sufficiently shown in what light they viewed the man who would undertake to be the stamp distributor. But, not content with this, the last night they again assembled in King's Street; where, after having kindled a fire, they proceeded, in two separate bodies, to attack the houses of two gentlemen of distinction, who, it had been suggested, were accessories to the present burthens; and did great damage in destroying their houses, furniture, &c., and irreparable damage in destroying their papers. Both parties, who before had acted separately, then unitedly proceeded to the Chief-Justice's house, who, not expecting them, was unattended by his friends, who might have

---

* These excerpts are reprinted from *Proceedings of the Massachusetts Historical Society*, 1st ser. 1791–1883 (20 vols., 1879–1884), vol. 4 (1858–1860), pp. 47–51.

assisted, or proved his innocence. In this situation, all his family, it is said, abandoned the house, but himself and his eldest daughter, whom he repeatedly begged to depart; but as he found all ineffectual, and her resolution fixed to stay and share his fate, with a tumult of passions only to be imagined, he took her in his arms and carried her to a place of safety, just before the incensed mob arrived. This filial affection saved, it is more than probable, his life. Thus unexpected, and nothing removed from the house, an ample field offered to satiate, if possible, this rage-intoxicated rabble. They beset the house on all sides, and soon destroyed every thing of value. . . . The destruction was really amazing; for it was equal to the fury of the onset. But what above all is to be lamented is the loss of some of the most valuable records of the country, and other ancient papers; for, as his Honor was continuing his history, the oldest and most important writings and records of the Province, which he had selected with great care, pains, and expense, were in his possession. This is a loss greatly to be deplored, as it is absolutely irretrievable.

The distress a man must feel on such an occasion can only be conceived by those who the next day saw his Honor the Chief-Justice come into court, with a look big with the greatest anxiety, clothed in a manner which would have excited compassion from the hardest heart, though his dress had not been striking contrasted by the other judges and bar, who appeared in their robes. Such a man in such a station, thus habited, with tears starting from his eyes, and a countenance which strongly told the inward anguish of his soul,—what must an audience have felt, whose compassion had before been moved by what they knew he had suffered, when they heard him pronounce the following words in a manner which the agitations of his mind dictated?

GENTLEMEN,—There not being a quorum of the court without me, I am obliged to appear. Some apology is necessary for my dress: indeed, I had no other. Destitute of every thing,—no other shirt; no other garment but what I have on; and not one in my whole family in a better situation than myself. The distress of a whole family around me, young and tender infants hanging about me, are infinitely more insupportable than what I feel for myself, though I am obliged to borrow part of *this* clothing.

Sensible that I am innocent, that all the charges against me are false, I can't help feeling: and though I am not obliged to give an answer to all the questions that may be put me by every lawless person, yet I call God to witness,—and I would not, for a thousand worlds, call my Maker to witness to falsehood,—I say, I call my Maker to witness, that I never, in New England or Old, in Great Britain or America, neither directly nor indirectly, was aiding, assisting, or supporting—in the least promoting or encouraging—what is commonly called the Stamp Act; but, on the contrary, did all in my power, and strove as much as in me lay, to prevent it. This is not declared through timidity; for I have nothing to fear. They can only take away my life, which is of but little value when deprived of all its comforts, all that was dear to me, and nothing surrounding me but the most piercing distress.

I hope the eyes of the people will be opened, that they will see how easy it is for some designing, wicked man to spread false reports, to raise suspicions and jealousies in the minds of the populace, and enrage them against the innocent; but, if guilty, this is not the way to proceed. The laws of our country are open to punish those who have offended. This destroying all peace and order of the community,—all will feel its effects; and I hope all will see how easily the people may be deluded, inflamed, and carried away with madness against an innocent man.

I pray God give us better hearts!

The court was then adjourned, on account of the riotous disorders of the preceding night, and universal confusion of the town, to the 15th of October following.

Learn wisdom from the present times! O ye sons of Ambition! beware lest a thirst of power prompt you to enslave your country! O ye sons of Avarice! beware lest the thirst for gold excite you to enslave your native country! O ye sons of Popularity! beware lest a thirst for applause move you ground-lessly to inflame the minds of the people! For the end of slavery is misery to the world, your country, fellow-citizens, and children; the end of popular rage, destruction, desolation, and ruin.

Who, that sees the fury and instability of the populace, but would seek protection under the arm of power? Who, that beholds the tyranny and oppression of arbitrary power, but would lose his life in defence of his liberty? Who, that marks the riotous tumult, confusion, and uproar of a democratic, the slavery and distress of a despotic, state,—the infinite miseries attendant on both,—but would fly for refuge from the mad rage of the one, and oppressive power of the other, to that best asylum, that glorious medium, the British Constitution? Happy people who enjoy this blessed constitution! Happy, thrice happy people, if ye preserve it inviolate! May ye never lose it through a licentious abuse of your invaluable rights and blood-purchased liberties! May ye never forfeit it by a tame and infamous submission to the yoke of slavery and lawless despotism!

> Remember, O my friends! the laws, the rights,
> The generous plan of power delivered down,
> From age to age, by your renowned forefathers,
> So dearly bought, the price of so much blood:
> Oh! let it never perish in your hands,
> But piously transmit it to your children.
> Do thou, great Liberty! inspire our souls,
> And make our lives in thy possession happy,
> Or our death glorious in thy just defence.

C. THE OFFICIAL COLONIAL PROTEST: THE DECLARATION OF THE STAMP ACT CONGRESS (OCT. 19, 1765)*

The members of this congress, sincerely devoted, with the warmest sentiments of affection and duty to his majesty's person and government; inviolably attached to the present happy establishment of the protestant succession, and with minds deeply impressed by a sense of the present and

* These excerpts are reprinted from Hezekiah Niles (ed.), *Principles and Acts of the Revolution in America* (1876), p. 163.

impending misfortunes of the British colonies on this continent; having considered as maturely as time would permit, the circumstances of the said colonies, esteem it our indispensable duty to make the following declarations, of our humble opinion, respecting the most essential rights and liberties of the colonists, and of the grievances under which they labor, by reason of several late acts of parliament.

1st. That his majesty's subjects in these colonies, owe the same allegiance to the crown of Great Britain, that is owing from his subjects born within the realm, and all due subordination to that august body, the parliament of Great Britain.

2d. That his majesty's liege subjects in these colonies are entitled to all the inherent rights and privileges of his natural born subjects within the kingdom of Great Britain.

3d. That it is inseparably essential to the freedom of a people, and the undoubted rights of Englishmen, that no taxes should be imposed on them, but with their own consent, given personally, or by their representatives.

4th. That the people of these colonies are not, and from their local circumstances, cannot be represented in the house of commons in Great Britain.

5th. That the only representatives of the people of these colonies, are persons chosen therein, by themselves; and that no taxes ever have been, or can be constitutionally imposed on them, but by their respective legislatures.

6th. That all supplies to the crown, being free gifts of the people, it is unreasonable and inconsistent with the principles and spirit of the British constitution, for the people of Great Britain to grant to his majesty the property of the colonists.

7th. That trial by jury is the inherent and invaluable right of every British subject in these colonies.

8th. That the late act of parliament, entitled, an act for granting and applying certain stamp duties, and other duties in the British colonies and plantations in America, etc., by imposing taxes on the inhabitants of these colonies, and the said act, and several other acts, by extending the jurisdiction of the courts of admiralty beyond its ancient limits, have a manifest tendency to subvert the rights and liberties of the colonists.

9th. That the duties imposed by several late acts of parliament, from their peculiar circumstances of these colonies, will be extremely burthensome and grievous, and from the scarcity of specie, the payment of them absolutely impracticable.

10th. That as the profits of the trade of these colonies ultimately centre in Great Britain, to pay for the manufactures which they are obliged to take from thence, they eventually contribute very largely to all supplies granted there to the crown.

11th. That the restrictions imposed by several late acts of parliament, on the trade of these colonies, will render them unable to purchase the manufactures of Great Britain.

12th. That the increase, prosperity and happiness of these colonies, depend on the full and free enjoyment of their rights and liberties, and an intercourse, with Great Britain, mutually affectionate and advantageous.

13th. That it is the right of the British subjects in these colonies, to petition the king or either house of parliament.

Lastly, That it is the indispensable duty of these colonies to the best of sovereigns, to the mother country, and to themselves, to endeavor by a loyal and dutiful address to his majesty, and humble application to both houses of parliament, to procure the repeal of the act for granting and applying certain stamp duties, of all clauses of any other acts of parliament, whereby the jurisdiction of the admiralty is extended as aforesaid, and of the other late acts for the restriction of the American commerce.

SELECTION

Repeal

By November 1, 1765, the date the Stamp Act was supposed to take effect, the Sons of Liberty had managed to nullify it in all of the old continental colonies except Georgia, where Governor James Wright actually managed to enforce it. During the fall committees of merchants in the major northern seaports entered into agreements not to import any European goods until the Stamp Act was repealed and some of the more objectionable features of the Sugar Act were modified. In addition to the suspension of commercial activity after November 1 that resulted from the refusal of American merchants to use the stamps required in most business transactions, these nonimportation agreements led to such a precipitous decline in consumption of British imports that British merchants became alarmed. Early in 1766, they petitioned the new ministry under the Marquis of Rockingham, who had succeeded George Grenville as First Minister in the summer of 1765 for reasons unrelated to American affairs, to repeal the Stamp Act and soften the terms of the Sugar Act. The petition from the London merchants, presented to Parliament on January 17, 1766, and reprinted below as Selection 7 A, was only one of many similar petitions which came from the merchants in most of the major British trading cities.

The Rockingham government responded favorably to the merchants, and when a new Parliament met on January 14 George III's address signified the intention of the government to repeal the Stamp Act. A debate followed in the House of Commons in which William Pitt (1708–1778), the political genius behind the great British victory in the Seven Years' War who had not been in office since October, 1761, praised the colonists for opposing the Stamp Act and, echoing the arguments of Daniel Dulany, advocated repeal on the grounds that Parliament could legislate for the colonies but could not tax them. He was opposed in this debate by George Grenville (1712–1770), who argued that taxation was merely a branch of legislation and that there was no limitation upon Parliament's authority over the colonies. Predicting revolution if Parliament yielded to the acts of violence in the colonies and repealed the Stamp Act, Grenville insisted upon its immediate enforcement. Portions of both of these speeches along with Pitt's reply to Grenville are reprinted here as Selection 7 B.

The Rockingham government, wishing to steer a course between the two extremes represented by Pitt and Grenville, sought to combine repeal of the Stamp Act with an assertion of Parliament's authority over the colonies. In pursuit of this objective, it called a number of men familiar with conditions in the colonies to testify before the House of Commons. One of the key testimonies, portions of which are reprinted here as Selection 7 C, was given by Benjamin Franklin (1706–1790). Perhaps by prearrangement with the ministry, which was eager not to draw attention to the extent of the colonists' denial of parliamentary authority in the colonies, Franklin was careful not to define the colonial position too precisely and confirmed, whether intentionally or not, a widespread impression among British politicians that the colonists objected to internal taxes but not to external taxes on trade. In fact, the Americans had made no such fine distinction but had objected to all taxes levied by Parliament for revenue while admitting Parliament's right to levy duties solely for the purpose of regulating trade.

In February the ministry introduced a series of resolutions calling for the simultaneous repeal of the Stamp Act and passage of a bill to declare the authority of Parliament to make laws for the colonies "in all cases whatsoever." On February 3, this declaratory bill sparked a high-level debate in the House of Lords, where Charles Pratt, Earl Camden (1714–1794), adherent of Pitt and Chief Justice of Common Pleas, argued that Parliament could not violate the laws of nature, that no taxation without representation was one of those laws, that Parliament could not, therefore, tax the colonies, and that the declaratory bill ought not to be passed because it gave Parliament "an absolute power of laying any tax upon America." In the most notable of the speeches made in answer to Camden, William Murray, Earl of Mansfield (1705–1793), Lord Chief Justice, adduced a variety of precedents to support his contention that there were no limitations upon Parliament's authority to legislate for all parts of the Crown's dominions. Although Camden maintained his ground in a long reply to his critics on March 7, the Declaratory Act passed the Lords as easily as it had passed the Commons and on March 18, along with a bill to repeal the Stamp Act, was signed into law. Excerpts from the speeches of Camden and Mansfield are reprinted here as Selection 7 D, and the Declaratory Act is reprinted in full as Selection 7 E.

Edmund S. Morgan and Helen M. Morgan, The Stamp Act Crisis: Prologue to Revolution *(1953), contains a full account of the repeal of the Stamp Act, though* C. H. McIlwain, The American Revolution: A Constitutional Interpretation *(1923), and Robert Livingston Schuyler,* Parliament and the British Empire: Some Constitutional Controversies concerning Imperial Legislative Jurisdiction *(1929), should be consulted for fuller discussions of the relative merits of the opposing arguments in Parliament over that body's right to tax the colonies.*

A. BRITISH MERCANTILE OPPOSITION: PETITION OF THE MERCHANTS OF LONDON, TRADING TO NORTH AMERICA (JAN. 17, 1766)*

That the petitioners have been long concerned in carrying on the trade between this country and the British colonies on the continent of North America; and that they have annually exported very large quantities of British manufactures, consisting of woollen goods of all kinds, cottons, linens, hardware, shoes, houshold furniture, and almost without exception of every

* Reprinted in full from William Cobbett (ed.), *The Parliamentary History of England* (36 vols., 1806–1820), vol. XVI (1765–1771), pp. 133–135.

other species of goods manufactured in these kingdoms, besides other articles imported from abroad, chiefly purchased with our manufactures and with the produce of our colonies; by all which, many thousand manufacturers, seamen, and labourers, have been employed, to the very great and increasing benefit of this nation; and that, in return for these exports, the petitioners have received from the colonies, rice, indico, tobacco, naval stores, oil, whale fins, furs, and lately pot-ash, with other commodities, besides remittances by bills of exchange and bullion, obtained by the colonists in payment for articles of their produce, not required for the British market, and therefore exported to other places; and that, from the nature of this trade, consisting of British manufactures exported, and of the import of raw materials from America, many of them used in our manufactures, and all of them tending to lessen our dependence on neighbouring states, it must be deemed of the highest importance in the commercial system of this nation; and that this commerce, so beneficial to the state, and so necessary for the support of multitudes, now lies under such difficulties and discouragement, that nothing less than its utter ruin is apprehended, without the immediate interposition of parliament; and that, in consequence of the trade between the colonies and the mother country, as established and as permitted for many years, and of the experience which the petitioners have had of the readiness of the Americans to make their just remittances to the utmost of their real ability, they have been induced to make and venture such large exportations of British manufactures, as to leave the colonies indebted to the merchants of Great Britain in the sum of several millions sterling; and that at this time the colonists, when pressed for payment, appeal to past experience, in proof of their willingness; but declare it is not in their power, at present, to make good their engagements, alledging, that the taxes and restrictions laid upon them, and the extension of the jurisdiction of vice admiralty courts established by some late acts of parliament, particularly by an act passed in the fourth year of his present Majesty, for granting certain duties in the British colonies and plantations in America, and by an act passed in the fifth year of his present Majesty, for granting and applying certain stamp duties, and other duties, in the British colonies and plantations in America, with several regulations and restraints, which, if founded in acts of parliament for defined purposes, are represented to have been extended in such a manner as to disturb legal commerce and harass the fair trader, have so far interrupted the usual and former most fruitful branches of their commerce, restrained the sale of their produce, thrown the state of the several provinces into confusion, and brought on so great a number of actual bankruptcies, that the former opportunities and means of remittances and payments are utterly lost and taken from them; and that the petitioners are, by these unhappy events, reduced to the necessity of applying to the House, in order to secure themselves and their families from impending ruin; to prevent a multitude of manufacturers from becoming a burthen to the community, or else seeking their bread in other countries, to the irretrievable loss of this kingdom; and to preserve the strength of this nation entire, its commerce flourishing, the revenues increasing, our navigation, the bulwark of the kingdom, in a state of growth and extension, and the colonies, from inclination, duty, and interest, firmly attached to the mother country; and therefore praying the consideration of the premises, and entreating such relief, as to the House shall seem expedient.

B. DEBATE IN THE HOUSE OF COMMONS: WILLIAM PITT VERSUS GEORGE GRENVILLE (JAN. 14, 1766)*

Mr. *Pitt* spoke next. As he always began very low, and as every body was in agitation at his first rising, his introduction was not heard, till he said, I came to town but to-day; I was a stranger to the tenor of his Majesty's Speech, and the proposed Address, till I heard them read in this House. Unconnected and unconsulted, I have not the means of information; I am fearful of offending through mistake, and therefore beg to be indulged with a second reading of the proposed Address. [The Address being read, Mr. Pitt went on:] He commended the King's Speech, approved of the Address in answer, as it decided nothing, every gentleman being left at perfect liberty to take such a part concerning America, as he might afterwards see fit. . . .

It is a long time, Mr. Speaker, since I have attended in parliament. When the resolution was taken in the House to tax America, I was ill in bed. If I could have endured to have been carried in my bed, so great was the agitation of my mind for the consequences! I would have solicited some kind hand to have laid me down on this floor, to have borne my testimony against it. It is now an act that has passed; I would speak with decency of every act of this House, but I must beg the indulgence of the House to speak of it with freedom.

I hope a day may be soon appointed to consider the state of the nation with respect to America. I hope gentlemen will come to this debate with all the temper and impartiality that his Majesty recommends, and the importance of the subject requires. A subject of greater importance than ever engaged the attention of this House! that subject only excepted, when near a century ago, it was the question whether you yourselves were to be bound, or free. In the mean time, as I cannot depend upon health for any future day, such is the nature of my infirmities, I will beg to say a few words at present, leaving the justice, the equity, the policy, the expediency of the act, to another time. I will only speak to one point, a point which seems not to have been generally understood, I mean to the right. Some gentlemen . . . seem to have considered it as a point of honour. If gentlemen consider it in that light, they leave all measures of right and wrong, to follow a delusion that may lead to destruction. It is my opinion, that this kingdom has no right to lay a tax upon the colonies. At the same time, I assert the authority of this kingdom over the colonies, to be sovereign and supreme, in every circumstance of government and legislation whatsoever. They are the subjects of this kingdom, equally entitled with yourselves to all the natural rights of mankind and the peculiar privileges of Englishmen. Equally bound by its laws, and equally participating of the constitution of this free country. The Americans are the sons, not the bastards, of England. Taxation is no part of the governing or legislative power. The taxes are a voluntary gift and grant of the Commons alone. In legislation the three estates of the realm are alike concerned, but the concurrence of the peers and the crown to a tax, is only necessary to close with the form of a law. The gift and grant is of the Commons alone. In ancient days, the crown, the barons, and the clergy

* These excerpts are reprinted from Cobbett (ed.), *The Parliamentary History of England,* vol. XVI, pp. 97–108.

possessed the lands. In those days, the barons and the clergy gave and granted to the crown. They gave and granted what was their own. At present, since the discovery of America, and other circumstances permitting, the Commons are become the proprietors of the land. The crown has divested itself of its great estates. The church (God bless it) has but a pittance. The property of the Lords, compared with that of the Commons, is as a drop of water in the ocean: and this House represents those Commons, the proprietors of the lands; and those proprietors virtually represent the rest of the inhabitants. When, therefore, in this House we give and grant, we give and grant what is our own. But in an American tax, what do we do? We, your Majesty's Commons of Great Britain, give and grant to your Majesty, what? Our own property? No. We give and grant to your Majesty, the property of your Majesty's commons of America. It is an absurdity in terms.

The distinction between legislation and taxation is essentially necessary to liberty. The Crown, the Peers, are equally legislative powers with the Commons. If taxation be a part of simple legislation, the Crown, the Peers, have rights in taxation as well as yourselves: rights which they will claim, which they will exercise, whenever the principle can be supported by power.

There is an idea in some, that the colonies are virtually represented in this House. I would fain know by whom an American is represented here? Is he represented by any knight of the shire, in any county in this kingdom? Would to God that respectable representation was augmented to a greater number! Or will you tell him, that he is represented by any representative of a borough—a borough, which perhaps, its own representative never saw. This is what is called, 'the rotten part of the constitution.' It cannot continue the century; if it does not drop, it must be amputated. The idea of a virtual representation of America in this House, is the most contemptible idea that ever entered into the head of a man; it does not deserve a serious refutation.

The Commons of America, represented in their several assemblies, have ever been in possession of the exercise of this, their constitutional right, of giving and granting their own money. They would have been slaves if they had not enjoyed it. At the same time, this kingdom, as the supreme governing and legislative power, has always bound the colonies by her laws, by her regulations, and restrictions in trade, in navigation, in manufactures, in every thing, except that of taking their money out of their pockets without their consent.

Here I would draw the line. . . .

Mr. *Grenville* next stood up. He began with censuring the ministry very severely, for delaying to give earlier notice to parliament of the disturbances in America. He said, They began in July, and now we are in the middle of January; lately they were only occurrences, they are now grown to disturbances, to tumults and riots. I doubt they border on open rebellion; and if the doctrine I have heard this day be confirmed, I fear they will lose that name to take that of revolution. The government over them being dissolved, a revolution will take place in America. I cannot understand the difference between external and internal taxes. They are the same in effect, and only differ in name. That this kingdom has the sovereign, the supreme legislative power over America, is granted. It cannot be denied; and taxation is a part of that sovereign power. It is one branch of the legislation. It is, it has been exercised, over those who are not, who were never represented. It is exercised over the India Company, the merchants of London, the proprietors of the stocks, and over many great manufacturing towns. It was exercised over the palatinate of Chester, and the bishopric of Durham, before they sent any representatives to parliament. . . . When I proposed to tax America, I asked the House, if any gentleman would object to the right; I repeatedly asked it, and no man would attempt to deny it. Protection and obedience are reciprocal. Great Britain protects America; America is bound to yield obedience. If not, tell me when the Americans were emancipated? When they want the protection of this kingdom, they are always very ready to ask it. That protection has always been afforded them in the most full and ample manner. The nation has run itself into an immense debt to give them their protection; and now they are called upon to contribute a small share towards the public expence, an expence arising from themselves, they renounce your authority, insult your officers, and break out, I might almost say, into open rebellion. The seditious spirit of the colonies owes its birth to the factions in this House. Gentlemen are careless of the consequences of what they say, provided it answers the purposes of opposition. We were told we trod on tender ground; we were bid to expect disobedience. What was this, but telling the Americans to stand out against the law, to encourage their obstinacy with the expectation of support from hence? Let us only hold out a little, they would say, our friends will soon be in power. Ungrateful people of America! Bounties have been extended to them. When I had the honour of serving the crown, while you yourselves were loaded with an enormous debt, you have given bounties on their lumber, on their iron, their hemp, and many other articles. You have relaxed, in their favour, the Act of Navigation, that palladium of the British commerce; and yet I have been abused in all the public papers as an enemy to the trade of America. I have been particularly charged with giving orders and instructions to prevent the Spanish trade, and thereby stopping the channel, by which alone North America used to be supplied with cash for remittances to this country. I defy any man to produce any such orders or instructions. I discouraged no trade but what was illicit, what was prohibited by act of parliament. . . .

[Mr. *Pitt* then answered,] Gentlemen, Sir, (to the Speaker) I have been charged with giving birth to sedition in America. They have spoken their sentiments with freedom, against this unhappy act, and that freedom has become their crime. Sorry I am to hear the liberty of speech in this House, imputed as a crime. But the imputation shall not discourage me. It is a liberty I mean to exercise. No gentleman ought to be afraid to exercise it. It is a liberty by which the gentleman who calumniates it might have profited. He ought to have profited. He ought to have desisted from his project. The gentleman tells us, America is obstinate; America is almost in open rebellion. I rejoice that America has resisted. Three millions of people, so dead to all the feelings of liberty, as voluntarily to submit to be slaves, would have been fit instruments to make slaves of the rest. I come not here armed at all points, with law cases and acts of parliament, with the statute-book doubled down in dogs-ears, to defend the cause of liberty: if I had, I myself would have cited the two cases of Chester and Durham. I would have cited them, to have shewn, that, even under any arbitrary reigns, parliaments were ashamed of taxing a people without their consent, and allowed them representatives. Why did the gentleman confine himself to Chester and Durham? He might have taken a higher example in Wales; Wales, that never was taxed by parliament, till it was incorporated. I would not debate a particular point of law with the gentleman: I know his abilities. I have been obliged to his diligent researches. But, for the defence of liberty upon a general principle, upon a constitutional principle, it is a ground on which I stand firm; on which I dare meet any man. The gentleman tells us of many who are taxed, and are not represented—The India company, merchants, stock-holders, manufacturers. Surely many of these are represented in other capacities, as owners of land, or as freemen of boroughs. It is a misfortune that more are not actually represented. But they are all inhabitants, and, as such, are virtually represented. Many have it in their option to be actually represented. They have connexions with those that elect, and they have influence over them. The gentleman mentioned the stockholders: I hope he does not reckon the debts of the nation as a part of the national estate. Since the accession of king William, many ministers, some of great, others of more moderate abilities, have taken the lead of government.

He then went through the list of them, bringing it down till he came to himself, giving a short sketch of the characters of each of them. None of these, he said, thought, or ever dreamed, of robbing the colonies of their constitutional rights. That was reserved to mark the æra of the late administration: not that there were wanting some, when I had the honour to serve his Majesty, to propose to me to burn my fingers with an American Stamp-Act. With the enemy at their back, with our bayonets at their breasts, in the day of their distress, perhaps the Americans would have submitted to the imposition; but it would have been taking an ungenerous, and unjust advantage. The gentleman boasts of his bounties to America! Are not those bounties intended finally for the benefit of this kingdom? If they are not, he has misapplied the national treasures. I am no courtier of America, I stand up for this kingdom. I maintain, that the parliament has a right to bind, to restrain America. Our legislative power over the colonies is sovereign and supreme. When it ceases to be sovereign and supreme, I would advise every gentleman to sell his lands, if he can, and embark for that country. When two countries are connected together, like England and her colonies, without being incorporated, the one must necessarily govern; the greater must rule the less; but so rule it, as not to contradict the fundamental principles that are common to both.

If the gentleman does not understand the difference between internal and external taxes, I cannot help it; but there is a plain distinction between taxes levied for the purposes of raising a revenue, and duties imposed for the regulation of trade, for the accommodation of the subject; although, in the consequences, some revenue might incidentally arise from the latter.

The gentleman asks, when were the colonies emancipated? But I desire to know, when they were made slaves? But I dwell not upon words. When I had the honour of serving his Majesty, I availed myself of the means of information, which I derived from my office: I speak, therefore, from knowledge. My materials were good. I was at pains to collect, to digest, to consider them; and I will be bold to affirm, that the profits to Great Britain from the trade of the colonies, through all its branches, is two millions a year. This is the fund that carried you triumphantly through the last war. The estates that were rented at two thousand pounds a year, threescore years ago, are at three thousand pounds at present. Those estates sold then from fifteen to eighteen years purchase; the same may be now sold for thirty. You owe this to America. This is the price that America pays you for her protection. And shall a miserable financier come with a boast, that he can fetch a pepper-corn into the exchequer, to the loss of millions to the nation! I dare not say, how much higher these profits may be augmented. Omitting the immense increase of people, by natural population, in the northern colonies, and the migration from every part of Europe, I am convinced the whole commercial system of America may be altered to advantage. You have prohibited, where you ought to have encouraged; and you have encouraged where you ought to have prohibited. Improper restraints have been laid on the conti-nent, in favour of the islands. You have but two nations to trade with in America. Would you had twenty! Let acts of parliament in consequence of treaties remain, but let not an English minister become a customhouse officer for Spain, or for any foreign power. Much is wrong, much may be amended for the general good of the whole. . . .

The Americans have not acted in all things with prudence and temper. They have been wronged. They have been driven to madness by injustice. Will you punish them for the madness you have occasioned? Rather let prudence and temper come first from this side. I will undertake for America, that she will follow the example. There are two lines in a ballad of Prior's, of a man's behaviour to his wife, so applicable to you and your colonies, that I cannot help repeating them:

> Be to her faults a little blind:
> Be to her virtues very kind.

Upon the whole, I will beg leave to tell the House what is really my opinion. It is, that the Stamp Act be repealed absolutely, totally, and im-mediately. That the reason for the repeal be assigned, because it was founded on an erroneous principle. At the same time, let the sovereign authority of this country over the colonies, be asserted in as strong terms as can be devised, and be made to extend to every point of legislation whatsoever. That we may bind their trade, confine their manufactures, and exercise every power whatsoever, except that of taking their money out of their pockets without their consent.

C EXAMINATION OF BENJAMIN FRANKLIN IN THE HOUSE OF COMMONS (FEB. 13, 1766)*

Q. What is your name, and place of abode?—*A.* Franklin, of Philadelphia. . . .

Are not the colonies, from their circumstances, very able to pay the stamp duty?—In my opinion, there is not gold and silver enough in the colonies to pay the stamp duty for one year.

Don't you know that the money arising from the stamps was all to be laid out in America?—I know it is appropriated by the act to the American service; but it will be spent in the conquered colonies, where the soldiers are, not in the colonies that pay it.

Is there not a balance of trade due from the colonies where the troops are

---

* These excerpts are reprinted from Cobbett (ed.), *The Parliamentary History of England,* vol. XVI, pp. 137–143, 145–149, 151–152, 155–156, 158–160.

posted, that will bring back the money to the old colonies?—I think not. I believe very little would come back. I know of no trade likely to bring it back. I think it would come from the colonies where it was spent directly to England; for I have always observed, that in every colony the more plenty of means of remittance to England, the more goods are sent for, and the more trade with England carried on. . . .

Do you think it right, that America should be protected by this country, and pay no part of the expence?—That is not the case. The colonies raised, clothed and paid, during the last war, near 25,000 men, and spent many millions.

Were you not reimbursed by parliament?—We were only reimbursed what, in your opinion, we had advanced beyond our proportion, or beyond what might reasonably be expected from us; and it was a very small part of what we spent. Pennsylvania, in particular, disbursed about 500,000*l.*, and the reimbursements, in the whole, did not exceed 60,000*l.* . . .

Do not you think the people of America would submit to pay the stamp duty, if it was moderated?—No, never, unless compelled by force of arms.

Are not the taxes in Pennsylvania laid on unequally, in order to burden the English trade, particularly the tax on professions and business?—It is not more burdensome in proportion than the tax on lands. It is intended, and supposed to take an equal proportion of profits.

How is the assembly composed? Of what kinds of people are the members, landholders or traders?—It is composed of landholders, merchants, and artificers.

Are not the majority landholders?—I believe they are.

Do not they, as much as possible, shift the tax off from the land, to ease that, and lay the burthen heavier on trade?—I have never understood it so. I never heard such a thing suggested. And indeed an attempt of that kind could answer no purpose. The merchant or trader is always skilled in figures, and ready with his pen and ink. If unequal burdens are laid on his trade, he puts an additional price on his goods; and the consumers, who are chiefly landholders, finally pay the greatest part, if not the whole.

What was the temper of America towards Great Britain before the year 1763?—The best in the world. They submitted willingly to the government of the crown, and paid, in all their courts, obedience to acts of parliament. Numerous as the people are in the several old provinces, they cost you nothing in forts, citadels, garrisons or armies, to keep them in subjection. They were governed by this country at the expence only of a little pen, ink, and paper. They were led by a thread. They had not only a respect, but an affection for Great Britain, for its laws, its customs and manners, and even a fondness for its fashions, that greatly increased the commerce. Natives of Britain were always treated with particular regard; to be an Old-England man was, of itself, a character of some respect, and gave a kind of rank among us.

And what is their temper now?—O, very much altered.

Did you ever hear the authority of parliament to make laws for America questioned till lately?—The authority of parliament was allowed to be valid in all laws, except such as should lay internal taxes. It was never disputed in laying duties to regulate commerce. . . .

In what light did the people of America use to consider the parliament of Great Britain?—They considered the parliament as the great bulwark and security of their liberties and privileges, and always spoke of it with the utmost respect and veneration. Arbitrary ministers, they thought, might possibly, at times, attempt to oppress them; but they relied on it, that the parliament, on application, would always give redress. They remembered, with gratitude, a strong instance of this, when a bill was brought into parliament, with a clause to make royal instructions laws in the colonies, which the House of Commons would not pass, and it was thrown out.

And have they not still the same respect for parliament?—No; it is greatly lessened.

To what causes is that owing?—To a concurrence of causes; the restraints lately laid on their trade, by which the bringing of foreign gold and silver into the colonies was prevented; the prohibition of making paper money among themselves; and then demand a new and heavy tax by stamps; taking away at the same time, trials by juries, and refusing to receive and hear their humble petitions.

Don't you think they would submit to the Stamp Act, if it was modified, the obnoxious parts taken out, and the duty reduced to some particulars, of small moment?—No; they will never submit to it. . . .

What is your opinion of a future tax, imposed on the same principle with that of the Stamp Act, how would the Americans receive it?—Just as they do this. They would not pay it.

Have not you heard of the resolution of this House, and of the House of Lords, asserting the right of parliament relating to America, including a power to tax the people there?—Yes, I have heard of such resolutions.

What will be the opinion of the Americans on those resolutions?—They will think them unconstitutional and unjust.

Was it an opinion in America before 1763, that the parliament had no right to lay taxes and duties there?—I never heard any objection to the right of laying duties to regulate commerce; but a right to lay internal taxes was never supposed to be in parliament, as we are not represented there.

On what do you found your opinion, that the people in America made any such distinction?—I know that whenever the subject has occurred in conversation where I have been present, it has appeared to be the opinion of every one, that we could not be taxed in a parliament where we were not represented. But the payment of duties laid by act of parliament, as regulations of commerce, was never disputed.

But can you name any act of assembly, or public act of any of your governments, that made such distinction?—I do not know that there was any; I think there was never an occasion to make any such act, till now that you have attempted to tax us; that has occasioned resolutions of assembly, declaring the distinction, in which I think every assembly on the continent, and every member in every assembly, have been unanimous. . . .

Considering the resolutions of parliament as to the right, do you think, if the Stamp Act is repealed, that the North Americans will be satisfied?—I believe they will.

Why do you think so?—I think the resolutions of right will give them very little concern, if they are never attempted to be carried into practice. The colonies will probably consider themselves in the same situation, in that respect, with Ireland; they know you claim the same right with regard to Ireland, but you never exercise it. And they may believe you never will exercise it in the colonies, any more than in Ireland, unless on some very extraordinary occasion.

But who are to be the judges of that extraordinary occasion? Is not the parliament?—Though the parliament may judge of the occasion, the people will think it can never exercise such right, till representatives from the colonies are admitted into parliament, and that whenever the occasion arises, representatives will be ordered. . . .

Can any thing less than a military force carry the Stamp Act into execution?—I do not see how a military force can be applied to that purpose.

Why may it not?—Suppose a military force sent into America, they will find nobody in arms; what are they then to do? They cannot force a man to take stamps who chuses to do without them. They will not find a rebellion; they may indeed make one.

If the act is not repealed, what do you think will be the consequences?—A total loss of the respect and affection the people of America bear to this country, and of all the commerce that depends on that respect and affection.

How can the commerce be affected?—You will find, that if the act is not repealed, they will take very little of your manufactures in a short time.

Is it in their power to do without them?—I think they may very well do without them.

Is it their interest not to take them?—The goods they take from Britain are either necessaries, mere conveniences, or superfluities. The first, as cloth, &c. with a little industry they can make at home: the second they can do without, till they are able to provide them among themselves; and the last, which are much the greatest part, they will strike off immediately. They are mere articles of fashion, purchased and consumed, because the fashion in a respected country, but will now be detested and rejected. The people have already struck off, by general agreement, the use of all goods fashionable in mournings, and many thousand pounds worth are sent back as unsaleable.

Is it their interest to make cloth at home?—I think they may at present get it cheaper from Britain, I mean of the same fineness and neatness of workmanship; but when one considers other circumstances, the restraints on their trade, and the difficulty of making remittances, it is their interest to make every thing.

Suppose an act of internal regulations connected with a tax, how would they receive it?—I think it would be objected to.

Then no regulation with a tax would be submitted to?—Their opinion is, that when aids to the crown are wanted, they are to be asked of the several assemblies according to the old established usage, who will, as they have always done, grant them freely. And that their money ought not to be given away, without their consent, by persons at a distance, unacquainted with their circumstances and abilities. The granting aids to the crown, is the only means they have of recommending themselves to their sovereign, and they think it extremely hard and unjust, that a body of men, in which they have no representatives, should make a merit to itself of giving and granting what is not its own, but theirs, and deprives them of a right they esteem of the utmost value and importance, as it is the security of all their other rights. . . .

If an excise was laid by parliament, which they might likewise avoid paying, by not consuming the articles excised, would they then not object to it?—They would certainly object to it, as an excise is unconnected with any service done, and is merely an aid which they think ought to be asked of them, and granted by them if they are to pay it, and can be granted for them, by no others whatsoever, whom they have not impowered for that purpose.

You say they do not object to the right of parliament, in laying duties on goods to be paid on their importation; now, is there any kind of difference between a duty on the importation of goods and an excise on their consumption?—Yes; a very material one; an excise, for the reasons I have just mentioned, they think you can have no right to lay within their country. But the sea is yours; you maintain, by your fleets, the safety of navigation in it, and keep it clear of pirates; you may have therefore a natural and equitable right to some toll or duty on merchandizes carried through that part of your dominions, towards defraying the expence you are at in ships to maintain the safety of that carriage. . . .

If the Stamp Act should be repealed, would not the Americans think they could oblige the parliament to repeal every external tax law now in force?— It is hard to answer questions what people at such a distance will think.

But what do you imagine they will think were the motives of repealing the Act?—I suppose they will think that it was repealed from a conviction of its inexpediency; and they will rely upon it, that while the same inexpediency subsists, you will never attempt to make such another.

What do you mean by its inexpediency?—I mean its inexpediency on several accounts; the poverty and inability of those who were to pay the tax; the general discontent it has occasioned; and the impracticability of enforcing it. . . .

Do you think the assemblies have a right to levy money on the subject there, to grant to the crown?—I certainly think so; they have always done it.

Are they acquainted with the Declaration of Rights; and do they know that by that statute, money is not to be raised on the subject but by consent of parliament?—They are very well acquainted with it.

How then can they think they have a right to levy money for the crown, or for any other than local purposes?—They understand that clause to relate to subjects only within the realm; that no money can be levied on them for the crown, but by consent of parliament. The colonies are not supposed to be within the realm; they have assemblies of their own, which are their parliaments, and they are, in that respect, in the same situation with Ireland. When money is to be raised for the crown upon the subject in Ireland, or in the colonies, the consent is given in the parliament or Ireland, or in the assemblies of the colonies. They think the parliament of Great Britain cannot properly give that consent till it has representatives from America; for the Petition of Right expressly says, it is to be by common consent in parliament, and the people of America have no representatives in parliament, to make a part of that common consent.

If the Stamp Act should be repealed, and an act should pass, ordering the assemblies of the colonies to indemnify the sufferers by the riots, would they obey it?—That is a question I cannot answer.

Suppose the King should require the colonies to grant a revenue, and the parliament should be against their doing it, do they think they can grant a revenue to the King, without the consent of the parliament of Great Britain?

—That is a deep question. As to my own opinion I should think myself at liberty to do it, and should do it, if I liked the occasion. . . .

Don't you know that there is, in the Pennsylvania charter, an express reservation of the right of parliament to lay taxes there?—I know there is a clause in the charter, by which the King grants that he will levy no taxes on the inhabitants, unless it be with the consent of the assembly, or by an act of parliament.

How then could the assembly of Pennsylvania assert, that laying a tax on them by the Stamp Act was an infringement of their rights?—They understand it thus: by the same charter, and otherwise, they are entitled to all the privileges and liberties of Englishmen; they find in the Great Charters, and the Petition and Declaration of Rights, that one of the privileges of English subjects is, that they are not to be taxed but by their common consent; they have therefore relied upon it, from the first settlement of the province, that the parliament never would, nor could, by colour of that clause in the charter, assume a right of taxing them, till it had qualified itself to exercise such right, by admitting representatives from the people to be taxed, who ought to make a part of that common consent.

Are there any words in the charter that justify that construction?—The common rights of Englishmen, as declared by Magna Charta, and the Petition of Right, all justify it.

Does the distinction between internal and external taxes exist in the words of the charter?—No, I believe not.

Then may they not, by the same interpretation, object to the parliament's right of external taxation?—They never have hitherto. Many arguments have been lately used here to shew them that there is no difference, and that if you have no right to tax them internally, you have none to tax them externally, or make any other law to bind them. At present they do not reason so, but in time they may possibly be convinced by these arguments.

Do not the resolutions of the Pennsylvania assemblies say, all taxes?—If they do, they mean only internal taxes; the same words have not always the same meaning here and in the colonies. By taxes they mean internal taxes; by duties they mean customs; these are the ideas of the language.

Have you not seen the resolutions of the Massachusett's Bay assembly? —I have.

Do they not say, that neither external nor internal taxes can be laid on them by parliament?—I don't know that they do; I believe not.

If . . . [they] should say neither tax nor imposition could be laid, does not that province hold the power of parliament can lay neither?—I suppose that by the word imposition, they do not intend to express duties to be laid on goods imported, as regulations of commerce.

What can the colonies mean then by imposition as distinct from taxes? —They may mean many things, as impressing of men, or of carriages, quartering troops on private houses, and the like; there may be great impositions that are not properly taxes. . . .

If the Stamp Act should be repealed, would it induce the assemblies of America to acknowledge the right of parliament to tax them, and would they erase their resolutions?—No, never.

Is there no means of obliging them to erase those resolutions?—None, that I know of; they will never do it, unless compelled by force of arms.

Is there a power on earth that can force them to erase them?—No power, how great soever, can force men to change their opinions. . . .

What used to be the pride of the Americans?—To indulge in the fashions and manufactures of Great Britain.

What is now their pride?—To wear their old clothes over again, till they can make new ones. . . .

D. DEBATE IN THE HOUSE OF LORDS: LORD CAMDEN VERSUS LORD MANSFIELD (FEB. 3, MAR. 7, 1766)*

Lord Camden.—I am very unhappy the first time of speaking in this House to differ from a lord of such superior abilities and learning, but the question before your lordships concerns the common rights of mankind; it is an abstract question, and will be judged of by your lordships gravely and deliberately, without any regard to the authority of any lord who speaks on either side of the question.

My lords; he who disputes the authority of any supreme legislature treads upon very tender ground. It is therefore necessary for me in setting out to lay in my claim to your lordships, and to desire that no inference may be drawn from any thing I shall advance. I disclaim that the consequence of my reasoning will be that the colonies can claim an independence on this country, or that they have a right to oppose acts of legislature in a rebellious manner, even though the legislature has no right to make such acts. In my own opinion, my lords, the legislature had no right to make this law.

The sovereign authority, the omnipotence of the legislature, my lords, is a favourite doctrine, but there are some things they cannot do. They cannot enact any thing against the divine law, and may forfeit their right. They cannot take away any man's private property without making him a compensation. A proof of which is the many private bills, as well as public, passed every session. They have no right to condemn any man by bill of attainder without hearing him.

But though the parliament cannot take any man's private property, yet every subject must make contribution. And this he consents to do by his representatives; when the people consented to be taxed they reserved to themselves a power of giving and granting by their representatives.

The Resolution now proposed is in my opinion too general, as it gives the legislature an absolute power of laying any tax upon America.

Notwithstanding the King, Lords, and Commons could in ancient times tax other persons, they never could tax the clergy. I have seen a record, 17 R. 2, of the Commons offering an aid to his majesty so as the clergy, who were possessed of a third part of the lands of the kingdom, would contribute a third part of the sum wanted. The clergy on that occasion said, that the parliament had no right to tax them, they might lay any part of the money wanted on the laity, and that they, the clergy, would then do what they saw just. And so late as in the year 1674 the clergy in convocation insisted on a right to tax themselves, and this right was recognized by the Commons.

* These excerpts are reprinted from Cobbett (ed.), *The Parliamentary History of England,* vol. XVI, pp. 168–170, 172–181.

At present the clergy have dropt that right; when, I cannot pretend to say, but when they did drop it they were melted down into the body of the country and are now electors of their own representatives.

The counties palatine were little feudal governments exercising regal authority. The method was, for the crown to require them by writ to tax themselves. Tyrrel mentions some records of writs of that kind directed to Chester. It appears, however, that afterwards the legislature took to itself the power of taxation over these counties palatine, but then when they petitioned to be represented the parliament readily granted them representatives.

It is observable, that at the close of the charter erecting Lancaster into a county palatine there is a salvo of the right to the parliament at large. And the great lord Hale, in a MS. never printed, which treats of the prerogative of the crown, observes, that this was a county palatine, without the requisites of Chester and Durham, particularly as to the power of taxing and pardoning.

Wales, my lords, was not taxed till it was united to England, when it was forthwith represented.

Calais and Berwick, when they were conquered, sent members to parliament. Guernsey, Jersey, and the Isle of Man are not yet a part of the realm of England, and have never yet been taxed.

Ireland was conquered originally, but was settled by the English. They tax themselves, and the parliament here has no right to tax them; lord Hale affirms this in the before-mentioned MS. where he says, that he thinks no acts here can bind the Irish in point of subsidies.

But, my lords, even supposing the Americans have no exclusive right to tax themselves, I maintain it would be good policy to give it them.—America feels she can do better without us, than we without her.

He spoke then to the expediency, and concluded that his opinion was, that the colonies had a right to tax themselves, and the parliament not. . . .

Lord *Mansfield*. I stand up to bring your lordships to the question before you, which is, whether the proposition made by the noble duke is, from what appears from our law and history, true or not true. . . . I shall . . . lay down two propositions:

1st, That the British legislature, as to the power of making laws, represents the whole British empire, and has authority to bind every part and every subject without the least distinction, whether such subjects have a right to vote or not, or whether the law binds places within the realm or without.

2nd, That the colonists, by the condition on which they migrated, settled, and now exist, are more emphatically subjects of Great Britain than those within the realm; and that the British legislature have in every instance exercised their right of legislation over them without any dispute or question till the 14th of January last.

As to the 1st proposition:

In every government the legislative power must be lodged somewhere, and the executive must likewise be lodged somewhere.

In Great Britain the legislative is in parliament, the executive in the crown.

The parliament first depended upon tenures. How did representation by election first arise? Why, by the favour of the crown. And the notion now taken up, that every subject must be represented by deputy, if he does not vote in parliament himself, is merely ideal.

At this day all the great companies here—the Bank, East India Company, and South Sea Company, have no representatives.

As to what has been said about the clergy—the fact is, that a demand made by them of a right to tax themselves was supported by the Pope; and the king and parliament of those times were weak enough to admit of it; but this admission is no proof of the right.

No distinction ought to be taken between the authority of parliament, over parts within or without the realm; but it is an established rule of construction, that no parts without the realm are bound unless named in the act. And this rule establishes the right of parliament; for unless they had a right to bind parts out of the realm, this distinction would never have been made.

As to Wales, it has been said that it was not part of the realm, and paid no taxes before it was united and represented. Now Wales, in statute *Walliæ*, 12 Edward I, is described as a part of the crown of England.

As to the parts beyond seas which were ceded to the crown of England; such as Guienne and Calais, they have been mentioned in, and bound by different statutes, before Calais ever sent a representative to parliament.

The Isle of Man is a very late instance of a part of the realm never represented, which came to the noble duke the proprietor, under a descent of 400 years; and his grace last session applied to the justice of parliament, and never was advised to dispute their right of laying taxes, &c.

As to the sound which has been thrown out, that no money can be raised without consent, the direct contrary is the truth; for if any number of people should agree to raise money for the King, it is unconstitutional.

By the Declaration of Right, 13 Car. 1, declaring it illegal to levy money except by act of parliament, the words are, 'by loan, gift, or benevolence,' and all such kind of levies are declared void.

Objection has been made, that Money Bills begin in the House of Commons, and have past here of course without amendment. I have read an able argument of lord Nottingham's on this subject, in the Journal of the House of Commons, when he managed the conference between the Houses, and to which I refer your lordships.

I shall now consider the demesnes of the crown; Counties palatine—it has been said they were not taxed till they were represented. The act in Henry 8th's time giving Chester a right to send representatives, recites, that they were liable to and bound by all the laws made by parliament, and therefore it was but just they should be represented.

The act, Car. 2, giving the right to Durham, recites, that they were then and before liable to taxes and subsidies. And therefore I think it clear, that the counties palatine were bound by acts of parliament in England, without being named, before they sent representatives.

As to Guienne and Calais, several acts were made here from the time they were first ceded, to lay interior regulations upon them. Calais and Berwick never sent members to parliament till the time of Henry 8, but several statutes past, binding these places from the time of Henry 6.

It has been said negatively, that Wales never paid taxes till it sent members to parliament. This was in 27 Henry 8. Now in several statutes for laying taxes before that period, Wales is *nominatim* excepted, and the reason given for that exception in the statutes is, that they paid *mises* (which was a tax) to the king; and it is in like manner excepted out of several statutes after 27 Henry 8, till these *mises* were taken away, and then it was taxed with the other part of the realm. But as a distinction has been taken between the power of laying taxes and making laws, I must declare, that after the most diligent searches on this head, I cannot find any distinction or difference whatever.

As to the second proposition I laid out,

It must be granted that they migrated with leave as colonies, and therefore from the very meaning of the word were, are, and must be subjects, and owe allegiance and subjection to their mother country.

My lords, there are three sorts of colonies in America:

King's Provinces; Proprietary Provinces, and Charter Provinces.

The King's provinces are governed by instructions sent to the governors, who after some time are directed to call assemblies, and they have a power to make bye laws for their interior government, &c.

The proprietary governments are Maryland and Pennsylvania: the first was granted to be held as the county of Durham, and that, before this county was represented in parliament, had by charter a subordinate power to make laws, so as the same were not contrary to the laws of England.

Pennsylvania was granted to W. Penn in 33 Car. 2.

The Pennsylvanians are among the loudest of those who complain of the Stamp Act. In the papers coming from them they use the King of Great Britain as they do their own proprietary king.

By their charter Mr. Penn has a power to raise money and make laws, &c. so as they be not repugnant to the laws of England. And it is provided, that a transcript of every law should be sent to Great Britain, and if repugnant to law here, shall be repealed. And an agent is to reside here to make satisfaction for all penalties; and if no satisfaction is made, the grant is to be void.

Charter governments are Virginia, Connecticut, Rhode Island, and Massachusets Bay.

These are all on the same footing as our great corporations in London. And it is worth remarking, that Massachusets Bay had a charter which in Charles 2's time was vacated in Chancery for their abuse of it. Now, is it possible to suppose that a legislature can exist with a sole power of laying taxes, which legislature may be destroyed here by a process in the courts of Chancery or King's-bench?

I find in the Journals of the House of Commons that, upon a Bill for a free fishery being brought into that House, 19 James 1, a doubt was thrown out, whether parliament had any thing to do in America. This doubt was immediately answered, I believe by Coke. The province is held of the manor of East Greenwich, and granted by charter under the great seal. This was thought a sufficient answer, and the Bill passed that House.

In the year 1650, during the Commonwealth, an act passed, avowing the subjection of the colonies to England.

The Act of Settlement is of England, &c. and all the dominions thereto belonging. If Americans are not subject to English statutes, the Act of Settlement does not bind them.

But there are many statutes laying taxes in America; I know no difference between laying internal and external taxes; but if such difference should be taken, are not the acts giving duties, customs, and erecting a post office, to be considered as laying an internal tax?

In 1724, the assembly of Jamaica refused to raise taxes for their necessary support. Application was made to the council by their agent here, and a reference to sir Clement Worge and Lord Hardwicke, to know whether the king could not lay a tax. They gave their opinion, that if Jamaica was to be considered as a conquered country, the king could lay taxes; if otherwise, the assembly must lay it, or it must be raised by act of parliament.

But this notion, my lords, is of a very modern date.

In December last the authority of parliament was not disputed; even on the 14th of Jan. no hint was given in this House, which was then very full, against that authority. This day is the first time we have heard of it in this House.

Before I conclude I will take the liberty of laying down one proposition, viz.

When the supreme power abdicates, the government is dissolved.

Take care, my lords, you do not abdicate your authority. In such an event, your lordships would leave the worthy and innocent, as well as the unworthy and guilty, to the same confusion and ruin.

His lordship has mentioned some quotations from lord chief justice Hale, whether this was wrote when his lordship was a student, barrister, or judge, does not appear, but at best it is but a quere of that learned judge on the power of England to lay taxes on Ireland. Molyneux, in his book, burnt by the hands of the common hangman, questioning the power of parliament, makes a distinction between Ireland and the colonies in this respect.

*   *   *

Lord *Camden*.

My lords; when I spoke last on this subject, I thought I had delivered my sentiments so fully, and supported them with such reasons, and such authorities, that I apprehended I should be under no necessity of troubling your lordships again. But I am now compelled to rise up, and to beg your farther indulgence: I find that I have been very injuriously treated; have been considered as the broacher of new-fangled doctrines, contrary to the laws of this kingdom, and subversive of the rights of parliament. My lords, this is a heavy charge, but more so when made against one stationed as I am in both capacities, as peer and judge, the defender of the law and the constitution. When I spoke last, I was indeed replied to, but not answered. In the intermediate time, many things have been said. As I was not present, I must now beg leave to answer such as have come to my knowledge. As the affair is of the utmost importance, and in its consequences may involve the fate of kingdoms, I took the strictest review of my arguments; I re-examined all my authorities; fully determined, if I found myself mistaken, publicly to own my mistake, and give up my opinion: but my searches have more and more convinced me, that the British parliament have no right to tax the Americans. I shall not therefore consider the Declaratory Bill now lying on your table; for to what purpose, but loss of time, to consider the particulars of a Bill, the very existence of which is illegal, absolutely illegal, contrary to the fundamental laws of nature, contrary to the fundamental laws of this constitution? A constitution grounded on the eternal and immutable laws of nature; a constitution whose foundation and centre is liberty, which sends liberty to every subject, that is or may happen to be within any part of its ample circumference. Nor, my lords, is the doctrine new, it is as old as the constitution; it grew up with it; indeed it is its support; taxation and representation are inseparably united; God hath joined them, no British parliament can separate them; to endeavour to do it, is to stab our very vitals. Nor is this the first time this doctrine has been mentioned; 70 years ago, my lords, a pamphlet was published, recommending the levying a parliamentary tax on one of the colonies; this pamphlet was answered by two others, then much read; these totally deny the power of taxing the colonies; and why? Because the colonies had no representatives in parliament to give consent; no answer, public or private, was given to these pamphlets, no censure passed upon them; men were not startled at the doctrine as either new or illegal, or derogatory to the rights of parliament. I do not mention these pamphlets by way of authority, but to vindicate myself from the imputation of having first broached this doctrine.

My position is this—I repeat it—I will maintain it to my last hour,—taxation and representation are inseparable;—this position is founded on the laws of nature; it is more, it is itself an eternal law of nature; for whatever is a man's own, is absolutely his own; no man hath a right to take it from him without his consent, either expressed by himself or representative; whoever attempts to do it, attempts an injury; whoever does it, commits a robbery, he throws down and destroys the distinction between liberty and slavery. Taxation and representation are coeval with and essential to this constitution. I wish the maxim of Machiavel was followed, that of examining a constitution, at certain periods, according to its first principles; this would correct abuses and supply defects. I wish the times would bear it, and that men's minds were cool enough to enter upon such a task, and that the representative authority of this kingdom was more equally settled. I am sure some histories, of late published, have done great mischief; to endeavour to fix the æra when the House of Commons began in this kingdom is a most pernicious and destructive attempt; to fix it in an Edward's or Henry's reign, is owing to the idle dreams of some whimsical, ill-judging antiquarians: but, my lords, this is a point too important to be left to such wrong-headed people. When did the House of Commons first begin? when, my lords? it began with the constitution, it grew up with the constitution; there is not a blade of grass growing in the most obscure corner of this kingdom, which is not, which was not ever, represented since the constitution began; there is not a blade of grass, which when taxed, was not taxed by the consent of the proprietor. There is a history written by one Carte, a history that most people now see through, and there is another favourite history, much read and admired. I will not name the author, your lordships must know whom I mean, and you must know from whence he pilfered his notions, concerning the first beginning of the House of Commons. My lords, I challenge any one to point out the time when any tax was laid upon any person by parliament, that person being unrepresented in parliament. My lords, the parliament laid a tax upon the palatinate of Chester and ordered commissioners to collect it there: as commissioners were ordered to collect it in other counties; but the palatinate refused to comply; they addressed the king by petition, setting forth, that the English parliament had no right to tax them, that they had a parliament of their own, that they had always taxed themselves, and therefore desired the king to order his commissioners not to proceed. My lords, the king received the petition; he did not declare them either seditious or rebellious, but allowed their plea, and they taxed themselves. Your lordships may see both the petition and the king's answer in the records in the Tower. The clergy taxed themselves; when the parliament attempted to tax them, they stoutly refused; said they were not represented there; that they had a parliament of their own, which represented the clergy; that they would tax themselves; they did so. Much stress has been laid upon Wales, before it was united as it now is, as if the King, standing in the place of their former princes of that country, raised money by his own authority; but the real fact is otherwise; for I find that, long before Wales was subdued, the northern counties of that principality had representatives, and a parliament or assembly. As to Ireland, my lords, before that kingdom had a parliament as it now has, if your lordships will examine the old records, you will find, that when a tax was to be laid on that country, the Irish sent over here representatives; and the same records will inform your lordships, what wages those representatives received from their constituents. In short, my lords, from the whole of our history, from the earliest period, you will find that taxation and representation were always united; so true are the words of that consummate reasoner and politician Mr. Locke. I before alluded to his book; I have again consulted him; and finding what he writes so applicable to the subject in hand, and so much in favour of my sentiments, I beg your lordships' leave to read a little of this book.

"The supreme power cannot take from any man, any part of his property, without his own consent;" and B. 2. p. 136–139, particularly 140. Such are the words of this great man, and which are well worth your serious attention. His principles are drawn from the heart of our constitution, which he thoroughly understood, and will last as long as that shall last; and, to his immortal honour, I know not to what, under providence, the Revolution and all its happy effects, are more owing, than to the principles of government laid down by Mr. Locke. For these reasons, my lords, I can never give my assent to any bill for taxing the American colonies, while they remain unrepresented; for as to the distinction of a virtual representation, it is so absurd as not to deserve an answer; I therefore pass it over with contempt. The forefathers of the Americans did not leave their native country, and subject themselves to every danger and distress, to be reduced to a state of slavery: they did not give up their rights; they looked for protection, and not for chains, from their mother country; by her they expected to be defended in the possession of their property, and not to be deprived of it: for, should the present power continue, there is nothing which they can call their own; or, to use the words of Mr. Locke, "What property have they in that, which another may, by right, take, when he pleases, to himself?"

E. REPEAL WITHOUT YIELDING IN PRINCIPLE: THE DECLARATORY ACT (MAR. 18, 1766)*

WHEREAS *several of the houses of representatives in his Majesty's colonies and plantations in* America, *have of late, against law, claimed to*

* These excerpts are reprinted from Danby Pickering (ed.), *Statutes at Large*, vol. XXVII, pp. 19–20.

*themselves, or to the general assemblies of the same, the sole and exclusive
right of imposing duties and taxes upon his Majesty's subjects in the said
colonies and plantations; and have, in pursuance of such claim, passed certain votes, resolutions, and orders, derogatory to the legislative authority of
parliament, and inconsistent with the dependency of the said colonies and
plantations upon the crown of* Great Britain: may it therefore please your
most excellent Majesty, that it may be declared; and be it declared by the
King's most excellent majesty, by and with the advice and consent of the
lords spiritual and temporal, and commons, in this present parliament
assembled, and by the authority of the same, That the said colonies and
plantations in *America* have been, are, and of right ought to be, subordinate
unto, and dependent upon the imperial crown and parliament of *Great
Britain;* and that the King's majesty, by and with the advice and consent
of the lords spiritual and temporal, and commons of *Great Britain,* in parliament assembled, had, hath, and of right ought to have, full power and
authority to make laws and statutes of sufficient force and validity to bind
the colonies and people of *America,* subjects of the crown of *Great Britain,*
in all cases whatsoever.

II. And be it further declared and enacted by the authority aforesaid,
That all resolutions, votes, orders, and proceedings, in any of the said
colonies or plantations, whereby the power and authority of the parliament
of *Great Britain,* to make laws and statutes as aforesaid, is denied, or drawn
into question, are, and are hereby declared to be, utterly null and void to
all intents and purposes whatsoever.

SELECTION

Polarization of Issues

*The Stamp Act crisis left no doubt that British and American political leaders
had markedly different views of the nature and constitutional structure of the
British Empire. The extent of the difference can be seen in the two selections
below. The conventional British view—that "what the parliament doth, no
authority upon earth can undo" and that the colonies were perforce subject to its
jurisdiction—was most succinctly and authoritatively expressed by Sir William
Blackstone (1723–1780), professor of English law at Oxford University, in the
passages printed below as Selection 8 A from his* Commentaries on the Laws of
England, *a series of lectures published between 1765 and 1769. At the other
extreme was the doctrine advanced by Richard Bland (1710–1776), Virginia
lawyer, planter, legislator, and antiquarian, early in 1766 in An* Inquiry into the
Rights of the British Colonies, *printed in part below as Selection 8 B. Whereas Blackstone's view assumed that in every polity, no matter how vast or loosely connected,
there had to be one supreme and sovereign legislative authority; Bland suggested*

that the legislative authority could be, and in fact was, divided in the British Empire. It was his contention that the colonies were "distinct" states, "independent, as to their internal *government, of the original kingdom, but united with her, as to their* external *polity, in the closest and most intimate LEAGUE AND AMITY, under the same allegiance, and enjoying the benefits of a reciprocal intercourse." It followed, therefore, that colonists had the "right . . . of directing their* internal *government by laws made with their own consent." Although Bland was not bold enough to say so explicitly, it also followed that Parliament's authority in the colonies was limited to the regulation of their external affairs and that it could neither tax them nor legislate on matters affecting their "internal polity." These arguments went well beyond the dominant American view at the time of the Stamp Act that Parliament could legislate for but not tax the colonists and indicated the direction Americans would take in formulating their constitutional position over the following decade.*

Daniel J. Boorstin, The Mysterious Science of the Law *(1941), is a comprehensive study of Blackstone and the* Commentaries, *and Clinton Rossiter,* Seedtime of the Republic: The Origin of the American Tradition of Political Liberty *(1953), pages 247–280, contains the fullest discussion of Bland.*

A. THE OMNIPOTENCE OF PARLIAMENT: SIR WILLIAM BLACKSTONE, "COMMENTARIES ON THE LAWS OF ENGLAND" (1765)*

BESIDES these adjacent islands, our more distant plantations in America, and elsewhere, are also in some respects subject to the English laws. Plantations, or colonies in distant countries, are either such where the lands are claimed by right of occupancy only, by finding them desart and uncultivated, and peopling them from the mother country; or where, when already cultivated they have been either gained by conquest, or ceded to us by treaties. And both these rights are founded upon the law of nature, or at least upon that of nations. But there is a difference between these two species of colonies, with respect to the laws by which they are bound. For it hath been held, that if an uninhabited country be discovered and planted by English subjects, all the English laws then in being, which are the birthright of every subject, are immediately there in force. But this must be understood with very many and very great restrictions. Such colonists carry with them only so much of the English law, as is applicable to their own situation and the condition of an infant colony; such, for instance, as the general rules of inheritance, and of protection from personal injuries. The artificial refinements and distinctions incident to the property of a great and commercial people, the laws of police and revenue, (such especially as are enforced by penalties) the mode of maintenance for the established clergy, the jurisdiction of spiritual courts, and a multitude of other provisions, are neither necessary nor convenient for them, and therefore are not in force. What shall be admitted and what rejected, at what times, and under what restrictions, must in case of dispute, be decided in the first instance by their own

* These excerpts are reprinted from the edition published in four volumes in Philadelphia in 1771–1772, vol. I, pp. 106–109, 160–162.

provincial judicature, subject to the revision and control of the king in council; the whole of their constitution being also liable to be new-modelled and reformed, by the general superintending power of the legislature in the mother country. But in conquered or ceded countries, that have already laws of their own, the king may indeed alter and change those laws; but, till he does actually change them, the antient laws of the country remain, unless such as are against the law of God, as in the case of an infidel country. Our American plantations are principally of this latter sort, being obtained in the last century either by right of conquest and driving out the natives (with what natural justice I shall not at present enquire) or by treaties. And therefore the common law of England, as such, has no allowance or authority there; they being no part of the mother country, but distinct (though dependent) dominions. They are subject however to the control of the parliament; though (like Ireland, Man, and the rest) not bound by any acts of parliament, unless particularly named.

WITH respect to their interior polity, our colonies are properly of three sorts. 1. Provincial establishments, the constitutions of which depend on the respective commissions issued by the crown to the governors, and the instructions which usually accompany those commissions; under the authority of which, provincial assemblies are constituted, with the power of making local ordinances, not repugnant to the laws of England. 2. Proprietary governments, granted out by the crown to individuals, in the nature of feudatory principalities, with all the inferior regalities, and subordinate powers of legislation, which formerly belonged to the owners of counties palatine: yet still with these express conditions, that the ends for which the grant was made be substantially pursued, and that nothing be attempted which may derogate from the sovereignty of the mother country. 3. Charter governments, in the nature of civil corporations, with the power of making by-laws for their own interior regulation, not contrary to the laws of England; and with such rights and authorities as are specially given them in their several charters of incorporation. The form of government in most of them is borrowed from that of England. They have a governor named by the king, (or in some proprietary colonies by the proprietor) who is his representative or deputy. They have courts of justice of their own, from whose decisions an appeal lies to the king in council here in England. Their general assemblies which are their house of commons, together with their council of state being their upper house, with the concurrence of the king or his representative the governor, make laws suited to their own emergencies. But it is particularly declared by statute 7 & 8 W. III. c. 22. that all laws, by-laws, usages, and customs, which shall be in practice in any of the plantations, repugnant to any law, made or to be made in this kingdom relative to the said plantations, shall be utterly void and of none effect. . . .

THE power and jurisdiction of parliament, says sir Edward Coke, is so transcendent and absolute, that it cannot be confined, either for causes or persons, within any bounds. . . . It hath sovereign and uncontrolable authority in making, confirming, enlarging, restraining, abrogating, repealing, reviving, and expounding of laws, concerning matters of all possible denominations, ecclesiastical, or temporal, civil, military, maritime, or criminal: this being the place where that absolute despotic power, which must in all governments reside somewhere, is entrusted by the constitution of these kingdoms. All mischiefs and grievances, operations and remedies, that transcend the ordinary course of the laws, are within the reach of this extraordinary tribunal. It can regulate or new model the succession to the crown; as was done in the reign of Henry VIII and William III. It can alter the established religion of the land; as was done in a variety of instances, in the reigns of king Henry VIII and his three children. It can change and create afresh even the constitution of the kingdom and of parliaments themselves; as was done by the act of union, and the several statutes for triennial and septennial elections. It can, in short, do every thing that is not naturally impossible; and therefore some have not scrupled to call it's power, by a figure rather too bold, the omnipotence of parliament. True it is, that what the parliament doth, no authority upon earth can undo. So that it is a matter most essential to the liberties of this kingdom, that such members be delegated to this important trust, as are most eminent for their probity, their fortitude, and their knowledge; for it was a known apothegm of the great lord treasurer Burleigh, "that England could never be ruined but by a parliament:" and, as sir Matthew Hale observes, this being the highest and greatest court, over which none other can have jurisdiction in the kingdom, if by any means a misgovernment should any way fall upon it, the subjects of this kingdom are left without all manner of remedy. . . .

IT must be owned that Mr Locke, and other theoretical writers, have held, that "there remains still inherent in the people "supreme power to remove or alter the legislative, when they find the legislative act contrary to the trust reposed in them: for when such trust is abused, it is thereby forfeited, and devolves to those who gave it." But however just this conclusion may be in theory, we cannot adopt it, nor argue from it, under any dispensation of government at present actually existing. For this devolution of power, to the people at large, includes in it a dissolution of the whole form of government established by that people; reduces all the members to their original state of equality; and, by annihilating the sovereign power, repeals all positive laws whatsoever before enacted. No human laws will therefore suppose a case, which at once must destroy all law, and compel men to build afresh upon a new foundation; nor will they make provision for so desperate an event, as must render all legal provisions ineffectual. So long therefore as the English constitution lasts, we may venture to affirm, that the power of parliament is absolute and without control.

B. THE CASE AGAINST PARLIAMENTARY AUTHORITY IN INTERNAL COLONIAL MATTERS: RICHARD BLAND, "AN ENQUIRY INTO THE RIGHTS OF THE BRITISH COLONIES" (1766)*

It is in vain to search into the civil constitution of *England* for directions in fixing the proper connection between the colonies and the mother-kingdom; I mean, what their reciprocal duties to each other are, and what obedience is due from the children to the general parent. The planting colonies from *Britain,* is but of recent date, and nothing relative to such plantation can be collected from the ancient laws of the kingdom; neither can we receive any

* These excerpts are reprinted from the London edition of 1769, pp. 11–13, 16–20.

better information, by extending our enquiry into the history of the colonies, established by the several nations, in the more early ages of the world. All the colonies (except those of *Georgia* and *Nova Scotia*) formed from the *English* nation in *North-America*, were planted in a manner, and under a dependence, of which there is not an instance in all the colonies of the ancients; and therefore I conceive, it must afford a good degree of surprize, to find an English civilian giving it as his sentiment, that the *English* colonies ought to be governed by the *Roman* laws; and for no better reason, than because the *Spanish* colonies, as he says, are governed by those laws. The *Romans* established their colonies, in the midst of vanquished nations, upon principles which best secured their conquests; the privileges granted to them were not always the same; their policy in the government of their colonies, and the conquered nations, being always directed by arbitrary principles to the end they aimed at, the subjecting the whole earth to their empire: but the colonies in *North-America*, except those planted within the present century, were founded by *Englishmen,* who, becoming private adventurers, established themselves, without any expence to the nation, in this uncultivated and almost uninhabited country; so that their case is plainly distinguishable from that of the *Roman,* or any other colonies of the ancient world.

As then we can receive no light from the laws of the kingdom, or from ancient history, to direct us in our enquiry, we must have recourse to the law of nature, and those rights of mankind which flow from it.

I have observed before, that when subjects are deprived of their civil rights, or are dissatisfied with the place they hold in the comunity, they have a natural right to quit the society of which they are members, and to retire into another country. Now when men exercise this right, and withdraw themselves from their country, they recover their natural freedom and independence: the jurisdiction and sovereignty of the state they have quitted, ceases; and if they unite, and by common consent take possession of a new country, and form themselves into a political society, they become a sovereign state, independent of the state from which they separated. If then the subjects of *England* have a natural right to relinquish their country; and by retiring from it, and associating together, to form a new political society and independent state, they must have a right, by compact with the sovereign of the nation, to remove into a new country, and to form a civil establishment upon the terms of the compact. In such a case, the terms of the compact must be obligatory and binding upon the parties; they must be the magna charta, the fundamental principles of government, to this new society; and every infringement of them must be wrong, and may be opposed. It will be necessary, then to examine, whether any such compact was entered into between the sovereign, and those *English* subjects who established themselves in *America*.

You have told us, that "before the first and great act of navigation, the inhabitants of *North-America* were but a few unhappy fugitives, who had wandered thither to enjoy their civil and religious liberties, which they were deprived of at home." If this was true, it is evident, from what has been said upon the law of nature, that they have a right to a civil independent establishment of their own, and that *Great-Britain* has no *right* to interfere in it. But you have been guilty of a gross anachronism in your chronology, and a great error in your account of the first settlement of the colonies in

North-America; for it is a notorious fact that they were not settled by fugitives from their native country, but by men who came over voluntarily, at their own expence, and under charters from the crown, obtained for that purpose, long before the first and great act of navigation. . . .

From [a review] . . . of the charters, and other acts of the crown, under which the first colony in *North-America* was established, it is evident, that "the colonists were not a few unhappy fugitives who had wandered into a distant part of the world to enjoy their civil and religious liberties, which they were deprived of at home," but had a regular government long before the first act of navigation, and were respected as a distinct state, independent, as to their *internal* government, of the original kingdom, but united with her, as to their *external* polity, in the closest and most intimate LEAGUE AND AMITY, under the same allegiance, and enjoying the benefits of a reciprocal intercourse.

But allow me to make a reflection or two upon the preceding account of the first settlement of an *English* colony in *North-America.*

America was no part of the kingdom of *England;* it was possessed by a savage people, scattered through the country, who were not subject to the *English* dominion, nor owed obedience to its laws. This independent country was settled by *Englishmen* at their own expence, under particular stipulations with the crown: these stipulations, then, must be the sacred band of union between *England* and her colonies, and cannot be infringed without injustice. But you object, that "no power can abridge the authority of parliament, which has never exempted any from the submission they owe to it; and no other power can grant such an exemption."

I will not dispute the authority of the parliament, which is, without doubt, supreme within the body of the kingdom, and cannot be abridged by any other power; but may not the king have prerogatives, which he has a right to exercise, without the consent of parliament? If he has, perhaps that of granting licence to his subjects to remove into a *new* country, and to settle therein upon particular conditions, may be one. If he has no such prerogative, I cannot discover how the royal engagements can be made good, that "the freedom and other benefits of the *British* constitution" shall be secured to those people who shall settle in a new country under such engagements; the freedom, and other benefits of the *British* constitution, cannot be secured to a people, without they are exempted from being taxed by any authority, but that of their representatives, chosen by themselves. This is an essential part of *British* freedom; but if the king cannot grant such an exemption, in right of his prerogative, the royal promises cannot be fulfilled; and all charters which have been granted by our former kings, for this purpose, must be deceptions upon the subjects who accepted them, which to say, would be a high reflection upon the honour of the crown. But there was a time, when some parts of *England* itself were exempt from the laws of parliament: the inhabitants of the county palatine of *Chester* were not subject to such laws *ab antiquo,* because they did not send representatives to parliament, but had their own *commune concilium;* by whose authority, with the consent of their earl, their laws were made. If this exemption was not derived originally from the crown, it must have arisen from that great principle in the *British* constitution, by which the freemen in the nation are not subject to any laws, but such as are made by representatives elected by themselves to parliament; so that in either case, it is an instance extremely applicable to the colonies, who contend for no other right, but that of directing their *internal* government by laws made with their own consent, which has been preserved to them by repeated acts and declarations of the crown.

The constitution of the colonies, being established upon the principles of *British* liberty, has never been infringed by the immediate act of the crown; but the powers of government, agreeably to this constitution, have been constantly declared in the king's commissions to their governors, which, as often as they pass the great seal, are *new* declarations and confirmations of the rights of the colonies. Even in the reign of *Charles* the second, a time by no means favourable to liberty, these rights of the colonies were maintained inviolate; for when it was thought necessary to establish a permanent revenue for the support of government in *Virginia,* the king did not apply to the *English* parliament, but to the general assembly; and sent over an act, under the great seal of *England,* by which it was enacted, "by the king's most excellent majesty, by and with the consent of the general assembly," that two shillings per hogshead upon all tobacco exported, one shilling and three-pence per ton upon shipping, and six-pence per poll for every person imported, not being actually a mariner in pay, were to be paid for ever as a revenue, for the support of the government in the colony.

I have taken notice of this act, not only because it shows the proper fountain from whence all supplies to be raised in the colonies ought to flow, but also as it affords an instance, that royalty itself did not disdain formerly to be named as a part of the legislature of the colony; though now, to serve a purpose destructive of their rights, and to introduce principles of despotism unknown to a free constitution, the legislature of the colonies are degraded even below the corporation of a petty borough in *England.* . . .

I have proved irrefragably, that the colonies are not represented in parliament, and . . . that no new law can bind them, that is made without the concurrence of their representatives; and if so, then every act of parliament that imposes *internal* taxes upon the colonies, is an act of *power,* and not of *right.* I must speak freely; I am considering a question which affects the *rights* of above two millions of as loyal subjects as belong to the *British* crown, and must use terms adequate to the importance of it; I say, that *power,* abstracted from *right,* cannot give a just title to dominion. If a man invades my property, he becomes an aggressor, and puts himself into a state of war with me: I have a right to oppose this invader; if I have not strength to repel him, I must submit; but he acquires no right to my estate which he has usurped. Whenever I recover strength, I may renew my claim, and attempt to regain my possession; if I am never strong enough, my son, or his son, may, when able, recover the natural right of his ancestor, which has been unjustly taken from him.

I hope I shall not be charged with insolence, in delivering the sentiments of an honest mind with freedom: I am speaking of the *rights* of a people: *rights* imply *equality,* in the instances to which they belong, and must be treated without respect to the dignity of the persons concerned in them. If "the *British* empire in *Europe* and in *America* is the same *power;*" if the "subjects in both are the same people, and all equally participate in the adversity and prosperity of the whole," what distinctions can the difference of their situations make, and why is this distinction made between them? Why is the trade of the colonies more circumscribed than the trade of *Britain?* And why are impositions laid upon the one, which are not laid upon the other? If the parliament "have a *right* to impose taxes of *every kind* upon the colonies," they ought in justice, as the same people, to have the same sources to raise them from: their commerce ought to be equally free with the commerce of *Britain,* otherwise it will be loading them with burthens, at the same time that they are deprived of strength to sustain them; it will be forcing them to make bricks without straw. I acknowledge the parliament is the sovereign legislative power of the *British* nation, and that by a full exertion of their power, they can deprive the colonists of the freedom, and other benefits of the *British* constitution, which have been secured to them by our kings; they can abrogate all their civil rights and liberties; but by what *right* is it, that the parliament can exercise such a power over the colonists, who have as natural a right to the liberties and privileges of *Englishmen,* as if they were actually resident within the kingdom? The colonies are subordinate to the authority of parliament; subordinate I mean in degree, but not absolutely so: for if by a vote of the *British* senate, the colonists were to be delivered up to the rule of a *French* or *Turkish* tyranny, they may refuse obedience to such a vote, and may oppose the execution of it by force. Great is the power of parliament, but, great as it is, it cannot, constitutionally, deprive the people of their *natural* rights; nor, in virtue of the same principle, can it deprive them of their *civil* rights, which are founded in compact, without their own consent. There is, I confess, a considerable difference between these two cases, as to the right of resistance: in the first, if the colonists should be dismembered from the nation, by act of parliament, and abandoned to another power, they have a natural right to defend their liberties by open force, and may lawfully resist; and, if they are able, repel the power to whose authority they are abandoned. But in the other, if they are deprived of their civil rights, if great and manifest oppressions are imposed upon them by the state on which they are dependent, their remedy is to lay their complaints at the foot of the throne, and to suffer patiently, rather than disturb the public peace, which nothing but a denial of justice can excuse them in breaking. But if this justice should be denied, if the most humble and dutiful representations should be rejected, nay, not even deigned to be received, what is to be done? To such a question, *Thucydides* would make the *Corinthians* reply, that if "a decent and condescending behaviour is shown on the part of the colonies it would be base in the mother-state to press too far on such moderation:" And he would make the *Corcyreans* answer, that "every colony, whilst used in a proper manner, ought to pay honour and regard to its mother state; but, when treated with injury and violence, is become an alien. They were not sent out to be the slaves, but to be the equals of those that remain behind." . . .

PART THREE

Internal Dissensions

Western Discontent in Pennsylvania:
The Declaration of the Injured Frontier Inhabitants (February, 1764)

Throughout the colonial period there were pockets of social and political conflict within the colonies. Mainly transitory in nature, they resulted, for the most part, from either the strain placed upon older institutions and values by the rapid influx of new immigrants or the demand of men with recently acquired wealth for a share of the political and social power previously monopolized by older, established families. These conflicts were usually brought out into the open by some immediate grievance and as a rule dissolved relatively quickly as the grievance was remedied, the new groups were assimilated into the old social and political structure, or the structure itself adjusted to meet the demands of the new groups. During the 1760s and 1770s there were a number of such conflicts, some of them stimulated by and in turn affecting the course of the contest with Britain.

One of the most dramatic was the march of the Paxton Boys on Philadelphia in February, 1764. For nearly twenty years through the last two intercolonial wars there had been sporadic discontent among the Scotch-Irish settlers on Pennsylvania's western frontiers because of the failure of the Pennsylvania Assembly, which was dominated by eastern Quakers, to provide adequate defenses against French and Indian attack. Prior to 1756, it was their pacifism that prevented the Quakers from acting; after that date it was their constant embroilment with the proprietor over the question of whether the Assembly could tax his unsettled proprietary lands. Whatever the reason, the Scotch-Irish could scarcely avoid the conclusion that the Pennsylvania government had little interest in them or their problems. They especially disliked the Quaker policy of providing protection and support for friendly Indians. From their perspective, such a policy— which was the logical result of the traditional Quaker insistence upon fair and generous treatment of the Indians—was indefensible. Indians in any guise, their experience had taught them, were enemies, and to treat them otherwise was to ignore the harsh realities of the frontier. When, therefore, the Assembly was slow in responding to Pontiac's Rebellion, a group of westerners from Paxton and Donegal took matters into their own hands and massacred several Conestoga Indians who were supposed to be under the protection of the Pennsylvania government. Further angered by the government's removal of other "friendly" Indians to Philadelphia for safeguarding and by rumors that the government was going to bring the Paxton Boys to Philadelphia for trial, a large group of westerners marched on Philadelphia in February, 1764. The purpose of the march, as revealed by the Declaration of the Injured Frontier Inhabitants, printed in full below from the Minutes of the Provincial Council of Pennsylvania *(ten volumes, 1852), volume IX (1762–1771), pages 142–145, was to defend the actions of the Paxton Boys and to demand that the government repudiate its traditional soft policy toward Indians and stop spending money to support and protect them. Alarmed by the militant mood of the westerners and by reports that they intended to defy the government and annihilate all of the friendly Indians under its protection, eastern politicians from both the Quaker and proprietary factions united and sent Benjamin Franklin to meet the group in Germantown. At Franklin's suggestion the westerners delegated two of their leaders, Matthew Smith and James Gibson, to present their grievances to the government and dispersed. In a subsequent document, Smith and Gibson expanded the demands of the frontiersmen to include more representatives in the Assembly, in which only ten of thirty-six representatives were elected by western counties. Although the Assembly neither changed its Indian policy nor gave the west more representatives, the subjugation of Pontiac and the subsequent lessening of the threat of Indian attack quieted the westerners. Although the frontiersmen, despite occasional demands from their leaders, did not secure a more equitable system of representatives until after the Declaration of Independence and the adoption of the Pennsylvania Constitution of 1776, the march of the Paxton Boys was the last instance of open conflict between east and west in Pennsylvania before the outbreak of the War for Independence.*

There is no detailed study of the Paxton affair or of the sectional tensions in Pennsylvania during the Revolutionary era, but Theodore Thayer, Pennsylvania Politics and the Growth of Democracy, 1740–1776 *(1953), and Brooke Hindle,* "The March of the Paxton Boys," William *and* Mary Quarterly, *third series, volume 3 (1946), pages 461–486, contain brief, general analyses.*

Inasmuch as the killing those Indians at Conestogoe Manor and Lancaster has been, and may be, the subject of much Conversation, and by invidious Representations of it, which some, we doubt not, will industriously spread, many unacquainted with the true state of Affairs may be led to pass a Severe Censure on the Authors of those Facts, and any others of the like nature, which may hereafter happen, than we are persuaded they would if matters were duly understood and deliberated. We think it, therefore, proper thus openly to declare ourselves, and render some brief hints of the reasons of our Conduct, which we must, and frankly do, confess, nothing but necessity itself could induce us to, or justify us in, as it bears an appearance of flying in the face of Authority, and is attended with much labour, fatigue, and expence.

Ourselves, then, to a Man, we profess to be loyal Subjects to the best of Kings, our rightful Sovereign George the third, firmly attached to his Royal Person, Interest, and Government, & of consequence, equally opposite to the Enemies of His Throne & Dignity, whether openly avowed, or more dangerously concealed under a mask of falsly pretended Friendship, and chearfully willing to offer our Substance & Lives in his Cause.

These Indians, known to be firmly connected in Friendship with our openly avowed embittered Enemies, and some of whom have, by several Oaths, been proved to be murderers, and who, by their better acquaintance with the Situation and State of our Frontier, were more capable of doing us mischief, we saw, with indignation, cherished and caressed as dearest Friends; But this, alas! is but a part, a small part, of that excessive regard manifested to Indians, beyond His Majesty's loyal Subjects, whereof we complain, and which, together with various other Grievances, have not only enflamed with resentment the Breasts of a number, and urged them to the disagreeable Evidence of it they have been constrained to give, but have heavily displeased by far the greatest part of the good Inhabitants of this Province.

Should we here reflect to former Treaties, the exorbitant presents and great Servility therein paid to Indians, have long been oppressive Grievances we have groaned under; and when at the last Indian Treaty held at Lancaster, not only was the Blood of our many murdered Brethren tamely covered, but our poor unhappy captivated Friends abandoned to slavery among the Savages, by concluding a Friendship with the Indians, and allowing them a plenteous trade of all kinds of Commodities, without those being restored, or any properly spirited Requisition made of them; How general Dissatisfaction those Measures gave, the Murmurs of all good People (loud as they dare to utter them) to this day declare, and had here infatuated Steps of Conduct, and a manifest Partiality in favour of Indians, made a final pause, happy had it been; We perhaps had grieved in silence for our abandoned, enslaved Brethren among the Heathen; but matters of a later Date are still more flagrant Reasons of Complaint. When last Summer His Majesty's Forces, under the Command of Colonel Bouquet, marched through this Province, and a demand was made by His Excellency General Amherst, of Assistance to escort Provisions, &ca., to relieve that important Post, Fort Pitt, yet not one man was granted, although never any thing appeared more reasonable or necessary, as the interest of the Province lay so much at stake, and the standing of the Frontier Settlements, in any manner, evidently depended, under God, on the almost despaired of success of His Majesty's little Army, whose Valour the whole Frontiers with gratitude acknowledge, and as the happy means of having saved from ruin great part of the Province; But when a number of Indians, falsely pretended Friends, and having among them some proved on Oath to have been guilty of Murder since this War begun, when they, together with others, known to be His Majesty's Enemies, and who had been in the Battle against Col. Bouquet, reduced to Distress by the Destruction of their Corn at the Great Island, and up the East branch of Susquehanna, pretend themselves Friends, and desire a Subsistance, they are openly caressed, & the Publick, that could not be indulged the liberty of contributing to His Majesty's assistance, obliged, as Tributaries to Savages, to support these Villians, these Enemies to our King & our Country; nor only so, but the hands that were closely shut, nor would grant His Majesty's General a single Farthing against a Savage Foe, have been liberally opened, and the Publick money basely prostituted to hire, at an exorbitant Rate, a mercenary Guard to protect His Majesty's worst of Enemies, those falsely pretended Indian friends, while, at the same time, Hundreds of poor distressed Families of His Majesty's Subjects, obliged to abandon their Possessions & fly for their lives at least, are left, except a small Relief at first, in the most distressing Circumstances, to starve neglected, save what the friendly hand of private Donations has contributed to their support, wherein they who are most profuse towards Savages, have carefully avoided having any part. When last Summer the Troops raised for Defence of the Province were limited to certain Bounds, nor suffered to attempt annoying our Enemies in their Habitations, and a number of brave Volunteers, equipped at their own Expence in September, up the Susquehanna, met and defeated their Enemy, with the loss of some of their number, and having others dangerously wounded, not the least thanks or acknowledgment was made them from the Legislature for the confessed Service they had done, nor only the least notice or Care taken of their wounded; Whereas, when a Seneca, who, by the Informany of many, as well as by his own Confession, had been, through the last War, our inveterate Enemy, had got a cut in his Head, last Summer, in a quarrel he had with his own Cousin, & it was reported in Philadelphia that his Wound was dangerous, a Doctor was immediately employed and sent to Fort Augusta to take care of him, and cure him if possible. To these may be added, that though it was impossible to obtain, through the Summer, or even yet, any Premium for Indian Scalps, or encouragement to excite Volunteers to go forth against them; Yet, when a few of them known to be the fast friends of our Enemies, and some of them murderers themselves, when these have been struck by a distressed, bereft, injured Frontier, a liberal reward is offered for apprehending the Perpetrators of that horrible Crime of Killing his Majesty's Cloaked Enemies, and their Conduct painted in the most atrocious Colours, while the horrid Ravages, cruel murders, and most shocking Barbarities, committed by Indians on his Majesty's Subjects, are covered over, and excused, under the charitable Term of this being their method of making War. But to recount the many repeated Grievances, whereof we might justly complain, and instances of a most violent attachment to Indians, were tedious beyond the patience of a Job to endure, nor can better be expected, nor need we be surprized at Indians insolence & Villainy, when it is considered, and which can be proved from the Publick Records of a certain County, that sometime before Conrad Weiser died, some Indians belonging to the Great Island or Wighalousing, assured him that Israel Pemberton (an ancient leader of that Faction, which for so long a time have found means to enslave the Province to Indians), together with others of the Friends, had given them a Rod to scourge the White People that were settled on the purchased Lands, for that Onas had cheated them out of a great deal of Land, or had not given near sufficient Price for what he had bought; and that the Traders ought also to be scourged, for that they defrauded the Indians, by selling Goods to them at too dear a rate; and that this Relation is matter of Fact, can easily be proved in the County of Berks. Such is our unhappy Situation, under the Villainy, Infatuation and Influence of a certain Faction, that have got the Political Reins in their hands, and tamely tyrannize over the other good Subjects of the Province. And can it be thought strange, that a Scene of such treatment as this, & the now adding, in this critical Juncture, to all our former Distresses, that disagreeable Burthen of supporting, in the very heart of the Province, at so great an Expence, between one and two hundred Indians, to the great Disquietude of the Majority of the good Inhabitants of this Province, should awaken the resentment of a people grossly abused, unrighteously burthened, and made Dupes and Slaves to Indians? And must not all well disposed people entertain a charitable Sentiment of those who, at their own great Expence and Trouble, have attempted or shall attempt, rescuing a labouring Land from a Weight so oppressive, unreasonable and unjust? It is this we design, it is this we are resolved to prosecute, though it is with great Reluctance we are obliged to adopt a Measure not so agreeable as could be desired, and to which Extremity alone compels.

GOD SAVE THE KING.

Regulator Movements in the Carolinas

Western discontent was also manifest later in the 1760s in the regulator movements in the two Carolinas. Though the two movements were similar in that they
were both partly the result of the failure of established institutions to meet the
demands of the vast number of new western settlers and produced severe tensions
between them and political leaders from the east, they were markedly dissimilar
in origin and purpose.

The South Carolina movement, which occurred first, was primarily an attempt
by respectable men of property in the west to establish a stable society where
persons and property would be safe from the wanton attacks of a numerous
banditti who had arisen out of the social and psychic dislocations caused by the
Cherokee War of 1760–1761 and who by 1766 were running unchecked all over the
backcountry. The only courts in the entire colony were in Charleston, and existing law enforcement agencies were simply too weak and too few to cope with the
situation. When petitions to the legislature—in which the backcountry with over
half of the free population of the colony had only six of fifty representatives—
failed to achieve immediate results, backcountry leaders took the law into their
own hands and in the summer of 1767 proceeded to set about the task of "regulating" the backcountry and bringing the outlaws to justice. Eventually, the regulators had to defy Charleston authorities to accomplish their purposes, but they
never displayed any deep-seated antagonism toward the low country. Their
central concern was always the internal regulation of the backcountry, and their
primary demand on Charleston was a court system which would provide the
foundation for an orderly society. At no point during their three-year domination
of the backcountry did low-country officials either oppose their social objectives
or make any concerted effort to suppress them. In fact, the legislature went out
of its way in making concessions to British authorities to secure imperial approval
of a court law that would satisfy regulator demands. When opposition did come
in 1769, it came from the moderators, a minority of leading backcountry men
who were shocked by the excesses of the regulators. With the truce between the
regulators and moderators in March, 1769, the subsequent establishment of
courts, and the pardon of the regulators by the royal governor, the regulator
movement collapsed. Content with the promise of law and order which these
developments brought, backcountry men put aside subsidiary demands that had
developed during the heat of the regulator movement for greater representation in the Assembly and a more equitable tax system, both of which were in
large part met after the establishment of an independent state government in
1776. Remonstrance of the Back Country, written by Charles Woodmason, an
itinerant Anglican clergyman, in November, 1767, and printed in part below as
Selection 10 A, contains a clear statement of regulator grievances early in the
movement.

In contrast, the North Carolina movement was primarily a protest by westerners against what they considered arbitrary and corrupt local government at the
county level. As with South Carolina, the western portions of North Carolina
were newly settled by the stream of immigrants who poured south from Pennsylvania and Virginia beginning in the 1730s and 1740s. Unlike the situation in South
Carolina, however, the North Carolina legislature had not neglected to provide

local government for the new western areas. The trouble was that local institutions in the west were dominated by eastern appointees who, discontented westerners claimed, were dishonest, money-grubbing rogues, interested only in their own enrichment and committing "civil robberies" under cover of their public offices. They charged with considerable justification that the sheriffs kept or temporarily "borrowed" much of the tax money for themselves and together with other local officials and lawyers charged exorbitant fees unwarranted by law. A scarcity of money, resentment over high taxes levied to build an expensive governor's palace in the east at New Bern, and a conviction that the west was inadequately represented in the provincial legislature added to the dissatisfaction, which resulted in the formation of the Regulator Association in 1768. The regulators began to interfere with the courts in several western counties and pledged to continue their activities until their grievances had been remedied, but a show of force and promises of reforms by Governor William Tryon in the summer of 1769 temporarily dampened their ardor. In 1769 several regulator leaders were elected to the Assembly and the regulators of Anson, Orange, and Rowan Counties drew up petitions asking for a number of reforms. Because of its opposition to British policy, however, the legislature was dissolved by Tryon before it could act upon the petitions, and violence again flared up in the west. In response, the Assembly passed a bill in January, 1771 declaring rioters guilty of treason, and Tryon led an army into the regulator area, where he defeated them on May 16, 1771, at the Battle of Alamance. Seven regulator leaders were executed, some fled, and over six thousand took an obligatory oath of allegiance to the government. Most of the regulators' grievances, including the underrepresentation of the western counties in the legislature, were eventually remedied, but a large residue of sectional animosity remained long after the regulator movement had been crushed. The nature and variety of the grievances of the North Carolina regulators may be seen in the petition of Anson County, October 9, 1769, reprinted in full below as Selection 10 B.

Richard Maxwell Brown, The South Carolina Regulators *(1963), provides a clear and comprehensive analysis of that group, while Hugh T. Lefler and Paul Wager (eds.),* Orange County, 1752–1952 *(1953), is the best study of the North Carolina movement. Richard J. Hooker (ed.),* The Carolina Backcountry on the Eve of the Revolution: The Journal and Other Writings of Charles Woodmason, Anglican Itinerant *(1953), contains some vivid descriptions of conditions in South Carolina during the regulation troubles.*

A. SOUTH CAROLINA: ''REMONSTRANCE OF THE BACK COUNTRY'' (NOVEMBER, 1767)*

Humbly Sheweth.

That for many Years past, the Back Parts of this Province hath been infested with an infernal Gang of Villains, who have committed such horrid Depredations on our Properties and Estates—Such Insults on the Persons of many Settlers and perpetrated such shocking Outrages thro'out the Back Settlements, as is past Description.

---

* These excerpts are reprinted from the Fulham Palace Transcripts, North Carolina, South Carolina, Georgia, No. 72, Library of Congress.

Our Large Stocks of Cattel are either stollen and destroy'd—Our Cow Pens are broke up—and All our valuable Horses are carried off—Houses have been burn'd by these Rogues, and families stripp'd and turn'd naked into the Woods—Stores have been broken open and rifled by them (wherefrom several Traders are absolutely ruin'd) Private Houses have been plunder'd; and the Inhabitants wantonly tortured in the Indian Manner for to be made confess where they secreted their Effects from Plunder. Married Women have been Ravished—Virgins deflowered, and other unheard of Cruelties committed by these barbarous Ruffians—Who, by being let loose among Us (and conniv'd at) by the Acting Magistrates, have hereby reduc'd Numbers of Individuals to Poverty—and for these three Years last past have laid (in a Manner) this Part of the Province under Contribution.

No Trading Persons (or others) or with Money or Goods, No responsible Persons and Traders dare keep Cash, or any Valuable Articles by them—Nor can Women stir abroad, but with a Guard, or in Terror—The Chastity of many beauteous Maidens have been threatned by these Rogues. Merchants Stores are oblig'd for to be kept constantly guarded (which enhances the Price of Goods) And thus We live not as under a British Government (ev'ry Man sitting in Peace and Security under his own Vine, and his own Fig Tree), But as if [we] were in *Hungary* or *Germany,* and in a State of War—continually exposed to the Incursions of *Hussars* and *Pandours;* Obliged to be constantly on the Watch, and on our Guard against these Intruders, and having it not in our Power to call what we possess our own, *not even for an Hour;* as being liable Daily and Hourly to be stripp'd of our Property.

Representations of these Grievances and Vexations have often been made by Us to those in Power—But without Redress—Our Cries must have pierc'd their Ears, tho' not enter'd into their Hearts—For, instead of Public justice being executed on many of these Notorious Robbers (who have been taken by us at much Labour and Expence and Committed) and on others (who with Great difficulty and Charge have been arraigned and convicted) We have to lament, that such have from Time to Time been *pardoned;* and *afresh* let loose among Us, to repeat their Villanies, and strip Us of the few remaining Cattle Horses and Moveables, which after their former Visits they had left us.

Thus distressed; Thus situated and unrelieved by Government, many among Us have been obliged to punish some of these Banditti and their Accomplices, in a proper Manner—Necessity (that first Principle) compelling them to Do, what was expected that the Executive Branch of the Legislature would *long ago,* have Done.

We are *Free-Men*—British Subjects—Not Born *Slaves*—We contribute our Proportion in all Public Taxations, and discharge our Duty to the Public, equally with our Fellow Provincials Yet We do not participate with them in the Rights and Benefits which they Enjoy, though equally Entituled to them.

Property is of no Value, except it be secure: How Ours is secured, appears from the foremention'd Circumstances, and from our now being obliged to defend our Families, by *our own Strength:* As *Legal Methods* are beyond our Reach—or not as yet *extended* to Us.

We may be deemed too bold in saying *"That the present Constitution of this Province is very defective, and become a Burden, rather than being beneficial to the Back-Inhabitants"*—For Instance—To have but *One* Place of Judicature in this Large and Growing Colony—And that seated *not Central,* but *in a Nook* by the SeaSide—The Back Inhabitants to travel Two, three hundred Miles to carry down Criminals, prosecute Offenders appear as Witnesses (though secluded to serve as Jurors) attend the Courts and Suits of Law—The Governor and Court of Ordinary—All Land Matters, and on evry Public Occasion are Great Grievances, and call loudly for *Redress* For 'til not only *Loss of Time* which the poor Settlers sustain therefrom, but the *Toil of Travelling,* and *Heavy-Expences* therefrom arising. Poor Suitors are often driven to great Distresses, Even to the spending their Last Shilling or to sell their *Only* Horse for to defray their traveling and Town Costs; After which, they are obliged to trudge home on foot, and beg for Subsistence by the Way: And after being Subpenaed, and then attending Court as Witnesses or as Constables, they oft are never called for On Trials but are put off to next Court, and then the same Services must be repeated. These are Circumstances experienced by no Individuals under British Government save those in South Carolina.

It is partly owing to these Burdens on our Shoulders, That the Gangs of Robbers who infest us, have so long reigned without Repression: For if a Party hath Twenty Cattle, or the best of his Stallions stollen from Him, The Time and Charge consequent on a Prosecution of the Offenders, is equal too, or Greater than his Loss—As, *To Prosecute,* would make Him Doubly a Sufferer; And Poor Persons have not Money to answer the Cravings of *Rapacious Lawyers*—As proceedings at Law are *now* managed, it may cost a Private person Fifty Pounds to bring a Villain to Justice— And in Civil Cases, the Recovery of *Twenty Pounds,* will frequently be attended with Seventy Pounds Costs—if not Treble that Sum. . . .

If we are thus insecure—If our Lives and Properties are thus at Stake— If we cannot be protected—If these Villains are suffered to range the Country uncontrouled, and no Redress to be obtained for our Losses, All of Us, and our families must quit the Province, and Retire, where there are Laws, Religion and Government. . . .

Nor can We be said to possess our Legal Rights as Freeholders, when We are so unequally represented in *Assembly*—The South Side of Santee River, electing 44 Members, and the North Side, with these Upper Parts of the Province (containing 2/3 of the White Inhabitants) returning but Six —It is to this Great Disproportion of Representatives on our Part, that our Interests have been so long neglected, and the Back Country disregarded. But it is the Number of *Free Men,* not *Black Slaves,* that constitute the Strength and Riches of a State.

The not laying out the Back Country into Parishes, is another most sensible Greivance. This Evil We apprehend to arise from the Selfish Views of those, whose Fortune and Estates, are in or near *Charlestown*—which makes them endeavour, That all Matters and Things shall center there, however detrimental to the Body Politic, Hence it arises, That Assemblies are kept sitting for six Months, when the Business brot before them might be dispatched in six Weeks—to oblige us (against Inclination) to chuse such Persons for Representatives, who live in or contiguous to *Charlestown;* and to render a Seat in the Assembly too heavy a Burden, for any Country Planter, of a small Estate, for to bear. From this our Non-Representation in the House, We conceive it is; That Sixty thousand Pounds Public Money, (of which we must pay the Greater Part, as being levyed on the Consumer) hath lately been voted, for to build an *Exchange* for the Merchants, and a *Ball-Room* for the Ladies of Charlestown; while near *Sixty thousand* of Us Back Settlers, have not a Minister, or a place of Worship to repair too! As if We were not worth even the Thought off, or deemed as *Savages,* and not *Christians!*

To leave our Native Countries, Friends, and Relations—the Service of God—the Enjoyment of our Civil and Religious Rights for to breathe here (as We hoped) a Purer Air of Freedom, and possess the *utmost Enjoyment* of *Liberty,* and *Independency*—And instead hereof, to be set adrift in the Wild Woods among *Indians,* and *Out Casts*—To live in a State of Heathenism—without Law, or Government or even, the *Appearance of Religion*— Exposed to the Insults of Lawless and Impudent Persons—To the Depredations of *Thieves & Robbers*—and to be treated by our Fellow Provincials who hold the Reins of Things, as Persons hardly worthy the Public Attention, Not so much as their Negroes:—These Sufferings have broken the Hearts of Hundreds of our New Settlers—Made others quit the Province, some return to *Europe* (and therefrom prevent others coming this Way) and deterred Numbers of Persons of Fortune and Character (both at Home, and in *America*) from taking up of Lands here, and settling this our Back Country, as otherwise they would have done. . . .

In our present unsettled Situation—When the Bands of Society and Government hang Loose and Ungirt about Us—When no regular Police is established, but every one left to Do as seemeth Him Meet, there is not the least Encouragement for any Individual to be Industrious—Emulous in Well Doing—or Enterprizing in any Attempt that is Laudable or public Spirited. Cunning; Rapine; Fraud and Violence, are now the Studies and persuits of the Vulgar: If We save a little Money for to bring down to Town Wherewith to purchase Slaves—should it be known, Our Houses are beset, and Robbers plunder Us, even of our Cloaths. If we buy Liquor for to Retail, or for Hospitality, they will break into our dwellings, and consume it. If We purchase Bedding, Linen, or Decent Furniture, they have early Notice, and we are certain for to be stripped of it. Should We raise Fat Cattle, or Prime Horses for the Market, they are constantly carried off though well Guarded—(As a small Force is insufficient for their Security). Of if we collect Gangs of Hogs for to kill, and to barrel up for Sale: Or plant Orchards or Gardens—the Rogues, and other Idle, worthless, vagrant People, with whom We are overrun, are continually destroying of them, and subsisting on the Stocks and Labours of the Industrious Planter. If we are in any wise injured in our Persons, Fame, or Fortune, What Remedy have We? What Redress can be obtained, without travelling Two hundred Miles to *Charlestown?* Where (through the Chicanry of Lawyers—Slowness of Law Proceedings and Expences thence arising), We are *greater Sufferers than before,* and only thereby add *Evil to Evil;* . . .

Property being thus insecure, No Improvements are attempted—No New Plans can take Place—Nothing out of the Common Road can be executed, till Legislation is extended to Us. A Damp is now put on all spirited Endeavours to make Matters run in their proper Channel—And (shameful to say) our Lands (some of the finest in *America*) lye useless and uncleared, being rendered of small Value from the many licentious Persons intermixed among Us, whom We cannot drive off without Force or Violence. . . .

By our urging of these Particulars, and thus bringing them home to the Attention of the Legislature, We do not presume to reflect on or to censure the Conduct, much less to prescribe or Dictate to those in Authority; But We humbly submit our Selves and our Cause to the Wisdom of our Superiors—professing our Selves Dutiful and Loyal Subjects to His Majesty King *George*—True Lovers of our Country—Zealous for its true Interests, the Rights and Liberties of the Subject, and the Stability of our present happy Constitution in Church and State: We only enumerate *Plain* and *Glaring Facts* And all We crave is—The Enjoyment of those *Native Rights*, which as Freeborn Subjects We are entituled unto, but at present are debarred off; And also the proper Establishment of Religion, and Dispensation of the Laws in the Upper Part of the Country All which our Petitions, We humbly beg leave (with the greatest Deference and Submission) to Sum up in the following Articles, Humbly Praying That the Legislature would be pleased to grant us such Relief as may be conducive to the Public Welfare—The Honour of the Crown—The Good of the Church, and the Peace and Prosperity of all His Majestys Leige People in this His Province.

With all due Respect, We humbly request

First)   That Circuit or County Courts, for the Due and speedy Administration of Justice be established in this, as is in the Neighbouring Provinces.

2d)   That some subordinate Courts (to consist of Justices and Freeholders) be erected in each Parish for the Trial of Slaves—Small and Mean Causes, and other Local Matters. And that (under the Governor) they may grant Probate of Wills, and Letters of Administration for all Effects under 100 £—Also To pass small Grants of Lands—Renew Warrants &c. (paying the Common fees—To prevent poor persons from travelling down to *Charlestown*, on Account of these, and other such Petty Matters.

3d)—That these Circuits or County Courts, may decide all Suits not exceeding 100 £ Currency without Appeal And that no *Nole Prosequi's* or *Traverses*, be filed against Informations made against Transgressors of the *Local*, or *Penal* Laws.

4th)   That the Clerk of the Circuit or County Court, may issue Writs, or Attachments for any Sum—All above 100 £ Currency to be made returnable to the Supreme Court in *Charlestown* and all under that Sum, returnable by the Sherif of each County to His particular Court—And that Justices of the Peace, or Clerk of the Court, may issue Attachments (as now they do Executions) for Sums under 20 £ Currency.

5th)   That the Poor Laws be amended, and some better Provision made for the Care of Poor Orphans and their Estates—Also of the Effects of Strangers Travellers and transient Persons dying within the Province.

6th)   That Court Houses, Goals, and Bridewells, be built in proper Places, and Coercive Laws framed for the Punishment of Idleness and Vice, and for the lessening the Number of Vagrant and Indolent Persons, who now prey on the Industrious—And that none such be allowed to traverse the Province without proper *Licences* or *Passes*.

7th)   That the Laws respecting Public Houses and Taverns be amended —and the Prices of Articles vended by them, for to be ascertained as to *Quality* and *Quantity*—And that none be permitted for to retail Liquors on the Public Roads, but such as can Lodge Travellers, and provide Entertainment for Man and Horse.

8th)   That the Laws concerning the Stealing and branding of Cattle—

Tolling of Horses—Taking up of Strays &c. be amended; That Hunters be put under some Restrictions, and obliged not to leave Carcasses unburied in the Woods; And that some few Regulations be made in Respect to Swine.

9th) That the provincial Laws be Digested into a Regular Code, and be printed as soon as possible.

10th) That Gentlemen, who may be Elected as Members of Assembly —Commissioners of the Roads, and into other public Offices, be obliged to *Serve,* or *Fine.*

11th) That the Interior and Upper Parts of the Province, and all beyond Black River, be laid out into Parishes, or Chapels, Churches, and Parsonages be founded among them.

12th) That Ministers be provided for these *New,* as well as Vacant Old Parishes—and that some Method be devised for an immediate Supply of Parishes with Ministers on the Death, or Cession of Incumbents—Also for the better Care (than at present) of Vacant Churches and Parsonages.

13th) That the Salaries of the Country Clergy be augmented and some Provision made for their Widows, thereby, that Learned and Goodly Men may be excited to come over to us, and not Profligates.

14th) That all Magistrates, Lay Persons, and Itinerant Preachers and Teachers, be inhibited from Marrying And the Mode, and Authenticity of Marriages be settled: And that Dissenting Teachers be obliged to register their Meeting Houses, and to take the State Oaths, agreeable to the Statute (1 William and Mary) And that none but such settled Pastors be allowed to teach or Preach among the People—

15th) That some Expedient be devised for His Majestys Attorneys General to put Recognizances in Suit—And that he may be empowered for to prosecute on all Recognizances given for the Observance of the Provincial Laws.

16th) That a proper Table of Fees be framed for all Ministers Ecclesiastical and Civil, to govern themselves by; And that the Length and enormous Expence of Law Suits be Moderated. This Province being harder rode at present by Lawyers, than Spain or Italy by Priests.

17th) That Juries be impannelled from, and all Offences tryed in that County, wherein Crimes, Trespasses and Damages have been committed, or Sustained—Agreeable to *Magna Charta.*

18th) That no Attorney be put into Commission of the Peace And that their Number be limited in the Commons House of Assembly.

19th) That some Public Schools be founded in the Back Settlements for training up of the Rising Generation in the true Principles of Things— that so they may become useful, and not pernicious Members of Society.

20th) That proper Premiums be annually distributed, for promoting Agriculture, the raising of Articles for Exportation, and establishing Usefull Arts, on the Plan of the Dublin Society, and that of Arts and Commerce in London.

21) That the Statute for Limitation of Actions, and that for preventing frivolous and vexatious Suits, be enforced and Elucidated; And that the Liberty of the Subject, as to Arrests, and Wrongful Imprisonments, be better secured.

22) That the Lines of the several Counties be run out from the Sea to the Cherokee Boundary—Also, that the Lines of Each Old and New Parish

be ascertained and known, that we may no longer wander in the Mazes of Supposition.

23)   Lastly We earnestly Pray That the Legislature would import a Quantity of Bibles, Common Prayers, and Devotional Tracts, to be distributed by the Ministers among the Poor, which will be of far greater Utility to the Province, than erecting the Statue of Mr. Pitt.

B. NORTH CAROLINA: PETITION
OF ANSON COUNTY (OCT. 9, 1769)*

HUMBLY SHEWETH

That the Province in general labour under general grievances, and the Western part thereof under particular ones; which we not only see, but very sensibly feel, being crouch'd beneath our sufferings: and notwithstanding our sacred priviledges, have too long yielded ourselves slaves to remorseless oppression.—Permit us to conceive it to be our inviolable right to make known our grievances, and to petition for redress; as appears in the Bill of Rights pass'd in the reign of King Charles the first, as well as the act of Settlement of the Crown of the Revolution. We therefore beg leave to lay before you a specimen thereof that your compassionate endeavours may tend to the relief of your injured Constituents, whose distressed condition calls aloud for aid. The alarming cries of the oppressed possibly may reach your Ears; but without your zeal how shall they ascend the throne—how relentless is the breast without sympathy, the heart that cannot bleed on a View of our calamity; to see tenderness removed, cruelty stepping in; and all our liberties and priviledges invaded and abridg'd (by as it were) domesticks: who are conscious of their guilt and void of remorse.—O how daring! how relentless! whilst impending Judgments loudly threaten and gaze upon them, with every emblem of merited destruction.

A few of the many grievances are as follows, (Viz.)

1. That the poor Inhabitants in general are much oppress'd by reason of disproportionate Taxes, and those of the western Counties in particular; as they are generally in mean circumstances.

2. That no method is prescribed by Law for the payment of the Taxes of the Western Counties in produce (in lieu of a Currency) as is in other Counties within this Province; to the Peoples great oppression.

3. That Lawyers, Clerks, and other pentioners; in place of being obsequious Servants for the Country's use, are become a nuisance, as the business of the people is often transacted without the last degree of fairness, the intention of the law evaded, exorbitant fees extorted, and the sufferers left to mourn under their oppressions.

4. That an Attorney should have it in his power, either for the sake of ease or interest, or to gratify their malevolence and spite, to commence suits to what Courts he pleases, however inconvenient it may be to the Defendant: is a very great oppression.

5. That all unlawful fees taken on Indictment, where the Defendant is

* Reprinted in full from William L. Saunders (ed.), *The Colonial Records of North Carolina* (10 vols., 1886–1890), vol. VIII (1769–1771), pp. 75–78.

acquitted by his Country (however customary it may be) is an oppression.

6. That Lawyers, Clerks, and others, extorting more fees than is intended by law; is also an oppression.

7. That the violation of the King's Instructions to his delegates, their artfulness in concealing the same from him; and the great Injury the People thereby sustains: is a manifest oppression.

And for remedy whereof, we take the freedom to recommend the following mode of redress, not doubting audience and acceptance; which will not only tend to our relief, but command prayers as a duty from your humble Petitioners.

1. That at all elections each suffrage be given by Ticket & Ballot.

2. That the mode of Taxation be altered, and each person to pay in proportion to the profits arising from his Estate.

3. That no future tax be laid in Money, untill a currency is made.

4. That there may be established a Western as well as a Northern and Southern District, and a Treasurer for the same.

5. That when a currency is made it may be let out by a Loan office (on Land security) and not to be call'd in by a Tax.

6. That all debts above 40s. and under £10 be tried and determined without Lawyers, by a jury of six freeholders, impanneled by a Justice, and that their verdict be enter'd by the said Justice, and be a final judgment.

7. That the Chief Justice have no perquisites, but a Sallary only.

8. That Clerks be restricted in respect to fees, costs, and other things within the course of their office.

9. That Lawyers be effectually Barr'd from exacting and extorting fees.

10. That all doubts may be removed in respect to the payment of fees and costs on Indictments where the Defendant is not found guilty by the jury, and therefore acquitted.

11. That the Assembly make known by Remonstrance to the King, the conduct of the cruel and oppressive Receiver of the Quit Rents, for omitting the customary easie and effectual method of collecting by distress, and pursuing the expensive mode of commencing suits in the most distant Courts.

12. That the Assembly in like manner make known that the governor and Council do frequently grant Lands to as many as they think proper without regard to Head Rights, notwithstanding the contrariety of His Majesties Instructions; by which means immense sums has been collected, and numerous Patents granted, for much of the most fertile lands in this Province, that is yet uninhabited and uncultivated, environed by great numbers of poor people who are necessitated to toil in the cultivation of bad Lands whereon they hardly can subsist, who are thereby deprived of His Majesties liberality and Bounty: nor is there the least regard paid to the cultivation clause in said Patent mentioned, as many of the said Council as well as their friends and favorites enjoy large Quantities of Lands under the above-mentioned circumstances.

13. That the Assembly communicates in like manner the Violation of His Majesties Instructions respecting the Land Office by the Governor and Council, and of their own rules, customs and orders, if it be sufficiently proved, that after they had granted Warrants for many Tracts of Land, and that the same was in due time survey'd and return'd, and the Patent fees timely paid into the said office; and that if a private Council was called on purpose to avoid spectators, and peremptory orders made that Patents should not be

granted; and Warrants by their orders arbitrarily to have Issued in the names of other Persons for the same Lands, and if when intreated by a solicitor they refus'd to render so much as a reason for their so doing, or to refund any part of the money by them extorted.

14. That some method may be pointed out that every improvement on Lands in any of the Proprietors part be proved when begun, by whom, and every sale made, that the eldest may have the preference of at least 300 Acres.

15. That all Taxes in the following Counties be paid as in other Counties in the Province (i e) in the produce of the Country and that ware Houses be erected as follows (Viz.)

In Anson County at Isom Haleys Ferry Landing on PeDee River,

Rowan and Orange at Cambleton in Cumberland County,

Mecklenburg at .... on the Catawba River, and in

Tryon County at .... on .... River.

16. That every denomination of People may marry according to their respective Mode Ceremony and custom after due publication or Licence.—

17. That Doctor Benjamin Franklin or some other known patriot be appointed Agent, to represent the unhappy state of this Province to his Majesty, and to solicit the several Boards in England: . . .

SELECTION

Challenging the Old Order: Alexander McDougall, "To the Betrayed Inhabitants of the City and Colony of New York" (1769)

Dissensions of a different sort developed during the 1760s within the older settled areas in several colonies. In Virginia, Maryland, Pennsylvania, New York, Rhode Island, Massachusetts, and New Hampshire men of new wealth protested against the domination of politics, social life, and, occasionally, some aspects of economic life by the older elite. Though their protests often took the form of a wholesale condemnation of all "aristocratic" tendencies within the society, they were fundamentally no more than demands for equal access of all men of wealth to public office, social standing, and the primary avenues to further enrichment. Where the older leadership did not readily accede to their demands, the new men in the decade before the War for Independence frequently assumed the leadership of the extra-legislative opposition to British policy.

A classic example of this process occurred in New York beginning in the late 1760s. Traditionally factional in nature, politics in New York was, nevertheless, largely the preserve of a rather narrow oligarchy, and the factionalism revolved around the competition among leading families for office, position, wealth, and power. There was little room at the top for men like Alexander McDougall (1732–

1786), son of a modest Scottish immigrant, successful sea captain during the Seven Years' War, and, by the end of the 1760s, a wealthy merchant. With economic success came political ambition, and, when McDougall found it difficult to fulfill this ambition in the usual manner, by securing a seat in the New York Assembly, he elbowed his way into political prominence by attacking that body for what he charged was its ready compliance with the Quartering Act. Threatened with suspension by an act of Parliament in 1767 for initially refusing to comply with the provisions of that act (see the introduction to Selection 12), the New York Assembly had eventually given in. But for over a year beginning in late 1768 it again refused compliance, only to reverse its position abruptly on December 15, 1769. The following day, a broadside, printed in full below from E. B. O'Callaghan (ed.), The Documentary History of the State of New York *(four volumes, 1850–51), volume III, pages 528–532, appeared anonymously. Written by McDougall who was backed by the recently defeated Livingston faction, it charged the members of the Assembly with betraying the trust reposed in them by their constituents in order to secure, it hinted darkly, the private advantage of the dominant De Lancey faction. Urging the "betrayed inhabitants" to assemble in the fields, McDougall proposed that they appoint a special committee to draw up "a state of the whole matter" to be distributed to the other colonies and to Britain so that "the whole world" would know the true sentiments of New York. In response to McDougall's call, 1,400 people assembled on December 17, voted that no money be provided for the troops, and selected a delegation to present their sentiments to the Assembly. But the Assembly refused to be thus intimidated and adopted a series of resolutions declaring McDougall's broadside "Subversive of the Fundamental Principles of our Happy Constitution" and offering a reward for anyone giving information about the author. Over the next month the situation was extremely tense, but public hostility was directed less at the Assembly than at the British soldiers who cut down the town's liberty pole on January 17, 1770, and who fought openly with a large number of citizens at the Battle of Golden Hill on January 19. On information given by printer James Parker, McDougall was arrested on February 8. Refusing to give bail, he remained in jail for eighty-one days, where in conscious imitation of the English patriot John Wilkes—whose "persecution" by the ministry and Parliament was followed closely in the colonies—he posed as the champion of liberty and attained great political popularity with the New York citizenry. Released from prison on April 29 after he had pleaded not guilty, McDougall was never brought to trial because of the death of the key witness, but he was subsequently called before the Assembly and imprisoned for over four months for contempt. This second imprisonment in no way diminished his popularity, however, and thereafter he was a force to be reckoned with in New York politics.*

Though now considerably out of date, the best study of the background and context of the McDougall affair and the political forces operative in New York in the 1760s and 1770s is Carl Lotus Becker, The History of Political Parties in the Province of New York, 1760–1776 *(1909).*

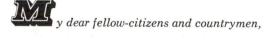

y dear fellow-citizens and countrymen,

In a day when the minions of tyranny and despotism in the mother country and the colonies, are indefatigable in laying every snare that their malevolent and corrupt hearts can suggest, to enslave a free people, when this unfortunate country has been striving under many disadvantages for three years past, to preserve their freedom; which to an Englishman is as dear as his life,—when the merchants of this city and the capital towns on the continent, have nobly and cheerfully sacrificed their private interest to the public good, rather than to promote the designs of the enemies of our happy constitution: It might justly be expected, that in this day of constitutional light, the representatives of this colony would not be so hardy, nor be so lost to all sense of duty to their constituents, (especially after the laudable example of the colonies of Massachusetts Bay and South Carolina before them) as to betray the trust committed to them. This they have done in passing the vote to give the troops a thousand pounds out of any monies that may be in the treasury, and another thousand out of the money that may be issued, to be put out on loan, which the colony will be obliged to make good, whether the bill for that purpose does or does not obtain the royal assent; and that they have betrayed the liberties of the people, will appear from the following consideration, to wit: That the ministry are waiting to see whether the colonies, under their distressed circumstances, will divide on any of the grand points which they are united in, and contending for, with the mother country; by which they may carry their designs against the colonies, and keep in administration.—For if this should not take place, the acts must be repealed; which will be a reflection on their conduct, and will bring the reproach and clamour of the nation on them, for the loss of trade to the empire, which their malconduct has occasioned.

Our granting money to the troops, is implicitly acknowledging the authority that enacted the revenue acts, and their being obligatory on us, as these acts were enacted for the express purpose of taking money out of our pockets without our consent; and to provide for the defending and support of government in America; which revenue we say by our grant of money, is not sufficient for the purpose aforesaid; therefore we supply the deficiency.

This was the point of view in which these acts were considered, by the Massachusetts and South Carolina Assemblies, and to prevent that dangerous construction, refuted it. On this important point we have differed with these spirited colonies, and do implicitly approve of all the tyrannical conduct of the ministry to the Bostonians, and by implication censure their laudable and patriotic denial. For if they did right (which every sensible American thinks they did) in refusing to pay the billeting money, surely we have done wrong, very wrong, in giving it. But our Assembly says, that they do their duty in granting money to the troops: Consequently the Massachusetts Assembly did not do theirs, in not obeying the ministerial mandate. If this is not a division in this grand point, I know not what is: And I doubt not but the ministry will let us know it is to our cost; for it will furnish them with arguments and fresh courage. Is this a grateful retaliation to that brave and sensible people, for the spirited and early notice they took of the suspending act? No, it is base ingratitude, and betraying the common cause of liberty.

To what other influence than the deserting the American cause, can the ministry attribute so pusillanimous a conduct, as this is of the Assembly; so repugnant and subversive of all the means we have used, and opposition that has been made by this and the other colonies, to the tyrannical conduct of the British Parliament! to no other. Can there be a more ridiculous farce to impose on the people than for the Assembly to vote their thanks to be given to the merchants for entering into an agreement not to import goods from Britain, until the revenue acts should be repealed, while they at the same time counteract it by countenancing British acts, and complying with ministerial requisitions, incompatible with our freedom? Surely they cannot.

And what makes the Assembly's granting this money the more grievous, is, that it goes to the support of troops kept here not to protect but to enslave us: Has not the truth of this remark been lately exemplified in the audacious, domineering and inhuman Major Pullaine, who ordered a guard to protect a sordid miscreant, that transgressed the laudable non-importation agreement of the merchants, in order to break that, which is the only means left them, under God to baffle the designs of their enemies to enslave this continent? This consideration alone ought to be sufficient to induce a free people, not to grant the troops any supply whatsoever, if we had no dispute with the mother country, that made it necessary not to concede anything that might destroy our freedom; reasons of economy and good policy suggest that we ought not to grant the troops money.

Whoever is the least acquainted with the English history, must know, that grants frequently made to the crown, is not to be refused, but with some degree of danger of disturbing the repose of the Kingdom or Colony. This evinces the expediency of our stopping these grants now, while we are embroiled with the mother country, that so we may not, after the grand controversy is settled, have a new bone of contention about the billeting money; which must be the case if we do not put an end to it at this time: for the colony, in its impoverished state, cannot support a charge which amounts to near as much per annum, as all the other expenses of the government besides.

Hence it follows that the assembly have not been attentive to the liberties of the continent, nor to the property of the good people of this colony in particular, we must therefore attribute this sacrifice of the public interest, to some corrupt source. This is very manifest in the guilt and confusion that covered the faces of the perfidious abettors of this measure, when the house was in debate on the subject. Mr. Colden knows from the nature of things, that he cannot have the least prospect to be in administration again; and therefore, that he may make hay while the sun shines, and get a full salary from the Assembly, flatters the ignorant members of it, with the consideration of the success of a bill to emit a paper currency; when he and his artful coadjutors must know, that it is only a snare to impose on the simple; for it will not obtain the royal assent. But while he is solicitous to obtain his salary, he must attend to his posterity, and as some of his children hold offices under the government, if he did not procure an obedience to his requisition, or do his duty in case the Assembly refused the billeting money, by dissolving them, his children might be in danger of losing their offices. If he dissolved the assembly they would not give him his salary.

The De Lancy family knowing the ascendancy they have in the present house of Assembly, and how useful that influence will be to their ambitious designs, to manage a new Governor, have left no stone unturned to prevent a dissolution. The Assembly, conscious to themselves, of having trampled on the liberties of the people, and fearing their just resentments on such an event, are equally careful to preserve their seats, expecting that if they can do it at this critical juncture, as it is imagined the grand controversy will be settled this winter, they will serve for seven years; in which time they hope the people will forget the present injuries done to them. To secure these several objects, the De Lancy family, like true politicians, although they were to all appearance at mortal odds with Mr. Colden, and represented him in all companies as an enemy to his country, yet a coalition is now formed in order to secure to them the sovereign lordship of this colony. The effect of which has given birth to the abominable vote, by which the liberties of the people are betrayed. In short, they have brought matters to such a pass, that all the checks resulting from the form of our happy constitution are destroyed. The Assembly might as well invite the council to save the trouble of formalities, to take their seats in the house of Assembly, and place the Lieut. Governor in the Speaker's chair, and then there would be no waste of time in going from house to house, and his honour would have the pleasure to see how zealous his former enemies are in promoting his interest to serve themselves. Is this a state to be rested in, when our all is at a stake? No, my countrymen, rouse! Imitate the noble example of the friends of liberty in England; who rather than be enslaved, contend for their right with k—g, lords and commons. And will you suffer your liberties to be torn from you, by your representatives? Tell it not in Boston; publish it not in the streets of Charles-Town! You have means yet left to preserve a unanimity with the brave Bostonians and Carolinians; and to prevent the accomplishment of the designs of tyrants. The house was so nearly divided, on the subject of granting the money in the way the vote passed, that one would have prevented it; you have, therefore, a respectable minority. What I would advise to be done is, to assemble in the fields, on Monday next, where your sense ought to be taken on this important point; notwithstanding the impudence of Mr. Jauncey, in his declaring in the house that he had consulted his constituents, and that they were for giving money. After this is done, go in a body to your members, and insist on their joining with the minority, to oppose the bill; if they dare refuse your just requisition, appoint a committee to draw up a state of the whole matter, and send it to the speakers of the several houses of assembly on the continent, and to the friends of our cause in England, and publish it in the news-papers, that the whole world may know your sentiments on this matter, in the only way your circumstance will admit. And I am confident it will spirit the friends of our cause and chagrin our enemies. Let the notification to call the people be so expressed, that whoever absents himself, will be considered as agreeing to what may be done by such as shall meet;—and that you may succeed, is the unfeigned desire of　　　　　　　　　　　A SON OF LIBERTY

PART FOUR

Renewal of Crisis, 1767–1770

Return to Strong Measures

In the summer of 1766, not long after the repeal of the Stamp Act, the Rockingham ministry, never very strong, gave way to a "broad bottom" government composed of members from all political factions and formed by William Pitt, who now became Earl of Chatham. With Chatham and Camden in the government and with William Petty, Earl of Shelburne, another man generally considered sympathetic to the colonies, as secretary of state for the southern department, the office chiefly responsible for the administration of the colonies, it seemed unlikely that the Chatham ministry would involve the British government in any further difficulties in the colonies. In fact, for a few months after it took office in August, 1766, prospects seemed bright for further concessions to the colonies in the form of relaxing the prohibition on the settlement of Western lands, easing the restrictions on legal-tender paper currency, and permitting colonial judges to hold office during good behavior instead of during the pleasure of the Crown.

But events in the colonies and the vagaries of British politics combined to produce a series of new legislative and executive enactments which the colonists found no less distasteful than the Stamp Act. In December, 1766, the New York Assembly flatly refused to comply with provisions in the Quartering Act of 1765 requiring the colonies to furnish provisions and other necessaries for troops stationed within their bounds. This action, taken by the Assembly because compliance with the Quartering Act could be interpreted as acquiescence in indirect taxation by Parliament, brought about an abrupt change in the attitudes of British political leaders during the early months of 1767. So direct a challenge to the authority of Parliament, they became convinced, had to be met with a vigorous exertion of parliamentary power in the colonies. At the same time, the physical and emotional indisposition of Chatham largely removed him from the political scene, and leadership of the ministry in large measure fell into the hands of Charles Townshend (1725–1767), Chancellor of the Exchequer and a long-time exponent of stricter control over the colonies. Goaded by George Grenville, then in opposition, into taking a strong stand in favor of parliamentary taxation of the colonies during a debate in the House of Commons on January 26, 1767, Townshend chided the Americans for their supposed distinction between internal taxes and external taxes and promised to introduce a scheme that, while humoring the Americans, would produce a considerable colonial revenue. Having taken this step spontaneously without the prior approval of the other ministers, Townshend finally convinced them to go along with him in late February after the country gentlemen in Parliament had forced through a considerable reduction of the land tax. This reduction, which promised to deprive the Treasury of £500,000 annually, made Townshend's talk of an American revenue sound overwhelmingly attractive. On May 13, 1767, he introduced the proposals that formed the basis for the Townshend Revenue Act, which became law on June 29. The taxes levied by this act, the main portions of which are reprinted below as Selection 12 A, were duties on all glass, red lead, white lead, painter's colors, paper, and tea imported into the colonies. All "external taxes" of the kind Americans had reputedly agreed to accept, these duties, Townshend estimated, would produce an annual revenue of £40,000, which was to be used to provide salaries for royal officials in the colonies and thus make them independent of colonial assemblies.

The Townshend Revenue Act was accompanied by two other laws designed to strengthen imperial control over the colonies. The first, portions of which are reprinted here as Selection 12 B, sought to increase the administrative efficiency of the customs by establishing a separate Board of Customs for the continental colonies. Previously, the customs service in America had been under the jurisdiction of the distant Board in London. With the new Board operating out of Boston, Townshend confidently expected to put an end to colonial evasion of the trade laws and to make sure that his Revenue Act would be strictly enforced. The second law, reprinted in part below as Selection 12 C, suspended the New York Assembly until it had complied with the Quartering Act. This measure, which was a direct challenge to the legislative rights of the Assembly, never went into effect because, unknown to authorities in Britain, the Assembly had already voted the money required on June 6, nearly a month before the passage of the Suspending Act. Although the Assembly's vote in no way recognized the validity of the Quartering Act or acknowledged Parliament's authority to require colonial assemblies to vote money for specific purposes, the ministry decided to let the matter drop and not to press for explicit compliance with the Quartering Act.

The tightening process represented by the three Townshend Acts continued over the next year. In September, 1767, imperial authorities tried to curtail the power of colonial lower houses of assembly and to deny their pretensions to be miniature Houses of Commons by issuing a general instruction (Selection 12 D) forbidding royal governors to assent to any laws whereby the lower houses attempted to change their constitutions or compositions. In July, 1768, the Privy Council sought to strengthen customs enforcement still further by creating by executive order (Selection 12 E) three new vice-admiralty courts at Boston, Philadelphia, and Charleston. Along with a fourth court previously established at Halifax in 1765, these new courts were to have both original and appellate jurisdiction over all cases arising under the trade laws and were intended to reinforce the provincial vice-admiralty courts that had been operating ineffectively in each of the colonies for over half a century.

John Brooke, The Chatham Administration 1766–1768 (1956), contains the best analysis of the general political conditions surrounding the passage of the Townshend Acts, and Sir Lewis Namier and John Brooke, Charles Townshend (1964), is a brief and penetrating biography of Townshend that explores the roots and nature of his American program. Nicholas Varga, "The New York Restraining Act: Its Passage and Some Effects, 1766–1768," New York History, volume XXXVII (July, 1956), pages 233–258, is the best discussion of the events surrounding the New York controversy over the Quartering Act; Jack P. Greene, The Quest for Power: The Lower Houses of Assembly in the Southern Royal Colonies, 1689–1776 (1963), analyzes the rationale behind and the colonial response to the General Instruction of 1767; and Carl Ubbelohde, The Vice-admiralty Courts and the American Revolution (1960), describes the changes in the vice-admiralty court system and their effect in the colonies.

A. A NEW SCHEME FOR TAXING THE COLONIES: THE TOWNSHEND REVENUE ACT (JUNE 29, 1767)*

WHEREAS *it is expedient that a revenue should be raised, in your Majesty's dominions in America, for making a more certain and adequate pro-*

---

* These excerpts are reprinted from Danby Pickering (ed.), *Statutes at Large,* vol. XXVII, pp. 505, 508–509, 511–512.

vision for defraying the charge of the administration of justice, and for the support of civil government, in such provinces where it shall be found necessary; and towards further defraying the expences of defending, protecting, and securing, the said dominions; . . . be it enacted . . . That from and after the twentieth day of *November,* one thousand seven hundred and sixty seven, there shall be raised, levied, collected, and paid, unto his Majesty, his heirs, and successors, for and upon the respective goods herein after mentioned, which shall be imported from *Great Britain* into any colony or plantation in *America* which now is, or hereafter may be, under the dominion of his Majesty, his heirs, or successors, the several rates and duties following . . . [upon glass, red lead, white lead, painter's colors, tea, and paper.]

IV. And it is hereby further enacted by the authority aforesaid, That the said rates and duties, charged by this act upon goods imported into any *British American* colony or plantation, shall be deemed, and are hereby declared to be, sterling money of *Great Britain;* and shall be collected, recovered, and paid, to the amount of the value which such nominal sums bear in *Great Britain;* and that such monies may be received and taken, according to the proportion and value of five shillings and six pence the ounce in silver . . . and that all the monies that shall arise by the said duties . . . shall be applied, in the first place, in such manner as is herein after mentioned, in making a more certain and adequate provision for the charge of the administration of justice, and the support of civil government, in such of the said colonies and plantations where it shall be found necessary; and that the residue of such duties shall be paid into the receipt of his Majesty's exchéquer, and shall be entered separate and apart from all other monies paid or payable to his Majesty, his heirs, or successors; and shall be there reserved, to be from time to time disposed of by parliament towards defraying the necessary expences of defending, protecting, and securing, the *British* colonies and plantations in *America.*

V. And be it further enacted by the authority aforesaid, That his Majesty and his successors shall be, and are hereby, impowered, from time to time, by any warrant or warrants under his or their royal sign manual or sign manuals, countersigned by the high treasurer, or any three or more of the commissioners of the treasury for the time being, to cause such monies to be applied, out of the produce of the duties granted by this act, as his Majesty, or his successors, shall think proper or necessary, for defraying the charges of the administration of justice, and the support of the civil government, within all or any of the said colonies or plantations. . . .

X. *And whereas by an act of parliament made in the fourteenth year of the reign of King* Charles *the Second, intituled,* An act for preventing frauds, and regulating abuses, in his Majesty's customs, *and several other acts now in force, it is lawful for any officer of his Majesty's customs, authorized by writ of assistance under the seal of his Majesty's court of exchequer, to take a constable, head-borough, or other public officer inhabiting near unto the place, and in the day-time to enter and go into any house, shop, cellar, warehouse, or room or other place, and, in case of resistance, to break open doors, chests, trunks, and other package there, to seize, and from thence to bring, any kind of goods or merchandize whatsoever prohibited or un-customed, and to put and secure the same in his Majesty's store-house next to the place where such seizure shall be made: and whereas by an act made in the seventh and eighth years of the reign of King* William *the Third,*

Return to Strong Measures

intituled, An act for preventing frauds, and regulating abuses, in the plantation trade, *it is, amongst other things, enacted, that the officers for collecting
and managing his Majesty's revenue, and inspecting the plantation trade, in*
America, *shall have the same powers and authorities to enter houses or
warehouses, to search for and seize goods prohibited to be imported or
exported into or out of any of the said plantations, or for which any duties
are payable, or ought to have been paid; and that the like assistance shall
be given to the said officers in the execution of their office; as, by the said
recited act of the fourteenth year of King* Charles *the Second, is provided
for the officers in* England: *but, no authority being expressly given by the
said act, made in the seventh and eighth years of the reign of King* William
*the Third, to any particular court to grant such writs of assistance for the
officers of the customs in the said plantations, it is doubted whether such
officers can legally enter houses and other places on land, to search for and
seize goods, in the manner directed by the said recited acts:* To obviate
which doubts for the future, and in order to carry the intention of the said
recited acts into effectual execution, be it enacted, and it is hereby enacted
by the authority aforesaid, That from and after the said twentieth day of
November, one thousand seven hundred and sixty seven, such writs of
assistance, to authorize and impower the officers of his Majesty's customs
to enter and go into any house, warehouse, shop, cellar, or other place, in
the *British* colonies or plantations in *America,* to search for and seize prohibited or uncustomed goods, in the manner directed by the said recited
acts, shall and may be granted by the said superior or supreme court of
justice having jurisdiction within such colony or plantation respectively. . . .

B. STRENGTHENING COLONIAL CUSTOMS
ENFORCEMENT: AMERICAN BOARD
OF CUSTOMS ACT (JUNE 29, 1767)*

WHEREAS *in pursuance of an act of parliament made in the twenty fifth
year of the reign of King* Charles *the Second, intituled,* An act for the
encouragement of the *Greenland* and *England* trades, and for the better
securing the plantation trade, *the rates and duties imposed by that, and
several subsequent acts of parliament, upon various goods imported into, or
exported from, the* British *colonies and plantation in* America, *have been
put under the management of the commissioners of the customs in* England
*for the time being, by and under the authority and directions of the high
treasurer, or commissioners of the treasury for the time being: and whereas
the officers appointed for the collection of the said rates and duties in*
America, *are obliged to apply to the said commissioners of the customs in*
England *for their special instructions and directions, upon every particular
doubt and difficulty which arises in relation to the payment of the said rates
and duties; whereby all persons concerned in the commerce and trade of
the said colonies and plantations, are greatly obstructed and delayed in the
carrying on and transacting of their business: and whereas the appointing*

* These excerpts are reprinted from Pickering (ed), *Statutes at Large,* vol.
XXVII, pp. 447–448.

*of commissioners to be resident in some convenient part of his Majesty's
dominions in* America, *and to be invested with such powers as are now
exercised by the commissioners of the customs in* England *by virtue of the
laws in being, would relieve the said merchants and traders from the said
inconveniencies, tend to the encouragement of commerce, and to the better
securing of the said rates and duties, by the more speedy and effectual
collection thereof:* be it therefore enacted . . . That the customs and other
duties imposed, by any act or acts of parliament, upon any goods or merchandizes brought or imported into, or exported or carried from, any *British*
colony or plantation in *America,* may, from time to time, be put under the
management and direction of such commissioners, to reside in the said
plantations, as his Majesty, his heirs, and successors, by his or their commission or commissions under the great seal of *Great Britain,* shall judge to
be most for the advantage of trade, and security of the revenue of the said
British colonies; any law, custom, or usage, to the contrary notwithstanding.

II. And it is hereby further enacted by the authority aforesaid, That the
said commissioners so to be appointed, or any three or more of them, shall
have the same powers and authorities for carrying into execution the several
laws relating to the revenues and trade of the said *British* colonies in
America, as were, before the passing of this act, exercised by the commissioners of the customs in *England,* by virtue of any act or acts of parliament
now in force: and it shall and may be lawful to and for his Majesty, his
heirs, and successors, in such commission or commissions, to make provision
for putting in execution the several laws relating to the customs and trade
of the said *British* colonies; any law, custom, or usage, to the contrary
notwithstanding. . . .

C. DISCIPLINING THE NEW YORK ASSEMBLY:
THE NEW YORK SUSPENDING ACT (JULY 2, 1767)*

WHEREAS *an act of parliament was made in the fifth year of his present
Majesty's reign, intituled,* An act to amend and render more effectual, in
his Majesty's dominions in *America,* an act passed in this present session of
parliament, intituled, *An act for punishing mutiny and desertion, and for the
better payment of the army and their quarters; wherein several directions
were given, and rules and regulations established and appointed, for the
supplying his Majesty's troops, in the* British *dominions in* America, *with
such necessaries as are in the said act mentioned during the continuance
thereof . . . and whereas the house of representatives of his Majesty's province of* New York *in* America *have, in direct disobedience of the authority
of the* British *legislature, refused to make provision for supplying the necessaries and in the manner required by the said act; and an act of assembly
hath been passed, within the said province, for furnishing the barracks in the
cities of* New York *and* Albany *with firewood and candles, and the other
necessaries therein mentioned, for his Majesty's forces, inconsistent with the*

* These excerpts are reprinted from Pickering (ed.), *Statutes at Large,* vol.
XXVII, pp. 609–610.

provisions, and in opposition to the directions, of the said act of parliament . . . That from and after the first day of *October*, one thousand seven hundred and sixty seven, until provision shall have been made by the said assembly of *New York* for furnishing his Majesty's troops within the said province with all such necessaries as are required by the said acts of parliament, or any of them, to be furnished for such troops, it shall not be lawful for the governor, lieutenant governor, or person presiding or acting as governor or commander in chief, or for the council for the time being, within the colony, plantation, or province, of *New York* in *America*, to pass, or give his or their assent to, or concurrence in, the making or passing of any act of assembly; or his or their assent to any order, resolution, or vote, in concurrence with the house of representatives for the time being within the said colony, plantation, or province; or for the said house of representatives to pass or make any bill, order, resolution, or vote, (orders, resolutions, or votes, for adjourning such house only, excepted) of any kind, for any other purpose whatsoever; and that all acts of assembly, orders, resolutions, and votes whatsoever, which shall or may be passed, assented to, or made, contrary to the tenor and meaning of this act, after the said first day of *October*, one thousand seven hundred and sixty seven, within the said colony, plantation, or province, before and until provision shall have been made for supplying his Majesty's troops with necessaries as aforesaid, shall be, and are hereby declared to be, null and void, and of no force or effect whatsoever.

II. Provided nevertheless, and it is hereby declared to be the true intent and meaning of this act, That nothing herein before contained shall extend, or be construed to extend, to hinder, prevent, or invalidate, the choice, election, or approbation, of a speaker of the house of representatives for the time being within the said colony, plantation, or province.

D. CURTAILING THE AUTHORITY OF COLONIAL LOWER HOUSES: THE CIRCULAR INSTRUCTION OF SEPT. 11, 1767 *

Whereas laws have at several times been passed in many of our colonies and plantations in America by which certain parishes and districts have been empowered and authorized to send representatives to the general assemblies of the respective colonies in which the said parishes and districts lie, and sundry other regulations have been introduced by those laws relative to the said assemblies; it is our will and pleasure and we do hereby require and command that you do not upon any pretense whatever give your assent to any law or laws to be passed in our province under your government by which the number of the assembly shall be enlarged or diminished, the duration of it ascertained, the qualification of the electors or the elected fixed or altered, or by which any regulations shall be established with respect thereto INCONSISTENT with our instructions to you our governor as prejudicial to that right or authority which you derive from us by virtue of our royal commission and instructions.

* Reprinted in full from Leonard Woods Labaree (ed.), *Royal Instructions to British Colonial Governors, 1670–1776* (1935), vol. I, p. 107.

E. REINFORCING THE VICE–ADMIRALTY SYSTEM: ORDER IN COUNCIL (JULY 6, 1768)*

Whereas by an Act Passed in the last Session of the last Parliament intitled an Act for the more easy and effectual Recovery of the Penalties and forfeitures inflicted by the Acts of Parliament relating to the Trade or Revenues of the British Colonies and Plantations in America, it is enacted that from and after the first day of September 1768, all forfeitures and Penalties inflicted by any Act or Acts of Parliament relating to the Trade or Revenues of the British Colonies or Plantations in America may be prosecuted, sued for and recovered in any Court of Vice Admiralty appointed or to be appointed, and which shall have Jurisdiction within the Colony Plantation or place where the Cause of such Prosecution shall have arisen, and that in all Cases where any prosecution or Suit shall be Commenced and Determined for any Penalty or forfeiture inflicted by any such Act or Acts of Parliament in any Court of Admiralty in the respective Colony or plantation where the offence shall be Committed, either party who shall think himself Aggrieved by such Determination, may appeal from such determination to any Court of Vice Admiralty appointed or to be Appointed, and which shall have Jurisdiction within such Colony Plantation or Place; And Whereas it will greatly Contribute to the due Collection of your Majesty's Revenue; and to the Prevention and Punishment of Frauds committed against the same, and will likewise tend to the more Speedy and effectual Administration of Justice within the said Colonies and Plantations, and be agreable to the Intention of the Legislature in passing the said Act that a sufficient Number of such Courts of Vice Admiralty be constituted and established at proper and convenient places within the said Colonies and Plantations; We humbly Submit to Your Majesty whether it may not be expedient and necessary for the Purposes above-mentioned to revoke the Commission appointing one only Court of Vice Admiralty over all America, and in lieu thereof, to establish four other Courts of Vice Admiralty the first at Halifax in the province of Nova Scotia; the Second at Boston in the province of New England; the third at Philadelphia in the Colony of Pensylvania, and the fourth at Charles Town in the Colony of South Carolina: the said Courts to have Jurisdiction within certain districts to be Allotted to them respectively by Your Majesty, [a plan of which districts is submitted], each of the Judges of the said Courts respectively to be allowed such Salary as Your Majesty shall think proper, to be paid, in the first Place, out of Your Majestys Moiety of the Money arising from any Penalties and Forfeitures to be levied within the said Colonies and Plantations and if this fund shall not be sufficient, out of the Money arising from the Sale of Old Naval Stores; and the said Judges to be expressly enjoined in their Commissions, upon pain of losing their offices, not to take any Fee, or gratuity whatsoever, for any Judgment given, or Business done, in their respective Courts. . . .

* These excerpts are reprinted from *Acts of the Privy Council, Colonial Series,* vol. V, pp. 151–153.

The Colonies Resist Again

Because the duties levied by the Townshend Revenue Act were "external taxes," British officials did not expect any major difficulty in enforcing them. The duties were, after all, similar in nature to the revised 1d duty on molasses that the colonists had been paying without serious protest since it went into effect on November 1, 1766. But the colonists, though considerably less precipitous in their opposition, found the Townshend Revenue Act no more palatable than the Stamp Act.

The call to resistance was sounded by John Dickinson, a conservatively inclined Pennsylvania lawyer who had served in the lower houses of both Delaware and Pennsylvania and had prepared the Declaration of Rights and Grievances adopted by the Stamp Congress. His Letters from a Farmer in Pennsylvania, *selections from which are reprinted here as Selection 13 A, were published all over the colonies between November, 1767, and January, 1768, first in serial form in the newspapers and then together as a pamphlet. Denying that the people of New York could "be legally deprived of the privilege of legislation" by Parliament, Dickinson strongly implied in his first letter that the New York Suspending Act was unconstitutional and warned residents of other colonies that it might serve as a precedent for a similar assault upon their legislative rights. But most of the* Letters *were devoted to a vigorous attack upon the constitutionality of the Townshend Revenue Act. The Stamp Act Congress, Dickinson pointed out, distinguished not between "internal and external taxes," as Townshend and British politicians seemed to think, but between taxes, internal or external, for the purpose of raising a revenue and duties for the purpose of regulating trade. Whether a parliamentary imposition was constitutional or not depended, then, entirely upon its intent. Dickinson freely admitted that Parliament could certainly levy duties to regulate trade for the general welfare of the entire British political community. What Parliament could never do without violating one of the colonists' most sacred rights as Englishmen was to tax them for revenue without the approval of their representatives.*

The Massachusetts House of Representatives spurred official resistance by the colonial assemblies with the Massachusetts Circular Letter. Drafted by Samuel Adams (1722–1803), one of the most popular and effective political leaders in Massachusetts, and formally approved by the House on February 11, 1768, this letter (Selection 13 B) was sent to the speakers of the lower houses in the other continental colonies. Declaring that the Townshend Revenue Act was unconstitutional, the letter called on the other legislatures to unite in protesting to George III against it. Although they admitted that Parliament was "the supreme legislative Power over the whole Empire," the Massachusetts legislators argued in the Circular Letter that the authority of every legislature was derived from and limited by the constitution and that one of the "fundamental Rules of the British Constitution" was that no man could have his property taken from him without his consent. Ruling out any possibility of American representation in Parliament, they also denounced the act for attempting to render royal officials "independent of the people" as dangerous to the "Happiness & Security of the Subject."

Dickinson and the Massachusetts House of Representatives had concentrated

121

their fire on the Townshend Revenue Act, but in Boston, where the new commissioners of the customs arrived in November, 1767, there was considerable resentment as well of the new Board and its vigorous efforts to perform its duties. Initially, this resentment was expressed through thinly veiled evasions of the trade laws. But on June 10, 1768, the antagonism to the commissioners turned into open defiance. On that day, Joseph Harrison (1709–1787), collector of the port of Boston, seized the Liberty, *a sloop owned by the wealthy merchant John Hancock (1737–1793), for allegedly having landed a cargo of Madeira wine on May 9 without payment of duties while a custom official, hitherto intimidated into keeping quiet, had been locked in a cabin below. As they attempted to leave the scene of the seizure, Harrison, along with his son and Benjamin Hallowell, the comptroller of customs, were physically attacked by an angry mob. They escaped without serious injury, but feeling against them was so intense that they and the customs commissioners fled for protection the next day to Castle William in Boston Harbor. This incident and the difficulties preceding it, which are described at length by Harrison below in a letter (Selection 13 C) to his patron, the Marquis of Rockingham, frightened the commissioners into calling for troops to protect them in performing their duties.*

The opposition to the American Board of Customs is analyzed at length by Oliver Morton Dickerson in The Navigation Acts and the American Revolution *(1951). Dickerson argues that the seizure of the* Liberty *was part of a plot by the customs commissioners to frame Hancock and thereby intimidate other merchants into complying with the trade laws—a view that is questioned by D. H. Watson (ed.), "Joseph Harrison and the* Liberty *Incident,"* William and Mary Quarterly, *third series, volume 20 (1963), pages 585–595. The standard study of Samuel Adams and the events surrounding the writing and adoption of the Massachusetts Circular Letter is John C. Miller,* Sam Adams: Pioneer in Propaganda *(1936). The early political career of John Dickinson may be followed in David L. Jacobson,* John Dickinson *(1965).*

A. "THOSE WHO ARE TAXED WITHOUT THEIR OWN CONSENT . . . ARE SLAVES": JOHN DICKINSON, "LETTERS FROM A FARMER IN PENNSYLVANIA . . ." (1767–1768)*

Letter I

I am a *Farmer*, settled, after a variety of fortunes, near the banks of the river *Delaware*, in the province of *Pennsylvania*. I received a liberal education, and have been engaged in the busy scenes of life; but am now convinced, that a man may be as happy without bustle, as with it. My farm is small; my servants are few, and good; I have a little money at interest; I wish for no more; my employment in my own affairs is easy; and with a contented grateful mind, (undisturbed by worldly hopes or fears, relating to myself,) I am completing the number of days allotted to me by divine goodness.

* These excerpts are reprinted from Paul Leicester Ford (ed.), The *Writings of John Dickinson* (1895), pp. 307–322, 328–335, 346–348, 355–357, 400, 405–406.

Being generally master of my time, I spend a good deal of it in a library, which I think the most valuable part of my small estate; and being acquainted with two or three gentlemen of abilities and learning, who honour me with their friendship, I have acquired, I believe, a greater knowledge in history, and the laws and constitution of my country, than is generally attained by men of my class, many of them not being so fortunate as I have been in the opportunities of getting information.

From my infancy I was taught to love *humanity* and *liberty*. Enquiry and experience have since confirmed my reverence for the lessons then given me, by convincing me more fully of their truth and excellence. Benevolence towards mankind, excites wishes for their welfare, and such wishes endear the means of fulfilling them. *These* can be found in liberty only, and therefore her sacred cause ought to be espoused by every man, on every occasion, to the utmost of his power. As a charitable, but poor person does not withhold his *mite,* because he cannot relieve *all* the distresses of the miserable, so should not any honest man suppress his sentiments concerning freedom, however small their influence is likely to be. Perhaps he "may touch some wheel," that will have an effect greater than he could reasonably expect.

These being my sentiments, I am encouraged to offer to you, my countrymen, my thoughts on some late transactions, that appear to me to be of the utmost importance to you. Conscious of my own defects, I have waited some time, in expectation of seeing the subject treated by persons much better qualified for the task; but being therein disappointed, and apprehensive that longer delays will be injurious, I venture at length to request the attention of the public, praying, that these lines may be *read* with the same zeal for the happiness of *British America,* with which they were *wrote.*

With a good deal of surprize I have observed, that little notice has been taken of an act of parliament, as injurious in its principle to the liberties of these colonies, as the *Stamp-Act* was: I mean the act for suspending the legislation of *New-York.*

The assembly of that government complied with a former act of parliament, requiring certain provisions to be made for the troops in *America,* in every particular, I think, except the articles of salt, pepper and vinegar. In my opinion they acted imprudently, considering all circumstances, in not complying so far as would have given satisfaction, as several colonies did: But my dislike of their conduct in that instance, has not blinded me so much, that I cannot plainly perceive, that they have been punished in a manner pernicious to *American* freedom, and justly alarming to all the colonies.

If the *British* parliament has a legal authority to issue an order, that we shall furnish a single article for the troops here, and to compel obedience to *that* order, they have the same right to issue an order for us to supply those troops with arms, cloths, and every necessary; and to compel obedience to *that* order also; in short, to lay *any burthens* they please upon us. What is this but *taxing* us at a *certain sum,* and leaving to us only the *manner* of raising it? How is this mode more tolerable than the *Stamp Act?* Would that act have appeared more pleasing to *Americans,* if being ordered thereby to raise the sum total of the taxes, the mighty privilege had been left to them, of saying how much should be paid for an instrument of writing on paper, and how much for another on parchment?

An act of parliament, commanding us to do a certain thing, if it has any validity, is a *tax* upon us for the expence that accrues in complying with it; and for this reason, I believe, every colony on the continent, that chose to give a mark of their respect for *Great-Britain,* in complying with the act relating to the troops, cautiously avoided the mention of that act, lest their conduct should be attributed to its supposed obligation.

The matter being thus stated, the assembly of *New-York* either had, or had not, a right to refuse submission to that act. If they had, and I imagine no *American* will say they had not, then the parliament had *no right* to compel them to execute it. If they had not *that right,* they had *no right* to punish them for not executing it; and therefore *no right* to suspend their legislation, which is a punishment. In fact, if the people of *New-York* cannot be legally taxed but by their own representatives, they cannot be legally deprived of the privilege of legislation, only for insisting on that exclusive privilege of taxation. If they may be legally deprived in such a case, of the privilege of legislation, why may they not, with equal reason, be deprived of every other privilege? Or why may not every colony be treated in the same manner, when any of them shall dare to deny their assent to any impositions, that shall be directed? Or what signifies the repeal of the *Stamp-Act,* if these colonies are to lose their *other* privileges, by not tamely surrendering *that* of taxation?

There is one consideration arising from this suspension, which is not generally attended to, but shews its importance very clearly. It was not *necessary* that this suspension should be caused by an act of parliament. The crown might have restrained the governor of *New-York,* even from calling the assembly together, by its prerogative in the royal governments. This step, I suppose, would have been taken, if the conduct of the assembly of *New-York* had been regarded as an act of disobedience *to the crown alone;* but it is regarded as an act of "disobedience to the authority of the BRITISH LEGISLATURE." This gives the suspension a consequence vastly more affecting. It is a parliamentary assertion of the *supreme authority* of the *British* legislature over these colonies, in *the point of taxation,* and is intended to COMPEL *New-York* into a submission to that authority. It seems therefore to me as much a violation of the liberty of the people of that province, and consequently of all these colonies, as if the parliament had sent a number of regiments to be quartered upon them till they should comply. For it is evident, that the suspension is meant as a *compulsion;* and the *method* of compelling is totally indifferent. It is indeed probable, that the sight of red coats, and the hearing of drums, would have been most alarming; because people are generally more influenced by their eyes and ears, than by their reason. But whoever seriously considers the matter, must perceive that a dreadful stroke is aimed at the liberty of these colonies. I say, of these colonies; for the cause of *one* is the cause of *all.* If the parliament may lawfully deprive *New-York* of any of *her* rights, it may deprive any, or all the other colonies of *their* rights; and nothing can possibly so much encourage such attempts, as a mutual inattention to the interests of each other. *To divide, and thus to destroy,* is the first political maxim in attacking those, who are powerful by their union. He certainly is not a wise man, who folds his arms, and reposes himself at home, viewing, with unconcern, the flames that have invaded his neighbour's house, without using any endeavours to extinguish them. When Mr. *Hampden's* ship money cause, for *Three Shillings* and *Four-pence,* was tried, all the people of *England,* with anxious expectations, interested themselves in the important decision; and when the slightest point, touching the freedom of *one* colony, is agitated, I earnestly wish, that *all the rest* may, with equal ardour, support their sister. Very much may be said on this subject; but I hope, more at present is unnecessary.

With concern I have observed, that *two* assemblies of this province have sat and adjourned, without taking any notice of this act. It may perhaps be asked, what would have been proper for them to do? I am by no means fond of inflammatory measures; I detest them. I should be sorry that any thing should be done, which might justly displease our sovereign, or our mother country: But a firm, modest exertion of a free spirit, should never be wanting on public occasions. It appears to me, that it would have been sufficient for the assembly, to have ordered our agents to represent to the King's ministers, their sense of the suspending act, and to pray for its repeal. Thus we should have borne our testimony against it; and might therefore reasonably expect that, on a like occasion, we might receive the same assistance from the other colonies.

> *Concordia res parvœ crescunt.*
> Small things grow great by concord.

Letter II

There is another late act of parliament, which appears to me to be unconstitutional, and as destructive to the liberty of these colonies, as that mentioned in my last letter; that is, the act for granting the duties on paper, glass, etc.

The parliament unquestionably possesses a legal authority to *regulate* the trade of *Great-Britain,* and all her colonies. Such an authority is essential to the relation between a mother country and her colonies; and necessary for the common good of all. He, who considers these provinces as states distinct from the *British Empire,* has very slender notions of *justice,* or of their *interests.* We are but parts of a *whole;* and therefore there must exist a power somewhere to preside, and preserve the connection in due order. This power is lodged in the parliament; and we are as much dependent on *Great-Britain,* as a perfectly free people can be on another.

I have looked over *every statute* relating to these colonies, from their first settlement to this time; and I find every one of them founded on this principle, till the *Stamp-Act* administration. *All before,* are calculated to regulate trade, and preserve or promote a mutually beneficial intercourse between the several constituent parts of the empire; and though many of them imposed duties on trade, yet those duties were always imposed *with design* to restrain the commerce of one part, that was injurious to another, and thus to promote the general welfare. The raising a revenue thereby was never intended. Thus the King, by his judges in his courts of justice, imposes fines which all together amount to a very considerable sum, and contribute to the support of government: But this is merely a consequence arising from restrictions, that only meant to keep peace, and prevent confusion; and surely a man would argue very loosely, who should conclude from hence, that the King has a right to levy money in general upon his subjects. Never

did the *British* parliament, till the period above mentioned, think of imposing duties in *America*, FOR THE PURPOSE OF RAISING A REVENUE. Mr. *Grenville*
first introduced this language, in the preamble to the 4th of *Geo.* III, Chap.
15, which has these words "And whereas it is just and necessary that A REVE-
NUE BE RAISED IN YOUR MAJESTY'S SAID DOMINIONS IN AMERICA, *for defraying
the expences of defending, protecting, and securing the same:* We your
Majesty's most dutiful and loyal subjects, THE COMMONS OF GREAT-BRITAIN,
in parliament assembled, being desirous to make some provision in this
present session of parliament, TOWARDS RAISING THE SAID REVENUE IN AMERICA,
have resolved to GIVE and GRANT unto your Majesty the several rates and
duties herein after mentioned," &c.

A few months after came the *Stamp-Act,* which reciting this, proceeds in
the same strange mode of expression, thus—"And whereas it is just and
necessary, that provision be made FOR RAISING A FURTHER REVENUE WITHIN
YOUR MAJESTY'S DOMINIONS IN AMERICA, *towards defraying the said expences,*
we your Majesty's most dutiful and loyal subjects, the COMMONS OF GREAT-
BRITAIN &c. GIVE and GRANT, &c. as before.

The last act, granting duties upon paper, &c. carefully pursues these
modern precedents. The preamble is, "Whereas it is expedient THAT A REVE-
NUE SHOULD BE RAISED IN YOUR MAJESTY'S DOMINIONS IN AMERICA, *for
making a more certain and adequate provision for defraying the charge of
the administration of justice, and the support of civil government in such
provinces, where it shall be found necessary; and towards the further
defraying the expences of defending, protecting and securing the said dominions,* we your Majesty's most dutiful and loyal subjects, the COMMONS
OF GREAT-BRITAIN, &c. GIVE and GRANT," &c. as before.

Here we may observe an authority *expressly* claimed and exerted to
impose duties on these colonies; not for the regulation of trade; not for the
preservation or promotion of a mutually beneficial intercourse between the
several constituent parts of the empire, heretofore the *sole objects* of parliamentary institutions; *but for the single purpose of levying money upon us.*

This I call an innovation; and a most dangerous innovation. It may perhaps be objected, that *Great-Britain* has a right to lay what duties she
pleases upon her exports, and it makes no difference to us, whether they are
paid here or there.

To this I answer. These colonies require many things for their use, which
the laws of *Great-Britain* prohibit them from getting any where but from her.
Such are paper and glass.

That we may legally be bound to pay any *general* duties on these commodities relative to the regulation of trade, is granted; but we being *obliged
by the laws* to take from *Great-Britain,* any *special* duties imposed on their
exportation *to us only, with intention to raise a revenue from us only,* are
as much *taxes,* upon us, as those imposed by the *Stamp-Act.*

What is the difference in *substance* and *right* whether the same sum is
raised upon us by the rates mentioned in the *Stamp-Act,* on the *use* of paper,
or by these duties, on the *importation* of it. It is only the edition of a former
book, shifting a sentence from the *end* to the *beginning.*

Suppose the duties were made payable in *Great-Britain.*

It signifies nothing to us, whether they are to be paid here or there. Had
the *Stamp-Act* directed, that all the paper should be landed at *Florida,* and
the duties paid there, before it was brought to the *British* colonies, would the

act have raised less money upon us, or have been less destructive of our rights? By no means: For as we were under a necessity of using the paper, we should have been under the necessity of paying the duties. Thus, in the present case, a like *necessity* will subject us, if this act continues in force, to the payment of the duties now imposed.

Why was the *Stamp-Act* then so pernicious to freedom? It did not enact, that every man in the colonies *should* buy a certain quantity of paper—No: It only directed, that no instrument of writing should be valid in law, if not made on stamped paper, &c.

The makers of that act knew full well, that the confusions that would arise from the disuse of writings, would COMPEL the colonies to use the stamped paper, and therefore to pay the taxes imposed. For this reason the *Stamp-Act* was said to be a law THAT WOULD EXECUTE ITSELF. For the very same reason, the last act of parliament, if it is granted to have any force here, WILL EXECUTE ITSELF, and will be attended with the very same consequences to *American* liberty.

Some persons perhaps may say, that this act lays us under no necessity to pay the duties imposed, because we may ourselves manufacture the articles on which they are laid; whereas by the *Stamp-Act* no instrument of writing could be good, unless made on *British* paper, and that too stamped.

Such an objection amounts to no more than this, that the injury resulting to these colonies, from the total disuse of *British* paper and glass, will not be *so afflicting* as that which would have resulted from the total disuse of writing among them; for by that means even the *Stamp-Act* might have been eluded. Why then was it universally detested by them as slavery itself? Because it presented to these devoted provinces nothing but a choice of calamities, imbittered by indignities, each of which it was unworthy of freemen to bear. But is no injury a violation of right but the *greatest* injury? If the eluding the payment of the taxes imposed by the *Stamp-Act*, would have subjected us to a more dreadful inconvenience, than the eluding the payment of those imposed by the late act; does it therefore follow, that the last is *no violation* of our rights, tho' it is calculated for the same purpose the other was, that is, *to raise money upon us*, WITHOUT OUR CONSENT.

This would be making *right* to consist, not in an exemption from *injury*, but from a certain *degree of injury*.

But the objectors may further say, that we shall suffer no injury at all by the disuse of *British* paper and glass. We might not, if we could make as much as we want. But can any man, acquainted with *America*, believe this possible? I am told there are but two or three *Glass-Houses* on this continent, and but very few *Paper-Mills;* and suppose more should be erected, a long course of years must elapse, before they can be brought to perfection. This continent is a country of planters, farmers, and fishermen; not of manufacturers. The difficulty of establishing particular manufactures in such a country, is almost insuperable. For one manufacture is connected with others in such a manner, that it may be said to be impossible to establish one or two, without establishing several others. The experience of many nations may convince us of this truth.

Inexpressible therefore must be our distresses in evading the late acts, by the disuse of *British* paper and glass. Nor will this be the extent of our misfortune, if we admit the legality of that act.

Great-Britain has prohibited the manufacturing *iron* and *steel* in these colonies, without any objection being made to her *right* of doing it. The *like* right she must have to prohibit any other manufacture among us. Thus she is possessed of an undisputed *precedent* on that point. This authority, she will say, is founded on the *original intention* of settling these colonies; that is, that we should manufacture for them, and that they should supply her with materials. The *equity* of this policy, she will also say, has been universally acknowledged by the colonies, who never have made the least objections to statutes for that purpose; and will further appear by the *mutual benefits* flowing from this usage ever since the settlement of these colonies.

Our great advocate, Mr. *Pitt,* in his speeches on the debate concerning the repeal of the *Stamp-Act,* acknowledged, that *Great-Britain* could restrain our manufactures. His words are these—"This kingdom, as the supreme governing and legislative power, has ALWAYS bound the colonies by her regulations and RESTRICTIONS in trade, in navigation, in MANUFACTURES—in every thing, *except that of taking their money out of their pockets,* WITHOUT THEIR CONSENT." Again he says, "We may bind their trade, CONFINE THEIR MANUFACTURES, and exercise every power whatever, *except that of taking their money out of their pockets,* WITHOUT THEIR CONSENT.

Here then, my dear countrymen, ROUSE yourselves, and behold the ruin hanging over your heads. If you ONCE admit, that *Great-Britain* may lay duties upon her exportations to us, *for the purpose of levying money on us only,* she then will have nothing to do, but to lay those duties on the articles which she prohibits us to manufacture—and the tragedy of *American* liberty is finished. We have been prohibited from procuring manufactures, in all cases, any where but from *Great-Britain* (excepting linens, which we are permitted to import directly from *Ireland*). We have been prohibited, in some cases, from manufacturing for ourselves; and may be prohibited in others. We are therefore exactly in the situation of a city besieged, which is surrounded by the works of the besiegers in every part *but one.* If *that* is closed up, no step can be taken, *but to surrender at discretion.* If *Great-Britain* can order us to come to her for necessaries we want, and can order us to pay what taxes she pleases before we take them away, or when we land them here, we are as abject slaves as *France* and *Poland* can shew in wooden shoes, and with uncombed hair. . . .

Upon the whole, the single question is, whether the parliament can legally impose duties to be paid *by the people of these colonies only,* FOR THE SOLE PURPOSE OF RAISING A REVENUE, *on commodities which she obliges us to take from her alone,* or, in other words, whether the parliament can legally take money out of our pockets, without our consent. If they can, our boasted liberty is but

> *Vox et præterea nihil.*
> A sound and nothing else.

Letter IV

An objection, I hear, has been made against my second letter, which I would willingly clear up before I proceed. "There is," say these objectors, "a material difference between the *Stamp-Act* and the *late Act* for laying a duty on paper, &c. that justifies the conduct of those who opposed the former, and yet are willing to submit to the latter. The duties imposed by the *Stamp-Act* were *internal* taxes; but the present are *external*, and therefore the parliament may have a right to impose them."

To this I answer, with a total denial of the power of parliament to lay upon these colonies any "tax" whatever.

This point, being so important to this, and to succeeding generations, I wish to be clearly understood.

To the word *"tax,"* I annex that meaning which the constitution and history of *England* require to be annexed to it; that is—that it is *an imposition on the subject, for the sole purpose of levying money.*

In the early ages of our monarchy, certain services were rendered to the crown *for the general good.* These were personal: But in process of time, such institutions being found inconvenient, *gifts* and *grants* of their own property were made by the people, under the several names of aids, tallages, tasks, taxes and subsidies, &c. These were made, as may be collected even from the names, *for public service* upon "need and necessity." All these sums were levied upon the people by virtue of their voluntary gift. Their design was to support the *national honor and interest.* Some of those grants comprehended duties arising from trade; being imposts on merchandizes. These Lord Chief Justice *Coke* classes under "subsidies," and "parliamentary aids." They are also called "customs." But whatever the *name* was, they were always considered as *gifts of the people to the crown, to be employed for public uses.*

Commerce was at a low ebb, and surprizing instances might be produced how little it was attended to for a succession of ages. The terms that have been mentioned, and, among the rest, that of *"tax,"* had obtained a national, parliamentary meaning, drawn from the principles of the constitution, long before any *Englishman* thought of *imposition of duties, for the regulation of trade.*

Whenever we speak of "taxes" among *Englishmen,* let us therefore speak of them with reference to the *principles* on which, and the *intentions* with which they have been established. This will give certainty to our expression, and safety to our conduct: But if, when we have in view the liberty of these colonies, we proceed in any other course, we pursue a *Juno** indeed, but shall only catch a cloud.

In the national, parliamentary sense insisted on, the word "tax" was certainly understood by the congress at *New-York,* whose resolves may be said to form the *American* "bill of rights."

The third, fourth, fifth, and sixth resolves, are thus expressed.

III. "That it is *inseparably essential to the freedom of a people,* and the *undoubted right* of *Englishmen,* that NO TAX be imposed on them, *but with their own consent,* given personally, or by their representatives."

IV. "That the people of the colonies are not, and from their local circumstances, cannot be represented in the house of commons in *Great-Britain.*"

V. "That the only representatives of the people of the colonies, are the persons chosen therein by themselves; and that NO TAXES ever have been,

---

* The Goddess of *Empire,* in the Heathen Mythology; according to an antient fable, *Ixion* pursued her, but she escaped in a cloud.

or can be constitutionally imposed on them, but by their respective legislatures."

VI. "That all *supplies to the crown,* being free gifts of the people, it is *unreasonable, and inconsistent with the principles and spirit of the* British *constitution,* for the people of *Great-Britain* to grant to his Majesty *the property of the colonies.*"

Here is no distinction made between *internal* and *external* taxes. It is evident from the short reasoning thrown into these resolves, that every imposition "to grant to his Majesty *the property of the colonies,*" was thought a "tax;" and that every such imposition, if laid any other way than "with their consent, given personally, or by their representatives," was not only "unreasonable, and inconsistent with the principles and spirit of the *British* constitution," but destructive "to the freedom of a people."

This language is clear and important. A "TAX" means an imposition to raise money. Such persons therefore as speak of *internal* and *external* "TAXES," I pray may pardon me, if I object to that expression, as applied to the privileges and interests of these colonies. There may be *internal* and *external* IMPOSITIONS, founded on *different principles,* and having *different tendencies,* every "tax" being an imposition, tho' every imposition is not a "tax." But *all taxes* are founded on the *same principles;* and have the *same tendency.*

External impositions, for the regulation of our trade, do not "grant to his Majesty *the property of the colonies.*" They only *prevent the colonies acquiring property,* in things not necessary, in a manner judged to be injurious to the welfare of the whole empire. But the last statute respecting us, "grants to his Majesty *the property of the colonies,*" by laying duties on the manufactures of *Great-Britain* which they MUST take, and which she settled on them, on purpose that they SHOULD take.

What *tax* can be more *internal* than this? Here is money drawn, *without their consent,* from a society, who have constantly enjoyed a constitutional mode of raising all money among themselves. The payment of their *tax* they have no possible method of avoiding; as they cannot do without the commodities on which it is laid, and they cannot manufacture these commodities themselves. Besides, if this unhappy country should be so lucky as to elude this act, by getting parchment enough, in the place of paper, or by reviving the antient method of writing on wax and bark, and by inventing something to serve instead of glass, her ingenuity would stand her in little stead; for then the parliament would have nothing to do but to prohibit such manufactures, or to lay a tax on *hats* and *woollen cloths,* which they have already prohibited the colonies *from supplying each other with;* or on instruments, and tools of *steel* and *iron,* which they have prohibited the provincials *from manufacturing at all:* And then, what little gold and silver they have, must be torn from their hands, or they will not be able, in a short time, to get an ax, for cutting their firewood, nor a plough, for raising their food. In what respect, therefore, I beg leave to ask, is the late act preferable to the *Stamp-Act,* or more consistent with the liberties of the colonies? For my own part, I regard them both with equal apprehensions; and think they ought to be in the same manner opposed.

Habemus quidem senatus consultum,—tanquam gladium in vagina repositum.
We have a statute, laid up for future use, like a sword in the scabbard.

Letter VI

It is true, that *impositions for raising a revenue,* may be hereafter called *regulations of trade:* But names will not change the nature of things. Indeed we ought firmly to believe, what is an undoubted truth, confirmed by the unhappy experience of many states heretofore free, that UNLESS THE MOST WATCHFUL ATTENTION BE EXERTED, A NEW SERVITUDE MAY BE SLIPPED UPON US, UNDER THE SANCTION OF USUAL AND RESPECTABLE TERMS.

Thus the *Cæsars* ruined the *Roman* liberty, under the titles of *tribunical* and *dictatorial* authorities, old and venerable dignities, known in the most flourishing times of freedom. In imitation of the same policy, *James* II. when he *meant* to establish popery, *talked* of liberty of conscience, the most sacred of all liberties; and had thereby almost deceived the Dissenters into destruction.

All artful rulers, who strive to extend their power beyond its just limits, endeavor to give to their attempts as much semblance of legality as possible. Those who succeed them may venture to go a little further; for each new encroachment will be strengthened by a former. "That which is now supported by examples, growing old, will become an example itself," and thus support fresh usurpations.

A free people therefore can never be too quick in observing, nor too firm in opposing the beginnings of *alteration* either in *form* or *reality,* respecting institutions formed for their security. The first kind of alteration leads to the last: Yet, on the other hand, nothing is more certain, than that the *forms* of liberty may be retained, when the *substance* is gone. In government, as well as in religion, "The *letter* killeth, but the *spirit* giveth life."

I will beg leave to enforce this remark by a few instances. The crown, by the constitution, has the prerogative of creating peers. The existence of that order, in due number and dignity, is essential to the constitution; and if the crown did not exercise that prerogative, the peerage must have long since decreased so much as to have lost its proper influence. Suppose a prince, for some unjust purposes, should, from time to time, advance so many needy, profligate wretches to that rank, that all the independence of the house of lords should be destroyed; there would then be a manifest violation of the constitution, *under the appearance of using legal prerogative.*

The house of commons claim the privilege of forming all money bills, and will not suffer either of the other branches of the legislature to add to, or alter them; contending that their power simply extends to an acceptance or rejection of them. This privilege appears to be just: but under pretence of this just privilege, the house of commons has claimed a licence of tacking to money bills, clauses relating to things of a totally different kind, and thus forcing them in a manner on the king and lords. This seems to be an abuse of that privilege, and it may be vastly more abused. Suppose a future house, influenced by some displaced, discontented demagogues—in a time of danger, should tack to a money bill, something so injurious to the king and peers, that they would not assent to it, and yet the commons should obstinately insist on it; the whole kingdom would be exposed to ruin by them, *under the appearance of maintaining a valuable privilege.*

In these cases it might be difficult for a while to determine, whether the king intended to exercise his prerogative in a constitutional manner or not; or whether the commons insisted on their demand factiously, or for the public good: But surely the conduct of the crown or of the house, would in time sufficiently explain itself.

Ought not the PEOPLE therefore to watch? to observe facts? to search into causes? to investigate designs? And have they not a right of JUDGING from the evidence before them, on no slighter points than their *liberty* and *happiness?* It would be less than trifling, wherever a *British* government is established, to make use of any arguments to prove such a right. . . .

Letter VII

From these remarks I think it evident, that we *must* use paper and glass; that what we use *must* be *British;* and that we *must* pay the duties imposed, unless those who sell these articles, are so generous as to make us presents of the duties they pay.

Some persons may think this act of no consequence, because the duties are so *small.* A fatal error. *That* is the very circumstance most alarming to me. For I am convinced, that the authors of this law would never have obtained an act to raise so trifling a sum as it must do, had they not intended by *it* to establish a *precedent* for future use. To console ourselves with the *smallness* of the duties, is to walk deliberately into the snare that is set for us, praising the *neatness* of the workmanship. Suppose the duties imposed by the late act could be paid by these distressed colonies with the utmost ease, and that the purposes to which they are to be applied, were the most reasonable and equitable that can be conceived, the contrary of which I hope to demonstrate before these letters are concluded; yet even in such a supposed case, these colonies ought to regard the act with abhorrence. For WHO ARE A FREE PEOPLE? Not *those,* over whom government is reasonably and equitably exercised, but *those,* who live under a government so *constitutionally checked* and *controuled,* that proper provision is made against its being otherwise exercised.

The late act is founded on the destruction of this constitutional security. If the parliament have a right to lay a duty of Four Shillings and Eightpence on a hundred weight of glass, or a ream of paper, they have a right to lay a duty of any other sum on either. They may raise the duty, as the author before quoted says has been done in some countries, till it "exceeds seventeen or eighteen times the value of the commodity." In short, if they have a right *to* levy a tax of *one penny* upon us, they have a right to levy *a million* upon us: For where does their right stop? At any given number of Pence, Shillings or Pounds? To attempt to limit their right, after granting it to exist at all, is as contrary to reason—as granting it to exist at all, is contrary to justice. If *they* have any right to tax *us*—then, whether *our own money* shall continue in *our own pockets* or not, depends no longer on *us,* but on *them.* "There is nothing which" we can call our own; or, to use the words of Mr. *Locke*—"WHAT PROPERTY HAVE WE IN THAT, WHICH ANOTHER MAY, BY RIGHT, TAKE, WHEN HE PLEASES, TO HIMSELF?"

These duties, which will inevitably be levied upon us—which are now levying upon us—are *expressly* laid FOR THE SOLE PURPOSE OF TAKING

MONEY. This is the true definition of *"taxes."* They are therefore *taxes*. This money is to be taken from *us*. *We* are therefore *taxed*. *Those* who are *taxed* without their own consent, expressed by themselves or their representatives, are *slaves*. *We are taxed* without our own consent, expressed by ourselves or our representatives. *We* are therefore—SLAVES.

> *Miserable vulgus*
> A miserable tribe.

Letter XII

Let these *truths* be indelibly impressed on our minds—*that we cannot be* HAPPY, WITHOUT *being* FREE—that we cannot be free, *without being secure in our property*—that *we* cannot be secure in our property, *if, without our consent, others may, as by right, take it away*—that *taxes imposed on us by parliament*, do thus take it away—that *duties laid for the sole purpose of raising money*, are taxes—that *attempts* to lay such duties *should be instantly and firmly opposed*—that this opposition can never be effectual, *unless it is the united effort of these provinces*—that therefore BENEVOLENCE *of temper towards each other*, and UNANIMITY *of councils*, are essential to the welfare of the whole—and lastly, that for this reason, every man amongst us, who in any manner would encourage either *dissension, diffidence*, or *indifference*, between these colonies, is an enemy to *himself*, and to *his country*.

.   .   .

To discharge this double duty to *yourselves*, and to your *posterity*, you have nothing to do, but to call forth into use the *good sense* and *spirit* of which you are possessed. You have nothing to do, but to conduct your affairs *peaceably—prudently—firmly—jointly*. By *these means* you will support the character of *freemen*, without losing that of *faithful subjects*—a good character in any government—one of the best under a *British* government—You will *prove*, that *Americans* have that true *magnanimity* of soul, that can resent injuries, without falling into rage; and that tho' your devotion to *Great-Britain* is the most affectionate, yet you can make PROPER DISTINCTIONS, and know what you owe *to yourselves*, as well as to her—You will, at the same time that you advance your *interests*, advance your *reputation*—You will convince the world of the *justice of your demands*, and the *purity of your intentions*.—While all mankind must, with unceasing applauses, confess, that YOU indeed DESERVE liberty, who so *well understand* it, so *passionately love* it, so *temperately enjoy* it, and so *wisely, bravely*, and *virtuously assert, maintain, and defend* it. . . .

For my part I am resolved to contend for the liberty delivered down to me by my ancestors; but whether I shall do it effectually or not, depends on you, my countrymen.

"How little soever one is able to write, yet when the liberties of one's country are threatened, it is still more difficult to be silent." . . .

B. ''IN ALL FREE STATES THE CONSTITUTION IS FIXD'': MASSACHUSETTS CIRCULAR LETTER (FEB. 11, 1768)*

SIR,

The House of Representatives of this Province have taken into their serious Consideration, the great difficultys that must accrue to themselves & their Constituents, by the operation of several acts of Parliament imposing Duties & Taxes on the American Colonys.

As it is a Subject in which every Colony is deeply interested they have no reason to doubt but your Assembly is deeply impressd with its Importance & that such constitutional measures will be come into as are proper. It seems to be necessary, that all possible Care should be taken, that the Representations of the several Assembly upon so delicate a point, should harmonize with each other: The House therefore hope that this letter will be candidly considerd in no other Light, than as expressing a Disposition freely to communicate their mind to a Sister Colony, upon a common Concern in the same manner as they would be glad to receive the Sentiments of your or any other House of Assembly on the Continent.

The House have humbly represented to the ministry, their own Sentiments that His Majestys high Court of Parliament is the supreme legislative Power over the whole Empire: That in all free States the Constitution is fixd; & as the supreme Legislative derives its Power & Authority from the Constitution, it cannot overleap the Bounds of it without destroying its own foundation: That the Constitution ascertains & limits both Sovereignty & allegiance, & therefore, his Majestys American Subjects who acknowlege themselves bound by the Ties of Allegiance, have an equitable Claim to the full enjoyment of the fundamental Rules of the British Constitution. That it is an essential unalterable Right in nature, ingrafted into the British Constitution, as a fundamental Law & ever held sacred & irrevocable by the Subjects within the Realm, that what a man has honestly acquird is absolutely his own, which he may freely give, but cannot be taken from him without his consent: That the American Subjects may therefore exclusive of any Consideration of Charter Rights, with a decent firmness adapted to the Character of free men & Subjects assert this natural and constitutional Right.

It is moreover their humble opinion, which they express with the greatest Deferrence to the Wisdom of the Parliament that the Acts made there imposing Duties on the People of this province with the sole & express purpose of raising a Revenue, are Infringements of their natural & constitutional Rights because as they are not represented in the British Parliament His Majestys Commons in Britain by those Acts grant their Property without their consent.

This House further are of Opinion that their Constituents considering their local Circumstances cannot by any possibility be represented in the Parliament, & that it will forever be impracticable that they should be equally represented there & consequently not at all; being seperated by an Ocean of a thousand leagues: and that his Majestys Royal Predecessors for

* Reprinted in full from Harry Alonzo Cushing (ed.), *The Writings of Samuel Adams* (1904–1908), vol. I, pp. 184–188.

this reason were graciously pleased to form a subordinate legislature here that their subjects might enjoy the unalienable Right of a Representation. Also that considering the utter Impracticability of their ever being fully & equally represented in parliament, & the great Expence that must unavoidably attend even a partial representation there, this House think that a taxation of their Constituents, even without their Consent, grievous as it is, would be preferable to any Representation that could be admitted for them there.

Upon these principles, & also considering that were the right in Parliament ever so clear, yet, for obvious reasons it would be beyond the rules of Equity that their Constituents should be taxed on the manufactures of Great Britain here, in Addition to the dutys they pay for them in England, & other Advantages arising to Great Britain from the Acts of trade, this House have preferrd a humble dutifull & loyal Petition to our most gracious Sovereign, & made such Representations to his Majestys Ministers, as they apprehended would tend to obtain redress.

They have also submitted to Consideration whether any People can be said to enjoy any degree of Freedom if the Crown in addition to its undoubted Authority of constituting a Governor, should also appoint him such a Stipend as it may judge proper without the Consent of the people & at their Expence; and whether while the Judges of the Land & other Civil officers hold not their Commission during good Behavior, their having salarys appointed for them by the Crown independent of the people hath not a tendency to subvert the principles of Equity & endanger the Happiness & Security of the Subject.

In addition to these measures the House have wrote a Letter to their Agent, Mr De Berdt, the Sentiments of which he is directed to lay before the ministry: wherein they take Notice of the hardships of the Act for preventing Mutiny & Desertion, which requires the Governor & Council to provide enumerated Articles for the Kings marching troops & the People to pay the Expences; & also of the Commission of the Gentlemen appointed Commissioners of the Customs to reside in America, which authorizes them to make as many Appointments as they think fit & to pay the Appointees what sum they please, for whose Mal Conduct they are not accountable— from whence it may happen that officers of the Crown may be multiplyd to such a degree as to become dangerous to the Liberty of the people by Virtue of a Commission which doth not appear to this House to derive any such Advantages to Trade as many have been led to expect.

These are the Sentiments & proceedings of this House; & as they have too much reason to believe that the Enemys of the Colonys have represented them to his Majestys Ministers & the parliament as factious disloyal & having a disposition to make themselves independent of the Mother Country, they have taken occasion in the most humble terms to assure his Majesty & his ministers that with regard to the People of this province & as they doubt not of all the colonies the charge is unjust.

The house is fully satisfyd that your Assembly is too generous and enlargd in sentiment, to believe, that this Letter proceeds from an Ambition of taking the Lead or dictating to the other Assemblys: They freely submit their opinions to the Judgment of others, & shall take it kind in your house to point out to them any thing further which may be thought necessary.

This House cannot conclude without expressing their firm Confidence in the King our common head & Father, that the united & dutifull Supplications of his distressed American Subjects will meet with his royal & favorable Acceptance.

C. OPPOSITION TO THE CUSTOMS COMMISSIONERS IN BOSTON: JOSEPH HARRISON TO THE MARQUIS OF ROCKINGHAM (JUNE 17, 1768)*

My Lord,

When I had the Honor of writing to Your Lordship by Mr. Rogers I was full of Apprehensions that some Tumults and Riots would be raised here on the arrival of the New Commissioners of the Customs, who landed here the beginning of November, and I afterwards wrote another Letter to inform Your Lordship that no open Violences had been committed on that Occasion but that the People had contented themselves in venting their ill Humors and Rancor against the late Parliamentary Regulations in Abuse and Invective only. Since then a dangerous and seditious Combination has been formed to resist the Execution of those Acts of Parliament and indeed of all others that impose any Duties payable in the Colonies. In order to effect this the News Papers have been employed all this last Winter in circulating a vast number of inflaming and seditious Publications tending to poison and incense the Minds of the People and alienate them from all regard and obedience to the Legislature of the Mother Country. Amongst these the most dangerous and alarming was a Series of Letters from a Farmer in Pennsylvania to the Inhabitants of the British Colonies written by one Dickinson a Lawyer in Philadelphia: At first they were retailed weekly in all the News Papers, and have since been published together in a Pamphlet, and dispersed throughout the whole Continent. I have been thus particular in mentioning these Letters as I believe they have been the principal means, of spreading this almost general Disaffection among the People, which has at last broke out in open Acts of Violence etc., but I will go on with my Narrative. About the time of these Publications it was easy to perceive that the Doctrines and Positions therein laid down and defended had taken deep Root and Effect in the Minds of the People. A general Discontent begun to prevail and soon shewed itself by an almost universal Clamor, against all Duties, Customs and Custom house Officers: even the penny a Gallon Duty on Molasses (which Your Lordship will remember, was admitted by the Americans themselves in 1766, as so proper and easy an Imposition, that no Objection could possibly be made to it) is now found out to be oppressive and illegal: the common Cry being, Pay no Duties,! save your Money and you save your Country!, so that running of Goods and Smuggling is become public Virtue and Patriotism. Thus far matters had advanced when the Season came on for the Arrival of Ships from England and other Places, with dutiable goods on board:- Judge then my Lord of the miserable Situation I was in being by my Office the Person who must levy all Duties, and stand the Shock of this Opposition and Clamor, and may aptly be compared to being placed between Two Fires.

* Reprinted in full from D. H. Watson (ed.), "Joseph Harrison and the *Liberty* Incident," *William and Mary Quarterly*, 3d ser., vol. 20 (1963), pp. 587–595.

The Commissioners on one Side requiring (as in duty bound) the Exaction of all Customs, and the People on the other disputing the payment of any and even objecting to the legality of them. However by a Steady, temperate and obliging behaviour and the Countenance of a few principal Merchants, (Friends to Government) I was enabled to surmount many Difficulties. But after the General Assembly had openly adopted the same Principles and published in the News Papers their petition and Remonstrances to the King and Ministry with their letters to some others of high Rank in England (among which was one to Your Lordship) the Spirit of Licentiousness had got to such a pitch that whole Cargoes of Dutiable Goods were clandestinely landed, and Smuggled, in the most open and audacious manner; and Merchants who were willing and desirous of rendering all due regard to Acts of Parliament were threatened by the Mob if they paid any Duties. By this time matters were concerting by the Sons of Liberty for an open Insurection, but it was given out that no Violences would take place till the Assembly had received an Answer to their Remonstrances: and then if those answers should prove unfavourable that is, if they had not positive Assurances from the Ministry that all Acts of Parliament imposing Duties on the Colonies should be immediately repealed, the Commissioners of the Customs and all other Officers dependent on them, should by force be obliged to deliver up and resign their Commissions, and be drove away out of the Country. . . . Thus affairs stood when News was received of the Mobs Riots and Tumults in England on account of Mr. Wilkes etc., which I believe have had a considerable Effect in hastening and precipitating the like Proceedings here, which I am next to give Your Lordship an Account of.

I mentioned before, that large Quantities of dutiable Goods had been smuggled in a most audacious manner but tho' publicly known and talked of Yet such is the Temper of the Times no legal Information could be obtained, so as to prosecute, or make any seizure of them. However an Affair of that Sort at last happened; of which we have the most authentic Evidence. A Vessel belonging to one of the Principal Merchants in this Town arrived lately from Madeira, went boldly to the Wharf, and in the Night a large number of People being collected together, they seized and confined the Tideswaiter that was on board, broke open the Hatches, and took out the greatest part of the Cargo of Wines. When the business was finished they released the Tidesman but with such Threats and Denunciations of Vengeance Death and Destruction in Case he divulged the Affair, that the poor man was so terrified, and intimidated that it was some time after before he ventured to make the Discovery. However at last, an Information upon Oath was given in of the whole Transaction which I immediately communicated to the Commissioners of the Customs and by them was referred to their Solicitor who gave his Opinion that the Vessel, a Sloop of about 90 Tuns, ought to be seized and the Chairman of the Board of Commissioners gave me Orders accordingly. The Owner of this Sloop is a Merchant of the largest property in this Town, and at this Time happens to be the Idol of the Mob, just as Mr. Wilkes is in England. Hancock and Liberty being the Cry here, as Wilkes and Liberty is in London! tho' in other respects Mr. Hancock is a generous benevolent Gentleman but unluckily subject to the influence of Otis and other Incendiaries. Under these Circumstances a Seizure must necessarily be attended with the utmost Risque and Danger to the Officer who should make the Attempt. However as I was judged to be the properest person to Effect it,

I was determined that no Danger should deter me from the Execution of my Duty, tho' I was then so ill as to be just able to stirr abroad. So after sending on board the Romney Man of Warr (which then lay in the Harbour) to request their assistance in case a Rescue should be attempted, I proceeded to execute my Orders; first informing my Brother Officer Mr. Hallowell the Comptroller of the Service I was going upon who generously declared that I should not singly be exposed to the fury of the Populace, but that he would share the danger with me, accordingly we set out together towards the Wharf where the Vessel lay and in our way thither my Son (about 18 Years of Age) accidentally joined us in the Street and went along with us. When we got down to the Wharf we found the Sloop lying there and after waiting till we saw the Man of Warrs Boat ready to put off the Comptroller and I, steped on board, seized the Vessel, and I put the Kings Mark on the Main Mast: By this time the People began to muster together on the Wharf, from all Quarters; and several Men had got on board in order to regain Possession just as the Man of Warrs Boat well Man'd and Armed had got along side: They soon drove the Intruders out and I delivered the Vessel into custody of the commanding Officer. We then went a Shore and walked off the Wharf without any Insult or Molestation from the People, who were eagerly engaged in a Scuffle with the Man of Warrs Men and endeavouring to detain the Sloop at the Wharf. But we had scarce got into the Street before we were pursued by the Mob which by this time was increased to a great Multitude. The onset was begun by throwing Dirt at me, which was presently succeeded by Volleys of Stones, Brickbatts, Sticks or anything that came to hand: In this manner I run the Gauntlet near 200 Yards, my poor Son following behind endeavouring to shelter his Father by receiving the strokes of many of the Stones thrown at him till at length he became equally an Object of their Resentment, was knocked down and then laid hold of by the Legs, Arms and Hair of his Head, and in that manner dragged along the Kennel in a most barbarous and cruel manner till a few compasionate people happening to see him in that Distress, formed a Resolution of attempting to rescue him out of the Hands of the Mob; which with much difficulty they effected, and got him into a House; tho' this pulling and hauling between Friends and Enemies had like to have been fatal to him. About this time I received a violent Blow on the Breast which had like to have brought me to the Ground, and I verily believe if I had fallen, I should never have got up again, the People to all appearance being determined on Blood and Murder. But luckily just at that critical moment a friendly Man came up and supported me; and observed that now was the time for my Escape as the whole Attention of the Mob was engaged in the Scuffle about my Son who he assured me would be taken out of their Hands by some Persons of his Acquaintance. He then bid me follow him, which I accordingly did, and by suddainly turning the corner of a Street, was presently out of Sight of the Crowd, and soon after got to a Friends House where I was kindly received and on whom I could depend for Safety and Protection: And in about an Hours time I had the satisfaction of hearing my Son was in Safety, and had been conducted home, by the Persons who rescued him from the Mob; but in a miserable Condition being much bruised and Wounded, tho' not dangerously, and I hope will soon get well again.

With regard to my friend the Comptroller he was a little Distance behind when the Assault first began and on his attempting to protect my Son, was himself beset in the same Manner, and would certainly have been murdered by the Mob, if some Persons had not rescued him out of their Hands: however he was very much hurt, having received two bad Contusions on his Cheek and the Back of his Head. All this happened about 7 o'Clock last Friday Afternoon [June 10] and it was hoped that the People would have dispersed without doing any further mischief, but instead of that, before 9 o'Clock the Mob had increased to such a prodigious Number that the whole Town was in the utmost Consternation and Confusion. When thus collected together, the first Attempt was on the Comptroller whose House they beset; but on being assured that he was not at Home, they contented themselves with breaking a few pains of Glass and then departed in order to pay a Visit to the Collector, But before they got to my House several principal Gentlemen of the Town had assembled there in order if possible to protect my Family, but before the Mob got there it was thought proper to send my Wife and Children to a House in the Neibourhood. On their Arrival the first Demand was for the Collector, but they were told that he was not there, upon which they attempted to enter the House but were prevented by the Gentlemen there whose kind Interposition in all probability prevented the Pillage and Destruction of all my Furniture. Finding this opposition within they concluded the Visit with breaking the Windows, and then marched off but in passing by the House of Mr. [John] Williams one of the Inspectors General of the Customs they served it in the same Manner. After this in all probability the Mob would have dispersed if some evil minded People had not informed them that I had a fine sailing pleasure Boat which I set great store by, that they lay in one the Docks, upon this Intelligence the whole Crowd posted down to the water side hauled the Boat out of the Water, and dragged her thro' the Streets to Liberty Tree (as it is called) where she was formally condemned, and from thence dragged up into the Common and there burned to Ashes. The Destruction of this Boat I must own is a very sensible mortification She being as celebrated here for Swift sailing as Bay Malton is in England for running and had just before been nicely fitted out to send a present to Sir Geo. Saville. With this Exploit they concluded the mischievous Labour of that Night; and soon after dispersed. The next Day (Saturday) it was said that another Mob would be assembled in the Evening; and that the Commissioners would be attacked; however on timely Notice of the Intention they very wisely took Refuge on Board the Romney Man of Warr, where they still remain, nor does it seem likely from the present Temper of the People that they will soon be permitted to return on Shore. This Afternoon a Negotiation was set on foot for putting the Sloop that had been seized in to the Possession of the Crown. Mr. Hancock on his giving security that she should be returned to me in case she should be condemned by a Decree of the Court of the Admiralty. This, it was said would quiet the Minds of the People and restore peace to the Town at least for the present; But it seems, The Sons of Liberty and Leaders of the Mob did not choose to let go their Hold of an affair so well adapted to keep up the Ferment. Mr. Hancock was very earnest and desirous that this Proposal should take place, but was over awed by some of those Firebrands who have the chief Direction of the Mob and so the Treaty was broke off on Sunday Night.

On this Occasion I can not help observing the unhappiness of Mr. Hancocks Situation: He is a Young Gentleman of the Largest Fortune in this

Town of a generous benevolent Disposition and very charitable to the Poor. These Qualities must necessarily render him extremely Popular and being unluckily connected with Otis and the other Ringleaders of the Faction they have artfully drawn him by little into all their Measures and have now placed him at the Head of their Party; tho' I verily believe in his own Mind he disapproves of their Proceedings, but being naturally of a timid pliable Temper is frequently bullied into a Compliance with them the contrary to his own Inclination.

The Negotiation for a Truce being thus broke off on Sunday Evening and it being the general Opinion that there would be another and more dangerous Riot the next Day. My Friends (and indeed I have found many) begun to be exceeding anxious for my safety; especially as I was the only principal Officer belonging to the Customs then remaining in the Town all the rest having taken Shelter either on board the Man of Warr or gone into the Country. I was so much hurt by the Mob that I had been obliged to keep my Bed Two Days but being now something better, it was resolved that I should attempt an Escape to the Castle (which is situated on an Island in the Harbour) where the Governor had very kindly offered me Protection with suitable accommodation for myself and my Family. Accordingly early on Monday morning we all set forward by land to a Place opposite to the Island; we got out of the Town before the People were stirring so met with no interruption: and at the Place appointed we found a Boat ready to carry us over to the Castle, where we landed safe, and were very kindly received by the Commanding Officer there; under whose protection we still remain.

I can give your Lordship but a very imperfect account of what has passed in the Town since I left it; only that on Tuesday there was a very numerous Meeting of the Inhabitants in order to concert measures for totally expelling the Commissioners of the Customs and several wild and strange Propositions for that Purpose were then made; but nothing more was done than appointing a Committee of 21 Persons to wait on the Governor with a Demand for the Redress of what they call Grievances. The Governor has since called several Councils and the People have had several Meetings, but what has been the result I have not yet heard.

How these things will end God only knows, at present affairs here wear a Dark and Gloomy Aspect, and I fear the worst is not over. The People are distracted and Liberty mad, and the Enthusiasm is spreading fast over the other Colonies; and if some prudent, judicious and effectual Measures are not immediately taken by the Ministry at Home to prevent it; I shall not be surprised if something like a general Rising of the People should take Place; at least they are certainly in a fit Temper and Disposition for such an Attempt.

It's astonishing to me: after the Warning and Experience of the Stamp Act Times; that any new Impositions should be laid on the Colonies, till the Powers of Government were strengthend, and a Reformation made in the Constitution of those, founded on the popular Plan; or at least, that some precautions should not have been previously taken, to preserve the Peace of the Country. Nor is it less surprizing that a Commission of such Importance as this for Establishing a New Board of Customs, at a Place where it was known to be generally obnoxious; should be sent over naked and defenceless, without even so much as a single Ship of Warr to accompany it. Governor Bernard has done everything in his Power to support the Commissioners;

But alas His Hands are too weak, and tho very able and clever, He finds it difficult enough to maintain even the Shaddow of Authority amongst such unruly and Licencious People.

As these disturbances here will undoubtedly make a great noise in England, and are indeed of an alarming nature I think it would not be unacceptable to Your Lordship to have the most early account of them; and that an exact Detail even to the Minute of every Circumstance so farr as I was concerned would not be improper; as many false Circumstances and Aggrevations are usually propagated on these Occasions. . . .

I am told that People in General at Boston, express much sorrow and Contrition for the cruel Treatment I have met with and would make any Attonement in their power, if I would return to Town again. The better Sort of People I verily believe are sincerely concerned for what has been done and highly resent the Insult; and I dare say would do all in their Power to prevent the like happening again. But so long as the Town continues to be governed by the Rabble, I shall be very cautious how I trust my self amongst them.

The beginning of last Winter I was in a fair way of recovering a confirmed state of Health. But since the arrival of the Commissioners they have oppressed me with such a Load of Business, over and above, what related to the usual Duty of my office that I have been worried and fatigued beyond Expression which at last brought on the former Disorder in my Head and Nerves. I was just recovering: and had got abroad again when this last unfortunate affair happened which has affected me so much that I am now as bad as ever. My present situation is indeed very distressing and truly pitiable. The Commissioners not very friendly (on account of my being an Advocate for temperate Measures till such Time as the Hands of Government shall be strengthened) and the Temper of the People such as to render it unsafe for me to be ashore, so that I am in a manner confined to a prison, which if it continues long must have a very bad effect on my health. I wish I could have permission to take a Voyage to England which I verily believe is the best thing I can do for my recovery. . . .

JOS. HARRISON

SELECTION

The Ministry Tries Firmness

Colonial opposition to the Townshend program only increased the determination of the British political community to uphold the authority of Parliament in the colonies. Wills Hill, Earl of Hillsborough (1718–1793), assumed responsibility for American affairs in January, 1768, after his appointment to the newly created post of secretary of state for the colonies. Long an advocate of a harder line toward the colonies, he responded, with the approval of the other members of the ministry, to the Massachusetts Circular Letter with a circular letter of his own on April 21, 1768. His letter, which was sent to each of the royal governors in the continental colonies and is printed below as Selection 14 A, directed each governor to persuade the lower house in his colony to ignore the Massachusetts Letter and to prorogue or dissolve that body if it took any favorable notice of the document. At the same time, Hillsborough ordered Governor Bernard to urge the Massachusetts House to rescind the letter and if it refused, to dissolve it immediately.

Hillsborough's directives only served to unify the colonies more firmly in opposition to the Townshend Revenue Act. Even the threat of parliamentary sanctions could not prevent the Massachusetts House from defying his commands, and on June 30 it voted by a large majority—ninety-two to seventeen—not to rescind the letter. Bernard promptly dissolved it, the ninety-two anti-rescinders became the heroes of the colonies, and most of the colonial legislatures who had not already done so expressed their approval of the contents of the Massachusetts Circular Letter at the first opportunity.

The opposition to the new American Board of Customs in Boston caused the ministry, even before the violent uprising that followed the seizure of the Liberty, to decide to use some of the troops stationed in the colonies as a police force in Boston. By a letter of June 8, 1768 (Selection 14 B), Hillsborough ordered General Thomas Gage (1721–1787), commander in chief of British forces in America, to use as many troops as he thought necessary—four regiments were ultimately transferred to Boston and its environs—to "enforce a due Obedience to the Laws, and protect and support the Civil Magistrates, and the Officers of the Crown, in the Execution of their Duty."

Thoroughly alarmed by the prospect of having a standing army in their midst, Boston patriots in a town meeting asked Governor Bernard to call the legislature into session to determine what should be done. When Bernard refused, the town meeting on September 12, 1768, in the most sweeping denial of parliamentary authority yet made by any public body in the colonies, voted that the colonists were not subject to any laws passed by any group in which they were not represented, declared that it was illegal to station troops in Boston without the approval of its inhabitants, and, in an extraordinarily bold step, called for a convention of representatives from the several towns in the colony to adopt such measures "as his Majesty's service, and the peace and safety of his Subjects in this Province may require." This popularly called convention, composed of representatives from ninety-six towns, met without the approval of Governor Bernard on September 22 in Boston and considered the possibility of armed resistance. When the troops arrived on October 1, however, they landed without opposition.

The response of Parliament to events in Massachusetts Bay in 1768 was a series of resolutions condemning the behavior of the "chief authors and instigators of the late disorders," especially their action in calling an extraconstitutional convention, and an address to George III recommending that they be arrested and, if they appeared to be guilty of treason, brought to Britain for trial under an old statute of the thirty-fifth year of the reign of Henry VIII. The resolutions are printed here as Selection 14 C.

Charles R. Ritcheson, British Politics and the American Revolution (1954), discusses the British response to the American opposition to the Townshend Acts; John Shy, Towards Lexington (1965), and John Richard Alden, General Gage in America (1948), contain accounts of the decision to send the troops to Boston and the colonial response; and John C. Miller, Sam Adams: Pioneer in Propaganda (1936), traces developments in Massachusetts.

A. RETALIATION: THE EARL OF HILLSBOROUGH'S CIRCULAR LETTER (APR. 21, 1768)*

Sir,

I have his Majesty's Commands to transmit to you the inclosed copy of a letter from the Speaker of the House of Representatives of the Colony of Massachusets Bay, adressed by order of that House to the Speaker of the Assembly of each Colony upon the Continent of North America.

As his Majesty considers this Measure to be of a most dangerous & factious tendency calculated to inflame the minds of his good Subjects in the Colonies, to promote an unwarrantable combination and to excite and encourage an open opposition to and denial of the Authority of Parliament, & to subvert the true principles of the constitution; It is his Majesty's pleasure that you should immediately upon the Receipt hereof exert your utmost influence to defeat this flagatious attempt to disturb the Public Peace by prevailing upon the Assembly of your Province to take no notice of it, which will be treating it with the contempt it deserves.

The repeated proofs which have been given by the Assembly of of their Reverence and respect for the laws, and of their faithful Attachment to the Constitution, leave little Room in his Majesty's Breast to doubt of their shewing a proper Resentment of this unjustifiable Attempt to revive those distractions which have operated so fatally to the prejudice of this Kingdom and the Colonies; and accordingly his Majesty has the fullest confidence in their Affections But if notwithstanding these expectations and your most earnest endeavours, there should appear in the Assembly of your Province a disposition to receive or give any Countenance to this Seditious Paper, it will be your duty to prevent any proceeding upon it, by an immediate Prorogation or Dissolution. . . .

HILLSBOROUGH

B. THE RESORT TO TROOPS: EARL OF HILLSBOROUGH TO GENERAL THOMAS GAGE (JUNE 8, 1768)†

Sir,

I transmit to You, for your private Information, Copies of a Letter from His Majesty's Commissioners of the Revenue to the Lords of the Treasury; of my Circular Letter to the several Governors upon the Continent in consequence of it, and of Governor Bernard's Three last Letters to my Office.

The Contents of these Papers will evince to you how necessary it is become that such Measures should be taken as will strengthen the Hands of Government in the Province of Massachusets Bay, enforce a due Obedience to the Laws, and protect and support the Civil Magistrates, and the Officers of the Crown, in the Execution of their Duty.

For these purposes I am to signify to you His Majesty's Pleasure that you

* Reprinted in full from *New York Colonial Documents,* vol. VIII, pp. 58–59.

† These excerpts are reprinted with permission from Clarence Edwin Carter (ed.), *The Correspondence of General Thomas Gage* (1931–1933), vol. II, pp. 68–69.

do forthwith Order, one Regiment, or such Force as you shall think necessary, to Boston, to be Quartered in that Town, and to give every legal assistance to the Civil Magistrate in the Preservation of the Public Peace; and to the Officers of the Revenue in the Execution of the Laws of Trade and Revenue. And, as this appears to be a Service of a delicate Nature, and possibly leading to Consequences not easily foreseen, I am directed by The King to recommend to you to make choice of an Officer for the Command of these Troops, upon whose Prudence, Resolution and Integrity, you can entirely rely.

The necessary Measures for quartering and providing for these Troops, must be entirely left to your Direction, but I would submit to you whether, as Troops will probably continue in that Town, and a Place of some Strength may in case of Emergency be of great Service, it would not be advisable to take Possession of, and Repair, if Repairs be wanting, the little Castle, or Fort, of William and Mary, which belongs to the Crown. . . .

HILLSBOROUGH

C. IN DEFENCE OF PARLIAMENTARY AUTHORITY: THE RESOLVES OF PARLIAMENT (FEB. 9, 1769)*

Resolved . . . That the Votes, Resolutions, and Proceedings of the House of Representatives of *Massachuset's Bay*, in the Months of *January* and *February* one thousand seven hundred and sixty-eight, respecting several late Acts of Parliament, so far as the said Votes, Resolutions, and Proceedings, do import a Denial of, or do draw into Question, the Power and Authority of His Majesty, by and with the Advice and Consent of the Lords Spiritual and Temporal, and Commons, in Parliament assembled, to make Laws and Statutes of sufficient Force and Validity to bind the Colonies and People of *America*, Subjects of the Crown of *Great Britain*, in all Cases whatsoever, are illegal, unconstitutional, and derogatory of the Rights of the Crown, and Parliament of *Great Britain*.

Resolved . . . That the Resolution of the said House of Representatives of the Province of *Massachuset's Bay*, to write Letters to the several Houses of Representatives of the *British* Colonies, on the Continent, desiring them to join with the said House of Representatives of the Province of *Massachuset's Bay*, in Petitions which do deny, or draw into Question, the Right of Parliament to impose Duties and Taxes upon His Majesty's Subjects in *America;* and in pursuance of the said Resolution, the writing such Letters, in which certain late Acts of Parliament, imposing Duties and Taxes, are stated to be Infringements of the Rights of His Majesty's Subjects of the said Province; are Proceedings of a most unwarrantable and dangerous Nature, calculated to inflame the Minds of His Majesty's Subjects in the other Colonies, tending to create unlawful Combination, repugnant to the Laws of *Great Britain*, and subversive of the Constitution . . .

Resolved . . . That it appears, that the Town of *Boston*, in the Province of *Massachuset's Bay*, has for some Time past been in a State of great Dis-

* These excerpts are reprinted from *Journals of the House of Commons*, vol. XXXII, pp. 185–186.

order and Confusion, and that the Peace of the said Town has at several Times been disturbed by Riots and Tumults of a dangerous Nature, in which the Officers of His Majesty's Revenue there have been obstructed, by Acts of Violence, in the Execution of the Laws, and their Lives endangered.

Resolved . . . That it appears, that neither the Council of the said Province of *Massachuset's Bay,* nor the ordinary Civil Magistrates, did exert their Authority, for suppressing the said Riots and Tumults.

Resolved . . . That in these Circumstances of the Province of the *Massachuset's Bay,* and of the Town of *Boston,* the Preservation of the public Peace, and the due Execution of the Laws became impracticable without the Aid of a Military Force to support and protect the Civil Magistrate and the Officers of His Majesty's Revenue.

Resolved . . . That the Declarations, Resolutions, and Proceedings, in the Town Meetings at *Boston,* on the 14th of *June,* and 12th *September,* were illegal and unconstitutional, and calculated to excite Sedition and Insurrections in His Majesty's Province of *Massachuset's Bay.*

Resolved . . . That the Appointment at the Town Meeting, on the 12th *September,* of a Convention to be held in the Town of *Boston,* on the 22d of that Month, to consist of Deputies from the several Towns and Districts in the Province of the *Massachuset's Bay,* and writing a Letter by the Select Men of the Town of *Boston,* to each of the said Towns and Districts, for the Election of such Deputies, were Proceedings subversive of His Majesty's Government, and evidently manifesting a Design in the Inhabitants of the said Town of *Boston,* to set up a new and unconstitutional Authority, independent of the Crown of *Great Britain . . .*

Resolved . . . That the Elections by several Towns and Districts in the Province of *Massachuset's Bay,* of Deputies to sit in the said Convention, and the Meeting of such Convention in consequence thereof, were daring Insults offered to His Majesty's Authority, and audacious Usurpations of the Powers of Government. . . .

SELECTION

American Intransigence

The presence of British troops operated to restore some semblance of acquiescence to British authority in Boston as the customs commissioners and other revenue officers once again proceeded about their duties, but British firmness only served to stiffen American resistance and to convince American leaders that the colonists were the victims of a ministerial plot to enslave them. The enslavement of the colonies, it was widely believed, was only the first step in an elaborate conspiracy by power-hungry ministers to corrupt the British constitution and destroy the freedom of Britons everywhere. To oppose the evil machinations of such men thus became a moral duty, and opposition to the Townshend Acts and the various measures taken to enforce them came to be conceived of not simply as a jurisdictional dispute between Parliament and the colonial lower houses of assembly but also, and vastly more important, as a struggle for "Law, Truth, and Justice, Liberty and Right" against "Ambition, and oppressive Might." John Dickinson, the ninety-two Massachusetts Anti-Rescinders, and others who took the lead in the colonial opposition were widely acclaimed for their patriotism—their devotion to their country's rather than their own selfish interests—and their virtue. This conception of the dispute and the assumptions that lay behind it were succinctly set forth by the anonymous poet Rusticus in the poem Liberty. *Dedicated to John Dickinson and published in Philadelphia in 1768, it is reprinted below in full as Selection 15 A.*

It was easy for Americans from Boston south to Charleston to identify their own difficulties with those of John Wilkes in Britain. Wilkes returned to London in early 1768 from Paris, where he had been in exile for four years since his conviction for seditious libel in the forty-fifth number of his antiministerial publication, The North Briton. *After obtaining election to Parliament for the county of Middlesex, Wilkes gave himself up for sentencing and was sent to prison for twenty-two months on June 18, 1768. Subsequently twice expelled by Parliament and twice reelected by Middlesex (Parliament set aside his second reelection), Wilkes became in the colonies as well as in England the hero of the contest against the supposed tyranny of the ministry. Colonial newspapers followed Wilkes's imprisonment in detail, and Sons of Liberty groups toasted "Wilkes & Liberty" and developed elaborate rituals of resistance employing the numbers 45 (the number of Wilkes's condemned publication) and 92 (the number of Massachusetts Anti-Rescinders). On April 18, 1770, the day of his release from prison, patriots up and down the colonial seaboard staged many celebrations and drank forty-five toasts to the cause of resistance. An important element in the colonial protest at every stage of the pre-Revolutionary debate, such toasts were especially effective, as John Adams remarked, in "cultivating the sensations of freedom" among rank-and-file colonists and, as one recent scholar has argued, provide a "sensitive index to shifting currents of thought and feeling." The nature and function of Revolutionary toasts as well as the colonial adulation of Wilkes can be surmised from Selection 15 B below, a newspaper account of the celebration in Charleston on the night of Wilkes's release from prison.*

To put some teeth into their opposition, American leaders moved to bring economic sanctions against Britain by entering into agreements not to import British goods until the Townshend Revenue Act had been repealed and other grievances redressed. Such a movement had been inaugurated in Boston as early as October, 1767. By the late spring of 1768, however, the movement seemed to be on the verge of collapse because the Philadelphia merchants refused to participate. But the continued refusal of the imperial government to back down gave the movement new life. On August 1, 1768, the Boston merchants entered into an independent agreement (Selection 15 C) which served as a stimulus for patriots elsewhere. By the end of 1769 every colony except New Hampshire had adopted nonimportation associations. So successful were they that in late 1768 and throughout 1769 British exports to the colonies fell by over one-third.

The colonists quickly came to conceive of these associations as a means not only to bring the British Parliament to heel but also to rescue American society from the corruption into which it seemed to be sinking. This impulse derived from widespread fears among the colonists that the falling away from old values and the precipitate decline in moral standards that they thought they saw all around them were the harbingers of a "general depravation of manners" and, perhaps even, the total ruin of American society. Expressive in part, at least, of deep-seated feelings of guilt and anxiety arising out of the relatively high level of prosperity in the colonies, such fears had been so often manifested in "times of troubles" throughout the colonial period that they seem to have been almost en-demic to colonial American society. Whatever their origins, however, they operated during the crisis over the Townshend Acts in such a way as to give the associating movement a powerful emotional appeal. By promoting industry and frugality and by discouraging "luxury and every kind of extravagance," the nonimportation associations promised to restore American virtue and to strengthen the moral fabric of American society. Wearing American-made homespuns instead of British finery and drinking American-made drinks instead of imported tea became the badges of American patriotism and the symbols of the campaign to eliminate corruption from the colonies. Newspapers were filled with schemes for developing American manufactures and exhortations to individuals to assist in bringing about an internal moral revolution by shunning British goods and thereby resisting the "temptations of ease and luxury" that they represented. Selection 15 D, an anonymous letter by Brutus printed in William Rind's Virginia Gazette *on June 1, 1769, illustrates these atavistic and cathartic elements in the nonimportation movement.*

Nonimportation was accompanied by further explicit denouncements of the unconstitutional behavior of Parliament by the colonial legislatures. On May 16, 1769, the Virginia House of Burgesses adopted a set of resolutions (Selection 15 E) in answer to Parliament's resolves of the previous February. Asserting the exclusive authority of the Burgesses to tax Virginians, the Burgesses censured Parliament's suggestion that leaders of American resistance be brought to Britain for trial as "highly derogatory of the Rights of British Subjects." Although the governor dissolved the Burgesses for this bold act, its resolutions served as a model for similar condemnations of parliamentary measures by lower houses in other colonies.

Up and down the colonial seaboard, in fact, resistance was stimulated by re-ports of happenings in the "glorious cause of Liberty" in other colonies and in Britain. "A Journal of the Times," portions of which are here reprinted as Selec-tion 15 F, provided a running account of events in Boston from the first arrival of British troops on October 1, 1768, until for unknown reasons it ceased publication on August 1, 1769. Serving both as a mirror of the fears of its anonymous writer or writers and as a warning to colonists elsewhere of the afflictions with which they might be visited if the cause of liberty were lost in Boston, the "Journal" edi-torialized about the dangers of a standing army and was published in newspapers all over the colonies.

Bernard Bailyn (ed.), Pamphlets of the American Revolution, 1750–1776 *(1965), volume I, discusses the development and nature of the colonial belief in a ministerial conspiracy. George F. Rudé,* Wilkes & Liberty: A Social Study of 1763 to 1774 *(1962), and Ian R. Christie,* Wilkes, Wyvill and Reform: The Parliamentary Reform Movement in British Politics 1760–1785 *(1962), are the most recent studies of the Wilkite enthusiasm in Britain, and Pauline Maier, "John Wilkes and American Disillusionment with Britain,"* William and Mary Quarterly, *third series, volume 20 (1963), pages 373–395, describes the American reception of and interpretation of the Wilkes episode. Richard J. Hooker, "The American Revolution Seen through a Wine Glass," ibid., volume 11 (1954), pages 52–77, analyzes the significance and changing content of Revolutionary toasts. Edmund S. Morgan, "The Puritan Ethic and the American Revolution," ibid.,*

*volume 24 (1967), pages 3–43, discusses the relationship between the nonimporta-
tion movements and colonial fears of internal corruption, and John Shy,* Toward
Lexington *(1965), treats the colonial reaction to imperial use of the army as an internal police force in Boston. Arthur Meier Schlesinger,* Prelude to Independence:
The Newspaper War on Britain, 1764–1776 *(1958), assesses the role of the newspapers in the pre-Revolutionary controversy.*

A. "THE CAUSE OF LIBERTY AND RIGHT": RUSTICUS, "LIBERTY" (1768)*

TRUTH long asleep, awoke immers'd in Tears,
Deprest by Anguish, and portending Fears;
Prophetic Doubts alarm'd her throbbing Breast,
Encreas'd her Terror and destroy'd her Rest,
Exulting SLAV'RY rear'd its baneful Head,
And almost utter'd----LIBERTY is dead!
Yet while corroding Thoughts assail'd the Mind,
While fell INJUSTICE ravag'd unconfin'd,
While trembling LIBERTY, involv'd in Care,
Foresaw the *Yoke* her Sons would shortly wear;
While pleasing Hope itself was almost fled,
"And FREEDOM hung suspended by a Thread;"
Then, even then, to chear desponding Grief,
MINERVA thus administer'd Relief.
  "Arise, ye *Colonists,* my Sons, arise,
"The servile Threats of lawless Force despise.
"To FREEDOM BORN your sacred Rights maintain,
"Nor let *Compulsion* one slight Purpose gain.
"*Power,* if at first it meets with no controul,
"Creeps by Degrees and quick subdues the Whole.
"Your Claim to FREEDOM is on *Virtue* built,
"To gain that Point your Parents' Blood was spilt;
"And will the Offspring of their worthy Race
"Contaminate their Blood by foul Disgrace?
"No, rather let Destruction swallow all,
"'Tis Time to suffer when oblig'd to fall!
"Tho' hostile Force should Devastation spread,
"And every Field show Mountains of the Dead;
"Tho' *Death* and *Carnage* should whole Cities sweep,
"And crimson Streams deface the briny Deep;
"E'en then, my Sons, undaunted rush to Death,
"Nor part with FREEDOM till you part with Breath.
"Mistaken Notions will mislead the Weak,
"And *Truth,* at all Times, is ashamed to speak;
"Yet when *Ambition,* and *oppressive Might,*
"Presume to rob a Subject of his *Right;*
"When the *Grand Charter* groans beneath the Weight

---

* Reprinted in full from *Liberty* (1768).

"Of all the machinating Wiles of State;
"When *Mi--st-rs* to feed insatiate Pride,
"Their *Truth*, their *Country* and their K--G misguide.
"By *Reason* prompted (if you must obey)
"Let *Truth* and FREEDOM only lead the Way,
  "BRITANNIA like yourselves my Int'rest claim,
"To serve ye both I from Olympia came;
"Yet mark the Mandate of omniscient Jove,
"Prompted by *Justice* and the *warmest Love*,
"Then thus, in short, the God his Will exprest,
"While Anger laboured in his sacred Breast.
  "Pallas, my Daughter, thither bend your Way,
"And tell the Colonists what here I say;
"Tell them, tho' lock'd in Fate, the Thund'rer sees
"Fair LIBERTY declining by Degrees,
"Encroaching *Slavery* lurking round the Land,
"And *Force despotic* stretching forth her Hand.
"Injurious Acts should once the Subject bear,
"Or tame Submission yield to groundless fear,
"*Tyrannic Measures*, and *imperious Sway*,
"Will force a thoughtless People to obey;
"A Violation from superior Might,
"Upon their *Laws*, their *Liberty* or *Right*,
"Tho' for a while thro' *Policy*, and Art,
"May gild the *Poison* and suspend the *smart*,
"Tho' it at first may not its End attain,
"*Compliance* loses all *Oppression's* Gain,
"Each Step is nigher to complete its Aim,
"And load the People with immortal Shame;
"FREEDOM once lost is not retriev'd again,
"The Wound is mortal, and acute the Pain;
"By sly Gradations Injuries encrease,
"Nor rush too sudden on the *Subject's* Peace;
"Yet when the Burden they are forced to bear,
"When forced to drag the galling Chain they wear;
"When *Mi--st-rs* are glutted with *Success*,
"And public Clamour echoes out---Redress;
"The frantic People mad'ning at their State,
"Exclaim in Rage---*Repentance* comes too late;
"In vain Experience would this *Truth* conceal,
"Some never think but *when compell'd* to *feel*.
"*True Greatness* must from real *Virtue* rise,
"An honest Action never wants Disguise.
"Would *Mi--st-rs* while at the Helm be just,
"And scorn for Lucre to betray their Trust;
"Would such consult the *Int'rest* of the State,
"And leave their own to undetermined Fate,
"Then would each Subject over-raptur'd bring
"His Mite to serve his *Country and his* KING;
"Yet while ignoble Deeds meet no Disgrace,
"And ev'ry *Knave* is huddled into Place;

"While *Merit* bleeds beneath so vile a Plan,
"And *Worth* is look'd upon no Part of Man,
"Well may the Bliss of LIBERTY decay,
"Since *Fools* and *Madmen* have a Right to sway.
"Attempts once made if not that Moment check'd,
"The Public suffers through its own Neglect;
"When once *Obedience* as a Duty reigns,
"Deluded People fasten on their Chains;
"Indignant Customs from Compliance flow,
"And ev'ry Day presents increasing Woe;
"Divided Notions soon the Soul possess,
"To prove a Scene of exquisite Distress;
"*Success* attends the crafty Courtiers Toil,
"And *Pride,* insatiate *Pride,* enjoys the Spoil.
     "Tread then secure the Paths your Fathers trod,
"The Road of *Justice* is the Road of GOD;
"Fear not the Issue of illicit Might,
"Heaven pleads the Cause of LIBERTY and RIGHT;
"Assert your Claims, to *Truth* and *Virtue* trust,
"Be to yourselves, your KING and COUNTRY just;
"Capricious Fancies will the Courtier guide;
"His Port *Preferment,* and his Pilot *Pride;*
"*Honor* and *Honesty* neglected rot,
"Those are the *Beggar*'s, not the *Statesman*'s Lot;
"When *Self* is once concern'd, the restless Great
"Deny their *Principles,* their *King* and *State;*
"*Ambition* agitates, corrupts the Mind,
"And *few* (if any) are to *Truth* confin'd.
     "Let then no Reasons urge a thoughtless Deed,
"*Power* never wants a *Reason* to succeed;
"Despoil'd of *Freedom* should *Injustice* sway,
"All then must truckle to the Word---*Obey;*
"All sink to *Bondage* from a freeborn State,
"And sweat beneath the heavy Yoke of Fate.
     "*Nature* and *Truth* in this grand Point agree,
"None can be happy but the Man that's FREE;
"None can the Bliss of LIBERTY ensure,
"But such who may their *Property* secure.
"*Taxes* impos'd will always more or less
"The Public's *Freedom* injure and oppress;
"Should *Br-t-h Pa-l-m--ts* usurp a Right,
"Demand your *Money,* and your CHARTER slight;
"All venal Acts reject with manly Scorn,
"Convince you *know* ye were to *Freedom born;*
"With honest Rage let every Bosom burn,
"And from your Souls the latent Poison spurn.
     "Yet some their are who guide the Helm of State,
"Deserving, virtuous, sensible and great;
"Some who would scorn from Honor's Path to swerve,
"Who draw their *Virtues* from the Prince they serve;
"But such, alas! are few---the Reason's plain,

"None long as *Mi-n-st-rs* must good remain,
"*Corruption, Art* and *Envy* spreads the Snare,
"And Bribes on Bribes the fatal Bait prepare;
"The Trap once laid, if Gold should not succeed,
"'Twould be, ye *Gods!* a *Miracle* indeed.
  "With modest Boldness make your Troubles known;
"The Way is shortest to address the Throne;
"To Jove, your CHARTER and your SOVEREIGN trust,
"He may be tardy, but he will be just;
"Of ev'ry noble Sentiment possest,
"*Injustice* reigns not in his royal Breast,
"Supremely good, compasionate and brave,
"None more than he detests the Sound of *Slave,*
"None more than he would feel unfeigned Joy,
"Your Griefs to *soften,* and your Wrongs *destroy.*
"Such is the Message from almighty Jove,
"The Voice of REASON, LIBERTY and LOVE:
"Yet e'er I seek yon distant azure Sky,
"And far from you to blest Elysium fly,
"Lest Tears for Errors past should not avail,
"By Way of Application hear a Tale.
  "A State once flourish'd ev'ry Blessing knew,
"Its Joys were many, and its Troubles few;
"No pungent Care the People's Peace destroy'd,
"VIRTUE and LIBERTY they long enjoy'd,
"Unknown to *Vice,* to *Slavery* or to *Shame,*
"They slept in *Freedom* and awoke the same;
"At length unworthy of so blest a Fate,
"They sought the Favour of the faithless Great;
"By Words delusive into *Folly* led,
"Their Eyes were open when their Freedom fled;
"Asham'd their Meanness and their Guilt to own,
"The penetential *Slaves* address'd the Throne.
"The Sovereign listened---pitied their Distress,
"Vouchsafed to answer, but would not redress;
"In Tears of Blood all then the Error wept,
"They wak'd in *Bondage,* but in *Freedom* slept.
  "Mark then, my Sons, the certain Fate of such
"Who think too little and believe too much.
"From their Example let this Maxim rise,
"Some may too late, but none too soon be wise."
She ceas'd---and cleaving thro' the ambient Air,
Dividing Clouds receiv'd the blue eyed Fair;
All streak'd in Gold in azure Vest array'd,
The opening Sky enshrin'd the heavenly Maid,
Harmonious Music as she took her Flight,
Hung on the Ear, and ravish'd with Delight.
  Minerva gone, attentive Crowds disperse,
Her Counsels honor, and her Words rehearse;
With Aspect modest, and Deportment meek,
The grateful Throng the holy Temple seek;

To Jove in fervent Prayer the People join,
And thus address the sacred Power divine.
    "Father of all, inimitably bright,
"Clad with the Glories of refulgent Light,
"Thou from whom ev'ry Consolation springs,
"Pure, holy, just, immortal King of *Kings,*
"Vouchsafe while now before thy Shrine we bend,
"To hear thy Suppliants and their Laws defend,
"By thee protected ev'ry Care shall cease,
"And all once more enjoy the Sweets of *Peace.*"
They ceas'd---when lo! Columbus, once the brave,
Brake thro' the gloomy Confines of the Grave;
To all the trembling Host (thro' Fear dismay'd)
Thus spake the godlike *venerable Shade.*
    "Wail not, my Sons, from yonder peaceful Tomb,
"Your Wrongs to mitigate, a Friend I come;
"Some Fifty Years in Silence have I slept,
"Nor should have woke, had Liberty not wept;
"But ah! when Frauds your precious *Freedom* shook,
"And Villains were for honest Men mistook;
"When all was sacrificed to *Int'rest's* Sake,
"'Twas Time, ye *Colonists,* the dead should wake;
"'Twas Time, when cunning plann'd your Overthrow,
"Yourselves to rouze, and stop the mortal Blow.
"But lest ye wonder how I quit my State,
"And stir one Space beyond the Verge of Fate;
"Unterrified with due Attention hear
"The artless dictates of a *Soul sincere.*
    "As *Gr-nv-lle* late by servile Art assay'd
"Your *Rights* to wound, and *Freedom* to invade;
"While he the Foe of Virtue and her Cause,
"Prepar'd the Poison to infect your Laws,
"To climes unknown the Fatal Rumour spread,
"And reach'd too soon the Mansions of the Dead;
"Your Fathers restless in the silent Grave,
"A Council called your Liberty to save;
"With Horror saw the black ignoble Deed,
"And shuddered lest *Injustice* should succeed;
"Among the Rest thus sumon'd to attend,
"Myself, your *Founder,* went, your *Chief* and *Friend;*
"From just Conclusions your Pretensions weigh'd,
"Your Troubles felt, and flew to lend you Aid;
"Yet hear me on---while *Gr-nv-lle* laid that Plan,
"Unworthy both the Minister and Man;
"While he and others bullied for the State,
"And *Stamps* were sent the *Harbingers* of Fate;
"Then venal B-rn--d, ever insincere,
"Perform'd the Functions of a *Gr-nv-lle* here,
"With open Zeal espous'd your injured Cause,
"Yet work'd in secret to subvert your Laws;
"But *Heaven* who ev'ry secret Action knows,

"Confus'd the plotting of your artful Foes;
"Your Troubles eas'd when most deprest by dread,
"And stop'd Perdition bursting o'er your Head.
"On *Care* and *Union* your *Success* depends,
"On *Negligence* and *Strife, Distress* attends;
"Let not *Divisions* damp the gen'rous Flame,
"But *all* and *one* demand your legal Claim;
"Unalter'd let your LIBERTIES remain,
"They want not mending which are *just* and *plain;*
"Oh! happy People, blest with Men of Parts,
"Endowed with Wisdom, and unfeigned Hearts,
"How my Soul gladdens at thy present State,
"Not long ago the Mark of envious Fate;
"Heavens! how exulting Raptures fill my Breast,
"Too long unknown to all the Joys of Rest.
  "Methinks I view when all seem'd lost indeed!
"*Virtue* and *Heaven* for gasping *Freedom* plead;
"SHARPE, like the Pylian Sage in Knowledge skill'd,
"Concern'd---the discontented Land beheld,
"In Silence sat, and tho' to speak was loath,
"His *Duty* knew, and prov'd a Friend to *both;*
"Nor did Heaven's Goodness in this Instance end,
"It rose the PATRIOT, COUNSELLOR and FRIEND:
"*Considerations* on your sinking Laws,
"Shone like a Meteor o'er your trembling Cause;
"There *Reason* pointed out with *Judgment* fraught,
"What you *ought not to do,* and what you *ought,*
"*Law, Truth,* and *Justice, Liberty* and *Right,*
"The able *Penman* brought to perfect light,
"Convey'd this Truth which laugh'd your Foes to scorn,
"Ye are the *Sons,* not *Slaves* of *Briton* born.
"Had I but Time his Character to scan,
"Or tell but half the Virtues of this *Man;*
"Could I, my Sons, his just Deserts proclaim,
"Or speak that *Worth* that soars above his Fame,
"E'en growling *Envy,* Foe to fair *Renown,*
"With ev'ry Virtue would the Author crown.
"*Another too* amidst the Storms of Fate,
"Foresaw the Troubles of a falling State,
"With Force energic cheer'd the drooping Mind,
"And *Truth* came mended from his Pen refin'd,
"With patriot Zeal your LIBERTY explain'd,
"Rever'd your CHARTER, and your *Rights* maintain'd,
"With splendid Brightness, like the spotless Sun,
"Burst thro' the FARMER and with Lustre shone;
"Each Line, each Word, soon reach'd the feeling Breast,
"The Man was valued, honor'd and carest.
  "Yet one Thing more, for short is now my Stay,
"The Gods have summon'd and I must obey.
"With *Resolution* still your Plan pursue,
"Support the glorious NUMBER NINETY-TWO;

"On that the *Basis* of your Bliss depends,
"On that the *Safety* of your *Lives* and *Friends;*
"Fresh Schemes are laying to disturb your *Peace,*
"Your *Rights* to wound, and *Injuries* encrease;
"Yet ev'ry Measure, ev'ry Act *defy,*
"They nobly *fall* who for their *Freedom* die,
"*Bribes, Threats,* and *Promises* will all employ,
"To stain your *Virtue,* and your *Truth* decoy;
"Yet thus in brief---Be *resolute* and *true,*
"And safely trust to NUMBER NINETY-TWO.
    He spake, when sudden all the *Temple* shook,
As thro' the Isle his Flight the *Vision* took;
Swift as the forked Lightning flies around,
The *Phantom* tripp'd the Surface of the Ground;
Enclos'd in Rays divinely pure and bright,
The manly *Fabrick* fled from human Sight.
    The gazing Strands with Admiration fraught,
To LIBERTY alone devote each Thought;
With grateful *Joy* the sacred Words retain,
Resolve their *Rights* and CHARTER to maintain,
Like *Cato's* Sons heroicly agree,
To lose their *Lives* before their LIBERTY.

B. "CULTIVATING THE SENSATIONS OF FREEDOM": THE CHARLESTON SONS OF LIBERTY TOAST THE RELEASE OF JOHN WILKES FROM PRISON (APR. 18, 1770)*

Yesterday being the Day on which JOHN WILKES, Esq., was to be released from an Imprisonment of *Two* and *Twenty*-Months; for having *republished* the 45th Number of a Paper called the NORTH-BRITON, wherein the *then* present Minister's Conduct was treated with that Freedom which Englishmen think the Constitution of their Country gives them a Right to use; the same was celebrated here by ringing of Bells, displaying of Colours, and abundant other Demonstrations of Satisfaction and Joy, by several Companies at different Houses; but particularly, by the Club NUMBER FORTY-FIVE, above *One Hundred* of whose Members (as loyal Subjects as any His Majesty King GEORGE the THIRD has, throughout his Dominions, and amongst them *many* Gentlemen of the first Rank and Property in the Province) met at the House of Mr. *Robert Dillon,* where they had a most elegant Entertainment, conducted by Six excellent Stewards, and spent the Evening in the most orderly and harmonious Manner that can be conceived; breaking up at 45 Minutes past 12, after drinking the following Toasts, viz.:

    1. *Our most gracious Sovereign, King George the Third.*
    2. *The Queen, and Prince of Wales.*
    3. *All the Royal Issue of the House of Brunswick.*
    4. *His Honour the Lieutenant Governor, and the Province.*

* Reprinted in full from the *South Carolina Gazette,* Apr. 19, 1770.

5. *The Speaker & present patriotic Commons House of Assembly.*
6. *The unanimous 26, of the late Assembly.*
7. *Lord Camden.*
8. *Earl of Chatham.*
9. *Marquis of Rockingham.*
10. *Marquis of Granby.*
11. *John Wilkes, Esq.*
12. *Earl Temple.*
13. *Serjeant Glynn.*
14. *May the Endeavours of John Wilkes, Esq; be rewarded as those of Junius were by the Romans.*
15. *The glorious Memory of William, late Duke of Cumberland.*
16. *A perpetual Separation of Military Force and Civil Power.*
17. *Christopher Gadsden, Esquire.*
18. *The truly Honourable Jonathan Bryan.*
19. *The as Honourable Henry Middleton.*
20. *Thomas Lynch, Esquire.*
21. *John Rutledge, Esquire.*
22. *Charles Pinckney, Esquire.*
23. *The immortal Pennsylvania Farmer.*
24. *Daniel Dulany, Esquire.*
25. *A constitutional Union between Great-Britain and her Colonies.*
26. *An inviolable Adherence in our Resolutions, 'till we are restored to our former Freedom.*
27. *Honour to the Sons of Liberty throughout the Globe; Confusion and Disgrace to all their Enemies.*
28. *The patriotic Supporters of the Bill of Rights.*
29. *Capt. Alexander McDougal of New-York, Mr. Bingley and all other Sufferers in the glorious Cause of Liberty.*
30. *The Liberty of the Press, in its utmost Extent.*
31. *The justly celebrated Mrs. Macauley.*
32. *Colonel Barré.*
33. *Mr. Burke.*
34. *The Patriot Junius.*
35. *Success to the Trade and Manufactures of Great-Britain and America.*
36. *James Otis, Esquire.*
37. *The patriotic self-denying Merchants throughout America.*
38. *The several Committees of Inspection throughout America.*
39. *The General Committee of this Province.*
40. *The 1292 unbiased Electors of the County of Middlesex.*
41. *The uncorrupted Minority of both Houses of Parliament in 1770.*
42. *May Great-Britain and America ever be supported by Strength, and guided by Reason.*
43. *The Brave, the Social, and the Virtuous.*
44. *A Speedy and effectual Redress of all Grievances.*
45. *Honour to the King, and Liberty to the Subject.*

C. ECONOMIC SANCTIONS: BOSTON NONIMPORTATION AGREEMENT (AUG. 1, 1768)*

THE merchants and traders in the town of Boston having taken into consideration the deplorable situation of the trade, and the many difficulties it

---

* Reprinted in full from *Annual Register*, vol. XII (1768), pp. 235–236.

at present labours under on account of the scarcity of money, which is daily increasing for want of the other remittances to discharge our debts in Great Britain, and the large sums collected by the officers of the customs for duties on goods imported; the heavy taxes levied tὂ discharge the debts contracted by the government in the late war; the embarrassments and restrictions laid on the trade by several late acts of parliament; together with the bad success of our cod fishery this season, and the discouraging prospect of the whale fishery, by which our principal sources of remittance are like to be greatly diminished, and we thereby rendered unable to pay the debts we owe the merchants in Great Britain, and to continue the importation of goods from thence;

We, the subscribers, in order to relieve the trade under those discouragements, to promote industry, frugality, and œconomy, and to discourage luxury, and every kind of extravagance, do promise and engage to and with each other as follows:

First, That we will not send for or import from Great Britain, either upon our own account, or upon commission, this fall, any other goods than what are already ordered for the fall supply.

Secondly, That we will not send for or import any kind of goods or merchandize from Great Britain, either on our own account, or on commissions, or any otherwise, from the 1st of January 1769, to the 1st of January 1770, except salt, coals, fish-hooks and lines, hemp, and duck bar lead and shot, wool-cards and card-wire.

Thirdly, That we will not purchase of any factor, or others, any kind of goods imported from Great Britain, from January 1769, to January 1770.

Fourthly, That we will not import, on our own account, or on commissions, or purchase of any who shall import from any other colony in America, from January 1769, to January 1770, any tea, glass, paper, or other goods commonly imported from Great Britain.

Fifthly, That we will not, from and after the 1st of January 1769, import into this province any tea, paper, glass, or painters colours, until the act imposing duties on those articles shall be repealed.

D. RESTORING COLONIAL VIRTUE: BRUTUS ON THE PROMISE OF THE NONIMPORTATION ASSOCIATIONS (JUNE 1, 1769)*

My dear countrymen,

THE times indeed are big with danger and alarm; and we stand upon the precipice of ruin and misery. We are therefore called upon by reason, prudence, and a tender regard for our posterity, to use the means which nature hath given us, to provide for our safety. Let us put on a resolution equal to the mighty occasion: Let us exert a spirit worthy of *Britons,* worthy of freemen, who deserve liberty. Let all those who have a common interest in the public safety, join in common measures to defend the public safety. We have now an opportunity of rescuing the constitution, and settling it upon a firm and solid basis. Let us not then cease our endeavours, until we

* Reprinted in full from William Rind (ed.), *Virginia Gazette,* June 1, 1769.

have accomplished that desirable end. We claim nothing new; we desire nothing more than the privileges of *British subjects,* the continuance of that constitution which we have long and peaceably enjoyed.

No government can long subsist, but by recurring often to its first principles. The prevailing principle of our government is, *virtue.* If we would be happy, we must be more attentive to it than we hitherto have been. By that only can liberty be preserved; and on the preservation of liberty depends our happiness. By *virtue,* I here mean a love for our country, which makes us pursue, with alacrity, such measures as tend to its preservation; and cheerfully resist the temptations of ease and luxury, with which liberty is incompatible. For luxury and idleness bring on a general depravation of manners, which sets us loose from all the restraints of both private and public virtue, and diverts our thoughts from examining the behaviour and politics of artful and designing men, who meditate our ruin, and would sacrifice their country for their private emolument. From immorality and excesses we fall into necessity, and this leads us to a servile dependence upon power, and fits us for the chains prepared for us.

Whilst we live at ease and luxury, we cannot be persuaded to see distant dangers, of which we feel no part. The conjunctures, then, proper for reformations in government, are when men are awakened by misfortunes, and sensible of the approach of present evils. Such, my countrymen, is the present conjuncture; and we may turn our misfortunes to our advantage, if we will consider our oppression as an opportunity given us by indulgent Providence to save ourselves. The measures, for this end, proposed by our late Representatives in their association, are wise and salutary. We should adopt them without hesitation. They should know that we approve their conduct; and our approbation of it cannot be too well manifested, as by pursuing the measures they have prescribed. Whoever will reflect on the means used to procure a repeal of the *Stamp-Act* and the good effects which resulted therefrom, will surely perceive the propriety of the present allocation and admit the necessity for such a conduct. Similar causes will undoubtedly produce like effects. If a regard to our own manufactures, and a resolution not to import those of Britain, until that act was repealed, did then avail us, the success of the present measure is warranted; and nothing more is requisite, but an unfeigned and unanimous exertion of our powers to execute it. Let the contention among us be, then, who shall most contribute to promote so salutary a purpose. Let us not foolishly neglect the invitation of Heaven to be happy. But let us from this moment pursue our real interest, and resolve to pay attention to the manufactures of our own country, which alone can continue us a free and happy people.

BRUTUS

E. DEFYING PARLIAMENT'S RESOLVES: THE VIRGINIA RESOLVES OF MAY 16, 1769*

Resolved, That it is the Opinion of this Committee, that the sole Right of imposing Taxes on the Inhabitants of this his Majesty's Colony and Do-

---

* These excerpts are reprinted from *Journals of the House of Burgesses, 1766–69,* p. 214.

minion of *Virginia*, is now, and ever hath been, legally and constitutionally vested in the House of Burgesses, lawfully convened according to the ancient and established Practice, with the Consent of the Council, and of his Majesty, the King of *Great-Britain*, or his Governor, for the Time being.

Resolved, That it is the Opinion of this Committee, that it is the undoubted Privilege of the Inhabitants of this Colony, to petition their Sovereign for Redress of Grievances; and that it is lawful and expedient to procure the Concurrence of his Majesty's other Colonies, in dutiful Addresses, praying the royal Interposition in Favour of the Violated Rights of *America*.

Resolved, That it is the Opinion of this Committee, that all Trials for Treason, Misprison of Treason, or for any Felony or Crime whatsoever, committed and done in this his Majesty's said Colony and Dominion, by any Person or Persons residing therein, ought of Right to be had, and conducted in and before his Majesty's Courts, held within the said Colony, according to the fixed and known Course of Proceeding; and that the seizing any Person or Persons, residing in this Colony, suspected of any Crime whatsoever, committed therein, and sending such Person, or Persons, to Places beyond the Sea, to be tried, is highly derogatory of the Rights of *British* Subjects; as thereby the inestimable Privilege of being tried by a Jury from the Vicinage, as well as the Liberty of summoning and producing Witnesses on such Trial, will be taken away from the Party accused.

Resolved, That it is the Opinion of this Committee, that an humble, dutiful, and loyal Address, be presented to his Majesty, to assure him of our inviolable Attachment to his sacred Person and Government; and to beseech his royal Interposition, as the Father of all his people, however remote from the Seat of his Empire, to quiet the Minds of his loyal Subjects of this Colony, and to avert from them, those Dangers and Miseries which will ensue, from the seizing and carrying beyond Sea, any Persons residing in *America*, suspected of any Crime whatsoever, to be tried in any other Manner, than by the ancient and long established Course of Proceeding.

F. THE DANGERS OF A STANDING ARMY: "A JOURNAL OF THE TIMES" (SEPT. 28, 1768–AUG. 1, 1769)*

September 28, 1768

ADVICE received that the men of war and transports from Halifax, with about 900 troops, collected from several parts of America, were safe arrived at Nantasket Harbour, having very narrowly escaped shipwreck on the back of Cape Cod, which disaster would have left the extensive sea coast of North America, almost bare of ships of war, and troops, but in no worse state than are the inland fortresses and settlements, from whence the garrisons had been before withdrawn.—Time must account for such extraordinary steps in our Ministry.

---

* These excerpts are reprinted from Oliver Morton Dickerson, *Boston under Military Rule (1768–1769)* (1936), pp. 1, 13, 15–16, 18, 28–29, 39–40, 71, 79.

September 29

The fleet was brought to anchor near Castle William, that evening there was throwing of sky rockets, and those passing in boats observed great rejoicings, and that the Yankey Doodle song was the capital piece in their band of music.—This day his Majesty's Council received a billet from Governor Bernard, requiring their attendance at Castle William, and informing them that the officers of his Majesty's fleet and army, would be present,—they attended accordingly, and notwithstanding all intimidations, adhered strictly to their votes, published in the last papers; the Governor's arts were ineffectual to induce them to give the least countenance to any troops being brought into Boston, as the barracks at Castle William were sufficient to receive the whole of them arrived from Halifax.—The treatment they received from his Excellency, during their tarry at the Castle, was very uncourtly, and even rude. . . .

October 28

In the morning it was known that the troops which lately occupied Fanueil-Hall, had been placed, or had quartered themselves in the buildings, which had been hired of James Murray, Esq; but owned by James Smith, Esq; of Brush-Hill, such a procedure in the face of an act of Parliament, may well surprise the inhabitants, and lead them to think that some gentlemen of the civil or military order have concluded that they have a right for *certain purposes,* of dispensing with those acts at their pleasure: However this may be, it is hoped that the people will soon have the satisfaction of knowing whether such steps can be taken by any with impunity; or whether every order and person among us is not equally held to the due observance of law.

The prints and letters brought by Capt. White, who arrived here yesterday from London, leads us to hope that American affairs will quickly take a new turn, as some late publications, had served to awaken the attention of the people to their own interest, which they now find has been ill consulted by those in power, who either by giving credit to the accounts received from hence, thro' interested and false mediums, or in order to answer purposes merely ministerial, had gone into such measures as have thrown the nation into the utmost confusion and distress, and if not changed must end in its total destruction.—A gentleman of this town now in London, writes that at an interview with L——d H——lls——gh, he was told that it was determined right or wrong to inforce an obedience to the late regulations. Several ministerial pieces justify G——l Amherst being displaced, and Lord Bottetourts being appointed in his room upon this principle, that every one who held any post from the Crown, ought to be ordered to their several stations in the colonies, in order to exert their whole influence to carry down the late regulations. *In pursuance of this ministerial plan of policy, we now behold a standing army and swarms of crown officers, placemen, pensioners and expectants, co-operating in order to subdue Americans to the yoke. Our hopes are that the people of Britain do now, or will soon fully perceive that they cannot have our monies in the way of a revenue, and trade both; that what the merchants and manufacturers receive, serves to increase the wealth and oppulence of the nation, while the other only tends to destroy trade and increase ministerial dependence. . . .*

October 29

The inhabitants of this town have been of late greatly insulted and abused by some of the officers and soldiers, several have been assaulted on frivolous pretences, and put under guard without any lawful warrant for so doing. A physician of the town walking the streets the other evening, was jostled by an officer, when a scuffle ensued, he was afterwards met by the same officer in the company with another, both as yet unknown, who repeated his blows, and as is supposed gave him a stroke with a pistol, which so wounded him as to endanger his life. A tradesman of this town on going under the rails of the Common in his way home, had a thrust in the breast with a bayonet from a soldier; another person passing the street was struck with a musket, and the last evening a merchant of the town was struck down by an officer who went into the coffee-house, several gentlemen following him in, and expostulating with the officers, were treated in the most ungenteel manner; but the most atrocious offence and alarming behaviour was that of a captain, the last evening, who in company with two other officers, endeavoured to persuade some Negro servants to ill-treat and abuse their masters, assuring them that the soldiers were come to procure their freedoms, and that with their help and assistance they should be able to drive all the Liberty Boys to the devil; with discourse of the like import, tending to excite an insurrection. Depositions are now taking before the magistrates, and prosecutions at common law are intended, the inhabitants being determined to oppose by the law such proceedings, apprehending it the most honourable as well as the most safe and effectual method of obtaining satisfaction and redress; at the same time they have a right to expect that General Gage will not remain an unconcerned spectator of such a conduct in any under his command.—*Here Americans you may behold some of the first fruits springing up from that root of bitterness a standing army. Troops are quartered upon us in a time of peace, on pretence of preserving order in a town that was as orderly before their arrival as any one large town in the whole extent of his Majesty's dominions; and a little time will discover whether we are to be governed by the martial or the common law of the land. . . .*

November 3

. . . This morning Mr. Arodi Thayer, marshal of the Court of Admiralty for three provinces, with a hanger at his side, came to the house of John Hancock, Esq; to serve him with a precept for £9000 sterling, and having arrested his person, demanded bail for £3000 sterling. Mr. Hancock offered him divers estates to the value thereof, which were absolutely refused; he then made him an offer of £3000 in money, and afterwards of £9000, which were also refused; Mr. Thayer alledging that such were his directions. Mr. Hancock . . . prudently determined to give bail, as did five other gentlemen arrested for the same sum, and on the same account from the like prudent motives. Thus the Commissioners of the Customs not satisfied with the seizing and forfeiture of the sloop Liberty, for a non-entry of a part of her cargo of Madeiria wines, which before the American Revenue Acts were duty free, have gone beyond every thing of the kind before heard of in America, in prosecuting the supposed owner and each person they imagined concerned in unloading the wines, for the value of the whole cargo and treble damages. —*The public will now impartially judge whether this conduct does not bear much the same complexion which his Majesty's Council expressly declared of the seizure of said sloop, namely to occasion a tumult, and thereby give the same colouring for a necessity of quartering the troops contrary to act of Parliament in the body of the town, instead of the barracks at Castle-Island, that was originally given for their being ordered here.* . . .

November 30

An honourable gentleman of his Majesty's Council, lately riding over Boston Neck in his coach, was stopped by some soldiers on guard, one of which had the assurance to open the door, and put in his head; upon being asked what had occasioned such freedom, he had the insolence to reply, that he was only examining whether any deserter was concealed there.

A number of gentlemen passing in the night by the Town-House, were hailed by the guards three several times, without answering; whereupon they were stopped and confined in the guard-house for a considerable time: A young gentleman in another part of town, having a lanthorn with him, was challenged by some soldiers, but not answering so readily as was expected, he was threatened with having his brains immediately blown out unless he stopped: A merchant of the town passing the grand guard this night about ten o'clock, was several times challenged by the soldiers, and upon telling them, that as an inhabitant he was not obliged to answer, nor had they any business with him; they replied that this was a garrison town, and accordingly they presented their bayonets to his breast, took and detained him a prisoner for above half an hour, when he was set free; having procured the names of those who had thus used him, he is prosecuting them for the same; and we may expect soon to have it determined, whether we are or are not a proper garrison town. *Perhaps by treating the most respectable of our inhabitants in this sort, it is intended to impress our minds with formidable ideas of a military government, that we may be induced the sooner to give up such trifling things as rights and privileges, in support of which we are now suffering such great insults and injuries.* . . .

December 25

One great objection to the quartering of troops in the body of a town, is the danger the inhabitants will be in of having their morals debauched; The ear being accustomed to oaths and imprecations, will be the less shockt at the profanity, and the frequent spectacles of drunkenness, exhibited in our streets, greatly countenances this shameful and ruinous vice. The officers of the army are not backward in resenting the smallest disrespect offered themselves by a soldier, and such offences are severely punished, but it seems the name of God may be dishonoured with horrid oaths and blasphemies, in their presence without their looking upon themselves as obliged to punish, or even reprove them for the same; perhaps they take this to be the duty of the civil magistrate, and indeed it appears highly reasonable, that the magistrates of the town should notice those offences, and exert themselves in all legal ways, to restrain the soldiery from such enormities, and check the progress of so terrible a contagion among the inhabitants.—Those who look upon the awful denunciations of God's word against sinners, not merely as bugbears to afrighten, but what will really be inflicted on all impenitents, cannot but compassionately wish that more pains were taken and better means used to reform the army. This set of men are generally made up of the most thoughtless and unprincipled of our youth; The common soldiers are in general destitute of Bibles and proper books of devotion; their pay so small as not to enable their procuring them, or else we might suppose stoppages for them as well as other articles; What a pity is it that the Society for Propagating the Gospel, do not spare a part of their charity for this purpose; and if together with this, due care was taken in the appointment of chaplains, and strict orders given them, diligently to pursue the duties of their office, by rebuking, exhorting, instructing, and daily praying with their regiments, might we not hope for such success, as that the reproach which has been too justly cast upon us by foreigners, "That our army has less appearance of religion among them than there is among any other in Europe," may be soon wiped away? . . .

February 27, 1769

Our former predictions of what would be the unhappy effects of quartering troops in this town, have been too fully verified: They are now most wretchedly debauched, and their licentiousness daily increasing; a particular enumeration of instances thereof, would be as tedious, as it is painful.—Two women the other evening, to avoid the *solicitations* and *insults* of a soldier, took refuge in a house, at the south end of the town; the soldier was so audacious, as to enter with them: The cries of distress, brought the master of the family into the entry with a candle; and before he could know the occasion of the noise, he received, a stroke from the soldier with his cutlass, which brought him to the ground, where he lay senseless for some time, and suffered the loss of a quart of his blood.—Another woman not happening to please some soldiers, received a considerable wound on her head with a cutlass; and a 3rd. woman presuming to scream, when laid hold of by a soldier, had a bayonet run through her cheek: A number of persons passing the north watch house, were hailed by the centry; on their refusing to answer, the watchmen went out, when they perceived three officers with drawn swords, who with bad language grossly insulted them.—Two other officers passing by the dock-watch, being hailed were so very profane and abusive in their language, that the watchmen went out to them, when one of those officers drew his sword, and swore he would run the man through that should come near; they soon came to blows, by one of which the spear of a watchman's pole was broken, however the officers soon fled, and the watchmen could not overtake them, neither have they been able to make a discovery who were the assailants. But a still more extraordinary insult upon the citizens, was made the other night: It seems that it was wrongly apprehended, that an officer's dog had been shot by one Mr. Hemmingway, living near Winisimmit Ferry: To revenge the death of this animal, upon the supposed murderer, Lieutenant M—t of the 14th. Regiment, with a number of armed soldiers, entered Hemmingway's house, which they searched and ransacked, threatning to be the death of any man they should find there, to the no small terror and distress of the women and children of the family: Those offenders have been apprehended, and taken before Richard Dana, and John Ruddock, Esqrs. two of his Majesty's justices of peace, and have by them, been bound over to the Court of Assize, to be held next month, then to answer to the charges which shall be brought against them—But not-withstanding those offenders were thus dealt with! It did not deter some soldiers the next, and several succeeding nights, from insulting said house with stones and brick bats, firing off guns, &c. thereby renewing the terror of those belonging to the family, and greatly disturbing the whole neighbour-hood. . . .

March 17

Instances of the licentious and outrageous behaviour of the *military con-servators* of the peace still multiply upon us, some of which are of such a nature, and have been carried to so great lengths, as must serve fully to evince that a late vote of this town, calling upon the inhabitants to provide themselves with arms for their defence, was a measure as *prudent* as it was *legal;* such violences are always to be apprehended from military troops, when quartered in the body of a populous city; but more especially so, when they are led to believe that they are *become necessary to awe a spirit of rebellion,* injuriously said to be existing therein. It is a natural right which the people have reserved to themselves, confirmed by the Bill of Rights, to keep arms for their own defence; and as Mr. Blackstone observes, it is to be made use of when the sanctions of society and law are found insufficient to restrain the violence of oppression.—We are however, pleased to find that the inhabitants of this town, under every insult and outrage, received from the soldiery, are looking up to the laws of the land, for redress; and if *any influence* should be powerful enough to *deprive* the meanest sub-ject of *this security;* the people will not be answerable for the *unhappy con-sequences* that may flow therefrom. . . .

SELECTION

The Boston Massacre

Continual friction between British troops and townspeople in Boston finally led to bloodshed in the Boston Massacre on the evening of March 5, 1770. The exact sequence of events has never been clear, but the incident seems to have resulted from a scuffle between a civilian and a soldier on one of the rope walks in the afternoon. Several brief fights between small groups of soldiers and townsmen followed. In the evening, a sentry in King Street, menaced by an angry mob of civilians, called for help from Captain Thomas Preston and the main guard, which, as the crowd grew increasingly militant, opened fire, killing five people. To avoid further bloodshed, Lieutenant Governor Thomas Hutchinson (1711–1780), who had succeeded Bernard as governor after the latter had been recalled to Britain the previous summer, acceded to the demands of patriot leaders that the troops be withdrawn from the town, and for the next three years there was only one regiment stationed in Massachusetts, at Castle William on an island in Boston Harbor.

The reaction of Massachusetts patriots to the Massacre can be seen in the two documents that follow. Selection 16 A is a graphic rendering of the event by Paul Revere (1735–1818), noted Boston silversmith and engraver who became famous for his ride to Lexington to warn Samuel Adams and John Hancock of the approach of British troops on the night of April 18, 1775. Selection 16 B consists of excerpts from the "official" version of the Massacre prepared by a committee of inquiry appointed by the town of Boston and headed by James Bowdoin (1726–1790), a successful merchant and a leading politician in the colony. Although the committee report, which summarizes the history of the troubles between the army and the town from the patriot point of view, attributes the Massacre to a conspiracy among the soldiery "to commit some outrage upon the inhabitants of the town indiscriminately," responsibility for the order to the troops to fire has never been fixed. The civil authorities arrested Preston and some of his men for murder. Brought to trial in October after the troops had been moved and passions had cooled, Preston and four soldiers were acquitted. Two others were convicted of manslaughter but were allowed to go free after they had pleaded benefit of clergy.

An analysis of the climate of opinion in Boston while the troops were there and its effect upon law enforcement will be found in Hiller B. Zobel, "Law under Pressure: Boston 1769–1771," in George Athan Billias (ed.), Law and Authority in Colonial America: Selected Essays *(1965), pages 187–208.*

A. "CARNAGE": PAUL REVERE, "THE BLOODY MASSACRE" (MAR. 5, 1770)*

* This engraving is reproduced from an original copy in the William L. Clements Library, University of Michigan.

B. "A MILITARY COMBINATION": REPORT OF A COMMITTEE OF THE TOWN OF BOSTON (1770)*

IT may be a proper introduction to this narrative, briefly to represent the state of things for some time previous to the said massacre; and this seems necessary in order to the forming a just idea of the causes of it.

At the end of the late war, in which this Province bore so distinguished a part, a happy union subsisted between Great-Britain and the Colonies. This was unfortunately interrupted by the Stamp-Act; but it was in some measure restored by the Repeal of it. It was again interrupted by other acts of parliament for taxing America; and by the appointment of a Board of Commissioners, in pursuance of an act, which by the face of it was made for the relief and encouragement of commerce, but which in its operation, it was apprehended, would have, and it has in fact had, a contrary effect. By the said act the said Commissioners were "to be resident in some convenient part of "his Majesty's dominions in America."—This must be understood to be in some part convenient for the whole.—But it does not appear, that in fixing the place of their residence, the convenience of the whole was at all consulted; for Boston being very far from the center of the colonies, could not be the place most convenient for the whole.—Judging by the act, it may seem this town was intended to be favoured, by the Commissioners being appointed to reside here; and that the consequence of that residence would be the relief and encouragement of commerce: but the reverse has been the constant and uniform effect of it; so that the commerce of the town, from the embarrassments in which it has been lately involved, is greatly reduced. For the particulars on this head, see the state of the trade not long since drawn up and transmitted to England by a committee of the merchants of Boston.

The residence of the Commissioners here has been detrimental not only to the commerce, but to the political interests of the town and province; and not only so, but we can trace from it the causes of the late horrid massacre.

Soon after their arrival here in November 1767, instead of confining themselves to the proper business of their office, they became partizans of Governor Bernard in his political schemes, and had the weakness and temerity to infringe upon one of the most essential rights of the house of commons of this province—that of giving their votes with freedom, and not being accountable therefor but to their constituents. One of the members of that house, Captain Timothy Folgier, having voted in some affair contrary to the mind of the said Commissioners, was for so doing dismissed from the office he held under them.

These proceedings of theirs, the difficulty of access to them on office-business, and a supercilious behaviour, rendered them disgustful to people in general, who in consequence thereof treated them with neglect. This probably stimulated them to resent it: and to make their resentment felt, they and their coadjutor Governor Bernard made such representations to his Majesty's ministers, as they thought best calculated to bring the displeasure of the nation upon the town and province: and in order that those representations might have the more weight, they are said to have contrived and executed plans for exciting disturbances and tumults, which otherwise would

---

* The following excerpts are reprinted from *A Short Narrative of the Horrid Massacre in Boston* (1770), pp. 5–12, 14–18, 21–25.

probably never have existed; and when excited, to have transmitted to the ministry the most exaggerated accounts of them.

These particulars of their conduct his Majesty's Council of this province have fully laid open in their proceeding in council, and in their address to General Gage in July and October 1768, and in their letter to Lord Hillsborough of the 15th of April 1769.—Unfortunately for us, they have been too successful in their said representations, which, in conjunction with Governor Bernard's, have occasioned his Majesty's faithful subjects of this town and province to be treated as enemies and rebels, by an invasion of the town by sea and land: to which the approaches were made with all the circumspection usual where a vigorous opposition is expected. While the town was surrounded by a considerable number of his Majesty's ships of war, two regiments landed and took possession of it; and to support these, two other regiments arrived some time after from Ireland, one of which landed at Castle-Island, and the other in the town.

Thus were we, in aggravation of our other embarrassments, embarrassed with troops, forced upon us contrary to our inclination—contrary to the spirit of Magna Charta—contrary to the very letter of the Bill of Rights, in which it is declared, that the raising or keeping a standing army within the kingdom in time of peace, unless it be with the consent of parliament, is against law—and without the desire of the civil magistrates, to aid whom was the pretence for sending the troops hither; who were quartered in the town in direct violation of an act of parliament for quartering troops in America: and all this in consequence of the representations of the said Commissioners and the said Governor, as appears by their memorials and letters lately published.

As they were the procuring cause of troops being sent hither, they must therefore be the remote and a blameable cause of all the disturbances and bloodshed that have taken place in consequence of that measure.

But we shall leave them to their own reflections, after observing, that as they had some months before the arrival of the troops, under pretence of safety to their persons, retired from town to the castle; so, after the arrival of the troops, and their being quartered in the town, they thought proper to return, having answered, as they doubtless thought, the purpose of their voluntary flight.

We shall next attend to the conduct of the troops, and to some circumstances relative to them.—Governor Bernard without consulting the Council, having given up the State-house to the troops at their landing, they took possession of the chambers, where the representatives of the province and the courts of law held their meetings, and (except the council-chamber) of all other parts of that house: in which they continued a considerable time, to the great annoyance of those courts while they sat, and of the merchants and gentlemen of the town, who had always made the lower floor of it their exchange. They had a right so to do, as the property of it was in the town; but they were deprived of that right by mere power. The said Governor soon after, by every stratagem and by every method, but a forcible entry, endeavoured to get possession of the manufactory-house, to make a barrack of it for the troops; and for that purpose caused it to be besieged by the troops, and the people in it to be used very cruelly; which extraordinary proceedings created universal uneasiness, arising from the apprehension that the troops under the influence of such a man would be employed to effect the most dangerous purposes: but failing in that, other houses were procured, in which, contrary to act of parliament, he caused the troops to be quartered. After their quarters were settled, the main guard was posted at one of the said houses, directly opposite to, and not 12 yards from the State-house (where the General Court, and all the Law Courts for the County were held) with two field pieces pointed to the State-house. This situation of the main guard and field pieces seemed to indicate an attack upon the constitution, and a defiance of law, and to be intended to affront the legislative and executive authority of the province.

The General Court, at the first Session after the arrival of the troops, viewed it in this light, and applied to Governor Bernard to cause such a nuisance to be removed; but to no purpose. Disgusted at such an indignity, and at the appearance of being under duresse, they refused to do business in such circumstances, and in consequence thereof were adjourned to Cambridge, to the great inconvenience of the members.

Besides this, the challenging the inhabitants by centinels posted in all parts of the town before the lodgings of officers, which (for about six months, while it lasted) occasioned many quarrels and great uneasiness.——

Captain Wilson's of the 59th, exciting the negroes of the town to take away their masters lives and property, and repair to the army for protection, which was fully proved against him.—The attack of a party of soldiers on some of the magistrates of the town—the repeated rescues of soldiers from peace officers—the firing of a loaded musket in a public street, to the endangering a great number of peaceable inhabitants—the frequent wounding of persons by their bayonets and cutlasses, and the numerous instances of bad behaviour in the soldiery, made us early sensible, that the troops were not sent here for any benefit to the town or province, and that we had no good to expect from such conservators of the peace.

It was not expected however, that such an outrage and massacre, as happened here on the evening of the fifth instant, would have been perpetuated. There were then killed and wounded, by a discharge of musquetry, eleven of his Majesty's subjects, viz.

Mr. Samuel Gray, killed on the spot by a ball entering his head.

Crispus Attucks, a molatto, killed on the spot, two balls entering his breast.

Mr. James Caldwell, killed on the spot, by two balls entering his back.

Mr. Samuel Maverick, a youth of 17 years of age, mortally wounded: he died the next morning.

Mr. Patrick Carr mortally wounded: he died the 14th instant.

Christopher Monk and John Clark, youths about 17 years of age, dangerously wounded; it is apprehended they will die.

Mr. Edward Payne, merchant, standing at his door, wounded.

Mess. John Green, Robert Patterson, and David Parker, all dangerously wounded.

The actors in this dreadful tragedy were a party of soldiers commanded by Captain Preston of the 29th regiment. This party, including the Captain, consisted of eight, who are all committed to gaol.

There are depositions in this affair, which mention that several guns were fired at the same time from the Custom-House; before which this shocking scene was exhibited. Into this matter inquisition is now making.——In the mean time it may be proper to insert here the substance of some of those depositions.

Benjamin Frizell, on the evening of the 5th of March, having taken his station near the west-corner of the Custom-House, in King-street, before and at the time of the soldiers firing their guns, declares, (among other things) that the first discharge was only of one gun, the next of two guns, upon which he the deponent thinks he saw a man stumble, the third discharge was of three guns, upon which he thinks he saw two men fall; and immediately after were discharged five guns, two of which were by soldiers on his right hand; *the other three, as appeared, to the deponent, were discharged from the balcony, or the chamber window of the* CUSTOM-HOUSE, *the flashes appearing on the left hand, and higher than the right hand flashes appeared to be, and of which the deponent was very sensible,* although his eyes were much turned to the soldiers, who were all on his right hand.

Gillam Bass, being in King-street at the same time, declares that they (the party of soldiers from the main guard) posted themselves between the Custom-House door, and the west corner of it; and in a few minutes began to fire upon the people: *Two or three of the flashes so high above the rest, that the deponent verily believes they must have come from the* CUSTOM-HOUSE *windows. . . .*

What gave occasion to the melancholy event of that evening seems to have been this. A difference having happened near Mr. Gray's ropewalk, between a soldier and a man belonging to it, the soldier challenged the ropemakers to a boxing match. The challenge was accepted by one of them, and the soldier worsted. He ran to the barrack in the neighbourhood, and returned with several of his companions. The fray was renewed, and the soldiers were driven off. They soon returned with recruits, and were again worsted. This happened several times, till at length a considerable body of soldiers was collected, and they also were driven off, the ropemakers having been joined by their brethren of the contiguous ropewalks. By this time Mr. Gray being alarmed interposed, and with the assistance of some gentlemen prevented any further disturbance. To satisfy the soldiers and punish the man who had been the occasion of the first difference, and as an example to the rest, he turned him out of his service; and waited on Col. Dalrymple, the commanding officer of the troops, and with him concerted measures for preventing further mischief. Though this affair ended thus, it made a strong impression on the minds of the soldiers in general, who thought the honour of the regiment concerned to revenge those repeated repulses. For this purpose they seem to have formed a combination to commit some outrage upon the inhabitants of the town indiscriminately; and this was to be done on the evening of the fifth instant, or soon after, as appears by the depositions of the following persons, viz.

William Newhall declares, that on Thursday night the first of March instant, he met four soldiers of the 29th regiment, and that he heard them say, *there were a great many that would eat their dinners on Monday next, that should not eat any on Tuesday.*

Daniel Calse declares, that on Saturday evening the 3d of March a campwoman, wife to James M'Deed a grenadier of the 29th, came into his father's shop, and the people talking about the affrays at the Ropewalks, and blaming the soldiers for the part they had acted in it, the woman said the soldiers were in the right; adding, *that before Tuesday or Wednesday night they would wet their swords or bayonets in New England people's blood.* . . .

Matthew Adams declares, that on Monday evening the 5th of March instant between the hours of seven and eight o'clock, he went to the house of corporal Pershall of the 29th regiment, near Quaker-lane, where he saw the corporal and his wife, with one of the fifers of the said regiments. When he had got what he went for, and was coming away, the corporal called him back, and desired him with great earnestness to go home to his master's house as soon as business was over, and not to be abroad on any account that night in particular, for *the soldiers were determined to be revenged on the ropewalk people, and that much mischief would be done.* Upon which the fifer (about 18 or 19 years of age) said, *he hoped in God they would burn the town down.* On this he left the house, and the said corporal called after him again, and begged he would mind what he said to him.

Caleb Swan declares, that on Monday night the 5th of March instant, at the time of the bells ringing for fire, he heard a woman's voice whom he knew to be the supposed wife of one Montgomery, a grenadier of the 29th regiment, standing at her door, *and heard her say, it was not fire; the town was too haughty and too proud; and that many of their arses would be laid low before the morning.* . . .

By the foregoing depositions it appears very clearly, there was a general combination among the soldiers, of the 29th regiment at least, to commit some extraordinary act of violence upon the town; that if the inhabitants attempted to repel it by firing even one gun upon those soldiers, the 14th regiment were ordered to be in readiness to assist him; and that on the late butchery in King-street they actually were ready for that purpose, had a single gun been fired on the perpetrators of it.

It appears by a variety of depositions, that on the same evening between the hours of six and half after nine (at which time the firing began) many persons, without the least provocation, were in various parts of the town insulted and abused by parties of armed soldiers patrolling the streets. . . .

Samuel Drowne declares, that about nine of the clock of the evening of the 5th of March current, standing at his own door in Cornhill, he saw about 14 or 15 soldiers of the 29th regiment, who came from Murray's barracks armed with naked cutlasses, swords, &c. and came upon the inhabitants of the town, then standing or walking in Cornhill, and abused some, and violently assaulted others as they met them; most of whom were without so much as a stick in their hand to defend themselves, as he very clearly could discern, it being moon-light, and himself being one of the assaulted persons. All or most of the said soldiers he saw go into King-street (some of them through Royal Exchange-lane) and there followed them, and soon discovered them to be quarrelling and fighting with the people whom they saw there, which he thinks were not more than a dozen, when the soldiers came there first, armed as aforesaid. Of those dozen people the most of them were gentlemen, standing together a little below the Town-house upon the Exchange. At the appearance of those soldiers so armed, the most of the twelve persons went off, some of them being first assaulted.

The violent proceedings of this party, and their going into King-street, "quarrelling and fighting with the people whom they saw there" (mentioned in Mr. Drowne's deposition) was immediately introductory to the grand catastrophe.

These assailants, who issued from Murray's barracks (so called) after attacking and wounding divers persons in Cornhill, as above mentioned, being armed, proceeded (most of them) up the Royal Exchange-lane, into King-street, where making a short stop, and after assaulting and driving away the few they met there, they brandished their arms, and cried out, Where are the boogers? where are the cowards? At this time there were very few persons in the street beside themselves.——This party in proceeding from Exchange-lane into King-street must pass the centry posted at the westerly corner of the Custom house, which butts on that lane and fronts on that street. This is needful to be mentioned, as near that spot and in that street the bloody tragedy was acted, and the street-actors in it were stationed, their station being but a few feet from the front side of the said Custom-house.——The outrageous behavior and the threats of the said party occasioned the ringing of the Meeting-house bell near the head of King-street; which bell ringing quick as for fire, it presently brought out a number of the inhabitants, who being soon sensible of the occasion of it, were naturally led to King-street, where the said party had made a stop but a little while before, and where their stopping had drawn together a number of boys round the centry at the Custom-house. Whether the boys mistook the centry for one of the said party, and thence took occasion to differ with him, or whether he first affronted them, which is affirmed in several depositions,—however that may be, there was much foul language between them; and some of them, in consequence of his pushing at them with his bayonet, threw snow-balls at him, which occasioned him to knock hastily at the door of the Custom-house. From hence two persons thereupon proceeded immediately to the main guard, which was posted (opposite to the State-house) at a small distance near the head of the said street. The officer on guard was Capt. Preston, who with seven or eight soldiers with fire arms, and charged bayonets, issued from the Guard-house, and in great haste posted himself and his soldiers in the front of the Custom-house near the corner aforesaid. In passing to this station the soldiers pushed several persons with their bayonets, driving through the people in so rough a manner, that it appeared they intended to create a disturbance. This occasioned some snow-balls to be thrown at them; which seems to have been the only provocation that was given. Mr. Knox (between whom and Capt. Preston there was some conversation on the spot) declares, that while he was talking with Capt. Preston, the soldiers of his detachment had attacked the people with their bayonets; and that there was not the least provocation given to Capt. Preston or his party; the backs of the people being towards them when the people were attacked. He also declares, that Capt. Preston seemed to be in great haste and much agitated; and that according to his opinion there were not then present in King-street above 70 or 80 persons at the extent.

The said party was formed into a half circle, and, within a short time after they had been posted at the Custom-house, began to fire upon the people.

Capt. Preston is said to have ordered them to fire, and to have repeated that order. One gun was fired first; then others in succession, and with deliberation, till ten or a dozen guns were fired, or till that number of discharges were made from the guns that were fired. By which means 11 persons were killed and wounded, as above represented. . . .

Soon after the firing, a drum with a party from the main guard went to

Murray's and the other barracks, beating an alarm as they went, which, with the firing, had the effect of a signal for action; whereupon all the soldiers of the 29th regiment, or the main body of them, appeared in King-street under arms, and seemed bent on a further massacre of the inhabitants, which was with great difficulty prevented. They were drawn up between the State-house and main guard, their lines extending across the street and facing down King-street, where the town-people were assembled. The first line kneeled; and the whole of the first platoon presented their guns ready to fire, as soon as the word should be given. They continued in that posture a considerable time; but by the good Providence of God they were restrained from firing. . . .

PART FIVE

"Period of Quiet," 1770–1773

The Wilkes Fund Controversy in South Carolina

On January 31, 1770, Frederick North, 2d Earl of Guildford (1732–1792), became First Minister, a post he would hold for over twelve years. As a conciliatory gesture, he promptly carried through Parliament a bill to repeal all of the Townshend duties except the 3d tax on tea, which was retained as a symbol of Parliament's authority to tax the colonies, and promised that Parliament would not lay any further taxes upon the colonies during his administration. Although diehard patriots insisted upon keeping up their resistance until the tea duty had also been repealed and other outstanding grievances redressed, North's gesture seriously undermined American opposition. One colony after another abandoned nonimportation until by July, 1771, the movement had completely collapsed. Some attempt was made to retain the boycott against tea, but as tempers cooled over the next three years an increasing amount of taxed tea found its way into American homes. The period between April 12, 1770, when the repeal went into effect, and May, 1773, when Parliament passed the Tea Act, is frequently designated as the "quiet period" because of the notable easing of tensions between the imperial government and the colonies and the tranquillity of the internal political life of most of the colonies. There were, however, some notable exceptions to this pattern.

One was South Carolina. In early 1769 some of the English friends of John Wilkes formed the Society of the Gentlemen Supporters of the Bill of Rights to "defend and maintain the legal constitutional Liberty of the subject" and, more immediately, to pay Wilkes's rather sizable debts. The society solicited funds from the colonies, but the only official governmental body to respond was the South Carolina Commons House of Assembly. On December 8, 1769, that body voted overwhelmingly to direct the treasurer to give £1,500 sterling (£10,500 South Carolina currency) to a committee for transmission to the Society. Imperial regulations had long prohibited the issuance of any money from colonial treasuries without the consent of the royal governors, but the South Carolina Commons had become so powerful through the middle decades of the eighteenth century that it had been able to secure the right to order money from the treasury without the governor's consent. Because no governor had been bold enough to complain about this development, authorities learned of it only when news of the grant to Wilkes had been published in London papers.

The ministry immediately moved both to force the Commons to rescind its grant —which had already been sent to the Society—and to put an end to so "unconstitutional" a method of disbursing public funds in the colony. By an additional instruction (Selection 17 A) to Lieutenant Governor William Bull the ministry placed the governor under strict regulations in the passage of money bills and threatened the treasurer with permanent exclusion from public office and a large fine if he issued any money from the treasury solely upon the Commons's order. A major controversy developed when the Commons on September 4, 1770, defied the "ministerial mandate" and passed a series of resolutions (Selection 17 B) asserting that its vote to Wilkes was "agreeable to the usage and practice both ancient and Modern of the Commons House of Assembly of this Province." When the ministry declined to withdraw the instruction, the South Carolina Commons refused to proceed to any public business. For five years beginning in December, 1769, the Wilkes grant was the central issue of South Carolina politics. No annual tax bill was passed in the colony after 1769 and no legislation at all after February, 1771. For all practical purposes, royal government in South Carolina broke down four years earlier than it did in any of the other colonies.

Jack P. Greene, "Bridge to Revolution: The Wilkes Fund Controversy in South Carolina, 1769–1775," Journal of Southern History, volume 29 (1963), pages 19–52, is a full account of the course and significance of this dispute.

A. MINISTERIAL MANDATE: ADDITIONAL INSTRUCTION OF APR. 14, 1770*

Whereas it hath been represented to us that our House of Representatives or lower house of assembly in our province of South Carolina in America have lately assumed to themselves a power of ordering without the concurrence of our governor and council the public treasurer of our said province to issue and advance out of the public treasury such sums of money and for such services as they have thought fit; and particularly that the said lower house of assembly did on the 8th day of December last past [1769] make an order upon the said public treasurer to advance the sum of ten thousand five hundred pounds currency out of any money in the treasury to be paid into the hands of Mr. Speaker, Mr. Gadsdon, Mr. Rutlidge, Mr. Parson, Mr. Ferguson, Mr. Dart, and Mr. Lynch, who were to remit the same to Great Britain for the support of the just and constitutional rights and liberties of the people of Great Britain and America; and whereas it is highly just and necessary that the most effectual measures be pursued for putting a stop to such dangerous and unwarrantable practices and for guarding for the future against such unconstitutional application of our treasure, cheerfully granted to us by our subjects in our said province of South Carolina for the public uses of the said province and for support of the government thereof; it is therefore our will and pleasure and you are hereby directed and required upon pain of our highest displeasure and of being forthwith removed from your government, not to give your assent to any bill or bills that shall be passed by our said lower house of assembly by which bill or bills any sum or sums of money whatsoever shall be appropriated to or provision made for defraying any expense incurred for services or purposes not immediately arising within or incident to our said province of South Carolina, unless upon special requisition from us, our heirs, and successors, nor to any bill or bills for granting any sum of money to us, our heirs, and successors, in which bill or bills it shall not be provided in express words that the money so to be granted, or any part thereof, shall not be issued or applied to any other services than those to which it is by the said bill appropriated, unless by act or ordinance of the general assembly of our said province; and it is our further will and pleasure and you are hereby directed and required upon pain of our highest displeasure as aforesaid not to give your assent to any bill or bills that shall be passed by our said lower house of assembly as aforesaid, by which any sum or sums of money whatever shall be granted to us, our heirs, and successors generally and without appropriation, unless there be a clause or clauses inserted in

* Reprinted in full from Leonard Woods Laboree (ed.), *Royal Instructions to British Colonial Governors, 1670–1776* (1935), vol. I, pp. 208–209.

the said bill or bills declaring and providing that the said money so to be granted shall remain in the treasury subject to such appropriation as shall thereafter be made by act or ordinance of the general assembly and not otherwise; and it is our further will and pleasure that you take especial care that in all and every bill and bills so to be passed by you as aforesaid for raising and granting public moneys a clause or clauses be inserted therein subjecting the public treasurer or any other persons or persons to whose custody public moneys may be committed, in case he or they shall issue or pay any such money otherwise than by express order contained in some act or ordinance of the general assembly, to a penalty in treble the sum so issued contrary thereto, and declaring him or them to be *ipso facto* incapable of holding the said office of treasurer or any other office civil or military within our said province; and it is our further will and pleasure that this our additional instruction to you be communicated to our council and lower house of assembly of our said province of South Carolina and entered upon the council books.

B. DEFYING THE MANDATE: RESOLVES OF THE SOUTH CAROLINA COMMONS HOUSE OF ASSEMBLY (SEPT. 4, 1770)*

Resolved, That this House hath an undoubted Right, which they have at all Times exercised, to give and grant Money to his Majesty, with or without a Requisition from the Crown, for any purpose whatsoever, whether local and Provincial or not, whenever they think it necessary or expedient for his service, of which they are the sole Judges.

Resolved, That in order to provide such Money, the House hath a Right, upon emergent Occasions and when the Money is immediately wanted, to borrow it upon the Public faith and Credit solemnly pledged by a Resolution of a House, to make good and repay the Money so borrowed; And that the House hath exercised this right whenever they have thought proper.

Resolved, That the House hath in such Cases, ordered the Public Treasurers, to advance the said Money, who hath accordingly done so, upon the Resolution of the House to make good the same; and that Provision for repaying it to him, hath always been made by the Tax Acts, which measure cannot be unknown to the Lieutenant Governor, whose Sanction, as well as that of his Predecessors it has often received.

Resolved, That the Order and Resolution of the House on the 8th day of December last (the said Order being never considered by this House but merely as a vote of Credit) are not unconstitutional but agreeable to the usage and practice both ancient and Modern of the Commons House of Assembly of this Province; That the Public Treasurer, having advanced the Money mentioned in the said Order in pursuance thereof on the Resolution of this House to repay the same did in his account charge it to the Public, and not to any particular Fund; And that in the schedule to the Tax Bill, the House inserted the Treasurer's Name as a Creditor of the Public for that sum, intending to repay it in the usual manner.

* Reprinted in full from *Journals of the Commons House of Assembly,* vol. XXXVIII, pp. 431–433.

Resolved, That the House hath never attempted by its single Authority, without the Concurrence of the Governor and Council, to issue out of the Treasury, Money appropriated by Law, and apply the same to other purposes than those for which it was granted.

Resolved, That the Order and Resolution of this House on the 8th day of December last, cannot be deemed dangerous or Unwarrantable, that the same would not have been so represented, or the power of this House on that point, drawn into Question, if the Money borrowed had not been applied towards frustrating the unjust and unconstitutional measures of an arbitrary and oppressive ministry. And his Honor the Lieutenant Governor, having assured the House, that all his Representations to his Majesty by his Ministers are made with the strictest regard to Truth.

Resolved, therefore, That the said Instruction cannot be supported by such Information, but is founded upon a false, partial and insidious Representation of the Proceedings of this House; False in asserting that the House had lately assumed a Power, when in Truth they only exercised an Ancient Right supported by constant usage; Partial in concealing its Resolution to repay the Money borrowed; and insidious in Artfully insinuating that the House had directed an Unconstitutional Application of the Public Treasure Granted to his Majesty in Ordering, by its single Vote; without the Concurrence of Governor or Council, Money appropriated by Law to be applied to other Purposes, And that the Censure contained in the said Instruction, is altogether Unmerited.

Resolved, That the Clauses and Provisions in the said Instruction relating to the Appropriation of such Monies as shall be granted by this House are unnecessary, every Law which grants Money sufficiently securing the appropriation thereof: And, as many Evils might arise to the Province from inserting the Clauses relative to the Treasurer, the House should not submit thereto.

Resolved, That a Ministers dictating how a Money Bill shall be framed, is an Infringement of the Privileges of this House; to whom alone it belongs to Originate and prepare the same, for the concurrence and assent of the Governor and Council without any Alteration or Amendment whatsoever.

Resolved, That whosoever made the false, partial and insidious Representation upon which the said Instruction is founded and advised such Instruction; are guilty of high misdemeanors and are Enemies to his Majesty and the Province.

SELECTION

Friction in Massachusetts

For Massachusetts, as for South Carolina, the years from 1770 to 1773 were anything but quiet. Although the situation never became so desperate as in South

Carolina and although there was a notable lessening of hostility to the imperial government, a series of running battles between Hutchinson and the House of Representatives kept Massachusetts politics in a constant broil. First, there was the question of the removal of the place of the meeting of the General Court from Boston to Cambridge. Bernard had taken this step in 1769, hoping thereby to lessen the influence of the more radical patriots in Boston upon both the House of Representatives and the Council. Although the House steadfastly refused to do any business until it was returned to its lawful place of meeting in Boston, Hutchinson, armed with a royal instruction empowering him to meet the legislature wherever he thought fit, continued to convene the General Court in Cambridge in 1770 and 1771. Both houses repeatedly protested the legality of the act and, during the protracted arguments that followed, attacked the growing and, from their point of view, unconstitutional use of instructions from the imperial government to alter ancient political practices in Massachusetts. Resentment against "government by instruction" was further intensified in August, 1770, when Hutchinson, again acting on instructions from home, turned Castle William, a provincial fort, over to the British Army and replaced the garrison of provincial troops with British troops.

Neither of these incidents created any widespread alarm outside the legislature, however, and it was not until after Hutchinson's announcements in the summer of 1772 that he and the judges would thenceforth receive their salaries from the Crown rather than from the colony that radical political leaders found an issue with broad appeal to the public at large. These announcements, which made it clear that the imperial government intended to remove both the executive and the judiciary from any financial dependence upon the House of Representatives, created considerable alarm in Boston, and on November 2, 1772, at the suggestion of Samuel Adams, the Boston town meeting approved the appointment of a standing committee of correspondence to prepare a statement of rights and grievances and to communicate it to the towns. This statement consisted of two parts, a "State of the Rights of the Colonists," written by Adams, and a "List of Infringements and Violations of Rights," written by Dr. Joseph Warren (1741–1775), who was rapidly emerging as one of the leading patriots in the Bay Colony. The latter, a comprehensive statement of grievances against the imperial government in both Massachusetts and Britain, is reprinted in large part below as Selection 18 A.

Other towns responded enthusiastically to these documents, establishing committees of correspondence and adopting similar statements of their own. Alarmed by the almost universal tendency of these statements to deny the authority of Parliament over the colonies, Hutchinson delivered a long speech to the General Court on January 6, 1773, in which he argued that Parliament had supreme authority over all British dominions. Because sovereignty could never be divided, he contended, there could only be one sovereign legislature in every state. It followed, therefore, that either Parliament was supreme over the colonies or they were independent states. To Hutchinson's chagrin, his strategy backfired as the House adopted a reply, prepared in part by John Adams (1735–1826), a rising lawyer from Braintree, that, as Edmund S. Morgan has remarked, "committed the whole province to the very position that Hutchinson had hoped to forestall, that Parliament had no authority in the colonies whatever." The Massachusetts House thus became the first colonial legislature to make so explicit and so comprehensive a claim to exemption from parliamentary control—a position that most colonists would not come to until after Parliament had issued a new challenge in the form of the Coercive Acts eighteen months later. Portions of Hutchinson's speech and of the House's reply are reprinted here as Selection 18 B.

The best accounts of Massachusetts in the "quiet period" may be found in John Cary, Joseph Warren: Physician, Politician, Patriot *(1961), and Robert E. Brown,* Middle-class Democracy and the Revolution in Massachusetts 1691–1780 *(1955). See also the brief discussion in Edmund S. Morgan,* The Birth of the Republic 1763–89 *(1956).*

A. A SPATE OF GRIEVANCES: BOSTON TOWN MEETING, ''LIST OF INFRINGEMENTS AND VIOLATIONS OF RIGHTS'' (NOV. 20, 1772)*

We cannot help thinking, that an enumeration of some of the most open infringments of our rights, will by every candid Person be Judged sufficient to Justify whatever measures have been already taken, or may be thought proper to be taken, in order to obtain a redress of the Grievances under which we labour. . . .

1st. The British Parliament have assumed the power of legislation for the Colonists in all cases whatsoever, without obtaining the consent of the Inhabitants, which is ever essentially necessary to the right establishment of such a legislative——

2d. They have exerted that assumed power, in raising a Revenue in the Colonies without their consent; thereby depriving them of that right which every man has to keep his own earnings in his own hands until he shall in person, or by his Representative, think fit to part with the whole or any portion of it. . . .

3d. A number of new Officers, unknown in the Charter of this Province, have been appointed to superintend this Revenue, whereas by our Charter the Great & General Court or Assembly of this Province has the sole right of appointing all civil officers, excepting only such officers, the election and constitution of whom is in said charter expressly excepted; among whom these Officers are not included.——

4th. These Officers are by their Commission invested with powers altogether unconstitutional, and entirely destructive to that security which we have a right to enjoy; and to the last degree dangerous, not only to our property; but to our lives: For the Commissioners of his Majestys customs in America, or any three of them, are by their Commission impowered, "by writing under their hands and seales to constitute and appoint inferior Officers in all and singular the Port within the limits of their commissions." Each of these petty officers so made is intrusted with power more absolute and arbitrary than ought to be lodged in the hands of any man or body of men whatsoever; for in the commission aforementioned, his Majesty gives & grants unto his said Commissioners . . . full power and authority . . . as well By Night as by day to enter and go on board any Ship, Boat, or other Vessel, riding lying or being within, or coming into any Port, Harbour, Creek or Haven . . . and also in the day time to go into any house, shop, cellar, or any other place where any goods wares or merchandizes lie concealed, or are *suspected* to lie concealed, whereof the customs & other duties, have not been, or shall not be, duly paid . . .

* These excerpts are reprinted from Harry Alonzo Cushing (ed.), *Writings of Samuel Adams,* vol. II, pp. 359–368.

Thus our houses and even our bed chambers, are exposed to be ransacked, our boxes chests & trunks broke open ravaged and plundered by wretches, whom no prudent man would venture to employ even as menial servants; whenever they are pleased to say they *suspect* there are in the house wares &c for which the dutys have not been paid. Flagrant instances of the wanton exercise of this power, have frequently happened in this and other sea port Towns. By this we are cut off from that domestick security which renders the lives of the most unhappy in some measure agreable. . . .

5th. Fleets and Armies have been introduced to support these unconstitutional Officers in collecting and managing this unconstitutional Revenue; and troops have been quarter'd in this Metropolis for that purpose. Introducing and quartering standing Armies in a free Country in times of peace without the consent of the people either by themselves or by their Representatives, is, and always has been deemed a violation of their rights as freemen . . .

6th. The Revenue arising from this tax unconstitutionally laid, and committed to the management of persons arbitrarily appointed and supported by an armed force quartered in a free City, has been in part applyed to the most destructive purposes. It is absolutely necessary in a mixt government like that of this Province, that a due proportion or balance of power should be established among the several branches of legislative. Our Ancestors received from King William & Queen Mary a Charter by which it was understood by both parties in the contract, that such a proportion or balance was fixed; and therefore every thing which renders any one branch of the Legislative more independent of the other two than it was originally designed, is an alteration of the constitution as settled by the Charter; and as it has been untill the establishment of this Revenue, the constant practise of the General Assembly to provide for the support of Government, so it is an essential part of our constitution, as it is a necessary means of preserving an *equilibrium,* without which we cannot continue a free state.——

In particular it has always been held, that the dependence of the Governor of this Province upon the General Assembly for his support, was necessary for the preservation of this *equilibrium;* nevertheless his Majesty has been pleased to apply fifteen hundred pounds sterling annually out of the American revenue, for the support of the Governor of this Province independent of the Assembly, whereby the ancient connection between him and this people is weakened, the confidence in the Governor lessened and the equilibrium destroyed, and the constitution essentially altered.——

And we look upon it highly probable from the best intelligence we have been able to obtain, that not only our Governor and Lieuvetenant Governor, but the Judges of the Superior Court of Judicature, as also the Kings Attorney and Solicitor General are to receive their support from this Grievous tribute. This will if accomplished compleat our slavery. For if taxes are raised from us by the Parliament of Great Britain without our consent, and the men on whose opinions and decisions our properties liberties and lives, in a great measure depend, receive their support from the Revenues arising from these taxes, we cannot, when we think on the depravity of mankind, avoid looking with horror on the danger to which we are exposed? . . .

7th. We find ourselves greatly oppressed by Instructions sent to our Governor from the Court of Great Britain, whereby the first branch of our legislature is made merely a ministerial engine. And the Province has already felt such effects from these Instructions, as We think Justly intitle us to say that they threaten an entire destruction of our liberties, and must soon, if not checked, render every branch of our Government a useless burthen upon the people. . . .

In consequence of Instructions, the Governor has called and adjourned our General Assemblies to a place highly inconvenient to the Members and grately disadvantageous to the interest of the Province, even against his own declared intention——

In consequence of Instructions, the Assembly has been prorogued from time to time, when the important concerns of the Province required their Meeting——

In obedience to Instructions, the General Assembly was Anno 1768 dissolved by Governor Bernard, because they would not consent to *rescind* the resolution of a *former* house, and thereby sacrifise the rights of their constituents.——

By an Instruction, the honourable his Majesty Council are forbid to meet and transact matters of publick concern as a Council of advice to the Governor, unless called by the Governor; and if they should from a zealous regard to the interest of the Province so meet at any time, the Governor is ordered to negative them at the next Election of Councellors. . . .

His Excellency has also pleaded Instructions for giving up the provincial fortress, Castle William into the hands of troops, over whom he had declared he had no controul (and that at a time when they were menaceing the Slaughter of the Inhabitants of the Town, and our Streets were stained with the blood which they had barbariously shed) . . .

8th. The extending the power of the Courts of Vice Admirality to so enormous a degree as deprives the people in the Colonies in a great measure of their inestimable right to tryals by *Juries:* which has ever been Justly considered as the grand Bulwark and security of English property.

This alone is sufficient to rouse our jealousy: And we are again obliged to take notice of the remarkable contrast, which the British Parliament has been pleased to exhibit between the Subjects in Great Britain & the Colonies. . . .

9th. The restraining us from erecting Stilling Mills for manufacturing our Iron the natural produce of this Country, Is an infringement of that right with which God and nature have invested us, to make use of our skill and industry in procuring the necessaries and conveniences of life. And we look upon the restraint laid upon the manufacture and transportation of Hatts to be altogether unreasonable and grievous. Although by the Charter all Havens Rivers, Ports, Waters, &c. are expressly granted the Inhabitants of the Province and their Successors, to their only proper use and behoof forever, yet the British Parliament passed an Act, whereby they restrain us from carrying our Wool, the produce of our own farms, even over a ferry; whereby the Inhabitants have often been put to the expence of carrying a Bag of Wool near an hundred miles by land, when passing over a River or Water of one quarter of a mile, of which the Province are the absolute Proprietors, would have prevented all that trouble.——

10th. The Act passed in the last Session of the British Parliament, intitled, *An Act for the better preserving his Majestys Dock Yards, Magazines, Ships, Ammunition and Stores*, is, as we apprehend a violent infringement of our Rights. By this Act any one of us may be taken from his Family, and carried to any part of Great Britain, there to be tried whenever it shall be pretended that he has been concerned in burning or otherwise destroying any Boat or Vessel, or any Materials for building &c. any Naval or Victualling Store &c. belonging to his Majesty. . . .

11th. As our Ancestors came over to this Country that they might not only enjoy their civil but their relegeous rights, and particularly desired to be free from the Prelates, who in those times cruilly persecuted all who differed in sentiment from the established Church; we cannot see without concern the various attempts, which have been made and are now making, to establish an American Episcopate. . . .

And we are further of Opinion, that no power on Earth can justly give either temporal or spiritual Jurisdiction within this Province, except the Great & General Court. We think therefore that every design for establishing the Jurisdiction of a Bishop in this Province, is a design both against our Civil and Religious rights. . . .

12th. Another Grievance under which we labour is the frequent alteration of the bounds of the Colonies by decisions before the King and Council, explanatory of former grants and Charters. This not only subjects Men to live under a constitution to which they have not consented, which in itself is a great Grievance; but moreover under color, that the *right of Soil* is affected by such declarations, some Governors, or Ministers, or both in conjunction, have pretended to Grant in consequence of a Mandamus many thousands of Acres of Lands appropriated near a Century past; and rendered valuable by the labors of the present Cultivators and their Ancestors. . . .

B. DEBATE OVER THE AUTHORITY OF PARLIAMENT: THE EXCHANGE BETWEEN GOVERNOR THOMAS HUTCHINSON AND THE HOUSE OF REPRESENTATIVES (JAN. 6, 26, 1773)*

The Governor's Speech

. . . When our predecessors first took possession of this plantation, or colony, under a grant and charter from the Crown of England, it was their sense, and it was the sense of the kingdom, that they were to remain subject to the supreme authority of Parliament. This appears from the charter itself, and from other irresistible evidence. This supreme authority has, from time to time, been exercised by Parliament, and submitted to by the colony, and hath been, in the most express terms, acknowledged by the Legislature, and, except about the time of the anarchy and confusion in England, which preceded the restoration of King Charles the Second, I have not discovered that it has been called in question, even by private or particu-

* These excerpts are reprinted from Alden E. Bradford (ed.), *Speeches of the Governors of Massachusetts from 1764 to 1775* (1818), pp. 337–340, 351–353, 357–358, 363–364.

lar persons, until within seven or eight years last past. Our provincial or local laws have, in numerous instances, had relation to acts of Parliament, made to respect the plantations in general, and this colony in particular, and in our Executive Courts, both Juries and Judges have, to all intents and purposes, considered such acts as part of our rule of law. Such a constitution, in a plantation, is not peculiar to England, but agrees with the principles of the most celebrated writers upon the law of nations, that "when a nation takes possession of a distant country, and settles there, that country, though separated from the principal establishment, or mother country, naturally becomes a part of the state, equally with its ancient possessions."

So much, however, of the spirit of liberty breathes through all parts of the English constitution, that, although from the nature of government, there must be one supreme authority over the whole, yet this constitution will admit of subordinate powers with Legislative and Executive authority, greater or less, according to local and other circumstances. Thus we see a variety of corporations formed within the kingdom, with powers to make and execute such by-laws as are for their immediate use and benefit, the members of such corporations still remaining subject to the general laws of the kingdom. We see also governments established in the plantations, which, from their separate and remote situation, require more general and extensive powers of legislation within themselves, than those formed within the kingdom, but subject, nevertheless, to all such laws of the kingdom as immediately respect them, or are designed to extend to them; and, accordingly, we, in this province have, from the first settlement of it, been left to the exercise of our Legislative and Executive powers, Parliament occasionally, though rarely, interposing, as in its wisdom has been judged necessary.

Under this constitution, for more than one hundred years, the laws both of the supreme and subordinate authority were in general, duly executed; offenders against them have been brought to condign punishment, peace and order have been maintained, and the people of this province have experienced as largely the advantages of government, as, perhaps, any people upon the globe; and they have, from time to time, in the most public manner expressed their sense of it, and, once in every year, have offered up their united thanksgivings to God for the enjoyment of these privileges, and, as often, their united prayers for the continuance of them.

At length the constitution has been called in question, and the authority of the Parliament of Great Britain to make and establish laws for the inhabitants of this province has been, by many, denied. What was at first whispered with caution, was soon after openly asserted in print; and, of late, a number of inhabitants, in several of the principal towns in the province, having assembled together in their respective towns, and have assumed the name of legal town meetings, have passed resolves, which they have ordered to be placed upon their own records, and caused to be printed and published in pamphlets and newspapers. I am sorry that it is thus become impossible to conceal, what I could wish had never been made public. I will not particularize these resolves or votes, and shall only observe to you in general, that some of them deny the supreme authority of Parliament, and so are repugnant to the principles of the constitution, and that others speak of this supreme authority, of which the King is a constituent part, and to every act of which his assent is necessary, in such terms as have a direct tendency to alienate the affections of the people from their Sovereign, who has ever been most tender of their rights, and whose person, crown, and dignity, we are under every possible obligation to defend and support. In consequence of these resolves, committees of correspondence are formed in several of those towns, to maintain the principles upon which they are founded.

I know of no arguments, founded in reason, which will be sufficient to support these principles, or to justify the measures taken in consequence of them. It has been urged, that the sole power of making laws is granted, by charter, to a Legislature established in the province, consisting of the King, by his Representative the Governor, the Council, and the House of Representatives; that, by this charter, there are likewise granted, or assured to the inhabitants of the province, all the liberties and immunities of free and natural subjects, to all intents, constructions and purposes whatsoever, as if they had been born within the realms of England; that it is part of the liberties of English subjects, which has its foundation in nature, to be governed by laws made by their consent in person, or by their representative; that the subjects in this province are not, and cannot be represented in the Parliament of Great Britain, and, consequently, the acts of that Parliament cannot be binding upon them.

I do not find, gentlemen, in the charter, such an expression as sole power, or any words which import it. The General Court has, by charter, full power to make such laws, as are not repugnant to the laws of England. A favorable construction has been put upon this clause, when it has been allowed to intend such laws of England only, as are expressly declared to respect us. Surely then this is, by charter, a reserve of power and authority to Parliament to bind us by such laws, at least, as are made expressly to refer to us, and consequently, is a limitation of the power given to the General Court. Nor can it be contended, that, by the limits of free and natural subjects, is to be understood an exemption from acts of Parliament, because not represented there, seeing it is provided by the same charter, that such acts shall be in force; and if they that make the objection to such acts, will read the charter with attention, they must be convinced that this grant of liberties and immunities is nothing more than a declaration and assurance on the part of the Crown, that the place, to which their predecessors were about to remove, was, and would be considered as part of the dominions of the Crown of England, and, therefore, that the subjects of the Crown so removing, and those born there, or in their passage thither, or in their passage from thence, would not become aliens, but would, throughout all parts of the English dominions, wherever they might happen to be, as well as within the colony, retain the liberties and immunities of free and natural subjects, their removal from, or not being born within the realm notwithstanding. If the plantations be part of the dominions of the Crown, this clause in the charter does not confer or reserve any liberties, but what would have been enjoyed without it, and what the inhabitants of every other colony do enjoy where they are without a charter. If the plantations are not the dominions of the Crown, will not all that are born here, be considered as born out of the liegeance of the King of England, and, whenever they go into any parts of the dominions, will they not be deemed aliens to all intents and purposes, this grant in the charter notwithstanding?

They who claim exemption from acts of Parliament by virtue of their rights as Englishmen, should consider that it is impossible the rights of English subjects should be the same, in every respect, in all parts of the dominions. It is one of their rights as English subjects, to be governed by laws made by persons, in whose election they have, from time to time, a voice; they remove from the kingdom, where, perhaps, they were in the full exercise of this right, to the plantations, where it cannot be exercised, or where the exercise of it would be of no benefit to them. Does it follow that the government, by their removal from one part of the dominions to another, loses its authority over that part to which they remove, and that they are freed from the subjection they were under before; or do they expect that government should relinquish its authority because they cannot enjoy this particular right? Will it not rather be said, that by this, their voluntary removal, they have relinquished for a time at least, one of the rights of an English subject, which they might, if they pleased, have continued to enjoy, and may again enjoy, whensoever they will return to the place where it can be exercised?

They who claim exemption, as part of their rights by nature, should consider that every restraint which men are laid under by a state of government, is a privation of part of their natural rights; and of all the different forms of government which exist, there can be no two of them in which the departure from natural rights is exactly the same. Even in case of representation by election, do they not give up part of their natural rights when they consent to be represented by such person as shall be chosen by the majority of the electors, although their own voices may be for some other person? And is it not contrary to their natural rights to be obliged to submit to a representative for seven years, or even one year, after they are dissatisfied with his conduct, although they gave their voices for him when he was elected? This must, therefore, be considered as an objection against a state of government, rather than against any particular form.

If what I have said shall not be sufficient to satisfy such as object to the supreme authority of Parliament over the plantations, there may something further be added to induce them to an acknowledgment of it, which, I think, will well deserve their consideration. I know of no line that can be drawn between the supreme authority of Parliament and the total independence of the colonies: it is impossible there should be two independent Legislatures in one and the same state; for, although there may be but one head, the King, yet the two Legislative bodies will make two governments as distinct as the kingdoms of England and Scotland before the union. . . .

Answer of the House of Representatives

We fully agree with your Excellency, that our own happiness, as well as his Majesty's service, very much depends upon peace and order; and we shall at all times take such measures as are consistent with our constitution, and the rights of the people, to promote and maintain them. That the government at present is in a very disturbed state, is apparent. But we cannot ascribe it to the people's having adopted unconstitutional principles, which seems to be the cause assigned for it by your Excellency. It appears to us, to have been occasioned rather by the British House of Commons assuming and exercising a power inconsistent with the freedom of the constitution, to give and grant the property of the colonists, and appropriate the same without their consent. . . .

You are pleased to say, that, "when our predecessors first took possession of this plantation, or colony, under a grant and charter from the Crown of England, it was their sense, and it was the sense of the kingdom, that they were to remain subject to the supreme authority of Parliament;" whereby we understand your Excellency to mean, in the sense of the declaratory act of Parliament . . . in all cases whatever. And, indeed, it is difficult, if possible, to draw a line of distinction between the universal authority of Parliament over the colonies, and no authority at all. It is, therefore, necessary for us to inquire how it appears, for your Excellency has not shown it to us, that when, or at the time that our predecessors took possession of this plantation, or colony, under a grant and charter from the Crown of England, it was their sense, and the sense of the kingdom, that they were to remain subject to the authority of Parliament. In making this inquiry, we shall, according to your Excellency's recommendation, treat the subject with calmness and candor, and also with a due regard to truth. . . .

The King, in the first charter to this colony, expressly grants, that it "shall be construed, reputed and adjudged in all cases, most favorably on the behalf and for the benefit and behoof of the said Governor and Company, and their successors—any matter, cause or thing, whatsoever, to the contrary notwithstanding." It is one of the liberties of free and natural subjects, born and abiding within the realm, to be governed, as your Excellency observes, "by laws made by persons, in whose elections they, from time to time, have a voice." This is an essential right. For nothing is more evident, than, that any people, who are subject to the unlimited power of another, must be in a state of abject slavery. It was easily and plainly foreseen, that the right of representation in the English Parliament, could not be exercised by the people of this colony. It would be impracticable, if consistent with the English constitution. And for this reason, that this colony might have and enjoy all the liberties and immunities of free and natural subjects within the realm, as stipulated in the charter, it was necessary, and a Legislative was accordingly constituted within the colony; one branch of which, consists of Representatives chosen by the people, to make all laws, statutes, ordinances, &c. for the well ordering and governing the same, not repugnant to the laws of England, or, as nearly as conveniently might be, agreeable to the fundamental laws of the English constitution. We are, therefore, still at a loss to conceive, where your Excellency finds it "provided in the same charter, that such acts," viz. acts of Parliament, made expressly to refer to us, "shall be in force" in this province. There is nothing to this purpose, expressed in the charter, or in our opinion, even implied in it. And surely it would be very absurd, that a charter, which is evidently formed upon a supposition and intention, that a colony is and should be considered as not within the realm; and declared by the very Prince who granted it, to be not within the jurisdiction of Parliament, should yet provide, that the laws which the same Parliament should make, expressly to refer to that colony, should be in force therein. Your Excellency is pleased to ask, "does it follow, that the government, by their (our ancestors) removal from one part of the dominions to another, loses its authority over that part to which they remove; and that they are freed from the subjection they were under before?" We answer, if that part of the King's dominions, to which they removed, was not then a part of the realm, and was never annexed to it, the Parliament lost no authority over it, having never had such authority; and the emigrations were consequently freed from the subjection they were under before their removal. The power and authority of Parliament, being constitutionally confined within the limits of the realm, and the nation collectively, of which alone it is the representing and Legislative Assembly. Your Excellency further asks, "will it not rather be said, that by this, their voluntary removal, they have relinquished, for a time, at least, one of the rights of an English subject, which they might, if they pleased, have continued to enjoy, and may again enjoy, whenever they return to the place where it can be exercised?" To which we answer; they never did relinquish the right to be governed by laws, made by persons in whose election they had a voice. The King stipulated with them, that they should have and enjoy all the liberties of free and natural subjects, born within the realm, to all intents, purposes and constructions, whatsoever; that is, that they should be as free as those, who were to abide within the realm: consequently, he stipulated with them, that they should enjoy and exercise this most essential right, which discriminates freemen from vassals, uninterruptedly, in its full sense and meaning; and they did, and ought still to exercise it, without the necessity of returning, for the sake of exercising it, to the nation or state of England. . . .

Your Excellency tells us, "you know of no line that can be drawn between the supreme authority of Parliament and the total independence of the colonies." If there be no such line, the consequence is, either that the colonies are the vassals of the Parliament, or that they are totally independent. As it cannot be supposed to have been the intention of the parties in the compact, that we should be reduced to a state of vassalage, the conclusion is, that it was their sense, that we were thus independent. "It is impossible," your Excellency says, "that there should be two independent Legislatures in one and the same state." May we not then further conclude, that it was their sense, that the colonies were, by their charters, made distinct states from the mother country? Your Excellency adds, "for although there may be but one head, the King, yet the two Legislative bodies will make two governments as distinct as the kingdoms of England and Scotland, before the union." Very true, may it please your Excellency; and if they interfere not with each other, what hinders, but that being united in one head and common Sovereign, they may live happily in that connection, and mutually support and protect each other? Notwithstanding all the terrors which your Excellency has pictured to us as the effects of a total independence, there is more reason to dread the consequences of absolute uncontroled power, whether of a nation or a monarch, than those of a total independence. It would be a misfortune "to know by experience, the difference between the liberties of an English colonist and those of the Spanish, French, and Dutch:" and since the British Parliament has passed an act, which is executed even with rigor, though not voluntarily submitted to, for raising a revenue, and appropriating the same, without the consent of the people who pay it, and have claimed a power of making such laws as they please, to order and govern us, your Excellency will excuse us in asking, whether you do not think we already experience too much of such a difference, and have not reason to fear we shall soon be reduced to a worse situation than that of the colonies of France, Spain, or Holland? . . .

After all that we have said, we would be far from being understood to have in the least abated that just sense of allegiance which we owe to the King of Great Britain, our rightful Sovereign; and should the people of this province be left to the free and full exercise of all the liberties and immunities granted to them by charter, there would be no danger of an independence on the Crown. Our charters reserve great power to the Crown in its Representative, fully sufficient to balance, analogous to the English constitution, all the liberties and privileges granted to the people. All this your Excellency knows full well; and whoever considers the power and influence, in all their branches, reserved by our charter, to the Crown, will be far from thinking that the Commons of this province are too independent.

SELECTION

The Burning of the "Gaspee"

The most dramatic interruption of the general calm that settled over imperial-colonial relations after 1770 occurred in Rhode Island. The British customs schooner Gaspee, *commanded by Lieutenant William Dudingston and stationed in Rhode Island waters since March 22, 1772, to help in enforcing the Navigation Acts and other imperial commercial regulations, ran aground on June 9 a few miles below Providence. Late that night several boatloads of men from Providence under the leadership of John Brown (1736–1803), one of the principal merchants of Rhode Island, boarded the ship, wounded Dudingston, sent the crew ashore, and burned the ship to the water's edge. These events are described in the two documents published below. The first, Selection 19 A, is the deposition of William Dickinson, midshipman of the* Gaspee. *The second is a letter of Rhode Island Governor Joseph Wanton to the Earl of Hillsborough in which Wanton tried to give Hillsborough some sense of the provocations that led to the destruction of the* Gaspee.*

The response of the ministry to this bold attack on one of the King's ships was the offer of a reward of £500 for the identification of the guilty parties and the appointment of a royal commission to inquire into the affair and send those responsible to Britain for trial. Despite the reward, the commission, which met at Newport in early 1773, failed to uncover sufficient evidence to warrant any arrests.

David S. Lovejoy, Rhode Island Politics and the American Revolution 1760–1776 *(1958), and William R. Leslie, "The Gaspee Affair: A Study of its Constitutional Significance,"* Mississippi *Valley Historical Review,* volume 39 *(1952), pages 233–256, trace the details and analyze the significance of the burning of the* Gaspee.

A. A BRITISH SAILOR DESCRIBES THE ATTACK: DEPOSITION OF WILLIAM DICKINSON (JUNE 11, 1772)*

William Dickinson, midshipman of His Majesty's schooner Gaspee, sayeth:
    That the said schooner was at single anchor about three leagues below

* Reprinted in full from John Russell Bartlett (ed.), *Records of the Colony of Rhode Island and Providence Plantations in New England* (10 vols., 1856–1865), vol. VII, pp. 82–84.

Providence, in Rhode Island government, 10th of June, 1772, and about half past twelve o'clock, in the night or morning, the watch gave the alarm that a number of boats were coming down the river, and very near us (being an exceeding dark night), we hailed them, and ordered them to keep off.

They instantly gave us three cheers; on which, we fired at them with muskets, which they immediately returned with a half a dozen muskets (or thereabouts). We then fired our pistols, on which they boarded us upon the starboard bow, and fired a number of small arms. Immediately Lieutenant Dudingston (her commander,) cried out, "Good God, I am done for." He was wounded in his groin and arm.

While we were disputing forward, relative to their boarding us, three other boats boarded us, upon the quarter. In the three boats which boarded us upon the quarter, there were thirty or forty men, at least; and in the whole, I suppose about one hundred and fifty in number, on which we thought proper (the lieutenant being wounded,) to surrender.

When they had got possession of the schooner, they used the people very ill, by pinioning of them, and throwing them into their boats, and refused the lieutenant and officers any necessaries but what they had on, and not even suffered the commanding officer to have his papers, and robbed his servant of several silver spoons, and throwed his linen and apparel overboard.

We were then sent ashore, in two different boats; the lieutenant and part of the men in one boat, and myself with the rest of the people in the other boat, at the distance of about two miles asunder, as we found at daylight. I remained on the beach; and about half past three o'clock, saw the schooner on fire; and about half past four, I saw three boats put off from her, full of men, and rowed up towards Providence; and an hour after, another boat came by her, and landed her men at Pawtuxet.

Questions by Admiral Montagu

Q.—How long had you been lying in Providence River?

A.—We came to an anchor there, at about four o'clock, in the afternoon of the 9th of June.

Q.—Had you sent any boat ashore?

A.—No; but employed sounding the harbor.

Q.—Had you been at Providence before, during the time you were upon that station?

A.—No.

Q.—Do you imagine that the people who boarded you, came from Providence?

A.—Yes; I believe the most part, but cannot say all, as one boat landed her men at Pawtuxet.

Q.—What distance is Pawtuxet from Providence, by land?

A.—Five miles.

Q.—What distance were the boats from the schooner, when they were first seen?

A.—I was not upon deck at first, myself; but when I saw them, they were about one hundred yards.

Q.—Why did you not fire your great guns at them?

A.—They boarded us upon the bows, and were so near to us, that we had not time to get our guns out at the bow ports.

Q.—Did any of the people that boarded you, appear like gentlemen?

A.—Yes; many of them appeared like men of credit and tradesmen; and but few like common men.

Q.—Did they make use of any opprobrious language?

A.—Yes; by threatening to put the lieutenant to death, and calling us piratical rascals.

Q.—Where did you leave the Beaver?

A.—Off Golden Island, in the mouth of Seaconnet Passage.

Q.—What distance from you?

A.—About twenty-five miles.

Q.—Could she be in sight when this happened?

A.—No; the main land is between.

Q.—Is there any thing more that you can recollect?

A.—Yes; one of the people took me by the collar, and said, "D—n you, where is your pilot Daggett?" I answered, he was discharged six weeks ago. He answered, "D—n your blood, you lie;" and said they would find him, and flee him alive.

Q.—Did they suffer the lieutenant to put on any clothes, after he was wounded?

A.—No; he was in his shirt, with his great coat over his shoulders, and a blanket round his body.

Q.—Was any other person wounded, except the lieutenant?

A.—Yes; one in the head.

And I further declare, that when Lieutenant Dudingston came on deck, I saw him go and stand by the starboard foreshrouds, in his shirt, with a pistol in one hand and a hanger in the other. After he was wounded, he got aft, and sat down by the cabin companion way, when the two ring-leaders, with a number following them, came to him, and said:

"Now, you piratical rascal, we have got you. D—n you, we will hang you all by the laws of Great Britain. D—n you, what made you fire, when we answered you that the head sheriff was in the boat?"

The captain (N. B. The head sheriff and captain are fictitious names that the ring-leaders went by) said, "Stand aside, let me dispatch the piratical dog."

He then lifted a handspike over Mr. Dudingston's head, who asked "if they would give no quarters?"

They answered "No."

He then desired they would let me bind up his wounds, for he was shot, and showed them the wound in his left arm.

They then said, "D—n your blood, you are shot by your own people."

He was then taken down into the cabin, by some of the mob. They then pinioned me, and put me into the boat, where I remained for half an hour; when one of the mob called to their people in the boat to loosen me, for the lieutenant wanted me. I went down in the cabin to him. He was laid on the after lockers, and one of the mob washing and binding up his wounds. The mob then got him on deck and put him into a boat, and put off.

Soon after, I was ordered into the boat again, and put off. In going on shore, I saw a negro with the lieutenant's hanger; being asked by another how he got it, he said he took it from the captain.

Being down in the cabin, with Lieutenant Dudingston, the ring-leaders, and some of the principal of the mob demanded his papers and orders for his proceeding in such piratical manner. I then showed them the commission from the lords of the admiralty, with all his orders and instructions that he had received from the admiral, which they took and carried away.

In going ashore, one of the mob that rowed the boat, said, that he and several more, would not have been there, but that they were taken out of a house by force, and compelled to go; that they beat a drum round the town of Providence, in the evening, to raise a mob.   W. DICKINSON

B. THE CASE AGAINST THE ''GASPEE'': GOVERNOR JOSEPH WANTON TO EARL OF HILLSBOROUGH (JUNE 16, 1772)*

My Lord:—I did myself the honor to write to Your Lordship on the 20th ultimo. I am now reduced to the necessity of addressing Your Lordship upon a most disagreeable subject; the destruction of the schooner Gaspee, under the command of Lieutenant William Dudingston, by persons unknown. The particulars relating to this unwarrantable transaction, so far as I have been able to collect them, are as follows:

On the 9th inst., she run aground on a point of land called Namquit, a little below Pawtuxet, on the Narragansett River, within this colony. About three-quarters of an hour after twelve o'clock, at night, there being but one hand on deck, six or seven boats, full of men, were by him discovered drawing towards said schooner; and before many of her hands had time to get upon deck, was boarded by the people in the boats, who, as soon as they had secured the possession of the schooner, took out the captain and all the people, and set them ashore on the main land; after which, they set fire to the schooner. In the attack, Mr. Dudingston was wounded by a ball through his arm, from whence it passed and lodged in some part of his body.

Mr. Sessions, the Deputy Governor of this colony, immediately upon hearing of this unhappy affair, went to Mr. Dudingston, and offered him all the help and assistance in his power; but Mr. Dudingston said he wanted no favors for himself.

The Deputy Governor then told him, that he came not only to offer him any relief his distressed circumstances might require, but also to gain a declaration from his own mouth respecting the destruction of the schooner under his command, that proper and rigorous measures might be taken to discover and bring the perpetrators to justice.

Mr. Dudingston answered, he would give him no account, because of his indisposition; and also, because it was his duty to forbear any thing of that kind, till he had done it to his commanding officer, at a court martial, to which, if he lived, he must be called; but if he died, he desired it might all die with him.

The Deputy Governor, with the consent of Mr. Dudingston, then pro-

*Reprinted in full from Bartlett (ed.), *Records of the Colony of Rhode Island and Providence Plantations in New England* (10 vols. 1856–1865), vol. VII, pp. 90–92.

ceeded to examine a number of his men, and, on the 11th, transmitted copies of the most material of the examinations to me; upon the receipt whereof, I immediately convened such of His Majesty's Council and the house of deputies as could be seasonably notified, and laid before them the proceedings of the Deputy Governor, which they highly approved of, and unanimously recommended my issuing a proclamation, with a reward of £100, sterling, for the discovery of any of the persons concerned in this violent insult upon government, which I cheerfully complied with, and sent them into the several towns within this colony.

This transaction gives me the utmost uneasiness; and Your Lordship may be assured, that the utmost vigilance of the civil authority will not be wanting, to bring the perpetrators to exemplary and condign punishment; and in justice to the inhabitants of the colony, I must not omit mentioning, that the conduct of those who committed this outrage, is, by them, universally condemned.

I wish, My Lord, those officers who have lately been sent into this colony, under a pretence of assisting trade, had conducted with that temper, prudence and discretion which persons entrusted with the execution of the laws ought, upon every occasion, to manifest.

In my last, I informed Your Lordship, that the inhabitants had been insulted without any just cause; and I am extremely sorry that I have still reason to say, that the trade of this colony is interrupted in a most unprecedented and oppressive manner, without contributing, in the least, to the service of the revenue. Inward bound vessels have been detained several days, without the least colorable pretext, and then delivered up.

One from South Kingstown, for having on board a small quantity of tobacco, of the growth of this colony, which the owner was transporting to Newport, for a market; another, for having only three or four dozen wine laid in by the captain, for sea stores. The small freight boats, plying between the several towns, with the produce of the colony, are, by the severity of these officers, subjected to great inconvenience, which very sensibly affects the whole colony; and particularly, the town of Newport, its metropolis, whose inhabitants are principally supplied with the necessaries of life by water; and the obstructions they now experience, have contributed not a little to enhance the price of fuel and provisions, to the great disadvantage of the town; and in my humble opinion, if such measures are permitted to be pursued, the colony will ere long be involved in the deepest calamity.

These, My Lord, are serious and important truths; and as Your Lordship, from your thorough knowledge of the colony, must be perfectly acquainted with the nature and extent of our trade, the profits of which, ultimately centering in Great Britain, for the purchase of her manufactures, I have no room to doubt of Your Lordship's interposition in behalf of this colony, that all cause of complaint against any of the King's officers stationed here, may be removed, and the inhabitants treated with that respect which is due to the subjects of His Britannic Majesty.

As a proof, My Lord, that the trade of this colony stands upon as fair and legal a footing as the trade of any part of His Majesty's dominions, out of two hundred sail of vessels which have entered this port since the 1st day of March last, only two in that number have been prosecuted and condemned for breach of acts of trade, one of which, belongs to the Massachusetts Bay, notwithstanding they have been searched and rummaged with the greatest severity. These two vessels, although seized and condemned here, were sent by Capt. Linzee, of the Beaver, and Lieut. Dudingston, to Boston, for sale, in direct opposition to the orders of the court of vice admiralty, within this colony; and the marshal of the said court prevented by force from libelling one of these vessels for payment of the mariners' wages.

These, My Lord, are but a few of the many grievances which the people of this colony have been for months past harrassed and perplexed with; but as the General Assembly will soon be convened, I make no doubt they will order a more particular remonstrance to be made.

In the mean time, permit me, My Lord, to implore your attention to the complaints of a much abused and injured people, whose loyalty and affection to their sovereign, claims Your Lordship's countenance and patronage.

J. WANTON

SELECTION

Establishment of Intercolonial Committees of Correspondence: The Virginia Resolves (Mar. 12, 1773)

If the royal commission to inquire into the destruction of the Gaspee *did not succeed in bringing the guilty parties to trial, its appointment did result in the extension of Samuel Adams's provincial system of committees of correspondence throughout the colonies. Taking the lead in this development was the Virginia House of* Burgesses. *Alarmed by the rumor that the commission was empowered to remove suspects to Britain for trial, the Burgesses adopted a set of resolves, reprinted in full below from the* Journals of the House of Burgesses 1772–76, *page 28. These resolves established a committee on March 12, 1773, to inquire into the matter and to establish a correspondence with other colonies about any "proceedings tending to deprive" the colonists "of their ancient, legal and constitutional Rights" and directed the speaker of the House to propose to the speakers in the other colonies that they recommend similar action by their lower houses. Over the following year every colonial legislature except those of North Carolina and Pennsylvania acted favorably on the Virginia proposal.*

Whereas, the minds of his Majesty's faithful Subjects in this Colony have been much disturbed, by various Rumours and Reports of proceedings tending to deprive them of their ancient, legal and constitutional Rights.

And *whereas,* the affairs of this Colony are frequently connected with those of *Great Britain,* as well as of the neighboring *Colonies,* which renders a Communication of Sentiments necessary; in Order therefore to remove the

Uneasinesses, and to quiet the minds of the People, as well as for the other good purposes above mentioned.

Be it *resolved,* that a standing Committee of Correspondence and inquiry be appointed to consist of eleven Persons, to wit, the Honourable *Peyton Randolph,* Esquire, *Robert Carter Nicholas, Richard Bland, Richard Henry Lee, Benjamin Harrison, Edmund Pendleton, Patrick Henry, Dudley Diggs, Dabney Carr, Archibald Cary,* and *Thomas Jefferson,* Esquires, any six of whom to be a Committee, whose business it shall be to obtain the most early and Authentic intelligence of all such Acts and *Resolutions* of the *British Parliament,* or proceedings *of* Administration, as may relate to or affect the British Colonies in America, and to keep up and maintain a Correspondence and Communication with our Sister Colonies, respecting these important Considerations; and the result of such their proceedings, from Time to Time, to lay before this House.

Resolved, that it be an instruction to the said Committee, that they do, without delay, inform themselves particularly of the principles and Authority, on which was constituted a *Court of inquiry,* said to have been lately held in *Rhode Island,* with Powers to transmit Persons, accused of Offences committed in *America,* to places beyond the Seas, to be tried. . . .

Resolved, that the Speaker of this House do transmit to the Speakers of the different Assemblys of the British Colonies, on the Continent, Copies of the said Resolutions, and desire that they will lay them before their respective Assemblies; and request them to appoint some Person or Persons, of their respective Bodies, to communicate, from Time to Time, with the said Committee.

The Tea Act Revives the Dispute

A Rescue Operation: The Tea Act (May 10, 1773)

It was not the isolated incidents in South Carolina, Massachusetts, and Rhode Island but Parliament's attempt to shore up the sagging fortunes of the East India Company by the Tea Act of 1773 that shattered the uneasy calm that had prevailed in imperial-colonial relations since the repeal of most of the Townshend duties in 1770. Not in any sense a punitive or a repressive measure, the Tea Act was intended simply to help the East India Company avoid bankruptcy by enabling it to dispose of part of 17 million pounds of surplus tea in America on unusually favorable terms. Formerly, East India Company tea had been sold only at public auction in London to wholesale merchants who in turn sold it to retail merchants in either Britain or the colonies. By enabling the East India Company to sell its tea directly to agents in the colonies, the Tea Act eliminated the costs involved in working through British wholesale merchants. By providing for the remission of all duties charged in Britain on tea that was reexported to the colonies, it further sought to make East India Company tea so cheap that even with the disadvantage of the 3d Townshend duty on tea—which was still in effect in the colonies—the Company could undersell all competitors in the colonial market, legitimate colonial tea merchants as well as the smugglers of Dutch tea who had been doing a thriving business throughout the early 1770s, especially in New York and Philadelphia. The East India Company immediately moved to take advantage of its new privileges. During the summer of 1773 it designated selected American firms in each major port as consignees and secured a license to export 600,000 pounds of tea to the colonies. The more important portions of the Tea Act are reprinted here from Danby Pickering (ed.), Statutes at Large, *volume XXX, pages 75–77.*

Excellent discussions of the events and considerations leading to passage of the Tea Act will be found in Benjamin Woods Labaree, The Boston Tea Party *(1964), and Bernard Donoughue,* British Politics and the American Revolution: The Path to War 1773–75 *(1964).*

. . . Be it enacted . . . [I.] That there shall be drawn back and allowed for all teas, which, from and after the tenth day of *May,* one thousand seven hundred and seventy-three, shall be sold at the publick sales of the said united [East India] company, or which shall be imported by licence . . . and which shall, at any time hereafter, be exported from this kingdom, as merchandise, to any of the *British* colonies or plantations in *America,* the whole of the duties of customs payable upon the importation of such teas . . . .

III. And be it further enacted by the authority aforesaid, That it shall and may be lawful for the commissioners of his Majesty's treasury, or any three or more of them, or for the high treasurer for the time being, upon application made to them by the said united company of merchants of *England* trading to the *East Indies* for that purpose, to grant a licence or licences to the said united company, to take out of their warehouses, without the same having been put up to sale, and to export to any of the *British* plantations in *America,* or to any parts beyond the seas, such quantity or quantities of tea as the said commissioners of his Majesty's treasury, or any three or more of them, or the high treasurer for the time being, shall think proper and expedient, without incurring any penalty or forfeiture for so doing . . .

IV. . . . That from and after the passing of this act, it shall and may be lawful for the commissioners of his Majesty's treasury, or any three or more of them, or the high treasurer for the time being, to grant a licence or licences to the said united company, to take out of their warehouses such quantities of tea as the said commissioners of the treasury, or any three or more of them, or the high treasurer for the time being, shall think proper, without the same having been exposed to sale in this kingdom; and to export such tea to any of the *British* colonies or plantations in *America,* or to foreign parts, discharged from the payment of any customs or duties whatsoever; any thing in the said recited act, or any other act to the contrary notwithstanding. . . .

SELECTION

Colonial Opposition to the Tea Act

The Tea Act had an unexpected reception in the colonies as colonial leaders interpreted it simply as a clever ruse to inveigle Americans into paying the 3d duty on tea and thereby openly admitting Parliament's right to tax the colonies. A secondary concern of special importance to colonial merchants in general and smugglers of Dutch tea in particular was the threat of monopoly. If Parliament could give the East India Company a virtual monopoly on the colonial tea market by legislative fiat, then it could do the same with any other commodity to the gross detriment of the colonial mercantile community. A mass meeting in Philadelphia on October 16, 1773, took the lead in opposing the act, adopting a set of resolves condemning the tax on tea and the regulations permitting the East India Company to send tea directly to America as part of a "ministerial plan" to "introduce arbitrary government and slavery" into the colonies, branded any one who "countenanced" the attempt "an enemy to his country," and appointed a committee to urge the merchants the East India Company had named as consignees in Philadelphia to resign. In the face of such pressure, the consignees did resign. Similar actions by the Sons of Liberty in New York were equally successful, but in Boston the tea consignees, who included two sons of Governor Hutchinson, steadfastly refused to resign.

The situation in Boston became critical after the arrival of the Dartmouth, *the first of three tea ships sent to that port, on November 27. The patriots, with wide public support, were determined that the tea should never be permitted to land and should be sent back to England without payment of the tea duty. With equal resolve, however, Hutchinson refused to permit the* Dartmouth *to leave the harbor until the duty had been paid. This impasse continued for twenty days until December 16, when the* Dartmouth, *according to law, became subject to seizure for non-payment of duties. To prevent the seizure, landing, and possible sale of the tea, about two hundred men dressed as Indians and cheered on by a crowd estimated to be as large as 8,000 people proceeded on the evening of the sixteenth to dump into Boston Harbor from the three vessels 342 chests of tea worth about £9,000. The* Boston Tea Party *was reenacted elsewhere in the colonies over the next year as the colonists successfully nullified the Tea Act either by destroying the tea, preventing its landing, or, as in Charleston, storing it until it was later sold by the Revolutionary government to raise funds for the War for Independence.*

The nature and intensity of colonial objections to the Tea Act and the measures taken to nullify it may be surmised from the two documents below. Selection 22 A is "The Association and Resolves of the New York Sons of Liberty" adopted on December 15, 1773, and Selection 22 B consists of three excerpts from letters of John Andrews, a Boston merchant, describing the Boston Tea Party and the events that preceded it.

Benjamin Woods Labaree, The Boston Tea Party (1964), contains a full account of the colonial opposition to the Tea Act.

A. THWARTING THE "DIABOLICAL PROJECT OF ENSLAVING AMERICA": "THE ASSOCIATION AND RESOLVES OF THE NEW YORK SONS OF LIBERTY" (DEC. 15, 1773)*

To the Public.

New York, December 15, 1773.

The following association is signed by a great number of the principal gentlemen of the city, merchants, lawyers, and other inhabitants of all ranks, and it is still carried about the city, to give an opportunity to those who have not yet signed to unite with their fellow-citizens, to testify their abhorrence to the diabolical project of enslaving America.

The Association of the Sons of Liberty of New York

It is essential to the freedom and security of a free people, that no taxes be imposed upon them but by their own consent, or their representatives. For "what property have they in that which another may, by right, take when he pleases tò himself?" The former is the undoubted right of Englishmen, to secure which they expended millions and sacrificed the lives of thousands. And yet, to the astonishment of all the world, and the grief of America, the commons of Great Britain, after the repeal of the memorable and detestable stamp-act, reassumed the power of imposing taxes on the American colonies; and, insisting on it as a necessary badge of parliamentary supremacy, passed a bill, in the seventh year of his present majesty's reign, imposing duties on all glass, painters' colors, paper and teas, that should, after the 20th of November, 1767, be "imported from Great Britain into any colony or plantation in America."—This bill, after the concurrence of the lords, obtained the royal assent. And thus they who, from time immemorial, have exercised the right of giving to, or withholding from the crown, their aids and subsidies, according to their *own free will and pleasure*, signified by their representatives in parliament, do, by the act in question, deny us, their brethren in America, the enjoyment of the same right. As this denial, and the execution of that act, involves our slavery, and would sap the foundation of our free-

* These excerpts are reprinted from Hezekiah Niles, *Principles and Acts of the Revolution*, pp. 169–170.

dom, whereby we should become slaves to our brethren and fellow subjects, born to no greater stock of freedom than the Americans—the merchants and inhabitants of this city, in conjunction with the merchants and inhabitants of the ancient American colonies, entered into an agreement to decline a part of their commerce with Great Britain, until the above mentioned act should be totally repealed. This agreement operated so powerfully to the disadvantage of the manufacturers of England that many of them were unemployed. To appease their clamors, and to provide the subsistence for them, which the non-importation had deprived them of, the parliament, in 1770, repealed so much of the revenue act as imposed a duty on glass, painters' colors, and paper, and left the duty on tea, as *a test of the parliamentary right to tax us*. The merchants of the cities of New York and Philadelphia, having strictly adhered to the agreement, so far as it is related to the importation of articles subject to an American duty, have convinced the ministry, that some other measures must be adopted to execute parliamentary supremacy over this country, and to remove the distress brought on the East India company, by the ill-policy of that act. Accordingly, to increase the temptation to the shippers of tea from England, an act of parliament passed the last session, which gives the whole duty on tea, the company were subject to pay, upon the importation of it into England, to the purchasers and exporters; and when the company have ten millions of pounds of tea, in their ware-houses exclusive of the quantity they may want to ship, they are allowed to export tea, discharged from the payment of that duty, with which they were before chargeable. In hopes of aid in the execution of this project, by the influence of the owners of the American ships, application was made by the company to the captains of those ships to take the tea on freight; but they virtuously rejected it. Still determined on the scheme, they have chartered ships to bring the tea to this country, which may be hourly expected, to make an important trial of our virtue. If they succeed in the sale of that tea, we shall have no property that we can call our own, and then we may bid adieu to American liberty.——Therefore, to prevent a calamity which, of all others, is the most to be dreaded—slavery, and its terrible concomitants—we, the subscribers, being influenced from a regard to liberty, and disposed to use all lawful endeavors in our power, to defeat the pernicious project, and to transmit to our posterity, those blessings of freedom which our ancestors have handed down to us; and to contribute to the support of the common liberties of America, which are in danger to be subverted, *do*, for those important purposes, agree to associate together, under the name and style of the *sons of New York*, and engage our honor to, and with each other faithfully to observe and perform the following *resolutions, viz.*

1st. *Resolved,* That whoever shall aid, or abet, or in any manner assist, in the introduction of tea, from any place whatsoever, into this colony, while it is subject, by a British act of parliament, to the payment of a duty, for the purpose of raising a revenue in America, he shall be deemed an enemy to the liberties of America.

2d. *Resolved,* That whoever shall be aiding, or assisting, in the landing, or carting of such tea, from any ship, or vessel, or shall hire any house, store-house, or cellar or any place whatsoever, to deposit the tea, subject to a duty as aforesaid, he shall be deemed an enemy to the liberties of America.

3d. *Resolved,* That whoever shall sell, or buy, or in any manner contribute to the sale, or purchase of tea, subject to a duty as aforesaid, or shall aid, or abet, in transporting such tea, by land or water, from this city, until the 7th George III.

chap. 46, commonly called the revenue act, shall be totally and clearly repealed, he shall be deemed an enemy to the liberties of America.

4th. *Resolved,* That whether the duties on tea, imposed by this act, be paid in Great Britain or in America, our liberties are equally affected.

5th. *Resolved,* That whoever shall transgress any of these resolutions, we will not deal with, or employ, or have any connection with him.

B. THE BOSTON TEA PARTY: JOHN ANDREWS TO WILLIAM BARRELL (NOV. 29, DEC. 1, DEC. 18, 1773)*

November 29th. Hall and Bruce arriv'd Saturday evening with each an hundred and odd chests of the detested Tea. What will be done with it, can't say: but I tremble for ye consequences should ye consignees still persist in their obstinacy and not consent to reship it. They have softened down so far as to offer it to the care of Council or the town, till such times as they hear from their friends in England, but am perswaded, from the present dispositions of ye people, that no other alternative will do, than to have it immediately sent back to London again. . . . Ye bells are ringing for a general muster, and a third vessel is now arriv'd in Nantasket road. Handbills are stuck up, calling upon Friends! Citizens! and Countrymen!

December 1st. Having just return'd from Fire Club, and am now, in company with the two Miss Masons and Mr. Williams of your place, at Sam. Eliot's, who has been dining with him at Col. Hancock's, and acquaints me that Mr. Palfrey sets off Express for New York and Philadelphia at five o'clock tomorrow morning, to communicate ye transactions of this town respecting the tea. . . . I acquainted you that Bruce and Hall had arrived, which was a mistake, as only Hall has arriv'd; which has caus'd ye most spirited and firm conduct to be observ'd that ever was known: the regularity and particulars of which proceedings Mr. Palfrey will be able to tell you. The consignees have all taken their residence at the Castle, as they still persist in their refusal to take the tea back. Its not only ye town, but the country are unanimous against the landing it, and at the Monday and Tuesday Meetings, they attended to the number of some hundreds from all the neighboring towns within a dozen miles:—'twould puzzle any person to purchase a pair of p—ls in town, as they are all bought up, with a full determination to repel force by force.

December 18th. However precarious our situation may be, yet *such* is the present calm composure of the people that a stranger would hardly think that ten thousand pounds sterling of the East India Company's *tea* was destroy'd the night, or rather the evening before last, yet its a serious truth; and if your's, together with ye other Southern provinces, should rest satisfied with *their* quota being stor'd, poor Boston will feel the whole weight of ministerial vengeance. However, its the opinion of most people that we stand an equal chance now, whether troops are sent in consequence of it or not; whereas, had it been stor'd, we should inevitably have had 'em, to enforce the sale of it.—The affair was transacted with the greatest regularity and despatch. Mr. Rotch finding he exposed himself not only to the loss of his

* These selections are reprinted from *Proceedings of the Massachusetts Historical Society,* 1st ser., vol. 8 (1864–1865), pp. 324–326.

ship but for ye value of the tea in case he sent her back with it, *without a clearance from the custom house,* as ye Admiral kept a ship in readiness to make a seizure of it whenever it should sail under *those circumstances;* therefore declin'd complying with his former promises, and absolutely declar'd his vessel should not carry it, without a *proper* clearance could be procur'd or he to be indemnified for the value of her:—when a general muster was assembled, from this and all ye neighbouring towns, to the number of five or six thousand, at 10 o'clock Thursday morning in the Old South Meeting house, where they pass'd a *unanimous* vote that the *Tea* should go out of the *harbour* that afternoon, and sent a committee with Mr. Rotch to ye Custom house to *demand* a clearance, which the collector told 'em was not in his power to give, without the duties being first paid. They then sent Mr. Rotch to Milton, to ask for a pass from ye Governor, who sent for answer, that "consistent with the rules of government and his duty to the King he could not grant one without they produc'd a previous clearance from the office."—By the time he return'd with this message the candles were light in [the] house, and upon reading it, such prodigious shouts were made, that induc'd me, while drinking tea at home, to go out and know the cause of it. The house was so crouded I could get no farther than ye porch, when I found the moderator was just declaring the meeting to be *dissolv'd,* which caused another general shout, out doors and in, and three cheers. What with that, and the consequent noise of breaking up the meeting, you'd thought that the inhabitants of the infernal regions had broke loose. For my part, I went contentedly home and finish'd my tea, but was soon inform'd what was going forward: but still not crediting it without ocular demonstration, I went and was *satisfied.* They muster'd, I'm told, upon Fort Hill, to the number of about two hundred, and proceeded, two by two, to Griffin's wharf, where Hall, Bruce, and Coffin lay, each with 114 chests of the *ill fated* article on board; the two former with *only* that article, but ye latter arriv'd at ye wharf only ye day before, was freighted with a large quantity of other goods, which they took the *greatest* care not to injure in the least, and before *nine* o'clock in ye evening, every chest from on board the three vessels was knock'd to pieces and flung over ye sides. They say the actors were *Indians* from *Narragansett.* Whether they were or not, to a transient observer they appear'd as *such,* being cloath'd in Blankets with the heads muffled, and copper color'd countenances, being each arm'd with a hatchet or axe, and pair pistols, nor was their *dialect* different from what I conceive these geniusses to *speak,* as their jargon was unintelligible to all but themselves. Not the least insult was offer'd to any person, save one Captain Conner, a letter of horses in this place, not many years since remov'd from *dear Ireland,* who had ript up the lining of his coat and waistcoat under the arms, and watching his opportunity had nearly fill'd 'em with tea, but being detected, was handled pretty roughly. They not only stripp'd him of his cloaths, but gave him a coat of mud, with a severe bruising into the bargain; and nothing but their utter aversion to make *any* disturbance prevented his being tar'd and feather'd.

Should not have troubled you with this, by this Post, hadn't I thought you would be glad of a more particular account of so *important a transaction,* than you could have obtain'd by common report; and if it affords my brother but a *temporary* amusement, I shall be more than repaid for the trouble of writing it. . . .

The Intolerable Acts

The British political community received the news of the Boston Tea Party with shock and anger. Hostility toward Massachusetts patriots was already high because of the attempts of the House of Representatives in the summer of 1773 first to impeach and then to persuade the Crown to remove Hutchinson and Lieutenant Governor Andrew Oliver for earlier having given "false" advice about the colony. This advice was contained in ten letters to Thomas Whateley that had somehow fallen into the hands of Benjamin Franklin, then agent for the House in London, after Whateley's death in 1772. Franklin sent the letters to Speaker Thomas Cushing with the admonition not to make them public, but Samuel Adams read them to the House in June, 1773, and later published them. The hearings before the Privy Council on the House's petition for removal were in progress when reports of the Tea Party first arrived in London in late January, 1774. The severe verbal lashing administered to Franklin for his part in the affair by Solicitor General Alexander Wedderburn before the Privy Council on January 29, along with the dismissal of Franklin from his post as Deputy Postmaster General for America on the following day, presaged the government response to the Tea Party.

There was almost universal sentiment, even among friends of the colonies such as Edmund Burke and the Earl of Chatham, that the time for temporizing was over and that firm measures had to be taken to bring the colony of Massachusetts Bay to a due obedience to the authority of Parliament. The ministry first considered the possibilities of handling the matter by executive action, thereby side-stepping the question of parliamentary authority, and of taking punitive action against only the parties responsible for the Tea Party. With the failure of the Gaspee commission fresh in mind, however, and the improbability of being able to discover the guilty parties and bring them to justice, the ministry eventually decided both to turn to Parliament and to take a series of blanket punitive actions against the whole town of Boston and the colony of Massachusetts Bay.

These actions were embodied in the decision to replace Hutchinson as governor with General Thomas Gage, commander in chief of British forces in North America, and in four Coercive Acts passed by Parliament in the spring of 1774. These acts consisted of the Boston Port Act, which closed the port of Boston beginning June 1, 1774, until the East India Company had been repaid for the losses it had suffered as a result of the Tea Party; the Administration of Justice Act, which empowered the Massachusetts governor to transfer either to Britain or to another colony for trial any official or soldier accused of a capital crime committed in the line of duty who could not expect a fair trial in Massachusetts; the Massachusetts Government Act, which altered the Massachusetts Charter in several important aspects by providing, among other things, that the Council would thenceforth be appointed by the Crown rather than elected by the House of Representatives and that town meetings (except for the annual election meeting) could not be held without the prior written approval of the governor; and the Quartering Act, which empowered every colonial governor to quarter troops by his own authority in any case in which there were no barracks and the colony neglected to provide quarters for as long as twenty-four hours. A fifth measure not explicitly related to the other four acts but lumped together with them by the colonists as the "Intolerable Acts" *was the Quebec Act, which was signed into law on June 22, 1774. This act sought to substitute for the temporary expedients that had been in operation since 1763 a more permanent system for administering the alien French population in Quebec and the region west of the Appalachian Mountains and north of the Ohio River. To that end, it provided for a civil government in Quebec without a representative assembly, toleration of Roman Catholics, the trial of civil cases without juries according to the French tradition, and the extension of the boundaries of Quebec west to the Mississippi River and south to the Ohio River. By depriving a number of Englishmen, even though they were largely French Englishmen without prior experience with representative institutions, of an assembly and trial by jury, opening the door to "popery," and extending so unconstitutional a system over much of the West, the Quebec Act, in association with the other four measures, seemed to the colonists especially ominous.*

How and why the British government decided upon each of these acts, the most important provisions of which are reprinted below in Selections 23 A to 23 E are explained in detail by Bernard Donoughue, British Politics and the American Revolution: The Path to War 1773–75 *(1964). Jack M. Sosin,* Whitehall in the Wilderness *(1961), is a discussion of British Western policy prior to 1775 and of the Quebec Act as a solution to the problems of governing the West. The background and reaction to the Quebec Act in Canada are discussed by Alfred LeRoy Burt,* The Old Province of Quebec *(1933) and Reginald Coupland,* The Quebec Act: A Study in Statesmanship *(1925).*

A. PUNISHING BOSTON: BOSTON PORT ACT (MAR. 31, 1774)*

WHEREAS *dangerous commotions and insurrections have been fomented and raised in the town of* Boston, *in the province of* Massachuset's Bay, *in* New England, *by divers ill-affected persons, to the subversion of his Majesty's government, and to the utter destruction of the publick peace, and good order of the said town; in which commotions and insurrections certain valuable cargoes of teas, being the property of the* East India Company, *and on board certain vessels lying within the bay or harbour of* Boston, *were seized and destroyed: And whereas, in the present condition of the said town and harbour, the commerce of his Majesty's subjects cannot be safely carried on there, nor the customs payable to his Majesty duly collected; and it is therefore expedient that the officers of his Majesty's customs should be forthwith removed from the said town* . . . That from and after the first day of *June,* one thousand seven hundred and seventy-four, it shall not be lawful for any person or persons whatsoever to lade put, or cause or procure to be laden or put, off or from any quay, wharf, or other place, within the said town of *Boston,* or in or upon any part of the shore of the bay, commonly called *The Harbour of Boston* . . . into any ship, vessel, lighter, boat, or bottom, any goods, wares, or merchandise whatsoever, to be transported or carried into any other country, province, or place whatsoever, or into any other part of the said province of the *Massachuset's Bay,* in *New England;*

---

* These excerpts are reprinted from Danby Pickering (ed), *Statutes at Large,* vol. XXX, pp. 336–338, 340.

or to take up, discharge, or lay on land, or cause or procure to be taken up, discharged, or laid on land, within the said town, or in or upon any of the places aforesaid, out of any boat, lighter, ship, vessel, or bottom, any goods, wares, or merchandise whatsoever, to be brought from any other country, province, or place, or any other part of the said province of the *Massachuset's Bay* in *New England,* upon pain of the forfeiture of the said goods, wares, and merchandise, and of the said boat, lighter, ship, vessel, or other bottom into which the same shall be put, or out of which the same shall be taken, and of the guns, ammunition, tackle, furniture, and stores, in or belonging to the same . . .

IV. Provided always, That nothing in this act contained shall extend, or be construed to extend, to any military or other stores for his Majesty's use, or to the ships or vessels whereon the same shall be laden, which shall be commissioned by, and in the immediate pay of, his Majesty, his heirs or successors; nor to any fuel or victual brought coastwise from any part of the continent of *America,* for the necessary use and sustenance of the inhabitants of the said town of *Boston* . . .

X. Provided also, and it is hereby declared and enacted, That nothing herein contained shall extend, or be construed, to enable his Majesty to appoint such port, harbour, creeks, quays, wharfs, places, or officers, in the said town of *Boston,* or in the said bay or islands, until it shall sufficiently appear to his Majesty that full satisfaction hath been made by or on behalf of the inhabitants of the said town of *Boston* to the united company of merchants of *England* trading to the *East Indies,* for the damage sustained by the said company by the destruction of their goods sent to the said town of *Boston,* on board certain ships or vessels as aforesaid; and until it shall be certified to his Majesty, in council, by the governor, or lieutenant governor, of the said province, that reasonable satisfaction hath been made to the officers of his Majesty's revenue, and others, who suffered by the riots and insurrections above mentioned, in the months of *November* and *December,* in the year one thousand seven hundred and seventy-three, and in the month of *January,* in the year one thousand seven hundred and seventy-four. . . .

B. ALTERING THE MASSACHUSETTS CONSTITUTION: THE MASSACHUSETTS GOVERNMENT ACT (MAY 20, 1774)*

WHEREAS *by letters patent under the great seal of* England, *made in the third year of the reign of their late majesties King* William *and Queen* Mary, *for uniting, erecting, and incorporating, the several colonies, territories, and tracts of land therein mentioned, into one real province, by the name of* Their Majesties Province of the *Massachuset's Bay,* in *New England; whereby it was, amongst other things, ordained and established, That the governor of the said province should, from thenceforth, be appointed and commissionated by their Majesties, their heirs and successors: It was, however, granted and ordained, That, from the expiration of the term for and*

* These excerpts are reprinted from Pickering (ed.), *Statutes at Large,* vol. XXX, pp. 381–384.

during which the eight and twenty persons named in the said letters patent were appointed to be the first counsellors or assistants to the governor of the said province for the time being, the aforesaid number of eight and twenty counsellors or assistants should yearly, once in every year, for ever thereafter, be, by the general court or assembly, newly chosen: And whereas the said method of electing such counsellors or assistants, to be vested with the several powers, authorities, and privileges, therein mentioned, although conformable to the practice theretofore used in such of the colonies thereby united, in which the appointment of the respective governors had been vested in the general courts or assemblies of the said colonies, hath, by repeated experience, been found to be extremely ill adopted to the plan of govern-ment established in the province of the Massachuset's Bay, *by the said letters patent herein-before mentioned, and hath been so far from contribut-ing to the attainment of the good ends and purposes thereby intended, and to the promoting of the internal welfare, peace, and good government, of the said province, or to the maintenance of the just subordination to, and con-formity with, the laws of* Great Britain, *that the manner of exercising the powers, authorities, and privileges aforesaid, by the persons so annually elected, hath, for some time past, been such as had the most manifest tendency to obstruct, and, in great measure, defeat, the execution of the laws; to weaken the attachment of his Majesty's well-disposed subjects in the said province to his Majesty's government, and to encourage the ill-disposed among them to proceed even to acts of direct resistance to, and defiance of, his Majesty's authority: And it hath accordingly happened, that an open resistance to the execution of the laws hath actually taken place in the town of* Boston, *and the neighbourhood thereof, within the said province: And whereas it is, under these circumstances, become absolutely necessary, in order to the preservation of the peace and good order of the said province, the protection of his Majesty's well-disposed subjects therein resident, the continuance of the mutual benefits arising from the commerce and correspondence between this kingdom and the said province, and the maintaining of the just dependance of the said province upon the crown and parliament of* Great Britain, *that the said method of annually electing the counsellors or assistants of the said province should no longer be suffered to continue, but that the appointment of the said counsellors or assistants should henceforth be put upon the like footing as is established in such other of his Majesty's colonies or plantations in* America, *the governors whereof are appointed by his Majesty's commission, under the great seal of* Great Britain: Be it therefore enacted . . . That from and after the first day of *August,* one thousand seven hundred and seventy-four, so much of the charter, granted by their majesties King *William* and Queen *Mary* to the inhabitants of the said province of the *Massachuset's Bay,* in *New England,* and all and every clause, matter, and thing, therein contained, which relates to the time and manner of electing the assistants or counsellors for the said province, be revoked, and is hereby revoked and made void and of none effect; and that the offices of all counsellors and assistants, elected and appointed in pursuance thereof, shall from thenceforth cease and determine: And that, from and after the said first day of *August,* one thousand seven hundred and seventy-four, the council, or court of assistants of the said province for the time being, shall be composed of such of the inhabitants or proprietors of lands within the same as shall be thereunto nominated and appointed by his Majesty, his heirs and successors, from time to time, by warrant under his or their signet or sign manual, and with the advice of the privy council, agreeable to the practice now used in respect to the appointment of counsellors in such of his Majesty's other colonies in *America,* the governors whereof are appointed by commission under the great seal of *Great Britain:* provided, that the number of the said assistants or counsellors shall not, at any one time, exceed thirty-six, nor be less than twelve.

II. And it is hereby further enacted, That the said assistants or counsellors, so to be appointed as aforesaid, shall hold their offices respectively, for and during the pleasure of his Majesty, his heirs or successors . . .

III. And be it further enacted . . . That from and after the first day of *July,* one thousand seven hundred and seventy-four, it shall and may be lawful for his Majesty's governor . . . to nominate and appoint, under the seal of the province, from time to time, and also to remove, without the consent of the council, all judges of the inferior courts of common pleas, commissioners of *Oyer* and *Terminer,* the attorney general, provosts, marshals, justices of the peace, and other officers to the council or courts of justice belonging . . .

V. And be it further enacted . . . That . . . it shall and may be lawful for his Majesty's governor . . . for the time being of the said province, from time to time, to nominate and appoint the sheriffs without the consent of the council, and to remove such sheriffs with such consent, and not otherwise. . . .

VII. *And whereas, by several acts of the general court, which have been from time to time enacted and passed within the said province, the freeholders and inhabitants of the several townships, districts, and precincts, qualified, as is therein expressed, are authorized to assemble together, annually, or occasionally, upon notice given, in such manner as the said acts direct, for the choice of select men, constables, and other officers, and for the making and agreeing upon such necessary rules, orders, and bye-laws, for the directing, managing, and ordering, the prudential affairs of such townships, districts, and precincts, and for other purposes: and whereas a great abuse has been made of the power of calling such meetings, and the inhabitants have, contrary to the design of their institution, been misled to treat upon matters of the most general concern, and to pass many dangerous and unwarrantable resolves:* for remedy whereof, be it enacted, That from and after the said first day of *August,* one thousand seven hundred and seventy-four, no meeting shall be called by the select men, or at the request of any number of freeholders of any township, district, or precinct, without the leave of the governor, or, in his absence, of the lieutenant-governor, in writing, expressing the special business of the said meeting, first had and obtained, except the annual meeting in the months of *March* or *May,* for the choice of select men, constables, and other officers, or except for the choice of persons to fill up the offices aforesaid, on the death or removal of any of the persons first elected to such offices, and also, except any meeting for the election of a representative or representatives in the general court; and that no other matter shall be treated of at such meetings, except the election of their aforesaid officers or representatives, nor at any other meeting, except the business expressed in the leave given by the governor, or, in his absence, by the lieutenant-governor.

VIII. *And whereas the method at present used in the province of* Massachuset's Bay, *in* America, *of electing persons to serve on grand juries, and other juries, by the freeholders and inhabitants of the several towns, affords occasion for many evil practices, and tends to pervert the free and impartial administration of justice:* for remedy whereof, be it further enacted by the authority aforesaid, That, from and after the respective times appointed for the holding of the general sessions of the peace in the several counties within the said province, next after the month of *September,* one thousand seven hundred and seventy-four, the jurors to serve at the superior courts of judicature, courts of assize, general gaol delivery, general sessions of the peace, and inferior court of common pleas, in the several counties within the said province, shall not be elected, nominated, or appointed, by the free-holders and inhabitants of the several towns within the said respective counties, nor summoned or returned by the constables of the said towns; but that, from thenceforth, the jurors to serve at the superior courts of judicature, courts of assize, general gaol delivery, general sessions of the peace, an inferior court of common pleas within the said province, shall be summoned and returned by the sheriffs of the respective counties within the said province . . .

C. "THE MURDER ACT": ADMINISTRATION OF JUSTICE ACT (MAY 20, 1774)*

WHEREAS *in his Majesty's province of* Massachuset's Bay, *in* New Eng-land, *an attempt hath lately been made to throw off the authority of the parliament of* Great Britain *over the said province, and an actual and avowed resistance, by open force, to the execution of certain acts of parliament, hath been suffered to take place, uncontrouled and unpunished, in defiance of his Majesty's authority, and to the utter subversion of all lawful government: and whereas, in the present disordered state of the said province, it is of the utmost importance to the general welfare thereof, and to the re-establishment of lawful authority throughout the same, that neither the magistrates acting in support of the laws, nor any of his Majesty's subjects aiding and assisting them therein, or in the suppression of riots and tumults, raised in opposition to the execution of the laws and statutes of this realm, should be discouraged from the proper discharge of their duty, by an apprehension, that in case of their being questioned for any acts done therein, they may be liable to be brought to trial for the same before persons who do not acknowledge the validity of the laws, in the execution thereof, or the authority of the magistrate in the support of whom, such acts had been done: in order therefore to remove every such discouragement from the minds of his Majesty's subjects, and to induce them, upon all proper occasions, to exert themselves in support of the public peace of the province, and of the authority of the King and parliament of* Great Britain *over the same;* be it enacted . . . That if any inquisition or indictment shall be found, or if any appeal shall be sued or preferred against any person, for murther, or other capital offence, in the province of the *Massachuset's Bay,* and it shall

---

* These excerpts are reprinted from Pickering (ed.), *Statutes at Large,* vol. XXX, pp. 367–369.

appear, by information given upon oath to the governor, or, in his absence, to the lieutenant-governor of the said province, that the fact was committed by the person against whom such inquisition or indictment shall be found, or against whom such appeal shall be sued or perferred, as aforesaid, either in the execution of his duty as a magistrate, for the suppression of riots, or in the support of the laws of revenue, or in acting in his duty as an officer of revenue, or in acting under the direction and order of any magistrate, for the suppression of riots, or for the carrying into effect the laws of revenue, or in aiding and assisting in any of the cases aforesaid; and if it shall also appear, to the satisfaction of the said governor, or lieutenant-governor respectively, that an indifferent trial cannot be had within the said province, in that case, it shall and may be lawful for the governor, or lieutenant-governor, to direct, with the advice and consent of the council, that the inquisition, indictment, or appeal, shall be tried in some other of his Majesty's colonies, or in *Great Britain;* and for that purpose, to order the person against whom such inquisition or indictment shall be found, or against whom such appeal shall be sued or preferred, as aforesaid, to be sent, under sufficient custody, to the place appointed for his trial, or to admit such person to bail, taking a recognizance, (which the said governor, or, in his absence, the lieutenant-governor, is hereby authorised to take), from such person, with sufficient sureties, to be approved of by the said governor, or, in his absence, the lieutenant-governor, in such sums of money as the said governor, or, in his absence, the lieutenant-governor, shall deem reasonable, for the personal appearance of such person, if the trial shall be appointed to be had in any other colony, before the governor, or lieutenant-governor, or commander in chief of such colony; and if the trial shall be appointed to be had in *Great Britain*, then before his Majesty's court of *King's Bench,* at a time to be mentioned in such recognizances; and the governor, or lieutenant-governor, or commander in chief of the colony where such trial shall be appointed to be had, or court of *King's Bench*, where the trial is appointed to be had in *Great Britain*, upon the appearance of such person, according to such recognizance, or in custody, shall either commit such person, or admit him to bail, until such trial; and which the said governor, or lieutenant-governor, or commander in chief, and court of *King's Bench,* are hereby authorized and impowered to do. . . .

D. STRENGTHENING THE HAND OF THE MILITARY: THE QUARTERING ACT (JUNE 2, 1774)*

WHEREAS *doubts have been entertained, whether troops can be quartered otherwise than in barracks, in case barracks have been provided sufficient for the quartering of all the officers and soldiers within any town, township, city, district, or place, within his Majesty's dominions in* North America: *And whereas it may frequently happen, from the situation of such barracks, that, if troops should be quartered therein, they would not be stationed where their presence may be necessary and required:* be it therefore enacted

* These excerpts are reprinted from Pickering (ed.), *Statutes at Large*, vol. XXX, p. 410.

. . . That, in such cases, it shall and may be lawful for the persons who now are, or may be hereafter, authorised by law, in any of the provinces within his Majesty's dominions in *North America*, and they are hereby respectively authorised, impowered, and directed, on the requisition of the officer who, for the time being, has the command of his Majesty's forces in *North America*, to cause any officers or soldiers in his Majesty's service to be quartered and billetted in such manner as is now directed by law, where no barracks are provided by the colonies.

II. And be it further enacted by the authority aforesaid, That if it shall happen at any time that any officers or soldiers in his Majesty's service shall remain within any of the said colonies without quarters, for the space of twenty-four hours after such quarters shall have been demanded, it shall and may be lawful for the governor of the province to order and direct such and so many uninhabited houses, out-houses, barns, or other buildings, as he shall think necessary to be taken, (making a reasonable allowance for the same), and make fit for the reception of such officers and soldiers, and to put and quarter such officers and soldiers therein, for such time as he shall think proper.

III. And be it further enacted by the authority aforesaid, That this act, and every thing herein contained, shall continue and be in force, in all his Majesty's dominions in *North America,* until the twenty-fourth day of *March,* one thousand seven hundred and seventy-six.

E. "OMINOUS PORTENT": THE QUEBEC ACT (JUNE 22, 1774)*

. . . Be it enacted . . . That all the territories, islands, and countries in *North America,* belonging to the crown of *Great Britain,* bounded on the south by a line from the bay of *Chaleurs,* along the high lands which divide the rivers that empty themselves into the river *Saint Lawrence* from those which fall into the sea, to a point in forty-five degrees of northern latitude, on the eastern bank of the river *Connecticut,* keeping the same latitude directly west, through the lake *Champlain,* until, in the same latitude, it meets the river *Saint Lawrence;* from thence up the eastern bank of the said river to the lake *Ontario;* thence through the lake *Ontario,* and the river commonly called *Niagara;* and thence along by the eastern and south-eastern bank of lake *Erie,* following the said bank, until the same shall be intersected by the northern boundary, granted by the charter of the province of *Pennsylvania,* in case the same shall be so intersected; and from thence along the said northern and western boundaries of the said province, until the said western boundary strike the *Ohio:* but in case the said bank of the said lake shall not be found to be so intersected, then following the said bank until it shall arrive at that point of the said bank which shall be nearest to the north-western angle of the said province of *Pennsylvania;* and thence, by a right line, to the said north-western angle of the said province; and thence along the western boundary of the said province, until it strike the river *Ohio;* and

---

* These excerpts are reprinted from Pickering (ed.), *Statutes at Large,* vol. XXX, pp. 549–554.

along the bank of the said river, westward, to the banks of the *Mississippi,* and northward to the southern boundary of the territory granted to the merchants adventurers of *England,* trading to *Hudson's Bay;* and also all such territories, islands, and countries, which have, since the tenth of *February,* one thousand seven hundred and sixty-three, been made part of the government of *Newfoundland,* be, and they are hereby, during his Majesty's pleasure, annexed to, and made part and parcel of the province of *Quebec,* as created and established by the said royal proclamation of the seventh of *October,* one thousand seven hundred and sixty-three. . . .

V. *And, for the more perfect security and ease of the minds of the inhabitants of the said province,* it is hereby declared, That his Majesty's subjects, professing the religion of the church of *Rome* of and in the said province of *Quebec,* may have, hold, and enjoy, the free exercise of the religion of the church of *Rome,* subject to the King's supremacy, declared and established by an act, made in the first year of the reign of Queen *Elizabeth,* over all the dominions and countries which then did, or thereafter should belong, to the imperial crown of this realm; and that the clergy of the said church may hold, receive, and enjoy, their accustomed dues and rights, with respect to such persons only as shall profess the said religion. . . .

VIII. And be it further enacted by the authority aforesaid, That his Majesty's *Canadian* subjects, within the province of *Quebec,* the religious orders and communities only excepted, may also hold and enjoy their property and possessions, together with all customs and usages relative thereto, and all other their civil rights, in as large, ample, and beneficial manner, as if the said proclamation, commissions, ordinances, and other acts and instruments, had not been made, and as may consist with their allegiance to his Majesty, and subjection to the crown and parliament of *Great Britain;* and that in all matters of controversy, relative to property and civil rights, resort shall be had to the laws of *Canada,* as the rule for the decision of the same . . .

XII. *And whereas it may be necessary to ordain many regulations for the future welfare and good government of the province of* Quebec, *the occasions of which cannot now be foreseen, nor, without much delay and inconvenience, be provided for, without intrusting that authority, for a certain time, and under proper restrictions, to persons resident there: and whereas it is at present inexpedient to call an assembly;* be it therefore enacted by the authority aforesaid, That it shall and may be lawful for his Majesty, his heirs and successors, by warrant under his or their signet or sign manual, and with the advice of the privy council, to constitute and appoint a council for the affairs of the province of *Quebec,* to consist of such persons resident there, not exceeding twenty-three, nor less than seventeen, as his Majesty, his heirs and successors, shall be pleased to appoint; and, upon the death, removal, or absence of any of the members of the said council, in like manner to constitute and appoint such and so many other person or persons as shall be necessary to supply the vacancy or vacancies; which council, so appointed and nominated, or the major part thereof, shall have power and authority to make ordinances for the peace, welfare, and good government, of the said province, with the consent of his Majesty's governor, or, in his absence, of the lieutenant-governor, or commander in chief for the time being.

XIII. Provided always, That nothing in this act contained shall extend to authorise or impower the said legislative council to lay any taxes or duties within the said province, such rates and taxes only excepted as the inhabitants of any town or district within the said province may be authorised by the said council to assess, levy, and apply, within the said town or district, for the purpose of making roads, erecting and repairing public buildings, or for any other purpose respecting the local convenience and oeconomy of such town or district.

XIV. Provided also, and be it enacted by the authority aforesaid, That every ordinance so to be made, shall, within six months, be transmitted by the governor, or, in his absence, by the lieutenant-governor, or commander in chief for the time being, and laid before his Majesty for his royal approbation; and if his Majesty shall think fit to disallow thereof, the same shall cease and be void from the time that his Majesty's order in council thereupon shall be promulgated at *Quebec*. . . .

SELECTION

The Emotional and Constitutional Grounds for Resistance

Intended to bring a swift halt to resistance to British authority in Massachusetts and, by serving as an example of what might happen to other colonies if they persisted in their opposition to Parliament, to drive a wedge between Massachusetts and the other colonies and thereby cut short the general colonial uprising against the Tea Act, the Coercive Acts had precisely the opposite effect. Far too severe a punishment for the offense, the acts, most American leaders concluded, could not possibly be simply a response to the Boston Tea Party. They could only be explained as part of that "settled fix'd plan" among the ministers "for inslaving the colonies . . . and indeed the [British] nation too" that, Americans had suspected for over a decade, had been at the root of most of their difficulties with the imperial government. No longer could there be much serious doubt that a malignant conspiracy among the ministers and a corrupt majority in Parliament was intent upon establishing an "arbitrary power" in the colonies, and because "such power will more surely intoxicate men than the strongest spirits" and turn the "best of men" into "monsters of cruelty" ever more dreadful measures could be expected to follow if the Coercive Acts were permitted to succeed. All over the colonies politicians, writers, and ministers in speeches, essays, and sermons enlarged upon this theme. The cause of Boston and Massachusetts Bay, they emphasized, was the cause of all. Nothing but the united resistance of all the colonies even by force of arms, if necessary, could preserve the liberty and property of Americans from total destruction by the ruthless acts of a corrupted imperial government. One of the clearest and most comprehensive statements of this interpretation of the Coercive Acts was written by Ebenezer Baldwin (1745–1776), a graduate from and former tutor at Yale College and pastor of the First Congregational Church in Danbury, Connecticut. Included as an appendix to a sermon delivered at a public fast on

August 31, 1774, by Samuel Sherwood, a minister at Fairfield, Baldwin's statement is reprinted in part below as Selection 24 A.

The Coercive Acts also forced Americans into a reformulation of their constitutional arguments. Previously, they had stood on the grounds laid down during the Stamp Act crisis: Parliament could legislate for the colonies but could not tax them for revenue. But the Coercive Acts, though not tax measures, seemed to Americans just as detrimental to colonial rights as the Stamp Act or the Townshend Revenue Act. Clearly, some new line of defense was needed. Richard Bland had shown the way in 1766 by implying that Parliament could neither tax nor legislate for the internal polity of the colonies and suggesting that the colonies were connected to Britain only through the Crown and not through Parliament. This doctrine, which had found expression in several isolated instances during the agitation over the Townshend Acts and had been openly advocated by the Massachusetts General Court in its debate with Hutchinson in January, 1773 (see Selection 18 B), now became the dominant colonial argument. The most famous and most systematic expression of it came from James Wilson (1742–1798), a Scotch-Irish lawyer who had migrated to the colonies in 1765, served as a tutor at the College of Philadelphia, studied law with John Dickinson, and was in 1774 a practicing attorney in Carlisle, Pennsylvania. In his Considerations on the Authority of Parliament, *first written in 1768 but not published until the summer of 1774 after he had made appropriate revisions, Wilson stated categorically that the colonies were "not bound by the acts of the British Parliament." Taking pains to refute all of the arguments advanced by British writers to prove the supremacy of Parliament over the colonies, Wilson contended that according to the constitution all legislation was inextricably dependent upon representation, that because Americans were not represented in Parliament they were not bound by its laws, and that "the only dependency, which they ought to acknowledge, is a dependency on the crown." The central portions of this pamphlet, which was widely read and had great influence upon American leaders, are reprinted below as Selection 18 B.*

Farther south in Virginia, Thomas Jefferson (1743–1826), another lawyer and a representative from Albemarle County to the House of Burgesses, had come to similar conclusions and had set them down in a series of proposed instructions to Virginia's delegates to a Continental Congress called by the Massachusetts House of Representatives to meet in Philadelphia in September. Jefferson intended to present his instructions to the Virginia Convention that met in August, 1774, to elect delegates to the Congress, but, when illness prevented his attendance, he sent them to friends who had them published in pamphlet form as A Summary View of the Rights of British America. *Like Baldwin, Jefferson concluded that the several "acts of power" by Parliament over the previous decade "too plainly" proved "a deliberate and systematical plan of reducing us to slavery"; like Wilson, he concluded as well that the colonies were distinct and independent governments bound to Britain only through their mutual allegiance to a common monarch and that the British Parliament had therefore "no right to exercise authority" over them. But Jefferson went significantly farther than either Baldwin or Wilson in pointing out that not just Parliament but George III acting in his executive capacity had been guilty of a "wanton exercise of . . . power" in the colonies. Charging the King with a long catalogue of oppressive acts against the colonists, Jefferson reminded him that kings were "the servants, not the proprietors of the people" and left him with a warning: If he persisted in "sacrificing the rights of one part of the empire to the inordinate desires of another," Jefferson implied, the colonists might be driven to a separation. Although Jefferson's views were far too radical to receive*

*the approval of either the Virginia Convention or the First Continental Congress,
they were important in indicating the direction of American thought. The text of*
A Summary View *is reprinted in full below as Selection 24 C.*

Randolph G. Adams, Political Ideas of the American Revolution *(1922), contains the fullest discussion of the constitutional position of the Americans in 1774.
Benjamin Woods Labaree,* The Boston Tea Party *(1964), is the best account of
the general American response to the Coercive Acts. In his introduction to* Pamphlets of the American Revolution *(1965), volume I, Bernard Bailyn calls attention
to the importance of the Baldwin tract and explores the nature and assesses the
importance of the colonial belief in a ministerial "conspiracy of power" against the
colonies. Charles Page Smith,* James Wilson, Founding Father 1742–1798 *(1956),
is a detailed biography of Wilson, and Dumas Malone,* Jefferson, the Virginian
(1948), the most comprehensive study of Jefferson's early career.

A. "A SETTLED FIX'D PLAN FOR INSLAVING THE COLONIES": EBENEZER BALDWIN, "AN APPENDIX STATING THE HEAVY GRIEVANCES THE COLONIES LABOR UNDER . . ." (AUG. 31, 1774)*

Indulge me a little longer while I endeavour to point out what we have *just*
reason to fear the consequences of these measures will be. If we view the
whole of the conduct of the ministry and parliament, I do not see how any
one can doubt but that there is a settled fix'd plan for *inslaving* the colonies,
or bringing them under arbitrary government, and indeed the nation too.
The present parliament have ever been (by all accounts) more devoted to
the interest of the ministry, than perhaps ever a parliament were. Now notwithstanding the excellency of the British constitution, if the ministry can
secure a majority in parliament, who will come into all their measures, will
vote as they bid them; they may rule as absolutely as they do in *France* or
Spain, yea as in *Turkey* or *India:* And this seems to be the present plan
to secure a majority of parliament, and thus enslave the nation with their
own consent. The more places or pensions the ministry have in their gift;
the more easily can they *bribe* a majority of parliament, by bestowing those
places on them or their friends. This makes them erect so many new and
unnecessary offices in America, even so as to swallow up the whole of the
revenue. The king is not at all the richer for these duties. But then by
bestowing these places---places of considerable profit and no labour, upon
the children or friends, or dependants of the members of parliament, the
ministry can secure them in their interest. This doubtless is the great thing
the ministry are driving at, to establish arbitrary government with the consent of parliament: And to keep the people of England still, the first exertions of this power are upon the colonies. If the parliament insist upon the
right of taxing the colonies at pleasure, the least we can expect is, to be
tax'd as heavily as we can possibly bear, and yet support our lives; for as
the members of parliament feel no burdens themselves by what they lay
upon us, and are under no danger of losing their places by taxing us, so

* These excerpts are reprinted from Samuel Sherwood, *A Sermon, Containing,
Scriptual Instructions to Civil Rulers and all Free-born Subjects* (1774), pp. 67–81.

long as they can persuade the people of England they are lightening their burdens thereby; they are under no motives of interest to abstain from loading us with taxes as heavy as we can possibly groan under. The Doubtless they will be cautious enough, to introduce these heavy taxes gradually, lest they excite too great commotions in this country: But let the *right* be once fix'd and established; it will be very easy to keep adding tax to tax; till the loads grow so heavy and are so fast bound, that we can never shake them off. Nothing most certainly but a principle of justice will keep them from it; and what can we expect from this quarter, when in open defiance of the *English* constitution, they claim a right to tax us, and thus deprive us of our dearest privileges?

In the mean time we must expect our *charters* will fall a sacrifice to these arbitrary claims. Charter governments have long been disagreable to the powers in Britain. The *free* constitution of these colonies makes them such nurseries of freemen as cannot fail to alarm an arbitrary ministry. They only wait a favourable opportunity to abolish their charters, as they have done that of the Massachusetts-Bay. We know the principle the parliament have adopted and openly profess to act upon, that they have a right to alter or annihilate charters when they judge it convenient: And we may depend upon it, whenever they shall think it can be done without raising too great commotions in the colonies, they will judge it convenient. Some may imagine it was the destroying the tea induced the parliament to change the government of the Massachusetts-Bay. If it was, surely 'tis very extraordinary to punish a whole province and their posterity thro' all ages, for the conduct of a few individuals. How soon will a riot or some disorder of a few individuals, afford them a pretext for the like treatment of all the other charter governments. I believe, however, it may be made very evident, that the destroying the tea was not the reason for altering the government of the Massachusetts-Bay; but that it was a fix'd plan long before, and they only waited a colourable pretext for carrying it into execution. It has been reported by gentlemen of unquestionable veracity, that they had incontestible evidence that the two bills for altering the government of the Massachusetts-Bay were ordered by the council to be drawn up by the crown lawyers more than two years ago. Now if this be true (as it undoubtedly is) 'tis quite certain the ministry were only waiting for some colourable pretext for carrying their design into execution. The charter governments are by this precedent reduced not merely to the greatest uncertainty of the continuance of their charters; but may be quite certain, if the present plan is prosecuted, they will be taken away, and these colonies reduced, (if nothing worse) to the state of the royal governments; their governors, councils, judges, &c. will be appointed from England, with high and extravagant salaries.

There is great reason to fear the next step will be the vacating all grants and patents of land from the king; that all our landed property may revert to his majesty; to be regranted under such *quit rents and services* as those in power shall see fit to impose: Nor will *this fear* appear chimerical to any one that duly considers what hath been already done, and what the plan is, which the ministry are doubtless pursuing. 'Twould be weak policy indeed for an arbitrary ministry to push with all their horns at first. But certainly it doth not require very great sagacity to see that their measures are tending to this. . . . Our fathers when they planted this wilderness, placed equal confidence in the royal word pledged in their charters; as in the patents by which they held their land: and deemed the privileges granted in the former of as much worth; as the property granted by the latter. The principle upon which the parliament proceeded in vacating the Massachusetts charter; will equally warrant them, whenever they shall see fit, to vacate all our grants of lands, i. e. when they shall judge it expedient, or for the good of the nation. If the parliament should once take it into their wise heads, that it is expedient, or for the general good, that all lands in America should revert to the crown, that they may be regranted all upon the same tenure,---upon large *quit-rents* to defray the charges of government; what will hinder their carrying it into execution? And indeed the Boston *port act* doth actually afford us a precedent of the exercise of this power: all their wharves and water-lots round the whole of Boston bay, are really *confiscated* to the king (as we have already shewn.) Now what is this but a vote of parliament to take away our landed property. And that power which hath been once exercised have we not all reason to fear will be exercised again.

And have we not just grounds to fear that all this will not be the completion of their oppressive plan, if the ministry find themselves successful in their first attempts? By the *Quebec-Act* we find the parliament claim a power to establish in *America*, the same arbitrary government that takes place in *France.*----To take away trials by juries:--- to set aside general assemblies:---to vest the king with a power to appoint legislative councils &c. Now this act not only respects the *French* inhabitants (who having been long used to slavish subjection, and not knowing the benefit of any other form of government, are possibly well eno' pleased with it, especially as the pill is gilded over with a full establishment of that religion, of which they are such bigotted professors;) but it respects thousands of *English*, who have settled there since the conquest, and all such as may settle any where within that vast extended province in future time. By the same right they could establish this form of government over the *English* in Canada; they may do it in the other provinces. In the province of the Massachusetts-Bay, the important privilege of being tried by a jury, is greatly *lessened* by setting aside the equitable and impartial method by which juries were wont to be panel'd. Viewing the things that have taken place, is it without foundation that I express my fears, that the British ministry will e'er long find our general assemblies troublesome things?---a hindrance to government and the like, and so set them aside, under a notion of their being *inexpedient*, and lodge the whole legislative power in a council appointed by the king. This is the very thing that took place in *Sir Edmond [Andros's]* time. The whole legislative power was lodged in him and his council. And since the previous steps are so like what took place then, why may we not expect the consequent ones will be so too? And very likely the ministry may find *juries* equally a bar to the government they mean to establish: and so may persuade the parliament, on the footing of expediency to abolish them likewise.

And when our civil rights and privileges shall have thus fallen a sacrifice to tyranny and oppression, our religious liberties cannot long survive: for where hath it ever been known that civil and ecclesiastical tyranny and despotism have not yet gone hand in hand together. The latter is so necessary to uphold and support the former, that arbitrary princes or ministers of state have ever found their interest in the encouragement of it. And should America be forced to yield in the present struggle for civil liberty, we have no reason to expect but ecclesiastical tyranny, in some shape or other, will like a mighty torrent overspread our land. Those princes on the British throne since the reformation, who have been most disposed to trample upon the rights of the people, and to rule in an arbitrary and despotic manner; have ever caressed the papists and shewn a favourable disposition towards the bloody religion of Rome, as that religion is the surest prop to tryanny and despotism. This is evident during the reigns of all the several kings of the house of *Stewart.* Papists shared in the royal favour and were sheltered under royal protection. Continual attempts were made to bring the church of England to a greater conformity to the despotic church of Rome; 'till James 2d. more adventurous than his predecessors boldly attempts to subvert the constitution both in state and in church;----to introduce both tyranny and popery: which so alarmed the nation that they dethroned the tyrant; and placed a confirmed protestant on the British throne. Some late transactions shew a very favourable disposition in the present ministry and parliament towards the religion of Rome; how far they may attempt to introduce into the English nation both in Britain and the colonies, God only knows. But thus much we may safely guess, without much danger of erring, that to introduce episcopacy with all those formidable powers with which it was clothed (which indeed were no obscure resemblance of the church of Rome) before the acts of parliament restraining and regulating prelative power and ecclesiastical courts, passed in consequence of the revolution, will be a darling object with the present ministry, if they see a prospect of being able to carry their designs into execution. For ecclesiastical government must be conformed to the civil, and nothing short of this would be in any measure suited to the genius of that civil policy they are evidently aiming to establish in the colonies. And tho' such an establishment might not introduce fire and faggots; yet depositions of the clergy, fines, imprisonment, disfranchisements, confiscations, &c. with various corporal penalties, you may depend upon it, will be its dire attendants.

All these things, I make no doubt, will take place one after another, as fast as the ministry can bring their measures to bear; unless something occur in God's providence to hinder them.

View now the situation of America: loaded with taxes from the British parliament, as heavy as she can possibly support under,---our lands charged with the most exorbitant quit-rents,---these taxes collected by foreigners, steeled against any impressions from our groans or complaints, with all the rapaciousness of Roman publicans---our charters taken away---our assemblies annihilated,---governors and councils, appointed by royal authority without any concurrence of the people, enacting such laws as their sovereign pleasure shall dictate--judges appointed from the same source, without any check from juries carrying their arbitrary laws into execution.---the lives and property of Americans entirely at the disposal of officers more than three thousand miles removed from any power to controul them---armies of soldiers quartered among the inhabitants, who know the horrid purpose for which they are stationed, in the colonies,---to subjugate and bear down the inhabitants---who know what a chance they stand for impunity, tho' they commit the greatest excesses. These will be ready, not only to execute every arbitrary mandate of their despotic masters; but self-moved (if like others of their profession) to commit every outrage upon the defenceless inhabitants. ---Robberies, rapes, murders, &c. will be but the wanton sport of such wretches without restraint let loose upon us.---These will be at hand by force and arms to quell every rising murmur, to crush every rising groan or complaint e'er it be uttered. And whenever the iron hand of oppression shall excite opposition or raise insurrections among the people: (which will ever be the case under arbitrary and despotic government, till long use has rendered their necks callous and insensible to the galling yoke) Blood-thirsty soldiers will be let loose upon them. Those who survive their murdering hands and have the misfortune to be taken captive by them, will soon be dragged, by the sentence of more merciless judges, to the place of execution.---Nothing shall then be heard of but executions, forfeitures of estates, families reduced to beggery, orphans crying for bread, and such like scenes of distress. The spirits of the people soon grow depress'd---Industry and public spirit die away----Learning, Virtue and Religion are soon extinguished.--No comfort or happiness to be enjoyed in social life, every one will be jealous and distrustful of his nearest friends and neighbours. To such a dreadful state as this, my countrymen, the present measures seem to be swiftly advancing. What free-born Englishman can view such a state of abject slavery as this, tho' at the greatest distance, without having his blood boil with indignation?

Some perhaps may be ready to think the issue of these measures cannot be so bad as has been described. No wonder men used to freedom cannot at once realize all the horrors of slavery. But this is no worse a state, than what now actually takes place in a great part of the world: and why will not the same government produce the same effects in America?

Others may think the British ministry cannot have so bad a scheme as this in view, that officers appointed by the crown cannot be so cruel and barbarous as hath been represented. Probably the ministry mayn't have it all in view at present: probably these officers would not at first be so cruel and barbarous, but there is no telling what men will soon become when entrusted with arbitrary power: such power will more surely intoxicate men than the strongest spirits: the best of men cannot be safely trusted with it. Many men amiable in private life have become monsters of cruelty when entrusted with arbitrary power: such were many of the Roman emperors. Should governors and councils appointed by the crown be entrusted with legislative power over the colonies, and be supported by armies of soldiers quartered among the people, I see not what (according to the ordinary course of things) would keep them from even greater excesses than I have mentioned.

Or should the colonies refuse to receive the chains prepared for them, and the present measures issue in a hostile rupture between Great Britain and the colonies, which God forbid, and which I wish the ministry may not have in view to promote, see what precautions they have early taken either to ruin us, or force us to subjection. To the Canadians who have been long inured to arbitrary government, and so are become fit tools for inslaving others, they have granted an establishment of their religion, the restoration of their former laws, &c. to attach them to their interest:---have continued Canada a military government that they may have store of forces at hand; that they may let loose these with all the force of Canada and all the northern tribes of Indians upon our exposed and helpless frontiers. What else can they have in view in trying so much to gratify the French inhabitants of that province?

Now if the British parliament and ministry continue resolved to prosecute the measures they have entered upon, it seems we must either submit to such a dreadful state of slavery as hath been shewn will be the probable issue of their measures, or must by force and arms stand up in defence of our liberties. The thoughts of either of which is enough to make our blood recoil with horror. Can any person survey the events that have taken place, and yet remain so stupid as not to be shocked at the dreadful prospect before us? Is there a wretch so unfeeling, as not to feel grieved and affected at the injured and violated liberties of America? Is there that tool of arbitrary power among the free-born sons of America, that will dare hold up his head in defence of such measures as these? If there be any such, I am sure I cannot find it in my heart to wish them worse, than to feel the iron rod of slavery, that is now shook over America, till they are brought to a sounder mind.

Having thus given a brief account of the late acts of the British parliament respecting the colonies;---of the grievances the colonies labour under therefrom, and of what the probable consequences of these measures will be. I will very briefly touch upon the last thing proposed viz. what can be done by us in such an alarming crisis.---Some perhaps may think me already too bold in speaking thus freely of the acts of the most respectable legislature in the British empire. But the more I consider the shocking tendency of them, the more difficult I find it to restrain myself within the bounds of decency.---I am sure however there is nothing *treasonable* in feeling oppression when oppressed---nor in groaning under the anguish of it---as yet I have done little more than express this.----Surely it cannot be *treason* to feel our burdens and weep and mourn and pray on account of them. To pray to God for redress is certainly innocent, and happy it is we have heaven to go to, tho' our prayers should be denied on earth. God hath once and again in answer to prayer wrought eminent deliverance for the oppressed. Remember how he delivered the Jews from Haman's cursed devices. Oft hath he delivered his people of old;---oft the people of New-England;---this affords great encouragement to be fervent in our supplications to the throne of grace. *The king's heart is in the hand of the Lord, as the rivers of water: he turneth it whithersoever he will.* But little will prayer avail us without unfeigned repentance and humiliation before God under the heavy frowns of his righteous providence. We have more reason to be afraid of the vice and wickedness that abounds among us, than of all the arms of Britain. These give us reason to fear lest we have not virtue enough to make use of the properest means of redress, and lest heaven should fight against us. Were a general reformation to take place I make no doubt heaven would find a way for our relief. The present alarming situation of things therefore loudly calls upon us to examine what sins in particular have provoked heaven thus to come out in judgment against us; and perhaps there cannot be a better rule of determining than to enquire what sins these calamities are properly retributive of, and by this rule will not the enslaving the poor *Africans* in the colonies stand forth in the front of the dreadful catalogue? Are not the colonies guilty of forcibly depriving them of their natural rights? Will not the arguments we use in defence of our own liberties against the claims of the British parliament, equally conclude in their favour? And is it not easy to see there is something retributive in the present judgments of heaven? We keep our fellow men in slavery---heaven is suffering others to enslave us. Again I must mention worldliness, covetousness, selfishness, dishonesty, disobedience to constitutional authority, and many other vices as contained in the dismal train, and for which we need to repent and humble ourselves before God . . .

But if ever we would hope for redress from the grievances we labour under; 'tis not only necessary that we repent, reform and pray; but that we unitedly prosecute the most firm and prudent measures for the attainment of it. A very little attention must convince every one of the necessity of our being united. If the colonies are divided or the people in the several colonies are very considerably divided, we are undone. Nothing but the united efforts of America can save us: and if united they must have that weight, which gives me the most sanguine hopes of success. It should then be the concern of every one to labour as far as his influence extends, to promote this necessary union. The determinations of the congress of delegates from the several colonies may be deemed the general voice of America. A concurrence with these we should every one labour to promote. If in every particular we should not be entirely suited; yet the dreadful consequences of disunion should make us cautious how we let it be known. The Congress we hear have come into a conclusion that we *import no* British goods. This is a measure for redress, of which we may very safely and easily make trial. We can with a little self-denial do without the superfluities we receive from Britain. This will doubtless be distressing to the Mother Country and may convince them of the necessity of continuing to us our dear bought rights and privileges. No friend of his country can hesitate a moment in such a cause to deny himself the superfluities of Britain. And should the Congress agree also upon *non-exportation*; and extend both this and the other, not only to Great-Britain but to Ireland and the West-Indies; a general compliance with which, will most certainly, according to the ordinary course of things, ensure us redress, and of which necessity most certainly will be a sufficient justification: Should this I say be agreed upon by the Congress; none I hope will be so inimical to his country, as to attempt to break the general union by refusing to comply therewith. But should there be any such; it becomes every one, that hath any regard to the liberties of his country, to treat with deserved neglect and abhorrence the wretch, that thus meanly seeks his own emolument upon the ruins of his country's liberties:----To break off all trade and dealings with such selfish miscreants; and make them sensible, that without injuring their lives or property, their injured country can make them feel the weight of her vengeance, and rue the day they ever suffered a selfish spirit to banish all love to their country from their breasts. Here is a sphere in which every one can contribute something to save his sinking country from ruin. Suffer me then to intreat you (of the western parts of the colony of Connecticut) in some proper way to shew your hearty concurrence with other parts of the continent in the cause of American liberty; and your resolution to concur with, and endeavour to carry into execution the conclusions of the American Congress; and to open your hearts to commiserate, and contribute to the relief of the suffering poor of the town of Boston. What hath been said I trust makes it sufficiently appear, that they are suffering in the common cause of American liberty. Allowing the conduct of those individuals who destroyed the tea as criminal as any are disposed to make it, yet the punishment is beyond all bounds disproportionate to the crime:---the innocent are involved with the guilty:---the requirements of the act are such, that it can never be known whether complied with or not:---The act is as compleat an instrument of tyranny as ever was formed.

---If the requirements of the act should be complied with; yet all their estates lying in wharves, water-lots, &c. will still lie at the king's mercy. So that the act cannot be complied with without giving up the struggle for liberty. The design in bearing thus hard upon one colony is evidently to divide the colonies; and thus to bring them one after another to submit to the arbitrary claims of parliament. All their means of subsistence depended on their trade, which by this act is wholly taken away. So that without assistance from the other colonies, they must inevitably yield, unless so very patriotic, as to be willing to starve to death. Our turn may soon come when we may want the like kind assistance from our brethren. Only apply the golden rule of "doing to others as we would that they should do unto us," and surely we cannot hesitate to contribute to their relief. . . . I wish the importance of contributing to the relief of Boston might be duly attended to, and that some measures might be come into in all our towns for trying the generosity of people for this purpose. I am sure they that have a sense of the worth of liberty and the importance of making a firm yet decent and harmless opposition to these oppressive measures, which are calculated to rivit the chains of slavery both upon us and our posterity, cannot hesitate a moment to contribute something generous for the relief of that suffering people. May Americans be united in a just sense of the worth of their civil rights and privileges, and in every laudable and righteous method for obtaining redress; and God grant their struggles in so glorious a cause may be crowned with happy success.

B. THE REJECTION OF PARLIAMENTARY AUTHORITY: JAMES WILSON, ''CONSIDERATIONS ON THE AUTHORITY OF PARLIAMENT'' (AUG. 17, 1774)*

But from what source does this mighty, this uncontrolled authority of the house of commons flow? From the collective body of the commons of Great Britain. This authority must, therefore, originally reside in them; for whatever they convey to their representatives, must ultimately be in themselves. And have those, whom we have hitherto been accustomed to consider as our fellow-subjects, an absolute and unlimited power over us? Have they a natural right to make laws, by which we may be deprived of our properties, of our liberties, of our lives? By what title do they claim to be our masters? What act of ours has rendered us subject to those, to whom we were formerly equal? Is British freedom denominated from the *soil*, or from the *people* of Britain? If from the latter, do they lose it by quitting the soil? Do those, who embark, freemen, in Great Britain, disembark, slaves, in America? Are those, who fled from the oppression of regal and ministerial tryanny, now reduced to a state of vassalage to those, who, then, equally felt the same oppression? Whence proceeds this fatal change? Is this the return made us for leaving our friends and our country—for braving the danger of the deep—for planting a wilderness, inhabited only by savage men and savage beasts—for extending the dominions of the British crown—for increasing the trade of the British merchants—for augmenting the rents of

* These excerpts are reprinted from James DeWitt Andrews (ed.), *The Works of James Wilson* (1896), vol. II, pp. 522–529, 531–542.

the British landlords—for heightening the wages of the British artificers? Britons should blush to make such a claim: Americans would blush to own it.

It is not, however, the ignominy only, but the danger also, with which we are threatened, that affects us. The many and careful provisions which are made by the British constitution, that the electors of members of parliament may be prevented from choosing representatives, who would betray them; and that the representatives may be prevented from betraying their constituents with impunity, sufficiently evince, that such precautions have been deemed absolutely necessary for securing and maintaining the system of British liberty.

How would the commons of Great Britain startle at a proposal, to deprive them of their share in the legislature, by rendering the house of commons independent of them! With what indignation would they hear it? What resentment would they feel and discover against the authors of it! Yet the commons of Great Britain would suffer less inconvenience from the execution of such a proposal, than the Americans will suffer from the extension of the legislative authority of parliament over them.

The members of parliament, their families, their friends, their posterity must be subject, as well as others, to the laws. Their interest, and that of their families, friends, and posterity, cannot be different from the interest of the rest of the nation. A regard to the former will, therefore, direct to such measures as must promote the latter. But is this the case with respect to America? Are the legislators of Great Britain subject to the laws which are made for the colonies? Is their interest the same with that of the colonies? If we consider it in a large and comprehensive view, we shall discern it to be undoubtedly the same; but few will take the trouble to consider it in that view; and of those who do, few will be influenced by the consideration. Mankind are usually more affected with a near though inferior interest, than with one that is superior, but placed at a greater distance. As the conduct is regulated by the passions, it is not to be wondered at, if they secure the former, by measures which will forfeit the latter. Nay, the latter will frequently be regarded in the same manner as if it were prejudicial to them. It is with regret that I produce some late regulations of parliament as proofs of what I have advanced. We have experienced what an easy matter it is for a minister with an ordinary share of art, to persuade the parliament and the people, that taxes laid on the colonies will ease the burthens of the mother country; which, if the matter is considered in a proper light, is, in fact, to persuade them, that the stream of national riches will be increased by closing up the fountain, from which they flow.

As the Americans cannot avail themselves of that check, which interest puts upon the members of parliament, and which would operate in favor of the commons of Great Britain, though they possessed no power over the legislature; so the love of reputation, which is a powerful incitement to the legislators to promote the welfare, and obtain the approbation, of those among whom they live, and whose praises or censures will reach and affect them, may have a contrary operation with regard to the colonies. It may become popular and reputable at home to oppress us. A candidate may recommend himself at his election by recounting the many successful instances, in which he has sacrificed the interests of America to those of Great Britain. A member of the house of commons may plume himself upon his ingenuity in inventing schemes to serve the mother country at the expense of the colonies; and may boast of their impotent resentment against him on that account.

Let us pause here a little.—Does neither the love of gain, the love of praise, nor the love of honor influence the members of the British parliament in favor of the Americans? On what principles, then—on what motives of action, can we depend for the security of our liberties, of our properties, of everything dear to us in life, of life itself? Shall we depend on their veneration for the dictates of natural justice? A very little share of experience in the world—a very little degree of knowledge in the history of men, will sufficiently convince us, that a regard to justice is by no means the ruling principle in human nature. He would discover himself to be a very sorry statesman, who would erect a system of jurisprudence upon that slender foundation. "He would make," as my Lord Bacon says, "imaginary laws for imaginary commonwealths; and his discourses, like the stars, would give little light, because they are so high."

But this is not the worst that can justly be said concerning the situation of the colonies, if they are bound by the acts of the British legislature. So far are those powerful springs of action, which we have mentioned, from interesting the members of that legislature in our favor, that, as has been already observed, we have the greatest reason to dread their operation against us. While the happy commons of Great Britain congratulate themselves upon the liberty which they enjoy, and upon the provisions—infallible, as far as they can be rendered so by human wisdom—which are made for perpetuating it to their latest posterity; the unhappy Americans have reason to bewail the dangerous situation to which they are reduced; and to look forward, with dismal apprehension, to those future scenes of woe, which, in all probability, will open upon their descendants.

What has been already advanced will suffice to show, that it is repugnant to the essential maxims of jurisprudence, to the ultimate end of all governments, to the genius of the British constitution, and to the liberty and happiness of the colonies, that they should be bound by the legislative authority of the parliament of Great Britain. Such a doctrine is not less repugnant to the voice of her laws. In order to evince this, I shall appeal to some authorities from the books of the law, which show expressly, or by a necessary implication, that the colonies are not bound by the acts of the British parliament; because they have no share in the British legislature.

The first case I shall mention was adjudged in the second year of Richard the Third. It was a solemn determination of all the judges of England, met in the exchequer chamber, to consider whether the people in Ireland were bound by an act of parliament made in England. They resolved, "that they were not, as to such things as were done in Ireland; but that what they did out of Ireland must be conformable to the laws of England, because they were the subjects of England. Ireland," said they, "has a parliament, who make laws; and our statutes do not bind them; *because they do not send knights to parliament:* but their persons are the subjects of the king, in the same manner as the inhabitants of Calais, Gascoigne, and Guienne." . . .

From this authority it follows, that it is by no means a rule, that the authority of parliament extends to all the subjects of the crown. The inhabitants of Ireland were the subjects of the king as of his crown of England; but it is expressly resolved, in the most solemn manner, that the inhabitants of Ireland are not bound by the statutes of England. Allegiance to the king and obedience to the parliament are founded on very different principles. The former is founded on protection; the latter, on representation. An inattention to this difference has produced, I apprehend, much uncertainty and confusion in our ideas concerning the connection, which ought to subsist between Great Britain and the American colonies.

The last observation which I shall make on this case is, that if the inhabitants of Ireland are not bound by acts of parliament made in England, *à fortiori*, the inhabitants of the American colonies are not bound by them. . . .

The American colonies are not bound by the acts of the British parliament, because they are not represented in it. But what reason can be assigned why they should be bound by those acts, in which they are specially named? Does naming them give those, who do them that honor, a right to rule over them? Is this the source of the supreme, the absolute, the irresistible, the uncontrolled authority of parliament? These positions are too absurd to be alleged; and a thousand judicial determinations in their favor would never induce one man of sense to subscribe his assent to them.

The obligatory force of the British statutes upon the colonies, when named in them, must be accounted for, by the advocates of that power, upon some other principle. In my Lord Coke's Reports, it is said, "that albeit Ireland be a distinct dominion, yet, *the title thereof being by conquest,* the same, by judgment of law, may be, by express words, bound by the parliaments of England." In this instance, the obligatory authority of the parliament is plainly referred to a title by conquest, as its foundation and original. . . . It is foreign to my purpose to inquire into the reasonableness of founding the authority of the British parliament over Ireland, upon the title of conquest, though I believe it would be somewhat difficult to deduce it satisfactorily in this manner. It will be sufficient for me to show, that it is unreasonable, and injurious to the colonies, to extend that title to them. How came the colonists to be a conquered people? By whom was the conquest over them obtained? By the house of commons? By the constituents of that house? If the idea of conquest must be taken into consideration when we examine into the title by which America is held, that idea, so far as it can operate, will operate in favor of the colonists, and not against them. Permitted and commissioned by the crown, they undertook, at their own expense, expeditions to this distant country, took possession of it, planted it, and cultivated it. Secure under the protection of their king, they grew and multiplied, and diffused British freedom and British spirit, wherever they came. Happy in the enjoyment of liberty, and in reaping the fruits of their toils; but still more happy in the joyful prospect of transmitting their liberty and their fortunes to the latest posterity, then inculcated to their children the warmest sentiments of loyalty to their sovereign, under whose auspices they enjoyed so many blessings, and of affection and esteem for the inhabitants of the mother country, with whom they gloried in being intimately connected. Lessons of loyalty to parliament, indeed, they never gave: they never suspected that such unheard-of loyalty would be required. They never suspected that their descendants would be considered and treated as a conquered people; and therefore they never taught them the submission and abject behavior suited to that character.

I am sufficiently aware of an objection, that will be made to what I have said concerning the legislative authority of the British parliament. It will be alleged, that I throw off all dependence on Great Britain. This objection will be held-forth, in its most specious colors, by those, who, from servility of soul, or from mercenary considerations, would meanly bow their necks to every exertion of arbitrary power: it may likewise alarm some, who entertain the most favorable opinion of the connection between Great Britain and her colonies; but who are not sufficiently acquainted with the nature of that connection, which is so dear to them. Those of the first class, I hope, are few; I am sure they are contemptible, and deserve to have very little regard paid to them: but for the sake of those of the second class, who may be more numerous, and whose laudable principles atone for their mistakes, I shall take some pains to obviate the objection, and to show that a denial of the legislative authority of the British parliament over America is by no means inconsistent with that connection, which ought to subsist between the mother country and her colonies, and which, at the first settlement of those colonies, it was intended to maintain between them; but that, on the contrary, that connection would be entirely destroyed by the extension of the power of parliament over the American plantations.

Let us examine what is meant by a *dependence* on Great Britain: for it is always of importance clearly to define the terms that we use. Blackstone, who, speaking of the colonies, tells us, that "they are no part of the mother country, but distinct (though dependent) dominions," explains dependence in this manner. "Dependence is very little else, but an obligation to conform to the will or law of that superior person or state, upon which the inferior depends. The original and true ground of this superiority, in the case of Ireland, is what we usually call, though somewhat improperly, the right of conquest; a right allowed by the law of nations, if not by that of nature; but which, in reason and civil policy, can mean nothing more, than that, in order to put an end to hostilities, a compact is either expressly or tacitly made between the conqueror and the conquered, that if they will acknowledge the victor for their master, he will treat them for the future as subjects, and not as enemies."

The original and true ground of the superiority of Great Britain over the American colonies is not shown in any book of the law, unless, as I have already observed, it be derived from the right of conquest. But I have proved, and I hope satisfactorily, that this right is altogether inapplicable to the colonists. The original of the superiority of Great Britain over the colonies is, then, unaccounted for; and when we consider the ingenuity and pains which have lately been employed at home on this subject, we may justly conclude, that the only reason why it is not accounted for, is, that it cannot be accounted for. The superiority of Great Britain over the colonies ought, therefore, to be rejected; and the dependence of the colonies upon her, if it is to be construed into "an obligation to conform to the will or law of the superior state," ought, in *this* sense, to be rejected also.

My sentiments concerning this matter are not singular. They coincide with the declarations and remonstrances of the colonies against the statutes imposing taxes on them. It was their unanimous opinion, that the parliament have no right to exact obedience to those statutes; and, consequently, that the colonies are under no obligation to obey them. The dependence of the colonies on Great Britain was denied, in those instances; but a denial of it in those instances is, in effect, a denial of it in all other instances. For, if dependence is an obligation to conform to the will or law of the superior state, any exceptions to that obligation must destroy the dependence. If, therefore, by a dependence of the colonies on Great Britain, it is meant, that they are obliged to obey the laws of Great Britain, reason, as well as the unanimous voice of the Americans, teaches us to disown it. Such a dependence was never thought of by those who left Britain, in order to settle in America; nor by their sovereigns, who gave them commissions for that purpose. Such an obligation has no correspondent right: for the commons of Great Britain have no dominion over their equals and fellow-subjects in America; they can confer no right to their delegates to bind those equals and fellow-subjects by laws.

There is another, and a much more reasonable meaning, which may be intended by the dependence of the colonies on Great Britain. The phrase may be used to denote the obedience and loyalty, which the colonists owe to the *kings* of Great Britain. If it should be alleged, that this cannot be the meaning of the expression, because it is applied to the kingdom, and not to the king, I give the same answer that my Lord Bacon gave to those who said that allegiance related to the kingdom and not to the king; because in the statutes there are these words—"born within the allegiance of England" —and again—"born without the allegiance of England." "There is no trope of speech more familiar," says he, "than to use the place of addition for the person. So we say commonly, the line of York, or the line of Lancaster, for the lines of the duke of York, or the duke of Lancaster. So we say the possessions of Somerset or Warwick, intending the possessions of the dukes of Somerset, or earls of Warwick. And in the very same manner, the statute speaks, allegiance of England, for allegiance of the king of England."

Dependence on the mother country seems to have been understood in this sense, both by the first planters of the colonies, and also by the most eminent lawyers, at that time, in England.

Those who launched into the unknown deep, in quest of new countries and habitations, still considered themselves as subjects of the English monarchs, and behaved suitably to that character; but it nowhere appears, that they still considered themselves as represented in an English parliament, or that they thought the authority of the English parliament extended over them. They took possession of the country in the *king's* name: they treated, or made war with the Indians by *his* authority: they held the lands under *his* grants, and paid *him* the rents reserved upon them: they established governments under the sanction of *his* prerogative, or by virtue of *his* charters:—no application for those purposes was made to the parliament: no ratification of the charters or letters patent was solicited from that assembly, as is usual in England with regard to grants and franchises of much less importance.

My Lord Bacon's sentiments on this subject ought to have great weight with us. His immense genius, his universal learning, his deep insight into the laws and constitution of England, are well known and much admired. Besides, he lived at that time when settling and improving the American plantations began seriously to be attended to, and successfully to be carried into execution. Plans for the government and regulation of the colonies were then forming: and it is only from the first general idea of these plans, that we can unfold, with precision and accuracy, all the more minute and intricate parts, of which they now consist. "The settlement of colonies," says he, "must proceed from the option of those who will settle them, else it sounds like an exile: they must be raised by the *leave,* and not by the *command* of the *king.* At their setting out, they must have their commission, or letters patent, from the *king,* that so they may acknowledge their *dependency upon the crown* of England, and under his protection." In another place he says, "that they still must be subjects of the realm." "In order to regulate all the inconveniences, which will insensibly grow upon them," he proposes, "that the king should erect a subordinate council in England, whose care and charge shall be, to advise, and put in execution, all things which shall be found fit for the good of those new plantations; who, upon all occasions, shall give an account of their proceedings, to the king or the council board, and from *them* receive such directions, as may best agree with the government of that place." It is evident, from these quotations, that my Lord Bacon had no conception that the parliament would or ought to interpose, either in the settlement or the government of the colonies. The only relation, in which he says the colonists must still continue, is that of subjects: the only dependency, which they ought to acknowledge, is a dependency on the crown.

This is a dependence, which they have acknowledged hitherto; which they acknowledge now; and which, if it is reasonable to judge of the future by the past and the present, they will continue to acknowledge hereafter. It is not a dependence, like that contended for on parliament, slavish and unaccountable, or accounted for only by principles that are false and inapplicable: it is a dependence founded upon the principles of reason, of liberty and of law. Let us investigate its sources.

The colonists ought to be dependent on the king, because they have hitherto enjoyed, and still continue to enjoy, his protection. Allegiance is the faith and obedience, which every subject owes to his prince. This obedience is founded on the protection derived from government: for protection and allegiance are the reciprocal bonds, which connect the prince and his subjects. Every subject, so soon as he is born, is under the royal protection, and is entitled to all the advantages arising from it. He therefore owes obedience to that royal power, from which the protection, which he enjoys, is derived. But while he continues in infancy and nonage, he cannot perform the duties which his allegiance requires. The performance of them must be respited till he arrive at the years of discretion and maturity. When he arrives at those years, he owes obedience, not only for the protection which he now enjoys, but also for that which from his birth, he has enjoyed; and to which his tender age has hitherto prevented him from making a suitable return. Allegiance now becomes a duty founded upon principles of gratitude, as well as on principles of interest: it becomes a debt, which nothing but the loyalty of a whole life will discharge. As neither climate, nor soil, nor time entitle a person to the benefits of a subject; so an alteration of climate, of soil, or of time cannot release him from the duties of one. An Englishman, who removes to foreign countries, however distant from England, owes the same allegiance to his king there which he owed him at home; and will owe it twenty years hence as much as he owes it now. Wherever he is, he is still liable to the punishment annexed by law to crimes against his allegiance; and still entitled to the advantages promised by law to the duties of it: it is not cancelled; and it is not forfeited. "Hence all children born in any part of the world, if they be of English parents continuing at that time as liege subjects to the king, and having done no act to forfeit the benefit of their allegiance, are *ipso facto* naturalized: and if they have issue, and their descendants intermarry among themselves, such descendants are naturalized to all generations." . . .

Now we have explained the dependence of the Americans. They are the subjects of the king of Great Britain. They owe him allegiance. They have a right to the benefits which arise from preserving that allegiance inviolate. They are liable to the punishments which await those who break it. This is a dependence, which they have always boasted of. The principles of loyalty are deeply rooted in their hearts; and there they will grow and bring forth fruit, while a drop of vital blood remains to nourish them. Their history is not stained with rebellious and treasonable machinations: an inviolable attachment to their sovereign, and the warmest zeal for his glory, shine in every page.

From this dependence, abstracted from every other source, arises a strict connection between the inhabitants of Great Britain and those of America. They are fellow-subjects; they are under allegiance to the same prince; and this union of allegiance naturally produces a union of hearts. It is also productive of a union of measures through the whole British dominions. To the king is intrusted the direction and management of the great machine of government. He therefore is fittest to adjust the different wheels, and to regulate their motions in such a manner as to co-operate in the same general designs. He makes war: he concludes peace: he forms alliances: he regulates domestic trade by his prerogative, and directs foreign commerce by his treaties with those nations, with whom it is carried on. He names the officers of government; so that he can check every jarring movement in the administration. He has a negative on the different legislatures throughout his dominions, so that he can prevent any repugnancy in their different laws.

The connection and harmony between Great Britain and us, which it is her interest and ours mutually to cultivate, and on which her prosperity, as well as ours, so materially depends, will be better preserved by the operation of the legal prerogatives of the crown, than by the exertion of an unlimited authority by parliament.

C. A WARNING TO THE KING: THOMAS JEFFERSON, "A SUMMARY VIEW OF THE RIGHTS OF BRITISH-AMERICA" (AUGUST, 1774)*

RESOLVED, that it be an instruction to the said deputies, when assembled in general congress with the deputies from the other states of British America, to propose to the said congress that an humble and dutiful address be presented to his Majesty, begging leave to lay before him, as Chief Magistrate of the British empire, the united complaints of his Majesty's subjects in America; complaints which are excited by many unwarrantable encroachments and usurpations, attempted to be made by the Legislature of one part of the empire, upon those rights which God and the laws have given equally and independently to all. To represent to his Majesty that these his states

* These selections are reprinted from the edition published in Philadelphia in 1774 by John Dunlap.

have often individually made humble application to his imperial throne to obtain, through its intervention, some redress of their injured rights, to none of which was ever even an answer condescended; humbly to hope that this their joint address, penned in the language of truth, and divested of those expressions of servility which would persuade his Majesty that we are asking favours, and not rights, shall obtain from his Majesty a more respectful acceptance. And this his Majesty will think we have reason to expect when he reflects that he is no more than the chief officer of the people, appointed by the laws, and circumscribed with definitive powers, to assist in working the great machine of government, erected for their use, and consequently subject to their superintendance. And in order that these our rights, as well as the invasions of them, may be laid more fully before his Majesty, to take a view of them from the origin and first settlement of these countries.

To remind him that our ancestors, before their emigration to America, were the free inhabitants of the British dominions in Europe, and possessed a right which nature has given to all men, of departing from the country in which chance, not choice, has placed them, of going in quest of new habitations, and of there establishing new societies, under such laws and regulations as to them shall seem most likely to promote public happiness. That their Saxon ancestors had under this universal law, in like manner left their native wilds and woods in the north of Europe, had possessed themselves of the island of Britain, then less charged with inhabitants, and had established there that system of laws which has so long been the glory and protection of that country. Nor was ever any claim of superiority or dependence asserted over them by that mother country from which they had migrated; and were such a claim made, it is believed that his Majesty's subjects in Great-Britain have too firm a feeling of the rights derived to them from their ancestors, to bow down the sovereignty of their state before such visionary pretensions. And it is thought that no circumstance has occurred to distinguish materially the British from the Saxon emigration. America was conquered, and her settlements made, and firmly established, at the expence of individuals, and not of the British public. Their own blood was spilt in acquiring lands for their settlement, their own fortunes expended in making that settlement effectual; for themselves they fought, for themselves they conquered, and for themselves alone they have right to hold. Not a shilling was ever issued from the public treasures of his Majesty, or his ancestors, for their assistance, till of very late times, after the colonies had become established on a firm and permanent footing. That then, indeed, having become valuable to Great-Britain for her commercial purposes, his Parliament was pleased to lend them assistance against an enemy, who would fain have drawn to herself the benefits of their commerce, to the great aggrandizment of herself, and danger of Great-Britain. Such assistance, and in such circumstances, they had often before given to Portugal, and other allied states, with whom they carry on a commercial intercourse; yet these states never supposed, that by calling in her aid, they thereby submitted themselves to her sovereignty. Had such terms been proposed, they would have rejected them with disdain, and trusted for better to the moderation of their enemies, or to a vigorous exertion of their own force. We do not, however, mean to under-rate those aids, which to us were doubtless valuable, on whatever principles granted; but we would shew that they cannot give a title to that authority which the British Parliament would arrogate over us, and that they may amply be repaid by our giving to the inhabitants of Great-Britain such exclusive privileges in trade as may be advantageous to them, and at the same time not too restrictive to ourselves. That settlements having been thus effected in the wilds of America, the emigrants thought proper to adopt that system of laws under which they had hitherto lived in the mother country, and to continue their union with her by submitting themselves to the same common Sovereign, who was thereby made the central link connecting the several parts of the empire thus newly multiplied.

But that not long were they permitted, however far they thought themselves removed from the hand of oppression, to hold undisturbed the rights thus acquired, at the hazard of their lives, and loss of their fortunes. A family of princes was then on the British throne, whose treasonable crimes against their people brought on them afterwards the exertion of those sacred and sovereign rights of punishment reserved in the hands of the people for cases of extreme necessity, and judged by the constitution unsafe to be delegated to any other judicature. While every day brought forth some new and unjustifiable exertion of power over their subjects on that side the water, it was not to be expected that those here, much less able at that time to oppose the designs of despotism, should be exempted from injury.

Accordingly that country, which had been acquired by the lives, the labours, and the fortunes of individual adventurers, was by these princes, at several times, parted out and distributed among the favourites and followers of their fortunes, and, by an assumed right of the crown alone, were erected into distinct and independent governments; a measure which it is believed his Majesty's prudence and understanding would prevent him from imitating at this day, as no exercise of such a power, of dividing and dismembering a country, has ever occurred in his Majesty's realm of England, though now of very ancient standing; nor could it be justified or acquiesced under there, or in any other part of his Majesty's empire.

That the exercise of a free trade with all parts of the world, possessed by the American colonists, as of natural right, and which no law of their own had taken away or abridged, was next the object of unjust encroachment. Some of the colonies having thought proper to continue the administration of their government in the name and under the authority of his Majesty King Charles the First, whom notwithstanding his late deposition by the commonwealth of England, they continued in the sovereignty of their state; the Parliament for the commonwealth took the same in high offence, and assumed upon themselves the power of prohibiting their trade with all other parts of the world, except the island of Great-Britain. This arbitrary act, however, they soon recalled, and by solemn treaty, entered into on the 12th day of March, 1651, between the said commonwealth by their commissioners, and the colony of Virginia by their house of burgesses, it was expressly stipulated, by the 8th article of the said treaty, that they should have "free trade as the people of England do enjoy to all places and with all nations, according to the laws of that commonwealth." But that, upon the restoration of his majesty king Charles the second, their rights of free commerce fell once more a victim to arbitrary power; and by several acts of his reign, as well as of some of his successors, the trade of the colonies was laid under such restrictions, as shew what hopes they might form from the justice of a British parliament, were its uncontrouled power admitted over these states. History has informed us that bodies of men, as well as individuals, are susceptible of the spirit of tyranny. A view of these acts of parliament for regulation, as it has been affectedly called, of the American trade, if all other evidence were removed out of the case, would undeniably evince the truth of this observation. Besides the duties they impose on our article of export and import, they prohibit our going to any markets northward of Cape Finisterre, in the kingdom of Spain, for the sale of commodities which Great Britain will not take from us, and for the purchase of others, with which she cannot supply us, and that for no other than the arbitrary purposes of purchasing for themselves, by a sacrifice of our rights and interests, certain privileges in their commerce with an allied state, who in confidence that their exclusive trade with America will be continued, while the principles and power of the British parliament be the same, have indulged themselves in every exorbitance which their avarice could dictate, or our necessities extort; have raised their commodities called for in America, to the double and treble of what they sold for before such exclusive privileges were given them, and of what better commodities of the same kind would cost us elsewhere, and at the same time give us much less for what we carry thither than might be had at more convenient ports. That these acts prohibit us from carrying in quest of other purchasers the surplus of our tobacoes remaining after the consumption of Great Britain is supplied; so that we must leave them with the British merchant for whatever he will please to allow us, to be by him reshipped to foreign markets, where he will reap the benefits of making sale of them for full value. That to heighten still the idea of parliamentary justice, and to shew with what moderation they are like to exercise power, where themselves are to feel no part of its weight, we take leave to mention to his majesty's certain other acts of British parliament, by which they would prohibit us from manufacturing for our own use the articles we raise on our own lands with our own labour. By an act passed in the 5th year of the reign of his late majesty king George the second, an American subject is forbidden to make a hat for himself of the fur which he has taken perhaps on his own soil; an instance of despotism to which no parallel can be produced in the most arbitrary ages of British history. By one other act passed in the 23d year of the same reign, the iron which we make we are forbidden to manufacture, and heavy as that article is, and necessary in every branch of husbandry, besides commission and insurance, we are to pay freight for it to Great Britain, and freight for it back again, for the purpose of supporting not men, but machines, in the island of Great Britain. In the same spirit of equal and impartial legislation is to be viewed the act of parliament passed in the 5th year of the same reign, by which American lands are made subject to the demands of British creditors, while their own lands were still continued unanswerable for their debts; from which one of these conclusions must necessarily follow, either that justice is not the same in America as in Britain, or else that the British parliament pay less regard to it here than there. But that we do not point out to his majesty the injustice of these acts, with intent to rest on that principle the cause of their nullity; but to shew that experience confirms the propriety of those political principles which exempt us from the jurisdiction of the British parliament. The true ground on which we declare these acts void is, that the British parliament has no right to exercise authority over us.

That these exercises of usurped power have not been confined to instances alone, in which themselves were interested, but they have also intermeddled with the regulation of the internal affairs of the colonies. The act of the 9th of Anne for establishing a post office in America seems to have had little connexion with British convenience, except that of accommodating his majesty's ministers and favourites with the sale of a lucrative and easy office.

That thus we have hastened through the reigns which preceded his majesty's, during which the violations of our right were less alarming, because repeated at more distant intervals than that rapid and bold succession of injuries which is likely to distinguish the present from all other periods of American story. Scarcely have our minds been able to emerge from the astonishment into which one stroke of parliamentary thunder has involved us, before another more heavy, and more alarming, is fallen on us. Single acts of tyranny may be ascribed to the accidental opinion of a day; but a series of oppressions begun at a distinguished period, and pursued, unalterably through every change of ministers, too plainly prove a deliberate and systematical plan of reducing us to slavery.

That the act, passed in the 4th year of his majesty's reign, entitled "An act for granting certain duties in the British colonies and plantations in America, &c."

One other act, passed in the 6th year of his reign, entituled "An act for the better securing the dependency of his majesty's dominions in America upon the crown and parliament of Great Britain;" and one other act, passed in the 7th year of his reign, entitled "An act for granting duties on paper, tea, &c." form that connected chain of parliamentary usurpation, which has already been the subject of frequent applications to his majesty, and the houses of lords and commons of Great Britain; and no answers having yet been condescended to any of these, we shall not trouble his majesty with a repetition of the matters they contained.

But that one other act, passed in the same 7th year of the reign, having been a peculiar attempt, must ever require peculiar mention; it is entituled "An act for suspending the legislature of New York." One free and independant legislature hereby takes upon itself to suspend the powers of another, free and independant as itself; thus exhibiting a phœnomenon unknown in nature, the creator and creature of its own power. Not only the principles of common sense, but the common feelings of human nature, must be surrendered up before his majesty's subjects here can be persuaded to believe that they hold their political existence at the will of a British parliament. Shall these governments be dissolved, their property annihilated, and their people reduced to a state of nature, at the imperious breath of a body of men, whom they never saw, in whom they never confided, and over whom they have no powers of punishment or removal, let their crimes against the American public be ever so great? Can any one reason be assigned why 160,000 electors in the island of Great Britain should give law to four millions in the states of America, every individual of whom is equal to every individual of them, in virtue, in understanding, and in bodily strength? Were this to be admitted, instead of being a free people, as we have hitherto supposed, and mean to continue ourselves, we should suddenly be found the slaves not of one but of 160,000 tyrants distinguished too from all others by this singular circumstance, that they are removed from the reach of fear, the only restraining motive which may hold the hand of a tyrant.

That by "an act to discontinue in such manner and for such time as are therein mentioned, the landing and discharging, lading or shipping, of goods, wares, and merchandize, at the town and within the harbour of Boston, in the province of Massachusetts Bay, in North America," which was passed at the last session of British parliament; a large and populous town, whose trade was their sole subsistence, was deprived of that trade, and involved in utter ruin. Let us for a while suppose the question of right suspended, in order to examine this act on principles of justice: An act of parliament had been passed imposing duties on teas, to be paid in America, against which act the Americans had protested as inauthoritative. The East India Company, who till that time had never sent a pound of tea to America on their own account, step forth on that occasion the assertors of parliamentary right, and send hither many ship loads of that obnoxious commodity. The masters of their several vessels, however, on their arrival in America, wisely attended to admonition, and returned with their cargoes. In the province of New England alone the remonstrances of the people were disregarded, and a compliance, after being many days waited for, was flatly refused. Whether in this the master of the vessel was governed by his obstinacy, or his instructions, let those who know say. There are extraordinary situations which require extraordinary interposition. An exasperated people, who feel that they possess power, are not easily restrained within limits strictly regular. A number of them assembled in the town of Boston, threw the tea into the ocean, and dispersed without doing any other act of violence. If in this they did wrong, they were known and were amenable to the laws of the land, against which it could not be objected that they had ever, in any instance, been obstructed or diverted from their regular course in favour of popular offenders. They should therefore not have been distrusted on this occasion. But that ill fated colony had formerly been bold in their enmities against the house of Stuart, and were now devoted to ruin by that unseen hand which governs the momentous affairs of this great empire. On the partial representations of a few worthless ministerial dependants, whose constant office it has been to keep that government embroiled, and who, by their treacheries, hope to obtain the dignity of the British knighthood, without calling for the party accused, without asking a proof, without attempting a distinction between the guilty and the innocent, the whole of that ancient and wealthy town is in a moment reduced from opulence to beggary. Men who had spent their lives in extending the British commerce, who had invested in that place the wealth their honest endeavours had merited, found themselves and their families thrown at once on the world for subsistence by its charities. Not the hundredth part of the inhabitants of that town had been concerned in the act complained of, many of them were in Great Britain and in other parts beyond sea, yet all were involved in one indiscriminate ruin, by a new executive power unheard of till then, that of a British parliament. A property, of the value of many millions of money, was sacrificed to revenge, not repay, the loss of a few thousands. This is administering justice with a heavy hand indeed! and when is this tempest to be arrested in its course? Two wharfs are to be opened again when his Majesty shall think proper. The residue, which lined the extensive shores of the bay of Boston, are forever interdicted the exercise of commerce. This little exception seems to have been thrown in for no other purpose than that of setting a precedent for investing his majesty with legislative powers. If the pulse of his people shall beat calmly under this experiment, another and another will be tried, till the measure of despotism be filled up. It would be an insult on common sense to pretend that this exception was made in order to restore its commerce to that great town. The trade which cannot be received at two wharfs alone must of necessity be transferred to some other place; to which it will soon be followed by that of the two wharfs. Considered in this light, it would be an insolent and cruel mockery at the annihilation of the town of Boston.

By the act for the suppression of riots and tumults in the town of Boston, passed also in the last session of parliament, a murder committed there is, if the governor pleases, to be tried in a court of King's Bench, in the island of Great Britain, by a jury of Middlesex. The witnesses, too, on receipt of such a sum as the governor shall think it reasonable for them to expend, are to enter into recognizance to appear at the trial. This is, in other words, taxing them to the amount of their recognizance, and that amount may be whatever a governor pleases; for who does his majesty think can be prevailed on to cross the Atlantic for the sole purpose of bearing evidence to a fact? His expences are to be borne, indeed, as they shall be estimated by a governor; but who are to feed the wife and children whom he leaves behind, and who have had no other subsistence but his daily labour? Those epidemical disorders too, so terrible in a foreign climate, is the cure of them to be estimated among the articles of expence, and their danger to be warded off by the almighty power of parliament? And the wretched criminal, if he happen to have offended on the American side, stripped of his privilege of trial by peers of his vicinage, removed from the place where alone full evidence could be obtained, without money, without counsel, without friends, without exculpatory proof, is tried before judges predetermined to condemn. The cowards who would suffer a countryman to be torn from the bowels of their society, in order to be thus offered a sacrifice to parliamentary tyranny, would merit that everlasting infamy now fixed on the authors of the act! A clause for a similar purpose had been introduced into an act passed in the twelfth year of his majesty's reign, entitled "An act for the better securing and preserving his majesty's dockyards, magazines, ships, ammunition and stores," against which, as meriting the same censures, the several colonies have already protested.

That these are acts of power, assumed by a body of men, foreign to our constitutions, and unacknowledged by our laws, against which we do, on behalf of the inhabitants of British America, enter this our solemn and determined protest; and we do earnestly entreat his majesty, as yet the only mediatory power between the several states of the British empire, to recommend to his parliament of Great Britain the total revocation of these acts, which, however nugatory they be, may yet prove the cause of further discontents and jealousies among us.

That we next proceed to consider the conduct of his majesty, as holding the executive powers of the laws of these states, and mark out his deviations from the line of duty: By the constitution of Great Britain, as well as of the several American states, his majesty possesses the power of refusing to pass into a law any bill which has already passed the other two branches of legislature. His majesty, however, and his ancestors, conscious of the impropriety of opposing their single opinion to the united wisdom of two houses of parliament, while their proceedings were unbiassed by interested principles, for several ages past have modestly declined the exercise of this power in that part of his empire called Great Britain. But by change of circumstances, other principles than those of justice simply have obtained an influence on their determinations; the addition of new states to the British empire has produced an addition of new, and sometimes opposite interests. It is now, therefore, the great office of his majesty, to resume the exercise of his negative power, and to prevent the passage of laws by any one legislature of the empire, which might bear injuriously on the rights and interests of another. Yet this will not excuse the wanton exercise of this power which we have seen his Majesty practice on the laws of the American legislatures. For the most trifling reasons, and sometimes for no conceivable reason at all, his majesty has rejected laws of the most salutary tendency. The abolition of domestic slavery is the great object of desire in those colonies, where it was unhappily introduced in their infant state. But previous to the enfranchisement of the slaves we have, it is necessary to exclude all further importations from Africa; yet our repeated attempts to effect this by prohibitions, and by imposing duties which might amount to a prohibition, have been hitherto defeated by his majesty's negative: Thus preferring the immediate advantages of a few African corsairs to the lasting interests of the American states, and to the rights of human nature deeply wounded by this infamous practice. Nay, the single interposition of an interested individual against a law was scarcely ever known to fail of success, though in the opposite scale were placed the interests of a whole country. That this is so shameful an abuse of a power trusted with his majesty for other purposes, as if not reformed, would call for some legal restrictions.

With equal inattention to the necessities of his people here has his majesty permitted our laws to lie neglected in England for years, neither confirming them by his assent, nor annulling them by his negative; so that such of them as have no suspending clause we hold on the most precarious of all tenures, his majesty's will, and such of them as suspend themselves till his majesty's assent be obtained, we have feared, might be called into existence at some future and distant period, when time and change of circumstances shall have rendered them destructive to his people here. And to render this grievance still more oppressive, his majesty by his instructions has laid his governors under such restrictions that they can pass no law of any moment unless it have such suspending clause; so that, however immediate may be the call for legislative interposition, the law cannot be executed till it has twice crossed the Atlantic, by which time the evil may have spent its whole force.

But in what terms, reconcileable to majesty, and at the same time to truth, shall we speak of a late instruction to his majesty's governor of the colony of Virginia, by which he is forbidden to assent to any law for the division of a county, unless the new county will consent to have no representative in assembly? That colony has as yet fixed no boundary to the westward. Their western counties, therefore, are of indefinite extent; some of them are actually seated many hundred miles from their eastern limits. Is it possible, then, that his majesty can have bestowed a single thought on the situation of those people, who, in order to obtain justice for injuries, however great or small, must, by the laws of that colony, attend their county court, at such a distance, with all their witnesses, monthly, till their litigation be determined? Or does his majesty seriously wish, and publish it to the world, that his subjects should give up the glorious right of representation, with all the benefits derived from that, and submit themselves the absolute slaves of his sovereign will? Or is it rather meant to confine the legislative body to their present numbers, that they may be the cheaper bargain whenever they shall become worth a purchase.

One of the articles of impeachment against Tresilian, and the other judges of Westminster-Hall, in the reign of Richard the second, for which they suffered death, as traitors to their country, was, that they had advised the king that he might dissolve his parliament at any time; and succeeding kings have adopted the opinion of these unjust judges. Since the establishment, however, of the British constitution, at the glorious revolution, on its free and antient principles, neither his majesty, nor his ancestors, have exercised such a power of dissolution in the island of Great Britain; and when his majesty was petitioned, by the united voice of his people there, to dissolve the present parliament, who had become obnoxious to them, his ministers were heard to declare, in open parliament, that his majesty possessed no such power by the constitution. But how different their language and his practice here! To declare, as their duty required, the known rights of their country, to oppose the usurpations of every foreign judicature, to disregard the imperious mandates of a minister or governor, have been the avowed causes of dissolving houses of representatives in America. But if such powers be really vested in his majesty, can he suppose they are there placed to awe the members from such purposes as these? When the representative body have lost the confidence of their constituents, when they have notoriously made sale of their most valuable rights, when they have assumed to themselves powers which the people never put into their hands, then indeed their continuing in office becomes dangerous to the state, and calls for an exercise of the power of dissolution. Such being the causes for which the representative body should, and should not, be dissolved, will it not appear strange to an unbiassed observer, that that of Great Britain was not dissolved, while those of the colonies have repeatedly incurred that sentence?

But your majesty, or your governors, have carried this power beyond every limit known, or provided for, by the laws: After dissolving one house of representatives, they have refused to call another, so that for a great length of time, the legislature provided by the laws has been out of existence. From the nature of things, every society must at all times possess within itself the sovereign powers of legislation. The feelings of human nature revolt against the supposition of a state so situated as that it may not in any emergency provide against dangers which perhaps threaten immediate ruin. While those bodies are in existence to whom the people have delegated the powers of legislation, they alone possess and may exercise those powers; but when they are dissolved by the lopping off one or more of their branches, the power reverts to the people, who may exercise it to unlimited extent, either assembling together in person, sending deputies, or in any other way they may think proper. We forbear to trace consequences further; the dangers are conspicuous with which this practice is replete.

That we shall at this time also take notice of an error in the nature of our land holdings, which crept in at a very early period of our settlement. The introduction of the feudal tenures into the kingdom of England, though ancient, is well enough understood to set this matter in a proper light. In the earlier ages of the Saxon settlement feudal holdings were certainly altogether unknown; and very few, if any, had been introduced at the time of the Norman conquest. Our Saxon ancestors held their lands, as they did their personal property, in absolute dominion, disencumbered with any superior, answering mearly to the nature of those possessions which the feudalists term allodial. William, the Norman, first introduced that system generally. The lands which had belonged to those who fell in the battle of Hastings, and in the subsequent insurrections of his reign, formed a considerable proportion of the lands of the whole kingdom. These he granted out, subject to feudal duties, as did he also those of a great number of his new subjects, who, by persuasions or threats, were induced to surrender them for that purpose. But still much was left in the hands of his Saxon subjects: held of no superior, and not subject to feudal conditions. These, therefore, by express laws, enacted to render uniform the system of military defence, were made liable to the same military duties as if they had been feuds; and the Norman lawyers soon found means to saddle them also with all the other feudal burthens. But still they had not been surrendered to the king, they were not derived from his grant, and therefore they were not holden of him. A general principle, indeed, was introduced, that "all lands in England were held either mediately or immediately of the crown," but this was borrowed from those holdings, which were truly feudal, and only applied to others for the purposes of illustration. Feudal holdings were therefore but exceptions out of the Saxon laws of possession, under which all lands were held in absolute right. These, therefore, still form the basis, or ground-work, of the common law, to prevail wheresoever the exceptions have not taken place. America was not conquered by William the Norman, nor its lands surrendered to him, or any of his successors. Possessions there are undoubtedly of the allodial nature. Our ancestors, however, who migrated hither, were farmers, not lawyers. The fictitious principle that all lands belong originally to the king, they were early persuaded to believe real; and accordingly took grants of their own lands from the crown. And while the crown continued to grant for small sums, and on reasonable rents, there was no inducement to arrest the error, and lay it open to public view. But his majesty has lately taken on him to advance the terms of purchase, and of holding to the double of what they were, by which means the acquisition of lands being rendered difficult, the population of our country is likely to be checked. It is time, therefore, for us to lay this matter before his majesty, and to declare that he has no right to grant lands of himself. From the nature and purpose of civil institutions, all the lands within the limits which any particular society has circumscribed around itself are assumed by that society, and subject to their allotment only. This may be done by themselves assembled collectively, or by their legislature, to whom they may have delegated sovereign authority; and if they are allotted in neither of these ways, each individual of the society may appropriate to himself such lands as he finds vacant, and occupancy will give him title.

That in order to enforce the arbitrary measures before complained of, his majesty has from time to time sent among us large bodies of armed forces, not made up of the people here, nor raised by the authority of our laws: Did his majesty possess such a right as this, it might swallow up all our other rights whenever he should think proper. But his majesty has no right to land a single armed man on our shores, and those whom he sends here are liable to our laws made for the suppression and punishment of riots, routs, and unlawful assemblies; or are hostile bodies, invading us in defiance of law. When in the course of the late war it became expedient that a body of Hanoverian troops should be brought over for the defence of Great Britain, his majesty's grandfather, our late sovereign, did not pretend to introduce them under any authority he possessed. Such a measure would have given just alarm to his subjects in Great Britain, whose liberties would not be safe if armed men of another country, and of another spirit, might be brought into the realm at any time without the consent of their legislature. He therefore applied to parliament, who passed an act for that purpose, limiting the number to be brought in, and the time they were to continue. In like manner is his majesty restrained in every part of the empire. He possesses, indeed, the the executive power of the laws in every state, but they are the laws of the particular state which he is to administer within that state, and not those of any one within the limits of another. Every state must judge for itself the number of armed men which they may safely trust among them, of whom they are to consist, and under what restrictions they shall be laid.

To render these proceedings still more criminal against our laws, instead of subjecting the military to the civil powers, his majesty has expressly made the civil subordinate to the military. But can his majesty thus put down all law under his feet? Can he erect a power superior to that which erected himself? He has done it indeed by force, but let him remember that force cannot give right.

That these are our grievances, which we have thus laid before his majesty, with that freedom of language and sentiment which becomes a free people claiming their rights, as derived from the laws of nature, and not as the gift of their chief magistrate: Let those flatter who fear, it is not an American art. To give praise which is not due might be well from the venal, but would ill beseem those who are asserting the rights of human nature. They know, and will therefore say, that kings are the servants, not the proprietors of the people. Open your breast, sire, to liberal and expanded thought. Let not the name of George the third be a blot in the page of history. You are surrounded by British counsellors, but remember that they are parties. You have no ministers for American affairs, because you have none taken from among us, nor amenable to the laws on which they are to give you advice. It behoves you, therefore, to think and to act for yourself and your people. The great principles of right and wrong are legible to every reader; to pursue them requires not the aid of many counsellors. The whole art of government consists in the art of being honest. Only aim to do your duty, and mankind will give you credit where you fail. No longer persevere in sacrificing the rights of one part of the empire to the inordinate desires of another; but deal out to all equal and impartial right. Let no act be passed by any one legislature which may infringe on the rights and liberties of another. This is the important post in which fortune has placed you, holding the balance of a great, if a well poised empire. This, sire, is the advice of your great American council, on the observance of which may perhaps depend your felicity and future fame, and the preservation of that harmony which alone can continue both to Great Britain and America the reciprocal advantages of their connection. It is neither our wish nor our interest to separate from her. We are willing, on our part, to sacrifice every thing which reason can ask to the restoration of that tranquillity for which all must wish. On their part, let them be ready to establish union and a generous plan. Let them name their terms, but let them be just. Accept of every commercial preference it is in our power to give for such things as we can raise for their use, or they make for ours. But let them not think to exclude us from going to other markets to dispose of those commodities which they cannot use, or to supply those wants which they cannot supply.—Still less let it be proposed that our properties within our own territories shall be taxed or regulated by any power on earth but our own. The God who gave us life gave us liberty at the same time; the hand of force may destroy, but cannot disjoin them. This, sire, is our last; our determined resolution; and that you will be pleased to interpose with that efficacy which your earnest endeavours may ensure to procure redress of these our great grievances, to quiet the minds of your subjects in British America, against any apprehensions of future encroachment, to establish fraternal love and harmony through the whole empire, and that these may continue to the latest ages of time, is the fervent prayer of all British America!

SELECTION

The Attempt at Compromise

Alarmed by the drift of events, a sizable number of Americans opposed the dominant stream of colonial thought and in one way or another attempted to reverse it. Some of these men simply believed that Parliament and the ministry were justified in punishing Massachusetts Bay; others were men of faint heart who thought it was folly to oppose the power of Britain; and still others tried to seek out some middle ground that would compromise the issues in dispute and put an end to the now seemingly chronic difficulties between Britain and the colonies. Representative of the last group and one of the few men from any of the three categories to be elected as a delegate to the First Continental Congress was Joseph Galloway (ca. 1731–1803), Philadelphia lawyer, nominal head of the Quaker political faction in Pennsylvania, speaker of the Pennsylvania Assembly, and long-time advocate of a moderate approach to the dispute with Britain. As he indicated in a letter, written less than a month before the convocation of the Congress and printed here as Selection 25 A, to Richard Jackson, an old friend and member of Parliament, he rejected the extreme position of both sides and was convinced that "both Countries should retreat a little" in order to find some compromise, some "constitutional" solution that would be acceptable to both parties. Increasingly coming to see himself as the one man who could work out such a compromise and thereby avert a permanent rupture between Britain and the colonies, Galloway prepared to lay before Congress his famous Plan of Union, printed below as Selection 25 B. Proposing to guarantee to each colony complete control over its internal affairs, this plan called for the creation of an "inferior and distinct branch of the British legislature" in the colonies to be composed of delegates from all of the continental colonies and presided over by a president general appointed by the King. The body was to have jurisdiction over general American affairs, but acceptance by both the

British and the American Parliament would be required before any measure respecting the colonies could go into effect.

The emergence in 1774 for the first time since the Stamp Act of an articulate opposition to whig leaders in the colonies is treated in William H. Nelson, The American Tory *(1961), which also contains a penetrating study of Galloway. On Galloway's Plan of Union see the discussion in Julian P. Boyd,* Anglo-American Union: Joseph Galloway's Plans to Preserve the British Empire, 1774–1788 *(1941). A biography of Galloway is Oliver C. Kuntzleman,* Joseph Galloway, Loyalist *(1941).*

A. THE SEARCH FOR A MIDDLE WAY: JOSEPH GALLOWAY TO RICHARD JACKSON (AUG. 10, 1774)*

. . . I have ever been of Opinion with You, that the Interest of Great Britain and her Colonies never can be separated upon any Principle of Policy or Good to either; but that their Happiness, their Dignity and Reputation among other Nations, with their common Safety, depend upon a solid political Union, to be formed on a Foundation very different from any that has been yet laid by the Friends and Advocates of either Country. In this Opinion I stand here almost alone; and perhaps, were I to remove to your great Capitol, where the most important Matters are decided, I should not be less so. However that might be, upon repeated Reviews of the Subject, and an impartial Examination of all that has been said and wrote upon it, I cannot say that I have had the least Reason to alter my Sentiments. Volumes have been written, and yet nothing is proposed, which carries with it the Appearance of a lasting Accommodation of the Dispute. On the one Side, the Advocates contend that the parliamentary Jurisdiction ought to be exercised over near 3,000,000 of People, none of whom have the least Participation in that Jurisdiction, or any Opportunity of communicating their Desires, Wants, and Necessities to it, which alone can enable it to form Regulations adapted to their Circumstances, or prevent those Regulations from being, in their Execution, attended with more Mischief than Benefit, and subversive of the End for which they were enacted. Certainly this Doctrine cannot be founded in Reason or Common Sense, in any Equity, or in the Nature, Policy, or Principles of the English Government. If not; is it unreasonable to expect the same Discontent will fill the Breasts of the Americans; which actuated the People of Wales, Chesire and Durham, when in the same unhappy Situation; when the like Doctrine was held and practised over them? And will not this Discontent be attended with Effects more mischievous and dangerous, where it takes Place in a People at the Distance, from the Seat of Power, of 3000 Miles, and more, especially as there is almost a moral Certainty, that their Numbers will increase tenfold in one Century? These Reasons induce me to wish, that the Politicians on your side the Water had condescended and taken the Matter up a little deeper at the End of the last War, and, instead of passing the Stamp-Act, they had cast their Thoughts upon the most proper Plan for cementing the two Countries together upon such Principles of Government and Policy, as would

---

* These excerpts are reprinted with the permission of the present Lord Dartmouth from the Dartmouth Papers, William Salt Library, Stafford, U.K.

have enabled them to obtain what they wanted, and secured to America the same Rights and Privileges as are enjoyed by the Subjects in Britain. A Plan of this Nature would in all Probability have succeeded in America at that Time, when the Omissions of Duty in the Colonies, the Deficiencies in their Contributions to the Expence which was necessary to the national Safety, the Inequality and Injustice of those Contributions among themselves, their weak and defenceless Situation arising from their Disunion, and heavy Sums, expended during War by the Mother State in their Defence, were obvious and had made deep Impressions of Gratitude and Affection. However this was not done. And perhaps it may be said, with some Reason, that such a Proposal should have originated in America, as she was inferior and the Party who sought Redress. I will not controvert such an Opinion. It was a Duty, as I thought, which America owed to herself as well as to Britain to do so; and I accordingly declared my Sentiments, but to no Purpose. For the American Advocates, instead of attending to the Want of a political Connection between the two Countries upon Principles of Equity, of Reason, and those Rights which were enjoyed by our Brethren in Britain, exerted all their Talents in denying the constitutional Authority of the British State to bind the Colonies, because they were not expressly represented in her Councils, and at the same Time declaring, that they will not accept of such Representation should it be offered to them; in tracing the American Rights up to Sources from which they never came, and where they never will be found, and in forming Lines of Jurisdiction most whimsical and novel; all which, instead of healing, had a manifest Tendency to widen the Breach, and to involve themselves and their Country in the severe Measures, which are now put in Practice towards them.

Is it not high Time, my dear Sir, that both Countries should retreat a little, and take other Ground, seeing That, which they are now upon, is likely to prove dangerous and distressing to Both? A thorough Conviction of the Truth of the two only essential Propositions in the Dispute will point out the Ground, which alone can ensure to them permanent Safety and Happiness. They are; that Great Britain ought not in Equity to exercise a Law-making Authority over the Colonies, while they are destitute of any Opportunity or constitutional Mode of communicating that Knowledge of their Circumstances, which is indispensably necessary to the right forming of Laws. And that the Colonies ought, as soon as possible, to be vested with a constitutional Power of communicating that Knowledge, as is the Case with the other Members of the British Government.

However disagreeable these Sentiments may be to the two Parties, I cannot think, that any other Remedy for their present Diseases will be lasting; and whenever it comes to be fully considered and digested, I am persuaded it will appear to others in the same Light. I mean to those, who have at heart, and are actuated by Motives, which lead to the Honor, Strength, and future Welfare of the Nation. I cannot find, that there is the least Disposition in the People of this Country to submit to the parliamentary Jurisdiction under the present System of Government and the Share they hold in it. And I believe, there will be no Change of Sentiments, untill there is a Change of Policy: And that seems very distant, as the Conduct on both Sides tends rather to divide and distract than to unite on those Principles of Government, which ever have and ever must be made use of to cement the different Parts of an Empire together. Under this dark Complexion, which the Face of Things now bears, what can be expected? Nothing but Confusion and Disorder. My ardent Wish is, that Wisdom and Moderation may take Place on both Sides; as from thence only we may hope for an Accommodation of the Difference upon a permanent Foundation.

A Congress of Delegates from the several Colonies will take Place in a few days at Philadelphia, to consider of these important Matters. I have consented to be one, greatly against my Inclination, at the earnest Solicitation of our Assembly: To do all the Good I can to both Countries is my sole Motive. I wish there was a Prospect of my doing a great Deal; but the Reverse is the Truth. What will be the Result of their Deliberations, it is hard, indeed impossible, to foretell. But it is more than probable, from present Appearances, that Commissioners will be appointed to come over and propose some Plan of Accommodation to the Parliament. But what that Plan will be, rests as yet in the greatest Uncertainty. . . .

B. A COMPROMISE SOLUTION:
THE GALLOWAY PLAN OF UNION (SEPT. 28, 1774)*

That a British and American legislature, for regulating the administration of the general affairs of America, be proposed and established in America, including all the said colonies; within, and under which government, each colony shall retain its present constitution, and powers of regulating and governing its own internal police, in all cases what[so]ever.

That the said government be administered by a President General, to be appointed by the King, and a grand Council, to be chosen by the Representatives of the people of the several colonies, in their respective assemblies, once in every three years.

That the several assemblies shall choose members for the grand council in the following proportions, viz.

New Hampshire.	Delaware Counties.
Massachusetts-Bay.	Maryland.
Rhode Island.	Virginia.
Connecticut.	North Carolina.
New-York.	South-Carolina.
New-Jersey.	Georgia.
Pennsylvania.	

Who shall meet at the city of   for the first time, being called by the President-General, as soon as conveniently may be after his appointment.

That there shall be a new election of members for the Grand Council every three years; and on the death, removal or resignation of any member, his place shall be supplied by a new choice, at the next sitting of Assembly of the Colony he represented.

That the Grand Council shall meet once in every year, if they shall think

* Reprinted from W. C. Ford et al. (eds.), *Journals of the Continental Congress* (1904–1937), vol. I, pp. 49–51.

it necessary, and oftener, if occasions shall require, at such time and place as they shall adjourn to, at the last preceding meeting, or as they shall be called to meet at, by the President-General, on any emergency.

That the grand Council shall have power to choose their Speaker, and shall hold and exercise all the like rights, liberties and privileges, as are held and exercised by and in the House of Commons of Great-Britain.

That the President-General shall hold his office during the pleasure of the King, and his assent shall be requisite to all acts of the Grand Council, and it shall be his office and duty to cause them to be carried into execution.

That the President-General, by and with the advice and consent of the Grand-Council, hold and exercise all the legislative rights, powers, and authorities, necessary for regulating and administering all the general police and affairs of the colonies, in which Great-Britain and the colonies, or any of them, the colonies in general, or more than one colony, are in any manner concerned, as well civil and criminal as commercial.

That the said President-General and the Grand Council, be an inferior and distinct branch of the British legislature, united and incorporated with it, for the aforesaid general purpose; and that any of the said general regulations may originate and be formed and digested, either in the Parliament of Great Britain, or in the said Grand Council, and being prepared, transmitted to the other for their approbation or dissent; and that the assent of both shall be requisite to the validity of all such general acts or statutes.

That in time of war, all bills for granting aid to the crown, prepared by the Grand Council, and approved by the President General, shall be valid and passed into a law, without the assent of the British Parliament.

SELECTION

The Rejection of Compromise

When delegates from all of the original thirteen colonies except Georgia met at Philadelphia on September 5, 1774, it quickly became clear that moderate counsels would probably not prevail. Numbered among the delegates were some of the most radical of colonial patriots, including Samuel Adams from Massachusetts, Patrick Henry and Richard Henry Lee (1732–1794) from Virginia, and Christopher Gadsden (1724–1805) from South Carolina. Charles Thomson (1729–1824), the leading Philadelphia radical who had been omitted from the conservative Pennsylvania delegation, was, to Joseph Galloway's chagrin, immediately chosen secretary. After almost two weeks of debate the Congress showed its colors by endorsing the Suffolk Resolves. Written by Joseph Warren and adopted by a convention in Suffolk County, Massachusetts, on September 9, these resolves not only declared the Coercive Acts unconstitutional and advocated economic sanctions against Great Britain but also advised the inhabitants of Massachusetts to form a new government to administer the colony until the Coercive Acts had been repealed and to arm themselves and elect officers of the militia. Introduced on September 28, Galloway's Plan of Union was only narrowly rejected by a vote of six colonies to five but it was expunged from the journal at the insistence of some of the more radical delegates on October 22.

These two acts—the endorsement of the Suffolk Resolves and the rejection of the Galloway Plan of Union—were harbingers of the eventual actions of the Congress. On October 14 Congress adopted a Declaration and Resolves, a bold statement of colonial rights and grievances prepared by a committee and reprinted here as Selection 26 A. Though the document was more moderate in tone and content than the more radical delegates would have wished, it explicitly denied that Parliament had any power to legislate for the colonies and offered to abide only by such acts of Parliament as were genuine regulations of the external commerce of the colonies designed for "securing the commercial advantages of the whole empire to the mother country, and the commercial benefits of its respective members." This offer, the Declaration emphasized, was made not out of any recognition of Parliament's right to make such regulations but only "from the necessity of the case." The Declaration also indicated the intention of Congress to enter into economic sanctions against Britain, and on October 18 it adopted the Continental Association (Selection 26 B), which committed the colonies represented to a nonimportation, nonexportation, and nonconsumption agreement until there was a change in British policy. Nonimportation of all British goods was to begin on December 1, 1774, and nonconsumption on March 1, 1775, but nonexportation, at the insistence of the southern staple colonies, was postponed for a year, until September 10, 1775. The Association further pledged the colonists to "encourage frugality, economy, and industry" and "discourage every species of extravagance and dissipation" and threatened any colony that did not adhere to the agreement with economic boycott. To enforce these regulations, the Association provided for the election of committees of safety in every "county, city, and town" to "observe the conduct of all persons touching the association," make public all violations, and "break off all dealings" with the violators. Following the adoption of two addresses, one to the King and another to the people of Britain and America, Congress voted to meet again on May 10, 1775, if colonial grievances had not been redressed and adjourned on October 22.

The standard study of the Continental Congress is Edmund Cody Burnett, The Continental Congress *(1941).*

A. DEMAND FOR THE REDRESS OF GRIEVANCES: DECLARATION AND RESOLVES OF THE FIRST CONTINENTAL CONGRESS (OCT. 14, 1774)*

Whereas, since the close of the last war, the British parliament, claiming a power of right to bind the people of America, by statute in all cases whatsoever, hath in some acts expressly imposed taxes on them, and in others, under various pretences, but in fact for the purpose of raising a revenue, hath imposed rates and duties payable in these colonies, established a board of commissioners, with unconstitutional powers, and extended the jurisdiction of courts of Admiralty, not only for collecting the said duties, but for the trial of causes merely arising within the body of a county.

* These selections are reprinted from *Journals of the Continental Congress*, vol. I, pp. 63–73.

And whereas, in consequence of other statutes, judges, who before held only estates at will in their offices, have been made dependant on the Crown alone for their salaries, and standing armies kept in times of peace:

And it has lately been resolved in Parliament, that by force of a statute, made in the thirty-fifth year of the reign of king Henry the eighth, colonists may be transported to England, and tried there upon accusations for treasons, and misprisons, or concealments of treasons committed in the colonies; and by a late statute, such trials have been directed in cases therein mentioned.

And whereas, in the last session of parliament, three statutes were made; one, intituled "An act to discontinue, in such manner and for such time as are therein mentioned, the landing and discharging, lading, or shipping of goods, wares & merchandise, at the town, and within the harbour of Boston, in the province of Massachusetts-bay, in North-America;" another, intituled "An act for the better regulating the government of the province of the Massachusetts-bay in New England;" and another, intituled "An act for the impartial administration of justice, in the cases of persons questioned for any act done by them in the execution of the law, or for the suppression of riots and tumults, in the province of the Massachusetts-bay, in New-England." And another statute was then made, "for making more effectual provision for the government of the province of Quebec, &c." All which statutes are impolitic, unjust, and cruel, as well as unconstitutional, and most dangerous and destructive of American rights.

And whereas, Assemblies have been frequently dissolved, contrary to the rights of the people, when they attempted to deliberate on grievances; and their dutiful, humble, loyal, & reasonable petitions to the crown for redress, have been repeatedly treated with contempt, by his majesty's ministers of state:

The good people of the several Colonies of New-hampshire, Massachusetts-bay, Rhode-island and Providence plantations, Connecticut, New-York, New-Jersey, Pennsylvania, Newcastle, Kent and Sussex on Delaware, Maryland, Virginia, North Carolina, and South Carolina, justly alarmed at these arbitrary proceedings of parliament and administration, have severally elected, constituted, and appointed deputies to meet and sit in general congress, in the city of Philadelphia, in order to obtain such establishment, as that their religion, laws, and liberties may not be subverted:

Whereupon the deputies so appointed being now assembled, in a full and free representation of these Colonies, taking into their most serious consideration, the best means of attaining the ends aforesaid, do, in the first place, as Englishmen, their ancestors in like cases have usually done, for asserting and vindicating their rights and liberties, declare,

That the inhabitants of the English Colonies in North America, by the immutable laws of nature, the principles of the English constitution, and the several charters or compacts, have the following Rights:

Resolved, N. C. D. 1. That they are entitled to life, liberty, & property, and they have never ceded to any sovereign power whatever, a right to dispose of either without their consent.

Resolved, N. C. D. 2. That our ancestors, who first settled these colonies, were at the time of their emigration from the mother country, entitled to all the rights, liberties, and immunities of free and natural-born subjects, within the realm of England.

Resolved, N. C. D. 3. That by such emigration they by no means forfeited, surrendered, or lost any of those rights, but that they were, and their descendants now are, entitled to the exercise and enjoyment of all such of them, as their local and other circumstances enable them to exercise and enjoy.

Resolved, 4. That the foundation of English liberty, and of all free government, is a right in the people to participate in their legislative council: and as the English colonists are not represented, and from their local and other circumstances, cannot properly be represented in the British parliament, they are entitled to a free and exclusive power of legislation in their several provincial legislatures, where their right of representation can alone be preserved, in all cases of taxation and internal polity, subject only to the negative of their sovereign, in such manner as has been heretofore used and accustomed. But, from the necessity of the case, and a regard to the mutual interest of both countries, we cheerfully consent to the operation of such acts of the British parliament, as are bona fide, restrained to the regulation of our external commerce, for the purpose of securing the commercial advantages of the whole empire to the mother country, and the commercial benefits of its respective members; excluding every idea of taxation, internal or external, for raising a revenue on the subjects in America, without their consent.

Resolved, N. C. D. 5. That the respective colonies are entitled to the common law of England, and more especially to the great and inestimable privilege of being tried by their peers of the vicinage, according to the course of that law.

Resolved, 6. That they are entituled to the benefit of such of the English statutes as existed at the time of their colonization; and which they have, by experience, respectively found to be applicable to their several local and other circumstances.

Resolved, N. C. D. 7. That these, his majesty's colonies, are likewise entitled to all the immunities and privileges granted & confirmed to them by royal charters, or secured by their several codes of provincial laws.

Resolved, N. C. D. 8. That they have a right peaceably to assemble, consider of their grievances, and petition the King; and that all prosecutions, prohibitory proclamations, and commitments for the same, are illegal.

Resolved, N. C. D. 9. That the keeping a Standing army in these colonies, in times of peace, without the consent of the legislature of that colony, in which such army is kept, is against law.

Resolved, N. C. D. 10. It is indispensably necessary to good government, and rendered essential by the English constitution, that the constituent branches of the legislature be independent of each other; that, therefore, the exercise of legislative power in several colonies, by a council appointed, during pleasure, by the crown, is unconstitutional, dangerous, and destructive to the freedom of American legislation.

All and each of which the aforesaid deputies, in behalf of themselves and their constituents, do claim, demand, and insist on, as their indubitable rights and liberties; which cannot be legally taken from them, altered or abridged by any power whatever, without their own consent, by their representatives in their several provincial legislatures.

In the course of our inquiry, we find many infringements and violations of the foregoing rights, which, from an ardent desire, that harmony and mutual intercourse of affection and interest may be restored, we pass over for the present, and proceed to state such acts and measures as have been adopted since the last war, which demonstrate a system formed to enslave America.

Resolved, N. C. D. That the following acts of Parliament are infringements and violations of the rights of the colonists; and that the repeal of them is essentially necessary in order to restore harmony between Great-Britain and the American colonies, viz:

The several acts of 4 Geo. 3. ch. 15, & ch. 34.—5 Geo. 3. ch. 25.—6 Geo. 3. ch. 52.—7 Geo. 3. ch. 41, & ch. 46.—8 Geo. 3. ch. 22, which impose duties for the purpose of raising a revenue in America, extend the powers of the admiralty courts beyond their ancient limits, deprive the American subject of trial by jury, authorize the judges' certificate to indemnify the prosecutor from damages, that he might otherwise be liable to, requiring oppressive security from a claimant of ships and goods seized, before he shall be allowed to defend his property, and are subversive of American rights.

Also the 12 Geo. 3. ch. 24, entituled "An act for the better securing his Majesty's dock-yards, magazines, ships, ammunition, and stores," which declares a new offence in America, and deprives the American subject of a constitutional trial by a jury of the vicinage, by authorizing the trial of any person, charged with the committing any offence described in the said act, out of the realm, to be indicted and tried for the same in any shire or county within the realm.

Also the three acts passed in the last session of parliament, for stopping the port and blocking up the harbour of Boston, for altering the charter & government of the Massachusetts-bay, and that which is entituled "An act for the better administration of Justice," &c.

Also the act passed in the same session for establishing the Roman Catholick Religion in the province of Quebec, abolishing the equitable system of English laws, and erecting a tyranny there, to the great danger, from so total a dissimilarity of Religion, law, and government of the neighbouring British colonies, by the assistance of whose blood and treasure the said country was conquered from France.

Also the act passed in the same session for the better providing suitable quarters for officers and soldiers in his Majesty's service in North-America.

Also, that the keeping a standing army in several of these colonies, in time of peace, without the consent of the legislature of that colony in which such army is kept, is against law.

To these grievous acts and measures, Americans cannot submit, but in hopes that their fellow subjects in Great-Britain will, on a revision of them, restore us to that state in which both countries found happiness and prosperity, we have for the present only resolved to pursue the following peaceable measures: . . .

1st. To enter into a non-importation, non-consumption, and non-exportation agreement or association.

2. To prepare an address to the people of Great-Britain, and a memorial to the inhabitants of British America, &

3. To prepare a loyal address to his Majesty; agreeable to Resolutions already entered into.

B. RENEWAL OF ECONOMIC SANCTIONS: CONTINENTAL ASSOCIATION (OCT. 20, 1774)*

WE, his majesty's most loyal subjects, the delegates of the several colonies of New-Hampshire, Massachusetts-Bay, Rhode-Island, Connecticut, New-York, New-Jersey, Pennsylvania, the three lower counties of New-Castle, Kent and Sussex, on Delaware, Maryland, Virginia, North-Carolina, and South-Carolina, deputed to represent them in a continental Congress, held in the city of Philadelphia, on the 5th day of September, 1774, avowing our allegiance to his majesty, our affection and regard for our fellow-subjects in Great-Britain and elsewhere, affected with the deepest anxiety, and most alarming apprehensions, at those grievances and distresses, with which his Majesty's American subjects are oppressed; and having taken under our most serious deliberation, the state of the whole continent, find, that the present unhappy situation of our affairs is occasioned by a ruinous system of colony administration, adopted by the British ministry about the year 1763, evidently calculated for inslaving these colonies, and, with them, the British empire. In prosecution of which system, various acts of parliament have been passed, for raising a revenue in America, for depriving the American subjects, in many instances, of the constitutional trial by jury, exposing their lives to danger, by directing a new and illegal trial beyond the seas, for crimes alleged to have been committed in America: and in prosecution of the same system, several late, cruel, and oppressive acts have been passed, respecting the town of Boston and the Massachusetts-Bay, and also an act for extending the province of Quebec, so as to border on the western frontiers of these colonies, establishing an arbitrary government therein, and discouraging the settlement of British subjects in that wide extended country; thus, by the influence of civil principles and ancient prejudices, to dispose the inhabitants to act with hostility against the free Protestant colonies, whenever a wicked ministry shall chuse so to direct them.

To obtain redress of these grievances, which threaten destruction to the lives, liberty, and property of his majesty's subjects, in North America, we are of opinion, that a non-importation, non-consumption, and non-exportation agreement, faithfully adhered to, will prove the most speedy, effectual, and peaceable measure: and therefore, we do, for ourselves, and the inhabitants of the several colonies, whom we represent, firmly agree and associate, under the sacred ties of virtue, honour and love of our country, as follows:

1. That from and after the first day of December next, we will not import, into British America, from Great-Britain or Ireland, any goods, wares, or merchandise whatsoever, or from any other place, any such goods, wares, or merchandise, as shall have been exported from Great-Britain or Ireland; nor will we, after that day, import any East-India tea from any part of the world; nor any molasses, syrups, paneles, coffee, or pimento, from the British plantations or from Dominica; nor wines from Madeira, or the Western Islands; nor foreign indigo.

2. We will neither import nor purchase, any slave imported after the first day of December next; after which time, we will wholly discontinue the slave trade, and will neither be concerned in it ourselves, nor will we hire

---

* Reprinted in full from *Journals of the Continental Congress*, vol. I, pp. 75–80.

our vessels, nor sell our commodities or manufactures to those who are concerned in it.

3. As a non-consumption agreement, strictly adhered to, will be an effectual security for the observation of the non-importation, we, as above, solemnly agree and associate, that, from this day, we will not purchase or use any tea, imported on account of the East-India company, or any on which a duty hath been or shall be paid; and from and after the first day of March next, we will not purchase or use any East-India tea whatever; nor will we, nor shall any person for or under us, purchase or use any of those goods, wares, or merchandise, we have agreed not to import, which we shall know, or have cause to suspect, were imported after the first day of December, except such as come under the rules and directions of the tenth article hereafter mentioned.

4. The earnest desire we have, not to injure our fellow-subjects in Great-Britain, Ireland, or the West-Indies, induces us to suspend a non-exportation, until the tenth day of September, 1775; at which time, if the said acts and parts of acts of the British parliament herein after mentioned are not repealed, we will not, directly or indirectly, export any merchandise or commodity whatsoever to Great-Britain, Ireland, or the West-Indies, except rice to Europe.

5. Such as are merchants, and use the British and Irish trade, will give orders, as soon as possible, to their factors, agents and correspondents, in Great-Britain and Ireland, not to ship any goods to them, on any pretence whatsoever, as they cannot be received in America; and if any merchant, residing in Great-Britain or Ireland, shall directly or indirectly ship any goods, wares or merchandise, for America, in order to break the said non-importation agreement, or in any manner contravene the same, on such unworthy conduct being well attested, it ought to be made public; and, on the same being so done, we will not, from thenceforth, have any commercial connexion with such merchant.

6. That such as are owners of vessels will give positive orders to their captains, or masters, not to receive on board their vessels any goods prohibited by the said non-importation agreement, on pain of immediate dismission from their service.

7. We will use our utmost endeavours to improve the breed of sheep, and increase their number to the greatest extent; and to that end, we will kill them as seldom as may be, especially those of the most profitable kind; nor will we export any to the West-Indies or elsewhere; and those of us, who are or may become overstocked with, or can conveniently spare any sheep, will dispose of them to our neighbours, especially to the poorer sort, on moderate terms.

8. We will, in our several stations, encourage frugality, economy, and industry, and promote agriculture, arts and the manufactures of this country, especially that of wool; and will discountenance and discourage every species of extravagance and dissipation, especially all horse-racing, and all kinds of gaming, cock-fighting, exhibitions of shews, plays, and other expensive diversions and entertainments; and on the death of any relation or friend, none of us, or any of our families, will go into any further mourning-dress, than a black crape or ribbon on the arm or hat, for gentlemen, and a black ribbon and necklace for ladies, and we will discontinue the giving of gloves and scarves at funerals.

9. Such as are venders of goods or merchandise will not take advantage of the scarcity of goods, that may be occasioned by this association, but will sell the same at the rates we have been respectively accustomed to do, for twelve months last past.—And if any vender of goods or merchandise shall sell any such goods on higher terms, or shall, in any manner, or by any device whatsoever violate or depart from this agreement, no person ought, nor will any of us deal with any such person, or his or her factor or agent, at any time thereafter, for any commodity whatever.

10. In case any merchant, trader, or other person, shall import any goods or merchandise, after the first day of December, and before the first day of February next, the same ought forthwith, at the election of the owner, to be either re-shipped or delivered up to the committee of the county or town, wherein they shall be imported, to be stored at the risque of the importer, until the non-importation agreement shall cease, or be sold under the direction of the committee aforesaid; and in the last-mentioned case, the owner or owners of such goods shall be reimbursed out of the sales, the first cost and charges, the profit, if any, to be applied towards relieving and employing such poor inhabitants of the town of Boston, as are immediate sufferers by the Boston port-bill; and a particular account of all goods so returned, stored, or sold, to be inserted in the public papers; and if any goods or merchandises shall be imported after the said first day of February, the same ought forthwith to be sent back again, without breaking any of the packages thereof.

11. That a committee be chosen in every county, city, and town, by those who are qualified to vote for representatives in the legislature, whose business it shall be attentively to observe the conduct of all persons touching this association; and when it shall be made to appear, to the satisfaction of a majority of any such committee, that any person within the limits of their appointment has violated this association, that such majority do forthwith cause the truth of the case to be published in the gazette; to the end, that all such foes to the rights of British-America may be publicly known, and universally contemned as the enemies of American liberty; and thenceforth we respectively will break off all dealings with him or her.

12. That the committee of correspondence, in the respective colonies, do frequently inspect the entries of their custom-houses, and inform each other, from time to time, of the true state thereof, and of every other material circumstance that may occur relative to this association.

13. That all manufactures of this country be sold at reasonable prices, so that no undue advantage be taken of a future scarcity of goods.

14. And we do further agree and resolve, that we will have no trade, commerce, dealings or intercourse whatsoever, with any colony or province, in North-America, which shall not accede to, or which shall hereafter violate this association, but will hold them as unworthy of the rights of freemen, and as inimical to the liberties of their country.

And we do solemnly bind ourselves and our constituents, under the ties aforesaid, to adhere to this association, until such parts of the several acts of parliament passed since the close of the last war, as impose or continue duties on tea, wine, molasses, syrups, paneles, coffee, sugar, pimento, indigo, foreign paper, glass, and painters' colours, imported into America, and extend the powers of the admiralty courts beyond their ancient limits, deprive the American subject of trial by jury, authorize the judge's certificate to indemnify the prosecutor from damages, that he might otherwise be liable to from a trial by his peers, require oppressive security from a claimant of ships or goods seized, before he shall be allowed to defend his property, are repealed.—And until that part of the act of the 12 G. 3. ch. 24, entitled "An act for the better securing his majesty's dock-yards, magazines, ships, ammunition, and stores," by which any persons charged with committing any of the offences therein described, in America, may be tried in any shire or county within the realm, is repealed—and until the four acts, passed the last session of parliament, viz. that for stopping the port and blocking up the harbour of Boston—that for altering the charter and government of the Massachusetts-Bay—and that which is entitled "An act for the better administration of justice, &c."—and that "for extending the limits of Quebec, &c." are repealed. And we recommend it to the provincial conventions, and to the committees in the respective colonies, to establish such farther regulations as they may think proper, for carrying into execution this association.

The foregoing association being determined upon by the Congress, was ordered to be subscribed by the several members thereof; and thereupon, we have hereunto set our respective names accordingly.

PART SEVEN

From Lexington to Independence

The Outbreak of Hostilities: Governor Thomas Gage Reports on the Battles of Lexington and Concord to the Earl of Dartmouth (Apr. 22, 1775)

Predictably, Congress's Declaration and Resolves got a cool reception in Britain when it was presented to Parliament on January 19, 1775. Like Galloway in Congress and with even less success, Chatham tried to secure approval of a conciliatory proposal that called for recognition of Congress and promise of exemption from parliamentary taxation in return for American acceptance of the general supremacy and superintending power of Parliament. But this plan, which scarcely went far enough to satisfy American leaders, went much too far to be acceptable to the vast majority of the members of Parliament, and on February 9 in an address to the throne both Houses declared Massachusetts to be in a state of rebellion, avowed their determination to support "the laws and constitution of Great Britain," and asked the King "to take the most effectual measures to enforce due obedience to the laws and authority of the supreme legislature." By this address both Houses of Parliament officially gave their approval to the use of force to secure compliance with the Coercive Acts in Massachusetts.

Actually the ministry had already decided upon such a course. On January 27 Lord Dartmouth, secretary of state for the colonies, had directed Governor Gage to use the forces under his command "to restore the vigour of Government" in Massachusetts. Gage received this directive on April 14, 1775, and immediately took steps to execute it. On the evening of April 18 he sent 700 men off to Concord to destroy military stores that the patriots had gathered there. Having learned of Gage's plans, Boston patriots sent Paul Revere and William Dawes to warn the countryside. Americans had been preparing for a clash of arms with the British since the previous fall, and there had been several confrontations between American militia and British troops during the winter, but they had not resulted in bloodshed. This time was different. At dawn on April 19 when the British force arrived in Lexington on its way to Concord, it encountered seventy Minutemen lined up on the town green. Firing broke out after the minutemen refused to put down their weapons, and eight Americans were killed. The British force then proceeded on to Concord and executed its mission. As they were preparing to leave, the British were attacked by a large American force that had gathered from nearby towns and were subjected to a murderous barrage all the way back to Boston. The Battles of Lexington and Concord, which cost the British over 250 casualties, turned the dispute into an armed conflict. The whole episode is described by Gage in his letter of April 22 to Dartmouth, which is reprinted from Clarence E. Carter (ed.), Correspondence of Thomas Gage, volume I, pages 396–397.

On the British decision to use force and the events that led to the Battles of Lexington and Concord see John R. Alden, General Gage in America (1948), Bernard Donoughue, British Politics and the American Revolution: The Path to War 1773–75 (1964), and B. D. Bargar, Lord Dartmouth and the American Revolution (1965). The battles themselves are fully described in Allen French, The Day of Concord and Lexington: The Nineteenth of April, 1775 (1923).

My Lord

. . . I am to acquaint your Lordship that having received Intelligence of a large Quantity of Military Stores being collected at Concord, for the avowed Purpose of Supplying a Body of Troops to act in opposition to His Majesty's Government, I got the Grenadiers and Light Infantry out of Town under the Command of Lieutenant Colonel Smith of the 10th Regiment and Major Pitcairne of the Marines with as much Secrecy as possible, on the 18th at Night and with Orders to destroy the said Military Stores; and Supported them the next Morning by Eight Companys of the 4th the same Number of the 23d, 47th and Marines, under the Command of Lord Percy. It appears from the Firing of Alarm Guns and Ringing of Bells that the March of Lieutenant Colonel Smith was discovered, and he was opposed by a Body of Men within Six Miles of Concord; Some few of whom first began to fire upon his advanced Companys which brought on a Fire from the Troops that dispersed the Body opposed to them; and they proceeded to Concord where they destroyed all the Military Stores they could find, on the Return of the Troops they were attacked from all Quarters where any Cover was to be found, from whence it was practicable to annoy them, and they were so fatigued with their March that it was with Difficulty they could keep out their Flanking Partys to remove the Enemy to a Distance, so that they were at length a good deal pressed. Lord Percy then Arrived opportunely to their Assisstance with his Brigade and two Pieces of Cannon, and Notwithstanding a continual Skirmish for the Space of Fifteen Miles, receiving Fire from every Hill, Fence, House, Barn, etc. His Lordship kept the Enemy off, and brought the troops to Charles-Town, from whence they were ferryed over to Boston. Too much Praise cannot be given Lord Percy for his remarkable Activity and Conduct during the whole Day, Lieutenant Colonel Smith and Major Pitcairn did every thing Men could do, as did all the Officers in general, and the Men behaved with their usual Intrepidity. I send your Lordship Lord Percy's and Lieutenant Colonel Smiths Letters to me on this Affair to which I beg Leave to referr your Lordship for a more Circumstantial Account of it. I have likewise the honour to transmit your Lordship a Return of the killed, wounded and Missing. The Loss sustained by those who attacked is said to be great.

The whole Country was assembled in Arms with Surprizing Expedition, and Several Thousand are now Assembled about this Town threatening an Attack, and getting up Artillery. And we are very busy in making Preparations to oppose them. . . .

SELECTION 28

War Is Declared

Like the Coercive Acts, the decision to use force in Massachusetts was based upon a patent misreading of the colonial temper. The assumption was that a show of force would throw the colonists into panic, put an end to all overt opposition, and drive them to accept Lord North's Conciliatory Proposition, by which Parliament on February 27, 1775, had offered not to tax any colony that would voluntarily tax itself to contribute to the common defense and provide for the cost of its own civil and judicial establishment. Instead, events at Lexington and Concord only served to solidify colonial opposition more firmly than ever by convincing even moderate American whigs that the charges of a ministerial conspiracy against colonial liberty were true, that the ministry and Parliament would go to any lengths, even the use of force, to achieve their evil designs. No longer, they believed, could there be any doubt that submission meant slavery, and, as group after group resolved and writer after writer proclaimed, in such a situation the only choice for freedom-loving Britons was to resist. When the Second Continental Congress convened at Philadelphia on May 10, 1775, just three weeks after Lexington and Concord, the delegates from the colonies were determined to counter force with force. On May 15 they voted to put the colonies into a state of defense. In mid-June, acting upon a proposal by the delegates of Massachusetts, they voted to take over the forces that had laid siege to Boston, made provisions for raising six companies of riflemen to join the siege, and named George Washington (1732–1799) commander in chief of the Continental Army. In late July they formally rejected North's Conciliatory Proposition. Congress also voted to make another attempt to negotiate the matters in dispute and on July 5 adopted John Dickinson's Olive Branch Petition, which professed loyalty to the King and asked him to intervene to bring about a reconciliation. But the mood and attitudes of Congress were more accurately revealed in its Declaration of the Causes and Necessities of Taking Up Arms, adopted on July 6. Written by Thomas Jefferson but subsequently toned down by Dickinson, this document, reprinted below as Selection 28 A, was both a formal justification of colonial military resistance and a masterful summary of the American case against Great Britain.

The determination of the colonists to resist was matched by the resolution of British officials to crush American resistance. The fighting at Lexington and Concord, the colonial siege of Boston, and the capture of Fort Ticonderoga on May 10 by a group of Connecticut and Vermont militia under the command of Ethan Allen (1738–1789) and Benedict Arnold (1741–1801) led to steps to augment British naval and land forces in the colonies. In addition, the news of the costly British victory at the Battle of Bunker Hill on June 17 led, on August 23, to a formal proclamation by George III declaring the colonies in rebellion and making it treason for anyone in Britain to aid them. This proclamation, reprinted here as Selection 28 B, effectively stifled the few British political leaders who still advocated making some concessions to the colonists in order to achieve a peaceful reconciliation and made the rejection of the Olive Branch Petition an absolute certainty.

For a description of the reaction of both sides to the outbreak of armed conflict see John Richard Alden, The American Revolution 1775–1783 *(1954). The work of the Second Continental Congress in the late spring and summer of 1775 can be followed in greater detail in Edmund Cody Burnett,* The Continental Congress *(1941).*

A. ''RESOLVED TO DYE FREE–MEN RATHER THAN LIVE SLAVES'': DECLARATION OF THE CAUSES AND NECESSITIES OF TAKING UP ARMS (JULY 6, 1775)*

If it was possible for men, who exercise their reason, to believe, that the Divine Author of our existence intended a part of the human race to hold an absolute property in, and an unbounded power over others, marked out by his infinite goodness and wisdom, as the objects of a legal domination never rightfully resistible, however severe and oppressive, the Inhabitants of these Colonies might at least require from the Parliament of Great Britain some evidence, that this dreadful authority over them, has been granted to that body. But a reverence for our great Creator, principles of humanity, and the dictates of common sense, must convince all those who reflect upon the subject, that government was instituted to promote the welfare of mankind, and ought to be administered for the attainment of that end. The legislature of Great Britain, however, stimulated by an inordinate passion for a power, not only unjustifiable, but which they know to be peculiarly reprobated by the very constitution of that kingdom, and desperate of success in any mode of contest, where regard should be had to truth, law, or right, have at length, deserting those, attempted to effect their cruel and impolitic purpose of enslaving these Colonies by violence, and have thereby rendered it necessary for us to close with their last appeal from Reason to Arms.—Yet, however blinded that assembly may be, by their intemperate rage for unlimited domination, so to slight justice and the opinion of mankind, we esteem ourselves bound, by obligations of respect to the rest of the world, to make known the justice of our cause.

Our forefathers, inhabitants of the island of Great Britain, left their native land, to seek on these shores a residence for civil and religious freedom. At the expence of their blood, at the hazard of their fortunes, without the least charge to the country from which they removed, by unceasing labor, and an unconquerable spirit, they effected settlements in the distant and inhospitable wilds of America, then filled with numerous and warlike nations of barbarians. Societies or governments, vested with perfect legislatures, were formed under charters from the crown, and an harmonious intercourse was established between the colonies and the kingdom from which they derived their origin. The mutual benefits of this union became in a short time so extraordinary, as to excite astonishment. It is universally confessed, that the amazing increase of the wealth, strength, and navigation of the realm, arose from this source; and the minister, who so wisely and successfully directed the measures of Great Britain in the late war, publicly declared, that these colonies enabled her to triumph over her enemies.—Towards the conclusion of that war, it pleased our sovereign to make a change in his counsels.—From that fatal moment, the affairs of the British empire began to fall into confusion, and gradually sliding from the summit of glorious prosperity, to which they had been advanced by the virtues and abilities of one man, are at length distracted by the convulsions, that now shake it to its deepest foundations. The new ministry finding the brave foes of Britain, though frequently defeated, yet still contending, took up the

* Reprinted in full from *Journals of the Continental Congress*, vol. II, pp. 140–157.

unfortunate idea of granting them a hasty peace, and then subduing her faithful friends.

These devoted colonies were judged to be in such a state, as to present victories without bloodshed, and all the easy emoluments of statuteable plunder.—The uninterrupted tenor of their peaceable and respectful behaviour from the beginning of colonization, their dutiful, zealous, and useful services during the war, though so recently and amply acknowledged in the most honorable manner by his majesty, by the late king, and by Parliament, could not save them from the meditated innovations.—Parliament was influenced to adopt the pernicious project, and assuming a new power over them, have, in the course of eleven years, given such decisive specimens of the spirit and consequences attending this power, as to leave no doubt concerning the effects of acquiescence under it. They have undertaken to give and grant our money without our consent, though we have ever exercised an exclusive right to dispose of our own property; statutes have been passed for extending the jurisdiction of courts of Admiralty and Vice-Admiralty beyond their ancient limits; for depriving us of the accustomed and inestimable privilege of trial by jury, in cases affecting both life and property; for suspending the legislature of one of the colonies; for interdicting all commerce to the capital of another; and for altering fundamentally the form of government established by charter, and secured by acts of its own legislature solemnly confirmed by the crown; for exempting the "murderers" of colonists from legal trial, and in effect, from punishment; for erecting in a neighboring province, acquired by the joint arms of Great Britain and America, a despotism dangerous to our very existence; and for quartering soldiers upon the colonists in time of profound peace. It has also been resolved in parliament, that colonists charged with committing certain offences, shall be transported to England to be tried.

But why should we enumerate our injuries in detail? By one statute it is declared, that parliament can "of right make laws to bind us IN ALL CASES WHATSOEVER." What is to defend us against so enormous, so unlimited a power? Not a single man of those who assume it, is chosen by us; or is subject to our controul or influence; but, on the contrary, they are all of them exempt from the operation of such laws, and an American revenue, if not diverted from the ostensible purposes for which it is raised, would actually lighten their own burdens in proportion as they increase ours. We saw the misery to which such despotism would reduce us. We for ten years incessantly and ineffectually besieged the Throne as supplicants; we reasoned, we remonstrated with parliament, in the most mild and decent language. But Administration, sensible that we should regard these oppressive measures as freemen ought to do, sent over fleets and armies to enforce them. The indignation of the Americans was roused, it is true; but it was the indignation of a virtuous, loyal, and affectionate people. A Congress of Delegates from the United Colonies was assembled at Philadelphia, on the fifth day of last September. We resolved again to offer an humble and dutiful petition to the King, and also addressed our fellow-subjects of Great Britain. We have pursued every temperate, every respectful measure: we have even proceeded to break off our commercial intercourse with our fellow-subjects, as the last peaceable admonition, that our attachment to no nation upon earth should supplant our attachment to liberty.—This, we flattered ourselves, was the ultimate step of the controversy: But subsequent events have shewn, how vain was this hope of finding moderation in our enemies.

Several threatening expressions against the colonies were inserted in his Majesty's speech; our petition, though we were told it was a decent one, and that his Majesty had been pleased to receive it graciously, and to promise laying it before his Parliament, was huddled into both houses amongst a bundle of American papers, and there neglected. The Lords and Commons in their address, in the month of February, said, that "a rebellion at that time actually existed within the province of Massachusetts bay; and that those concerned in it, had been countenanced and encouraged by unlawful combinations and engagements, entered into by his Majesty's subjects in several of the other colonies; and therefore they besought his Majesty, that he would take the most effectual measures to enforce due obedience to the laws and authority of the supreme legislature."—Soon after the commercial intercourse of whole colonies, with foreign countries, and with each other, was cut off by an act of Parliament; by another, several of them were entirely prohibited from the fisheries in the seas near their coasts, on which they always depended for their sustenance; and large re-inforcements of ships and troops were immediately sent over to General Gage.

Fruitless were all the entreaties, arguments, and eloquence of an illustrious band of the most distinguished Peers, and Commoners, who nobly and strenuously asserted the justice of our cause, to stay, or even to mitigate the heedless fury with which these accumulated and unexampled outrages were hurried on.—Equally fruitless was the interference of the city of London, of Bristol, and many other respectable towns in our favour. Parliament adopted an insidious manœuvre calculated to divide us, to establish a perpetual auction of taxations where colony should bid against colony, all of them uninformed what ransom would redeem their lives; and thus to extort from us, at the point of the bayonet, the unknown sums that should be sufficient to gratify, if possible to gratify, ministerial rapacity, with the miserable indulgence left to us of raising, in our own mode, the prescribed tribute. What terms more rigid and humiliating could have been dictated by remorseless victors to conquered enemies? In our circumstances to accept them, would be to deserve them.

Soon after the intelligence of these proceedings arrived on this continent, General Gage, who in the course of the last year had taken possession of the town of Boston, in the province of Massachusetts Bay, and still occupied it as a garrison, on the 19th day of April, sent out from that place a large detachment of his army, who made an unprovoked assault on the inhabitants of the said province, at the town of Lexington, as appears by the affidavits of a great number of persons, some of whom were officers and soldiers of that detachment, murdered eight of the inhabitants, and wounded many others. From thence the troops proceeded in warlike array to the town of Concord, where they set upon another party of the inhabitants of the same province, killing several and wounding more, until compelled to retreat by the country people suddenly assembled to repel this cruel aggression. Hostilities, thus commenced by the British troops, have been since prosecuted by them without regard to faith or reputation.—The inhabitants of Boston being confined within that town by the General their Governor, and having, in order to procure their dismission, entered into a treaty with him, it was stipulated that the said inhabitants having deposited their arms with their own magistrates, should have liberty to depart, taking with them their other effects. They accordingly delivered up their arms, but in open violation of honor, in defiance of the obligation of treaties, which even savage nations esteemed sacred, the Governor ordered the arms deposited as aforesaid, that they might be preserved for their owners, to be seized by a body of soldiers; detained the greatest part of the inhabitants in the town, and compelled the few who were permitted to retire, to leave their most valuable effects behind.

By this perfidy wives are separated from their husbands, children from their parents, the aged and the sick from their relations and friends, who wish to attend and comfort them; and those who have been used to live in plenty and even elegance, are reduced to deplorable distress.

The General, further emulating his ministerial masters, by a proclamation bearing date on the 12th day of June, after venting the grossest falsehoods and calumnies against the good people of these colonies, proceeds to "declare them all, either by name or description, to be rebels and traitors, to supersede the course of the common law, and instead thereof to publish and order the use and exercise of the law martial."—His troops have butchered our countrymen, have wantonly burnt Charles-Town, besides a considerable number of houses in other places; our ships and vessels are seized; the necessary supplies of provisions are intercepted, and he is exerting his utmost power to spread destruction and devastation around him.

We have received certain intelligence that General Carleton, the Governor of Canada, is instigating the people of that province and the Indians to fall upon us; and we have but too much reason to apprehend, that schemes have been formed to excite domestic enemies against us. In brief, a part of these colonies now feels, and all of them are sure of feeling, as far as the vengeance of administration can inflict them, the complicated calamities of fire, sword, and famine.—We are reduced to the alternative of chusing an unconditional submission to the tyranny of irritated ministers, or resistance by force.— The latter is our choice.—We have counted the cost of this contest, and find nothing so dreadful as voluntary slavery.—Honor, justice, and humanity, forbid us tamely to surrender that freedom which we received from our gallant ancestors, and which our innocent posterity have a right to receive from us. We cannot endure the infamy and guilt of resigning succeeding generations to that wretchedness which inevitably awaits them, if we basely entail hereditary bondage upon them.

Our cause is just. Our union is perfect. Our internal resources are great, and, if necessary, foreign assistance is undoubtedly attainable.—We gratefully acknowledge, as signal instances of the Divine favour towards us, that his Providence would not permit us to be called into this severe controversy, until we were grown up to our present strength, had been previously exercised in warlike operation, and possessed of the means of defending ourselves.—With hearts fortified with these animating reflections, we most solemnly, before God and the world, declare, that, exerting the utmost energy of those powers, which our beneficent Creator hath graciously bestowed upon us, the arms we have been compelled by our enemies to assume, we will, in defiance of every hazard, with unabating firmness and perseverance, employ for the preservation of our liberties; being with our [one] mind resolved to dye Free-men rather than live Slaves.

Lest this declaration should disquiet the minds of our friends and fellow-subjects in any part of the empire, we assure them that we mean not to dissolve that Union which has so long and so happily subsisted between us, and which we sincerely wish to see restored.—Necessity has not yet driven us into that desperate measure, or induced us to excite any other nation to war against them.—We have not raised armies with ambitious designs of separating from Great Britain, and establishing independent states. We fight not for glory or for conquest. We exhibit to mankind the remarkable spectacle of a people attacked by unprovoked enemies, without any imputation or even suspicion of offence. They boast of their privileges and civilization, and yet proffer no milder conditions than servitude or death.

In our own native land, in defence of the freedom that is our birth-right, and which we ever enjoyed till the late violation of it—for the protection of our property, acquired solely by the honest industry of our fore-fathers and ourselves, against violence actually offered, we have taken up arms. We shall lay them down when hostilities shall cease on the part of the aggressors, and all danger of their being renewed shall be removed, and not before.

With an humble confidence in the mercies of the supreme and impartial Judge and Ruler of the universe, we most devoutly implore his divine goodness to protect us happily through this great conflict, to dispose our adversaries to reconciliation on reasonable terms, and thereby to relieve the empire from the calamities of civil war.

By order of Congress,

JOHN HANCOCK, *President.*

Attested,

CHARLES THOMPSON, *Secretary.*

B. TO SUPPRESS "REBELLION AND SEDITION": ROYAL PROCLAMATION OF REBELLION (AUG. 23, 1775)*

Whereas many of Our Subjects in divers Parts of Our Colonies and Plantations in North America, misled by dangerous and ill-designing Men, and forgetting the Allegiance which they owe to the Power that has protected and sustained them, after various disorderly Acts committed in Disturbance of the Publick Peace, to the Obstruction of lawful Commerce, and to the Oppression of Our loyal Subjects carrying on the same have at length proceeded to an open and avowed Rebellion, by arraying themselves in hostile Manner to withstand the Execution of the Law, and traitorously preparing, ordering, and levying War against Us; And whereas there is Reason to apprehend that such Rebellion hath been much promoted and encouraged by the traitorous Correspondence, Counsels, and Comfort of divers wicked and desperate Persons within this Realm: To the End therefore that none of Our Subjects may neglect or violate their Duty through Ignorance thereof, or through any Doubt of the Protection which the Law will afford to their Loyalty and Zeal; We have thought fit, by and with the Advice of Our Privy Council, to issue this Our Royal Proclamation, hereby declaring that not only all Our Officers Civil and Military are obliged to exert their utmost

* Reprinted in full from Clarence S. Brigham (ed.), *British Royal Proclamations Relating to America, 1603–1783* (1911), pp. 228–229.

Endeavours to suppress such Rebellion, and to bring the Traitors to Justice;
but that all Our Subjects of this Realm and the Dominions thereunto
belonging are bound by Law to be aiding and assisting in the Suppression
of such Rebellion, and to disclose and make known all traitorous Conspiracies and Attempts against Us, Our Crown and Dignity; And We do
accordingly strictly charge and command all Our Officers as well Civil as
Military, and all other Our obedient and loyal Subjects, to use their utmost
Endeavours to withstand and suppress such Rebellion, and to disclose and
make known all Treasons and traitorous Conspiracies which they shall
know to be against Us, Our Crown and Dignity; and for that Purpose, that
they transmit to One of Our Principal Secretaries of State, or other proper
Officer, due and full Information of all Persons who shall be found carrying
on Correspondence with, or in any Manner or Degree aiding or abetting the
Persons now in open Arms and Rebellion against Our Government within
any of Our Colonies and Plantations in North America, in order to bring
to condign Punishment the Authors, Perpetrators, and Abettors of such
traitorous Designs. . . .

SELECTION

Opposing Perceptions of Events

The wave of martial enthusiasm that swept the colonies in the weeks after Lexing-
ton and Concord was accompanied among thoughtful men of all shades of political
opinion by a searching analysis of the causes and meaning of so extraordinary a
turn of events, an attempt to explain to themselves and their fellows exactly what
had brought this grave misfortune down upon them. For almost a decade American
whigs had been attributing the difficulties of the colonies to a conspiracy of corrupt
and power-thirsty ministers in Britain, and the resort to arms by Britain only
seemed to reveal the depth of that conspiracy and the extent to which the ministers
were willing to go to achieve their sordid ends. But many American whigs were
nagged by an uneasy sense that it was not simply British corruption but their own
sins that were ultimately responsible for their troubles. Earlier revealed in the
colonial response to nonimportation during the crisis over the Townshend Acts
(see Selection 15 D) and in the reaction to the Coercive Acts (see especially the
closing paragraphs of Selection 24 A), the feeling that the ministry, Parliament,
and now the British Army were the agencies of God's punishment for the colonists'
impiety and moral degeneration was widely manifest in the months immediately
after Lexington and Concord as well as later in the war. One of the dominant
themes in public sermons, this feeling was expressed through the traditional
Protestant philosophy of the jeremiad, which held that humiliation before God,
acknowledgment of sins, and a sincere determination to inaugurate and carry
through a moral reformation were absolutely necessary before God would intervene

to help in removing the source of the afflictions. As Perry Miller has remarked, the vindication of American rights and privileges and the success of American arms thus became "inextricably dependent upon moral renovation" within American society. Following precedents established by several of the Revolutionary governments in the colonies, the Second Continental Congress gave national and official expression to this feeling by setting aside July 20, 1775, as a day of humiliation, fasting, and prayer on which the colonists were in unison to begin the work of social regeneration. The nature of the sins for which Americans thought they were being punished and the procedures necessary for removing them and once again securing Divine favor may be seen in Selection 28 A, an excerpt from "The American Vine," a sermon preached in Philadelphia to the members of Congress by Jacob Duché (1738–1798), an Anglican clergyman and chaplain to Congress, on the day of humiliation, fasting, and prayer. Although Duché became a loyalist in 1776 and went to England the following year, "The American Vine" was thoroughly representative of patriot sentiment in mid-1775.

The American tories had quite a different explanation for the conflict. In general, they agreed with those whigs who suggested that it was the Americans who were responsible, but they found the root of the troubles not in the internal corruption of American society but in the "ancient republican independent Spirit" that the colonists had brought with them from England in the early seventeenth century and, more immediately, in the ambitions and designs of turbulent demagogues and selfish leaders who by "Bubbling the undiscerning Multitude" had created that social "Dementia" that made Americans think that they could successfully resist the might of the British state. Not British ministers, then, but American whigs were the ones guilty of conspiracy. Representative of the tory view is the letter, reprinted in part below as Selection 28 B, from Jonathan Sewall (1728–1796) to General Frederick Haldimand, written less than six weeks after Lexington and Concord. Sewall, a native of Massachusetts and a close friend of John Adams and other patriots in the colony, held several lucrative Crown offices in the 1760s and 1770s. Forced to flee his home in Cambridge as British officials along with the British Army were forced to take refuge in Boston after Lexington and Concord, Sewall left for Britain in 1775, staying there until 1788, when he migrated to New Brunswick, where he died.

Perry Miller, "From the Covenant to the Revival," in James Ward Smith and A. Leland Jamison (eds.), The Shaping of American Religion *(1961), pages 322–368, and Alan Heimert,* Religion and the American Mind from the Great Awakening to the Revolution *(1966), stress the importance of American religious ideas and the fear of internal corruption in shaping the colonial response to the developing Revolutionary situation. William H. Nelson,* The American Tory *(1961), is the fullest examination of the tory response, though Douglass Adair and John A. Shutz (eds.),* Peter Oliver's Origin & Progress of the American Rebellion: A Tory View *(1961), should also be consulted.*

A. THE WHIG VIEW: JACOB DUCHÉ, "THE AMERICAN VINE" (JULY 20, 1775)*

I. GREAT and astonishing have been the blessings of Providence, by which these American colonies have been distinguished from their very first settle-

* These selections are reprinted from the original edition (1775), pp. 16–34.

ments to the present period. They have indeed been a VINEYARD PLANTED BY THE LORD'S RIGHT HAND. And though some gloomy scenes have now and then shaded the brightness of the prospect, yet even these have greatly contributed to their prosperity and enlargement.

IF we look back a little into the annals of America, we shall find, that this very spot, on which our large and populous city now stands, was, less than a century ago, a wild uncultivated desart. The arts and customs of civilized life were here unknown. Nought else was visible, but the sad effects of ignorance, superstition and idolatry. The untutor'd savage roamed the wood, like a beast of prey, stranger to the comforts and advantages of mental culture, involved in Pagan darkness, with scarcely one ray of heavenly truth to irradiate the gloom of nature.

SUCH was the dark and dreary prospect, when Providence conducted our Forefathers to this new world. He took the tender slip from the PARENT VINE. HE CAST OUT THE HEATHEN AND PLANTED IT. THE HILLS WERE SOON COVERED WITH THE SHADOW OF IT, AND THE BOUGHS THEREOF WERE LIKE THE GOODLY CEDARS. SHE SENT OUT HER BOUGHS UNTO THE SEA, AND HER BRANCHES UNTO THE RIVER.—From NORTH to SOUTH he stretched the extensive line.—From EAST to WEST he had the prospect open——THE WILDERNESS AND SOLITARY PLACE WERE MADE GLAD, AND THE DESART REJOICED AND BLOSSOMED LIKE THE ROSE.

OUR sober Ancestors brought over with them, not only the several useful arts and improvements, of which the natives were ignorant, but a treasure of infinitely greater value, even the charter of TEMPORAL FREEDOM, and the records of ETERNAL TRUTH. The banners of CHRISTIAN and BRITISH Liberty were at once unfolded, and these remote parts of the earth were thereby added to the MESSIAH's kingdom.

NUMBERLESS, indeed, were the toils, difficulties, and dangers, to which the first founders of these colonies, as well as their successors were exposed, before they arrived at their present height of opulence and splendor. So remarkable, however, were the interpositions of Providence, that the most inattentive mind must have frequently discerned them.

SCARCELY is there recorded in the annals of history a more rapid series of successes of every kind in the settlement and population of any country on the globe. Whilst favoured with the nurturing care and protection of the mother country, whose fleets and armies, in conjunction with our own, have ever been faithfully and successfully employed in our defence, our common enemies have looked with astonishment and envy upon our rising glory, nor have dared for years to interrupt a repose, purchased, under the smiles of Heaven, by virtue, industry, and British and American valour.

AND happy, my dear brethren, should we still remain, if the parent would be satisfied with such returns from the children, as filial duty would always prompt them to pay, and not exact such an illegal and unrighteous tribute, as by weakening and distressing them, must in the end weaken and distress the parent too.

HERE then our present calamities commence. Our MORNING JOYS are past —and a NIGHT OF HEAVINESS succeeds—THE HEDGES OF LIBERTY, by which we hoped our VINEYARD was secured, ARE BROKEN DOWN, and THEY THAT PASS BY THE WAY, ARE seeking to PLUCK OUR GRAPES.

'TIS not indeed THE WILD BOAR OUT OF THE WOOD, OR THE WILD BEAST

OF THE FIELD, that are ready to WASTE AND DEVOUR IT. 'Tis not now a foreign enemy, or the savages of our own wilderness, that have made the cruel and unrighteous assault—But it is even, thou, BRITAIN, that with merciless and unhallowed hands, wouldst cut down and destroy this BRANCH of thine own VINE, the very BRANCH which Providence HATH MADE STRONG even for THYSELF!

II. INJURED and oppressed as we are, unmeriting the harsh and rigorous treatment, which we have received from such an unexpected quarter, let us, however, look up to an higher cause for the awful infliction; and whilst we are faithfully persevering in the defence of our TEMPORAL RIGHTS, let us humble ourselves before God, lay our hands upon our hearts, and seriously and impartially enquire, what returns we have made to Heaven for its past favours, and whether its present chastisements have not been drawn down upon us by a gross neglect of our SPIRITUAL PRIVILEGES.

HATH OUR RIGHTEOUSNESS, then, SHONE FORTH AS THE LIGHT, AND OUR JUST DEALINGS AS THE NOON DAY?—Hath a sense of GOD's unnumbered and unmerited mercies awakened in our souls an ardent affection for our divine Benefactor? Have we been more zealous for the honour of his government and the observance of his laws? Have we testified our zeal by a correspondent practice? By works of piety, beneficence, and public virtue? Have our heads of families been careful to set good examples to their children and servants, by a punctual attendance at the house of GOD, by a decent and devout behaviour in our solemn assemblies, and by regular, daily, grateful addresses to their heavenly Father in their closets at home?

HAVE we been careful to check that overweening fondness of gaiety and pleasure, which frequently discovers itself in the dispositions of our children?—to check it did I say—yea, to endeavour to root it out of their hearts, and plant and nourish in its room the love of GOD and of goodness?—In a word, have we been industrious, in our several stations and according to our respective abilities, in propagating the gospel of JESUS CHRIST, as well in sound doctrine as in sound practice? Hath our LIGHT for this purpose, so SHONE BEFORE MEN, THAT THEY SEEING OUR GOOD WORKS, have been led TO GLORIFY OUR FATHER WHICH IS IN HEAVEN?—

ALAS! my brethren, have we not rather been so far carried away by the stream of prosperity, as to be forgetful of the source from whence it was derived? So elevated by the prospect, which peace and a successful commerce have opened to us, as to neglect those impressions of goodness, which former afflictions had left upon our hearts? Have not luxury and vice, the common attendants of wealth and grandeur, too soon made their appearance amongst us, and begun to spread a dangerous infection through our hitherto healthy and thriving state? Amid the hurry and tumult of the passions, hath not conscience fallen asleep? Hath not a false security gained ground? And a worldly spirit too generally prevailed?

AND is it not for this, that the ALMIGHTY hath bared his arm against us?——Is it not for this, that he now speaks to us in thunder? And, as we would not be drawn by the cords of his love, that he is now chastising us with the rods of his wrath? Is it not for this, that the flames of an UNNATURAL WAR have burst forth in the very bowels of our native land? And that our garments have been already stained with kindred blood?———

O MY GOD! let this suffice!—let MERCY interpose, and stay the avenging hand of JUSTICE!

For behold! we now desire to TURN UNTO THEE WITH ALL OUR HEART, WITH FASTING, AND WITH WEEPING AND WITH MOURNING! We know, that MERCY is thy darling attribute, and that JUDGMENT is a STRANGE WORK to thee!—RETURN then, we BESEECH THEE, O GOD OF HOSTS! LOOK DOWN FROM HEAVEN! And once more BEHOLD AND VISIT THIS VINE!

III. BUT WHEREWITHAL, my dear brethren, SHALL WE COME BEFORE THE LORD, AND BOW OURSELVES BEFORE THE HIGH GOD? With what sacrifice shall we approach his altar? With what language, or by what conduct shall we invite him to return?

THE SACRIFICE OF GOD IS A BROKEN SPIRIT: A BROKEN AND A CONTRITE HEART, O GOD, THOU WILT NOT DESPISE. PRAYER and SUPPLICATION, is a language, which he will not refuse to hear: And REPENTANCE and REFORMATION of life, through the redeeming power of his EVER-BLESSED SON, is the only conduct, that will reinstate us in his favour.

LET us adore, then, the divine wisdom and goodness, for putting it into the hearts of that Honourable Assembly, now entrusted with the great cause of American Liberty, to call upon the whole people, whom they represent, in the most solemn and affectionate manner, to join in deprecating the Divine displeasure, by one general act of religious humiliation. Heaven be praised, that they have hereby shewn their attention and zeal for our eternal as well as temporal welfare.

Go on, ye chosen band of Christian Patriots! Testify to the world, by your example as well as by your counsels, that ye are equally the foes of VICE and of SLAVERY——Banish the Syren LUXURY, with all her train of fascinating pleasures, idle dissipation, and expensive amusements from our borders. Call upon honest industry, sober frugality, simplicity of manners, plain hospitality and christian benevolence to throw down the usurpers, and take possession of their seats. Recommend every species of reformation, that will have a tendency to promote the glory of GOD, the interest of the Gospel of JESUS, and all those private and public virtues, upon the basis of which alone, the superstructure of true Liberty can be erected.

To second your virtuous attempts, let the MINISTERS of the everlasting gospel, the embassadors of JESUS CHRIST, step forth with fresh zeal and courage to their duty. Let them remember, that they are not only answerable for their own souls, but for the souls of those under their care. "They are set as watchmen over the house of Israel."—Let them, therefore, CRY ALOUD AND SPARE NOT: let them LIFT UP THEIR VOICE AS A TRUMPET, AND SHEW ISRAEL THEIR TRANSGRESSION, AND THE HOUSE OF JACOB THEIR SIN.

FROM these let the MAGISTRATES take the alarm—Let them boldly rebuke vice—Let them punish immorality and profaneness without respect to rank or fortune—Let them become MINISTERS of the GOSPEL as well as MINISTERS of JUSTICE—Let them inculcate the knowledge and practice of true religion and virtue, as far as their influence and authority extends.

WHEN MAGISTRATES and MINISTERS shall ardently conspire for such pious and benevolent purposes—Heaven will surely smile upon their labours of love; and the people committed to their charge will GROW IN GRACE, and become eminent examples of every divine and social virtue.

WE cannot expect, my dear brethren, that the GOD OF HOSTS WILL RETURN, LOOK DOWN FROM HEAVEN, AND BEHOLD AND VISIT OUR VINE; that he will cause his sun to shine, and his refreshing dews and rains to descend upon it, unless we are careful to cultivate and improve the soil, and to root out every useless noxious weed, that will impede its growth. By neglecting this, we shall be in danger of incurring the dreadful sentence denounced against the barren fig-tree, CUT IT DOWN: WHY CUMBERETH IT THE GROUND?

BUT whilst I am recommending in general those essential branches of a true reformation, piety and gratitude to GOD, repentance and humiliation for past neglects, together with the revival of every private and public virtue, which can adorn and dignify the citizen and the christian, let me not forget to remind you, at this awful season in particular, of the great gospel duty of CHARITY, which will ever prompt us to sympathize with the distresses, and to relieve the wants of our brethren.

WHILE prosperity stretches her silken banner over our heads, and administers a continual supply of the comforts and enjoyments of life, let us not be content to repose at ease beneath her friendly shade, and selfishly and solitarily reach forth our hands to take her cup of bliss, whilst thousands are suffering, neglected beside us, and ten thousands at our right-hand. In these calamitous times at least, let us deem it BETTER TO GO TO THE HOUSE OF MOURNING THAN TO THE HOUSE OF FEASTING. Let us chearfully sacrifice our hours of entertainment and convivial mirth, and be willing to contract our usual expences, that we may have leisure TO WEEP WITH THEM THAT WEEP, and have somewhat to spare for the relief of them that want.

FOR, alas! if arms must decide the unnatural contest, and Heaven should even smile upon our righteous cause, our success cannot be purchased without many a tear, on the part of the victor as well as the vanquished. An anxious parent may be afflicted with the melancholy tidings of the death of an only Son—A fond wife may be plunged into all the bitterness of woe, upon reading the name of her affectionate spouse among the number of the slain—A beloved child may listen with an heart-felt anguish to the sad story of his father's fall—And all this load of misery may be dreadfully accumulated by the languors of disease, and the frowns of poverty.

OUR fasting and humiliation, therefore, will stand us in no stead, unless, whilst we are seeking TO LOOSE THE BANDS OF WICKEDNESS in our own hearts, we endeavour likewise TO UNDO THE HEAVY BURDENS OF OTHERS, AND TO LET THE OPPRESSED GO FREE—unless WE DEAL OUR BREAD TO THE HUNGRY, AND BRING THE POOR THAT ARE CAST OUT INTO OUR HOUSES—WHEN WE SEE THE NAKED, THAT WE COVER HIM, AND HIDE NOT OURSELVES FROM OUR OWN FLESH.

IF our hearts and hands are employed in such deeds of beneficence and love, OUR LIGHT SHALL BREAK FORTH AS THE MORNING, AND OUR HEALTH SHALL SPRING FORTH SPEEDILY: OUR RIGHTEOUSNESS SHALL GO BEFORE US: THE GLORY OF THE LORD SHALL BE OUR REAR-WARD.

IN a word, if we would wish THE GOD OF HOSTS TO RETURN, TO LOOK DOWN FROM HEAVEN AND BEHOLD AND VISIT our American VINE, we must be prepared to meet him by such heavenly tempers and dispositions, as alone can testify our vital union and communion with him. Happy, if we find him a reconciled GOD in CHRIST JESUS! Thrice happy, if our faith has fixed us to the ROCK OF AGES! Then indeed the rude winds may blow, the billows of public or private adversity may rise and rage: But we shall stand collected and secure, like the stately cedars of the mountain, amid the general storm.

B. THE TORY VIEW: JONATHAN SEWALL
TO GENERAL FREDERICK HALDIMAND (MAY 30, 1775)*

Sir

. . . It is now become too plain to be any longer doubted, that a Union is formed by a great Majority, almost throughout this whole Continent, for opposing the Supremacy, and even the lowest Degree of legislative Jurisdiction, of the British Parliament, over the British Colonies—that an absolute unlimited Independence, is the Object in View—and that, to obtain this End, preparations for War are made, and making, with a Vigor, which the most imminent Dangers from a foreign Enemy, could never inspire. It should seem astonishing, that a Country of Husbandmen, possessed every one, almost, of a sufficient Share of landed property, in one of the finest Climates in the World; living under the mildest Government, enjoying the highest portion of civil and religious Liberty that the Nature of human Society admits, and protected in the Enjoyment of these, and every other desirable Blessing in Life, upon the easiest Terms, by the only Power on Earth capable of affording that protection—that a people so scituated for Happiness, should throw off their rural Simplicity, quit the peaceful Sweets and Labours of Husbandry, bid open Defiance to the gentle Intreaties and the angry Threats of that powerful parent State which nursed their tender Years, and rush to Arms with the Ferocity of Savages, and with the fiery Zeal of Crusaders!—and all this, for the Redress of Chimerical Grievances— to oppose a claim of Parliament, made explicitly, exercised uniformly over, and quietly acquiesced in by, the Colonies from their earliest Origin! It is, I say, so truly astonishing, so entirely out of the Course of Nature, so repugnant to the known principles which most forceably actuate the human mind, that we must search deeper for the grand and more hidden Spring which causes so wonderful a movement in the Machine. And this, in my Opinion, is no other than that ancient republican independent Spirit, which the first Emigrants to America brought out with them; and which the Forms of Government, unhappily given to the New England Colonies, instead of checking, have served to cherish and keep alive. This is the Seed, which, being planted together with the Colonies, early took deep root; and being nourished by the Beams of civil and ecclesiastical Government, though, at some Seasons, it has appeared withered and almost dead, yet accidental Causes, like Showers in the natural World, have, from Time to Time, revived and given it fresh Growth; but never before, with that Luxuriance with which we now see it spread. The immediate Causes, which brought it to its present Enormity, lie obvious to every observing Eye here; they originated in the disappointed Ambition of one Man, of great Influence and no principle of publick or private Virtue—the Occasion did not escape the Notice of those watchful turbulent Spirits which are ever to be found in all Governments partaking of Democracy; by the help of the single Word, *Liberty,* they conjured up the most horrid Phantoms in the Minds of the common people, ever, an easy prey to such specious Betrayers—the Merchants, from a Desire of a free and unrestrained Trade, the sure and easy Means of arriving at a Superiority in Wealth, joined in Bubbling the undiscerning

* These selections are reprinted from the Dartmouth Papers, William Salt Library, Stafford, U.K.

Multitude—the Clergy, from that restless Spirit and Lust of Dominion, which, with a melancholy Notoriety, mark the Character of the priesthood in all Ages and Nations; from a genuine republican Temper, and from a rooted Enmity against the Church of England, opined, as Leaders of the pack, upon those never failing Topics of Tyranny and Popery—the simple unmeaning Mechanics, peasants and Labourers, who had really no Interest in the Matters of Controversy, hoodwinked, inflamed and goaded on by their Spiritual Drivers, fancied they saw civil and religious Tyranny advancing with hasty Strides; and by the Help of kindred Spirits on the other Side the Atlantic it has at length spread through the Continent.

It had been happy for us, if the British Administration had early attended to that wise Maxim in politics, *obsta principiis*. Till within about eighteen months, Words only, delivered in a firm Tone, would have quelled the rising Mischief. I have seen several periods, within the last ten Years, when two Regiments might have done, what, perhaps Thirty will not be more than sufficient to effect now. Great Britain is at length reduced to this simple Alternative; either to renounce her Claim to Supremacy over the Colonies, or, in support of it, to conquer them, and establish such a Form of Government for them as shall be, in itself, a specific Remedie for the inbred Disease. She must *now* make her Election; if she chooses to give up her Colonies, the sooner she does it, the better it will be for herself, and for all the King's loyal Subjects among them: if she resolves to maintain her Supremacy, which I must suppose, she must exert herself with her native Vigor. It is in vain to think any longer of drawing them—to such a pitch is the Frenzy now raised, that the Colonists will never yield Obedience to the Laws of the parent State, till, by Experience, they are taught to fear her power. Such is the Infatuation, that, like madmen, they are totally incapable of attending to the Dictates of reason, and will remain so till the passion of Fear is awakened; this will never be effected by Threats, or by the Appearance of a Force with which they imagine themselves able to contend. I am far from considering the Colonists, either by Nature or Habit, in the Light of a warlike people; but there is an Enthusiasm in politics, like that which religious Notions inspire, that drive Men on with an unnatural Impetuosity, that baffles and confounds all Calculation grounded upon rational principles. Liberty, among Englishmen, is a Word, whose very Sound carries a fascinating charm. The Colonists fancy this precious Jewel is in Danger of being ravished from them; and however ill-founded this Apprehension may be, while it continues, the Effect on their Minds is the same as moral Certainty would produce. They will not, they cannot examine or question the Truth of it, untill they are frightened; then, and not till then, they will pause, reflect, look back and look forward—they will examine the Grounds of their Jealousy; question the propriety of their Conduct: attentively view the certain Evils upon which they will find themselves to be rushing, see the Impossibility of arriving at their darling Independence; and reason will again resume her Seat to direct and govern their Ideas and Actions. I am so well convinced that my Countrymen, at least a Majority of them, act under the power of mere Delusion, rather than from positive vicious Intentions, that I most ardently wish to see them brought back to a Sense of their Duty, with as little Havock and Bloodshed as may be; to this End, I wish to see Great Britain rise with a power that shall strike Terror through the Continent, and leave it no longer problematical whether she is in earnest or not. . . .

I believe a very great Majority of Merchants and Traders throughout the continent, heartily anathematise this destructive Measure; and could they be protected in a Neutrality, and a peaceable prosecution of their Business, would gladly remain quiet—though they at first joined in the Opposition, yet they always intended to stop short of the point to which Matters are now brought—they proposed to gain some Advantages in Trade, and with this View, by the means of desparate Demagogues, an unweildy ill-proportioned House of Representatives, Town Meetings, Committees of Correspondence, Congresses and pulpit Declaimers, they raised that old republican Spirit in the Country people which, like a Torrent, bears them along with irresistable Rapidity; and now many are intimidated by the Threats of their Countrymen, and a Dispair of protection, into an involuntary Compliance with this strange Measure, in order to save their Lives, with the Loss of their only Means of supporting them; while others seized with the Dementia of the Times, make a voluntary Sacrifice of themselves, their Wives, Children and Fortunes, at the Shrine of Liberty; and fondly imagine they recommend themselves to Heaven and posterity, by thus heroically preferring poverty and Distress, to the most inconsiderable Abridgment of, what they call, English Liberty. . . .

SELECTION

The Road to Independence

Congress in its Declaration of the Causes and Necessities of Taking Up Arms had specifically and sincerely denied that the colonies had any desire to seek independence, and in the Olive Branch Petition it had expressed the hope, albeit a slim, and many thought, a futile one, that George III might rise above the wicked advice of his ministers and somehow bring about a harmonious end to the conflict. But the King's refusal to entertain the Olive Branch Petition, his address to Parliament from the throne in October explicitly accusing the colonists of aiming at independence, the continued buildup of British naval and military forces, and Parliament's prohibition of all American trade in December with the American Prohibitory Act convinced an increasing number of patriot leaders both that independence was desirable and that the King himself must all along have been a party to the conspiracy against colonial liberty. The most forceful exposition of this view and the most widely reprinted and effective tract to come out of the debate with Britain was a pamphlet, Common Sense, *published anonymously in Philadelphia on January 10, 1776, and written, as it turned out, by Thomas Paine (1737–1809), a brilliant polemicist who had just migrated to the colonies in the fall of 1774. Paine began with a frontal assault upon two institutions that most colonists held in highest veneration: the British constitution and hereditary monarchy. The former, which he described as "the base remains of two ancient tyrannies, compounded with* some new republican materials," was too complex and too easily corrupted to be properly responsive to the people, and the latter was "the means of misery to mankind." Far from being the "FATHER OF HIS PEOPLE" in the colonies, George III, Paine charged, was a "Royal Brute," a "hardened, sullen-tempered Pharoah" who would bring nothing but trouble to the colonies. Challenging the advocates of reconciliation to show "a single advantage that this continent can reap, by being connected with Great-Britain," he brought forth a spate of reasons for separation and called for an immediate declaration of independence and the creation of a continental government. The most important portions of this pamphlet are republished here as Selection 30 A.

Precisely because it put the case so powerfully for what for both practical and emotional reasons was rapidly becoming an absolute necessity, Common Sense had a strong impact upon the American political community. During the winter of 1775–1776 several "blood-thirsty" acts—especially the attempt by Lord Dunmore, royal governor of Virginia, to incite a slave rebellion in that colony, rumors that British agents were urging the Indians in the West to descend upon the frontiers of the colonies, and the decision in Britain to employ foreign mercenaries against the colonists—helped to shatter whatever emotional ties still bound Americans to Britain, and by early 1776 many prominent American leaders were openly advocating independence. Only by lifting the fight with Britain out of the category of a civil war, they realized, could they hope to secure the foreign aid necessary for ultimate victory, and only by destroying the last shreds of authority still retained by the old colonial governments could they clarify the ambiguous political situation and establish the governmental machinery capable of coping with the problems of maintaining internal order and fighting the war. In pursuit of this last objective, New Hampshire and South Carolina both adopted temporary constitutions during the first months of 1776, and on May 10 Congress formally recommended (Selection 30 B) that the inhabitants of all of the colonies withdraw their support of the old colonial governments and formally create new governments.

An important step toward independence, these actions were accompanied by official votes in several colonies in favor of independence. The North Carolina Convention authorized its representatives in Congress to vote for independence on April 12, 1776, the Rhode Island legislature formally declared that state independent of Great Britain on May 4, and the Virginia Convention instructed its delegates to Congress to propose independence to Congress and to support whatever steps Congress thought necessary to form foreign alliances and a Confederation of the Colonies. Acting upon these instructions (Selection 30 C), Richard Henry Lee, on June 7, 1776, presented formal resolutions (Selection 30 D) to Congress. After considerable debate, Congress decided on June 11 to postpone final consideration on Lee's resolutions for three weeks until sentiment for independence in the middle colonies had had time to ripen. At the same time, however, Congress appointed one committee of five—Thomas Jefferson, John Adams, Benjamin Franklin, Robert Livingston, and Roger Sherman—to draft a Declaration of Independence and a second committee, headed by John Dickinson and consisting of one delegate from each colony, to draft a plan for a confederation.

The movement for independence is described briefly and clearly in John R. Alden, American Revolution (1954). A more detailed study stressing the central role of George Washington is Curtis P. Nettels, George Washington and American Independence (1951). Alfred Owen Aldridge, Man of Reason: The Life of Thomas Paine (1959), is a recent biography of Paine, while Cecelia M. Kenyon, "Where Paine Went Wrong," American Political Science Review, volume 45 (1951), pages

1086–1099, is the most penetrating analysis of Paine's political ideas and their re-lation to the thought of other Revolutionary leaders.

A. THE CALL FOR INDEPENDENCE: THOMAS PAINE, ''COMMON SENSE'' (1776)*

SOME writers have so confounded society with government, as to leave little or no distinction between them; whereas they are not only different, but have different origins. Society is produced by our wants, and government by our wickedness; the former promotes our happiness *positively* by uniting our affections, the latter *negatively* by restraining our vices. The one encourages intercourse, the other creates distinctions. The first is a patron, the last a punisher.

Society in every state is a blessing, but government even in its best state is but a necessary evil; in its worst state an intolerable one; for when we suffer, or are exposed to the same miseries *by a government,* which we might expect in a country *without government,* our calamity is heightened by reflecting that we furnish the means by which we suffer. Government, like dress, is the badge of lost innocence; the palaces of kings are built on the ruins of the bowers of paradise. For were the impulses of conscience clear, uniform, and irresistably obeyed, man would need no other lawgiver; but that not being the case, he finds it necessary to surrender up a part of his property to furnish means for the protection of the rest; and this he is induced to do by the same prudence which in every other case, advises him out of two evils to chuse the least. *Wherefore* security being the true design and end of government, it unanswerably follows, that whatever *form* thereof appears most likely to insure it to us, with the least expence and greatest benefit, is preferable to all others.

In order to gain a clear and just idea of the design and end of government, let us suppose a small number of persons settled in some sequestred part of the earth, unconnected with the rest: they will then represent the first peopling of any country, or of the world. In this state of natural liberty, society will be their first thought. A thousand motives will excite them thereto, the strength of one man is so unequal to his wants, and his mind so unfitted for perpetual solitude, that he is soon obliged to seek assistance and relief of another, who in his turn requires the same. Four or five united would be able to raise a tolerable dwelling in the midst of a wilderness; but *one* man might labour out the common period of life without accomplishing any thing; when he had felled his timber he could not remove it, nor erect it after it was removed; hunger in the mean time would urge him from his work, and every different want call him a different way. Disease, nay even misfortune would be death: for tho' neither might be mortal, yet either would disable him from living, and reduce him to a state in which he might rather be said to perish than to die.

Thus necessity, like a gravitation power, would soon form our newly-

* These excerpts are reprinted from the London edition of J. Almon (1776), pp. 1–7, 10–12, 14–23, 25–29, 39–40. The sentences and phrases in brackets were printed in all American editions but deleted from the London edition.

arrived emigrants into society, the reciprocal blessings of which, would supersede, and render the obligations of law and government unnecessary while they remained perfectly just to each other. But, as nothing but heaven is impregnable to vice, it will unavoidably happen, that in proportion as they surmount the first difficulties of emigration, which bound them together in a common cause, they will begin to relax in their duty and attachment to each other; and this remissness will point out the necessity of establishing some form of government to supply the defect of moral virtue.

Some convenient tree will afford them a State-House, under the branches of which, the whole colony may assemble to deliberate on public matters. It is more than probable that their first laws will have the title only of REGULATIONS, and be inforced by no other penalty than public disesteem. In this first parliament every man, by natural right, will have a seat.

But as the colony increases, the public concerns will increase likewise, and the distance at which the members may be separated, will render it too inconvenient for all of them to meet on every occasion as at first, when their number was small, their habitations near, and the public concerns few and trifling. This will point out the convenience of their consenting to leave the legislative part to be managed by a select number chosen from the whole body, who are supposed to have the same concerns at stake which those have who appointed them, and who will act in the same manner as the whole body would act, were they present. If the colony continue increasing, it will become necessary to augment the number of the representatives, and that the interest of every part of the colony may be attended to, it will be found best to divide the whole into convenient parts, each part sending its proper number; and that the *elected* might never form to themselves an interest separate from the *electors,* prudence will point out the necessity of having elections often; because as the *elected* might by that means return and mix again with the general body of the *electors* in a few months, their fidelity to the public will be secured by the prudent reflection of not making a rod for themselves. And as this frequent interchange will establish a common interest with every part of the community, they will mutually and naturally support each other, and on this (not on the unmeaning name of king) depends the *strength of government and the happiness of the governed.*

Here then is the origin and rise of government; namely, a mode rendered necessary by the inability of moral virtue to govern the world; here too is the design and end of government, viz. freedom and security. And however our eyes may be dazzled with show, or our ears deceived by sound; however prejudice may warp our wills, or interest darken our understanding; the simple voice of nature and of reason will say, it is right.

I draw my idea of the form of government from a principle in nature, which no art can overturn, viz. that the more simple any thing is, the less liable it is to be disordered, and the easier repaired when disordered; and with this maxim in view, I offer a few remarks on the so much boasted constitution of England. That it was noble for the dark and slavish times in which it was erected, is granted. When the world was over-run with tyranny, the least remove therefrom was a glorious rescue. But that it is imperfect, subject to convulsions, and incapable of producing what it seems to promise, is easily demonstrated.

Absolute governments, (tho' the disgrace of human nature) have this advantage with them, that they are simple; if the people suffer, they know the head from which their suffering springs, know likewise the remedy, and are not bewildered by a variety of causes and cures. But the constitution of England is so exceedingly complex, that the nation may suffer for years together without being able to discover in which part the fault lies; some will say in one and some in another, and every political physician will advise a different medicine.

I know it is difficult to get over local or long standing prejudices, yet if we will suffer ourselves to examine the component parts of the English constitution, we shall find them to be the base remains of two ancient tyrannies, compounded with some new republican materials.

First.—The remains of monarchical tyranny in the person of the king.

Secondly.—The remains of aristocratical tyranny in the persons of the peers.

Thirdly.—The new republican materials in the persons of the commons, on whose virtue depends the freedom of England.

The two first, by being hereditary, are independent of the people; wherefore in a *constitutional sense* they contribute nothing towards the freedom of the state.

To say that the constitution of England is a *union* of three powers reciprocally *checking* each other, is farcical, either the words have no meaning, or they are flat contradictions.

To say that the commons are a check upon the king, presupposes two things:

First.—That the king is not to be trusted without being looked after, or in other words, that thirst for absolute power is the natural disease of monarchy.

Secondly.—That the commons, by being appointed for that purpose, are either wiser or more worthy of confidence than the crown.

But as the same constitution which gives the commons a power to check the king by withholding the supplies, gives afterwards the king a power to check the commons by empowering him to reject their other bills; it again supposes that the king is wiser than those whom it has already supposed to be wiser than him. A mere absurdity!

There is something exceedingly ridiculous in the composition of monarchy; it first excludes a man from the means of information, yet empowers him to act in cases where the highest judgment is required. The state of a king shuts him from the world, yet the business of a king requires him to know it thoroughly; wherefore the different parts, by unnaturally opposing and destroying each other, prove the whole character to be absurd and useless.

Some writers have explained the English constitution thus: The king, say they, is one, the people another; the peers are an house in behalf of the king, the commons in behalf of the people. But this hath all the distinctions of an house divided against itself; and though the expressions be pleasantly arranged, yet when examined, they appear idle and ambiguous; and it will always happen, that the nicest construction that words are capable of when applied to the description of something which either cannot exist, or is too incomprehensible to be within the compass of description, will be words of sound only, and tho' they may amuse the ear, they cannot inform the mind, for this explanation includes a previous question, viz. *How came the king by a power which the people are afraid to trust, and always obliged to check?* Such a power could not be the gift of a wise people, neither can any power, *which needs checking,* be from God; yet the provision, which the constitution makes, supposes such a power to exist.

But the provision is unequal to the task; the means either cannot or will not accomplish the end, and the whole affair is a *felo de se;* for as the greater weight will always carry up the less, and as all the wheels of a machine are put in motion by one, it only remains to know which power in the constitution has the most weight, for that will govern; and tho' the others, or a part of them, may clog, or, as the phrase is, check the rapidity of its motion, yet so long as they cannot stop it, their endeavours will be ineffectual; the first moving power will at last have its way, and what it wants in speed, is supplied by time.

That the crown is this overbearing part in the English constitution, needs not be mentioned, and that it derives its whole consequence merely from being the giver of places and pensions, is self-evident; wherefore, though we have been wise enough to shut and lock a door against absolute monarchy, we at the same time have been foolish enough to put the crown in possession of the key.

The prejudice of Englishmen in favour of their own government by kings, lords and commons, arises as much or more from national pride than reason. Individuals are undoubtedly safer in England than in some other countries, but the *will* of the king is as much the *law* of the land in Britain as in France, with this difference, that instead of proceeding directly from his mouth, it is handed to the people under the more formidable shape of an act of parliament. For the fate of Charles the First hath only made kings more subtle—not more just.

Wherefore, laying aside all national pride and prejudice in favour of modes and forms, the plain truth is, that *it is wholly owing to the constitution of the people, and not to the constitution of the government,* that the crown is not as oppressive in England as in Turkey.

An inquiry into the *constitutional errors* in the English form of government is at this time highly necessary; for as we are never in a proper condition of doing justice to others, while we continue under the influence of some leading partiality, so neither are we capable of doing it to ourselves while we remain fettered by any obstinate prejudice. And as a man, who is attached to a prostitute, is unfitted to choose or judge of a wife, so any prepossession in favour of a rotten constitution of government will disable us from discerning a good one.

Of Monarchy and Hereditary Succession

MANKIND being originally equals in the order of creation, the equality could only be destroyed by some subsequent circumstances; the distinction of rich and poor may in a great measure be accounted for, and that without having recourse to the harsh, ill-founding names of oppression and avarice. Oppression is often the *consequence,* but seldom or never the *means* of riches; and though avarice will preserve a man from being necessitously poor, it generally makes him too timorous to become wealthy.

But there is another and greater distinction, for which no truly natural or religious reason can be assigned, and that is, the distinction of men into

KINGS and SUBJECTS. Male and female are the distinctions of nature, good and bad the distinction of heaven; but how a race of men came into the world so exalted above the rest, and distinguished like some ne· species, is worth enquiring into, and whether they are the means of happiness or of misery to mankind.

In the early ages of the world, according to the scripture chronology, there were no kings; the consequence of which was, there were no wars; it is the pride of kings which throws mankind into confusion. Holland without a king hath enjoyed more peace for this last century than any of the monarchical governments in Europe. Antiquity favours the same remark; for the quiet and rural lives of the first patriarchs hath a happy something in them, which vanishes away when we come to the history of Jewish royalty. . . .

To the evil of monarchy we have added that of hereditary succession; and as the first is a degradation and lessening of ourselves, so the second, claimed as a matter of right, is an insult and an imposition on posterity. For all men being originally equals, no *one* by *birth* could have a right to set up his own family in perpetual preference to all others for ever, and though himself might deserve *some* decent degree of honours of his cotemporaries, yet his descendants might be far too unworthy to inherit them. One of the strongest *natural* proofs of the folly of hereditary right in kings, is, that nature disapproves it, otherwise she would not so frequently turn it into ridicule by giving mankind an *Ass for a Lion*.

Secondly, as no man at first could possess any other public honors than were bestowed upon him, so the givers of those honors could have no right to give away the right of posterity. And though they might say, "We choose you for *our* head," they could not, without manifest injustice to their children, say, "that your children, and your children's children shall reign over *ours* for ever. Because such an unwise, unjust, unnatural compact might (perhaps) in the next succession put them under the government of a rogue or a fool. Most wise men, in their private sentiments, have ever treated hereditary right with contempt; yet it is one of those evils which, when once established, is not easily removed; many submit from fear, others from superstition, and the more powerful part shares with the king the plunder of the rest.

This is supposing the present race of kings in the world to have had an honourable origin; whereas it is more than probable, that could we take off the dark covering of antiquity, and trace them to their first rise, that we should find the first of them nothing better than the principal ruffian of some restless gang, whose savage manners, or pre-eminence in subtility obtained him the title of chief among plunderers; and who by increasing in power, and extending his depredations, over-awed the quiet and defenceless to purchase their safety by frequent contributions. Yet his electors could have no idea of giving hereditary right to his descendants, because such a perpetual exclusion of themselves was incompatible with the free and unrestrained principles they professed to live by. Wherefore hereditary succession in the early ages of monarchy could not take place as a matter of claim, but as something casual or complimental; but as few or no records were extant in those days, and traditionary history stuffed with fables, it was very easy, after the lapse of a few generations, to trump up some superstitious tale, conveniently timed, Mahomet like, to cram hereditary right down the throats of the vulgar. Perhaps the disorders which threatened, or seemed to threaten, on the decease of a leader, and the choice of a new one, (for elections among ruffians could not be very orderly) induced many at first to favor hereditary pretensions; by which means it happened, as it hath happened since, that what at first was submitted to as a convenience, was afterwards claimed as a right.

England, since the conquest, hath known some few good monarchs, but groaned beneath a much larger number of bad ones; yet no man in his senses can say that their claim under William the Conqueror is a very honourable one. A French bastard landing with an armed banditti, and establishing himself king of England against the consent of the natives, is in plain terms a very paltry rascally original. It certainly hath no divinity in it. However, it is needless to spend much time in exposing the folly of hereditary right; if there are any so weak as to believe it, let them promiscuously worship the ass and the lion, and welcome. I shall neither copy their humility, nor disturb their devotion. . . .

In short, monarchy and succession have laid (not this or that kingdom only) but the world in blood and ashes. 'Tis a form of government which the word of God bears testimony against, and blood will attend it. . . .

The nearer any government approaches to a republic the less business there is for a king. It is somewhat difficult to find a proper name for the government of England. Sir William Meredith calls it a republic; but in its present state it is unworthy of the name, because the corrupt influence of the crown, by having all the places in its disposal, hath so effectually swallowed up the power, and eaten out the virtue of the house of commons (the republican part of the constitution) that the government of England is nearly as monarchical as that of France or Spain. Men fall out with names without understanding them. For it is the republican and not the monarchical part of the constitution of England which Englishmen glory in, viz. the liberty of choosing an house of commons from out of their own body—and it is easy to see that when republican virtue fails, slavery ensues. Why is the constitution of England sickly, but because monarchy hath poisoned the republic, the crown hath engrossed the commons? . . .

Thoughts on the Present State of American Affairs

IN the following pages I offer nothing more than simple facts, plain arguments, and common sense; and have no other preliminaries to settle with the reader, than that he will divest himself of prejudice and prepossession, and suffer his reason and his feelings to determine for themselves; that he will put *on*, or rather that he will not put *off* the true character of a man, and generously enlarge his views beyond the present day.

Volumes have been written on the subject of the struggle between England and America. Men of all ranks have embarked in the controversy, from different motives, and with various designs: but all have been ineffectual, and the period of debate is closed. Arms, as the last resource, decide the contest; the appeal was the choice of the king, and the continent hath accepted the challenge.

It hath been reported of the late Mr. Pelham (who tho' an able minister was not without his faults) that on his being attacked in the house of commons, on the score, that his measures were only of a temporary kind, replied *"they will last my time."* Should a thought so fatal and unmanly possess the colonies in the present contest, the name of ancestors will be remembered by future generations with detestation.

The sun never shone on a cause of greater worth. 'Tis not the affair of a city, a country, a province, or a kingdom, but of a continent—of at least one eighth part of the habitable globe. 'Tis not the concern of a day, a year, or an age; posterity are virtually involved in the contest, and will be more or less affected, even to the end of time, by the proceedings now. Now is the feed-time of continental union, faith and honor. The least fracture now will be like a name engraved with the point of a pin on the tender rind of a young oak; the wound will enlarge with the tree, and posterity read in it full grown characters.

By referring the matter from argument to arms, a new æra for politicks is struck; a new method of thinking hath arisen. All plans, proposals, &c. prior to the nineteenth of April, *i. e.* to the commencement of hostilities, are like the almanacks of the last year; which though proper then are superseded and useless now. Whatever was advanced by the advocates on either side of the question then; terminated in one and the same point, viz. a union with Great-Britain; the only difference between the parties was the method of effecting it; the one proposing force, the other friendship; but it hath so far happened that the first hath failed, and the second hath withdrawn her influence.

As much hath been said of the advantages of reconciliation, which, like an agreeable dream, hath passed away and left us as we were, it is but right, that we should examine the contrary side of the argument, and enquire into some of the many material injuries which these colonies sustain, and always will sustain, by being connected with, and dependant on Great Britain. To examine that connection and dependance, on the principles of nature and common sense, to see what we have to trust to, if separated, and what we are to expect, if dependant,

I have heard it asserted by some, that as America hath flourished under her former connection with Great-Britain, that the same connection is necessary towards her future happiness, and will always have the same effect. Nothing can be more fallacious than this kind of argument. We may as well assert that because a child has thriven upon milk, that it is never to have meat, or that the first twenty years of our lives is to become a precedent for the next twenty. But even this is admitting more than is true, for I answer roundly, that America would have flourished as much, and probably much more, had no European power had any thing to do with her. The commerce by which she hath inriched herself, are the necessaries of life, and will always have a market while eating is the custom of Europe.

But she has protected us, say some. That she has engrossed us is true, and defended the continent at our expence as well as her own, is admitted, and she would have defended Turkey from the same motive, viz. the sake of trade and dominion.

Alas, we have been long led away by ancient prejudices, and made large sacrifices to superstition. We have boasted the protection of Great Britain, without considering that her motive was *interest* not *attachment;* that she did not protect us from *our enemies* on *our account,* but from *her enemies* on *her own account,* from those who had no quarrel with us on any *other account,* and who will always be our enemies on the *same account.* Let Britain wave her pretensions to the continent, or the continent throw off the dependance, and we should be at peace with France and Spain were they at war with Britain. The miseries of Hanover last war ought to warn us against connexions.

It has lately been asserted in parliament, that the colonies have no relation to each other but through the parent country, i. e. that Pennsylvania and the Jerseys, and so on for the rest, are sister colonies by the way of England; this is certainly a very round-about way of proving relationship, but it is the nearest and only true way of proving enemyship if I may so call it. France and Spain never were, nor perhaps ever will be our enemies as *Americans,* but as our being the *subjects of Great Britain.*

But Britain is the parent country, say some. Then the more shame upon her conduct. Even brutes do not devour their young, nor savages make war upon their families; wherefore the assertion, if true, turns to her reproach; but it happens not to be true, or only partly so, and the phrase *parent* or *mother country* hath been jesuitically adopted by the [king] and his parasites, with a low papistical design of gaining an unfair bias on the credulous weakness of our minds. Europe, and not England, is the parent country of America. This new world hath been the asylum for the persecuted lovers of civil and religious liberty from *every part* of Europe. Hither have they fled, not from the tender embraces of the mother, but from the cruelty of the monster; and it is so far true of England, that the same tyranny which drove the first emigrants from home, pursues their descendants still.

In this extensive quarter of the globe, we forget the narrow limits of three hundred and sixty miles (the extent of England) and carry our friendship on a larger scale; we claim brotherhood with every European Christian, and triumph in the generosity of the sentiment.

It is pleasant to observe by what regular gradations we surmount the force of local prejudice, as we enlarge our acquaintance with the world. A man born in any town in England divided into parishes, will naturally associate most with his fellow-parishioners (because their interests in many cases will be common) and distinguish him by the name of *neighbour;* if he meet him but a few miles from home, he drops the narrow idea of a street, and salutes him by the name of *townsman;* if he travel out of the country, and meet him in any other, he forgets the minor divisions of street and town, and calls him *countryman,* i. e. *countyman;* but if in their foreign excursions they should associate in France, or any other part of *Europe,* their local remembrance would be enlarged into that of *Englishmen.* And by a just parity of reasoning, all Europeans meeting in America, or any other quarter of the globe, are *countrymen;* for England, Holland, Germany, or Sweden, when compared with the whole, stand in the same places on the larger scale, which the divisions of street, town, and county do on the smaller ones; distinctions too limited for continental minds. Not one-third of the inhabitants, even of this province, are of English descent. Wherefore I reprobate the phrase of parent or mother country applied to England only, as being false, selfish, narrow, and ungenerous.

But admitting, that we were all of English descent, what does it amount to? Nothing. Britain, being now an open enemy, extinguishes every other name and title: And to say that reconciliation is our duty, is truly farcical.

The first king of England, of the present line (William the Conqueror) was a Frenchman, and half the Peers of England are descendants from the same country; wherefore, by the same method of reasoning, England ought to be governed by France.

Much hath been said of the united strength of Britain and the colonies, that in conjunction they might bid defiance to the world. But this is mere presumption; the fate of war is uncertain, neither do the expressions mean any thing; for this continent would never suffer itself to be drained of inhabitants, to support the British arms in either Asia, Africa, or Europe.

Besides what have we to do with setting the world at defiance? Our plan is commerce, and that, well attended to, will secure us the peace and friendship of all Europe; because, it is the interest of all Europe to have America a *free port*. Her trade will always be a protection, and her barrenness of gold and silver secure her from invaders.

I challenge the warmest advocate for reconciliation, to shew, a single advantage that this continent can reap, by being connected with Great-Britain. I repeat the challenge, not a single advantage is derived. Our corn will fetch its price in any market in Europe, and our imported goods must be paid for buy them where we will.

But the injuries and disadvantages we sustain by that connection, are without number; and our duty to mankind at large, as well as to ourselves, instruct us to renounce the alliance: Because, any submission to, or dependance on Great-Britain, tends directly to involve this continent in European wars and quarrels; and set us at variance with nations, who would otherwise seek our friendship, and against whom we have neither anger nor complaint. As Europe is our market for trade, we ought to form no partial connection with any part of it. It is the true interest of America to steer clear of European contentions, which she never can do, while by her dependance on Britain, she is made the make-weight in the scale of British politics.

Europe is too thickly planted with kingdoms to be long at peace, and whenever a war breaks out between England and any foreign power, the trade of America goes to ruin, *because of her connection with Britain*. The next war may not turn out like the last, and should it not, the advocates for reconciliation now, will be wishing for separation then, because, neutrality in that case, would be a safer convoy than a man of war. Every thing that is right or natural pleads for separation. The blood of the slain, the weeping voice of nature cries, 'TIS TIME TO PART. Even the distance at which the Almighty hath placed England and America, is a strong and natural proof, that the authority of the one, over the other, was never the design of Heaven. The time likewise at which the continent was discovered, adds weight to the argument, and the manner in which it was peopled encreases the force of it. The reformation was preceded by the discovery of America, as if the Almighty graciously meant to open a sanctuary to the persecuted in future years, when home should afford neither friendship nor safety.

The authority of Great-Britain over this continent, is a form of government, which sooner or later must have an end: and a serious mind can draw no true pleasure by looking forward, under the painful and positive conviction, that what is called "the present constitution" is merely temporary. As parents, we can have no joy, knowing that *this government* is not sufficiently lasting to ensure any thing which we may bequeath to posterity: And by a plain method of argument, as we are running the next generation into debt, we ought to do the work of it, otherwise we use them meanly and pitifully. In order to discover the line of our duty rightly, we should take our children in our hand, and fix our station a few years farther into life; that eminence will present a prospect, which a few present fears and prejudices conceal from our sight.

Though I would carefully avoid giving unnecessary offence, yet I am inclined to believe, that all those who espouse the doctrine of reconciliation, may be included within the following descriptions. Interested men, who are not to be trusted; weak men, who *cannot* see; prejudiced men, who *will not* see; and a certain set of moderate men, who think better of the European world than it deserves; and this last class, by an ill-judged deliberation, will be the cause of more calamities to this continent, than all the other three.

It is the good fortune of many to live distant from the scene of sorrow; the evil is not sufficiently brought to *their* doors to make *them* feel the precariousness with which all American property is possessed. But let our imaginations transport us for a few moments to Boston, that seat of wretchedness will teach us wisdom, and instruct us for ever to renounce a power in whom we can have no trust. The inhabitants of that unfortunate city, who but a few months ago were in ease and affluence, have now, no other alternative than to stay and starve, or turn out to beg. Endangered by the fire of their friends if they continue within the city, and plundered by the soldiery if they leave it. In their present condition they are prisoners without the hope of redemption, and in a general attack for their relief, they would be exposed to the fury of both armies.

Men of passive tempers look somewhat lightly over the offences of Britain, and still hoping for the best, are apt to call out, *"Come, come, we shall be friends again, for all this."* But examine the passions and feelings of mankind, bring the doctrine of reconciliation to the touchstone of nature, and then tell me, whether you can hereafter love, honour, and faithfully serve the power that hath carried fire and sword into your land? If you cannot do all these, then are you only deceiving yourselves, and by your delay bringing ruin upon posterity. Your future connexion with Britain, whom you can neither love nor honour, will be forced and unnatural, and being formed only on the plan of present convenience, will in a little time fall into a relapse more wretched than the first. But if you say, you can still pass the violations over, then I ask, Hath your house been burnt? Hath your property been destroyed before your face? Are your wife and children destitute of a bed to lie on, or bread to live on? Have you lost a parent or a child, by their hands, and yourself the ruined and wretched survivor? If you have not, then are you not a judge of those who have. But if you have, and still can shake hands with the murderers, then are you unworthy the name of husband, father, friend, or lover, and whatever may be your rank or title in life, you have the heart of a coward, and the spirit of a sycophant.

This is not inflaming or exaggerating matters, but trying them by those feelings and affections which nature justifies; and without which, we should be incapable of discharging the social duties of life, or enjoying the felicities of it. I mean not to exhibit horror for the purpose of provoking revenge, but to awaken us from fatal and unmanly slumbers, that we may pursue determinately some fixed object. It is not in the power of Britain or of Europe to conquer America, if she do not conquer herself by *delay* and *timidity*. The present winter is worth an age, if rightly employed, but if neglected, the whole continent will partake of the misfortune; and there is no punishment which that man will not deserve, be he who, or what, or where he will, that may be the means of sacrificing a season so precious and useful.

It is repugnant to reason, to the universal order of things, to all examples from former ages, to suppose, that this continent can longer remain subject to any external power. The most sanguine in Britain does not think so. The utmost stretch of human wisdom cannot, at this time, compass a plan short of separation, which can promise the continent even a year's security. Reconciliation is *now* a fallacious dream. Nature hath deserted the connexion, and art cannot supply her place. For, as Milton wisely expresses, "Never can true reconcilement grow, where wounds of deadly hate have pierc'd so deep."

Every quiet method for peace hath been ineffectual. Our prayers have been rejected with disdain; and only tended to convince us, that nothing flatters vanity, or confirms obstinacy in Kings more than repeated petitioning—and nothing hath contributed more than that very measure to make the Kings of Europe absolute: Witness Denmark and Sweden. Wherefore, since nothing but blows will do, for God's sake, let us come to a final separation, and not leave the next generation to be cutting throats, under the violated unmeaning names of parent and child.

To say, they will never attempt it again is idle and visionary, we thought so at the repeal of the stamp-act, yet a year or two undeceived us; as well may we suppose that nations, which have been once defeated, will never renew the quarrel.

As to government matters, it is not in the power of Britain to do this continent justice: The business of it will soon be too weighty, and intricate, to be managed with any tolerable degree of convenience, by a power so distant from us, and so very ignorant of us; for if they cannot conquer us, they cannot govern us. To be always running three or four thousand miles with a tale or a petition, waiting four or five months for an answer, which when obtained requires five or six more to explain it in, will in a few years be looked upon as folly and childishness—There was a time when it was proper, and there is a proper time for it to cease.

Small islands, not capable of protecting themselves, are the proper objects for kingdoms to take under their care; but there is something very absurd in supposing a continent to be perpetually governed by an island. In no instance hath nature made the satellite larger than its primary planet, and as England and America, with respect to each other, reverses the common order of nature, it is evident they belong to different systems; England to Europe, America to itself.

I am not induced by motives of pride, party, or resentment to espouse the doctrine of separation and independence; I am clearly, positively, and conscientiously persuaded, that it is the true interest of this continent to be so; that every thing short of *that* is mere patchwork, that it can afford no lasting felicity,----that it is leaving the sword to our children, and shrinking back at a time, when, a little more, a little farther, would have rendered this continent the glory of the earth.

As Britain hath not manifested the least inclination towards a compromise, we may be assured that no terms can be obtained worthy the acceptance of the continent, or any ways equal to the expence of blood and treasure we have been already put to.

The object contended for, ought always to bear some just proportion to the expence. The removal of North, or the whole detestable junto, is a matter unworthy the millions we have expended. A temporary stoppage of trade, was an inconvenience, which would have sufficiently ballanced the repeal of all the acts complained of, had such repeals been obtained; but if the whole continent must take up arms, if every man must be a soldier, it is scarcely worth our while to fight against a contemptible ministry only. Dearly, dearly, do we pay for the repeal of the acts, if that is all we fight for; for in a just estimation, it is as great a folly to pay a Bunker-hill price for law as for land. As I have always considered the independency of this continent as an event which sooner or later must arrive, so from the late rapid progress of the continent to maturity, the event could not be far off. Wherefore, on the breaking out of hostilities, it was not worth while to have disputed a matter which time would have finally redressed, unless we meant to be in earnest; otherwise it is like wasting an estate on a suit at law, to regulate the trespasses of a tenant, whose lease is just expiring. No man was a warmer wisher for reconciliation than myself before the fatal nineteenth of April, 1775, but the moment the event of that day was made known, [I rejected the hardened sullen-tempered Pharaoh of England for ever; and disdain the wretch, that with the pretended title of FATHER OF HIS PEOPLE can unfeelingly hear of their slaughter, and composedly sleep with their blood upon his soul] . . . .

But the most powerful of all arguments, is, that nothing but independance, i. e. a continental form of government, can keep the peace of the continent and preserve it inviolate from civil wars. I dread the event of a reconciliation with Britain now, as it is more than probable, that it will be followed by a revolt somewhere or other, the consequences of which may be far more fatal than all the malice of Britain. . . .

The colonies have manifested such a spirit of good order and obedience to continental government, as is sufficient to make every reasonable person easy and happy on that head. No man can assign the least pretence for his fears, on any other grounds than such as are truly childish and ridiculous, viz. that one colony will be striving for superiority over another.

Where there are no distinctions, there can be no superiority; perfect equality affords no temptation. The republics of Europe are all (and we may say always) in peace. Holland and Switzerland are without wars, foreign or domestic: monarchical governments, it is true, are never long at rest; the crown itself is a temptation to enterprising *ruffians* at *home;* and that degree of pride and insolence ever attendant on regal authority, swells into a rupture with foreign powers, in instances where a republican government, by being formed on more natural principles, would negociate the mistake.

If there is any true cause of fear respecting independance, it is because no plan is yet laid down. Men do not see their way out—Wherefore, as an opening into that business, I offer the following hints; . . .

LET the assemblies be annual, with a President only.----The representation more equal. Their business wholly domestic, and subject to the authority of a Continental Congress. . . .

But as there is a peculiar delicacy, from whom, or in what manner this business must first arise, and as it seems most agreeable and consistent, that it should come from some intermediate body between the governed and the governors, that is, between the Congress and the people, let a CONTINEN- TAL CONFERENCE be held . . . to frame a CONTINENTAL CHARTER, or CHARTER of the United Colonies; (answering to what is called the Magna Charta of England) fixing the number and manner of choosing members of Congress, members of Assembly, with their date of sitting, and drawing the line of business and jurisdiction between them: (Always remembering, that our strength is continental, not provincial:) Securing freedom and property to all men, and above all things, the free exercise of religion, according to the dictates of conscience: with such other matter as is necessary for a charter to contain. Immediately after which, the said Conference to dissolve, and the bodies which shall be chosen conformable to the said charter, to be the legislators and governors of this continent for the time being. . . .

But where, say some, is the King of America? I'll tell you, Friend, he reigns above, and doth not make havoc of mankind [like the Royal Brute of Great Britain.] Yet that we may not appear to be defective even in earthly honours, let a day be solemnly set apart for proclaiming the charter; let it be brought forth placed on the divine law, the word of God; let a crown be placed thereon, by which the world may know that so far we approve of monarchy, that in America THE LAW IS KING. For as in absolute governments the King is law, so in free countries the law *ought* to be King; and there ought to be no other. But lest any ill use should afterwards arise, let the crown, at the conclusion of the ceremony, be demolished, and scattered among the people whose right it is.

A government of our own is our natural right: And when a man seriously reflects on the precariousness of human affairs, he will become convinced, that it is infinitely wiser and safer, to form a constitution of our own in a cool deliberate manner, while we have it in our power, than to trust such an interesting event to time and chance, . . .

To CONCLUDE, however strange i may appear to some, or however unwill- ing they may be to think so, matters not, but many strong, and striking reasons may be given, to shew, that nothing can settle our affairs so expe- ditiously as an open, and determined declaration for independance. Some of which are,

First. It is the custom of nations, when any two are at war, for some other powers, not engaged in the quarrel, to step in as mediators, and bring about the preliminaries of a peace: but while America calls herself the subject of Great- Britain, no power, however well disposed she may be, can offer her mediation. Wherefore, in our present state we may quarrel on for ever.

Secondly. It is unreasonable to suppose, that France or Spain will give us any kind of assistance, if we mean only to make use of that assistance for the purpose of repairing the breach, and strengthening the connection between Britain, and America; because, those powers would be sufferers by the consequences.

Thirdly. While we profess ourselves the subjects of Britain, we must, in the eye of foreign nations, be considered as rebels. The precedent is somewhat dangerous to *their peace,* for men to be in arms under the name of subjects; we, on the spot, can solve the paradox: but to unite resistance, and subjection, requires an idea much too refined for common understanding.

Fourthly. Were a manifesto to be published, and dispatched to foreign courts, setting forth the miseries we have endured, and the peaceable methods we have ineffectually used for redress; declaring at the same time, that not being able, any longer, to live happily or safely under the cruel disposition of the British court, we had been driven to the necessity of breaking off all connection with her; at the same time, assuring all such courts of our peaceable disposition towards them, and of our desire of entering into trade with them: such a memorial would produce more good effects to this Continent, than if a ship were freighted with petitions to Britain.

Under our present denomination of British subjects, we can neither be received nor heard abroad: The custom of all courts is against us, and will be so, until, by an independance, we take rank with other nations.

These proceedings may at first appear strange and difficult; but, like all other steps which we have already passed over, will in a little time become familiar, and agreeable; and, until an independance is declared, the Continent will feel itself like a man who continues putting off some unpleasant business from day to day, yet knows it must be done; hates to act about it, wishes it over, and is continually haunted with the thoughts of its necessity.

B. TOWARD THE CREATION OF INDEPENDENT STATE GOVERNMENTS: THE RESOLVES AND RECOMMENDATIONS OF CONGRESS (MAY 10, 15, 1776)*

Whereas his Britannic Majesty, in conjunction with the lords and commons of Great Britain, has, by a late act of Parliament, excluded the inhabitants of these United Colonies from the protection of his crown; And whereas, no answer, whatever, to the humble petitions of the colonies for redress of grievances and reconciliation with Great Britain, has been or is likely to be given; but, the whole force of that kingdom, aided by foreign mercenaries, is to be exerted for the destruction of the good people of these colonies; And whereas, it appears absolutely irreconcileable to reason and good Conscience, for the people of these colonies now to take the oaths and affirmations necessary for the support of any government under the crown of Great Britain, and it is necessary that the exercise of every kind of authority under the said crown should be totally suppressed, and all the powers of government exerted, under the authority of the people of the colonies, for the preservation of internal peace, virtue, and good order, as well as for the defence of their lives, liberties, and properties, against the hostile invasions and cruel depredations of their enemies; therefore . . .

Resolved, That it be recommended to the respective assemblies and conventions of the United Colonies, where no government sufficient to the exigencies of their affairs have been hitherto established, to adopt such government as shall, in the opinion of the representatives of the people, best conduce to the happiness and safety of their constituents in particular, and America in general.

* These excerpts are reprinted from *Journals of the Continental Congress,* vol. IV, pp. 342, 357–358.

C. VIRGINIA DECIDES FOR INDEPENDENCE: RESOLVES OF THE VIRGINIA CONVENTION (MAY 15, 1776)*

Forasmuch as all the endeavours of the United Colonies, by the most decent representations and petitions to the King and Parliament of *Great Britain,* to restore peace and security to *America* under the *British* Government, and a reunion with that people upon just and liberal terms, instead of a redress of grievances, have produced, from an imperious and vindictive Administration, increased insult, oppression, and a vigorous attempt to effect our total destruction:—By a late act all these Colonies are declared to be in rebellion, and out of the protection of the *British* Crown, our properties subjected to confiscation, our people, when captivated, compelled to join in the murder and plunder of their relations and countrymen, and all former rapine and oppression of *Americans* declared legal and just; fleets and armies are raised, and the aid of foreign troops engaged to assist these destructive purposes; the King's representative in this Colony hath not only withheld all the powers of Government from operating for our safety, but, having retired on board an armed ship, is carrying on a piratical and savage war against us, tempting our slaves by every artifice to resort to him, and training and employing them against their masters. In this state of extreme danger, we have no alternative left but an abject submission to the will of those overbearing tyrants, or a total separation from the Crown and Government of *Great Britain,* uniting and exerting the strength of all *America* for defence, and forming alliances with foreign Powers for commerce and aid in war:— Wherefore, appealing to the Searcher of hearts for the sincerity of former declarations expressing our desire to preserve the connection with that nation, and that we are driven from that inclination by their wicked councils, and the eternal law of self-preservation:

Resolved, unanimously, That the Delegates appointed to represent this Colony in General Congress be instructed to propose to that respectable body to declare the United Colonies free and independent States, absolved from all allegiance to, or dependance upon, the Crown of Parliament of *Great Britain;* and that they give the assent of this Colony to such declaration, and to whatever measures may be thought proper and necessary by the Congress for forming foreign alliances, and a Confederation of the Colonies, at such time and in the manner as to them shall seem best: *Provided,* That the power of forming Government for, and the regulations of the internal concerns of each Colony, be left to the respective Colonial Legislatures. . . .

D. INDEPENDENCE MOVED IN CONGRESS: RICHARD HENRY LEE, RESOLVES FOR INDEPENDENCE (JUNE 7, 1776)†

Resolved, That these United Colonies are, and of right ought to be, free and independent States, that they are absolved from all allegiance to the British

* These excerpts are reprinted from Peter Force (ed.), *American Archives* (1837–1853), 4th ser., vol. VI, p. 1524.

† These excerpts are reprinted from *Journals of the Continental Congress,* vol. V, p. 425.

Crown, and that all political connection between them and the State of Great Britain is, and ought to be, totally dissolved.

That it is expedient forthwith to take the most effectual measures for forming foreign Alliances.

That a plan of confederation be prepared and transmitted to the respective Colonies for their consideration and approbation.

SELECTION

The Uncertain Prospects of Independence

Within the American political community there was a wide range of reactions to the approach of independence. For the high tories and loyal adherents to Britain, most of whom had already either fled to Britain or resolved to keep quiet until the unhappy dispute had been resolved, independence meant total alienation from their native or adopted country and probably exile. For a second category of men who saw merits and demerits in the behavior of both sides and fervently hoped for an eventual reconciliation, it was a major catastrophe. With all hopes of reconciliation gone, they found themselves in a tragic dilemma, uncertain how they should behave and, now that some choice was paramount, which side to choose. Such a man was William Smith, Jr. (1728–1793), chief justice and member of the royal Council of New York, who, unable to commit himself to either side, had largely withdrawn from active political life after the passage of the Coercive Acts in early 1774. Written just after learning of the vote for independence by the Virginia Convention, his tortured attempt to explain for himself how and why each side had contributed to bring things to such a state and to determine how he should behave is reprinted below as Selection 31 A. His continued refusal to take sides led to his confinement at Livingston Manor in 1777 and to his banishment the next year. Remaining in New York City until the British evacuated it in 1783, he became chief justice of Quebec in 1786 after a three-year exile in Britain.

For many patriots as well, independence was not viewed as an unmixed blessing. No matter how apparently heinous the actions of the imperial government had been, it was not easy even for staunch whigs to renounce forever all allegiance to a country and a system of government they had only a few years before held in the highest veneration. Some, like the wealthy Virginia planter Landon Carter (1710–1778), who, having once been prominent in Virginia counsels, had retired from all but local political activity, were afraid that social chaos and political despotism might follow the dissolution of the old bonds of authority. Carter revealed his doubts in the passages of his diary reprinted here as Selection 31 B. Others, such as John Dickinson, who, like Carter, accepted independence once it had been declared, were simply temperamentally unable to bring themselves to join wholeheartedly in such a radical step. Profoundly cautious, Dickinson in a last-minute plea before Congress, reprinted here as Selection 31 C, adduced all of the arguments he could think of against independence and in favor of a more prudent course. His remarks revealed the mistrust of France and Spain and the fears of the divisive effects of internal rivalries among the states upon the success of the American cause that were widespread among those reluctant patriots who opposed independence.

If patriots like Carter and Dickinson had to be compelled to independence, however, there were others, like John Adams, who thought that it had been delayed far too long, hailed it as a "mighty revolution," and were convinced that it would be "celebrated by succeeding generations" as a "memorable epocha in the history of America." Adams recorded his ecstatic reaction to Congress's vote on July 2, 1776, to accept Richard Henry Lee's resolutions for independence in a letter to his wife Abigail written the following day and reprinted here as Selection 31 D.

There is no comprehensive or thorough analysis of the mixed reactions to and the emotional and political effects of the decision for independence upon the several segments of the American political community, though the appropriate sections of William H. Nelson, The American Tory *(1961), Merrill Jensen,* The Articles of Confederation: An Interpretation of the Social-Constitutional History of the American Revolution 1774–1781 *(1940), Moses Coit Tyler,* The Literary History of the American Revolution, 1763–1783 *(1897), and John C. Miller,* Origins of the American Revolution *(1943), may be consulted with profit. There is no adequate biographical treatment of Smith, though L. F. S. Upton (ed.),* The Diary and Selected Papers of Chief Justice William Smith, 1784–1793 *(1963), and William H. W. Sabine,* Historical Memoirs of William Smith *(1956–1958), contain useful sketches. On Carter see the introduction to Jack P. Greene (ed.),* The Diary of Colonel Landon Carter of Sabine Hall 1752–1778 *(1965), and on Adams, Page Smith,* John Adams *(1962).*

A. THE DILEMMA OF THE UNDECIDED: WILLIAM SMITH, JR., "THOUGHTS AS A RULE FOR MY OWN CONDUCT" (JUNE 9, 1776)*

I now set down—My Thoughts as a Rule for my own Conduct, at this melancholy Hour of approaching Distress.—

I   Every Nation has Authority to frame such a Government for itself as will without Injury to others, be most conducive to its own Felicity.

II   The Legislative Power of a Nation, whether trusted by the People to one or more Persons or however modelled, is absolute; for no State can exist if any of its Members may by Force or Fraud, act against it with Impunity; and therefore all Governments punish Treason, or the Attempt to subvert the Constitution, as the highest Crime of which a Subject can be guilty.

III   No Man will be innocent, even *Foro conscientiae* [in the court of conscience], in an Endeavor to overturn the Government of his Country, if the meditated Revolution, tends to light up a Civil War, and the Miseries of it will probably exceed those, which the People have been accustomed to endure.

IV   The Establishments made in the American Colonies, by English

* These excerpts are reprinted from William H. W. Sabine (ed), *Historical Memoirs of William Smith* (1956–1958), vol. I, pp. 271–277.

Emigrants and their Associates, might in their early Days and weak States, have been prevented or subverted by the Mother Country.

V   The Lords and Commons of England, being conversant of the Grants and Charters of their Kings and Queens, for the Encouragement of the Colonies, and of the Transactions under them; And afterwards co-operating for regulating the Plantations, rendring them secure against foreign Invasions, and useful to Great Britain, they are therefore not meerly royal and crown-created, but National and parliamentary Establishments.

VI   The Grants of Charters to the Colonies, and the posterior Settlements, Regulations and Usages by the Permission, and with the knowledge or Privity, and without the Interdiction of Parliament, are incontestable Proofs of a great National Covenant, between the Mother Country and the Colonies; for her Favors (which undeniably have been many and great) by inspiring the Colonists with Confidence, and exposing them to hazardous and expensive Undertakings, created Rights; And Gratitude never obliges to Returns and Surrenders, incompatible with those Rights, which are essential to the Felicity of the Receiver of the Benefit.

VII   Before the Year 1764 The Kings Lords and Commons, or Legislators of the *Mother* Country, were the acknowledged supreme Lawgivers of the *whole* Empire; of which the English Colonies were Members.

VIII   The National Covenant bound the Parent Country, to protect and promote the Colonies, according to the good Faith inspired by the Grants and Charters and other royal and national Acts in their Favor, consistant with the Weal of both Countries; And it obliged the Plantations to submit to her Authority, in all Cases not repugnant to their Grants, Charters and established Privileges; and to contribute to the common Felicity and Defence of the Empire.

IX   Neither of the contracting Parties may dissolve this Compact, as long as their joint Aim in the union, to wit their mutual Prosperity, can be attained by it.

X   As no Provision was made for constituting an Impartial Judge between them, to bridle or correct the Partiality or Infidelity of either of the Parties, their Controversies are therefore to be decided by Negotiation and Treaty, or on an Appeal to the Lord of Hosts by Battle; for neither is obliged to surrender its essential Rights at the Will of the other; & each may lawfully exert its own self-preserving Powers.

XI   Since amongst imperfect Beings Offences are inevitable, the Contractors are by the Laws of a Judge who cannot be deceived reciprocally bound upon Exceptions taken, to pursue every Measure of a conciliatory Nature consistant with the original End of the Union, and to such Mutual Condescensions, as tend to the Re Establishment of the General Felicity, Peace and Harmony: And this is more especially their Duty, since the Empire consists of Branches, who have offended neither of the Parties at Strife, & yet will be ruined, if the Controversy terminates in a Disunion. . . .

To the Application of our Principle, we shall make several . . . particular Remarks

(1) That the present Animosities are imputable to the Pride & Avarice of Great Britain, in assuming an Authority, inconsistant with the Compact by which the Empire has been so long prosperously united. The Colonies have the Merit of returning to their Submission, the instant she disharmed them of the Stamp Duties, notwithstanding her irritating Avowal of a Right to

unlimited Sovereignty. They remained quiet, till Mr Townsend revived the Imposition, by the Duties upon Paper Paint and Glass in 1767, for raising a Revenue, subversive of the Colony Legislatures and the Old Customs of the Empire.

(2) That the Colonies were justifiable, in resisting the new Law devised to execute the Tea Duty Act; for that aiming to inforce the Claim of absolute Supremacy, they were driven to the alternative of open Violence, or an unconditional Submission. The Mother Country had contemned all their Petitions and Remonstrances, & Force was inevitable agt. the Dutied Article, since a meer Disswasion from the Purchase of Tea, might expose to Prosecution, ruinous to the patriotic Diswader, unless his Countrymen would make Exertions agt. the Government for his Redemption—And it was therefore more eligible immediately to destroy the Commodity, than afterwards to break Jails, and overturn the Colony Government, to defeat the regular Course of Law.

(3) That the Resentment of Great Britain on the Destruction & Expulsion of the Tea, manifested in the hostile Measures of 1774, by altering the Charter of the Massachusetts Bay, extinguishing the Commerce of Boston, collecting an Army there, rendring the Soldiery dispunishable even for Blood wasted, and by Modelling the Province of Quebec, favorable to the Designs of Compulsion & Violence, was utterly unjustifiable & an Infraction of the League; which obliged Great Britain to protect the Colonies. And these Severities were the more inexcusable, since to that Moment her Sovereignty in all Cases (the Matter of Taxation excepted) had not been denied by the Colonies, but was supported by all our Courts and Judicatures. *Jam domiti ut paveant,* as Tacitus said of our British ancestors, *nondum ut serviant*—Subjects not Slaves.

(4) That the Continental Congress now formed in September 1774, might with Justice have resorted to Arms, in Defence of the Massachusetts Bay, agt. the little Army collected there, for the avowed Design of inforcing a Principle destructive of the common Safety of the Provinces.

(5) That it was the Duty of the American Assemblies, and of that Congress, as acting for the whole Continent, to render a Plan to the Mother Country for restoring Peace, consistant with the Compact, by which the Parliament of Great Britain, was to injoy a Supremacy not incompatible with the Common Felicity of the Empire—And consequently that the Declaration they then made, of the Right of the Colonies to an *exclusive* Legislation, not only in all laws of Taxation, but of *internal Polity,* subject only to the negative of their Sovereign, was a Departure in Terms, from the Original Covenant; since it left no Authority to the Parliament of Great Britain, over the Plantations, except for the Regulation of external Commerce, and countenanced a Jealousy, excited by the Mis-Representations of their Enemies, of a Design to maintain a Union only with the Kings, and not with the Legislature of Great Britain—And that the Intimation of that Congress, of the Willingness of the Colonies, to acquiesce in their Condition prior to the Year 1763, gave Great Britain no sufficient Ground, to expect their Submission to the antient, acknowledged Claims of her Parliament; since her Repeal of the offending Statutes, unless we retracted our Denial of her Legislative Authority in Matters of internal Polity, would establish by fair Implication, the Congress's Declaration as the Basis of Peace, and that thenceforth America was to be considered as the Ally of Great Britain, &

not a Member of the Empire—So it struck me on the first Publication of that Declaration; & Mr. Hutchinson & others who had slandered the Colonies to Administration, must have exulted in this Proof of the Truth of what they wrote, & long afterwards, applied to the great Mass, were malignant Calumnies.

(6) That it would not have been inconsistant with the Dignity of Great Britain, instead of declaring War against the Colonies, as she did by the joint Address of the Lords & Commons to the King in Jany 1775 to have animadverted upon the Denial of her Authority in all Cases respecting their internal Polity, *as an Error;* And to have specified, in what Particulars America should be restored to a *uti possedetis* [a situation in which each party retains what he possesses.], relative to their Charters, Patents, Assemblies, Elections and Modes of Government, on Condition of her contributing to the Necessities of the Empire—And that the Parliamentary Vote of the 20 Feby 1775, would have been a rational Foundation for a Treaty of Reconciliation, if it had explicitly asserted, that the Right reserved by Parliament, of approving the Quantum of the Colony Contributions towards the common Defence, was not claimed, upon any Supposition, that the Parliament might authoritatively *command* Levies, but only judge of the Exercize or Defect of a due Sympathy in any Branch of the Empire to the general Necessities of the whole Body—And especially if G Britain had also intimated a Readiness to consent to such Checks, Limitations and Restraints, upon the Disposition of the Contributions, as might be necessary to insure the Application of them to the End for which they were given, and had promised with these, a Restitution of Rights, and an Act of Oblivion.

(7) That Great Britain is justly blamable, for issuing that Proposal, in Terms countenancing a haughty Attachment to the Principles of unlimited Submission, and accompanying it with Acts for Augmenting her Force at Boston, and restraining the Fishery and Commerce of the Colonies; and for neglecting to command a Cessation of Arms, until the Colonies, had an opportunity to deliberate with Composure of Mind, upon her Proposal; and more especially for her irritating Sally to Concord & Lexington on the 19t April, when no Governor but Mr. Gage was then possessed of the Parliamentary Resolve, & he had concealed it even from the People committed to his Care.

(8) That as that Vote under those Circumstances, and the partial Direction of her Wrath against the New England Colonies, countenanced the Opinion of its being contrived to decieve and divide the Colonies, the Congress of 1775 had some Pretext for flying to Arms, to repel the further Incursions of the British Troops, till the Government gave them an opportunity, in a Condition less alarming, to explain their Declaration of Sept 1774, into a Consistancy with the antient, acknowledged Supremacy of Parliament, and to state the Limitations requisite for their Safety, in Answer to the February Resolve.

(9) That the total Rejection of the Parliamentary Proposal of 1775, and the neglect of the Congress to recal or explain the Declaration of 1774, tended to exasperate the British Nation; especially as the Successes of the Continental Operations in Canada, and the inefficacious Condition of the British Army at Boston, did leave America in a Condition for a more deliberate Consideration of the Controversy, than could be expected immediately after the bloody Scenes at Lexington Concord and Charles Town

—And that both Countries ought then to have tendered conciliatory Propositions to each other, and sent Agents to explain and inculcate their mutual Requisitions.

(10) That the sanguinary Orders to the Navy of Great Britain in June 1775, to sack every Town in America, which should prepare for Defence; and her Neglect to stay Hostilities after the Petition of the Congress preferred in August by Mr. Richd. Penn, to his Majesty, submitting it to his Wisdom to point to some Plan, for the Restoration of Harmony, greatly inhances the Guilt, with which she stands chargeable, for commencing an unnecessary War to maintain an illiberal Dominion.

(11) That every partial View, whether of Great Britain to aggrandize herself, by extortionate Exactions from the Plantations, regardless of their Felicity; or of America to figure among the Nations, as an independent Power, on the Ruins of Great Britain, Ireland, and the other Colonies, is unrighteous in the Sight of God; and upon the Supposition of the Manifestation of his Justice in the Government of Nations, will expose to the Correction & Chastisement of his irresistible and unerring Hand.

(12) That both Countries continue still chargeable, with a guilty Neglect of the Obligations they were under to pursue the Measures requisite to a Reconciliation—Great Britain having begun the War for an unconditional Submission; and when she deigned to make the Proposals of Feby 1775, uttered herself in a Form, & pursued such a Conduct, as had a natural Tendency to render them abortive, especially as the Kings Ministers affected to confine their Indignation to the more formidable Colonies in New England —Whilst America on the other Hand, instead of tendering a Plan of Peace, consistant with the Union, rejected the British Offers, without proposing any qualifying Clauses or Emendations tending to a friendly Negotiation upon the Subject of their Differences; and has to this Moment adhered to her Denial in 1774 of the whole Authority of Parliament, respecting the internal Polity of the Provinces—And turned a deaf Ear to the Overtures of last Winter by Lord Drummond & Mr. Elliot, from which much might I think have been hoped, if we had instantly dispatched Commissioners to meet the Ministry, in their own secret Way of feeling each others Pulses, without National Credentials, that might give an Alarm to the Jealousies of the Multitude and the Misrepresentations of Faction & Party on either Side of the Atlantic.

(13) That when Terms are proposed, consistant with the original Compact, neither Party can reject them and be innocent; tho' they offer no Reimbursement for the Charges of the War, not any Hostages or Surrenders for Security agt a future Apostacy; because the Controversy sprang from the Neglect of both Countries in early Days, to concert such specific Stipulations, as were necessary to prevent Strife, and reconcile their Safety with the general Supremacy cf Parliament; & because the Exaction of Hostages or Surrenders, or any Thing beyond an explicit and definitive Treaty, will partake, as I concieve, of the Nature of a Cession of Rights, contrary to the Design of a Restitution to their primitive Condition—A Condition to America, after another prosperous half Century, perfectly safe, from her inevitable Growth.—And to Great Britain least dangerous because from the Predispositions of God's Providence, she seems to have no other Choice than of a Civil War, which will quicken her Fall, or the Resort to a wise and liberal System of Administration for retarding that Catastrophe

until the gradual Transfer of her Wealth & Inhabitants has reared an Empire for her in the Western Hemisphere superior to what she enjoys in the East, and that to such a distant Aera, as tho' offensive to her Pride, may not be really injurious to the *present* Possessors of the antient Emporium nor even to their Posterity within the Sphere of human and rational Attachmts.

(14) That the Approval being made by the Sword to the omniscient Judge of Heaven, who will decide between the contending Parties with unerring Rectitude, and the War daily wasting the Blood and Treasure of both Countries, and tending to a separation, ruinous to millions who have taken no Part in the Quarrel, it concerns those who have excited, or contributed to it, by the Calls and Ties of Justice, Humanity, Patriotism, Benevolence, Honor, Religion, and Interest, to cultivate Concord, and a Return to their antient Union, according to that Compact, which so eminently advanced the Prosperity of the Empire, antecedent to the year 1764 —For no End however in itself desirable and laudable, is to expect Success by a perfidious & ambitious Violation of that Covenant, under which the Providence of God placed us and our Fathers, be the Prospect of our accelerating it, never so flattering to our Zeal for the Civil or religious Interests of Mankind; it being our indispensible Duty to seek for temporal as well as eternal Felicity, *in the way of well doing;* trusting it to the great Creator & Manager of the Universe to accomplish his benevolent Designs, relating both to Church & State, according to his own infinite Wisdom & irresistible Sovereignty; for the Principle that Evil may be done that good may come of it, is beyond all Controversy a satanical Maxim, which has often deluded both priests and People, into Practices, professedly aiming at the Advancement of the Glory of God & the Benefit of Mankind, but in Reality dishonoring Religion, & deluging the World with human Blood. . . .

B. FEAR OF SOCIAL CHAOS: LANDON CARTER, DIARY (MAY 1, 29, 1776)*

[May 1]   I have just heard A certain G. R., when asked to lend his fire lock to go against the tender, asked the People if they were such fools to go to protect the Gentlemen's houses on the river side; he thought it would be the better if they were burnt down. This it seems a Gentleman heard and told to a Committee man; and though we have had a Committee since no Notice was ever taken of it. The old deligates were left out, for this very Purpose and these new ones chose for this Very Purpose of an intire independence in which no Gentleman should have the least share. Hurray for Independancy, Sedition, and Confusion.

If this Mr. G. R. had been mentioned to the Committee I should then as Chairman have represented how conspicuous their notice of him would have made him even to this disgrace of the rest of the County and would have recommended to them to take no notice of him. For my observation on Such people's behaviour, has generally turned out, that they only want to be taken notice of, that they may have some grounds to represent to those like them-

* These selections are reprinted from Jack P. Greene (ed.), *The Diary of Colonel Landon Carter of Sabine Hall 1752–1778* (1965), vol. II, pp. 1030–1031, 1046.

selves, what persecution they endure by resisting the rich or, as they call them, the Gentlemen. . . .

[May 29] I can with truth say, and bless my God for it, that although I from the beginning abominated this present contest which Great Britain certainly began with America by attempting to tax her out of the constitutional road, yet I was so convinced of the Romanticness of her intention to come 3,000 miles and subdue above 3 million of People to her arbitrary rule of enslaving, that I never once entertained the least Possibility of her success in it; and I do suppose from a confidence in the success of our cause, by applying my leisure hours and devoting my most serious thoughts to the throne of mercy, I can say that I have never been moved with the least fear or apprehension as to the success of the dispute. But really my only dread has been on account of this separation which she, her King, her ministry and her Parliament have barbarously driven us into, least from the secret inclination of some to an arbitrary sway themselves we might fall into a worse situation from internal oppression and commotions than might have been obtained by a serious as well as cautious reconciliation. Therefore, I have always wondered at the prodigious rash Praise which has been given to that most nonsensical of all Pamphlets, *Common Sense,* in which I could not deduce one just Sentiment, according to any Sense whatever. From whence I still conclude that the support which it has met with must have been through a latent desire in every body that has contenanced it, to be as arbitrary as possible; and they have therefore resolved to run every risk rather than not indulge this innate disposition to rule. Certainly then it behooves him who admires Peace, order, and moderation in Government to be cautious of such People, for it is morally certain that there are such, and without the utmost timely care they will work themselves into the Hydra of Power. I don't expect to live to see it but mark the conclusion.

C. THE CALL FOR PRUDENCE: JOHN DICKINSON, "ARGUMENTS AGAINST THE INDEPENDENCE OF THE COLONIES . . ." (JULY 1, 1776)*

The Consequences involvd in the Motion now lying before You are of such Magnitude, that I tremble under the oppressive Honor of sharing in its Determination. I feel Myself unequal to the Burthen assigned Me. I believe, I had almost said, I rejoice, that the Time is approaching, when I shall be relieved from its Weight. . . . My Conduct, this Day, I expect will give the finishing Blow to my once too great, and . . . too diminish'd Popularity. It will be my Lott to know, that I had rather vote away the Enjoyment of that dazzling display, that pleasing Possession, than the Blood and Happiness of my Countrymen—too fortunate, amidst their Calamities, if I prove . . . that I had rather they should hate Me, than that I should hurt them. I might indeed, practise an artful, an advantageous Reserve upon this Occasion. But thinking as I do on the Subject of Debate, Silence would be guilt. I

* These excerpts are reprinted from *The Pennsylvania Magazine of History and Biography,* vol. 65 (1941), pp. 468–476, 478–481, without the extensive editorial apparatus included by the discoverer and original editor of the document, John H. Powell.

despise its Arts, I detest its Advantages. I must speak, tho I should lose my Life, tho I should lose the Affections of my Country. Happy at present, however, I shall esteem Myself, if I can so far rise to the Height of this great argument as to offer to this Honorable Assembly in a full & clear Manner, those Reasons, that have so invariably fix'd my own Opinion.

It was a Custom in a wise and virtuous State, to preface Propositions in Council, with a Prayer, that they might redound to the public Benefit. I beg Leave to imitate the laudable Example—And I do most humbly implore Almighty God, with whom dwells Wisdom itself, so to enlighten the Members of this House, that their Decision may be such as will best promote the Liberty Safety and Prosperity of these Colonies—and for Myself, that his Divine Goodness may be graciously pleased to enable Me, to speak the Precepts of Sound Policy on the important Question that now engages our Attention.

Sir, Gentlemen of very distinguished Abilities and Knowledge differ widely in their Sentiments upon the Point now agitated. They all agree, that the utmost Prudence is required in forming our Decisions, But immediately disagree in their Notion of that Prudence. Some cautiously insist, that We ought to obtain that previous Information which we are likely quickly to obtain, and to make those previous Establishments that are acknowledged to be necessary. Others strenuously assert, that tho regularly such Information & Establishment ought to precede the Measure proposed, yet confiding in our Fortune more boldly than Caesar himself, we ought to brave the Storm in a Skiff made of Paper.

In all such Cases, where every Argument is adorn'd with an Eloquence that may please and yet mislead, it seems to me the proper method of discovering the right Path, to enquire, which of the parties is probably, the most warm'd by Passion. Other Circumstances being equal or nearly equal, that Consideration would have Influence with Me. I fear the Virtue of Americans. Resentment of the Injuries offered to their Country, may irritate them to Counsels & to Actions that may be detrimental to the Cause, they would dye to advance.

What advantages could it be claimed would follow from the adoption of this resolution? 1 It might animate the People. 2 It would Convince foreign Powers of our Strength & Unanimity & we would receive their aid in consequence thereof. As to the 1st point—it is Unnecessary. The preservation of Life Liberty & Property is a sufficient Motive to animate the People. The General Spirit of America is animated.

As to the 2d foreign Powers will not rely on Words.

The Event of the Campaign will be the best Evidence of our strength and unanimity. This Properly the first Campaign. Who has received Intelligence that such a Proof of our Strength & daring Spirit will be agreable to France—? What must She expect from a People that begin their Empire in so high a stile, when on the Point of being invaded by the whole Power of Great Britain aided by formidable afor[?] aid—unconnected with foreign Powers—She & Spain must Perceive the immediate Danger of their Colonies lying at our Doors—Their Seat of Empire is in another World . . .

It would be More respectful to act in Conformity to the Views of France. Let us Take advantage of their Pride, let us Give them Reason to believe that We confide in them—that we desire to act in Conjonction with their Policies & Interests. Let us Know how they would regard this Stranger in

the States of the World. People are fond of what they have attaind in producing; they Regard it as a Child, A Cement of Affection exists between
them. Let us Allow them the Glory of appearing the Vindicators of Liberty.
It will please them.

It is treating them with Contempt to act otherwise. Especially after the
application made to France. Which by this Time has reach'd them. . . .
Consider the Abilities of the persons sent. What will they think, if now so
quickly afterwards without waiting for their Determination, totally slighting
their Sentiments on such a prodigous issue, We haughtily pursue our own
Measures?

May they not say to Us, Gentlemen, You falsely pretended to consult Us,
& disrespectfully proceeded without waiting our Resolution. You must abide
the Consequences. We are not ready for a Rupture; You should have negotiated till We were. We will not be hurried by your Impetuosity. We know
it is our Interest to support You, But We shall be in no haste about it. Try
your own Strength & Resources in which You have such Confidence. We
know now You dare not look back. Reconciliation is impossible without
declaring independence, now that you have reached the stage you have.
Yours is the most rash & at the same Time the most contemptible Senate
that ever existed on Earth!

Suppose on this Event Great Britain should offer Canada to France &
Florida to Spain with an Extension of the old Limits. Would not France &
Spain accept them? Gentlemen say the Trade of all america is more valuable
to France than Canada. I grant it; but suppose She may get both? If She
is politick, & none doubts that, I averr She has the easiest Game to play for
attaining both, that ever presented itself to a Nation.

When We have bound ourselves to a stern Quarrel with Great Britain by
a Declaration of Independence, France has nothing to do but to hold back
& intimidate Great Britain till Canada is put into her Hands, then to
intimidate Us into a most disadvantageous Grant of our Trade. It is my
firm Opinion these Events will take Place, & arise naturally from our declaring Independance.

As to Aid from foreign Powers: our Declaration can procure Us none
during this present Campaign though made today. It is impossible.

Now let us consider, if all the Advantages expected from foreign Powers
cannot be attained in a more unexceptional manner. Is there no way of
giving Notice of a Nation's Resolution, than by proclaiming it to all the
World? Let Us in the most solemn Manner inform the House of Bourbon,
at least France, that We wait only for her Determination to declare our
Independence. We must not talk generally of foreign Powers but only of
those We expect to favor Us. Let Us assure Spain that We never will give
any Assistance to her Colonies. Let France become guarantee For us in
arrangements of this Kind.

Besides, first we ought to Establish our governments & take the Regular
Form of a State—These preventive Measures will shew Deliberation, Wisdom, Caution & Unanimity.

It is Our Interest to keep Great Britain in the Opinion that We mean
Reconciliation as long as possible—. . . . The Wealth of London &c is
por'd into the Treasury. The whole Nation is ardent against Us. We oblige
her by our attitude to persevere in Her Spirit. See the last petition of
London.

Suppose we shall ruin her. France must rise on her Ruins. Her Ambition. Her Religion. Our Dangers from thence. We shall weep at our [?] We shall be Overwhelm'd with Debt. I Compute that Debt at 6 Millions of Pennsylvania Money a Year.

The War will be carried on with more Severity. The Burning of Towns, the Setting Loose of Indians on our Frontiers, has Not yet been done. Boston might have been burnt though it was not.

What Advantage is to be expected from a Declaration? 1—The Animating of our Troops? I answer, it is unnecessary. 2—Union of the Colonies? I answer, this is also unnecessary. It may weaken that Union, when the People find themselves engaged in a cause rendered more cruel by such a Declaration without Prospect of an End to their Calamities, by a Continuation of the War.

People are changeable. In Bitterness of Soul they may complain against our Rashness & ask why We did not apply first to foreign Powers, Why We did not settle Differences among ourselves, why we did not Take Care to secure unsettled Lands for easing their Burthens instead of leaving them to particular Colonies, Why we did not wait till we were better prepar'd, or till We had made an Experiment of our Strength.

3—A third advantage to be expected from a Declaration is said to be the Proof it would furnish of our Strength of Spirit. But This is possibly only the first Campaign of the war. France & Spain may be alarm'd & provoked with each other; Masserano was an insult to France. There is Not the least Evidence of her granting Us favorable Terms. Her probable Conditions The Glory of recovering Canada will be enough for her. She will get that & then dictate Terms to Us.

A PARTITION of these Colonies will take Place if Great Britain cant conquer Us. To escape from the protection we have in British rule by declaring independence would be like Destroying a House before We have got another, In Winter, with a small Family; Then asking a Neighbour to take Us in and finding He is unprepared.

4th   It is claimed that The Spirit of the Colonies calls for such a Declaration. I Answer, that the spirit of the colonies is Not to be relied on. Not only Treaties with foreign powers but among Ourselves should precede this Declaration. We should know on what Grounds We are to stand with Regard to one another. We ought to settle the issues raised by the Declaration of Virginia about Colonists in *their Limits*. And, too, The Committee on Confederation dispute almost every Article—Some of Us totally despair of any reasonable Terms of Confederation.

We cannot look back. Men generally sell their Goods to most Advantage when they have several Chapmen. We have but two to rely on. We exclude one by this Declaration without knowing what the other will give.

Great Britain after one or more unsuccessful Campaigns may be induc'd to offer Us such a share of Commerce as would satisfy Us, to appoint Councillors during good Behaviour, to withdraw her armies, to protect our Commerce, Establish our Militias—in short to redress all the Grievances complain'd of in our first Petition. Let Us know, if We can get Terms from France that will be more beneficial than these. If we can, let Us declare Independence. If We cannot, let Us at least withold that Declaration, till We obtain Terms that are tolerable.

We have many Points of the utmost Moment to settle with France—

Canada, Acadia and Cape Breton. What will content her? Trade or Territory? What Conditions of Trade? Barbary Pirates, Spain, Portugal? Will she demand an Exclusive Trade as a Compensation, or grant Us Protection against piratical States only for a Share of our Commerce?

When our Enemies are pressing Us so vigorously, When We are in so wretched a State of Preparation, When the Sentiments & Designs of our expected Friends are so unknown to Us, I am alarm'd at this Declaration being so vehemently presented. A worthy Gentleman told Us, that people in this House have had different Views for more than a 12 month. This is Amazing after what they have so repeatedly declared in this House & private Conversations, that they meant only Reconciliation. But since they can conceal their Views so dextrously, I should be glad to read a little more in the Doomsday Book of America—Not all—that like the Book of Fate might be too dreadful. . . . I should be glad to know whether in 20 or 30 Years this Commonwealth of Colonies may not be thought too unwieldy, & Hudson's River be a proper Boundary for a separate Commonwealth to the Northward. I have a strong Impression on my Mind that this will take Place.

D. THE PROMISE OF INDEPENDENCE: JOHN ADAMS TO ABIGAIL ADAMS (JULY 3, 1776)*

Yesterday, the greatest question·was decided, which ever was debated in America, and a greater, perhaps, never was nor will be decided among men. A resolution was passed without one dissenting colony, "that these United Colonies are, and of right ought to be, free and independent States, and as such they have, and of right ought to have, full power to make war, conclude peace, establish commerce, and to do all other acts and things which other States may rightfully do." You will see in a few days a Declaration setting forth the causes which have impelled us to this mighty revolution, and the reasons which will justify it in the sight of God and man. A plan of confederation will be taken up in a few days.

When I look back to the year 1761, and recollect the argument concerning writs of assistance in the superior court, which I have hitherto considered as the commencement of this controversy between Great Britain and America, and run through the whole period, from that time to this, and recollect the series of political events, the chain of causes and effects, I am surprised at the suddenness as well as greatness of this revolution. Britain has been filled with folly, and America with wisdom. At least, this is my judgment. Time must determine. It is the will of Heaven that the two countries should be sundered forever. It may be the will of Heaven that America shall suffer calamities still more wasting, and distresses yet more dreadful. If this is to be the case, it will have this good effect at least. It will inspire us with many virtues, which we have not, and correct many errors, follies and vices which threaten to disturb, dishonor, and destroy us. The furnace of affliction produces refinement, in States as well as individuals. And the new governments we are assuming in every part will require a purification from our vices, and

* The following excerpts are reprinted from Charles Francis Adams (ed.), *The Works of John Adams* (1854), vol. IX, pp. 418–420.

an augmentation of our virtues, or they will be no blessings. The people will have unbounded power, and the people are extremely addicted to corruption and venality, as well as the great. But I must submit all my hopes and fears to an overruling Providence, in which, unfashionable as the faith may be, I firmly believe.

Had a Declaration of Independency been made seven months ago, it would have been attended with many great and glorious effects. We might, before this hour, have formed alliances with foreign States. . . .

But, on the other hand, the delay of this declaration to this time has many great advantages attending it. The hopes of reconciliation, which were fondly entertained by multitudes of honest and well-meaning, though weak and mistaken people, have been gradually and, at last, totally extinguished. Time has been given for the whole people maturely to consider the great question of independence, and to ripen their judgment, dissipate their fears, and allure their hopes, by discussing it in newspapers and pamphlets, by debating it in assemblies, conventions, committees of safety and inspection, in town and county meetings, as well as in private conversations, so that the whole people, in every colony of the thirteen, have now adopted it as their own act. This will cement the union, and avoid those heats, and perhaps convulsions, which might have been occasioned by such a declaration six months ago.

But the day is past. The second day of July, 1776, will be the most memorable epocha in the history of America. I am apt to believe that it will be celebrated by succeeding generations as the great anniversary festival. It ought to be commemorated, as the day of deliverance, by solemn acts of devotion to God Almighty. It ought to be solemnized with pomp and parade, with shows, games, sports, guns, bells, bonfires, and illuminations, from one end of this continent to the other, from this time forward, forevermore.

You will think me transported with enthusiasm, but I am not. I am well aware of the toil, and blood, and treasure, that it will cost us to maintain this declaration, and support and defend these States. Yet, through all the gloom, I can see the rays of ravishing light and glory. I can see that the end is more than worth all the means, and that posterity will triumph in that day's transaction, even although we should rue it, which I trust in God we shall not.

SELECTION

"That These United Colonies Are, and of Right Ought to Be Free and Independent States": The Declaration of Independence (July 4, 1776)

By July 1, 1776, the date set for the further consideration of Richard Henry Lee's motion of June 7 for independence, sentiment for the motion among the delegates from the middle colonies had ripened considerably. A preliminary vote in committee found nine colonies in favor of the motion, two (South Carolina and Pennsylvania) opposed, one (Delaware) divided, and one (New York) abstaining. At the final vote on July 2, however, both the South Carolina and Pennsylvania delegations switched their votes, and the arrival of a third delegate from Delaware put that colony into the affirmative column. Only the New York delegation, adhering to instructions from the New York Provincial Congress, did not vote on the motion, which passed with twelve affirmative and no negative votes. During the remainder of July 2 and on July 3 Congress considered the Declaration of Independence, which with the exception of a few amendments by Adams and Franklin was the work of Thomas Jefferson. An eloquent justification of the actions of the colonies in declaring independence and a powerful assertion of man's natural right of revolution, the Declaration also contained a long list of charges against George III and "others" (the ministry and Parliament) that stand as a superb statement of the substantive issues of the American Revolution as the dominant whig group saw them in 1776. After making some further amendments, Congress formally accepted the Declaration of July 4 by a vote of twelve to nothing with New York again abstaining. With the endorsement of the Declaration by the New York Provincial Congress on July 9 the decision for independence became unanimous. The Declaration is reprinted in full below from Francis Newton Thorpe (ed.), The Federal and State Constitutions, and Other Organic Laws *(seven volumes, 1909), vol I, pages 3–7.*

The classic study of the Declaration is Carl Becker, The Declaration of Independence: A Study in the History of Political Ideas *(1922), though it should be supplemented by Edward Dumbauld,* The Declaration of Independence and What It Means Today *(1950), which contains a more careful evaluation of the list of grievances in the Declaration.*

The Unanimous Declaration of the Thirteen United States of America

WHEN in the Course of human events, it becomes necessary for one people to dissolve the political bands which have connected them with another, and to assume among the Powers of the earth, the separate and equal station to which the Laws of Nature and of Nature's God entitle them, a decent respect to the opinions of mankind requires that they should declare the causes which impel them to the separation.

We hold these truths to be self-evident, that all men are created equal, that they are endowed by their Creator with certain unalienable Rights, that among these are Life, Liberty and the pursuit of Happiness. That to secure these rights, Governments are instituted among Men, deriving their just powers from the consent of the governed, That whenever any Form of Government becomes destructive of these ends, it is the Right of the People to alter or to abolish it, and to institute new Government, laying its foundation on such principles and organizing its powers in such form, as to them shall seem most likely to effect their Safety and Happiness. Prudence, indeed will dictate that Governments long established should not be changed for light and transient causes; and accordingly all experience hath shown, that mankind are more disposed to suffer, while evils are sufferable, than to right themselves by abolishing the forms to which they are accustomed. But when a long train of abuses and usurpations, pursuing invariably the same

Object evinces a design to reduce them under absolute Despotism, it is their right, it is their duty, to throw off such Government, and to provide new Guards for their future security.—Such has been the patient sufferance of these Colonies; and such is now the necessity which constrains them to alter their former Systems of Government. The history of the present King of Great Britain is a history of repeated injuries and usurpations, all having in direct object the establishment of an absolute Tyranny over these States. To prove this, let Facts be submitted to a candid world.

He has refused his Assent to Laws, the most wholesome and necessary for the public good.

He has forbidden his Governors to pass Laws of immediate and pressing importance, unless suspended in their operation till his Assent should be obtained; and when so suspended, he has utterly neglected to attend to them.

He has refused to pass other Laws for the accommodation of large districts of people, unless those people would relinquish the right of Representation in the Legislature, a right inestimable to them and formidable to tyrants only.

He has called together legislative bodies at places unusual, uncomfortable, and distant from the depository of their Public Records, for the sole purpose of fatiguing them into compliance with his measures.

He has dissolved Representative Houses repeatedly, for opposing with manly firmness his invasions on the rights of the people.

He has refused for a long time, after such dissolutions, to cause others to be elected; whereby the Legislative Powers, incapable of Annihilation, have returned to the People at large for their exercise; the State remaining in the mean time exposed to all the dangers of invasion from without, and convulsions within.

He has endeavoured to prevent the population of these States; for that purpose obstructing the Laws for Naturalization of Foreigners; refusing to pass others to encourage their migration hither, and raising the conditions of new Appropriations of Lands.

He has obstructed the Administration of Justice, by refusing his Assent to Laws for establishing Judiciary Powers.

He has made Judges dependent on his Will alone, for the tenure of their offices, and the amount and payment of their salaries.

He has erected a multitude of New Offices, and sent hither swarms of Officers to harrass our People, and eat out their substance.

He has kept among us, in times of peace, Standing Armies without the Consent of our legislature.

He has affected to render the Military independent of and superior to the Civil Power.

He has combined with others to subject us to a jurisdiction foreign to our constitution, and unacknowledged by our laws; giving his Assent to their Acts of pretended Legislation:

For quartering large bodies of armed troops among us:

For protecting them, by a mock Trial, from Punishment for any Murders which they should commit on the Inhabitants of these States:

For cutting off our Trade with all parts of the world:

For imposing Taxes on us without our Consent:

For depriving us in many cases, of the benefits of Trial by Jury:

For transporting us beyond Seas to be tried for pretended offences:

For abolishing the free System of English Laws in a neighbouring Province, establishing therein an Arbitrary government, and enlarging its Boundaries so as to render it at once an example and fit instrument for introducing the same absolute rule into these Colonies:

For taking away our Charters, abolishing our most valuable Laws, and altering fundamentally the Forms of our Governments:

For suspending our own Legislatures, and declaring themselves invested with Power to legislate for us in all cases whatsoever.

He has abdicated Government here, by declaring us out of his Protection and waging War against us.

He has plundered our seas, ravaged our Coasts, burnt our towns, and destroyed the Lives of our people.

He is at this time transporting large Armies of foreign Mercenaries to compleat the works of death, desolation and tyranny, already begun with circumstances of Cruelty & perfidy scarcely paralleled in the most barbarous ages, and totally unworthy the Head of a civilized nation.

He has constrained our fellow Citizens taken Captive on the high Seas to bear Arms against their Country, to become the executioners of their friends and Brethren, or to fall themselves by their Hands.

He has excited domestic insurrections amongst us, and has endeavoured to bring on the inhabitants of our frontiers, the merciless Indian Savages, whose known rule of warfare, is an undistinguished destruction of all ages, sexes and conditions.

In every stage of these Oppressions We have Petitioned for Redress in the most humble terms: Our repeated Petitions have been answered only by repeated injury. A Prince, whose character is thus marked by every act which may define a Tyrant, is unfit to be the ruler of a free People.

Nor have We been wanting in attention to our British brethren. We have warned them from time to time of attempts by their legislature to extend an unwarrantable jurisdiction over us. We have reminded them of the circumstances of our emigration and settlement here. We have appealed to their native justice and magnanimity, and we have conjured them by the ties of our common kindred to disavow these usurpations, which, would inevitably interrupt our connections and correspondence. They too have been deaf to the voice of justice and of consanguinity. We must, therefore, acquiesce in the necessity, which denounces our Separation, and hold them, as we hold the rest of mankind, Enemies in War, in Peace Friends.

We, therefore, the Representatives of the united States of America, in General Congress, Assembled, appealing to the Supreme Judge of the world for the rectitude of our intentions, do, in the Name, and by Authority of the good People of these Colonies, solemnly publish and declare, That these United Colonies are, and of Right ought to be Free and Independent States; that they are Absolved from all Allegiance to the British Crown, and that all political connection between them and the State of Great Britain, is and ought to be totally dissolved; and that as Free and Independent States, they have full Power to levy War, conclude Peace, contract Alliances, establish Commerce, and to do all other Acts and Things which Independent States may of right do. And for the support of this Declaration, with a firm reliance on the Protection of Divine Providence, we mutually pledge to each other our Lives, our Fortunes and our sacred Honor.

JOHN HANCOCK.

New Hampshire

JOSIAH BARTLETT,

WM. WHIPPLE,

MATTHEW THORNTON.

Massachusetts Bay

SAML. ADAMS,

JOHN ADAMS,

ROBT. TREAT PAINE,

ELBRIDGE GERRY.

Rhode Island

STEP. HOPKINS,

WILLIAM ELLERY.

Connecticut

ROGER SHERMAN,

SAM'EL HUNTINGTON,

WM. WILLIAMS,

OLIVER WOLCOTT.

New York

WM. FLOYD,

PHIL. LIVINGSTON,

FRANS. LEWIS,

LEWIS MORRIS.

New Jersey

RICHD. STOCKTON,

JNO. WITHERSPOON,

FRAS. HOPKINSON,

JOHN HART,

ABRA. CLARK.

Pennsylvania

ROBT. MORRIS,

BENJAMIN RUSH,

BENJA. FRANKLIN,

JOHN MORTON,

GEO. CLYMER,

JAS. SMITH,

GEO. TAYLOR,

JAMES WILSON,

GEO. ROSS.

Delaware

CÆSAR RODNEY,

GEO. READ,

THO. M'KEAN.

Maryland

SAMUEL CHASE,

WM. PACA,

THOS. STONE,

CHARLES CARROLL of Car-
rollton.

Virginia

GEORGE WYTHE,

RICHARD HENRY LEE,

TH JEFFERSON,

BENJA. HARRISON,

THOS. NELSON, jr.,

FRANCIS LIGHTFOOT LEE,

CARTER BRAXTON.

North Carolina

WM. HOOPER,

JOSEPH HEWES,

JOHN PENN.

South Carolina

EDWARD RUTLEDGE,

THOS. HEYWARD, Junr.,

THOMAS LYNCH, Junr.,

ARTHUR MIDDLETON.

Georgia

BUTTON GWINNETT,

LYMAN HALL,

GEO. WALTON.

PART EIGHT

Reconstituting the Polity

Prescriptions for Government

*Perhaps the most revealing fact about the American Revolution is that the break-
down of royal government and the Declaration of Independence were followed not
by the social chaos or the popular or military despotism some fainthearted whigs
had predicted but by the firm establishment of stable and popular constitutional
governments, first in the states and then in the nation. Such a development was
completely without precedent in modern history, and American leaders had to feel
their way. Because they had no ready-made manuals on constitution making to
guide them, they proceeded to produce their own, and a series of proposals found
their way into print throughout 1776. More clearly even than the constitutions
themselves, these plans reveal the character of the concerns—the fear of human
nature and the distrust of power—that drove American leaders to insist upon the
immediate adoption of written constitutions, the intense seriousness with which
they approached the task, and their assumptions about the function of government and its relationship to society.*

*In general, these plans represented an attempt to reduce to a systematic body
of concrete proposals the central elements of the inherited traditions and practical
political experience of the colonists. There was thus a strong preference for a
mixed or balanced constitution similar to the British. This preference is clearly
revealed in John Adams's Thoughts on Government, which is printed in full below
as Selection 33 A. The most influential of all the proposals published in 1776, this
pamphlet was prepared by Adams in late 1775 and early 1776 at the request of
William Hooper (1742–1790) and John Penn (1740–1788), two of his fellow delegates to the Second Continental Congress from North Carolina. It was intended
to serve as a model for the framers of the state constitutions and as an antidote to
the proposals for an "unrestrained democracy" enunciated by Thomas Paine in
Common Sense. Like the vast majority of American leaders, Adams wanted a
government that would both reflect the will of the public and, because of the
imperfections of man and, more important, his inability to resist the temptations
of power, embody the principle of counterpoise. In Adams's "mixed republic" this
principle was to operate in two ways. First, the three functions of government—
legislative, executive, and judicial—were to be assigned to three distinct and counter-
vailing branches. Second, the legislative power was to be apportioned among three
separate institutions, each counterbalancing the other two. Thus, a representative
assembly that was to be "in miniature an exact portrait of the people at large"
was to be subjected to the "controlling power" of a second house of the legislature
elected by the assembly and having "a free and independent exercise of its judgment" and to a governor with a veto power who was to be chosen by both houses.
By such a division of powers along with other devices such as rotation of office
Adams hoped to prevent any segment of the government from engrossing all power
and introducing some form of tyranny and thereby to guarantee that "impartial
and exact execution of the laws" that was the distinguishing feature of an ideal
government.*

*Adams's Thoughts on Government represented the dominant strain of political
thought among American leaders in 1776, but there was a wide range of dissenting
proposals. Some of the most interesting and original of these came out of Pennsylvania, where there was a vigorous and prolonged discussion preceding the adop-*

tion of a constitution in September. Sentiment in Pennsylvania ran strongly against the traditional bicameral form of government. That form in Britain was thought to derive from the division of society into two separate orders—the nobility and the commons—and the central problem facing the proponents of bicameralism during the Revolutionary era was to discover some basis for justifying a second branch of the legislature in a society that was obviously composed of only one order. Adams was noticeably silent on this question, and no other advocate of bicameralism seemed sure about just what the upper house was supposed to represent. It became a commonplace that the lower house should represent opinion and the upper house judgment, but, as Bernard Bailyn has pointed out, no one was able to suggest exactly how judgment "could be recognized publicly, isolated, and recruited into a particular branch of government." It was to avoid this and other more obvious difficulties that several Pennsylvania tracts argued in favor of a unicameral legislature.

Two of the most interesting of these tracts, Four Letters on Interesting Subjects and The Interest of America, both of which were published anonymously in 1776, are reprinted in part below as Selection 33 B (1) and Selection 33 B (2) respectively. Assuming that the "simplest mode of legislation is certainly best," the writers of both pieces insisted that "One branch of Legislature is much preferable to more than one." A bicameral legislature, they argued, only created delays, fostered potentially disastrous rivalries between the two houses, and was needlessly expensive. Moreover, a bicameral system did not correspond with social realities in America. There was no need for an upper house, the author of The Interest of America declared, because "we have not, and hope never shall have, a hereditary nobility, different from the general body of the people," and to "admit different branches of the Legislature" only increased the danger that such a nobility might "in time" develop. In a much more radical departure from the traditional lines of constitutional thought, the author of Four Letters discussed political and social divisions in terms of interests rather than social orders. He identified two broad interest groups, the landed and the commercial, and contended that they should not be segregated in different houses but thrown together into one house so that the conflicts between them could be more easily and quickly resolved. Neither writer wanted to place all authority in the hands of a single-house legislature, however. No less fearful of the corrupting influences of power than their contemporaries, they both wanted a distinct separation of functions between the legislature and the executive, frequent elections, and rotation in office. More important, the writer of Four Letters, who made a much sharper distinction between a constitution and a government than most of his contemporaries, thought that the constitution should set the limits of governmental power and, in a novel suggestion, called for the creation of a "Provincial Jury" to be elected periodically to make sure that the government had not exceeded the power given it by the constitution. To achieve the same ends, the author of The Interest of America wanted to keep as much authority as possible in the hands of the towns and counties and to give to the state and national governments only those powers that could not be properly handled at the local level.

How wide the spectrum of proposals was may be seen in Selection 33 C, Address to the Convention of the Colony and Ancient Dominion of Virginia, and 33 D, The People the Best Governors. Usually attributed to Carter Braxton (1736–1797), a wealthy Virginia planter, legislator, and delegate to the Continental Congress, the Address reflected the fear of social anarchy that derived from the fluid political situation following the destruction of the old colonial governments and gripped so *many American political leaders during the spring and summer of 1776. To re-establish order, clarify the lines of political authority, and prevent the "tumult and riot incident to" the "simple Democracy" advocated by others, Braxton wanted to "adopt and perfect that system which England has suffered to be grossly abused, and the experience of ages has taught us to venerate." To make the Virginia Constitution correspond as closely as possible to the English, he proposed that the governor hold office not for any set term but during good behavior and that the members of the upper house of the legislature be elected for life by the lower house. If Braxton's ideas were far too "aristocratical" to appeal to a very broad segment of American political leadership,* The People the Best Governors, *coming probably out of western New England but with no indication either of its place of publication or of its author, was much too "democratical." Probably the most extreme plea for popular government published in 1776, it advanced a series of partially contradictory arguments and proposals based upon the predication that the "people best know their own wants and necessities, and therefore are best able to rule themselves."*

The most comprehensive and penetrating discussion of the various constitutional proposals of 1776 is in the introduction to Bernard Bailyn (ed.), Pamphlets of the American Revolution *(1965). Bailyn's remarks may be supplemented by Elisha P. Douglass,* Rebels and Democrats: The Struggle for Equal Political Rights and Majority Rule during the American Revolution *(1955), and Merrill Jensen, "Democracy and the American Revolution,"* Huntington Library Quarterly, *volume 20 (August, 1957), pages 321–341.*

A. A MIXED POPULAR FORM: JOHN ADAMS, ''THOUGHTS ON GOVERNMENT'' (1776)*

My DEAR SIR,—If I was equal to the task of forming a plan for the government of a colony, I should be flattered with your request, and very happy to comply with it; because, as the divine science of politics is the science of social happiness, and the blessings of society depend entirely on the constitutions of government, which are generally institutions that last for many generations, there can be no employment more agreeable to a benevolent mind than a research after the best.

Pope flattered tyrants too much when he said,

> For forms of government let fools contest,
> That which is best administered is best.

Nothing can be more fallacious than this. But poets read history to collect flowers, not fruits; they attend to fanciful images, not the effects of social institutions. Nothing is more certain, from the history of nations and nature of man, than that some forms of government are better fitted for being well administered than others.

We ought to consider what is the end of government, before we determine which is the best form. Upon this point all speculative politicians will agree,

* Reprinted from Charles Francis Adams (ed.), *The Works of John Adams* (1854), vol. IV, pp. 193–200.

that the happiness of society is the end of government, as all divines and moral philosophers will agree that the happiness of the individual is the end of man. From this principle it will follow, that the form of government which communicates ease, comfort, security, or, in one word, happiness, to the greatest number of persons, and in the greatest degree, is the best.

All sober inquirers after truth, ancient and modern, pagan and Christian, have declared that the happiness of man, as well as his dignity, consists in virtue. Confucius, Zoroaster, Socrates, Mahomet, not to mention authorities really sacred, have agreed in this.

If there is a form of government, then, whose principle and foundation is virtue, will not every sober man acknowledge it better calculated to promote the general happiness than any other form?

Fear is the foundation of most governments; but it is so sordid and brutal a passion, and renders men in whose breasts it predominates so stupid and miserable, that Americans will not be likely to approve of any political institution which is founded on it.

Honor is truly sacred, but holds a lower rank in the scale of moral excellence than virtue. Indeed, the former is but a part of the latter, and consequently has not equal pretensions to support a frame of government productive of human happiness.

The foundation of every government is some principle or passion in the minds of people. The noblest principles and most generous affections in our nature, then, have the fairest chance to support the noblest and most generous models of government.

A man must be indifferent to the sneers of modern Englishmen, to mention in their company the names of Sidney, Harrington, Locke, Milton, Nedham, Neville, Burnet, and Hoadly. No small fortitude is necessary to confess that one has read them. The wretched condition of this country, however, for ten or fifteen years past, has frequently reminded me of their principles and reasonings. They will convince any candid mind, that there is no good government but what is republican. That the only valuable part of the British constitution is so; because the very definition of a republic is "an empire of laws, and not of men." That, as a republic is the best of governments, so that particular arrangement of the powers of society, or, in other words, that form of government which is best contrived to secure an impartial and exact execution of the laws, is the best of republics.

Of republics there is an inexhaustible variety, because the possible combinations of the powers of society are capable of innumerable variations.

As good government is an empire of laws, how shall your laws be made? In a large society, inhabiting an extensive country, it is impossible that the whole should assemble to make laws. The first necessary step, then, is to depute power from the many to a few of the most wise and good. But by what rules shall you choose your representatives? Agree upon the number and qualifications of persons who shall have the benefit of choosing, or annex this privilege to the inhabitants of a certain extent of ground.

The principal difficulty lies, and the greatest care should be employed, in constituting this representative assembly. It should be in miniature an exact portrait of the people at large. It should think, feel, reason, and act like them. That it may be the interest of this assembly to do strict justice at all times, it should be an equal representation, or, in other words, equal interests among the people should have equal interests in it. Great care should be taken to effect this, and to prevent unfair, partial, and corrupt elections. Such regulations, however, may be better made in times of greater tranquillity than the present; and they will spring up themselves naturally, when all the powers of government come to be in the hands of the people's friends. At present, it will be safest to proceed in all established modes, to which the people have been familiarized by habit.

A representation of the people in one assembly being obtained, a question arises, whether all the powers of government, legislative, executive, and judicial, shall be left in this body? I think a people cannot be long free, nor ever happy, whose government is in one assembly. My reasons for this opinion are as follow:—

1. A single assembly is liable to all the vices, follies, and frailties of an individual; subject to fits of humor, starts of passion, flights of enthusiasm, partialities, or prejudice, and consequently productive of hasty results and absurd judgments. And all these errors ought to be corrected and defects supplied by some controlling power.

2. A single assembly is apt to be avaricious, and in time will not scruple to exempt itself from burdens, which it will lay, without compunction, on its constituents.

3. A single assembly is apt to grow ambitious, and after a time will not hesitate to vote itself perpetual. This was one fault of the Long Parliament; but more remarkably of Holland, whose assembly first voted themselves from annual to septennial, then for life, and after a course of years, that all vacancies happening by death or otherwise, should be filled by themselves, without any application to constituents at all.

4. A representative assembly, although extremely well qualified, and absolutely necessary, as a branch of the legislative, is unfit to exercise the executive power, for want of two essential properties, secrecy and despatch.

5. A representative assembly is still less qualified for the judicial power, because it is too numerous, too slow, and too little skilled in the laws.

6. Because a single assembly, possessed of all the powers of government, would make arbitrary laws for their own interest, execute all laws arbitrarily for their own interest, and adjudge all controversies in their own favor.

But shall the whole power of legislation rest in one assembly? Most of the foregoing reasons apply equally to prove that the legislative power ought to be more complex; to which we may add, that if the legislative power is wholly in one assembly, and the executive in another, or in a single person, these two powers will oppose and encroach upon each other, until the contest shall end in war, and the whole power, legislative and executive, be usurped by the strongest.

The judicial power, in such case, could not mediate, or hold the balance between the two contending powers, because the legislative would undermine it. And this shows the necessity, too, of giving the executive power a negative upon the legislative, otherwise this will be continually encroaching upon that.

To avoid these dangers, let a distinct assembly be constituted, as a mediator between the two extreme branches of the legislature, that which represents the people, and that which is vested with the executive power.

Let the representative assembly then elect by ballot, from among themselves or their constituents, or both, a distinct assembly, which, for the sake of perspicuity, we will call a council. It may consist of any number you please, say twenty or thirty, and should have a free and independent exercise of its judgment, and consequently a negative voice in the legislature.

These two bodies, thus constituted, and made integral parts of the legislature, let them unite, and by joint ballot choose a governor, who, after being stripped of most of those badges of domination, called prerogatives, should have a free and independent exercise of his judgment, and be made also an integral part of the legislature. This, I know, is liable to objections; and, if you please, you may make him only president of the council, as in Connecticut. But as the governor is to be invested with the executive power, with consent of council, I think he ought to have a negative upon the legislative. If he is annually elective, as he ought to be, he will always have so much reverence and affection for the people, their representatives and counsellors, that, although you give him an independent exercise of his judgment, he will seldom use it in opposition to the two houses, except in cases the public utility of which would be conspicuous; and some such cases would happen.

In the present exigency of American affairs, when, by an act of Parliament, we are put out of the royal protection, and consequently discharged from our allegiance, and it has become necessary to assume government for our immediate security, the governor, lieutenant-governor, secretary, treasurer, commissary, attorney-general, should be chosen by joint ballot of both houses. And these and all other elections, especially of representatives and counsellors, should be annual, there not being in the whole circle of the sciences a maxim more infallible than this, "where annual elections end, there slavery begins."

These great men, in this respect, should be, once a year,

> Like bubbles on the sea of matter borne,
> They rise, they break, and to that sea return.

This will teach them the great political virtues of humility, patience, and moderation, without which every man in power becomes a ravenous beast of prey.

This mode of constituting the great offices of state will answer very well for the present; but if by experiment it should be found inconvenient, the legislature may, at its leisure, devise other methods of creating them, by elections of the people at large, as in Connecticut, or it may enlarge the term for which they shall be chosen to seven years, or three years, or for life, or make any other alterations which the society shall find productive of its ease, its safety, its freedom, or, in one word, its happiness.

A rotation of all offices, as well as of representatives and counsellors, has many advocates, and is contended for with many plausible arguments. It would be attended, no doubt, with many advantages; and if the society has a sufficient number of suitable characters to supply the great number of vacancies which would be made by such a rotation, I can see no objection to it. These persons may be allowed to serve for three years, and then be excluded three years, or for any longer or shorter term.

Any seven or nine of the legislative council may be made a quorum, for doing business as a privy council, to advise the governor in the exercise of the executive branch of power, and in all acts of state.

The governor should have the command of the militia and of all your armies. The power of pardons should be with the governor and council.

Judges, justices, and all other officers, civil and military, should be nominated and appointed by the governor, with the advice and consent of council, unless you choose to have a government more popular; if you do, all officers, civil and military, may be chosen by joint ballot of both houses; or, in order to preserve the independence and importance of each house, by ballot of one house, concurred in by the other. Sheriffs should be chosen by the freeholders of counties; so should registers of deeds and clerks of counties.

All officers should have commissions, under the hand of the governor and seal of the colony.

The dignity and stability of government in all its branches, the morals of the people, and every blessing of society depend so much upon an upright and skilful administration of justice, that the judicial power ought to be distinct from both the legislative and executive, and independent upon both, that so it may be a check upon both, as both should be checks upon that. The judges, therefore, should be always men of learning and experience in the laws, of exemplary morals, great patience, calmness, coolness, and attention. Their minds should not be distracted with jarring interests; they should not be dependent upon any man, or body of men. To these ends, they should hold estates for life in their offices; or, in other words, their commissions should be during good behavior, and their salaries ascertained and established by law. For misbehavior, the grand inquest of the colony, the house of representatives, should impeach them before the governor and council, where they should have time and opportunity to make their defence; but, if convicted, should be removed from their offices, and subjected to such other punishment as shall be thought proper.

A militia law, requiring all men, or with very few exceptions besides cases of conscience, to be provided with arms and ammunition, to be trained at certain seasons; and requiring counties, towns, or other small districts, to be provided with public stocks of ammunition and intrenching utensils, and with some settled plans for transporting provisions after the militia, when marched to defend their country against sudden invasions; and requiring certain districts to be provided with field-pieces, companies of matrosses, and perhaps some regiments of light-horse, is always a wise institution, and, in the present circumstances of our country, indispensable.

Laws for the liberal education of youth, especially of the lower class of people, are so extremely wise and useful, that, to a humane and generous mind, no expense for this purpose would be thought extravagant.

The very mention of sumptuary laws will excite a smile. Whether our countrymen have wisdom and virtue enough to submit to them, I know not; but the happiness of the people might be greatly promoted by them, and a revenue saved sufficient to carry on this war forever. Frugality is a great revenue, besides curing us of vanities, levities, and fopperies, which are real antidotes to all great, manly, and warlike virtues.

But must not all commissions run in the name of a king? No. Why may they not as well run thus, "The colony of   to A. B. greeting," and be tested by the governor?

Why may not writs, instead of running in the name of the king, run thus, "The colony of   to the sheriff," &c., and be tested by the chief justice?

Why may not indictments conclude, "against the peace of the colony of   and the dignity of the same?"

A constitution founded on these principles introduces knowledge among the people, and inspires them with a conscious dignity becoming freemen; a general emulation takes place, which causes good humor, sociability, good manners, and good morals to be general. That elevation of sentiment inspired by such a government, makes the common people brave and enterprising. That ambition which is inspired by it makes them sober, industrious, and frugal. You will find among them some elegance, perhaps, but more solidity; a little pleasure, but a great deal of business; some politeness, but more civility. If you compare such a country with the regions of domination, whether monarchical or aristocratical, you will fancy yourself in Arcadia or Elysium.

If the colonies should assume governments separately, they should be left entirely to their own choice of the forms; and if a continental constitution should be formed, it should be a congress, containing a fair and adequate representation of the colonies, and its authority should sacredly be confined to these cases, namely, war, trade, disputes between colony and colony, the post-office, and the unappropriated lands of the crown, as they used to be called.

These colonies, under such forms of government, and in such a union, would be unconquerable by all the monarchies of Europe.

You and I, my dear friend, have been sent into life at a time when the greatest lawgivers of antiquity would have wished to live. How few of the human race have ever enjoyed an opportunity of making an election of government, more than of air, soil, or climate, for themselves or their children! When, before the present epocha, had three millions of people full power and a fair opportunity to form and establish the wisest and happiest government that human wisdom can contrive? I hope you will avail yourself and your country of that extensive learning and indefatigable industry which you possess, to assist her in the formation of the happiest governments and the best character of a great people. For myself, I must beg you to keep my name out of sight; for this feeble attempt, if it should be known to be mine, would oblige me to apply to myself those lines of the immortal John Milton, in one of his sonnets:—

> I did but prompt the age to quit their clogs
> By the known rules of ancient liberty,
> When straight a barbarous noise environs me
> Of owls and cuckoos, asses, apes, and dogs.

B.   A SIMPLE POPULAR FORM

1. "Four Letters on Interesting Subjects" (1776)*

AMONG the many publications which have appeared on the subject of political Constitutions, none, that I have seen, have properly defined what is meant by *a Constitution,* that word having been bandied about without any determinate sense being affixed thereto. A Constitution, and a form of government, are frequently confounded together, and spoken of as synonimous

* These excerpts are from the fourth letter and are reprinted from the original edition (1776), pp. 18–24.

things; whereas they are not only different, but are established for different purposes: All countries have some form of government, but few, or perhaps none, have truly a Constitution. The form of government in England is by a king, lords and commons; but if you ask an Englishman what he means when he speaks of the English Constitution, he is unable to give you any answer. The truth is, the English have no fixed Constitution. The prerogative of the crown, it is true, is under several restrictions; but the legislative power, which includes king, lords and commons, is under none; and whatever acts *they* pass, are laws, be they ever so oppressive or arbitrary. England is likewise defective in Constitution in three other material points, viz. The crown, by virtue of a patent from itself, can increase the number of the lords (one of the legislative branches) at his pleasure. . . . The crown can likewise, by a patent, incorporate any town or village, small or great, and empower it to send members to the house of commons, and fix what the precise number of the electors shall be. And an act of the legislative power, that is, an act of king, lords, and commons, can again diminish the house of commons to what number they please, by disfranchising any county, city or town.

IT is easy to perceive that individuals by agreeing to erect forms of government, (for the better security of themselves) must give up some part of their liberty for that purpose; and it is the particular business of a Constitution to mark out *how much* they shall give up. In this sense it is easy to see that the English have no Constitution, because they have given up every thing; their legislative power being unlimited without either condition or controul, except in the single instance of trial by Juries. No country can be called *free* which is governed by an absolute power; and it matters not whether it be an absolute royal power or an absolute legislative power, as the consequences will be the same to the people. That England is governed by the latter, no man can deny, their being, as is said before, no Constitution in that country which says to the legislative powers, "Thus far shalt thou go, and no farther." There is nothing to prevent them passing a law which shall exempt themselves from the payment of taxes, or which shall give the house of commons power to sit for life, or to fill up the vacancies by appointing others, like the Corporation of Philadelphia. In short, an act of parliament, to use a court phrase, can do any thing but make a man a woman.

A Constitution, when completed, resolves the two following questions: First, What shall the form of government be? And secondly, What shall be its power? And the last of these two is far more material than the first. The Constitution ought likewise to make provision in those cases where it does not empower the legislature to act.

THE forms of government are numerous, and perhaps the simplest is the best. The notion of checking by having different houses, has but little weight with it, when inquired into, and in all cases it tends to embarrass and prolong business; besides, what kind of checking is it that one house is to receive from another? or which is the house that is most to be trusted to? They may fall out about forms and precedence, and check one another's honour and tempers, and thereby produce petulances and ill-will, which a more simple form of government would have prevented. That some kind of convenience might now and then arise from having two houses, is granted, and the same may be said of twenty houses; but the question is, whether such a mode would not produce more hurt than good. The more houses the more parties; and perhaps the ill consequence to this country would be, that the landed interest would get into one house, and the commercial interest into the other; and by that means a perpetual and dangerous opposition would be kept up, and no business be got through: Whereas, were there a large, equal and annual representation in one house *only*, the different parties, by being thus blended together, would hear each others arguments, which advantage they cannot have if they sit in different houses. To say, there ought to be two houses, because there are two sorts of interest, is the very reason why there ought to be but one, and *that one* to consist of every sort. The lords and commons in England formerly made but one house; and it is evident, that by separating men you lessen the quantity of knowledge, and increase the difficulties of business. However, let the form of government be what it may, in this, or other provinces, so long as it answers the purpose of the people, and they approve it, they will be happy under it. That which suits one part of the Continent may not in every thing suit another; and when each is pleased, however variously, the matter is ended. No man is a true republican, or worthy of the name, that will not give up his single voice to that of the public: his private opinion he may retain; it is obedience only that is his duty.

THE chief convenience arising from two houses is, that the second may sometimes amend small imperfections which would otherwise pass; yet, there is nearly as much chance of their making alterations for the worse as the better; and the supposition that a single house may become arbitrary, can with more reason be said of two; because their strength is greater. Besides, when all the supposed advantages arising from two houses are put together, they do not appear to balance the disadvantage. A division in one house will not retard business, but serves rather to illustrate; but a difference between two houses may produce serious consequences. In queen Ann's reign a quarrel arose between the upper and lower house, which was carried to such a pitch that the nation was under very terrifying apprehensions, and the house of commons was dissolved to prevent worse mischief. A like instance was nearly happening about six years ago, when the members of each house very affrontingly turned one another by force out of doors: The two best bills in the last sessions in England were entirely lost by having two houses; the bill for encreasing liberty of conscience, by taking off the necessity of subscription to the thirty-nine articles, Athanasian creed, &c. after passing the lower house by a very great majority, was thrown out by the upper one; and at the time that the nation was starving with the high price of corn, the bill for regulating the importation and exportation of grain, after passing the lower house, was lost by a *difference* between the two, and when returned from the upper one was thrown on the floor by the commons, and indignantly trampled under foot.---Perhaps most of the Colonies will have two houses, and it will probably be of benefit to have some little difference in the forms of government, as those which do not like one, may reside in another, and by trying different experiments, the best form will the sooner be found out, as the preference at present rests on conjecture.

GOVERNMENT is generally distinguished into three parts, Executive, Legislative and Judicial; but this is more a distinction of words than things. Every king or governor in giving his assent to laws acts legislatively, and not executively: The house of lords in England is both a legislative and judicial body. In short, the distinction is perplexing, and however we may refine and define, there is no more than two powers in any government, viz. the power to make laws, and the power to execute them; for the judicial power is only a branch of the executive, the CHIEF of every country being the first magistrate.

A CONSTITUTION should lay down some permanent ratio, by which the representation should afterwards encrease or decrease with the number of inhabitants; for the right of representation, which is a natural one, ought not to depend upon the will and pleasure of future legislatures. And for the same reason perfect liberty of conscience; security of person against unjust imprisonments, similar to what is called the Habeas Corpus act; the mode of trial in all law and criminal cases; in short, all the great rights which man never mean, nor ever ought, to lose, should be *guaranteed,* not *granted,* by the Constitution; for at the forming a Constitution we ought to have in mind, that whatever is left to be secured by law only, may be altered by another law. That Juries ought to be judges of law, as well as fact, should be clearly described; for though in some instances Juries may err, it is generally from tenderness, and on the right side. A man cannot be *guilty* of a *good* action, yet if the fact only is to be proved (which is Lord Mansfield's doctrine) and the Jury not empowered to determine in their own minds, whether the fact proved to be done is a crime or not, a man may hereafter be found guilty of going to church or meeting.

THERE is one circumstance respecting trial by Juries which seems to deserve attention; which is, whether a Jury of Twelve persons, which cannot bring in a verdict unless they are all of one mind, or appear so; or, whether a Jury of not less than Twenty-five, a majority of which shall make a verdict, is the safest to be trusted to? The objections against an Jury of Twelve are, that the necessity of being unanimous prevents the freedom of speech, and causes men sometimes to conceal their own opinions, and follow that of others; that it is a kind of terrifying men into a verdict, and that a strong hearty obstinate man who can bear starving twenty-four or forty-eight hours, will distress the rest into a compliance; that there is no difference, in effect, between hunger and the point of a bayonet, and that under such circumstances a Jury is not, nor can be free. In favour of the latter it is said, that the least majority is thirteen; that the dread of the consequences of disagreeing being removed, men will speak freer, and that justice will thereby have a fairer chance.

IT is the part of a Constitution to fix the manner in which the officers of government shall be chosen, and determine the principal outlines of their power, their time of duration, manner of commissioning them, &c. The line, so far as respects their election, seems easy, which is, by the representatives of the people; provincial officers can be chosen no other way, because the whole province cannot be convened, any more than the whole of the Associators could be convened for choosing generals. Civil officers for towns and countries may easily be chosen by election. The mode of choosing delegates for Congress deserves consideration, as they are not officers but legislators. Positive provincial instructions have a tendency to disunion, and, if admitted, will one day or other rend the Continent of America. A continental Constitution, when fixed, will be the best boundaries of Congressional power, and in matters for the general good, they ought to be as free as assemblies. The notion, which some have, of excluding the military from the legislature is unwise, because it has a tendency to make them form a distinct party of their own. Annual elections, strengthened by some kind of periodical exclusion, seem the best guard against the encroachments of power; suppose the exclusion was triennial, that is, that no person should be returned a member of assembly for more than three succeeding years, nor be capable of being returned again till he had been absent three years. Such a mode would greatly encrease the circle of knowledge, make men cautious how they acted, and prevent the disagreeableness of giving offence, by removing some, to make room for others of equal, or perhaps superior, merit. Something of the same kind may be practised respecting Presidents or Governors, not to be eligible after a certain number of returns; and as no person, after filling that rank, can, consistent with character, descend to any other office or employment; and as it may not always happen that the most wealthy are the most capable, some decent provision therefore should be made for them in their retirement, because it is a retirement from the world. Whoever reflects on this, will see many good advantages arising from it.

MODEST and decent honorary titles, so as they be neither hereditary, nor convey legislative authority, are of use in a state; they are, when properly conferred, the badges of merit. The love of the public is the chief reward which a generous man seeks; and, surely! if *that* be an honour, the mode of conferring it must be so likewise.

NEXT to the forming a good Constitution, is the means of perserving it. If once the legislative power breaks in upon it, the effect will be the same as if a kingly power did it. The Constitution, in either case, will receive its death wound, and "the outward and visible sign," or mere form of government only will remain. "I wish," says Lord Camden, "that the maxim of Machiavel was followed, that of examining a Constitution, at certain periods, according to its first principles; this would correct abuses, and supply defects." The means here pointed out for preserving a Constitution are easy, and some article in the Constitution may provide, that at the expiration of every seven or any other number of years a *Provincial Jury* shall be elected, to enquire if any inroads have been made in the Constitution, and to have power to remove them; but not to make alterations, unless a clear majority of all the inhabitants shall so direct. . . .

I shall . . . conclude with remarking, that perfection in government, like perfection in all other earthly things, is not to be hoped for. A single house, or a duplication of them, will alike have their evils; and the defect is incurable, being founded in the nature of man, and the instability of things.

2. "The Interest of America" (1776)*

The important day is come, or near at hand, that *America* is to assume a form of Government for herself. We should be very desirous to know what form is best; and that surely is best which is most natural, easy, cheap, and which best secures the rights of the people. We should always keep in mind that great truth, viz: that the good of the people is the ultimate end of civil Government. As we must (some Provinces at least) in a short time assume some new mode of Government, and the matter cannot be deferred so long as to canvass, deliberately weigh, and fully adjust everything that may

* These excerpts are reprinted from Peter Force (ed.), *American Archives* (1837–1853), 4th ser., vol. VI, pp. 840–843.

hereafter appear necessary, we should leave room to alter for the better in time to come. Every Province should be viewed as having a right, either with or without an application to the Continental Congress, to alter their form of Government in some particulars; and that without being liable to raise a clamour, by some who would be glad to say that it was contrary to the Constitution that they first formed upon; that it was overturning the original plan, and leaving people at uncertainties as to the foundation they are upon, and the like. As the Government is for the people, the people, when properly represented, have a right to alter it for their advantage.

The affair now in view is the most important that ever was before *America*. In my opinion, it is the most important that has been transacted in any nation for some centuries past. If our civil Government is well constructed and well managed, *America* bids fair to be the most glorious State that has ever been on earth. We should now, at the beginning, lay the foundation right. Most, if not all, other Governments have had a corrupt mixture in their very Constitution; they have generally been formed in haste, or out of necessity, or tyrannically, or in a state of ignorance; and, being badly formed, the management of them has been with difficulty. But we have opportunity to form with some deliberation, with free choice, with good advantages for knowledge; we have opportunity to observe what has been right and what wrong in other States, and to profit by them. The plan of *American* Government should, as much as possible, be formed to suit all the variety of circumstances that people may be in—virtuous or vicious, agreeing or contending, moving regularly or convulsed by the intrigues of aspiring men; for we may expect a variety of circumstances in a course of time, and we should be prepared for every condition. We should assume that mode of Government which is most equitable and adapted to the good of mankind, and trust Providence for the event; for *God,* who determines the fate of Governments, is most like to prosper that which is most equitable; and I think there can be no doubt that a well-regulated Democracy is most equitable. An annual of frequent choice of magistrates, who, in a year, or after a few years, are again left upon a level with their neighbours, is most likely to prevent usurpation and tyranny, and most likely to secure the privileges of the people. If rulers know that they shall, in a short term of time, be again out of power, and, it may be, liable to be called to an account for misconduct, it will guard them against maladministration. A truly popular Government has, I believe, never yet been tried in the world. The most remarkable Government that has ever been, viz: the *Roman* Republick, was something near it, but not fully so; and the want of it being fully so, kept a continual contest between the Senate and Plebeians.

America must consist of a number of confederate Provinces, Cantons, Districts, or whatever they may be called. These must be united in a General Congress; but each Province must have a distinct Legislature, and have as much power within itself as possible. The General Congress should not interfere or meddle with Provincial affairs more than needs must. Every Province should be left to do as much within itself as may be; and every Province should allow each County, yea, and each Town, to do as much within themselves as possible. Small bodies manage affairs much easier and cheaper than large ones. If every County and Town manage as much business as may be within themselves, people will be better satisfied, and the Provincial Congress saved much trouble. Our Counties and Towns have heretofore been left to manage many of their own affairs; and it has been a great privilege, and their business has been managed to great advantage. Each County should now choose their own officers, which were heretofore appointed by the Crown. These matters may now be adjusted with much ease. Every Province should be allowed such full power within itself, and receive such advantages by a general union or confederation, that it would choose to continue in that union. The connection of the Provinces should be made to be for the interest of each, and be agreeable to each. This will keep them quiet and peaceable; and nothing will tend so much to this, as to let every Province have as much power and liberty within itself as will consist with the good of the whole. Neither the Continental Congress, nor any other number of men, should assume or use any power or office for their own sake, but for the good of the whole. Let *America* increase ever so much, there must never be any power like a Kingly power; no power used for its own sake, or for the advantage or dignity of any number of men, as distinct from the good of the whole; and while things are thus managed, a general union will be agreeable, and people will not complain.

Notwithstanding every Province should have all possible power within itself, yet some things must be left to the General Congress; as, 1. Making and managing war and making peace. 2. Settling differences between Provinces. 3. Making some maritime laws, or general regulations respecting trade; otherwise one Province might unjustly interfere with another. 4. Ordering a currency for the whole Continent; for it would be best that, as soon as may be, there should be one currency for the whole; the General Congress might order the quota for each Province. 5. The forming of new Provinces. 6. The sale of new lands. 7. Treaties with other nations; consequently some general directions of our *Indian* affairs.

As we are now to assume a new mode of Government, I think it ought properly to be new. Some are for keeping as near the old form of Government in each Province as can well be. But I think it is entirely wrong; it is mistaken policy. It is probable that some who propose it mean well; but I humbly conceive they have not thoroughly considered the thing. Others who propose it may have self-interest at bottom, hoping thereby to retain, or obtain, places of profit or honour. We must come as near a new form of Government as we can, without destroying private property. So far as private property will allow, we must form our Government in each Province just as if we had never any form of Government before. It is much easier to form a new Government than to patch up one partly old and partly new, because it is more simple and natural. I speak chiefly with respect to Legislature. We should by all means avoid several branches of Legislature.

One branch of Legislature is much preferable to more than one, because a plurality causes perpetual contention and waste of time. It was so in *Rome;* it has been so in *Great Britain;* and has been remarkably so in these Provinces in times past. The ever-memorable Congress now in *America* has done business infinitely better than if there had been several orders of Delegates to contest, interrupt, and be a negative one upon another.

A patched Government, consisting of several parts, has been the difficulty, I may call it the disease, of some of the best civil Governments that have been in the world—I mean the *Roman* Republick and the Government of *Great Britain.* Had the *Romans* been a true Democracy, without a Senate, or body different from the Plebeians, they might have avoided those jars and contentions which continually subsisted between those two bodies. Should we admit different branches of Legislature, it might give occasion in time to degenerate into that form of Government, or something like that, which has been so oppressive in our nation. It might open a door for ill-disposed aspiring men to destroy the State. Our having several branches of Legislature heretofore is an argument against, rather than for it, in time to come, because it is a word that not only has been abused, but in its nature tends to abuse. The simplest mode of legislation is certainly best. The *European* nations have, for some centuries past, derived most of their knowledge from the *Greeks* and *Romans*. The *Romans*, especially, have been, in a sort, an example, being excellent in many things. We have been ready to view them so in all things. We are very apt to take in, or imitate, the imperfections as well as the excellencies of those that are excellent. Hence, I suppose, it is that most, if not all, the Republicks in *Europe* have a body of Senators in their form of Government. I doubt not it will be an argument with many, that we in *America* must have something like a Senate, or Council, or Upper House, because the *Romans* and other Republicks have had. But the argument is the other way; it was their imperfection, it was a source of trouble, it was a step towards arbitrary power, and therefore to be avoided. Free Government can better, must better, subsist without it. Different branches of Legislature cause much needless expense, two ways: First, as there are more persons to maintain; and, second, as they waste time, and prolong a session by their contentions. Besides, it is a great absurdity that one branch of a Legislature, that can negative all.the rest, should be the principal Executive power in the State. There can be but little chance for proper freedom, where the making and executing the laws of a State lie in the same hand, and that not of the people in general, but of a single person. The Legislative and Executive power in every Province ought to be kept as distinct as possible. Wise, experienced, and publick-spirited persons should be in places of power, and if so, they must be sought out, chosen, and introduced. For this reason there ought not to be a number that are hereditary, for wisdom is not a birthright; nor a number put in place for life, for men's abilities and manners may change. Rulers should be frequently chose to their office. A Provincial Congress is the whole Province met by Representatives; and there is no need of a representative of a King, for we have none; nor can there be need of a Council to represent the House of Lords, for we have not, and hope never shall have, a hereditary nobility, different from the general body of the people; but if we admit different branches of the Legislature, there is danger that there may be in time.

C. A PERFECT MODEL OF THE ENGLISH CONSTITUTION: [CARTER BRAXTON], ''ADDRESS TO THE CONVENTION OF THE COLONY AND ANCIENT DOMINION OF VIRGINIA'' (1776)*

GENTLEMEN: When despotism had displayed her banners, and with unremitting ardour and fury scattered here engines of oppression through this

---

* These excerpts are reprinted from Force (ed.), *American Archives* (1837–1853), 4th ser., vol. VI, pp. 748–753.

wide extended continent, the virtuous opposition of the people to its progress relaxed the tone of Government in almost every Colony, and occasioned in many instances a total suspension of law. These inconveniences, however, were natural, and the more readily submitted to, as there was then reason to hope that justice would be done to our injured country, the same laws, executed under the same authority, soon regain their former use and lustre, and peace, raised on a permanent foundation, bless this our native land.

But since these hopes have hitherto proved delusive, and time, instead of bringing us relief, daily brings forth new proofs of *British* tyranny, and thereby separates us farther from that reconciliation we so ardently wished; does it not become the duty of you, and every other Convention, to assume the reins of Government, and no longer suffer the people to live without the benefit of law, and order the protection it affords? Anarchy and riot will follow a continuance of its suspension, and render the enjoyment of our liberties and future quiet at least very precarious.

Presuming that this object will, ere long, engage your attention, and fully persuaded that when it does it will be considered with all the candour and deliberation due to its importance, I have ventured to collect my sentiments on the subject, and in a friendly manner offer them to your consideration. . . .

Taking for granted, therefore, the necessity of instituting a Government capable of affording all the blessings of which the most cruel attempts have been made to deprive us, the first inquiry will be, which of the various forms is best adapted to our situation, and will in every respect most probably answer our purpose? . . .

Although all writers agree in the object of Government, and admit that it was designed to promote and secure the happiness of every member of society; yet their opinions as to the system most productive of this general benefit have been extremely contradictory. As all these systems are said to move on separate and distinct principles, it may not be improper to analyze them, and by that means show the manner of their operations.

Government is generally divided into two parts: *Its mode or form of Constitution,* and the *principle* intended to direct it.

The simple forms of Government are Despotism, Monarchy, Aristocracy, and Democracy. Out of these an infinite variety of combinations may be deduced. The absolute unlimited control of one man describes Despotism, whereas Monarchy compels the Sovereign to rule agreeable to certain fundamental laws. Aristocracy vests the sovereignty of a State in a few nobles; and Democracy allows it to reside in the body of the people, and is thence called a popular Government.

Each of these forms are actuated by different principles. The subjects of an unlimited despotick Prince, whose will is their only rule of conduct, are influenced by the principle of fear. In a Monarchy limited by laws, the people are insensibly led to the pursuit of honour; they feel an interest in the greatness of their Princes; and, inspired by a desire of glory, rank, and promotion, unite in giving strength and energy to the whole machine. Aristocracy and Democracy claim for their principle publick virtue, or a regard for the publick good independent of private interest.

Let us inquire from which of these several vines we should take a scion to ingraft on our wild one; see which is most congenial to our soil, and by the extent and strength of its branches best calculated to shelter the people from the rage of those tempests which often darken the political hemisphere.

I will not deny, whatever others may do, that individuals have enjoyed a certain degree of happiness under all these forms. Content, and consequently happiness, depend more on the state of our minds than external circumstances, and some men are satisfied with fewer enjoyments than others. Upon these occasions the inclinations of men, which are often regulated by what they have seen and experienced, ought to be consulted. It cannot be wise to draw them further from their former institutions than obvious reasons and necessity will justify. Should a form of Government directly opposite to the ancient one under which they have been happy, be introduced and established, will they not, on the least disgust, repine at the change, and be disposed even to acts of violence in order to regain their former condition? Many examples in the history of almost every country prove the truth of this remark.

What has been the Government of *Virginia,* and in a revolution how is its spirit to be preserved, are important questions. The better to discuss these points, we should take a view of the Constitution of *England,* because by that model ours was constructed, and under it we have enjoyed tranquillity and security. Our ancestors, the *English,* after contemplating the various forms of Government, and experiencing, as well as perceiving the defects of each, wisely refused to resign their liberties either to the single man, the few, or the many. They determined to make a compound of each the foundation of their Government, and of the most valuable parts of them all to build a superstructure that should surpass all others, and bid defiance to time to injure, or anything, except national degeneracy and corruption, to demolish.

In rearing this fabrick, and connecting its parts, much time, blood, and treasure, were expended. By the vigilance, perseverance, and activity, of innumerable martyrs, the happy edifice was at length completed, under the auspices of the renowned King *William* in the year 1688. They wisely united the hereditary succession of the Crown with the good behaviour of the Prince; they gave respect and stability to the Legislature, by the independence of the Lords, and security, as well as importance to the People, by being parties with their Sovereign in every act of legislation. Here, then, our ancestors rested from their long and laborious pursuit, and saw many good days in the peaceable enjoyment of the fruit of their labours. Content with having provided against the ills which had befallen them, they seemed to have forgotten that although the seeds of destruction might be excluded from their Constitution, they were, nevertheless, to be found in those by whom their affairs were administered.

Time, the improver as well as destroyer of all things, discovered to them that the very man who had wrought their deliverance was capable of pursuing measures leading to their destruction. Much is it to be lamented that this magnanimous Prince, ascending a throne beset with uncertainty and war, was induced, by the force of both, to invent and practise the art of funding to supply his wants, and create an interest that might support him in possession of his Crown. He succeeded to his wish, and thereby established a moneyed interest, which was followed by levying of taxes, by a host of tax-gatherers, and a long train of dependants on the Crown. The practice grew into system, till at length the Crown found means to break down those barriers which the Constitution had assigned to each branch of the Legislature, and effectually destroyed the independence of both Lords and Commons. These breaches, instead of being repaired as soon as discovered, were, by the supineness of the nation, permitted to widen by daily practice, till, finally, the influence of the Crown pervaded and overwhelmed the whole people, and gave birth to the many calamities which we now bewail, and for the removal of which the united efforts of *America* are at this time exerted.

Men are prone to condemn the whole because a part is objectionable; but certainly it would, in the present case, be more wise to consider whether, if the Constitution was brought back to its original state, and its present imperfections remedied, it would not afford more happiness than any other. If the independence of the Commons could be secured, and the dignity of the Lords preserved, how can a Government be better formed for the preservation of freedom? And is there anything more easy than this? If placemen and pensioners were excluded a seat in either House, and elections made triennial, what danger could be apprehended from prerogative? I have the best authority for asserting, that with these improvements, added to the suppression of boroughs, and giving the people an equal and adequate representation, *England* would have remained a land of liberty to the latest ages.

Judge of the *principle* of this Constitution by the great effects it has produced. Their code of laws, the boast of *Englishmen* and of freedom; the rapid progress they have made in trade, in arts and sciences; the respect they commanded from their neighbours; then gaining the empire of the sea; are all powerful arguments of the wisdom of that Constitution and Government which raised the people of that island to their late degree of greatness. But though I admire their perfections, I must mourn their faults; and though I would guard against, and cast off their oppression, yet would I retain all their wise maxims, and derive advantage from their mistakes and misfortunes. The testimony of the learned *Montesquieu* in favor of the *English* Constitution is very respectable: "There is (says he) one nation in the world that has for the direct end of its Constitution political liberty." Again he says, "It is not my business to examine whether the *English* actually enjoy this liberty or not; sufficient it is for my purpose to observe that it is established by their laws, and I inquire no further."

This Constitution and these laws have also been those of *Virginia*, and let it be remembered, that under them she flourished and was happy. The same principles which led the *English* to greatness animates us. To that principle our laws, our customs, and our manners, are adapted; and it would be perverting all order to oblige us, by a novel Government, to give up our laws, our customs, and our manners.

However necessary it may be to shake off the authority of arbitrary *British* dictators, we ought, nevertheless, to adopt and perfect that system which *England* has suffered to be grossly abused, and the experience of ages has taught us to venerate. This, like almost everything else, is perhaps liable to objections, and probably the difficulty of adopting a limited Monarchy will be largely insisted on. Admit this objection to have weight, and that we cannot in every instance assimilate a Government to that, yet no good reason can be assigned why the same principle, or spirit, may not in a great measure be preserved. But honourable as this spirit is, we daily see it calumniated by advocates for popular Governments, and rendered obnoxious to all whom their artifices can influence or delude. The systems recommended to the Colonies seem to accord with the temper of the times, and are fraught with all the tumult and riot incident to simple Democracy —systems which many think it their interest to support, and without doubt will be industriously propagated among you. The best of these systems exist only in theory, and were never confirmed by the experience even of those who recommend them. I flatter myself, therefore, that you will not quit a substance actually enjoyed, for a shadow or phantom, by which, instead of being benefited, many have been misled and perplexed.

Let us examine the principles they assign to their Government, and try its merits by the unerring standard of truth. In a late pamphlet it is thus stated: The happiness of man, as well as his dignity, consists in virtue: if there be a form of Government, then, whose principle is virtue, will not every sober man acknowledge it better calculated to promote the general happiness of society than any other form? Virtue is the principle of a Republick, therefore a Republick is the best form of Government.

The author, with what design I know not, seems to have cautiously blended private and publick virtue, as if for the purpose of confounding the two, and thereby recommending his plan under the amiable appearance of courting virtue. It is well known that private and publick virtue are materially different. The happiness and dignity of man, I admit, consists in the practice of private virtues, and to this he is stimulated by the rewards promised to such conduct. In this he acts for himself, and with a view of promoting his own particular welfare. Publick virtue, on the other hand, means a disinterested attachment to the publick good, exclusive and independent of all private and selfish interest, and which, though sometimes possessed by a few individuals, never characterized the mass of the people in any state. And this is said to be the principle of democratical Governments, and to influence every subject of it to pursue such measures as conduce to the prosperity of the whole. A man, therefore, to qualify himself for a member of such a community, must divest himself of all interested motives, and engage in no pursuits which do not ultimately redound to the benefit of society. He must not, through ambition, desire to be great, because it would destroy that equality on which the security of the Government depends; nor ought he to be rich, lest he be tempted to indulge himself in those luxuries which, though lawful, are not expedient, and might occasion envy and emulation. Should a person deserve the esteem of his fellow-citizens and become popular, he must be neglected, if not banished, lest his growing influence disturb the equilibrium. It is remarkable that neither the justice of *Aristides* nor the bravery of *Themistocles* could shield them from the darts of envy and jealousy; nor are modern times without examples of the same kind.

To this species of Government everything that looks like elegance and refinement is inimical, however necessary to the introduction of manufactures and the cultivation of arts and sciences. Hence, in some ancient Republicks, flowed those numberless sumptuary laws, which restrained men to plainness and familiarity in dress and diet, and all the mischiefs which attend agrarian laws, and unjust attempts to maintain their idol equality by an equal division of property.

Schemes like these may be practicable in countries so sterile by nature as to afford a scanty supply of the necessaries, and none of the conveniences of life; but they can never meet with a favourable reception from people who inhabit a country to which Providence has been more bountiful. They will always claim a right of using and enjoying the fruits of their honest industry, unrestrained by any ideal principles of Government, and will gather estates for themselves and children without regarding the whimsical impropriety of being richer than their neighbours. These are rights which freemen will never consent to relinquish; and after fighting for deliverance from one species of tyranny, it would be unreasonable to expect they should tamely acquiesce under another.

The truth is, that men will not be poor from choice or compulsion, and these Governments can exist only in countries where the people are so from necessity. In all others they have ceased almost as soon as erected, and in many instances been succeeded by despotism, and the arbitrary sway of some usurper, who had before perhaps gained the confidence of the people by eulogiums on liberty, and possessing no property of his own, by most disinterestedly proposing depredations on that of his neighbours.

The most considerable state in which the shadow of Democracy exists (for it is far from being purely so) is that of the United Provinces of *Holland, &c.* Their territories are confined within narrow limits, and the exports of their own produce very inconsiderable. Trade is the support of that people, and, however said to be considerable, will not admit of luxury. With the greatest parsimony and industry, they, as a people, can but barely support themselves, although individuals among them may amass estates. I own they have exhibited to mankind an example of perseverance and magnanimity that appeared like a prodigy. By the profits of their trade they maintained large armies, and supported a navy equal to the first in the day of warfare; but their military strength, as well as the form of their Government, have long since given way. Their navy has dwindled into a few ships of war, and their Government into an Aristocracy, as unhappy and despotick as the one of which we complain.

The State of *Venice*, once a Republick, is now governed by one of the worst of despotisms. In short, I do not recollect a single instance of a nation who supported this form of Government for any length of time, or with any degree of greatness; which convinces me, as it has many others, that the principle contended for is ideal, and a mere creature of a warm imagination.

One of the first staples of our country, you know, is esteemed by many to be one of the greatest luxuries in the world, and I fancy it will be no easy matter to draw you into measures that would exclude its culture, and deprive you of the wealth resulting from its exportation.

That I may not tire your patience, I will now proceed to delineate the method in which I would distribute the powers of Government, so as to devise the best code of laws, engage their due execution, preserve the strength of the Constitution, and secure the liberties of the people. It is agreed by most writers on this subject, that this power should be divided into three parts, each independent of, but having connection with each other. Let the people in the first place choose their usual number of Representatives, and let this right return to them every third year.

Let these Representatives, when convened, elect a Governour, to continue in authority during his good behaviour, of which the two Houses of Council of State and Assembly should jointly be the judges, and by majority of voices supply any vacancy in that office, which may happen by dismission, death, or resignation.

Let the Representatives also choose out of the Colony at large twenty-four proper persons to constitute a Council of State, who should form a distinct or intermediate branch of the Legislature, and hold their places for life, in order that they might possess all the weight, stability, and dignity, due to the importance of their office. Upon the death or resignation of any of the members, let the Assembly appoint another to succeed him.

Let no member of either House, except the Treasurer, hold a post of profit in the Government.

Let the Governour have a Privy Council of seven to advise him, though they should not be members of either House.

Let the Judges of the Courts of Common Law and Chancery be appointed by the Governour, with the advice of his Privy Council, to hold their offices during their good behaviour, but should be excluded a seat in either House.

Let the Treasurer, Secretary, and other great officers of State, be chosen by the lower House, and proper salaries assigned to them, as well as to the Judges, &c.

Let all military officers be appointed by the Governour, and all other inferior civil ones.

Let the different Courts appoint their own Clerks. The Justices in each County should be paid for their services, and required to meet for the despatch of business every three months. Let five of them be authorized to form a Court to hear and determine causes, and the others empowered to keep the peace, &c.

These are the outlines of a Government which would, I think, preserve the principle of our Constitution, and secure the freedom and happiness of the people better than any other.

The Governour will have dignity to command necessary respect and authority, to enable him to execute the laws, without being deterred by the fear of giving offence; and yet be amenable to the other branches of the Legislature for every violation of the rights of the people. If this great officer was exposed to the uncertain issue of frequent elections, he would be induced to relax and abate the vigorous execution of the laws whenever such conduct would increase his popularity. Should he, by discharging his duty with impartiality, give offence to men of weight and influence, he would be liable to all the opposition, threats, and insults, which resentment could suggest, and which few men in such a dependant state would have sufficient resolution to neglect and despise; and hence it would follow, that the apprehensions of losing his election would frequently induce him to court the favour of the great, at the expense of the duties of his station and the publick good. For these, and a variety of other reasons, this office should be held during good behaviour.

The Council of State, who are to constitute the second branch of the Legislature, should be for life. They ought to be well informed of the policy and laws of other States, and therefore should be induced, by the permanence of their appointment, to devote their time to such studies as may best qualify them for that station. They will acquire firmness from their independency, and wisdom from their reflection and experience, and appropriate both to the good of the State. Upon any disagreement between the Governour and lower House, this body will mediate and adjust such difference; will investigate the propriety of laws, and often propose such as may be of publick utility for the adoption of the Legislature. Being secluded from offices of profit, they will not be seduced from their duty by pecuniary considerations.

The Representatives of the people will be under no temptation to swerve from the design of their institution by bribery or corruption, all lucrative posts being denied them. And should they, on any occasion, be influenced by improper motives, the short period of their duration will give their constituents an opportunity of depriving them of power to do injury. The Governour, and the members of the Council of State, should be restrained from intermeddling further in the elections of Representatives than merely by giving their votes. . . .

A NATIVE

D. AN EXTREME POPULAR FORM:
"THE PEOPLE THE BEST GOVERNORS" (1776)*

The Preface

It was observed by Sir William Temple, that none can be said to know things well, who do not know them in the beginnings. There are many very noisy about liberty, but are aiming at nothing more than personal grandeur and power. Are not many, under the delusive character of Guardians of their country, collecting influence and honour only for oppression? Behold Caesar! at first a patriot, a consul, and commander of the Roman Army. How apparently noble his intentions, and how specious his conduct! But unbounded in his ambition, by these means he became, at length, a perpetual dictator, and an unlimited commander.

God gave mankind freedom by nature, made every man equal to his neighbor, and has virtually enjoined them to govern themselves by their own laws. The government which he introduced among his people the Jews abundantly proves it, and they might have continued in that state of liberty had they not desired a king. The people best know their own wants and necessities, and therefore are best able to rule themselves. Tent-makers, cobblers, and common tradesmen composed the legislature at Athens. "Is not the body (said Socrates) of the Athenian people composed of men like these?" That I might help in some measure to eradicate the notion of arbitrary power, heretofore drank in, and to establish the liberties of the people of this country upon a more generous footing, is the design of the following impartial work, now dedicated by the Author to the honest farmer and citizen.

The People *the Best* Governors, etc.

THE just power of a free people respects first the making and secondly the executing of laws. The liberties of a people are chiefly, I may say entirely guarded by having the controul of these two branches in their own hands.

MANY have been the disputes as to the best way of civil government. The

---

* These excerpts are reprinted from Frederick Chase, *A History of Dartmouth College and the Town of Hanover, New Hampshire* (John K. Lord [ed.], 2 vols., 1891), vol. I, pp. 654–663.

Athenians boasted of their popular assemblies; the Aetolians of their representatives, whom they termed the Panaetolium; and as for the Romans, they had a more complicated plan: viz., their consuls, the senate, and plebeians.

I AM not to examine into the advantages of a popular, or a representative government—in this case we are to consult the situation and number of the inhabitants. Were the people of the different counties numerous and wealthy enough, with that degree of knowledge which is common in many parts of the continent, every freeman might then have a hand in making laws to govern himself by, as well as in appointing the person to execute them; but the people of these States are very unequally and thinly settled, which puts us upon seeking some mode of governing by a representative body. The freemen give up in this way just so much of their natural right as they find absolutely convenient, on account of the disadvantages in their personal acting. The question now arises, how far they can with safety deposit this power of theirs into other hands. To this I answer: that where there are representatives who hold the legislature, their power ought never to extend any further than barely the making of laws. For what matters it, whether they themselves execute the laws, or appoint persons to do it in their stead, since these very persons, being only creatures of their own appointment, will be induced by interest to act agreeable to their will and pleasure. Indeed upon this plan the greatest corruption may take place,—for should there be in some important affairs very unjust decisions, where could the injury gain redress? Iniquity might be supported by the executioners of it; they out of the reach of the people, from whom they do not derive their authority; and the legislative body, as they are not the immediate perpetrators, may be often skreened from just reproach.

PERHAPS it will be said by some that the people are sufficiently guarded against infringements of this nature, as their representatives are chosen only for a certain time, may be called to an account for any misconduct in their business, and withal are liable to be turned out by their constituents at any time. There is indeed something plausible in all this; but it will vanish when we consider that these representatives, while they act as such, being supreme in legislation, and [in] the appointing and supporting the executors of law, may by these advantages assume to themselves a lasting, unlimited power. And I beg of any one to tell me what will prevent it, if they have only art, and are generally agreed among themselves.

BUT it seems there is another objection started by some: That the common people are not under so good advantages to choose judges, sheriffs, and other executive officers as their representatives are. This is a mere delusion, which many have taken in, and, if I may be allowed a vulgar expression, the objectors in this instance put the cart before the horse. For they say that the people have wisdom and knowledge enough to appoint proper persons through a State to make laws, but not to execute them. It is much easier to execute, than to make and regulate the system of laws, and upon his single consideration the force of the objection fails: The more simple, and the more immediately dependent . . . , the authority is upon the people the better, because it must be granted that they themselves are the best guardians of their own liberties.

2dly. UPON the above principles we will proceed farther, and say that if there be a distinct negative power over those that enact the laws, it can by no means derive [it] from them as representatives of the people, and for these reasons: As far as there is any power over the rights of the people, so far they themselves are divested of it. Now, by chusing representatives to make laws for them, they put that power out of their own hands; yet they do not deposit it into the hands of their representatives to give to others, but to exercise it in their room and stead.—Therefore, I say, for the representatives to appoint a council with a negative authority, is to give away that power, which they have no right to do, because they themselves derived it from the people.

Again, there is a palpable contradiction implied; for this negative power, if it cannot be called legislative, has at least such weight in the legislature as to be the unlimited *sine qua non* (a restraining power). Those therefore who act as a council or negative body make use of a power in the room of the people, and consequently represent them so far as their power extends. In fine, to say that the legislative body can appoint them is as absurd as to say that the representatives have a right to appoint the representatives of the people.

3dly. IT appears now that the representatives have no right to enlarge their power which they have received, nor to alter or put any incumbrance upon it, by making a negative body. The common people, and consequently their representatives, may not happen to be so learned and knowing as some others in a State; and as the latter are bound to their constituents to act by the best light they can get, they may, if they please, chuse a council, barely to give advice, and to prepare matters for their consideration; but not to negative, which is a contradiction in terms. Agreeable to this observation was the government at Athens; the council consisted of 400 persons, and, in a legislative capacity, could devise, and prepare matters for the consideration of the people.

BUT it will be enquired whether the inhabitants themselves, through a State, cannot consistently make a negativing body over those that form the laws? To this I answer that there is no real absurdity in their taking such a step: But upon this plan those that are called representatives have only a partial right as such; for they have a delegated power from the people to act no farther than this negative body concurs. Now this said negative body are likewise virtually the representatives of the people, and derive just so much authority from them as will make up the defect of the others, viz., that of confirming. They have been generally named a council in our American States, though they have really acted in a legislative capacity, and seem rather to answer the idea of a *senate*, which was hereditary at Rome, but here elective.

WHERE there is such a body of men appointed, it is best that these should be but few in number, and chosen by the people at large through the government. At least that there should not be destricts marked out and the plan fixed, that the inhabitants in the respective counties may choose just so many, only in proportion to their present number, without any regard to the future increase of the people—rather let the same principles of an equal partition of land settling, and settled, take place in this matter, as we shall point out under the next head, when we speak of representation.

To conclude, I do not say that it is expedient to choose a Senate, if I may so call it, with such a negative power as before mentioned; but rather propose, whether a council of advice would not answer better purposes, and that inequality be thereby prevented, which is sometimes occasioned by two destinct fountains of power.

4thly. WE will next lay open the nature and right of jurisdiction more clearly in examining the best standard by which representation may be regulated. In the first place, it is asserted by some that representation ought to be enlarged or diminished in proportion to the amount of taxes in the different parts of a State; but such a procedure would be very unreasonable. For taxation only respects property, without regard to the liberties of a person; and if representation should be wholly limited by that, the man who owns six times as much as another would consequently have six times the power, though their natural right to freedom is the same. Nature itself abhors such a system of civil government, for it will make an inequality among the people and set up a number of lords over the rest. In the next place, it is said that representation should be determined entirely according to the number of inhabitants. But to have a State represented adequately upon this plan would puzzle the brain of a philosopher. Indeed, to effect it some townships must be cut to pieces, others tacked together,—and at best many parts would remain defective. And if we look into this matter critically, we shall find it still more egregious. It is an old observation that *political bodies should be immortal.* A government is not founded for a day or a year, and for that very reason should be erected upon some invariable principles. Grant, for a moment, that the number of people is the only measure of representation; as often then as the former increases or diminishes, the latter must, of consequence; as often as the inhabitants in a State vary their situation the weight of legislation changes; and accordingly the balance of power is subject to continual and frequently unforeseen alterations. Turn which way we will upon this plan, we shall find unsurmountable difficulties; so that those who have adopted this measure are either too short-sighted to see the future interests of society, or so secret and designing as to take the advantage of such undeterminate principles. The question now comes in, how shall we find an *invariable* free mode of representation? This I own is a delicate point; yet if we enter into the matter, doubt not but that we shall fix upon something useful.

Every government is necessarily confined to some extent of territory. It may happen by some peculiar circumstances that some parts of the land in a State may be at first much more peopled than others. Yet in time (excepting the metropolis and some places of trade) they become generally alike settled. We find that this was the case in the old republics of Greece, as likewise at present in Switzerland; indeed, it is commonly so through the civilized kingdoms of Europe and Asia. The reasons for this are handy. The God of nature has formed the different situations of land through a government mostly with equal advantages. Some parts are proper for agriculture, others for trade and commerce; some produce one sort of commodity, and some another. By this means it is that people have intercourse together, and are at length equally diffused within the limits of a State. We will now come nearer to the point before us. It has been said that a government should be formed, if possible, upon so solid a foundation as to be liable to no alterations on account of its internal defects. A well-regulated representation is the only security of our liberties. We have seen that it cannot depend upon taxation, nor the number of inhabitants solely, without being subject to changes and innovations; and to have it depend on both taken together, will render it intirely capricious. Land is the most solid estate that can be taxed, and is the only permanent thing. Let that therefore be divided into equal convenient parts in a State, as is the case with our townships, and let the inhabitants possessing the said parts or townships be severally and distinctly represented. By this means the plan of the legislature will be fixed, and an earnest of it handed down to posterity, for whom politicians were rather made, than for those who live in their time.

But it may be objected by some that live in a government where towns are very unequally settled that there is no right or justice in the inhabitants having the same advantage as to representation, since those that live in the larger towns must not only support their own but also help to support the representatives of the smaller ones. The objection is trifling. Every government is an entire body politic, and therefore each particular member in the legislature does not represent any distinct part, but the whole of the said body. Blackstone's words are these: "For it is to be observed that though every member is chosen by a particular county or borough, yet, as is justly observed by Lord Cooke and others, when in parliament he serves for the whole nation." The consequence is, that if every incorporate town, small as well as large, has a right to chuse a representative, he does when chosen represent the whole government; and therefore ought to be paid by it. Besides, the inhabitants of the smaller towns do upon this plan pay their proportion for representation, and a small sum may be as much for a poor man as a large sum for a rich man, agreeable to what the Scripture observes of the widow that cast her mite into the treasury. Again, shall we sacrifice a free constitution barely to avoid the trifling expense of a free government? But is there not enough said yet to satisfy the objectors? Then let every town support its own representative, but in consideration of that, place the seat of government in the centre of the State. This inequality will last but for a few years; the smaller towns are growing. Nor does it become patriots to study their own ease, at the expense of embroiling their children.

WHAT has been proposed I cannot but think to be the only sure foundation to form a legislature upon,—all others are wavering and uncertain.

5thly. THE question now that closes the whole arises, what it is that ought to be the qualification of a representative. In answer, we observe that fear is the principle of a despotic, honour of a kingly, and virtue is the principle of a republican government. Social virtue and knowledge, I say then, is the best and only necessary qualification of the person before us. But it will be said that an estate of two hundred, four hundred pounds, or some other sum, is essential. So sure as we make interest necessary in this case, as sure we root out virtue; and what will then become of the genuine principle of freedom? This notion of an estate has the directest tendency to set up the avaricious over the heads of the poor, though the latter are ever so virtuous. Let it not be said in future generations that money was made by the founders of the American States an essential qualification in the rulers of a free people. It never was known among the Antients; and we find many of their best leaders in very needy circumstances. Witness the Athenians Cimon and Aristides; the Romans Numa, Cato, and Regulus. Thus I have gone through what I had to say on some interesting points of government; and it is proposed with more cheerfulness, as many of the sentiments oppose the present regulations of most of our States.

Now is the time for the people to be critical in establishing a plan of government. For they are now planting a seed which will arise with boughs, either extended to shelter the liberty of succeeding ages, or only to skreen the designs of crafty usurpers.

THAT this short treatise may not be left imperfect, I will only propose for the consideration of the people a concise plan, founded on the principles that have been laid down.

IT is observed then, in the first place, that the freemen of each incorporated town through a State shall chuse by ballot, at an annual meeting, one person respectively, whom they shall think suitable to represent them in a general assembly.

2dly. THAT, if the metropolis, and some particular large places, may require an additional number of representatives, it may be granted them by the general assembly as the latter shall think proper.

3dly. THAT the general assembly should meet at certain times twice every year, and that if the State is extensive, there may be two seats of government, in which case the said assembly are to convene at them, once in their turns.

4thly. THAT the people chuse annually by ballot in their town meetings a council consisting of twelve persons, through the government at large, whose business shall be to help in preparing matters for the consideration of the assembly, to assist them with their advice; And lastly it shall be their duty to inquire into every essential defect in the regulations of government, and to give the people seasonable notice in a public way, with their opinion respecting the matter.

5thly. THAT they likewise chuse annually a first executive officer, without any concern in the legislature; but it shall be his duty to transact such occasional business as the assembly may devolve upon him; And that he be the general commander of the militia, and in these capacities the people, if they please, may stile him a governor—and in case of his incapacity a lieutenant, &c., may be appointed as before, to act occasionally in his stead.

6thly. THE said governor, with advice of any three of his council, may at any time call a special assembly on extraordinary business.

7thly. THAT the freemen vote annually, in their town meetings respectively, for the judges of the superior court, at large through the government.

8thly. THAT the judges of the inferior court, attorneys general, probate judges, registers, &c., be chosen, in manner before mentioned, by the inhabitants of each respective county: And that the justices of the peace be also chosen by the people of each respective town in proportion to the representatives.

9thly. THAT there be one general proxy day agreed upon for the people through the government to vote for the officers as aforesaid, and that the representatives likewise fix upon one day of election, to be annual, at which time the votes are to be brought in from the different towns and examined; and the persons for governors, a council, judges, registers, sheriffs, &c., are to be then published through the State.

10thly. THAT all the resolves of every assembly be conveyed from time to time by the representatives to each respective town, and there enrolled for the inhabitants to see, in order to instruct their said representatives.

11thly. THAT no person shall hold too [two] public offices in a State at the same time.

12thly. THAT no person shall be capable of holding any public office except he possesses a belief of one only invisible God, that governs all things; and that the bible is his revealed word; and that he be also an honest, moral man.

13thly. THAT any freeman through the government may freely enter, a complaint of defect or misdemeanor to the general assembly against any of the executive State officers, and if the assembly think there is just grounds for the said complaint, they may suspend the person so complained of in his office, appoint another for the present in his stead—but be obliged to publish in the superior or county courts, according as the person sustained his said office, their proceeding in that matter, with all their reasons for them; that the people if they please may drop the said person or persons, in their next annual election.

14thly. THAT the assembly may have power to negative any of their members a seat; but, should they do it, be obliged to inform the town or towns that sent him or them so negatived, with their reasons for such proceedure, that the inhabitants may have an opportunity to chuse another or others as soon as conveniently may be, which second choice it shall not be in the power of the said assembly to negative.

15thly. THAT the particular town officers be chosen yearly by the inhabitants, as usual; and that each town clerk be the recorder of deeds.

16thly. THAT any orderly free male of ordinary capacity, and more than 21 years of age, having resided one year in a town, may be a legal voter during his continuance; but if he should be absent afterwards steadily more than a year, that he should be divested then of the privilege of voting in said town as if he never had resided there; PROVIDED he has not a real estate in the aforesaid town of at least one hundred pounds lawful money.

17thly. THAT any legal voter shall be capable of holding any office, unless something that has been said to the contrary.

IT is a darling principle of freedom that those who make laws ought not to execute them; but notwithstanding should it be enquired whether there may be a proper course of appeals in some important matters from the superior court to the general assembly, I would answer affirmatively. The cases between man & man together with their circumstances are so infinite in number that it is impossible for them all to be specified by the letter of the law. The judges therefore, in many cases, are obliged not to adhere to the letter, but to put such a construction on matters as they think most agreeable to the spirit and reason of the law. Now so far as they are reduced to this necessity, they assume what is in fact the prerogative of the legislature, for those that made the laws ought to give them a meaning when they are doubtful. To make then the application: It may happen that some very important cases may be attended with such circumstances as are exceptions from the written law, agreeable to the old maxim, . . . *extreme right is extreme wrong;* or they may come under doubtful constructions. In either of these instances the person that is cast by the verdict makes his appeal from the court to the general assembly; that they would virtually in deciding his case, make a regulation, or rather in a legislative capacity put a lasting construction on the written law, respecting affairs of that particular nature. Thus, by examining the principles of such appeals, we find they imply not that the legislative act in an executive capacity.

LASTLY, let every government have an equal weight in the general congress, and let the representatives of the respective states be chosen by the people annually by ballot in their stated town meetings; the votes to be carried in and published at the appointed election as with respect to a governor, council, &c., in manner aforesaid; and the assemblies of the respective states may have power to instruct the said representatives from time to time as they shall think proper.

It appears that the forms of government that have hitherto been proposed since the breach with Great Britain, by the friends of the American States, have been rather too arbitrary. The people are now contending for freedom; and would to God they might not only obtain, but likewise keep it in their own hands. I own myself a friend to a popular government; have freely submitted my reasons upon it. And although the plan here proposed might not ever [have] been adopted as yet, nevertheless those as free have alone secured the liberties of former ages, and a just notion of them has guarded the people against the sly insinuations and proposals of those of a more arbitrary turn, whose schemes have a tendency to deprive mankind of their natural rights.

SELECTION

The Limits of Governmental Power: The First Bill of Rights, Virginia (June 12, 1776)

Most of the state constitutions adopted during the Revolution included or were accompanied by a formal declaration of rights. Drawing heavily upon the English Bill of Rights of 1689 and the various colonial statements of rights and grievances generated by the debate with Britain over the previous twelve years, these declarations sought to establish the limits of governmental power by enumerating the fundamental and inviolable principles upon which government was supposed to operate and by spelling out the basic and inalienable rights of citizens upon which it could never encroach. The first of these bills of rights was the Virginia Declaration of Rights adopted by the Virginia Convention on June 12, 1776, and reprinted below from Francis Newton Thorpe (ed.), The Federal and State Constitutions, Colonial Charters, and Other Organic Laws *(seven vols., 1909), volume VII, pages 3812–3814. Mostly the work of George Mason (1725–1792), a planter from Fairfax County and a towering figure in the process of constitution making during the Revolutionary era, the Virginia Declaration served as a model for the other states, each of which had issued a similar statement by the spring of 1784.*

Robert Allen Rutland, The Birth of the Bill of Rights, 1776–1791 *(1955), describes the origin and adoption of each of these bills of rights in the various states, and Benjamin Fletcher Wright,* Consensus and Continuity, 1776–1787 *(1958), the rationale behind them.*

A declaration of rights made by the representatives of the good people of Virginia, assembled in full and free convention; which rights do pertain to them and their posterity, as the basis and foundation of government.

SECTION 1. That all men are by nature equally free and independent, and have certain inherent rights, of which, when they enter into a state of society, they cannot, by any compact, deprive or divest their posterity; namely, the enjoyment of life and liberty, with the means of acquiring and possessing property, and pursuing and obtaining happiness and safety.

SEC. 2. That all power is vested in, and consequently derived from, the people; that magistrates are their trustees and servants, and at all times amenable to them.

SEC. 3. That government is, or ought to be, instituted for the common benefit, protection, and security of the people, nation, or community; of all the various modes and forms of government, that is best which is capable of producing the greatest degree of happiness and safety, and is most effectually secured against the danger of maladministration; and that, when any government shall be found inadequate or contrary to these purposes, a majority of the community hath an indubitable, inalienable, and indefeasible right to reform, alter, or abolish it, in such manner as shall be judged most conducive to the public weal.

SEC. 4. That no man, or set of men, are entitled to exclusive or separate emoluments or privileges from the community, but in consideration of public services; which, not being descendible, neither ought the offices of magistrate, legislator, or judge to be hereditary.

SEC. 5. That the legislative and executive powers of the State should be separate and distinct from the judiciary; and that the members of the two first may be restrained from oppression, by feeling and participating the burdens of the people, they should, at fixed periods, be reduced to a private station, return into that body from which they were originally taken, and the vacancies be supplied by frequent, certain, and regular elections, in which all, or any part of the former members, to be again eligible, or ineligible, as the laws shall direct.

SEC. 6. That elections of members to serve as representatives of the people, in assembly, ought to be free; and that all men, having sufficient evidence of permanent common interest with, and attachment to, the community, have the right of suffrage, and cannot be taxed or deprived of their property for public uses, without their own consent, or that of their representives so elected, nor bound by any law to which they have not, in like manner, assembled, for the public good.

SEC. 7. That all power of suspending laws, or the execution of laws, by any authority, without consent of the representatives of the people, is injurious to their rights, and ought not to be exercised.

SEC. 8. That in all capital or criminal prosecutions a man hath a right to demand the cause and nature of his accusation, to be confronted with the accusers and witnesses, to call for evidence in his favor, and to a speedy trial by an impartial jury of twelve men of his vicinage, without whose unanimous consent he cannot be found guilty; nor can he be compelled to give evidence against himself; that no man be deprived of his liberty, except by the law of the land or the judgment of his peers.

SEC. 9. That excessive bail ought not to be required, nor excessive fines imposed, nor cruel and unusual punishments inflicted.

SEC. 10. That general warrants, whereby an officer or messenger may be commanded to search suspected places without evidence of a fact committed, or to seize any person or persons not named, or whose offence is not particularly described and supported by evidence, are grievous and oppressive, and ought not to be granted.

SEC. 11. That in controversies respecting property, and in suits between man and man, the ancient trial by jury is preferable to any other, and ought to be held sacred.

SEC. 12. That the freedom of the press is one of the great bulwarks of liberty, and can never be restrained but by despotic governments.

SEC. 13. That a well-regulated militia, composed of the body of the people, trained to arms, is the proper, natural, and safe defence of a free State; that standing armies, in time of peace, should be avoided, as dangerous to liberty; and that in all cases the military should be under strict subordination to, and governed by, the civil power.

SEC. 14. That the people have a right to uniform government; and, therefore, that no government separate from, or independent of the government of Virginia, ought to be erected or established within the limits thereof.

SEC. 15. That no free government, or the blessings of liberty, can be preserved to any people, but by a firm adherence to justice, moderation, temperance, frugality, and virtue, and by frequent recurrence to fundamental principles.

SEC. 16. That religion, or the duty which we owe to our Creator, and the manner of discharging it, can be directed only by reason and conviction, not by force or violence; and therefore all men are equally entitled to the free exercise of religion, according to the dictates of conscience; and that it is the mutual duty of all to practice Christian forbearance, love, and charity towards each other.

SELECTION

Two Early Constitutions

By 1777 all of the states except Massachusetts had either adopted new constitutions or, in the cases of Connecticut and Rhode Island, adapted their colonial charters by removing all references to British authority. New Hampshire and South Carolina acted first in the early months of 1776 well before the Declaration of Independence, but their constitutions were avowedly temporary, and Virginia was the first state to attempt to establish a permanent constitution in May and

June, 1776. This constitution, formally adopted by the Virginia Convention on June 29, 1776, and reprinted in part below as Selection 35 A, was, like the Virginia Declaration of Rights, largely the handiwork of George Mason, though it bore a striking resemblance to and was much influenced by the suggestions of John Adams in his Thoughts on Government. *The government provided for was to have a bicameral legislature, separation of powers, frequent elections, rotation in office, and election of state officers including the governor and the judiciary by the joint action of the two houses of the legislature. The apportionment of representation to the lower house and the property qualifications for voting remained the same as they had been under the Crown, and, contrary to Adams's suggestion, the governor, though elected for a three-year term, was to be almost completely dependent on the legislature. Although they varied considerably in detail, most of the other state constitutions written in 1776 and 1777 followed the Virginia example in their general outlines.*

The major exception was the Pennsylvania Constitution, which was modeled after the proposals set forth in Four Letters *and* The Interest of America, *was the most innovative of all of the early constitutions, and is printed in part below as Selection 35 B. Adopted on September 28, 1776, it appears to have been primarily the work of a small coterie of radical political thinkers including James Cannon (1740–1782), tutor in mathematics at the College of Philadelphia, Timothy Matlack (ca. 1736–1829), a Philadelphia merchant, David Rittenhouse (1732–1796). the noted astronomer, and three men who were not even members of the convention that framed the document: George Bryan (1731–1791), an Irish Presbyterian merchant from Philadelphia; Dr. Thomas Young (1732–1777), a former New Englander; and Thomas Paine (1737–1809). A unicameral legislature was only the most striking of a number of novel provisions which distinguished the Pennsylvania Constitution from those of most of the other states. Others included a plural executive elected directly by the public, a broad franchise that included all male taxpayers and sons of taxpayers over twenty-one years of age, and apportionment of legislative seats on the basis of the number of taxables. The government established by the constitution was more popular than that of any other state, and the popularly elected unicameral legislature had enormous power. It was not, however, an unrestrained power because the constitution stipulated both that legislative acts would not ordinarily become law until they had been published for perusal by the public and repassed at the succeeding legislature and, implementing the suggestion of the author of* Four Letters, *that a council of censors would be elected every seven years to review the conduct of the legislature and make sure that no violations of the constitution had occurred. During the Revolutionary era only Georgia and later Vermont wrote constitutions based on the Pennsylvania model and providing for a unicameral legislature.*

On the adoption and provisions of the first state constitutions Allan Nevins, The American States during and after the Revolution, 1775–1789 *(1924), offers the fullest and most comprehensive coverage. Elisha P. Douglass,* Rebels and Democrats: The Struggle for Equal Political Rights and Majority Rule during the American Revolution *(1955); Benjamin Fletcher Wright,* Consensus and Continuity, 1776–1787 *(1958); Fletcher M. Green,* Constitutional Development in the South Atlantic States, 1776–1860: A Study in the Evolution of Democracy *(1930); and, for the Pennsylvania Constitution, J. Paul Selsam,* The Pennsylvania Constitution of 1776: A Study in Revolutionary Democracy *(1936), should also be consulted.*

A. EXPERIMENT WITH A MIXED FORM: THE VIRGINIA CONSTITUTION OF (JUNE 29) 1776*

We . . . the delegates and representatives of the good people of Virginia, having maturely considered the premises, and viewing with great concern the deplorable conditions to which this once happy country must be reduced, unless some regular, adequate mode of civil polity is speedily adopted, and in compliance with a recommendation of the General Congress, do ordain and declare the future form of government of Virginia to be as followeth:

The legislative, executive, and judiciary department, shall be separate and distinct, so that neither exercise the powers properly belonging to the other: nor shall any person exercise the powers of more than one of them, at the same time; except that the Justices of the County Courts shall be eligible to either House of Assembly.

The legislative shall be formed of two distinct branches, who, together, shall be a complete Legislature. They shall meet once, or oftener, every year, and shall be called, *The General Assembly of Virginia.* One of these shall be called, *The House of Delegates,* and consist of two Representatives, to be chosen for each county, and for the district of West-Augusta, annually, of such men as actually reside in, and are freeholders of the same, or duly qualified according to law, and also of one Delegate or Representative, to be chosen annually for the city of Williamsburgh, and one for the borough of Norfolk, and a Representative for each of such other cities and boroughs, as may hereafter be allowed particular representation by the legislature; but when any city or borough shall so decrease, as that the number of persons, having right of suffrage therein, shall have been, for the space of seven years successively, less than half the number of voters in some one county in Virginia, such city or borough thenceforward shall cease to send a Delegate or Representative to the Assembly.

The other shall be called *The Senate,* and consist of twenty-four members, of whom thirteen shall constitute a House to proceed on business; for whose election, the different counties shall be divided into twenty-four districts; and each county of the respective district, at the time of the election of its Delegates, shall vote for one Senator, who is actually a resident and freeholder within the district, or duly qualified according to law, and is upwards of twenty-five years of age; and the Sheriffs of each county, within five days at farthest, after the last county election in the district, shall meet at some convenient place, and from the poll, so taken in their respective counties, return, as a Senator, the man who shall have the greatest number of votes in the whole district. To keep up this Asssembly by rotation, the districts shall be equally divided into four classes and numbered by lot. At the end of one year after the general election, the six members, elected by the first division, shall be displaced, and the vacancies thereby occasioned supplied from such class or division, by new election, in the manner aforesaid. This rotation shall be applied to each division, according to its number, and continued in due order annually.

The right of suffrage in the election of members for both Houses shall

---

* These excerpts are reprinted from Francis Newton Thorpe (ed.), *The Federal and State Constitutions, and Other Organic Laws* (7 vols., 1909), vol. VII, pp. 3815–3819.

remain as exercised at present; and each House shall choose its own Speaker, appoint its own officers, settle its own rules of proceeding, and direct writs of election, for the supplying intermediate vacancies.

All laws shall originate in the House of Delegates, to be approved of or rejected by the Senate, or to be amended, with consent of the House of Delegates; except money-bills, which in no instance shall be altered by the Senate, but wholly approved or rejected.

A Governor, or chief magistrate, shall be chosen annually by joint ballot of both Houses (to be taken in each House respectively) deposited in the conference room; the boxes examined jointly by a committee of each House, and the numbers severally reported to them, that the appointments may be entered (which shall be the mode of taking the joint ballot of both Houses, in all cases) who shall not continue in that office longer than three years successively, nor be eligible, until the expiration of four years after he shall have been out of that office. An adequate, but moderate salary shall be settled on him, during his continuance in office; and he shall, with the advice of a Council of State, exercise the executive powers of government, according to the laws of this Commonwealth; and shall not, under any pretence, exercise any power or prerogative, by virtue of any law, statute or custom of England. But he shall, with the advice of the Council of State, have the power of granting reprieves or pardons, except where the prosecution shall have been carried on by the House of Delegates or the law shall otherwise particularly direct; in which cases, no reprieve or pardon shall be granted, but by resolve of the House of Delegates.

Either House of the General Assembly may adjourn themselves respectively. The Governor shall not prorogue or adjourn the Assembly, during their sitting, nor dissolve them at any time; but he shall, if necessary, either by advice of the Council of State, or on application of a majority of the House of Delegates, call them before the time to which they shall stand prorogued or adjourned.

A Privy Council, or Council of State, consisting of eight members, shall be chosen, by joint ballot of both Houses of Assembly, either from their own members or the people at large, to assist in the administration of government. They shall annually choose, out of their own members, a President, who, in case of death, inability, or absence of the Governor from the government, shall act as Lieutenant-Governor. Four members shall be sufficient to act, and their advice and proceedings shall be entered on record, and signed by the members present, (to any part whereof, any member may enter his dissent) to be laid before the General Assembly, when called for by them. This Council may appoint their own Clerk, who shall have a salary settled by law, and take an oath of secrecy, in such matters as he shall be directed by the board to conceal. A sum of money, appropriated to that purpose, shall be divided annually among the members, in proportion to their attendance; and they shall be incapable, during their continuance in office, of sitting in either House of Assembly. Two members shall be removed, by joint ballot of both Houses of Assembly, at the end of every three years, and be ineligible for the three next years. These vacancies, as well as those occasioned by death or incapacity, shall be supplied by new elections, in the same manner.

The Delegates for Virginia to the Continental Congress shall be chosen annually, or superseded in the mean time, by joint ballot of both Houses of Assembly.

The present militia officers shall be continued, and vacancies supplied by appointment of the Governor, with the advice of the Privy-Council, on recommendations from the respective County Courts; but the Governor and Council shall have a power of suspending any officer, and ordering a Court Martial, on complaint of misbehaviour or inability, or to supply vacancies of officers, happening when in actual service.

The Governor may embody the militia, with the advice of the Privy Council; and when embodied, shall alone have the direction of the militia, under the laws of the country.

The two Houses of Assembly shall, by joint ballot, appoint Judges of the Supreme Court of Appeals, and General Court, Judges in Chancery, Judges of Admiralty, Secretary, and the Attorney-General, to be commissioned by the Governor, and continue in office during good behaviour. In case of death, incapacity, or resignation, the Governor, with the advice of the Privy Council, shall appoint persons to succeed in office, to be approved or displaced by both Houses. These officers shall have fixed and adequate salaries, and, together with all others, holding lucrative offices, and all ministers of the gospel, of every denomination, be incapable of being elected members of either House of Assembly or the Privy Council.

The Governor, with the advice of the Privy Council, shall appoint Justices of the Peace for the counties; and in case of vacancies, or a necessity of increasing the number hereafter, such appointments to be made upon the recommendation of the respective County Courts. The present acting Secretary in Virginia, and Clerks of all the County Courts, shall continue in office. In case of vacancies, either by death, incapacity, or resignation, a Secretary shall be appointed, as before directed; and the Clerks, by the respective Courts. The present and future Clerks shall hold their offices during good behaviour, to be judged of, and determined in the General Court. The Sheriffs and Coroners shall be nominated by the respective Courts, approved by the Governor, with the advice of the Privy Council, and commissioned by the Governor. The Justices shall appoint Constables; and all fees of the aforesaid officers be regulated by law.

The Governor, when he is out of office, and others, offending against the State, either by mal-administration, corruption, or other means, by which the safety of the State may be endangered, shall be impeachable by the House of Delegates. Such impeachment to be prosecuted by the Attorney-General, or such other person or persons, as the House may appoint in the General Court, according to the laws of the land. If found guilty, he or they shall be either forever disabled to hold any office under government, or be removed from such office *pro tempore,* or subjected to such pains or penalties as the laws shall direct.

If all or any of the Judges of the General Court should on good grounds (to be judged of by the House of Delegates) be accused of any of the crimes or offences above mentioned, such House of Delegates may, in like manner, impeach the Judge or Judges so accused, to be prosecuted in the Court of Appeals; and he or they, if found guilty, shall be punished in the same manner as is prescribed in the preceding clause.

Commissions and grants shall run, *"In the name of the Commonwealth of Virginia,"* and bear test by the Governor, with the seal of the Commonwealth annexed. Writs shall run in the same manner, and bear test by the

Clerks of the several Courts. Indictments shall conclude, *"Against the peace and dignity of the Commonwealth."*

A Treasurer shall be appointed annually, by joint ballot of both Houses.

All escheats, penalties, and forfeitures, heretofore going to the King, shall go to the Commonwealth, save only such as the Legislature may abolish, or otherwise provide for.

The territories, contained within the Charters, erecting the Colonies of Maryland, Pennsylvania, North and South Carolina, are hereby ceded, released, and forever confirmed, to the people of these Colonies respectively, with all the rights of property, jurisdiction and government, and all other rights whatsoever, which might, at any time heretofore, have been claimed by Virginia, except the free navigation and use of the rivers Patomaque and Pokomoke, with the property of the Virginia shores and strands, bordering on either of the said rivers, and all improvements, which have been, or shall be made thereon. The western and northern extent of Virginia shall, in all other respects, stand as fixed by the Charter of King James I. in the year one thousand six hundred and nine, and by the public treaty of peace between the Courts of Britain and France, in the year one thousand seven hundred and sixty-three; unless by act of this Legislature, one or more governments be established westward of the Alleghany mountains. And no purchases of lands shall be made of the Indian natives, but on behalf of the public, by authority of the General Assembly.

In order to introduce this government, the Representatives of the people met in the convention shall choose a Governor and Privy Council, also such other officers directed to be chosen by both Houses as may be judged necessary to be immediately appointed. The Senate to be first chosen by the people, to continue until the last day of March next, and the other officers until the end of the succeeding session of Assembly. In case of vacancies, the Speaker of either House shall issue writs for new elections.

B. EXPERIMENT WITH A SIMPLE FORM: THE PENNSYLVANIA CONSTITUTION OF (SEPT. 28) 1776 *

SECTION 1. The commonwealth or state of Pennsylvania shall be governed hereafter by an assembly of the representatives of the freemen of the same, and a president and council, in manner and form following—

SECT. 2. The supreme legislative power shall be vested in a house of representatives of the freemen of the commonwealth or state of Pennsylvania.

SECT. 3. The supreme executive power shall be vested in a president and council.

SECT. 4. Courts of justice shall be established in the city of Philadelphia, and in every county of this state.

SECT. 5. The freemen of this commonwealth and their sons shall be trained and armed for its defence under such regulations, restrictions, and exceptions as the general assembly shall by law direct, preserving always to the

* These excerpts are reprinted from Thorpe (ed.), *The Federal and State Constitutions and Other Organic Laws,* vol. V, pp. 3084–3092.

people the right of choosing their colonels and all commissioned officers under that rank, in such manner and as often as by the said laws shall be directed.

SECT. 6. Every freeman of the full age of twenty-one years, having resided in this state for the space of one whole year next before the day of election for representatives, and paid public taxes during that time, shall enjoy the right of an elector: Provided always, that sons of freeholders of the age of twenty-one years shall be intitled to vote although they have not paid taxes.

SECT. 7. The house of representatives of the freemen of this commonwealth shall consist of persons most noted for wisdom and virtue, to be chosen by the freemen of every city and county of this commonwealth respectively. And no person shall be elected unless he has resided in the city or county for which he shall be chosen two years immediately before the said election; nor shall any member, while he continues such, hold any other office, except in the militia.

SECT. 8. No person shall be capable of being elected a member to serve in the house of representatives of the freemen of this commonwealth more than four years in seven.

SECT. 9. The members of the house of representatives shall be chosen annually by ballot, by the freemen of the commonwealth, on the second Tuesday in October forever, (except this present year,) and shall meet on the fourth Monday of the same month, and shall be stiled, *The general assembly of the representatives of the freemen of Pennsylvania,* and shall have power to choose their speaker, the treasurer of the state, and their other officers; sit on their own adjournments; prepare bills and enact them into laws; judge of the elections and qualifications of their own members; they may expel a member, but not a second time for the same cause; they may administer oaths or affirmations on examination of witnesses; redress grievances; impeach state criminals; grant charters of incorporation; constitute towns, boroughs, cities, and counties; and shall have all other powers necessary for the legislature of a free state or commonwealth: But they shall have no power to add to, alter, abolish, or infringe any part of this constitution. . . .

SECT. 13. The doors of the house in which the representatives of the freemen of this state shall sit in general assembly, shall be and remain open for the admission of all persons who behave decently, except only when the welfare of this state may require the doors to be shut.

SECT. 14. The votes and proceedings of the general assembly shall be printed weekly during their sitting, with the yeas and nays, on any question, vote or resolution, where any two members require it, except when the vote is taken by ballot; and when the yeas and nays are so taken every member shall have a right to insert the reasons of his vote upon the minutes, if he desires it.

SECT. 15. To the end that laws before they are enacted may be more maturely considered, and the inconvenience of hasty determinations as much as possible prevented, all bills of public nature shall be printed for the consideration of the people, before they are read in general assembly the last time for debate and amendment; and, except on occasions of sudden necessity, shall not be passed into laws until the next session of assembly; and for the more perfect satisfaction of the public, the reasons and motives for making such laws shall be fully and clearly expressed in the preambles. . . .

SECT. 17. The city of Philadelphia and each county of this commonwealth respectively, shall on the first Tuesday of November in this present year, and on the second Tuesday of October annually for the two next succeeding years, *viz.* the year one thousand seven hundred and seventy-seven, and the year one thousand seven hundred and seventy-eight, choose six persons to represent them in general assembly. But as representation in proportion to the number of taxable inhabitants is the only principle which can at all times secure liberty, and make the voice of a majority of the people the law of the land; therefore the general assembly shall cause complete lists of the taxable inhabitants in the city and each county in the commonwealth respectively, to be taken and returned to them, on or before the last meeting of the assembly elected in the year one thousand seven hundred and seventy-eight, who shall appoint a representation to each, in proportion to the number of taxables in such returns; which representation shall continue for the next seven years afterwards at the end of which, a new return of the taxable inhabitants shall be made, and a representation agreeable thereto appointed by the said assembly, and so on septennially forever. The wages of the representatives in general assembly, and all other state charges shall be paid out of the state treasury.

SECT. 18. In order that the freemen of this commonwealth may enjoy the benefit of election as equally as may be until the representation shall commence, as directed in the foregoing section, each county at its own choice may be divided into districts, hold elections therein, and elect their representatives in the county, and their other elective officers, as shall be hereafter regulated by the general assembly of this state. And no inhabitant of this state shall have more than one annual vote at the general election for representatives in assembly.

SECT. 19. For the present the supreme executive council of this state shall consist of twelve persons chosen in the following manner: The freemen of the city of Philadelphia, and of the counties of Philadelphia, Chester, and Bucks, respectively, shall choose by ballot one person for the city, and one for each county aforesaid, to serve for three years and no longer, at the time and place for electing representatives in general assembly. The freemen of the counties of Lancaster, York, Cumberland, and Berks, shall, in like manner elect one person for each county respectively, to serve as counsellors for two years and no longer. And the counties of Northampton, Bedford, Northumberland and Westmoreland, respectively, shall, in like manner, elect one person for each county, to serve as counsellors for one year, and no longer. And at the expiration of the time for which each counsellor was chosen to serve, the freemen of the city of Philadelphia, and of the several counties in this state, respectively, shall elect one person to serve as counsellor for three years and no longer; and so on every third year forever. By this mode of election and continual rotation, more men will be trained to public business, there will in every subsequent year be found in the council a number of persons acquainted with the proceedings of the foregoing years, whereby the business will be more consistently conducted, and moreover the danger of establishing an inconvenient aristocracy will be effectually prevented. All vacancies in the council that may happen by death, resignation, or otherwise, shall be filled at the next general election for representatives in general assembly, unless a particular election for that purpose shall be sooner appointed by the president and council. No member of the general assembly or delegate in congress, shall be chosen a member of the council. The president and vice-president shall be chosen annually by the joint ballot of the general assembly and council, of the members of the council. Any person having served as a counsellor for three successive years, shall be incapable of holding that office for four years afterwards. Every member of the council shall be a justice of the peace for the whole commonwealth, by virtue of his office.

In case new additional counties shall hereafter be erected in this state, such county or counties shall elect a counsellor, and such county or counties shall be annexed to the next neighbouring counties, and shall take rotation with such counties.

The council shall meet annually, at the same time and place with the general assembly.

The treasurer of the state, trustees of the loan office, naval officers, collectors of customs or excise, judge of the admirality, attornies general, sheriffs, and prothonotaries, shall not be capable of a seat in the general assembly, executive council, or continental congress.

SECT. 20. The president, and in his absence the vice-president, with the council, five of whom shall be a quorum, shall have power to appoint and commissionate judges, naval officers, judge of the admiralty, attorney general and all other officers, civil and military, except such as are chosen by the general assembly or the people, agreeable to this frame of government, and the laws that may be made hereafter; and shall supply every vacancy in any office, occasioned by death, resignation, removal or disqualification, until the office can be filled in the time and manner directed by law or this constitution. They are to correspond with other states, and transact business with the officers of government, civil and military; and to prepare such business as may appear to them necessary to lay before the general assembly. They shall sit as judges, to hear and determine on impeachments, taking to their assistance for advice only, the justices of the supreme court. And shall have power to grant pardons, and remit fines, in all cases whatsoever, except in cases of impeachment; and in cases of treason and murder, shall have power to grant reprieves, but not to pardon, until the end of the next sessions of assembly; but there shall be no remission or mitigation of punishments on impeachments, except by act of the legislature; they are also to take care that the laws be faithfully executed; they are to expedite the execution of such measures as may be resolved upon by the general assembly; and they may draw upon the treasury for such sums as shall be appropriated by the house: They may also lay embargoes, or prohibit the exportation of any commodity, for any time, not exceeding thirty days, in the recess of the house only: They may grant such licences, as shall be directed by law, and shall have power to call together the general assembly when necessary, before the day to which they shall stand adjourned. The president shall be commander in chief of the forces of the state, but shall not command in person, except advised thereto by the council, and then only so long as they shall approve thereof. The president and council shall have a secretary, and keep fair books of their proceedings, wherein any counsellor may enter his dissent, with his reasons in support of it. . . .

SECT. 22. Every officer of state, whether judicial or executive, shall be liable to be impeached by the general assembly, either when in office, or after his resignation or removal for mal-administration: All impeachments shall be before the president or vice-president and council, who shall hear and determine the same.

SECT. 23. The judges of the supreme court of judicature shall have fixed salaries, be commissioned for seven years only, though capable of re-appointment at the end of that term, but removable for misbehaviour at any time by the general assembly; they shall not be allowed to sit as members in the continental congress, executive council, or general assembly, nor to hold any other office civil or military, nor to take or receive fees or perquisites of any kind. . . .

SECT. 25. Trials shall be by jury as heretofore: And it is recommended to the legislature of this state, to provide by law against every corruption or partiality in the choice, return, or appointment of juries.

SECT. 26. Courts of sessions, common pleas, and orphans courts shall be held quarterly in each city and county; and the legislature shall have power to establish all such other courts as they may judge for the good of the inhabitants of the state. All courts shall be open, and justice shall be im-partially administered without corruption or unnecessary delay: All their officers shall be paid an adequate but moderate compensation for their services: And if any officer shall take greater or other fees than the law allows him, either directly or indirectly, it shall ever after disqualify him from holding any office in this state. . . .

SECT. 28. The person of a debtor, where there is not a strong presump-tion of fraud, shall not be continued in prison, after delivering up, *bona fide,* all his estate real and personal, for the use of his creditors, in such manner as shall be hereafter regulated by law. All prisoners shall be bailable by sufficient sureties, unless for capital offences, when the proof is evident, or presumption great.

SECT. 29. Excessive bail shall not be exacted for bailable offences: And all fines shall be moderate.

SECT. 30. Justices of the peace shall be elected by the freeholders of each city and county respectively. . . .

SECT. 31. Sheriffs and coroners shall be elected annually in each city and county, by the freemen. . . .

SECT. 35. The printing presses shall be free to every person who under-takes to examine the proceedings of the legislature, or any part of govern-ment.

SECT. 36. As every freeman to preserve his independence, (if without a sufficient estate) ought to have some profession, calling, trade or farm, whereby he may honestly subsist, there can be no necessity for, nor use in establishing offices of profit, the usual effects of which are dependence and servility unbecoming freemen, in the possessors and expectants; faction, contention, corruption, and disorder among the people. But if any man is called into public service, to the prejudice of his private affairs, he has a right to a reasonable compensation: And whenever an office, through increase of fees or otherwise, becomes so profitable as to occasion many to apply for it, the profits ought to be lessened by the legislature.

SECT. 37. The future legislature of this state, shall regulate intails in such a manner as to prevent perpetuities.

SECT. 38. The penal laws as heretofore used shall be reformed by the legislature of this state, as soon as may be, and punishments made in some cases less sanguinary, and in general more proportionate to the crimes.

SECT. 39. To deter more effectually from the commission of crimes, by continued visible punishments of long duration, and to make sanguinary punishments less necessary; houses ought to be provided for punishing by hard labour, those who shall be convicted of crimes not capital; wherein the criminals shall be imployed for the benefit of the public, or for reparation of injuries done to private persons: And all persons at proper times shall be admitted to see the prisoners at their labour. . . .

SECT. 41. No public tax, custom or contribution shall be imposed upon, or paid by the people of this state, except by a law for that purpose: And before any law be made for raising it, the purpose for which any tax is to be raised ought to appear clearly to the legislature to be of more service to the community than the money would be, if not collected; which being well observed, taxes can never be burthens.

SECT. 42. Every foreigner of good character who comes to settle in this state, having first taken an oath or affirmation of allegiance to the same, may purchase, or by other just means acquire, hold, and transfer land or other real estate; and after one year's residence, shall be deemed a free denizen thereof, and entitled to all the rights of a natural born subject of this state, except that he shall not be capable of being elected a representative until after two years residence. . . .

SECT. 44. A school or schools shall be established in each county by the legislature, for the convenient instruction of youth, with such salaries to the masters paid by the public, as may enable them to instruct youth at low prices: And all useful learning shall be duly encouraged and promoted in one or more universities.

SECT. 45. Laws for the encouragement of virtue, and prevention of vice and immorality, shall be made and constantly kept in force, and provision shall be made for their due execution: And all religious societies or bodies of men heretofore united or incorporated for the advancement of religion or learning, or for other pious and charitable purposes, shall be encouraged and protected in the enjoyment of the privileges, immunities and estates which they were accustomed to enjoy, or could of right have enjoyed, under the laws and former constitution of this state. . . .

SECT. 47. In order that the freedom of the commonwealth may be preserved inviolate forever, there shall be chosen by ballot by the freemen in each city and county respectively, on the second Tuesday in October, in the year one thousand seven hundred and eighty-three, and on the second Tuesday in October, in every seventh year thereafter, two persons in each city and county of this state, to be called the COUNCIL OF CENSORS; who shall meet together on the second Monday of November next ensuing their election; the majority of whom shall be a quorum in every case, except as to calling a convention, in which two-thirds of the whole number elected shall agree: And whose duty it shall be to enquire whether the constitution has been preserved inviolate in every part; and whether the legislative and executive branches of government have performed their duty as guardians of the people, or assumed to themselves, or exercised other or greater powers than they are intitled to by the constitution: They are also to enquire whether the public taxes have been justly laid and collected in all parts of this commonwealth, in what manner the public monies have been disposed of, and whether the laws have been duly executed. For these purposes they shall have power to send for persons, papers, and records; they shall have authority to pass public censures, to order impeachments, and to recommend to the legislature the repealing such laws as appear to them to have been enacted contrary to the principles of the constitution. These powers they shall continue to have, for and during the space of one year from the day of their election and no longer: The said council of censors shall also have power to call a convention, to meet within two years after their sitting, if there appear to them an absolute necessity of amending any article of the constitution which may be defective, explaining such as may be thought not clearly expressed, and of adding such as are necessary for the preservation of the rights and happiness of the people: But the articles to be amended, and the amendments proposed, and such articles as are proposed to be added or abolished, shall be promulgated at least six months before the day appointed for the election of such convention, for the previous consideration of the people, that they may have an opportunity of instructing their delegates on the subject. . . .

SELECTION **36**

The People as Constituent Power: Constitution Making in Massachusetts

Because of a prolonged and extremely complex internal political struggle Massachusetts, in contrast to the other states, did not adopt a constitution until 1780, and one of the results of the delay was the discovery of what, most historians are agreed, was the most distinctive political contribution of the American Revolution. American constitutional thought revolved around two basic ideas: that all power derived from the people and that there was a sharp distinction between fundamental law as embodied in a constitution and statutory law as represented by legislative enactments. In the process of writing constitutions in 1776 and 1777, however, none of the states had succeeded in finding a way to put either of these ideas into practical effect. Every one of the early constitutions was written and adopted by Revolutionary conventions or provincial congresses that also acted in a legislative capacity before, during, and after the writing of the constitutions. This confusion between legislative and constitution-making powers meant that the constitutions in fact rested upon no higher authority than ordinary laws. Moreover, it was by no means certain in any of the states that the "people," however defined, had actually exercised their rightful authority to make a constitution. Only a few of the Revolutionary bodies that wrote the constitutions had been elected specifically for that purpose, and none of the early constitutions had been submitted to the people for their approval. What was needed was some procedure by which the people could exercise their sovereign power to constitute their own governments and the constitution-making powers could be kept separate from and be elevated above ordinary legislative powers.

Such a procedure was gradually worked out in Massachusetts between 1776 and 1780. As early as December, 1775, a group known as the Constitutionalists from Berkshire County in the extreme west of Massachusetts had questioned the authority of the provincial congresses that had been governing the colony since October, 1774, and by the middle of 1776 there were widespread demands for the adoption of a new and, the opponents of the existing government insisted, legitimate government. On September 17, 1776, the Massachusetts lower house in opposition to the wishes of the Council, whose members wanted to postpone the task of constitution making until the popular political enthusiasms of mid-1776 had subsided, asked the towns to empower the General Court (both houses acting together) to prepare and adopt a constitution. It was in response to this request that the Concord town meeting, arguing strongly that a legislature was "by no means a Body proper to form . . . a Constitution," first suggested in the resolutions reprinted here as Selection 36 A that a special convention be called for the sole purpose of writing a constitution. In addition, several other towns insisted that, however a constitution was written, it should be submitted for ratification to the people. A vast majority of the towns, however, voted to authorize the legislature to write the constitution, and on June 15, 1777, after an initial resolution calling for a special convention was defeated, both houses resolved themselves into a convention to draft a constitution to be referred to the people for acceptance or rejection. The constitution prepared by this convention was formally approved by the convention on February 28, 1778, and submitted to the towns on March 4. After a vigorous, and in many instances extraordinarily sophisticated, discussion, the towns, each voting separately, rejected the constitution of 1778 by a margin of about five to one. Many towns submitted specific proposals for amendments; others prepared elaborate statements containing a mixture of theory, concrete objections to the constitution, and recommendations for a new one. Among the most important of the latter was the document that came out of the convention held in Essex County. Almost entirely the work of a young lawyer, Theophilus Parsons (1750–1813), the Essex Result was most remarkable for its suggestion of one possible solution to the problem that had plagued the advocates of bicameralism in preparing the state constitutions: how to achieve a separate base for each of the two houses. The lower house, the Essex Convention recommended in the portion of the Result reprinted below as Selection 36 B, should represent persons and the upper house property— a recommendation that was actually incorporated into the constitution of 1780.

In rejecting the constitution of 1778 three towns—Concord, Lexington, and Beverly—called for a specially elected convention to prepare a new constitution, and in June, 1779, after considerable pressure from the western towns and a favorable response from the towns to a resolution by the General Court asking for power to call a constitutional convention, the General Court called a convention to meet in Cambridge on September 1, 1779. The convention assigned the task of drafting a constitution to a committee of thirty, which in turn handed it over to a subcommittee composed of James Bowdoin (1727–1790), a wealthy merchant, president of the convention, and later governor; Samuel Adams; and John Adams. John Adams seems to have written most of the constitution, which was the most elaborate of all of the early state constitutions and was approved by the convention and submitted to the towns in the late winter of 1780. To prevent the constitution of 1780 from suffering the same fate as its predecessor, the convention adopted An Address . . . to Their Constituents, reprinted here as Selection 36 C. Often attributed to Samuel Adams, the Address explained the theory behind the constitution and tried to anticipate possible objections. Though almost every town either objected to indi-

*vidual clauses or suggested new provisions, each clause seems to have received the
necessary two-thirds majority, and the entire constitution, having been declared
duly ratified by the reconvened convention in June, went into effect on October 25, 1780.*

*The procedure employed by Massachusetts with a convention chosen by the
people solely for the purpose of writing a constitution and the ancillary device of
popular ratification of the convention's work thus provided for the first time an
acceptable means for putting the idea of the people as constituent power into
practice and making the clear and crucial distinction between fundamental law and
statutory law. Institutionalized in the process of writing the Federal Constitution
of 1787, it has subsequently come to serve as a model for much of the rest of the
world.*

Allan Nevins, The American States during and after the Revolution, 1775–1789
(1924), and Elisha P. Douglass, Rebels and Democrats: The Struggle for Equal
Political Rights and Majority Rule during the American Revolution *(1955), describe the process of constitution making in Massachusetts, as does Robert J. Taylor
(ed.),* Massachusetts, Colony to Commonwealth: Documents on the Formation of
Its Constitution, 1775–1780 *(1961), a useful documentary collection enriched by a
series of skillful introductions. Oscar and Mary Handlin,* The Popular Sources
of Political Authority: Documents on the Massachusetts Constitution of 1780
*(1966), provides a more complete documentary record for the constitution of 1780.
The last stages of the constitution-making process are recounted in more detail in
Samuel Eliot Morison, "The Struggle over the Adoption of the Constitution of
Massachusetts, 1780,"* Proceedings of the Massachusetts Historical Society, *volume 50, pages 353–411, while R. R. Palmer,* The Age of the Democratic Revolution, *volume One,* The Challenge *(1959), assesses the importance of the Massachusetts contribution to the world's stock of constitutional procedures.*

A. PROPOSAL FOR A CONSTITUTIONAL CONVENTION: THE RESOLVES OF THE CONCORD TOWN MEETING (OCT. 21, 1776)*

At a meeting of the Inhabitants of the Town of Concord being free & twenty
one years of age and upwards met by adjournment on the twenty first Day
of October to take into Consideration a Resolve of the Honorable House
of Representatives of this State on the 17th of September Last the Town
Resolved as follows—

Resolve 1st. That this State being at Present destitute of a Properly
established form of Government, it is absolutely necessary that one should
be immediately formed and established.

Resolved 2. That the Supreme Legislative, either in their Proper Capacity,
or in Joint Committee, are by no means a Body proper to form & Establish
a Constitution, or form of Government; for Reasons following. First Because
we Conceive that a Constitution in its Proper Idea intends a System of
Principles Established to Secure the Subject in the Possession & enjoyment

---

* These excerpts are reprinted from the facsimile edition of the original manuscript included as a frontispiece in The Commonwealth of Massachusetts, *A Manual
for the Constitutional Convention 1917* (1917).

of their Rights and Priviliges, against any Encroachments of the Governing Part. 2d Because the Same Body that forms a Constitution have of Consequence a power to alter it. 3d Because a Constitution alterable by the Supreme Legislature is no Security at all to the Subject against any Encroachment of the Governing part on any, or on all of their Rights and privileges.

Resolve 3d. That it appears to this Town highly necessary & Expedient that a Convention, or Congress be immediatly Chosen, to form & establish a Constitution, by the Inhabitants of the Respective Towns in this State, being free & of twenty one years of age, and upwards, in Proportion as the Representatives of this State formerly were Chosen; the Convention or Congress not to Consist of a greater number then the house of assembly of this State heretofore might Consist of, Except that each Town & District shall have Liberty to Send one Representative, or otherwise as shall appear meet to the Inhabitants of this State in General.

Resolve 4th. that when the Convention, or Congress have formed a Constitution they adjourn for a Short time, and Publish their Proposed Constitution for the Inspection & Remarks of the Inhabitents of this State.

Resolved 5ly. that the Honorable house of assembly of this State be Desired to Recommend it to the Inhabitents of the State to Proceed to Chuse a Convention or Congress for the Purpas abovesaid as soon as Possable.

B. OBJECTIONS TO THE CONSTITUTION OF 1778: [THEOPHILUS PARSONS], "RESULT OF THE CONVENTION OF DELEGATES HOLDEN AT IPSWICH IN THE COUNTY OF ESSEX" (MAY 12, 1778)*

THE Committee have purposely been as concise as possible in their observations upon the Constitution proposed by the Convention of this State— Where they thought it was non-conformable to the principles of a free republican government, they have ventured to point out the non-conformity —Where they thought it was repugnant to the original social contract, they have taken the liberty to suggest that repugnance—And where they were persuaded it was founded in political injustice, they have dared to assert it.

THE Committee, in obedience to the direction of this body, afterwards proceeded to delineate the general outlines of a Constitution, conformable to what have been already reported by them, as the principles of a free republican government, and as the natural rights of mankind.

THEY first attempted to delineate the legislative body. It has already been premised, that the legislative power is to be lodged in two bodies, composed of the representatives of the people. That representation ought to be equal. And that no law affecting the person and property of the members of the state ought to be enacted, without the consent of a majority of the members, and of those also who hold a major part of the property.

IN forming the first body of legislators, let regard be had only to the representation of persons, not of property. This body we call the house of representatives. Ascertain the number of representatives. It ought not to be

---

* These excerpts are reprinted from the original edition published in Newburyport in 1778, pp. 48–57.

so large as will induce an enormous expence to government, nor too unwieldy to deliberate with coolness and attention; nor so small as to be unacquainted with the situation and circumstances of the state. One hundred will be large enough, and perhaps it may be too large. We are persuaded that any number of men exceeding that, cannot do business with such expedition and propriety a smaller number could. However let that at present be considered as the number. Let us have the number of freemen in the several counties in the state; and let these representatives be apportioned among the respective counties, in proportion to their number of freemen. The representation yet remains equal. Let the representatives for the several counties be elected in this manner. Let the several towns in the respective counties, the first wednesday in May annually, choose delegates to meet in county convention on the thursday next after the second wednesday in May annually, and there elect the representatives for the county—Let the number of delegates each town shall send to the county convention be regulated in this manner. Ascertain that town which hath the smallest number of freemen; and let that town send one. Suppose the smallest town contains fifty. All the other towns shall then send as many members as they have fifties. If after the fifties are deducted, there remains an odd number, and that number is twenty five, or more, let them send another, if less, let no notice be taken of it. We have taken a certain for an uncertain number. Here the representation is as equal as the situation of a large political society will admit. No qualification should be necessary for a representative, except residence in the county the two years preceeding his election, and the payment of taxes those years. Any freeman may be an elector who hath resided in the county the year preceeding. The same qualification is requisite for a delegate, that is required of a representative. The representatives are designed to represent the persons of the members, and therefore we do not consider a qualification in point of property necessary for them.

THESE representatives shall be returned from the several parts of the county in this manner—Each county convention shall divide the county into as many districts as they send representatives, by the following rule—As we have the number of freemen in the county, and the number of county representatives, by dividing the greater by the less we have the number of freemen entitled to send one representative. Then add as many adjoining towns together as contain that number of freemen, or as near as may be, and let those towns form one district, and proceed in this manner through the county. Let a representative be chosen out of each district, and let all the representatives be elected out of the members who compose the county convention. In this house we find a proportionate representation of persons. If a law passes this house it hath the consent of a majority of the freemen; and here we may look for political honesty, probity and upright intentions to the good of the whole. Let this house therefore originate money-bills, as they will not have that inducement to extravagant liberality which an house composed of opulent men would, as the former would feel more sensibly the consequences. This county convention hath other business to do, which shall be mentioned hereafter. We shall now only observe, that this convention, upon a proper summons, is to meet again, to supply all vacancies in it's representation, by electing other representatives out of the district in which the vacancy falls. The formation of the second body of legislators next came under consideration, which may be called the senate. In electing the members for this body, let the representation of property be attended to. The senators may be chosen most easily in a county convention, which may be called the senatorial convention. Ascertain the number of senators. Perhaps thirty three will be neither too large nor too small. Let seven more be added to the thirty three which will make forty—these seven will be wanted for another purpose to be mentioned hereafter—Apportion the whole number upon the several counties, in proportion to the state-tax each county pays. Each freeman of the state, who is possessed of a certain quantity of property, may be an elector of the senators. To ascertain the value of a man's estate by a valuation is exceedingly difficult if possible, unless he voluntarily returns a valuation—To ascertain it by oath would be laying snares for a man's conscience, and would be a needless multiplication of oaths if another method could be devised—To fix his property at any certain sum, would be vague and uncertain, such is the fluctuation of even the best currency, and such the continual alteration of the nominal value of property—Let the state-tax assessed on each freeman's estate decide it—That tax will generally bear a very just proportion to the nominal value of a currency, and of property. Let every freeman whose estate pays such a proportion of the state-tax that had been last assessed previous to his electing, as three pounds is to an hundred thousand pounds, be an elector—The senatorial convention may be composed of delegates from the several towns elected in this manner. Ascertain the town which contains the smallest number of freemen whose estates pay such tax, and ascertain that number. Suppose it to be thirty. Let that town send one, and let all the other towns in the county send as many delegates as they have thirties. If after the thirties are deducted, there remains an odd number, and that number is fifteen, or more, let them send another, if it is less than fifteen let no notice be taken of it. Let the delegates for the senatorial convention be chosen at the same time with the county delegates, and meet in convention the second wednesday in May annually, which is the day before the county convention is to meet—and let no county delegate be a senatorial delegate the same year—We have here a senate (deducting seven in the manner and for the purpose hereafter to be mentioned) which more peculiarly represents the property of the state; and no act will pass both branches of the legislative body, without having the consent of those members who hold a major part of the property of the state. In electing the senate in this manner, the representation will be as equal as the fluctuation of property will admit of, and it is an equal representation of property so far as the number of senators are proportioned among the several counties. Such is the distribution of interstate estates in this country, the inequality between the estates of the bulk of the property holders is so inconsiderable, and the tax necessary to qualify a man to be an elector of a senator is so moderate, it may be demonstrated, that a law which passes both branches will have the consent of those persons who hold a majority of the property in the state. No freeman should be a delegate for the senatorial convention unless his estate pays the same tax which was necessary to qualify him to elect delegates for that convention; and no freeman shall be an elector of a delegate for that convention, nor a delegate therefore, unless he has been an inhabitant of the county for the two years next preceeding. No person shall be capable of an election into the senate unless he has been an inhabitant of the county for three years next preceeding his election—His qualification in point of estate is also to be considered. Let the state tax which was assessed upon his estate for the three years next preceeding his election be upon an average, at the rate of six pounds in an hundred thousand annually.

THIS will be all the duty of the senatorial convention unless there should be a vacancy in the senate when it will be again convened to fill up the vacancy. These two bodies will have the execution of the legislative power; and they are composed of the necessary members to make a just proportion of taxes among the several counties. This is all the discretionary power they will have in apportioning the taxes.

ONCE in five years at least, the legislative body shall make a valuation for the several counties in the State, and at the same time each county shall make a county valuation, by a county convention chosen for that purpose only, by the same rules which the legislative body observed in making the State valuation—and whenever a State valuation is made, let the several county valuations be also made. The legislative body after they have proportioned the State tax among the several counties, shall also proportion the tax among the several plantations and towns, agreeably to the county valuation, to be filed in the records of the General Court for that purpose. It may be observed that this county valuation will be taken and adjusted in county convention, in which persons only are to be equally represented: and it may also be objected that property ought also to be represented for this purpose. It is answered that each man in the county will pay at least a poll tax, and therefore ought to be represented in this convention—that it is impracticable in one convention to have persons and property both represented, with any degree of equality, without great intricacy—and that, where both cannot be represented without great intricacy, the representation of property should yield the preference to that of persons. The counties ought not to be compelled to pay their own representatives—if so, the counties remote from the seat of government would be at a greater charge than the other counties, which would be unjust—for they have only an equal influence in legislation with the other counties, yet they cannot use that influence but at a greater expence——They therefore labor under greater disadvantages in the enjoyment of their political liberties, than the other counties. If the remote counties enjoyed a larger proportional influence in legislation than the other counties, it would be just they should pay their own members, for the enhanced expence would tend to check this inequality of representation.

ALL the representatives should attend the house, if possible, and all the senators the senate. A change of faces in the course of a session retards and perplexes the public business. No man should accept of a seat in the legislative body without he intends a constant attendance upon his duty. Unavoidable accidents, necessary private business, sickness and death may, and will prevent a general attendance: but the numbers requisite to constitute a quorum of the house and senate should be so large as to admit of the absence of members, only for the reasons aforesaid. If members declined to attend their duty they should be expelled, and others chosen who would do better. Let seventy five constitute a quorum of the house, and twenty four of the senate. However no law ought to be enacted at any time, unless it has the concurrence of fifty one representatives, and seventeen senators.

WE have now the legislative body (deducting seven of the senators.) Each branch hath a negative upon the other—and either branch may originate any bill or propose any amendment, except a money bill, which should be concurred or non-concurred by the senate in the whole. The legislative body is so formed and ballanced that the laws will be made with the greatest wisdom and the best intentions; and the proper consent thereto is obtained. Each man enjoys political liberty, and his civil rights will be taken care of. And all orders of men are interested in government, will put confidence in it, and struggle for it's support. As the county and senatorial delegates are chosen the same day throughout the State, as all the county conventions are held at the same time, and all the senatorial conventions on one day, and as these delegates are formed into conventions on a short day after their election, elections will be free, bribery will be impracticable, and party and factions will not be formed. As the senatorial conventions are held the day before the county conventions, the latter will have notice of the persons elected senators, and will not return them as representatives—The senatorial convention should after it's first election of senators be adjourned without day, but not dissolved, and to be occasionally called together by the supreme executive officer to keep the senate full, should a senator elected decline the office, or afterwards resign, be expelled, or die. The county convention in the same way are to keep the representation full, and also supply all vacancies in the offices they will be authorised to appoint to and elect as will be presently mentioned. By making provision in the constitution that recourse be had to these principles of representation every twenty years, by taking new lists of the freemen for that purpose, and by a new distribution of the number of representatives agreeably thereto, and of the senators in proportion to the State tax, representation will be always free and equal. These principles easily accommodate themselves to the erection of new counties and towns. Crude and hasty determinations of the house will be revised or controuled by the senate; and those views of the senate which may arise from ambition or a disregard to civil liberty will be frustrated. Government will acquire a dignity and firmness, which is the greatest security of the subject: while the people look on, and observe the conduct of their servants, and continue or withdraw their favour annually, according to their merit or demerit. . . .

C. SUBMITTING THE CONSTITUTION OF 1780 TO THE PEOPLE: ''AN ADDRESS OF THE CONVENTION . . . TO THEIR CONSTITUENTS'' (1780)*

Friends and Countrymen,

Having had your Appointment and Instruction, we have undertaken the arduous Task of preparing a civil Constitution for the People of the Massachusetts Bay; and we now submit it to your candid Consideration. It is your *Interest* to revise it with the greatest Care and Circumspection, and it is your undoubted *Right*, either to propose such Alterations and Amendments as you shall judge proper, or, to give it your own Sanction in its present Form, or, totally to reject it.

In framing a Constitution, to be adapted as far as possible to the Circum-

---

* These excerpts are reprinted from *An Address of the Convention, for Framing a New Constitution of Government, for the State of Massachusetts-Bay, to Their Constituents* (1780), pp. 5–18.

stances of Posterity yet unborn, you will conceive it to be exceedingly difficult, if not impracticable, to succeed in every part of it, to the full Satisfaction of all. Could the *whole Body* of the People have Conven'd for the same Purpose, there might have been equal Reason to conclude, that a perfect Unanimity of Sentiments would have been an Object not to be obtain'd. In a Business so universally interesting, we have endeavor'd to act as became the Representatives of a wise, understanding and free People; and, as we have Reason to believe you would *yourselves* have done, we have open'd our Sentiments to each other with Candor, and made such mutual Concessions as we could consistently, and without marring the only Plan, which in our most mature Judgment we can at present offer to you.

The Interest of the Society is common to all its Members. The great Enquiry is, wherein this Common Interest consists. In determining this Question, an Advantage may arise from a Variety of Sentiments offer'd to public Examination concerning it. But wise Men are not apt to be obstinately tenacious of their own Opinions: They will always pay a due Regard to those of other Men and keep their minds open to Conviction. We conceive, that in the present Instance, by accommodating ourselves to each other, and individually yielding particular and even favorite Opinions of smaller moment, to essential Principles, and Considerations of general Utility, the public Opinion of the Plan now before you may be consolidated.—But without such mutual Condescention in unimportant Matters, we may almost venture to predict, that we shall not soon, if ever, be bless'd with such a Constitution as those are intitled to, who have struggled hard for Freedom and Independence. You will permit us on this Occasion, just to hint to you our own Apprehension, that there may be amongst us, some Persons disaffected to that great Cause for which we are contending, who may be secretly instructed by our common Enemy to divide and distract us; in hopes of preventing our Union in any Form of Government whatever, and by this Means of depriving us of the most honorable Testimony, as well as the greatest Security of our Freedom and Independence.—If there be such Men, it is our Wisdom to mark them, and guard ourselves against their Designs.

We may not expect to agree in a perfect System of Government: This is not the Lot of Mankind. The great End of Government, is, to promote the Supreme Good of human Society: Every social Affection should therefore be interested in the Forming of a Government and in judging of one when it is Formed. Would it not be prudent for Individuals to cast out of the Scale, smaller Considerations and fall in with an evident Majority, unless in Matters in which their Consciences shall constrain them to determine otherwise? Such a Sacrifice, made for the sake of Union, would afford a strong Evidence of public Affection; and Union, strengthened by the social Feeling, would promise a greater Stability to any Constitution, and, in its operation, a greater Degree of Happiness to the Society. It is here to be remembered, that on the Expiration of Fifteen Years a new Convention may be held, in order that such Amendments may be made in the Plan you may now agree to, as Experience, that best Instructor, shall then point out to be expedient or necessary.

A Government without Power to exert itself, is at best, but an useless Piece of Machinery. It is probable, that for the want of Energy, it would speedily lose even the Appearance of Government, and sink into Anarchy. Unless a due Proportion of Weight is given to each of the Powers of Government, there will soon be a Confusion of the whole. An Overbearing of any one of its Parts on the rest, would destroy the Balance and accelerate its Dissolution and Ruin: And, a Power without *any* Restraint is Tyranny. The Powers of Government must then be balanced: To do this accurately requires the highest Skill in political Architecture. Those who are to be invested with the Administration, should have such Powers given to them, as are requisite to render them useful in their respective Places; and such *Checks* should be added to every Branch of Power as may be sufficient to prevent its becoming formidable and injurious to the Common wealth. If we have been so fortunate as to succeed in this point of the greatest Importance, our Happiness will be compleat, in the Prospect of having laid a good Foundation for many Generations. *You* are the Judges how far we have succeeded; and whether we have raised our Superstructure, agreeably to our profess'd Design, upon the Principles of a *Free Common Wealth*.

In order to assist your Judgments, we have thought it necessary, briefly to explain to you the Grounds and Reasons upon which we have formed our Plan. In the third article of the Declaration of Rights, we have, with as much Precision as we were capable of, provided for the free exercise of *the Rights of Conscience:* We are very sensible that our Constituents hold those Rights infinitely more valuable than all others; and we flatter ourselves, that while we have considered Morality and the public Worship of GOD, as important to the happiness of Society, we have sufficiently guarded the rights of Conscience from every possible infringement. This Article underwent long debates, and took Time in proportion to its importance; and we feel ourselves peculiarly happy in being able to inform you, that though the debates were managed by persons of various denominations, it was finally agreed upon with much more Unanimity than usually takes place in disquisitions of this Nature. We wish you to consider the Subject with Candor, and Attention. Surely it would be an affront to the People of Massachusetts Bay to labour to convince them, that the Honor and Happiness of a People depend upon Morality; and that the Public Worship of GOD has a tendency to inculcate the Principles thereof, as well as to preserve a People from forsaking Civilization, and falling into a state of Savage barbarity.

In the form now presented to you, there are no more Departments of Government than are absolutely necessary for the free and full Exercise of the Powers thereof. The House of Representatives is intended as the Representative of the Persons and the Senate, of the property of the Common Wealth. These are to be annually chosen, and to sit in separate Bodies, each having a Negative upon the Acts of [the] other. This Power of a Negative in each must ever be necessary; for all Bodies of Men, assembled upon the same occasion and united by one common Interest of Rank, Honor, or Estate, are liable, like an individual, to mistake bias and prejudice. These two Houses are vested with the Powers of Legislation, and are to be chosen by the Male Inhabitants who are Twenty one Years of age, and have a Freehold of the small annual income of Three Pounds or Sixty Pounds in any Estate. Your Delegates considered that Persons who are Twenty one Years of age, and have no Property, are either those who live upon a part of a Paternal estate, expecting the Fee thereof, who are but just entering into business, or those whose Idleness of Life and profligacy of manners will forever bar them from acquiring and possessing Property. And we will submit it to the former Class, whether they would not think it safer for them to have their right of Voting for a Representative suspended for small space of Time, than forever hereafter to have their Privileges liable to the control of Men, who will pay less regard to the Rights of Property because they have nothing to lose.

The Power of Revising, and stating objections to any Bill or Resolve that shall be passed by the two Houses, we were of opinion ought to be lodged in the hands of some *one* person; not only to perserve the Laws from being unsystematical and innaccurate, but that a due balance may be preserved in the three capital powers of Government. The Legislative, the Judicial and Executive Powers naturally exist in every Government: And the History of the rise and fall of the Empires of the World affords us ample proof, that when the same Man or Body of Men enact, interpret and execute the Laws, property becomes too precarious to be valuable, and a People are finally borne down with the force of corruption resulting from the Union of those Powers. The Governor is emphatically the Representative of the whole People, being chosen not by one Town or County, but by the People at large. We have therefore thought it safest to rest this Power in his hands; and as the Safety of the Common wealth requires, that there should be one Commander in Chief over the Militia, we have given the Governor that Command for the same reason, that we thought him the only proper Person that could be trusted with the power of revising the Bills and Resolves of the General Assembly; but the People may if they please choose their own Officers.

You will observe that we have resolved, that Representation ought to be founded on the Principle of equality; but it cannot be understood thereby that each Town in the Commonwealth shall have Weight and importance in a just proportion to its Numbers and property. An exact Representation would be unpracticable even in a System of Government arising from the State of Nature, and much more so in a state already divided into nearly three hundred Corporations. But we have agreed that each Town having One hundred and fifty Rateable Poles shall be entitled to send one Member, and to prevent an advantage arising to the greater Towns by their numbers, have agreed that no Town shall send two unless it hath three hundred and seventy five Rateable Poles, and then the still larger Towns are to send one Member for every two hundred and twenty-five Rateable Polls over and above Three hundred and seventy-five. This method of calculation will give a more exact Representation when applied to all the Towns in the State than any that we could fix upon.

We have however digressed from this Rule in admiting the small Towns now incorporated to send Members. There are but a few of them which will not from their continual increase, be able to send one upon the above plan in a very little Time. And the few who will never probably have that number have been heretofore in the exercise of this privilege, and will now be very unwilling to relinquish it.

To prevent the governor from abusing the Power which is necessary to be put into his hands we have provided that he shall have a Council to advise him at all Times and upon all important Occasions, and he with the advice of his Council is to have the Appointment of Civil Officers. This was very readily agreed to by your Delegates, and will undoubtedly be agreeable to their Constituents; for if those Officers who are to interpret and execute the Laws are to be dependent upon the Election of the people it must forever keep them under the Controul of ambitious, artful and interested men, who can obtain most Votes for them.—If they were to be Appointed by the Two Houses or either of them, the persons appointing them would be too numerous to be accountable for putting weak or wicked Men into Office. Besides the House is designed as the Grand Inquest of the Common Wealth, and are to impeach Officers for male Conduct, the Senate are to try the Merits of such impeachments; it would be therefore unfit that they should have the Creation of those Officers which the one may impeach and the other remove: but we conceive there is the greatest propriety in Vesting the Governor with this Power, he being as we have before observed, the compleat representative of all the People, and at all Times liable to be impeached by the House before the Senate for male Administration. And we would here observe that all the Powers which we have given the Governor are necessary to be lodged in the hands of one Man, as the General of the Army and first Magistrate, and none can be entitled to it but he who has the Annual and United Suffrages of the whole Common Wealth.

You will readily conceive it to be necessary for your own Safety, that your Judges should hold their Offices during good behaviour; for Men who hold their places upon so precarious a Tenure as annual or other frequent Appointments will never so assiduously apply themselves to study as will be necessary to the filling their places with dignity. Judges should at all Times feel themselves independent and free.

Your Delegates have further provided that the Supreme Judicial Department, by fixed and ample Salaries, may be enabled to devote themselves wholly to the Duties of their important Office. And for this reason, as well as to keep this Department separate from the others in Government have excluded them from a Seat in the Legislature; and when our Constituents consider that the final Decision of their Lives and Property must be had in this Court, we conceive they will universally approve the measure. The Judges of Probate and those other officers whose presence is always necessary in their respective Counties are also excluded.

We have attended to the inconveniences suggested to have arisen from having but one Judge of Probate in each County; but the erecting and altering Courts of Justice being a mere matter of Legislation, we have left it with your future Legislature to make such Alterations as the Circumstances of the several Counties may require.

Your Delegates did not conceive themselves to be vested with Power to set up one Denomination of Christians above another; for Religion must at all Times be a matter between GOD and individuals: But we have, nevertheless, found ourselves obliged by a Solemn Test, to provide for the exclusion of those from Offices who will not disclaim those Principles of Spiritual Jurisdiction which Roman Catholicks *in some Countries* have held, and which are subversive of a free Government established by the People. We find it necessary to continue the former Laws, and Modes of proceeding in Courts of Justice, until a future Legislature shall alter them: For, unless this is done, the title to Estates will become precarious, Law-suits will be multiplied, and universal Confusion must take place. And least the Commonwealth for want of a due Administration of Civil Justice should be involved in Anarchy, we have proposed to continue the present Magistrates and Officers until new Appointments shall take place.

Thus we have, with plainness and sincerity, given you the Reasons upon which we founded the principal parts of the System laid before you, which appeared to us as most necessary to be explained: And we do most humbly beseech the Great Disposer of all Events, that we and our Posterity may be established in and long enjoy the Blessings of a well-ordered and free Government.

SELECTION

Criticisms of the Early Constitutions

Most of the early constitutions had been made in haste and sometimes, as in the case of New York, on the run. Not surprisingly, they were defective in many parts, inconsistent and contradictory from one clause to another, and in many instances completely unworkable. From the point of view of men committed to the doctrine of separation of powers—and the number of such men was very great among the politically significant elements in American society—the most glaring defect of the constitutions was the overwhelming power they gave to the lower houses of the legislature. In virtually every state the executive and judicial branches of the government were to varying degrees dependent upon and consequently subordinate to the legislative with the result that there was no effective way to check the power of the legislatures. This and other defects were quickly spotted by contemporaries, and within a year critics in almost every state were demanding the amendment or replacement of the original instruments. The literature they produced, represented by the two selections below, helped to refine and enlarge the available body of constitutional theory and revealed the continuing preoccupation with and emphasis upon constitutional questions during the later stages of the Revolution.

In Pennsylvania, where there were powerful and articulate advocates of bicameralism who were adamantly opposed to the unicameral legislature and other innovative features of the constitution, a bitter and prolonged debate between constitutionalists and anticonstitutionalists began as soon as the constitution was published. One of the most comprehensive statements of the case for the anticonstitutionalists, written by Dr. Benjamin Rush (1745–1813), noted Philadelphia physician and advocate of various humanitarian reforms, appeared in pamphlet form in 1777 under the title Observations upon the Present Government of Pennsylvania. *In this pamphlet, the major portions of which are reprinted below as Selection 37 A, Rush objected to the constitution primarily because it placed too much power in the hands of the unicameral legislature. Far from preventing the development of an "aristocratical and monarchical power" in the state, as its proponents contended, a unicameral legislature, Rush argued, laid the "foundation . . . for the most complete aristocracy that ever existed in the world" both because a single house could be all the more easily captured by the wealthy, who had "always been an overmatch for the poor in all contests for power," and because the executive and judiciary were so completely dependent upon the legislature that there was no certain way to prevent it from making itself all powerful and overturning the constitution. Rush also thought it unsafe to give such "supreme and uncontrouled power" to the council of censors, which because it only met every seven years would not in any case be an effective check upon the unicameral legislature, and unwise to give the public at large a share of the executive power by entrusting them with the task of electing civil magistrates and militia officers below the rank of brigadier general. That "all power is* derived *from the people," he insisted, did not imply "that all power is* seated *in the people" who, in the view of Rush, should never be permitted to choose directly the officers of government they were obliged to obey. Thus, even the power of the people had to be restrained, and, Rush predicted, unless the constitution was revised so that adequate checks were placed upon the legislature and the council of censors Pennsylvania would "most certainly" become "the most miserable spot upon the surface of the globe." Despite Rush's dire predictions, however, the constitutionalists were able to head off any movement for altering the constitution until 1790, when a new constitution providing for a bicameral legislature was adopted.*

In Virginia there was no organized opposition to the constitution, but there were numerous proponents of reform, among them Thomas Jefferson, who as governor of the state from 1779 to 1781 had witnessed the defects of the constitution from the place in the governmental structure at which they were most obvious. Jefferson's objections to the constitution were first published in 1785 in his Notes on the State of Virginia *and are reprinted in large part below as Selection 37 B. Although he was upset by inequities in the system of representation and by the failure of the constitution to make a clear distinction between the function and composition of the upper house and that of the lower house, Jefferson was primarily concerned about the concentration of power in the legislature. "An* elective despotism," *he declared, "was not the government we fought for," and, he warned, unless proper barriers were erected among the "legislative, executive, and judiciary departments, the legislature may seize the whole," especially because the constitution had been written by an ordinary legislative body and could therefore be abridged, suspended, or amended by any legislature intent upon establishing a tyranny. To rescue themselves from so perilous a situation, Jefferson declared, Virginians needed a special convention "to fix the constitution." Despite frequent complaints from others, however, the "very capital defects" pointed out by Jefferson were not removed until 1830, when the constitution of 1776 was finally replaced by a new one.*

There is no comprehensive or adequate study of the movement for constitutional reform in the states in the 1770s and 1780s, though some information will be found in Allan Nevins, The American States during and after the Revolution, 1775–1789 *(1924); Fletcher M. Green,* Constitutional Development in the South Atlantic States, 1776–1860: A Study in the Evolution of Democracy *(1930); and Merrill Jensen,* The New Nation: A History of the United States During the Confederation, 1781–1789 *(1950). Developments in Pennsylvania may be followed in Robert L. Brunhouse,* The Counter-Revolution in Pennsylvania, 1776–1790 *(1942).*

A. DEFECTS OF THE PENNSYLVANIA CONSTITUTION: [BENJAMIN RUSH], ''OBSERVATIONS UPON THE PRESENT GOVERNMENT OF PENNSYLVANIA ... '' (1777)*

Letter I

EVERY free government should consist of three parts, viz. I. A BILL OF RIGHTS. II. A CONSTITUTION, And III. LAWS.

I. The BILL OF RIGHTS should contain the great principles of *natural* and *civil liberty*. It should be unalterable by any human power.

II. The CONSTITUTION is the executive part of the Bill of Rights. It should contain the division and distribution of the power of the people.----The modes and forms of making laws, of executing justice, and of transacting business: Also the limitation of power, as to time and jurisdiction. It should be unalterable by the legislature, and should be changed only by a representation of the people, chosen for that purpose.

III. LAWS are the executive part of a constitution. They cease to be binding whenever they transgress the principles of Liberty, as laid down in the Constitution and Bill of Rights.

Let us now apply these principles to the Bill of Rights, Constitution and Laws of Pennsylvania. . . .

I. The Bill of Rights has confounded *natural* and *civil* rights in such a manner as to produce endless confusion in society.

II. The Constitution in the gross is exceptionable in the following particulars:

1. No regard is paid in it to the ancient habits and customs of the people of Pennsylvania in the distribution of the supreme power of the state, nor in the forms of business, or in the stile of the Constitution. The suddenness of the late revolution, the attachment of a large body of the people to the old Constitution of the state, and the general principles of human nature made an attention to ancient forms and prejudices a matter of the utmost importance to this state in the present controversy with Great-Britain. Of so much consequence did the wise Athenians view the force of ancient habits and customs in their laws and government, that they punished all *strangers* with death who interfered in their politics. They well knew the effects of novelty upon the minds of the people, and that a more fatal stab could not be given to the peace and safety of their state than by exposing its laws and government to frequent or *unnecessary* innovations.

2. The Constitution is wholly repugnant to the principles of action in man, and has a direct tendency to check the progress of genius and virtue in human nature. It supposes perfect equality, and an equal distribution of property, wisdom and virtue, among the inhabitants of the state.

3. It comprehends many things which belong to a Bill of Rights, and to Laws, and which form no part of a Constitution.

4. It is contrary, in an important article, to the Bill of Rights. By the second article of the Bill of Rights, "no man can be abridged of any *civil* right, who acknowledges the being of a GOD;" but by the Constitution, no man can take his

---

* These excerpts are reprinted from the original Philadelphia edition, pp. 3–5, 7–20.

seat in the Assembly, who does not "acknowledge the Scriptures of the Old and New Testament to be given by divine inspiration."

5. It is deficient in point of perspicuity and method. Instead of reducing the legislative, executive and judicial parts of the constitution, with their several powers and forms of business, to distinct heads, the whole of them are jumbled together in a most unsystematic manner.

6. It fixes all these imperfections upon the people for seven years, by precluding them from the exercise of their own power to remove them at any other time, or in any other manner than by a septennial convention, called by a Council of Censors.

III. The laws and proceedings of the Assembly of Pennsylvania are in many particulars contrary to the constitution. Only one half of the Members took the oath of allegiance, prescribed in the tenth section of the constitution. The Speaker of the House issued writs for the election of Members of Assembly and of Counsellors, notwithstanding this power is lodged, by the 19th section of the constitution, *only* in the President and Council. Two gentlemen were appointed Members of Congress, who held offices under the Congress, which is expressly forbidden in the 11th section of the constitution. The constitution requires further in the 40th section, that every military officer should take the oath of allegiance, before he enters upon the execution of his office; but the Assembly have dispensed with this oath in their Militia Law. The 15th section of the constitution declares, that no law shall be passed, unless it be previously published for the consideration of the People; but the Assembly passed all the laws of their late session, without giving the People an opportunity of seeing them, till they were called upon to obey them. These proceedings of the Assembly lead to one, and perhaps to all the three following conclusions: First, That the Assembly have violated the principles of the constitution; secondly, that the constitution is so formed, that it could not be executed by the Assembly, consistent with the safety of the State; lastly, that none of their laws are binding, inasmuch as they are contrary to the superior and radical laws of the constitution. These considerations are all of a most alarming nature. Farewel to Liberty, when the sacred bulwarks of a constitution can be invaded by a legislature! And if the constitution cannot be executed in all its parts, without endangering the safety of the State, and if all our late laws must be set aside in a court of justice, because they were not assented to by the People, previous to their being enacted, is it not high time for the People to unite and form a more effectual, and more practicable system of government? . . .

Letter II

I SHALL now proceed to say a few words upon particular parts of the Constitution.

In the second section, "the supreme legislature is vested in a *'single'* House of Representatives of the Freemen of the Commonwealth." By this section we find, that the supreme, absolute, and uncontrouled power of the whole State is lodged in the hands of *one body* of men. Had it been lodged in the hands of one man, it would have been less dangerous to the safety and liberties of the community. Absolute power should never be trusted to man. It has perverted the wisest heads, and corrupted the best hearts in the world. I should be afraid to commit my property, liberty and life to a body of angels for one whole year. The Supreme Being alone is qualified to possess supreme power over his creatures. It requires the wisdom and goodness of a Deity to controul, and direct it properly. . . .

I might . . . shew, that all the dissentions of Athens and Rome, so dreadful in their nature, and so fatal in their consequences, originated in single Assemblies possessing all the power of those commonwealths; but this would be the business of a volume, and not of a single essay.---I shall therefore pass on, to answer the various arguments that have been used in Pennsylvania, in support of a single legislature.

1. We are told, that the perfection of every thing consists in its simplicity, ---that all mixtures in government are impurities, and that a single legislature is perfect, because it is simple.---To this I answer, that we should distinguish between simplicity in principles, and simplicity in the application of principles to practice. What can be more simple than the principles of mechanics, and yet into how many thousand forms have they been tortured by the ingenuity of man. A few simple elementary bodies compose all the matter of the universe, and yet how infinitely are they combined in the various forms and substances which they assume in the animal, vegetable, and mineral kingdoms. In like manner a few simple principles enter into the composition of all free governments. These principles are perfect security for property, liberty and life; but these principles admit of extensive combinations, when reduced to practice:---Nay more, they require them. A despotic government is the most simple government in the world, but instead of affording security to property, liberty or life, it obliges us to hold them all on the simple will of a capricious sovereign. I maintain therefore, that all governments are safe and free in proportion as they are compounded in a certain degree, and on the contrary, that all governments are dangerous and tyrannical in proportion as they approach to simplicity.

2. We are told by the friends of a single legislature, that there can be no danger of their becoming tyrannical, since they must partake of all the burdens they lay upon their constituents. Here we forget the changes that are made upon the head and heart by arbitrary power, and the cases that are recorded in history of *annual* Assemblies having refused to share with their constituents in the burdens which they had imposed upon them. If every elector in Pennsylvania is capable of being elected an assembly-man, then agreeably to the sixth section of the constitution, it is possible for an Assembly to exist who do not possess a single foot of property in the State, and who can give no other evidence of a common interest in, or attachment to, the community than having paid "public taxes," which may mean poor-taxes. Should this be the case, (and there is no obstacle in the constitution to prevent it) surely it will be in the power of such an Assembly to draw from the State the whole of its wealth in a few years, without contributing any thing further towards it than their proportion of the trifling tax necessary to support the poor.----But I shall shew in another place equal dangers from another class of men, becoming a majority in the Assembly.

3. We are told of instances of the House of Lords, in England, checking the most salutary laws, after they had passed the House of Commons, as a proof of the inconvenience of a compound legislature. I believe the fact to be true, but I deny its application in the present controversy. The House of Lords, in England, possess privileges and interests, which do not belong to the House of Commons. Moreover they derive their power from the crown

and not from the people. No wonder therefore they consult their own interests, in preference to those of the People. In the State of Pennsylvania we
wish for a council, with *no one* exclusive privilege, and we disclaim every
idea their possessing the smallest degree of power, but what is derived from
the *annual* suffrages of the people. A body thus chosen could have no object
in view but the happiness of their constituents. It is remarkable in Connecticut, that the legislative council of that State has in no one instance made
amendments, or put a negative upon the acts of their Assembly, in the course
of above one hundred years, in which both have not appeared to the people
in a few months to have been calculated to promote their liberty and
happiness.

4. We are told, that the Congress is a single legislature, therefore a single
legislature is to be preferred to a compound one.---The objects of legislation
in the Congress relate only to peace and war, alliances, trade, the Post-
Office, and the government of the army and navy. They never touch the
liberty, property, nor life of the individuals of any State in their resolutions,
and even in their ordinary subjects of legislation, they are liable to be
checked by *each* of the Thirteen States.

5. We have been told, that a legislative council or governor lays the
foundation for aristocratical and monarchical power in a community. However ridiculous this objection to a compound legislature may appear, I have
more than once heard it mentioned by the advocates for a single Assembly.
Who would believe, that the same fountain of pure water should send forth,
at the same time, wholesome and deadly streams? Are not the Council and
Assembly both formed alike by the *annual* breath of the people? But I will
suppose, that a legislative Council aspired after the honors of hereditary
titles and power, would they not be *effectually* checked by the Assembly?

I cannot help commending the zeal that appears in my countrymen
against the power of a King or a House of Lords. I concur with them in all
their prejudices against hereditary titles, honour and power. History is little
else than a recital of the follies and vices of kings and noblemen, and it is
because I dread so much from them, that I wish to exclude them for ever
from Pennsylvania, for notwithstanding our government has been called a
simple democracy, I maintain, that a foundation is laid in it for the most
complete aristocracy that ever existed in the world.

In order to prove this assertion, I shall premise two propositions, which
have never been controverted: First, where there is wealth, there will be
power; and, secondly, the rich have always been an over-match for the poor
in all contests for power.

These truths being admitted, I desire to know what can prevent our single
representation being filled, in the course of a few years, with a majority of
rich men? Say not, the people will not choose such men to represent them.
The influence of wealth at elections is irresistible. It has been seen and felt
in Pennsylvania, and I am obliged in justice to my subject to say, that there
are poor men among us as prepared to be influenced, as the rich are prepared to influence them. The fault must be laid in both cases upon human
nature. The consequence of a majority of rich men getting into the legislature
is plain. Their wealth will administer fuel to the love of arbitrary power that
is common to all men. The present Assembly have furnished them with
precedents for breaking the Constitution. Farewel now to annual elections!
Public emergencies will sanctify the most daring measures. The clamours of

their constituents will be silenced, and Pennsylvania will be inhabited like most of the countries in Europe, with only two sorts of animals, tyrants and slaves.

It has often been said, that there is but one rank of men in America, and therefore, that there should be only one representation of them in a government. I agree, that we have no artificial distinctions of men into noblemen and commoners among us, but it ought to be remarked, that superior degrees of industry and capacity, and above all, commerce, have introduced inequality of property among us, and these have introduced natural distinctions of rank in Pennsylvania, as certain and general as the artificial distinctions of men in Europe. This will ever be the case while commerce exists in this country. The men of middling property and poor men can never be safe in a mixed representation with the men of over-grown property. Their liberties can only be secured by having exact bounds prescribed to their power, in the fundamental principles of the Constitution. By a representation of the men of middling fortunes in one house, their *whole* strength is collected against the influence of wealth. Without such a representation, the most violent efforts of individuals to oppose it would be divided and broken, and would want that system, which alone would enable them to check that lust for dominion which is always connected with opulence. The government of Pennsylvania therefore has been called most improperly a government for poor men. It carries in every part of it a poison to their liberties. It is impossible to form a government more suited to the passions and interests of rich men.

6. But says the advocate for a single legislature, if one of the advantages of having a Legislative Council arises from the Counsellors possessing more wisdom than the Assembly, why may not the members of the Council be thrown into the Assembly, in order to instruct and enlighten them? If sound reasoning always prevailed in popular Assemblies, this objection to a Legislative Council might have some weight. The danger in this case would be, that the Counsellors would partake of the passions and prejudices of the Assembly, by taking part in their debates; or, if they did not, that they would be so inconsiderable in point of numbers, that they would be constantly out-voted by the members of the Assembly.

7. But would you suffer twenty or thirty men in a Legislative Council to controul seventy or eighty in an Assembly? Yes, and that for two reasons: First, I shall suppose that they will consist of men of the most knowledge and experience in the State: Secondly, that their obligations to wisdom and integrity will be much stronger than the Assembly's can be, because fewer men will be answerable for unjust or improper proceedings at the bar of the public. But I beg pardon of any readers for introducing an answer to an objection to a small number of men controuling the proceedings of a greater. The friends of the present Constitution of Pennsylvania cannot urge this objection with any force, for in the 47th section of the Constitution I find twenty-four men called a COUNCIL OF CENSORS, invested with a supreme and *uncontroule*d power to revise and to censure all the laws and proceedings of not a single Assembly, but of all the Assemblies that shall exist for seven years, which Assemblies may contain the united wisdom of five hundred and four Assembly-men. They are moreover, invested with more wisdom than the Convention that is to be chosen by their recommendation; for this Convention, which is to consist of seventy-two men, is to make no *one* alteration in the Constitution but what was suggested to them by the Council of Censors.

I can easily conceive, that two houses consisting of an unequal number of members, both viewing objects through the same medium of time and place, may agree in every thing essential, and disagree in matters only of doubtful issue to the welfare of the state; but I am sure, a body of twenty-four men sitting in judgment upon the proceedings of a body of men defunct in their public capacity seven years before them, cannot fail of committing the most egregious mistakes from the obscurity which time, and their ignorance of a thousand facts and reasonings must throw upon all their deliberations. But more of the arbitrary power of the Censors hereafter.

8. We are told that the state of Pennsylvania has always been governed by a single legislature, and therefore, that part of our Constitution is not an innovation. There is a short way of confuting this assertion by pronouncing it without any foundation. The Governor always had a negative power upon our laws, and was a distinct branch of our legislature. It is true, he some-times exercised his power to the disadvantage of the people; for he was the servant of a King who possessed an interest distinct from that of his people, and in some cases the Governor himself possessed an interest incompatible with the rights of the people. God forbid that ever we should see a resurrec-tion of his power in Pennsylvania, but I am obliged to own, that I have known instances in which the *whole* state have thanked him for the inter-position of his negative and amendments upon the acts of the Assembly. Even the Assembly-men themselves have acknowledged the justice of his conduct upon these occasions, by condemning in their cooler hours their own hasty, and ill-digested resolutions.

9. But why all these arguments in favor of checks for the Assembly? The Constitution (says the single legislative-man) has provided no less than four for them. First, Elections will be annual. Secondly, The doors of the Assembly are to be always open. Thirdly, All laws are to be published for the consideration and assent of the people: And, Fourthly, The Council of Censors will punish, by their censures, all violations of the Constitution, and the authors of bad laws. I shall examine the efficacy of each of these checks separately.

I hope, for the peace of the state, that we shall never see a body of men in power more attached to the present Constitution than the present Assembly, and if, with all their affection for it, they have broken it in many articles, it is reasonable to suppose that future Assemblies will use the same freedoms with it. They may, if they chuse, abolish annual elections. They may tell their constituents that elections draw off the minds of the people from neces-sary labour; or, if a war should exist, they may shew the impossibility of holding elections when there is a chance of the militia being called into the field to oppose a common enemy: Or lastly, they may fetter elections with oaths in such a manner as to exclude nine-tenths of the electors from voting. Such stratagems for perpetual power will never want men nor a *society* of men to support them; for the Assembly possesses such a plenitude of power from the influence of the many offices of profit and honour that are in their gift, that they may always promise themselves support from a great part of the state. But I will suppose that no infringement is ever made upon annual elections. In the course of even one year a single Assembly may do the most irreparable mischief to a state. Socrates and Barnevelt were both put to death by Assemblies that held their powers at the election of the people. The same Assemblies would have shed oceans of tears to have recalled those illustrious citizens to life again, in less than half a year after they imbrued their hands in their blood.

I am highly pleased with having the doors of our Assembly kept constantly open; but how can this check the proceedings of the Assembly, when none but a few citizens of the town or county, where the Assembly sits, or a few travelling strangers, can ever attend or watch them?

I shall take no notice of the delays of business, which must arise from publishing all laws for the consideration and assent of the people; but I beg to be informed *how long* they must be published before they are passed? For I take it for granted, that each county has a right to equal degrees of time to consider of the laws. In what manner are they to be circulated? How are the sentiments of the people, scattered over a county fifty or sixty miles in extent, to be collected? Whether by ballot, or by voting in a tumultuary manner? These are insurmountable difficulties in the way of the people at *large* acting as a check upon the Assembly. But supposing an attempt should be made to restrain the single legislature in this manner, are we sure the disapprobation of the people would be sufficient to put a negative upon improper or arbitrary laws? Would not the Assembly, from their partiality to their own proceedings, be apt to pass over the complaints of the people in silence? to neglect or refuse to enter their petitions or remonstrances upon their Journals? or to raise the hue and cry of a fostered junto upon them, as "tories," or "*apostate whigs*," or "*an aristocratic faction?*"

To talk of the Council of Censors, as a check upon the Assembly, is to forget that a man or a body of men may deceive, rob, and enslave the public for seven years, and then may escape the intended efficacy of the censures of the Council by death, or by flying into a neighbouring state.

10. We are informed that a single legislature was supported in the Convention by Dr. Franklin, and assented to by Mr. Rittenhouse; gentlemen distinguished for their uncommon abilities, and deservedly dear for their virtues to every lover of human nature. The only answer, after what has been said, that I shall give to this argument, is that Divine Providence seems to have permitted them to *err* upon this subject, in order to console the world for the very great superiority they both possess over the rest of mankind in every thing else, except the science of government.

Thus have I answered all the arguments that ever I have heard offered in favour of a single legislature, and I hope, silenced all the objections that have been made to a double representation of the people. I might here appeal further to the practice of our courts of law in favour of repeated deliberations and divisions. In a free government, the most inconsiderable portion of our liberty and property cannot be taken from us, without the judgment of two or three courts; but, by the Constitution of Pennsylvania, the whole of our liberty and property, and even our lives, may be taken from us, by the hasty and passionate decision of a single Assembly.

I shall conclude my observations upon this part of the Constitution, by summing up the advantages of a compound or double legislature.

1. There is the utmost *freedom* in a compound legislature. The decisions of two legislative bodies cannot fail of coinciding with the wills of a great majority of the community.

2. There is *safety* in such a government, in as much as each body possesses a free and independant power, so that they mutually check ambition and usurpation in each other.

3. There is the greatest *wisdom* in such a government. Every act being obliged to undergo the revision and amendments of two bodies of men, is necessarily strained of every mixture of folly, passion, and prejudice.

4. There is the longest *duration* of freedom in such a government.

5. There is the most *order* in such a government. By order, I mean obedience to laws, subordination to magistrates, civility and decency of behaviour, and the contrary of every thing like mobs and factions.

6. Compound governments are most agreeable to *human nature,* inasmuch as they afford the greatest scope for the expansion of the powers and virtues of the mind. Wisdom, learning, experience, with the most extensive benevolence, the most unshaken firmness, and the utmost elevation of soul, are all called into exercise by the opposite and different duties of the different representations of the people.

Letter III

THE powers of government have been very justly divided into legislative, executive and judicial. Having discussed the legislative power of the government of Pennsylvania, I shall proceed now to consider the executive and judicial.

It is agreed on all hands that the executive and judicial powers of government should be *wholly independant* of the legislative. The authors of the Pennsylvania Constitution *seem* to have given their sanction to this opinion, by separating those powers from the powers of the Assembly.---It becomes us to enquire whether they have made them so independant of the Assembly as to give them the free exercise of their own judgments.

The insignificant figure the President and Council make in the Constitution from not having a negative upon the laws of the Assembly, alone would soon have destroyed their authority and influence in the State. But the authors of the Constitution have taken pains to throw the whole power of the Council at once into the hands of the Assembly, by rendering the former dependant upon the latter in the two following particulars,

1. The President is chosen by the joint ballot of the Assembly and Council. The Assembly being to the Council, in point of numbers, as five are to one, of course chuse the President. Each member will expect in his turn to fill the first chair in the State, and hence the whole Council will yield themselves up to the will of the Assembly.

2. The salaries of the President and of each of the Counsellors are fixed by the Assembly. This will necessarily render them dependant upon them. It is worthy of notice here, that a rotation is established in the 19th section of the Constitution, to "prevent the danger of an inconvenient aristocracy." ---From what abuse of power can this aristocracy arise? Are they not the creatures of the Assembly? But there is a magic terror in the sound of a Counsellor. Call a man an Assemblyman, or a Censor, and he becomes an innocent creature, though you invest him with the despotism of an eastern monarch. If the Council are dependant upon the Assembly, it follows of course that the Judges, who are appointed by the Council, are likewise dependant upon them. But in order more fully to secure their dependance upon the will of the Assembly, they are obliged to hold their salaries upon the tenure of their will. In vain do they hold their commissions for seven years. This is but the shadow of independance. They cannot live upon the air, and their absolute dependance upon the Assembly gives that body a

transcendent influence over all the courts of law in the State. Here then we have discovered the legislative, executive and judicial powers of the State all blended together.---The liberty, the property and life of every individual in the State are laid prostrate by the Constitution at the feet of the Assembly. This combination of powers in one body has in all ages been pronounced a tyranny. To live by one man's will became the cause of all men's misery; but better, far better, would it be to live by the will of one man, than to live, or rather to die, by the will of a body of men. Unhappy Pennsylvania! Methinks I see the scales of justice broken in thy courts.---I see the dowry of the widow and the portion of the orphans unjustly taken from them, in order to gratify the avarice of some demagogue who rules the Assembly by his eloquence and arts.---I see the scaffolds streaming with the blood of the wisest and best men in the State.---I see the offices of government------But the prospect is too painful, I shall proceed to take notice of some other parts of the Constitution.

It was not sufficient to contaminate justice at its fountain, but its smallest streams are made to partake of impurity by the Convention. In the 30th section of the Constitution "all Justices of the Peace are to be elected by the freeholders of each city and county." The best observations that can be made on this part of the Constitution is to inform the public, that not above one half the people of the State chose magistrates agreeable to the laws of the Assembly for that purpose; that more than one half of those that were chosen have refused to accept of commissions, and that many of those who act are totally disqualified from the want of education or leisure for the office.---It has been said often, and I wish the saying was engraven over the doors of every statehouse on the Continent, that "all power is *derived* from the people," but it has never yet been said that all power is *seated* in the people. Government supposes and requires a delegation of power: It cannot exist without it. And the idea of making the people at large judges of the qualifications necessary for magistrates, or judges of laws, or checks for Assemblies proceeds upon the supposition that mankind are all alike wise, and just, and have equal leisure. It moreover destroys the necessity for all government. What man ever made himself his own attorney? And yet this would not be more absurd than for the people at *large* to pretend to give up their power to a set of rulers, and afterwards reserve the right of making and of judging of all their laws themselves. Such a government is a monster in nature. It contains as many Governors, Assemblymen, Judges and Magistrates as there are freemen in the State, all exercising the same powers and at the same time. Happy would it be for us, if this monster was remarkable only for his absurdity; but alas! he contains a tyrant in his bowels. All history shews us that the people soon grow weary of the folly and tyranny of one another. They prefer one to many masters, and stability to instability of slavery. They prefer a Julius Cæsar to a Senate, and a Cromwell to a perpetual parliament.

I cannot help thinking a mistake lays rather in words than ideas when we talk of the rights of the people. Where is the difference between my chusing a Justice of Peace, and my chusing an Assemblyman and a Counsellor, by whose joint suffrages a Governor is chosen, who appoints a Justice for me? I am still the first link of the sacred chain of the power of the State. But are there no cases in which I may be bound by acts of a single, or of a body of magistrates in the State, whom I have had no hand in chusing? Yes, there are. Here then I am bound contrary to the principles of liberty (which consist in a man being governed by men chosen by himself), whereas if all the magistrates in the State were appointed by the Governor, or executive part of the State, it would be impossible for me to appear before the bar of a magistrate any where who did not derive his power *originally* from me.

By the 5th section all militia officers below the rank of a Brigadier General are to be chosen by the people. Most of the objections that have been mentioned against magistrates being chosen by the people, apply with equal force against the people's chusing their military officers. . . .

But, is there no power lodged in the Constitution to alter these imperfections? Has our Convention monopolized all the wisdom of succeeding years, so as to preclude any improvements being made in the infant science of government? Must we groan away our lives in a patient submission to all the evils in the Constitution which have been described? Let the 47th and last section of the Constitution answer these questions. By this section it is declared, that after the expiration of seven years, there shall "be chosen two men from each city and county, (a majority of whom shall be a quorum in every case, except as to *calling a Convention*) who shall be called a Council of Censors, and who shall have power to call a Convention within two years after their sitting, if there appears to them an absolute necessity of amending any article of the Constitution which may be defective, explaining such as may be thought not clearly expressed, and of adding such as are necessary for the preservation of the rights and happiness of the people." . . .

They are empowered . . . "to enquire, whether the *Constitution* has been preserved *inviolate* in *every* part? and whether the legislative and executive branches of government have performed their duty, as guardians of the people; or assumed to themselves, or exercised *other* or greater powers than they are entitled to by the Constitution: They are also to enquire, whether the public taxes have been justly laid and collected in all parts of this commonwealth;----in what manner the public monies have been disposed of, and whether the laws have been duly executed: For these purposes they shall have power to send for persons, papers and records; they shall have authority to pass public censures, and to recommend to the legislature, the repealing such laws as appear to them to have been enacted contrary to the principles of the Constitution: These powers they shall continue to have for, and during the space of one year, from the day of their election, and no longer."

Is this the commission of the Grand Turk? or is it an extract from an act of the British Parliament, teeming with vengeance against the liberties of America?----No.----It is an epitome of the powers of the Council of Censors established by the late Convention of Pennsylvania. Innocence has nothing to fear from justice, when it flows through the regular channels of law; but where is the man who can ensure himself a moment's safety from a body of men, invested with absolute power for one whole year to censure and condemn, without judge or jury, every individual in the State. . . .

But perhaps the Constitution has provided a remedy for its defects, without the aid of the Council of Censors? No---this cannot be done; for every Member of Assembly, before he takes his seat, is obliged, by the 10th section of the Constitution to swear that he will not "do nor consent to any act whatever, that shall have a tendency to lessen or abridge their rights and privileges as declared *in the Constitution of this State*," as also, "that he will not directly or indirectly do or consent to any act or thing prejudicial or injurious to the Constitution or Government thereof, as *established by the Convention*," agreeably to the 40th section of the Constitution. These oaths of infallibility and passive obedience to the form of the Constitution, effectually preclude every man, who holds an office under it, from attempting to procure the least amendment in any part of it. . . .

Had the Constitution appeared to me to have been unexceptionable in every part, and had it been the result of the united wisdom of men and angels, I would not have taken an oath of passive obedience to it, for seven or nine years. The constant changes in human affairs, and in the dispositions of a people, might render occasional alterations, in that time, necessary in the most perfect Constitution. But to take an oath of allegiance to a Constitution,---full of experiments,---a Constitution that was indeed a new thing under the sun,----that had never been tried in some of its parts in *any* country,---and that had produced misery in other of its parts in *every* country.---I say to swear to support or even to submit, for seven or nine years, to such a Constitution, is to trifle with all morality, and to dishonour the sacred name of GOD himself. . . .

It is to no purpose to talk here of the many excellent articles in the Bill of Rights; such as religious toleration,---the habeas corpus act,---trials by juries,---the rotation of office, &c. None of them can flourish long in the neighbourhood of a single Assembly, and a Council of Censors possessing all the powers of the State.------These inestimable privileges in the Constitution of Pennsylvania resemble a tree loaded with the most luscious fruit, but surrounded with thorns, in such a manner, as to be for ever inaccessible to the hungry traveller.

Perhaps, while the government is upon its good behaviour, and while the passions of the State are directed against a cruel and common enemy, we may not experience all the calamities that have been demonstrated to flow from the Constitution.------But the revolution of a few years, and the return of peace, will most certainly render Pennsylvania, under her present Constitution, the most miserable spot upon the surface of the globe. . . .

B. WEAKNESSES OF THE VIRGINIA CONSTITUTION: THOMAS JEFFERSON, "NOTES ON THE STATE OF VIRGINIA" (1781–1782)*

This constitution was formed when we were new and unexperienced, in the science of government. It was the first too which was formed in the whole United States. No wonder then that time and trial have discovered very capital defects in it.

1. The majority of the men in the state, who pay and fight for its support, are unrepresented in the legislature, the roll of freeholders entitled to vote, not including generally the half of those on the roll of the militia, or of the tax-gatherers.

2. Among those who share the representation, the shares are very unequal. Thus the county of Warwick, with only 100 fighting men, has an equal

* These excerpts are reprinted from the eighth American edition (1801), pp. 171–178, 183–185, 188–190.

representation with the county of Loudon, which has 1746. So that every man in Warwick has as much influence in the government as 17 men in Loudon. But lest it should be thought that an equal interspersion of small among large counties, through the whole state, may prevent any danger of injury to particular parts of it, we will divide it into districts, and show the proportions of land, of fighting men, and of representation in each.

	Square miles	Fighting men	Dele- gates	Sena- tors
Between the sea-coast and falls of the rivers	11,205	19,012	71	12
Between the falls of the rivers and the Blue ridge of mountains	18,759	18,828	46	8
Between the Blue ridge and the Alleghaney	11,911	7,673	16	2
Between the Alleghaney and Ohio	79,650	4,458	16	2
Total	121,525	49,971	149	24

An inspection into this table will supply the place of commentaries on it. It will appear at once that 19,000 men, living below the falls of the rivers possess half the senate, and want four members only of possessing a majority of the house of delegates; a want more than supplied by the vicinity of their situation to the seat of our government, and of course the greater degree of convenience and punctuality with which their members may add will attend in the legislature. These 19,000 therefore, living in one part of the country, give law to upwards of 30,000 living in another, and appoint all their chief officers executive and judiciary. From the difference of their situation and circumstances, their interests will often be very different.

3. The senate, by its constitution, too homogenious with the house of delegates. Being chosen by the same electors at the same time, and out of the same subjects, the choice falls of course on men of the same description. The purpose of establishing different houses of legislation is to introduce the influence of different interests or different principles. Thus in Great-Britain it is said their constitution relies on the house of commons for honesty, and the lords for wisdom; which would be a rational reliance if honesty were to be bought with money, and if wisdom were hereditary. In some of the American states the delegates and senators are so chosen, as that the first represent the persons, and the second the property of the state. But with us, wealth and wisdom have equal chance for admission into both houses. We do not therefore derive from the separation of our legislature into two houses, those benefits which a proper complication of principles is capable of producing, and those which alone can compensate the evils which may be produced by their dissentions.

4. All the powers of government, legislative, executive, and judiciary, result to the legislative body. The concentrating these in the same hands is precisely the definition of despotic government. It will be no alleviation that these powers will be exercised by a plurality of hands, and not by a single one: 173 despots would surely be as oppressive as one. Let those who doubt it turn their eyes on the republic of Venice. As little will it avail us that they are chosen by ourselves. An *elective despotism* was not the government

we fought for; but one which should not only be founded upon free principles, but in which the powers of government should be so divided and balanced among several bodies of magistracy, as that no one could transcend their legal limits, without being effectually checked and restrained by the others. For this reason that convention, which passed the ordinance of government, laid its foundation on this basis, that the legislative, executive and judiciary departments should be separate and distinct, so that no person should exercise the powers of more than one of them at the same time. But no barrier was provided between these several powers. The judiciary and executive members were left dependant on the legislative for their subsistence in office, and some of them for their continuance in it. If therefore the legislature assumes executive and judiciary powers, no opposition is likely to be made; nor, if made, can it be effectual; because in that case they may put their proceedings into the form of an act of assembly, which will render them obligatory on the other branches. They have accordingly, in many instances, decided rights which should have been left to judiciary controversy: and the direction of the executive, during the whole time of their session, is becoming habitual and familiar. And this is done with no ill intention. The views of the present members are perfectly upright. When they are led out of their regular province, it is by art in others, and inadvertence in themselves. And this will probably be the case for some time to come. But it will not be a very long time. Mankind soon learn to make interested uses of every right and power which they possess or may assume. The public money and public liberty, intended to have been deposited with three branches of magistracy but found inadvertently to be in the hands of one only, will soon be discovered to be sources of wealth and dominion to those who hold them; distinguished too by this tempting circumstance, that they are the instrument, as well as the object of acquisition. With money we will get men, said Cæsar, and with men we will get money. Nor should our assembly be deluded by the integrity of their own purposes, and conclude that these unlimited powers will never be abused, because themselves are not disposed to abuse them. They should look forward to a time, and that not a distant one, when corruption in this, as in the country from which we derived our origin, will have seized the heads of government, and be spread by them through the body of the people; when they will purchase the voices of the people, and make them pay the price. Human nature is the same on every side of the Atlantic, and will be alike influenced by the same causes. The time to guard against corruption and tyranny, is before they shall have gotten hold on us. It is better to keep the wolf out of the fold, than to trust to drawing his teeth and talons after he shall have entered. To render these considerations the more cogent, we must observe in addition.

5. That the ordinary legislature may alter the constitution itself. On the discontinuance of the assemblies, it became necessary to substitute in their place some other body, competent to the ordinary business of government, and to the calling forth the powers of the state for the maintenance of our opposition to Great-Britain. Conventions were therefore introduced, consisting of two delegates from each county, meeting together and forming one house, on the plan of the former house of burgesses, to whose places they succeeded. These were at first chosen anew for every particular session. But in March 1775 they recommended to the people to choose a convention, which should continue in office a year. This was done accordingly in April

1775, and in the July following that convention passed an ordinance for the election of delegates in the month of April annually. It is well known, that in July 1775, a separation from Great-Britain and establishment of republican government had never yet entered into any person's mind. A convention therefore chosen under that ordinance, cannot be said to have been chosen for the purposes which certainly did not exist in the minds of those who passed it. Under this ordinance, at the annual election in April 1776, a convention for the year was chosen. Independence, and the establishment of a new form of government, were not even yet the objects of the people at large. One extract from the pamphlet called Common Sense had appeared in the Virginia papers in February, and copies of the pamphlet itself had got into a few hands. But the idea had not been opened to the mass of the people in April, much less can it be said that they had made up their minds in its favor. So that the electors of April 1776, no more than the legislators of July 1775, not thinking of independence and a permanent republic, could not mean to vest in these delegates powers of establishing them, or any authorities other than those of the ordinary legislature. So far as a temporary organization of government was necessary to render our opposition energetic, so far their organization was valid. But they received in their creation no powers but what were given to every legislature before and since. They could not therefore pass an act transcendant to the powers of other legislatures. If the present assembly pass an act, and declare it shall be irrevocable by subsequent assemblies, the declaration is merely void, and the act repealable, as other acts are. So far, and no farther authorised, they organized the government by the ordinance entitled a constitution or form of government. It pretends to no higher authority than the other ordinances of the same session; it does not say that it shall be perpetual; that it shall be unalterable by other legislatures; that it shall be transcendant above the powers of those, who they knew would have equal power with themselves. Not only the silence of the instrument is a proof they thought it would be alterable, but their own practice also; for this very convention, meeting as a house of delegates in general assembly with the senate in the autumn of that year, passed acts of assembly in contradiction to their ordinance of government: and every assembly from that time to this has done the same. I am safe therefore in the position, that the constitution itself is alterable by the ordinary legislature. . . .

6. That the assembly exercises a power of determining a quorum of their own body which may legislate for us. After the establishment of the new form they adhere to the *Lex majoris partis,* founded in common law as well as common right. It is the natural law of every assembly of men, whose numbers are not fixed by any other law. They continued for some time to require the presence of a majority of their whole number, to pass an act. But the British parliament fixes its own quorum: our former assemblies fixed their own quorum: and one precedent in favor of power is stronger than an hundred against it. The house of delegates therefore have lately voted that, during the present dangerous invasion, forty members shall be a house to proceed to business. They have been moved to this by the fear of not being able to collect a house. But this danger could not authorise them to call that a house which was none: and if they may fix it at one number, they may at another, till it loses its fundamental character of being a representative body. As this vote expires with the present invasion, it is probable the

former rule will be permitted to revive: because at present no ill is meant. The power however of fixing their own quorum has been avowed, and a precedent set. From forty it may be reduced to four, and from four to one: from a house to a committee, from a committee to a chairman or speaker, and thus an oligarchy or monarchy be substituted under forms supposed to be regular. . . . When therefore it is considered, that there is no legal obstacle to the assumption by the assembly of all the powers legislative, executive, and judiciary, and that these may come to the hands of the smallest rag of delegation, surely the people will say, and their representatives, while yet they have honest representatives, will advise them to say, that they will not acknowledge as laws any acts not considered and assented to by the major part of their delegates.

In enumerating the defects of the constitution, it would be wrong to count among them what is only the error of particular persons. In December 1776, our circumstances being much distressed, it was proposed in the house of delegates to create a *dictator,* invested with every power legislative, executive and judiciary, civil and military, of life and death, over our persons and over our properties: and in June 1781, again under calamity, the same proposition was repeated, and wanted a few votes only of being passed. One who entered into this contest from a pure love of liberty, and a sense of injured rights, who determined to make every sacrifice, and to meet every danger, for the re-establishment of those rights on a firm basis, who did not mean to expend his blood and substance for the wretched purpose of changing this master for that, but to place the powers of governing him in a plurality of hands of his own choice, so that the corrupt will of no one man might in future oppress him, must stand confounded and dismayed when he is told that a considerable portion of that plurality had meditated the surrender of them into a single hand, and, in lieu of a limited monarchy, to deliver him over to a despotic one! How must we find his efforts and sacrifices abused and baffled, if he may still by a single vote be laid prostrate at the feet of one man? In God's name from whence have they derived this power? . . .

The advocates for this measure . . . had been seduced in their judgment by the example of an ancient republic, whose constitution and circumstances were fundamentally different. They had sought this precedent in the history of Rome, where alone it was to be found, and where at length too it had proved fatal. They had taken it from a republic rent by the most bitter factions and tumults, where the government was of a heavy-handed unfeeling aristocracy, over a people ferocious, and rendered desperate by poverty and wretchedness; tumults which could not be allayed under the most trying circumstances, but by the omnipotent hand of a single despot. Their constitution therefore allowed a temporary tyrant to be erected, under the name of a dictator; and that temporary tyrant after a few examples became perpetual.—They misapplied this precedent to a people, mild in their dispositions, patient under their trial, united for the public liberty, and affectionate to their leaders. But if from the constitution of the Roman government there resulted to their senate a power of submitting all their rights to the will of one man, does it follow, that the assembly of Virginia, have the same authority? What clause in our constitution has substituted that of Rome, by way of residuary provision, for all cases not otherwise provided for? Or if they may step ad libitum into any other form of government for precedents to rule us by, for what oppression may not a precedent be found in this world . . . ?—Searching for the foundations of this proposition, I can find none which may pretend a color of right or reason, but the defect before developed, that there being no barrier between the legislature, executive, and judiciary departments, the legislature may seize the whole: that having seized it, and possessing a right to fix their own quorum, they may reduce that quorum to one, whom they may call a chairman, speaker, dictator, or by any other name they please.—Our situation is indeed perilous, and I hope my countrymen will be sensible of it, and will apply, at a proper season the proper remedy; which is a convention to fix the constitution, to amend its defects, to bind up the several branches of government by certain laws, which when they transgress their acts shall become nullities; to render unnecessary an appeal to the people, or in other words a rebellion, on every infraction of their rights, on the peril that their acquiescence shall be construed into an intention to surrender those rights.

PART NINE

Transformation: The Revolution in Ideals

SELECTION  **38**

"The Perfection and Happiness of Mankind": Samuel Williams, "A Discourse on the Love of Our Country" (Dec. 15, 1774)

If most American Revolutionary leaders were uneasy about the internal state of American society and concerned to establish constitutional safeguards to protect that society from both the British and their own imperfect natures, there was a significant minority, largely on the fringes of political life and especially numerous among the evangelical clergy, who had a much more optimistic view of the current and future state of American life. Representative of this group was Samuel Williams (1743–1817), pastor of the First Church in Bradford, Massachusetts, whose sermon A Discourse on the Love of Our Country *was delivered on December 15, 1774, a day of thanksgiving set aside by Congress, and is reprinted in part below from the original edition (1775), pages 5–10, 12–18, 20–29.*

Most of the early portions of this sermon were simply a restatement of conventional social theory about the obligations of citizens to their country, but in a final section dealing with the "particular reasons and motives" Americans had to love their country Williams attempted to show how the development of the colonies was a standing proof of the thesis he advanced in his first sentence: that God had "made the human race capable of continual advances towards a state of perfection and happiness." The high degree of "Toleration and Liberty of Conscience" in religion, the "free and equal . . . system of civil government," and the great amount of social freedom enjoyed by the colonists were all compelling reasons for the deep attachment of every American to his "native country" and an unmistakable indication that the extraordinary prosperity and virtue already attained by the colonists were only the first step in the fulfillment of God's designs for America, a certain sign "that the perfection and happiness of mankind is to be carried further in America, than it has ever yet been in any place." With the rest of the world rapidly sinking under the "yoke of universal slavery" into a state of corruption, misery, and despair, the "North-American provinces" remained "the country of free men: The Asylum" in which the oppressed of Europe could find sanctuary and the instrument by which God would lead "the way to a more perfect and happy state." By requiring a vigorous exertion of moral energy and a "steady regard to the rules . . . of personal and social virtue," by forcing the colonists to exorcise whatever "fatal arts of luxury and corruption" had found their way into the American social fabric, the contest with Britain, Williams strongly implied, could only hasten the arrival of the "new æra." The preservation of American liberty was moreover absolutely necessary if human nature was ever to regain "its first and original dignity." On the success of American resistance thus rested the fate of mankind.

The millenarian character of such thinking—the sense of mission, the expectation of not just material but moral progress, the suggestion that human nature itself might ultimately be restored to its original perfect state in the new American Eden—gave the Revolution some distinctly radical intellectual undertones. It would be another fifty years before these early impulses would be transformed into fully articulated articles of belief and gradually transferred from the edges to the center of American intellectual life. Considerable evidence during the Revolution itself, however, indicated that that transformation and transfer were already underway.

Though it is limited almost entirely to a discussion of religious literature, the

376

most penetrating and comprehensive study of the millenarian thought of the Revolution is Alan Heimert, Religion and the American Mind from the Great Awakening to the Revolution *(1966).*

IF I forget thee, O Jerusalem, let my right hand forget her cunning. If I do remember thee, let my tongue cleave to the roof of my mouth; if I prefer not Jerusalem above my chief joy.

PSALM cxxxvii. 5, 6.

THE wise and benevolent Author of nature has made the human race capable of continual advances towards a state of perfection and happiness. All those religious institutions which God has appointed among mankind, are evidently designed and adapted to promote this end. And this is what human wisdom has been aiming at by the various methods of education, instruction, laws, and government. To a virtuous mind, nothing can yield a more rational or benevolent pleasure, than to see this great design taking place, in the increase and progress of human happiness: To all the friends of mankind, such views and prospects cannot but prove one of their chief joys. And the same benevolence that leads us to rejoice in human happiness, will make us feel for mankind on the approach of their adversities and sufferings: Feelings which become strong and painful, in proportion to the degree and extent of the miseries and calamities of our fellow men.

IN what manner they will operate on such occasions, you have a natural and beautiful description in that passage of holy scripture which has now been read. It is designed to represent the language and the affections of the children of Israel, when they were carried from their native country. Infinite wisdom had seen fit to put that people under a more excellent constitution of government, than any other nation has ever had. God himself was their King. And they might have been long happy under a government, in which, the Ruler of the world condescended himself to execute the office of Chief-Magistrate. But such was their impiety and folly, that in many instances they greatly abused and perverted the privileges they were favoured with. As the just punishment of their sin and folly, God gave them up to the power of their enemies. Nebuchadnezzar king of Babylon prevailed over them in battle. Being brought under his power, they soon found what the insolence of victory, and what the fate of a conquered people generally is. From liberty, peace, and plenty, in their own land, they were carried away to endure all the miseries of subjection and slavery, in a kingdom where no other law or liberty was known to them, but the arbitrary will of a proud, cruel, despotic monarch.

ON such an occasion and in such a state, Nature felt her aversion to slavery, and her love of freedom. As the unhappy people "sat down by the rivers of Babylon they wept when they remembered" their native country "Zion." In vain did their new masters call them to be pleased with the condition they had assigned to them; or to put forth songs of joy under their new constitution. Nature felt for, and she acted like herself, in this unhappy people. The idea of their former happy days, was constantly returning to their minds. But amidst all their gloomy prospects, the interest and welfare of their country lay nearest to their hearts. With a beauty, force, and energy, that nothing but this noble patriotic passion could inspire, the author in the psalm, in the language of his own feelings, thus expresseth the love, regard, and attachment, they *all* bore to her,—*If I forget thee, O Jerusalem, let my right hand forget her cunning. If I do not remember thee, let my tongue cleave to the roof of my mouth; if I prefer not Jerusalem above my chief joy.* q. d. "Wheresoever I am carried, or whatever I endure, I shall never forget my native country. The right hand might as well forget her motions; the tongue might as well lie dumb, as that I should cease to remember and love her. For in her welfare and prosperity, my chief joy and pleasure lies."

Such was the regard God's people of old, bore to their native country. And verily, my Brethren, if we except the Love of God, a nobler principle never entered the heart of man. To love our friends, to love our neighbours, is the character of a benevolent mind: But how much more extensive and worthy of praise, is that benevolence that reaching out to all mankind, takes in and embraces her country, in the most strong and affectionate manner? . . .

And here it is to be observed, that Love to our country supposes that there is a proper community, or public society formed. Were there no other associations among mankind, but those of lawless, desperate, and designing men, joined together for the purposes of fraud, rapine, and oppression; such an assembly would not be a society, which, as such, would deserve our regard: But ought rather to be esteemed a body injurious to the interests of mankind; and which, as the friends of human happiness, we must wish to see dissolved, and broken in pieces. The same may be said of uncivilized tribes; of all combinations among tyrants and robbers; and of all the unnatural associations that have, or may take place, among the enemies of mankind. In such cases there is no *Public*, there is no *State*, or *Country*, which as a society or body politic, ought to be esteemed or regarded. We must therefore first of all suppose, a real and proper community, or state of civil society, to have taken place.

As our Maker designed us for such a state, he has given us natures adapted to, and tending towards it. The disadvantages of a solitary state are so many and obvious, that they must have been early, and unavoidably felt. To avoid these, and with a view to enjoy the many advantages no otherwise to be had, mankind naturally fell into the practice of resolving themselves into a social state: Combining together in some form of society, for the purposes of mutual benefit, protection, and defence. And as they early found the necessity of forming themselves into a social state, they must also have soon found the necessity of some general rules and measures to regulate and govern their conduct towards each other. This unavoidably lead them to form laws and rules of action; and of consequence to appoint some to see that these laws and rules were duly observed. And hence government and order arose. Time and necessity ripened the first, rude, unfinished plan. And in the revolutions of time, wisdom gathered from their own errors, wants, necessities and experience, and from the conduct and measures of others; rendered that tolerably well adjusted, and proportioned, which at first was in a very indigested imperfect state. In a way somewhat similar to this, we may suppose mankind were lead into those social combinations, which in a long series of ages, under gradual improvements, grew up to the form of large, powerful, well-regulated states.

Such a state of society constituted by *common reason*, and formed on the plan of a *common interest,* is one of the most necessary and useful regulations that ever took place among mankind. We have many affections which a solitary life would give us little room to exercise or cultivate. We have many wants and necessities belonging to our condition, which nothing can tolerably well supply, but an extensive intercourse between man and man. There are many dangers to which we are exposed, against which no defence can be made, without more power and strength than our own. And there are many difficulties against which we cannot guard, without the council, wisdom, and help of others. We cannot therefore either improve or enjoy ourselves as God designed, but in a state of society. And a state of society will necessarily bring in some constitution and form of government, some general plan and system of laws; which on the one hand, will point out the office and power of rulers; and on the other, the privileges and duty of subjects. Every such society will also have some general dominions to be defended; wants, to be provided for; interests, to be promoted; and dangers, to be guarded against. And that which can alone constitute the security, defence, and protection of every part; is the common wisdom, strength, and safety of the whole.

AND from this, we may collect what is the *nature* and *ground* of Love to our country. The great community of which we are a part, is such a body politic, or well-regulated society. And to this society we are joined, by many and strong connections. We live in her dominions; we believe in her religion; we think her laws and government are best suited to our state, disposition, temper, and climate; and we partake in all her calamities and prosperity.— Joined to our country by such numerous, extensive, and lasting ties, she becomes the object of our attention, veneration, reverence, and regard. And that regard or affection which is our duty to her, extends to all her interests and connections: It takes in her dominions, her religious interests, her constitution, her laws, her liberties, her people, and her happiness. In a word, it takes in her general and particular interests, welfare, and good. By the Love of our country then, we are to understand a regard and affection to the *common good;* to the interest and welfare of that community, or body politic, of which we are a part. . . .

As society is combined together for the purposes of mutual benefit and advantage, *the common good* of the whole, greatly depends on individuals being subject to the laws of their country, and faithfully performing the business and duties of their station. This only makes them good members of society. One great point therefore, which all wise rulers must ever have in view, is to effect this: To find out such principles, and to make use of such arts, as tend to bind together the various parts of which the body politic consists; and to give such a direction to the views and conduct of individuals, as shall make them subject and useful to the state. As different governments are founded on different principles, and moved by different springs, the ways and methods by which rulers aim to effect this, are very different. In *a despotic government,* the only principle by which the Tyrant who is to move the whole machine, means to regulate and manage the people, is *Fear;* by a servile dread of his power. But *a free government,* which of all others is far the most preferable, cannot be supported without *Virtue.* This virtue is the Love of our country. And after all the devices that sound policy or the most refined corruption have, or can suggest; this is the most efficacious principle to hold the different parts of an empire together, and to make men good members of the society to which they belong. Other principles of political obedience if they are unconnected with this, will in a course of time interfere, clash, oppose, and destroy each other's influence: Or else, and which is more likely and infinitely worse, they will jointly operate to destroy virtue, and to produce universal vice and oppression. But Virtue, like gravitation, will ever draw towards the common centre. And so long as this can be kept up, the rulers and the people, by its influence, will be kept in that place, and move in that course, which the laws of their country have assigned to them. And this is the only way to have the state prosperous, and the members good subjects of it.

THERE are no people but what seem to be in some degree attached to their native country. But there are none among mankind, that have more just and weighty reasons for it, than we.   Thus,

1. THE *Religion of our country* may be named as a primary and important consideration, which cannot but greatly endear our country to us. Religion is one of those concerns, that will always be of great importance to the state. The operations of this principle, though often silent, are generally of the most extensive and powerful kind. When it inspires men with reverence to the Deity, and with benevolence to each other, it proves one of the main pillars and springs of a free and equal government. But when it degenerates into enthusiasm, fanaticism, and extravagance, it produces a spirit of *levelism* and fierceness; which, with a blind fiery zeal, pulls down government, rulers, church, state, science, and morals, into one general and common ruin. It is therefore of the greatest importance to societies, that their religion be such, that while it leads men to be looking for perfect felicity in another life, it should promote their peace, order, comfort, and happiness, in this.—And such is the *religion* that we profess. What Christianity aims to form us to, is the love of God, and man. Towards the Deity, it enjoins love, reverence, and veneration: Towards men, it teaches righteousness, justice, benevolence, and every social virtue. Towards rulers, it requires respect, submission, and obedience, so long as they continue the ministers of God for the public good. Nothing can be better adapted than such a religion to give life, energy, and force, to all useful civil institutions and regulations.——Among the various *forms* and *constitutions* in which it is established, we think nothing is more agreeable to its nature, or less liable to inconveniences, than that every one should be left to his own freedom and choice. It was the happiness of our fathers to be descended from ancestors who lived in the most enlightned part of the old world; and at a time when the human understanding began to exert itself. Their situation enabled them to profit by the errors and mistakes, as well as from the wisdom and knowledge of the mother-country. Time and sufferings fully taught them what must be the effect of endeavouring to inforce *uniformity,* in doctrine or discipline. This, with the gradual improvement of the human mind that has since taken place, has been leading these colonies into that truly righteous and catholic principle, *Universal Toleration, and Liberty of Conscience;* which, if not already perfect, we are in the sure path to. We have indeed the various names of *Episcopalians, Presbyterians, Congregationalists, Baptists, Friends, &c.* The fierce and bigotted of each party, may be inflamed with a desire of establishing themselves, upon the destruction of the rest. But whatever temporary enthusiasm this may occasion in the minds of a few, it can never succeed. The different parties among us will subsist, and grow up into more large and respectable bodies. And the mutual interests and wisdom of all, cannot fail to perfect that universal toleration and liberty of conscience, which is so generally and well begun. . . . If we are to judge of the spirit and forms of a religion by the effect they have on the *morals* of a people, though we have reason for deep humiliation before God on account of our sins, yet modesty will allow us to say, among all the relations we can

find of the present state of mankind, we can find none in which the state of their morals is represented as being better than it is with us. The poor instead of being sunk into that general licentiousness, profligacy and dissoluteness of manners, of which there is so much complaint in the ancient countries; are, for the most part, industrious, frugal, and honest. We have few so corrupted with riches, as to be above all other pursuits but those of luxury, indolence, amusement, and pleasure. Chastity is yet the common virtue, boast, and glory of the one sex: Industry, sobriety, and hospitality, make part of the general character of the other.. . .

2. NEXT to religion, the most important concern to mankind, is to have a wise and good *civil Government* established among them: And this is another of those reasons and motives, that may well attach us to our native country. Much has been said by political writers to point out the advantages and disadvantages, that arise from, or are connected with, the several forms of government. That government must upon the whole be esteemed best for a people, which is best suited to their temper and genius; to the nature of their soil, and climate; to their situation, extent, connections, dangers, and wants: the ways of subsistance, the occupations, and employments, that nature has assigned to them.—On such, and on all accounts, *a free and equal government* is best suited to our infant and rising state. And such was the system of civil government that took place in these colonies, with a few exceptions, till the close of the last war. If in some parts of it, and in some of the colonies, it was less perfect than it might have been, and than time and encreasing knowledge and experience would have made it; taken together, it was such as we were content with, and happy under.—If we compare this system of government with the situation, state and wants of the colonies, it will appear to have been wisely adapted to promote their interest. It gave to the people here a share in their own government; and put us in the happy situation of being ruled by laws, to which we had consented, by representatives chosen from among ourselves. It secured us from oppression and plunder, by preserving to us the right of giving and granting our own money, for the support of government, and defence of the state; of both which the inhabitants of a country, must be the best judges. It provided for the administration of justice by means of that wisest and best of all civil regulations, *a trial by jury.* It made provision for improvements in knowledge, arts, and science, (which infant colonies greatly need) by the freedom of the press. But without entering into every particular, "this government carried prosperity along with it." We found its happy effects, in a rapid increase of our numbers; in a universal spirit of industry; in a gradual increase of wealth; and in a settled peace, quietness, and good order, among ourselves.. . .

SUCH has been the spirit and tendency of our civil government. We cannot but be attached to it, because we found ourselves prosperous and happy under it. We cannot but value it, because it attached and connected us so long and so firmly with Britain, the country of our friends and ancestors. And while we still look with veneration and reverence to that country, we cannot but bear the most affectionate regard to this; for we have found ourselves satisfied and happy, under the influence of her laws and government.

3. To these great blessings of religion and government we may add that of *Freedom* or *Liberty,* as another that must also lead us to love this our native country. In a state of nature all men are equal and free. By entering into society they give up many of their natural rights, in order to obtain those civil privileges without which they could not well subsist. "In every human society, there is an effort continually tending to confer on one part, the height of power and happiness; and to reduce the other, to the extreme of weakness and misery." And hence, many governments by force and fraud, have gradually extended their influence and power; till they have brought the people into such a total subjection to their rulers, as to leave them wholly at their mercy for whatever they enjoy. This is the case with far the greatest part of the human race. All *Asia* is over-run with this plague. Her amazing

numbers, fertility, and wealth, are not allowed to minister to the ease and comfort of her inhabitants; but only to the will and pleasure of her *imperial tyrants, and European plunderers and oppressors.*—To such a degree of abasement and degradation are her wretched inhabitants reduced, that the very idea of Liberty is unknown among them. In *Africa,* scarce any human beings are to be found but barbarians, tyrants, and slaves: All equally remote from the true dignity of human nature, and from a well-regulated state of society. Nor is *Europe* free from the curse. Most of her nations are forced to drink deep of the bitter cup. And in those in which freedom seem to have been established, the vital flame is going out. Two kingdoms, those of *Sweden* and *Poland,* have been betrayed and enslaved in the course of one year. The free towns of *Germany* can remain free, no longer than their potent neighbours shall please to let them. *Holland* has got the forms, if she lost the spirit of a free country: *Switzerland* alone is in the full and safe possession of her freedom. In *Britain,* next to that of self-preservation, political liberty is the main aim and end of her constitution. And yet her senators and historians are repeatedly predicting, that the time will come, when continued corruption and standing armies will prove mortal distempers in her constitution.

To our own country then we must look for the biggest part of that liberty and freedom, that yet remains, or is to be expected, among mankind. And such has been our constitution and form of government, that till of late, she seemed to be deeply rooted, and firmly fixed here. The foundation was laid for it, by preserving to the colonies that first and fundamental right, a share in their own legislative council. It was preserved for a long time, by having the business of Taxation lodged wholly in our own hands. It was confirmed by that wisest and best principle of British jurisprudence, which appoints that trials for life, liberty, or property, shall be by a jury of our peers. It was made sure by the tenure on which we held our lands. And it was designed to be guarded and strengthened, by the liberty of the press.—On such firm and solid foundations, Freedom has been established in North-America. And this is one of those reasons that may well lead us to value and love this country. For while the greatest part of the nations of the earth, are held together under the yoke of universal slavery, the North-American provinces yet remain *the country of free men:* The *asylum,* and the last, to which such may yet flee from the common deluge.

4. As what should further confirm our attachment to our native country, it bids the fairest of any to promote *the perfection and happiness of mankind.* We have but few principles from which we can argue with certainty, what will be the state of mankind in future ages. But if we may judge of the designs of providence, by the number and power of the causes that are already at work, we shall be lead to think that the perfection and happiness of mankind is to be carried further in America, than it has ever yet been in any place.—From the weak beginnings of private adventurers, so amazingly rapid has been our growth and progress, that in a century and an half, we are become more than *three millions* of inhabitants. The period of doubling in these colonies, is not more than 25 years. And to accelerate our increase, Britain and other parts of Europe are every year pouring large numbers of their inhabitants into these provinces. Tired out with the miseries they are doomed to at home, they croud to us as the only country in which they can find food, raiment, and rest.—In that vast extent of country which reaches from *Labrador* to *Florida,* there is a climate adapted to health, vigour, industry, liberty, genius, and happiness. Our soil is adapted to the most useful kinds of produce; and our situation is not unfriendly to commerce. That vigour and industry which is the natural growth of our own climate, applied to the soil, never fails to give the labourer what neither Europe nor Asia will afford him, a comfortable support for the wages of his work.—The fatal arts of luxury and corruption are but comparatively beginning among us. Security and wealth had indeed began in our larger towns to enervate, and introduce luxury, vanity, and various kinds of unnecessary expence; which were

gradually diffusing the poison all around. But the late measures have effectually cured us for the present, of this kind of folly. Nor is corruption yet established as the common principle in public affairs. Our representatives are not chosen by bribing, corrupting, or buying the votes of the electors. Nor does it take one half of the revenue of a province, to manage her house of commons. Public integrity was sufficient to secure a large majority, during all our happy days of peace and concord.—We have been free also from the burthen and danger of standing armies. The powers of Europe are undoing themselves, and one another, with the exorbitant number of their forces. With all the wealth and power of the world at their command, they are multiplying their taxes and debts, and thus ruining their kingdoms, that they may increase their standing armies. The nature, and tendency of this evil, till within a few years have been unknown among us. Our defence has been our *Militia*. With this we have all along repelled our numerous savage enemies, aided by France. With this we subdued *Nova-Scotia* in 1690. And with this we conquered *Cape-Breton* in 1745; by which conquest, Britain was enabled to make the peace of *Aix-la-Chapelle*. But instead of keeping up our armies, when war has ceased, our officers and soldiers like the old *Romans* have laid down their arms, and returned to their fields and farms, to cultivate the more useful arts of peace.—Nor have the arts and sciences been unattended to. In infant states it is not to be expected that much should be done this way. They cannot have the numbers, wealth, or literary establishments of ancient states; to form, ripen, and expand the genius of their country. And yet no country with so few advantages, and such small revenues, has done so much for the cause of science. Almost every province has its public *Academy;* some of which are nearly as ancient as the state, and grown up to the form of the ancient universities. Physical and philosophical foundations are taking place. And there are two *capital discoveries** of which America can already boast. From such promising beginnings, the fairest hopes and prospects arise. The forms of our government will naturally lead us to cultivate the arts of eloquence and speaking. The controversies with our mother-country, though full of mischief in other respects, will be attended with this advantage, they will turn our attention to matters of history, jurisprudence, and policy. The natural productions of this vast continent, are a treasure yet untouched; which in time cannot fail to afford ample matter for improvements in commerce, philosophy, and the medicinal art. It seems as if necessity must force us to find out some better methods of preserving a proper regard to public worship, morals, rulers, laws, liberty, public revenues and æconomy, than the ancient countries have done. And why may we not imagine that some of those great Geniuses which occasionally rise up to enlighten mankind, may be born here? One such† we have already had: And what is there that forbids us to hope for more? But however this may be, the situation in which we are placed, the time when our political state began, the improvements we are receiving from the ancient countries, with the general operation of things among ourselves, indicate strong tendencies towards a state of greater perfection and happiness than mankind has yet seen.

THUS many and powerful causes are already at work, which if we may judge from the common methods of providence, are leading the way to a more perfect and happy state. The prospect and probability is, that things will operate this way in America, for many centuries yet to come. Our present difficulties may retard the event; but they cannot finally defeat the tendencies and preparations of nature and providence: Tendencies and preparations which will naturally operate to increase the perfection and

* In *Electricity* and *Inoculation*.
† Dr. FRANKLIN.

happiness of mankind; and of consequence to attach us to that country, in which alone we can look for such a state.

WHAT has been said on the Love of our country, will naturally turn our thoughts to the present unhappy and critical state of the North-American colonies. Amidst all the pleasure a benevolent mind must receive from the growth, progress, and general tendency of the colonies; the unhappy disputes we are engaged in with our mother-country, seem to cast a shade over all other prospects. Both countries were long happily united in mutual affection, friendship, and confidence. We looked upon her as a wise and tender parent: And she regarded us as her friends and children. And this mutual affection was the honor, comfort, strength, and safety of both. But instead of our former peace and friendship, what fears, murmurs, and unusual commotions now prevail from one end of the *American* continent to the other? From what *Innovations* these disputes and difficulties began, or to what a dangerous height late measures have carried them, no one need to be informed. We seem to be on the eve of some great and unusual events: Events, which it is not improbable, may form a new æra, and give a new turn to human affairs. The state of both countries is critical and dangerous to the last degree. A few more alarming measures on either side, and all public confidence will cease. While both countries are preparing to proceed, may Heaven interpose, and prevent the sword from engaging in that which ignorance and folly first began!——The cause of *America* seems indeed to be much the better cause. It is not the cause of a mob, of a party, or a faction that *America* means to plead. May these things to which some have been unhappily driven, but which are unnatural productions in this country, cease forever from among us. Nor is it the cause of independency that we have in view. It is the cause of *Self-Defence,* of *Public Faith,* and of the *Liberties of Mankind,* that America is engaged in. And we have every thing that is dear, valuable, and precious to attach us to it. "In our destruction, Liberty itself expires; and human nature will despair of evermore regaining its first and original dignity."——To oppose Britain by force and violence, is an extreme to which all wise and good men among us, most ardently pray we may never be forced. But to give up to her the management of taxes, is to give up all that we have. Dreadful extremes! May the wise and good on both sides, instead of increasing the difficulty, join to find out some happy expedient for restoring such mutual justice, friendship and union, as shall leave this country free, and set that at the head of human affairs for many ages yet to come.

THE subject we have been considering, should lead us to shew our love to our country, in every way in which we can promote its good. It is not the business of the pulpit to determine measures of state, or to invade the office or power of civil rulers; but to inculcate that public and private virtue which is agreeable to the laws of God, and adapted to promote the interest and welfare of mankind.—The surest way we can take to promote the good of our country, is to attend to this. It should lead us to repent of all the vice, wickedness, and moral evils that are among us. It is our interest to renounce whatever is contrary to the rules of religion, to purity of morals, and the prosperity of the state. It is our duty to reform every kind of extravagance, superfluity, and unnecessary expence. It would be our wisdom to put on the most strict frugality, œconomy, and self-denial, in all unnecessary articles of food, raiment, convenience and pleasure.—Such virtue will naturally tend to promote the good of our country. And this is what the united councils and voice of America now call us to. If therefore, my brethren, you have any value for your own interest, any feeling for the love of your country, or any regard for the generations that are to come; if you are *Americans* any more than by name, if you have the spirit, or desire to have the privileges of *Free-men*, you must now vigorously exert yourselves in this way, for the interest and welfare of your country.

IN the present singular situation of this province, it may not be unseasonable to caution you against loosing your regard to good laws and government. It is an unhappy necessity which forces our attention so much to matters of state. But while we see every thing in a state of disorder and confusion around us, it is of the last importance that we keep up a steady regard to the rules of righteousness, of personal and social virtue. Now is the time, my brethren, when our enemies expect that we shall run wild and mad, for want of something to guide us. The extremes of power, and the wanton abuse of liberty, you may assure yourselves will always end alike, in absolute tyranny at last.——God give you firmness to adhere to your liberties, with prudence and discretion at the same time, to maintain quiet and peaceable lives in all godliness and honesty. Government is a wise, a necessary, and a sacred thing. And while you see it abused by men of high, and of low degree; instead of wishing to be free from its necessary restraints, let us be looking to the Ruler of all nations to put us again upon a good foundation, that duty and interest may both lead us to be subject to the ordinances of man.——From the collected wisdom of your country, you will judge what measures are proper for you to take, in the present exigency of public affairs. The business of the pulpit is to enjoin whatsoever things are true, honest, just, pure, lovely, and of good report. If there be any virtue, and if there be any praise, shew to the nations of the earth (what will indeed be a most singular phenomenon) amidst all the jarring interests, subtlety, and rage of politics—you had virtue enough to think of, and to practice these things.

AND while we are thus anxious for the welfare of our country, let us praise God's holy name for the blessings we yet enjoy in it. These, amidst all our gloomy prospects, are neither few nor small things. We yet enjoy the means of grace, and the rights of conscience. We are blessed with general health, food, raiment, and all the necessaries of life. We have been favoured in the seasons of the year, and in the produce of the earth. Such a spirit of benevolence has been shewn towards that part of this province which is suffering the vengeance of power, as was not to be expected among mankind. And what must be ascribed to the influence of heaven, the very measures that were designed to divide, have proved the means of establishing a firm and solid union among the colonies. To all these mercies we may add, the life of our sovereign Lord the King has been preserved: To his family and throne, it is our duty and interest to bear a steady allegiance; and in whose royal favour and protection, we hope this country will find peace, safety and happiness, for many ages yet to come. For these and all other mercies, let us return sincere thanks to almighty God; whose providence has always appeared for our help and protection, in all the difficulties we have passed through.——One way, my brethren, in which we should express our gratitude to God for his mercies, should be by unfeigned repentance for all our past sins: And this, with prayer and supplication, is the proper way to seek his favour for the time to come. Let us return then to the Almighty, that he may build us up. Let us return to that sober sense of piety and religion, which animated and encouraged our Fathers in that noblest enterprize of public virtue, laying the foundation of these colonies. Then shall we have reason to expect that heaven and earth will once more join to remove our difficulties and fears, and to make us a free, a grateful, and a happy people. To this then, repentance and reformation, we are now called by all that is holy in religion, by all that is important to our country, and by all that is valuable to mankind. And may God arise and have mercy upon Zion: May the time to favour her, yea, may the set time now come.

SELECTION

Disestablishment of Religion

Among the indications that there was an active, if largely unorganized, effort during the Revolution to make American society conform to the social ideals of the new era was the abolition of certain feudal relics including quitrents, entail, primogeniture, and titles of honor. Because these items had long before ceased to serve any necessary social function in the colonies, their abolition produced no serious disruption of society or encountered any serious opposition. As Bernard Bailyn has pointed out, their elimination represented no more than an attempt to end a long-standing divergence between social reality in the colonies and traditional institutional forms and habits of mind that had been brought over from Britain. Other proposed reforms, however, challenged institutions and practices that were still, or at least to dominant segments of colonial society appeared to be, integral to colonial life. These frequently resulted in bitter political contests and, when they were successful, tangible and revolutionary social changes.

One of the most important of these proposed reforms was the demand for the disestablishment of religion. As Samuel Williams suggested (Selection 38), a high degree of practical religious toleration of Protestants existed in most of the colonies throughout the eighteenth century. But the Congregational Church was established in most of the New England colonies and the Anglican Church in a part of New York and all of the colonies from Maryland south to Georgia. Establishment usually meant support by public taxes levied alike upon all inhabitants regardless of their religious affiliation and such establishments obviously discriminated against dissenters. Although lax enforcement of establishment laws in some colonies and the de facto or legal exemption of dissenters from them in others tended to make these laws less onerous than they might otherwise have been, the religious fragmentation that grew out of the Great Awakening resulted, especially in New England, in wide-

spread demands for either complete legal exemption for all dissenters from payment of taxes to support the established church or total disestablishment. These demands were intensified in the 1760s and 1770s as dissenters began to apply to the ecclesiastical realm the arguments employed against British measures in the civil.

Representative of this trend was the sermon "Freedom from Civil and Ecclesiastical Slavery, the Purchase of Christ," delivered in 1774 in commemoration of the Boston Massacre by Jonathan Parsons (1705–1776), minister of the Presbyterian Church at Newbury, Massachusetts, and partially reprinted here as Selection 39 A. Arguing that civil liberty and ecclesiastical liberty were both legacies purchased by Christ's blood, he declared that each should be forever preserved inviolate and called on the members of the Massachusetts House of Representatives "to put an end to all civil and ecclesiastical oppression" and grant "all denominations of protestants" the "liberty to seek their edification in those worshipping assemblies with which they agree in sentiment, and be discharged from ministerial taxes to any but where they attend." It was absolutely inconsistent for men to plead for civil liberty while condoning or actively advocating ecclesiastical slavery. Surely, Parsons insisted, there ought to "be as great freedom in the Church as we plead for in the state."

The campaign of the dissenters resulted during the Revolution in the disestablishment of the Anglican Church in every colony in which it had been established. In states such as New York and North Carolina where the establishment was weak, disestablishment was accomplished with relative ease; in states such as Virginia and South Carolina where powerful segments of the population were strongly attached to the church, disestablishment came only after constant and prolonged pressure from its proponents. Because of the popular and political strength of the Congregational Church, the movement for disestablishment was least successful in New England, where, though dissenters were exempted from paying taxes to support the established church, the church continued to be legally established in Connecticut, Massachusetts, and New Hampshire well into the nineteenth century.

For the most part, the dissenters had been interested in securing complete religious freedom only for Protestants. But the arguments for freedom for all Protestants, an increasing number of thinkers pointed out, could be applied with equal force in behalf of complete religious toleration. Among the most devoted advocates of universal toleration was Thomas Jefferson, who along with James Madison, George Mason, and other allies waged a vigorous battle to achieve complete separation of church and state in Virginia. Despite major opposition from both Episcopalians and dissenters, the efforts of these men finally achieved success in January, 1786, with the passage of the Virginia Statute for Religious Freedom. Printed in full below as Selection 39 B, this statute vigorously denounced and made illegal any form of civil interference with private religious opinions. Jefferson ranked it along with the Declaration of Independence and the establishment of the University of Virginia as one of his three most important accomplishments.

Alan Heimert, Religion and the American Mind from the Great Awakening to the Revolution *(1966), and Bernard Bailyn,* Pamphlets of the American Revolution *(1965), contain the fullest and most revealing discussions of the demand for religious disestablishment during the Revolution, and J. Franklin Jameson,* The American Revolution Considered as a Social Movement *(1926), and Allan Nevins,* American States during and after the Revolution, 1775–1789 *(1924), describe the general process of disestablishment. For Virginia developments see George M. Brydon,* Virginia's Mother Church and the Political Conditions under Which It Grew *(two volumes, 1947–1952).*

A. "THE CHURCH AS WELL AS THE STATE MUST BE FOUNDED ON PRINCIPLES OF JUSTICE": JONATHAN PARSONS, "FREEDOM FROM CIVIL AND ECCLESIASTICAL SLAVERY, THE PURCHASE OF CHRIST" (1774)*

I WISH and earnestly pray that our patriotic House of Representatives may be inspired to exert themselves, in the wisest and most effectual way, to put an end to all civil and ecclesiastical oppression, and to make liberty equal to all men inhabiting the province.—This, this would immortalize their names, and all the sons of liberty would rise up and call them blessed. When that time commences it will be a token for good that justice will run down our streets as waters, and righteousness as a mighty stream.

BUT whether success attends our endeavours or not, it becomes us, as men and christians, to assert our natural and constitutional privileges—never to give them up, but if possible to recover and defend them against all malicious claims of haughty and covetous tools of arbitrary power, they are a legacy left us by Christ, the purchase of his blood. And will any tamely submit to be entangled with the yoke of bondage, now Christ has made us free!

SURELY, *My Friends and Townsmen,* you will be very jealous for the defence for our excellent constitution, and where a breach is made upon it you will earnestly contend for its being healed. Neither the high notions of the British Parliament, nor the groundless prejudices in this Province, should intimidate your minds. Where is the brave spirits of our Fore-fathers that ventured life and all that was dear to them, rather, than give up their privileges to the pleasure of *Sir Edmund Androse* and his creatures! Sure, in this enlightned age of liberty, you will not readily yield to slavery. Now natural and constitutional rites are so well understood, and appear so reasonable you cannot desert the cause, nor grow indifferent about it. I perswade myself, that you, in combination with our brethren, will be more successful than our mother country has sometimes been, in preserving that reverance and authority which is due to christian liberty.

I PITY rather than hate the British parliament, in their tyrannical sentiments respecting the Colonies. We chuse to be as one body—like *Jerusalem,* as a City COMPACT together. We desire to live in connection with Great-Britain, in a sweet harmony, and are grieved to see the dispotism that is breaking us asunder. I pity the place-men and pensioners in this Province, who are striving by public measures among ourselves, and private letters to men abroad, to keep up and increase the alienation between us and our mother country. I wish the bleeding wounds may be thoroughly healed, and the true interests of Church and state may govern all denominations in their future contests, and regulate all their claims: They were designed to be mutual benefits; and if they were cordially united in the truth, we might be led forth in the right way of peace, by the hand of *Moses* and *Aaron.* May the virtuous on both sides endeavour, by all probable means, to remove all grounds of complaint, and restore equal liberties—If every one uprightly considered his own happiness as a part of the whole, and inseperable from it, he would feel no disposition to enslave any. All would chearfully submit to a righteous government in church and state; for they would find all turn

* These excerpts are reprinted from the original Newburyport edition, pp. 10–16.

to general good, friendship and gratitude would be restored between Great-Britain and her Colonies, love and peace between the various denominations of protestant christians.—Church and state would be mutual helps in this province; and as we are beautiful for situation, we should soon be the joy of the whole land. None would be taxed without his consent, to support a ministry he conscientiously dissented from. The enemies would not roar in parishes, nor break down the carved work with axes and hammers; the same public spirit would reign in all orders and conditions of men, which reigned in Christ Jesus.—If a spirit of Christian benevolence was properly cultivated in all the different classes, *parish lines* would not bind any one to pay their money to support a worship which they esteemed corrupt, but where they could with peace and comfort set down with their brethren; and this would not lessen the extent of good order and pleasure nor shorten their duration.

BUT when shall this happy *æra* commence! Not in the STATE, as long as fleets and armies are palmed upon us, to threaten distruction in a time of peace—Not as long as the parliament of Great-Britain strive to tax us without our consent.

THE shocking effects of these violent measures we have already felt by the ever memorable tragical scene at *Boston* four years ago! We mourn with our brethren, that the sons of violence and blood were ever suffered to parade the streets of our Metropolis! We feel for them, who saw their streets stained with INNOCENT BLOOD, by worse than butchering Soldiers! Should the Lord arraign the blood-thirsty crew as he did *Cain,* they might add rebellion to their other sin, as he did: But if they should hear GOD say, "What have you done! The voice of your brethren's blood crieth unto me from the ground;" they would be ready to cry, "Our punishment is greater than we can bear:" They would feel themselves cut off from the church, and forbid to bring any more vain oblations, unpardoned guilt would fill their souls with continual terror. May .the awful catastrophe of that evening be ever deeply engraven upon our hearts as it is this day!

I READILY own that I feel upon my mind a great aversion to all enslaving measures, and a strong desire for public liberty. I wish to see all those fetters which parliaments have endeavoured to fix upon us, done away. When will the time come, that fleets and armies shall be recalled, and better employed than to threaten us with bondage and death! I could also wish for the peace and happiness of the church; and therefore, that all denominations of protestants might be at liberty to seek their edification in those worshiping assemblies with which they agree in sentiment, and be discharged from ministerial taxes to any but where they attend, as it is in this town, through the benevolent application of its inhabitants. We see many sad consequences of violence in the church; we have tried force long enough to convince us that we have no reason to be proud of the experiment. Methinks a *collector* has as much reason to tremble at the face of an honest man when he demands his money or property in such a case, as a thief would have at the sight of a sheriff. What benefit has ever accrued to people by the plunder of honest men, who soberly dissent from their brethren—the consequence of so much injustice has been to excite people to devise several schemes to get rid of their fetters. Besides, it is attended with a general loss of credit and confidence in one another. It requires no great degree of virtue and wisdom in a court to put a stop to such gains of ungodliness.

BUT a spirit of liberty is wanting, even among those that are pleading for

liberty, and dread slavery. The Church as well as the State must be founded
on principles of justice, benevolence and moderation, or there can be no
peace. The wisdom that is from above is first PURE, then *peaceable*—but envy
and strife arise from beneath.

I PRESUME not to dictate the legislators of the people: But it is our duty
as Ministers of Christ, to open the nature of justice and oppression. We
have a right to say that what any man can call *his,* must remain his, till
he agrees to part with it; and if it is taken away by *force,* it is an act of
injustice. Justice will regulate the happiness of church and state; but oppression will promote their misery. By what bond society and social happiness
will be promoted, I know not, as long as they bite and devour one another.

RIGHTEOUSNESS and mercy are due to all men, especially to those with
whom we are nearly connected. The law of nature and the written law of
God, ought to be the great maxims of all civil and ecclesiastical policy. It is
truely surprising to observe, how *Slowly* the principles of freedom prevail
respecting the Church in a land so warmly engaged for liberty in the *State.*
It has been the policy of some, who are zealous for liberty, to lay their
brethren under the severest restrictions on religious accounts, though doubtless if proper freedom was granted, the whole body would feel the blessings
of it; for the most effectual method of receiving good from others is to do
good to them. Equal liberties granted to all denominations, would naturally
tend to beget affectionate union. The time I am perswaded will come, when
the restraints laid upon some christians, and the violence used towards them
will cease, and there will be as great freedom in the Church as we plead for
in the state. It would be a noble effect of laudable ambition in our whole
legislative body, if they should follow their neighbours in this matter, or
fix upon some better plan for relief. O that court and country may break
through the prejudices and selfishness of the age! O that all may be led
into the right path to promote truth and social happiness! The path that
would make the province peaceful among themselves, and respectable among
others! But force and fraud will never effect this blessing, though love and
friendship might. And then we should, with a better grace, plead the merits
of our cause, whenever called thereto, though it should be at the expence
of life and treasure—the evidence in our favour would shine the brighter in
the view of all wise and good men. It would be a good means to convince
them that we are contending for our rights and liberties, with a benevolent
and christian spirit—by the armour of righteousness on the right hand and
on the left, through the manifestation of the truth; and that we dread the
defence of liberty by external force—that nothing but meer necessity shall
draw us into it. . . .

B. "ALL MEN SHALL BE FREE TO PROFESS . . . THEIR OPINION IN MATTERS OF RELIGION": VIRGINIA STATUTE FOR RELIGIOUS FREEDOM (JAN. 16, 1786)*

I. WHEREAS Almighty God hath created the mind free; that all attempts
to influence it by temporal punishments or burthens, or by civil incapacita-

* Reprinted in full from William Waller Hening (ed.), *The Statutes at Large*
(13 vols., 1809–1823), vol. XII, pp. 84–86.

tions, tend only to beget habits of hypocrisy and meanness, and are a departure from the plan of the Holy author of our religion, who being Lord both of body and mind, yet chose not to propagate it by coercions on either, as was in his Almighty power to do; that the impious presumption of legislators and rulers, civil as well as ecclesiastical, who being themselves but fallible and uninspired men, have assumed dominion over the faith of others, setting up their own opinions and modes of thinking as the only true and infallible, and as such endeavouring to impose them on others, hath established and maintained false religions over the greatest part of the world, and through all time; that to compel a man to furnish contributions of money for the propagation of opinions which he disbelieves, is sinful and tyrannical; that even the forcing him to support this or that teacher of his own religious persuasion, is depriving him of the comfortable liberty of giving his contributions to the particular pastor, whose morals he would make his pattern, and whose powers he feels most persuasive to righteousness, and is withdrawing from the ministry those temporary rewards, which proceeding from an approbation of their personal conduct, are all additional incitement to earnest and unremitting labours for the instruction of mankind; that our civil rights have no dependence on our religious opinions, any more than our opinions in physics or geometry; that therefore the proscribing any citizen as unworthy the public confidence by laying upon him an incapacity of being called to offices of trust and emolument, unless he profess or renounce this or that religious opinion, is depriving him injuriously of those privileges and advantages to which in common with his fellow-citizens he has a natural right; that it tends only to corrupt the principles of that religion it is meant to encourage, by bribing with a monopoly of wordly honours and emoluments, those who will externally profess and conform to it; that though indeed these are criminal who do not withstand such temptation, yet neither are those innocent who lay the bait in their way; that to suffer the civil magistrate to intrude his powers into the field of opinion, and to restrain the profession or propagation of principles on supposition of their ill tendency, is a dangerous fallacy, which at once destroys all religious liberty, because he being of course judge of that tendency will make his opinions the rule of judgment, and approve or condemn the sentiments of others only as they shall square with or differ from his own; that it is time enough for the rightful purposes of civil government, for its officers to interfere when principles break out into overt acts against peace and good order; and finally, that truth is great and will prevail if left to herself, that she is the proper and sufficient antagonist to error, and has nothing to fear from the conflict, unless by human interposition disarmed of her natural weapons, free argument and debate, errors ceasing to be dangerous when it is permitted freely to contradict them:

II. *Be it enacted by the General Assembly,* That no man shall be compelled to frequent or support any religious worship, place, or ministry whatsoever, nor shall be enforced, restrained, molested, or burthened in his body or goods, nor shall otherwise suffer on account of his religious opinions or belief; but that all men shall be free to profess, and by argument to maintain, their opinion in matters of religion, and that the same shall in no wise diminish, enlarge, or affect their civil capacities.

III. And though we well know that this assembly elected by the people for the ordinary purposes of legislation only, have no power to restrain the acts of succeeding assemblies, constituted with powers equal to our own, and that therefore to declare this act to be irrevocable would be of no effect in law; yet we are free to declare, and do declare, that the rights hereby asserted are of the natural rights of mankind, and that if any act shall be hereafter passed to repeal the present, or to narrow its operation, such act will be an infringement of natural right.

SELECTION **40**

Attack on Chattel Slavery

The arguments employed against the establishment of religion were even more obviously applicable to the institution of chattel slavery, and during the long debate with Britain colonial opponents of slavery, who were especially numerous among the members of the Society of Friends, seized the opportunity to intensify their attacks upon the "horrid demon" of slavery. One of the most direct and moving statements of the antislavery position was included by Richard Wells, a Quaker merchant from Philadelphia, in 1774 in his pamphlet A Few Political Reflections *and is reprinted below as Selection 40 A. To the traditional religious and humanitarian arguments against slavery Wells added another and, in the situation, more compelling one that an increasing number of commentators were beginning to make: that the "exercise of SLAVERY" could not possibly be reconciled "with our professions of freedom." If freedom was indeed " 'founded on the law of God and nature, and the common rights of mankind,' " as Americans were asserting in their objections to British violations of colonial rights, then it had to be the inherent right of all men, black as well as white; and for men to contend for civil liberty upon such grounds while they were at that very time "keeping their fellow creatures in perpetual bondage" was obviously totally inconsistent. If, indeed, "ALL the inhabitants of America" were "entitled to the privileges of the inhabitants of Great-Britain," then, Wells declared in an obvious reference to and paraphrase of Lord Mansfield's famous decision in the Somerset case in England two years earlier, "the instant a Negro sets his foot in America, he is as free as if he had landed in England." Calling for immediate steps to end the slave trade and provide for manumission of the slaves, Wells even suggested that the struggle with Britain would never come to a successful conclusion "till this barbarous inhuman practice is driven from our borders."*

The rising crescendo of voices against slavery was not limited to the middle and northern colonies, where slavery was scarcely an important institution. During the 1770s and 1780s an increasing number of southerners, many of them slaveholders, who lived in Virginia and Maryland, where slavery was considerably less profitable economically than it had been three or four decades earlier, joined in the chorus. Even in South Carolina and Georgia, where slavery was growing at an accelerated rate and generally considered essential to the successful cultivation of their staple crops of rice and indigo, there were a few isolated utterances in opposition to slavery. One of these came from Henry Laurens (1724–1792), Charleston merchant and owner of several rich plantations and slaves valued at over £20,000. Having earlier made a huge mercantile fortune in part by dealing in slaves, Laurens had apparently always "disliked" slavery and had actually given up the slave trade in the years just before Independence. On August 14, 1776, just twelve days after he had first read the Declaration of Independence with its blanket assertion that "all men are created equal" he wrote to his son John expressing again his abhorrence of slavery and his determination in spite of the "Laws & Customs of my Country, my own & the avarice of my Country Men" to devise means for manumitting many of his slaves and "cutting off the entail of Slavery." With Wells, Laurens thought that Americans could not "dare trust in Providence for defence & security of their own Liberty while they enslave & wish to continue in Slavery, thousands who are as well intitled to freedom as themselves." Although his son strongly approved of his stand on slavery, Laurens suffered such heavy financial losses during the war that he did not attempt to carry out his plan when the war was over. The portions of his letter relating to slavery are reprinted here as Selection 40 B.

Thomas Jefferson was another southern slaveholder who had long been opposed to slavery. Jefferson had earlier been one of the sponsors of an unsuccessful request to the Crown for permission to pass a law prohibiting the importation of slaves into Virginia, and during the Revolution he came, like many other Virginia slaveholders, to advocate "a total emancipation." As he explained in a passage originally published in his Notes on the State of Virginia *and reprinted below as Selection 40 C, Jefferson opposed slavery not simply because of the "miserable condition" and the rank injustice of slavery but also because it corrupted the manners and morals of the slaveholders. "The whole commerce between master and slave is a perpetual exercise of the most boisterous passions," he declared with an insight born of experience, "the most unremitting despotism on the one part, and degrading submissions on the other." The salvation of the masters as well as the necessity of doing justice to the slaves, Jefferson thus implied, required the elimination of slavery.*

The results of the agitation against slavery during the Revolution included the prohibition or heavy taxation of the slave trade in every state except South Carolina and Georgia, the abolition of slavery in Massachusetts and New Hampshire, and the requirement of gradual emancipation of all slaves in Pennsylvania, Rhode Island, and Connecticut.

Bernard Bailyn, Pamphlets of the American Revolution *(1965), contains the best discussion of the development of antislavery thought during the Revolution and its relationship to the debate with Britain; David Brion Davis,* The Problem of Slavery in Western Culture *(1966), Allan Nevins,* American States during and after the Revolution, 1775–1789 *(1924), and J. Franklin Jameson,* American Revolution Considered as a Social Movement *(1926), describe the steps taken to eliminate slavery, and David Duncan Wallace,* The Life of Henry Laurens *(1915), traces the development of Laurens's attitudes toward slavery.*

A. "THE INCONSISTENT PRACTICE OF KEEPING . . . FELLOW CREATURES IN PERPETUAL BONDAGE": RICHARD WELLS, "A FEW POLITICAL REFLECTIONS" (AUG. 4, 1774)*

Now, my brethren, I will beg leave to come close to the point, and call for an examination of our own conduct—Let us try if it will square with our

---

* These excerpts are reprinted from the original Philadelphia edition, pp. 79–85.

pretensions, whether we can reconcile the *exercise of* SLAVERY with our *professions of freedom, "founded on the law of God and nature, and the common rights of mankind"*——I beseech you, brethren, with dispassionate and disinterested minds to survey the subject—Can we suppose that the people of England will grant the force of our reasoning, when they are told, that *every colony* on the continent is deeply involved in the inconsistent practice of *keeping their fellow creatures* in *perpetual bondage?* So much has been wrote on this subject by abler pens, that it may be difficult to set it in so new and striking a point of light as to gain your attention; but whilst the evil remains, the same arguments will necessarily arise; nor will they ever lose their force. In vain shall we contend for *liberty,* as an *"essential in our constitution,"* till this barbarous inhuman practice is driven from our borders. Let him who claims an exemption from the controul of Parliamentary power, shew to the world, by what right, human or divine, he keeps in cruel slavery his *fellow man.* We declare with a joint voice, that ALL *the inhabitants of America* are entitled to the privileges of the inhabitants of Great-Britain; if so, by what right do we support slavery?—the instant a slave sets his foot in England he claims the protection of the laws, and puts his master at defiance; if British rights extend to America, *who* shall detain him in bondage? If his pretended owner can shew no personal contract with the unfortunate African, is there a court on the continent, that would unrighteously declare him a slave? You say you bought them of those who had a right to sell.——I dispute it——on behalf of the injured Blacks, I dispute it, and call on you to shew your title. When a servant is offered for sale in the colonies, are we contented with the Captain's asseverations?——no——we call for the indenture, the personal contract; if *that* is not to be produced, where is the man who will be hardy enough to sell him? If he is indebted for his passage, he is at liberty to make his own bargain with the purchaser, and enters into a voluntary temporary servitude; even if he be a *convict,* and has *forfeited his life* to the laws of his country, and is respited for transportation, I presume no Captain ever came over unprovided with authentic documents from the records of Newgate; though many contend, that servitude is no part of their sentence, as being inconsistent with the liberty of an Englishman, and I have been assured that some, on their landing in America, have demanded their liberty.—If this be the case—if the English constitution guards the liberties of men, who have been condemned to die for the breach of their own country's laws, how comes it that *we* undertake to inflict so barbarous a punishment upon the natives of Africa, for *their* transgressions in Guinea, which is the last wretched argument of refuge, which the advocates for slavery insist on; and that not content with *gloriously* taking up the cause of an Ethiopian savage government, and *nobly* becoming their *honourable executions,* we visit the sins of the fathers to the latest generations; but if we admit the propriety of the argument, I request on behalf of the injured and distressed, that you produce the records of their courts, or the proofs of their crimes; if you do neither, what better testimony do you shew for your possession than the house-breaker or highway-man?—Wherever a man claims and supports his property, he shall undoubtedly recover it. Now every slave, by his personal appearance, makes *that* claim,—he for ever carries about him the strongest proofs in nature of his *original right*---he is the first grand link, and unless his pretended owner shall deduce a regular chain of conveyance, I contend that, by the laws of the English constitution, and by our *own declarations,* the instant a Negro sets his foot in America, he is as free as if he had landed in England. If *force* and *power* are the only important links in the title, what arguments can we advance in *their* favour, which will not militate against ourselves, whilst England remains superior by land and by sea.

SHALL a climate, a colour, or a country, determine the miserable inhabitants as slaves and vassals to the rest of the world; or from what quarter shall we derive our reasonings, to prove and support our tyrannizing power? —Is there such a thing with Englishmen---high claiming Englishmen---as *partial* liberty? Has the Almighty decreed *us* their masters, and degrading the workmanship of his hands, stamped slave to eternity on their foreheads? By what law has he thus vested us with barbarous and cruel sway? Is it possible we can sit down in the cool of the day, and laying our hands on our bosoms, say we believe they were formed for our servants? On the other hand I would ask, Is there a single argument to be adduced in support of *our* right to their services, which would not equally hold in favour of *their* enslaving *us,* if we were trepanned into their country? But why need I argue on the point? I cannot consent to believe that there is a single slave holder on the continent, who is from principle a tyrant. Their interests are so nearly connected with the subject, that their judgments are misled. With such men it is hard to contend; their reason lies buried and concealed; when called forth it appears with reluctance, and urges its efforts with enervated force. Yet many there are in the several colonies, who are earnestly concerned in this important cause.---To *you,* my brethren---*you* genuine sons of liberty, they look for support. Let us set foot to foot and shoulder to shoulder, to expel this horrid demon from our land.---How oft is my heart sunk into sorrowing sympathy with these poor and unfortunate wretches. When I hear of the brutal cruelties exercised over them, by their inhuman owners, when I view these usurpers of human freedom, basking in the beams of success, and bowling through life with undaunted career, I look up with wondering eye to the great and Almighty Author of our being and am lost in contemplating the dispensations of his Providence.

THE noble, spirited and virtuous Assembly of Virginia, not long ago petitioned his Majesty for leave to pass an act to prohibit the importation of slaves, as inconsistent with the principles of humanity; but the petition was rejected. Yet should the colonies, with their joint voice at the Congress, make a forcible remonstrance against the iniquity of the slave trade, it would breathe such an independant spirit of liberty, and so corroborate our own claims, that I should dare to hope for an intervening arm of Providence to be extended in our favour. Should the colonies gain permission to pass prohibitory acts against future importations, I should then, with expectant joy, look forward for the glorious dawning of a day of liberty.

UNIMPORTANT as this may seem to some, I hesitate not to pronounce, that the true interests and welfare of America are more intimately connected with it, than with the repeal of every act which now agitates the continent---*one* we might probably out grow in a series of years, but *the other* would "strengthen with our strength," and involve us in endless perplexities. If a stop could be put to the importation, the grand difficulty would be over. Means might soon be devised to discharge this unhappy race amongst us, and wear out the monstrous badge of unrighteousness. To the Congress I would earnestly urge this weighty point, and to the internal policy of every government I would press the necessity of removing every legal obstruction, which stands as a bar to their freedom. I am unacquainted with the general laws of emancipation in the southern and the eastern colonies, but those of Maryland, Pennsylvania and New-Jersey have fallen within my knowledge. In the first, any slave holder may set his slaves at liberty without charge or encumbrance, provided they are not aged or infirm, but in Pennsylvania the law requires a bond of indemnification of thirty pounds, to prevent the slave becoming a burthen to the township, and the law is so worded as to admit of a doubt, whether such bond totally discharges the master's estate; and in some cases the courts, before whom such emancipation is to be declared, have so far exerted their power, as to refuse admitting the security, though undoubtedly good, and the slaves intended for freedom healthy and young; by which means, they were kept in bondage against the inclinations of their owners. In New-Jersey, the law requires a security of two hundred pounds, but the assembly of that province, at their last session, took up the matter on virtuous principles, and made an essay towards *"an act for the more equitable manumission of slaves,"* by which any person declaring his Negro free, before proper authority, at the age of twenty one, may do it without charge or encumbrance, and for every year exceeding that age, the owner so intending to set him free, is to pay into the hands of the overseers of the poor, the sum of twenty shillings, which shall be a total discharge: This with a few discretionary restrictions is published in their votes, for the inspection of their constituents, and it is hoped by every lover of liberty, that it will pass into a law at the next sessions.

WERE the colonies as earnest for the preservation of liberty, upon its *true* and *genuine* principles, as they are to oppose the supremacy of an English parliament, they would enter into a virtuous and *perpetual* resolve neither to import, nor to purchase any slaves introduced among them after the meeting of the Congress. A resolve so replete with liberty, so truly noble, would indelibly convey to future ages a memorable record of disinterested virtue; whilst thousands, ten thousands yet unborn, might bless them in their native shades, carving on the smooth bark of every tree, NOBLE AMERICANS. With grateful hearts might they look up *"to the unknown God,* and urge this ardent prayer————*Great and Almighty ruler of the Universe, shower down the choicest of thy blessings on yon western climes. . . .*

B. "I ABHOR SLAVERY": HENRY LAURENS TO JOHN LAURENS (AUG. 14, 1776)*

My Negroes . . . all to a Man are strongly attached to me, so are all of mine in this Country, hitherto not one of them has attempted to desert on the contrary those who are more exposed hold themselves always ready to fly from the Enemy in case of a sudden descent—many hundreds of that Colour have been stolen & decoyed by the Servants of King George the third—Captains of British Ships of War & Noble Lords have busied themselves in such inglorious pilferage to the disgrace of their Master & disgrace

* These excerpts are reprinted from *A Letter From Henry Laurens to His Son John Laurens* (1964), pp. 20–21.

of their Cause.—these Negroes were first enslaved by the English—Acts of Parliament have established the Slave Trade in favour of the home residing English & almost totally prohibited the Americans from reaping any share of it—Men of War Forts Castles Governors Companies & Committees are employed & authorized by the English Parliament to protect regulate & extend the Slave Trade—Negroes are brought by English Men & sold as Slaves to Americans—British Liverpoole Manchester Birmingham &c. &c. live upon the Slave Trade—the British Parliament now employ their Men of War to steal those Negroes from the Americans to whom they had sold them, pretending to set the poor wretches free but basely trepan & sell them into ten fold worse Slavery in the West Indies, where probably they will become the property of English-Men again & of some who sit in Parliament; what meanness! what complicated wickedness appears in this scene! O England, how changed! how fallen!

You know my Dear Sir. I abhor Slavery, I was born in a Country where Slavery had been established by British Kings & Parliaments as well as by the Laws of that Country Ages before my existence, I found the Christian Religion & Slavery growing under the same authority & cultivation—I nevertheless disliked it—in former days there was no combatting the prejudices of Men supported by Interest, the day I hope is approaching when from principles of gratitude as well justice every Man will strive to be foremost in shewing his readiness to comply with the Golden Rule; not less than £20000. Stg. would all my Negroes produce if sold at public Auction tomorrow I am not the Man who enslaved them. they are indebted to English Men for that favour, nevertheless I am devising means for manumitting many of them & for cutting off the entail of Slavery—great powers oppose me, the Laws & Customs of my Country, my own & the avarice of my Country Men—What will my Children say if I deprive them of so much Estate? these are difficulties but not insuperable

I will do as much as I can in my time & leave the rest to a better hand.

I am not one of those who arrogate the peculiar care of Providence in each fortunate event, nor one of those who dare trust in Providence for defence & security of their own Liberty while they enslave & wish to continue in Slavery, thousands who are as well intitled to freedom as themselves.—I perceive the work before me is great. I shall appear to many as a promoter not only of strange but of dangerous doctrines, it will therefore be necessary to proceed with caution, you are apparently deeply Interested in this affair but as I have no doubts concerning your concurrence & approbation I most sincerely wish for your advice & assistance & hope to receive both in good time. . . .

C. "AN UNHAPPY INFLUENCE ON THE MANNERS OF OUR PEOPLE": THOMAS JEFFERSON, "NOTES ON THE STATE OF VIRGINIA" (1781–1782)*

It is difficult to determine on the standard by which the manners of a nation may be tried, whether *catholic,* or *particular*. It is more difficult for a native

* These excerpts are reprinted from the eighth American edition (1801), pp. 240–242.

to bring to that standard the manners of his own nation, familiarized to him by habit. There must doubtless be an unhappy influence on the manners of our people produced by the existence of slavery among us. The whole commerce between master and slave is a perpetual exercise of the most boisterous passions, the most unremitting despotism on the one part, and degrading submissions on the other. Our children see this, and learn to imitate it; for man is an imitative animal. This quality is the germ of all education in him. From his cradle to his grave he is learning to do what he sees others do. If a parent could find no motive either in his philanthropy or his self-love, for restraining the intemperance of passion towards his slave, it should always be a sufficient one that his child is present. But generally it is not sufficient. The parent storms, the child looks on, catches the lineaments of wrath, puts on the same airs in the circle of smaller slaves, gives a loose to the worst of passions, and thus nursed, educated, and daily exercised in tyranny, cannot but be stamped by it with odious peculiarities. The man must be a prodigy who can retain his manners and morals undepraved by such circumstances. And with what execration should the statesman be loaded, who permitting one half the citizens thus to trample on the rights of the other, transforms those into despots, and these into enemies, destroys the morals of the one part, and the amor patriæ of the other. For if a slave can have a country in this world, it must be any other in preference to that in which he is born to live and labor for another: in which he must lock up the faculties of his nature, contribute as far as depends on his individual endeavors to the evanishment of the human race, or entail his own miserable condition on the endless generations proceeding from him. With the morals of the people, their industry also is destroyed. For in a warm climate, no man will labor for himself who can make another labor for him. This is so true, that of the proprietors of slaves a very small proportion indeed are ever seen to labor. And can the liberties of a nation be thought secure when we have removed their only firm basis, a conviction in the minds of the people that these liberties are of the gift of God? That they are not to be violated but with his wrath? Indeed I tremble for my country when I reflect that God is just; that his justice cannot sleep for ever: that considering numbers, nature and natural means only, a revolution of the wheel of fortune, an exchange of situation is among possible events: that it may become probable by supernatural interference! The Almighty has no attribute which can take side with us in such a contest.—But it is impossible to be temperate and to pursue this subject through the various considerations of policy, of morals, of history natural and civil. We must be contented to hope they will force their way into every one's mind. I think a change already perceptible, since the origin of the present revolution. The spirit of the master is abating, that of the slave is rising from the dust, his condition mollifying, the way I hope preparing, under the auspices of heaven, for a total emancipation, and that this is disposed, in the order of events, to be with the consent of the masters, rather than by their extirpation.

The Necessity and Promise of Education: Benjamin Rush, "Thoughts upon the Mode of Education Proper in a Republic" (1786)

The Revolution gave considerable impetus to the establishment of schools in the several states. During the colonial period, primary responsibility for educating the young had rested with the family, church, and community, but during the early and middle decades of the eighteenth century there had been a sharp increase in the number of schools, town schools in New England and private schools in New England and the rest of the colonies. Because, as all writers agreed, the animating principle of republican government was public virtue and public virtue depended in large measure upon an enlightened citizenry, a number of men began to argue after the Declaration of Independence that the success of the republican experiment in America might very well depend upon the establishment of some form of public school system. Thus between 1779 and 1786 Thomas Jefferson tried to persuade the Virginia legislature to establish free public schools, and in 1786 Dr. Benjamin Rush published A Plan for the Establishment of Public Schools and the Diffusion of Knowledge in Pennsylvania. *The rationale behind these proposals can be surmised from Rush's* Thoughts upon the Mode of Education Proper in a Republic, *which was published as an appendix to his plan and is reprinted in part here from the original Philadelphia edition, pages 13–16, 20–25, 27–32, 34. On the avowed assumption that with the proper education men might be converted into "republican machines," Rush advocated a form of education and a curriculum that would through religious, moral, and political instruction at once inculcate the young with a sense of obligation to the republic and devotion to the duties required of all citizens of republics and provide them with the equipment and understanding necessary to enable them to meet the demands imposed upon them by free government. Unlike some later writers, Rush was by no means certain that an extensive system of public education would automatically bring about a general moral improvement in man and usher in that new era envisioned by Samuel Williams. Still, there was no telling to what "degrees of happiness and perfection . . . mankind may be raised" by the "combined and reciprocal influence of religion, liberty and learning upon the morals, manners and knowledge of individuals, of these, upon government, and of government, upon individuals." Whether or not education would bring about that "golden age, so much celebrated by the poets," its promise, Rush was thoroughly persuaded, was enormous.*

J. Franklin Jameson, The American Revolution Considered as a Social Movement *(1926), and Evarts Boutell Greene,* The Revolutionary Generation, 1763–1790 *(1943), contain discussions of the effect of the Revolution upon educational thought in the United States. Bernard Bailyn,* Education in the Forming of American Society *(1960), is an excellent brief treatment of education during the colonial period, and Frederick Rudolph (ed.),* Essays on Education in the Early Republic *(1965), reprints a number of late eighteenth-century tracts and proposals on various aspects of education.*

THE business of education has acquired a new complexion by the independence of our country. The form of government we have assumed, has created a new class of duties to every American. It becomes us, therefore, to examine our former habits upon this subject, and in laying the foundations for nurseries of wise and good men, to adapt our modes of teaching to the peculiar form of our government.

The first remark that I shall make upon this subject is, that an education in our own, is to be preferred to an education in a foreign country. The principle of patriotism stands in need of the reinforcement of *prejudice,* and it is well known that our strongest prejudices in favour of our country are formed in the first one and twenty years of our lives. The policy of the Lacedamonians is well worthy of our imitation. When Antipater demanded fifty of their children as hostages for the fulfilment of a distant engagement, those wise republicans refused to comply with his demand, but readily offered him double the number of their adult citizens, whose habits and prejudices could not be shaken by residing in a foreign country. Passing by, in this place, the advantages to the community from the early attachment of youth to the laws and constitution of their country, I shall only remark, that young men who have trodden the paths of science together, or have joined in the same sports, whether of swimming, scating, fishing, or hunting, generally feel, thro' life, such ties to each other, as add greatly to the obligations of mutual benevolence.

I conceive the education of our youth in this country to be peculiarly necessary in Pennsylvania, while our citizens are composed of the natives of so many different kingdoms in Europe. Our Schools of learning, by producing one general, and uniform system of education, will render the mass of the people more homogeneous, and thereby fit them more easily for uniform and peaceable government.

I proceed, in the next place, to enquire, what mode of education we shall adopt so as to secure to the state all the advantages that are to be derived from the proper instruction of youth; and here I beg leave to remark that the only foundation for a useful education in a republic is to be laid in RELIGION. Without this, there can be no virtue, and without virtue there can be no liberty, and liberty is the object and life of all republican governments.

Such is my veneration for every religion that reveals the attributes of the Deity, or a future state of rewards and punishments, that I had rather see the opinions of Confucius or Mahomed inculcated upon our youth, than see them grow up wholly devoid of a system of religious principles. But the religion I mean to recommend in this place, is the religion of JESUS CHRIST.

It is foreign to my purpose to hint at the arguments which establish the truth of the Christian revelation. My only business is to declare, that all its doctrines and precepts are calculated to promote the happiness of society, and the safety and well being of civil government. A Christian cannot fail of being a republican. The history of the creation of man, and of the relation of our species to each other by birth, which is recorded in the Old Testament, is the best refutation that can be given to the divine right of kings, and the strongest argument that can be used in favour of the original and natural equality of all mankind. A Christian, I say again, cannot fail of being a republican, for every precept of the Gospel inculcates those degrees of humility, self-denial, and brotherly kindness, which are directly opposed to the pride of monarchy and the pageantry of a court. A Christian cannot fail of being useful to the republic, for his religion teacheth him that no man "liveth to himself." And lastly, a Christian cannot fail of being wholly inoffensive, for his religion teacheth him, in all things to do to others what he would wish, in like circumstances, they should do to him. . . .

NEXT to the duty which young men owe to their Creator, I wish to see a SUPREME REGARD TO THEIR COUNTRY, inculcated upon them. When the Duke of Sully became prime minister to Henry the IVth of France, the first thing he did, he tells us, "Was to subdue and forget his own heart." The same duty is incumbent upon every citizen of a republic. Our country includes family, friends and property, and should be preferred to them all. Let our pupil be taught that he does not belong to himself, but that he is public property. Let him be taught to love his family, but let him be taught, at the same time, that he must forsake and even forget them, when the welfare of his country requires it. He must watch for the state as if its liberties depended upon his vigilance alone, but he must do this in such a manner as not to defraud his creditors, or neglect his family. He must love private life, but he must decline no station, however public or responsable it may be, when called to it by the suffrages of his fellow-citizens. He must love popularity, but he must despise it when set in competition with the dictates of his judgement, or the real interest of his country. He must love character, and have a due sense of injuries, but he must be taught to appeal only to the laws of the state, to defend the one, and punish the other. He must love family honour, but he must be taught that neither the rank nor antiquity of his ancestors can command respect, without personal merit. He must avoid neutrality in all questions that divide the state, but he must shun the rage, and acrimony of party spirit. He must be taught to love his fellow creatures in every part of the world, but he must cherish with a more intense and peculiar affection, the citizens of Pennsylvania and of the United States. I do not wish to see our youth educated with a single prejudice against any nation or country; but we impose a task upon human nature, repugnant alike to reason, revelation and the ordinary dimensions of the human heart, when we require him to embrace, with equal affection, the whole family of mankind. He must be taught to amass wealth, but it must be only to encrease his power of contributing to the wants and demands of the state. He must be indulged occasionally in amusements, but he must be taught that study and business should be his principal pursuits in life. Above all he must love life, and endeavour to acquire as many of its conveniences as possible by industry and œconomy, but he must be taught that this life "Is not his own," when the safety of his country requires it. These are practicable lessons, and the history of the commonwealths of Greece and Rome show, that human nature, without the aids of Christianity, has attained these degrees of perfection.

While we inculcate these republican duties upon our pupil, we must not neglect, at the same time, to inspire him with republican principles. He must be taught that there can be no durable liberty but in a republic, and that government, like all other sciences, is of a progressive nature. The chains which have bound this science in Europe are happily unloosed in America. *Here* it is open to investigation and improvement. While philosophy has protected us by its discoveries from a thousand natural evils, government has unhappily followed with an unequal pace. It would be to dishonour human genius only to name the many defects which still exist in the best systems of legislation. We daily see matter of a perishable nature rendered durable by certain chemical operations. In like manner, I conceive, that it is possible to analyze and combine power in such a manner as not only to encrease the happiness, but to promote the duration of republican forms of government far beyond the terms limited for them by history, or the common opinions of mankind. . . .

In the education of youth, let the authority of our masters be as *absolute* as possible. The government of schools like the government of private families, should be *arbitrary*, that it may not be *severe*. By this mode of education, we prepare our youth for the subordination of laws, and thereby qualify them for becoming good citizens of the republic. I am satisfied that the most useful citizens have been formed from those youth who have never known or felt their own wills till they were one and twenty years of age, and I have often thought that society owes a great deal of its order and happiness to the deficiencies of parental government, being supplied by those habits of obedience and subordination which are contracted at schools.

I cannot help bearing a testimony, in this place, against the custom, which prevails in some parts of America, (but which is daily falling into disuse in Europe) of crouding boys together under one roof for the purpose of education. The practice is the gloomy remains of monkish ignorance, and is as unfavourable to the improvements of the mind in useful learning, as monasteries are to the spirit of religion. I grant this mode of secluding boys from the intercourse of private families, has a tendency to make them scholars, but our business is to make them men, citizens and christians. . . .

From the observations that have been made it is plain, that I consider it as possible to convert men into republican machines. This must be done, if we expect them to perform their parts properly, in the great machine of the government of the state. That republic is sophisticated with monarchy or aristocracy that does not revolve upon the wills of the people, and these must be fitted to each other by means of education before they can be made to produce regularity and unison in government.

Having pointed out those general principles, which should be inculcated alike in all the schools of the state, I proceed now to make a few remarks upon the method of conducting, what is commonly called a liberal or learned education in a republic.

I shall begin this part of my subject by bearing a testimony against the common practice of attempting to teach boys the learned languages, and the arts and sciences too early in life. The first twelve years of life are barely sufficient to instruct a boy in reading, writing and arithmetic. With these, he may be taught those modern languages which are necessary for him to *speak*. The state of the memory, in early life, is favourable to the acquisition of languages, especially when they are conveyed to the mind through the ear. It is, moreover, in early life only, that the organs of speech yield in such a manner as to favour the just pronounciation of foreign languages.

I do not wish the LEARNED OR DEAD LANGUAGES, as they are commonly called, to be reduced below their present just rank in the universities of Europe, especially as I consider an acquaintance with them as the best foundation for a correct and extensive knowledge of the language of our country. Too much pains cannot be taken to teach our youth to read and write our American language with propriety and elegance. The study of the Greek language constituted a material part of the literature of the Athenians, hence the sublimity, purity and immortality of so many of their writings. The advantages of a perfect knowledge of our language to young men intended for the professions of law, physic or divinity are too obvious to be mentioned, but in a state which boasts of the first commercial city in

America, I wish to see it cultivated by young men, who are intended for the compting house, for many such, I hope, will be educated in our colleges. The time is past when an academical education was thought to be unnecessary to qualify a young man for merchandize. I conceive no profession is capable of receiving more embellishments from it.

Connected with the study of our own language is the study of ELOQUENCE. It is well known how great a part it constituted of the Roman education. It is the first accomplishment in a republic, and often sets the whole machine of government in motion. Let our youth, therefore, be instructed in this art. We do not extol it too highly when we attribute as much to the power of eloquence as to the sword in bringing about the American revolution.

With the usual arts and sciences that are taught in our American colleges, I wish to see a regular course of lectures given upon HISTORY and CHRONOLOGY. The science of government, whether it relates to constitutions or laws, can only be advanced by a careful selection of facts, and these are to be found chiefly in history. Above all, let our youth be instructed in the history of the ancient republics, and the progress of liberty and tyranny in the different states of Europe. I wish likewise to see the numerous facts that relate to the origin and present state of COMMERCE, together with the nature and principles of MONEY, reduced to such a system as to be intelligible and agreeable to a young man. If we consider the commerce of our metropolis only as the avenue of the wealth of the state, the study of it merits a place in a young man's education; but, I consider commerce in a much higher light when I recommend the study of it in republican seminaries. I view it as the best security against the influence of hereditary monopolies of land, and, therefore, the surest protection against aristocracy. I consider its effects as next to those of religion in humanizing mankind, and lastly, I view it as the means of uniting the different nations of the world together by the ties of mutual wants and obligations.

CHEMISTRY by unfolding to us the effects of heat and mixture, enlarges our acquaintance with the wonders of nature, and the mysteries of art, hence it has become, in most of the universities of Europe, a necessary branch of a gentleman's education. In a young country, where improvements in agriculture and manufactures are so much to be desired, the cultivation of this science, which explains the principles of both of them, should be considered as an object of the utmost importance.

In a state where every citizen is liable to be a soldier and a legislator, it will be necessary to have some regular instruction given upon the ART OF WAR and upon PRACTICAL LEGISLATION. These branches of knowledge are of too much importance in a republic to be trusted to solitary study, or to a fortuitous acquaintance with books. Let mathematical learning, therefore, be carefully applied, in our colleges, to gunnery and fortification, and let philosophy be applied to the history of those compositions which have been made use of for the terrible purposes of destroying human life. These branches of knowledge will be indispensably necessary in our republic, if unfortunately war should continue hereafter to be the unchristian mode of arbitrating disputes between Christian nations. Again, let our youth be instructed in all the means of promoting national prosperity and independence, whether they relate to improvements in agriculture, manufactures, or inland navigation. Let him be instructed further in the general principles of legislation, whether they relate to revenue, or to the preservation of life, liberty or property. Let him be directed frequently to attend the courts of justice, where he will have the best opportunities of acquiring habits of arranging and comparing his ideas by observing the secretion of truth, in the examination of witnesses, and where he will hear the laws of the state explained, with all the advantages of that species of eloquence which belongs to the bar. Of so much importance do I conceive it to be, to a young man, to attend occasionally to the decisions of our courts of law, that I wish to see our colleges and academies established, only in county towns. . . .

From the combined and reciprocal influence of religion, liberty and learning upon the morals, manners and knowledge of individuals, of these, upon government, and of government, upon individuals, it is impossible to measure the degrees of happiness and perfection to which mankind may be raised. For my part, I can form no ideas of the golden age, so much celebrated by the poets, more delightful, than the contemplation of that happiness which it is now in the power of the legislature of Pennsylvania to confer upon her citizens, by establishing proper modes and places of education in every part of the state. . . .

PART TEN

The War for Independence

The Home Front: Thomas Paine, "The American Crisis" (1776–1783)

The most pressing and difficult problem facing Americans between 1775 and 1783 was not of course reconstituting the polity or transforming society but defeating the British army. The initial burst of military ardor that sent 14,000 men, some of them from as far south as Virginia, to the defense of Massachusetts in the weeks immediately after Lexington and Concord and set colonists elsewhere to preparing against the threat of British invasion quickly cooled, and by the end of 1776, as the American army suffered one minor defeat after another and won no striking victories, it had become clear both that the war would not be a short one and that maintaining an army in the field and keeping up the interest and patriotism of the public would be difficult tasks. To counter the apathy and discouragement that seem at least in retrospect to have been almost as formidable an enemy to the American cause as British military and naval might, Thomas Paine wrote a series of sixteen papers beginning in late 1776 which he published throughout the war under the title The American Crisis. *In these papers, brief selections from which are reprinted here from Moncure Daniel Conway (ed.),* The Writings of Thomas Paine *(four volumes, 1894–1896), volume I, pages 170, 173–174, 301–302, 304, Paine played upon hatred of the tories and British and used cajolery, intimidation, and exhortation to stir the public into new exertions of patriotism. A superb example of Paine's skill as a propagandist,* The American Crisis *reveals as clearly as any other contemporary document the nature and extent of the difficulties encountered by American leaders in trying to secure sufficient popular support to win a war that dragged on for over seven years and had to be fought over a broad expanse of territory by an army of citizen soldiers.*

For discussions of the home front during the War for Independence see especially John Richard Alden, The American Revolution, 1775–1783 *(1954); Evarts Boutell Greene,* The Revolutionary Generation, 1763–1790 *(1943); and Edmund Cody Burnett,* The Continental Congress *(1941).*

THESE are the times that try men's souls. The summer soldier and the sunshine patriot will, in this crisis, shrink from the service of their country; but he that stands it *now*, deserves the love and thanks of man and woman. Tyranny, like hell, is not easily conquered; yet we have this consolation with us, that the harder the conflict, the more glorious the triumph. What we obtain too cheap, we esteem too lightly: it is dearness only that gives every thing its value. Heaven knows how to put a proper price upon its goods; and it would be strange indeed if so celestial an article as FREEDOM should not be highly rated. Britain, with an army to enforce her tyranny, has declared that she has a right (*not only to* TAX) but "to BIND us in ALL CASES WHATSOEVER," and if being *bound in that manner*, is not slavery, then is there not such a thing as slavery upon earth. Even the expression is impious; for so unlimited a power can belong only to God. . . .

Why is it that the enemy have left the New-England provinces, and made these middle ones the seat of war? The answer is easy: New-England is not infested with tories, and we are. I have been tender in raising the cry against these men, and used numberless arguments to show them their danger, but it will not do to sacrifice a world either to their folly or their baseness. The period is now arrived, in which either they or we must change our sentiments, or one or both must fall. And what is a tory? Good God! what is he? I should not be afraid to go with a hundred whigs against a thousand tories, were they to attempt to get into arms. Every tory is a coward; for servile, slavish, self-interested fear is the foundation of toryism; and a man under such influence, though he may be cruel, never can be brave.

But, before the line of irrecoverable separation be drawn between us, let us reason the matter together: Your conduct is an invitation to the enemy, yet not one in a thousand of you has heart enough to join him. Howe is as much deceived by you as the American cause is injured by you. He expects you will all take up arms, and flock to his standard, with muskets on your shoulders. Your opinions are of no use to him, unless you support him personally, for 'tis soldiers, and not tories, that he wants. . . .

*   *   *

HAD America pursued her advantages with half the spirit that she resisted her misfortunes, she would, before now, have been a conquering and a peaceful people; but lulled in the lap of soft tranquillity, she rested on her hopes, and adversity only has convulsed her into action. Whether subtlety or sincerity at the close of the last year induced the enemy to an appearance for peace, is a point not material to know; it is sufficient that we see the effects it has had on our politics, and that we sternly rise to resent the delusion.

The war, on the part of America, has been a war of natural feelings. Brave in distress; serene in conquest; drowsy while at rest; and in every situation generously disposed to peace; a dangerous calm, and a most heightened zeal have, as circumstances varied, succeeded each other. Every passion but that of despair has been called to a tour of duty; and so mistaken has been the enemy, of our abilities and disposition, that when she supposed us conquered, we rose the conquerors. The extensiveness of the United States, and the variety of their resources; the universality of their cause, the quick operation of their feelings, and the similarity of their sentiments, have, in every trying situation, produced a *something,* which, favored by providence, and pursued with ardor, has accomplished in an instant the business of a campaign. We have never deliberately sought victory, but snatched it; and bravely undone in an hour the blotted operations of a season.

The reported fate of Charleston, like the misfortunes of 1776, has at last called forth a spirit, and kindled up a flame, which perhaps no other event could have produced. If the enemy has circulated a falsehood, they have unwisely aggravated us into life, and if they have told us the truth, they have unintentionally done us a service. We were returning with folded arms from the fatigues of war, and thinking and sitting leisurely down to enjoy repose. The dependence that has been put upon Charleston threw a drowsiness over America. We looked on the business done—the conflict over—the matter settled—or that all which remained unfinished would follow of itself. In this state of dangerous relaxation, exposed to the poisonous infusions of the enemy, and having no common danger to attract our attention, we were extinguishing, by stages, the ardor we began with, and surrendering by piece-meals the virtue that defended us.

Afflicting as the loss of Charleston may be, yet if it universally rouse us from the slumber of twelve months past, and renew in us the spirit of former days, it will produce an advantage more important than its loss. America ever *is* what she *thinks* herself to be. Governed by sentiment, and acting her own mind, she becomes, as she pleases, the victor or the victim.

It is not the conquest of towns, nor the accidental capture of garrisons, that can reduce a country so extensive as this. The sufferings of one part can never be relieved by the exertions of another, and there is no situation the enemy can be placed in that does not afford to us the same advantages which he seeks himself. By dividing his force, he leaves every post attackable. It is a mode of war that carries with it a confession of weakness, and goes on the principle of distress rather than conquest. . . .

At a crisis, big, like the present, with expectation and events, the whole country is called to unanimity and exertion. Not an ability ought now to sleep, that can produce but a mite to the general good, nor even a whisper to pass that militates against it. The necessity of the case, and the importance of the consequences, admit no delay from a friend, no apology from an enemy. To spare now, would be the height of extravagance, and to consult present ease, would be to sacrifice it perhaps forever. . . .

SELECTION

A Critical American Victory at Saratoga: The Report of "The Annual Register" (1777)

The year 1776 was on the whole a discouraging one for the American cause. British forces under the command of General William Howe abandoned Boston in March, and another force led by General Henry Clinton was defeated in an attempt to capture Charleston, South Carolina. But Sir Guy Carleton repulsed an American attempt to take Canada, and during the summer and fall Howe drove Washington out of New York and harried the main American force all the way across New Jersey. Victories by Washington at Trenton and Princeton over advanced segments of Howe's forces in late December and early January, 1777, helped to restore American confidence, but the British were planning a major offensive in 1777 that they confidently expected would bring an end to the rebellion.

That offensive was to be directed by General John Burgoyne, who hoped to isolate New England from the rest of the colonies by seizing and holding a line running along the Hudson River and Lake Champlain from New York to Montreal. The plan called for a three-pronged attack with Burgoyne's force moving south from Canada, Howe's army moving north from New York, and a smaller force attacking eastward from Oswego on Lake Ontario down the Mohawk River Valley. The three armies were to meet and crush the American Army in the vicinity of Albany. This plan went awry largely because Howe was also intent upon taking Philadelphia from Washington. That project took him most of the summer and he could not come to the aid of Burgoyne, who extended his supply lines too far and permitted his army to be trapped and defeated by a larger American force under the command of General Horatio Gates (ca. 1728–1806) at the Battle of Saratoga on October 13, 1777. This first great American victory cost the British the services of most of their 7,700-man northern army, 5,700 of whom were taken prisoner, stimulated many people in Britain to demand a peace settlement, and thoroughly revived American hopes of bringing the war to a successful conclusion. The pessimistic evaluation of the defeat at Saratoga by the compilers of The Annual Register *in their review of the year's events is reprinted below from the volume for 1777, first edition (1778), pages 175–176.*

Excellent short accounts of the military history of the Revolution are to be found in John Richard Alden, The American Revolution, 1775–1783 *(1954), Willard M. Wallace,* Appeal to Arms: A Military History of the American Revolution *(1951), and Howard H. Peckham,* The War for Independence: A Military History *(1958). Other, more extended, treatments are Christopher Ward,* The War of the Revolution *(John Richard Alden [ed.], two volumes, 1952), and Piers Mackesy,* The War for America, 1775–1783 *(1964), the latter being especially valuable for its account of British strategy prior to Saratoga. The best analysis of the British failure in 1777 is in William B. Willcox,* Portrait of a General: Sir Henry Clinton in the War of Independence *(1964).*

Such was the unfortunate issue of the northern campaign: The event of an expedition which was undertaken with the most confident hopes, and for some time pursued with very flattering appearances of success. It was supposed the principal means for the immediate reduction of the colonies; but it has only served, in conjunction with other operations, which in the first instance have succeeded better, to demonstrate the difficulties attending the subjugation of a numerous people at a great distance, in an extensive country marked with strong lines, and abounding in strong natural defences, if the resources of war are not exceedingly deficient, and that the spirit of the people is in any degree proportioned to their situation. It may now, whatever it was in the beginning, be a matter of doubt, whether any superiority of power, of wealth, and of discipline, will be found to overbalance such difficulties.

It would not be easy at present, as many things necessary to be known have not yet been fully explained, and improper, as the whole is still a subject of public investigation, to attempt forming any judgment upon the general plan or system of this campaign. The general conduct of the war this year has already undergone much censure; and undoubtedly, the sending of the grand army at such a distance to the southward, whilst the inferior was left struggling with insurmountable difficulties in the north, when it would seem that their junction or co-operation would have rendered them greatly superior to any force which could have been possibly brought to oppose their progress, seems, in this view of things, not to be easily accounted for. . . .

The French Alliance: The Treaty of Feb. 6, 1778

The most significant result of the American victory at Saratoga was the stimulus it gave to the conclusion of a treaty of alliance with France. The French, who were anxious to avenge their humiliating defeat at the hands of the British in the Seven Years' War, had been secretly aiding the Americans with money, munitions, and military stores since March, 1776, and Silas Deane (1737–1789), Arthur Lee (1740–1792), and Benjamin Franklin had been in Paris throughout 1777 trying, under a commission from Congress, to secure foreign aid and conclude treaties of amity and commerce with France and other European powers. Upon learning of the events at Saratoga, the French, fearing the possibility that the British might try to bring about a reconciliation with the colonies, finally decided to recognize the independence of the United States in December, 1777, and on February 6, 1778, the French concluded a treaty of amity and commerce and a treaty of alliance with the American commissioners. The treaty of alliance, which pledged the French to work for American independence and was to take effect with the inauguration of hostilities between France and Britain, is printed in large part below from William M. Malloy (ed.), Treaties, Conventions, International Acts, Protocols, and Agreements between the United States and other Powers, 1776–1909 *(two volumes, 1910), volume I, pages 479–482. The French formally entered the war after a naval engagement with the British on June 17, 1778, and French naval and military aid were of enormous importance in the ultimate American victory.*

Samuel Flagg Bemis, The Diplomacy of the American Revolution *(1935), is the standard account of the negotiation of the French treaties and the early diplomacy of the Revolution, and Weldon A. Brown,* Empire or Independence: A Study in the Failure of Reconciliation, 1774–1783 *(1941), is a full description of British attempts at reconciliation. Carl Van Doren,* Benjamin Franklin *(1938), describes Franklin's important role in bringing about the French alliance.*

The Most Christian King and the United States of North America, to wit: New Hampshire, Massachusetts Bay, Rhodes Island, Connecticut, New York, New Jersey, Pennsylvania, Delaware, Maryland, Virginia, North Carolina, South Carolina, and Georgia, having this day concluded a treaty of amity and commerce, for the reciprocal advantage of their subjects and citizens, have thought it necessary to take into consideration the means of strengthening those engagements, and of rendering them useful to the safety and tranquility of the two parties; particularly in case Great Britain, in resentment of that connection and of the good correspondence which is the object of the said treaty, should break the peace with France, either by direct hostilities, or by hindering her commerce and navigation in a manner contrary to the rights of nations, and the peace subsisting between the two Crowns. And His Majesty and the said United States, having resolved in that case to join their councils and efforts against the enterprises of their common enemy, the respective Plenipotentiaries impowered to concert the clauses and conditions proper to fulfil the said intentions, have, after the most mature deliberation, concluded and determined on the following articles:

410

Article I

If war should break out between France and Great Britain during the continuance of the present war between the United States and England, His Majesty and the said United States shall make it a common cause and aid each other mutually with their good offices, their counsels and their forces, according to the exigence of conjunctures, as becomes good and faithful allies.

Article II

The essential and direct end of the present defensive alliance is to maintain effectually the liberty, sovereignty, and independance absolute and unlimited, of the said United States, as well in matters of government as of commerce.

Article III

The two contracting parties shall each on its own part, and in the manner it may judge most proper, make all the efforts in its power against their common enemy, in order to attain the end proposed.

Article IV

The contracting parties agree that in case either of them should form any particular enterprise in which the concurrence of the other may be desired, the party whose concurrence is desired, shall readily, and with good faith, join to act in concert for that purpose, as far as circumstances and its own particular situation will permit; and in that case, they shall regulate, by a particular convention, the quantity and kind of succour to be furnished, and the time and manner of its being brought into action, as well as the advantages which are to be its compensation.

Article V

If the United States should think fit to attempt the reduction of the British power, remaining in the northern parts of America, or the islands of Bermudas, those countries or islands, in case of success, shall be confederated with or dependant upon the said United States.

Article VI

The Most Christian King renounces forever the possession of the islands of Bermudas, as well as of any part of the continent of North America, which before the treaty of Paris in 1763, or in virtue of that treaty, were acknowledged to belong to the Crown of Great Britain, or to the United States, heretofore called British Colonies, or which are at this time, or have lately been under the power of the King and Crown of Great Britain.

Article VII

If His Most Christian Majesty shall think proper to attack any of the islands situated in the Gulph of Mexico, or near that Gulph, which are at present under the power of Great Britain, all the said isles, in case of success, shall appertain to the Crown of France.

Article VIII

Neither of the two parties shall conclude either truce or peace with Great Britain without the formal consent of the other first obtained; and they mutually engage not to lay down their arms until the independence of the United States shall have been formally or tacitly assured by the treaty or treaties that shall terminate the war.

Article IX

The contracting parties declare, that being resolved to fulfil each on its own part the clauses and conditions of the present treaty of alliance, according to its own power and circumstances, there shall be no after claim of compensation on one side or the other, whatever may be the event of the war.

Article X

The Most Christian King and the United States agree to invite or admit other powers who may have received injuries from England, to make common cause with them, and to accede to the present alliance, under such conditions as shall be freely agreed to and settled between all the parties.

Article XI

The two parties guarantee mutually from the present time and forever against all other powers, to wit: The United States to His Most Christian Majesty, the present possessions of the Crown of France in America, as well as those which it may acquire by the future treaty of peace: And His Most Christian Majesty guarantees on his part to the United States their liberty, sovereignty and independence, absolute and unlimited, as well in matters of government as commerce, and also their possessions, and the additions or conquests that their confederation may obtain during the war, from any of the dominions now, or heretofore possessed by Great Britain in North America, conformable to the 5th and 6th articles above written, the whole as their possessions shall be fixed and assured to the said States, at the moment of the cessation of their present war with England.

Article XII

In order to fix more precisely the sense and application of the preceding article, the contracting parties declare, that in case of a rupture between

France and England the reciprocal guarantee declared in the said article shall have its full force and effect the moment such war shall break out; and if such rupture shall not take place, the mutual obligations of the said guarantee shall not commence until the moment of the cessation of the present war between the United States and England shall have ascertained their possessions.

Article XIII

The present treaty shall be ratified on both sides, and the ratifications shall be exchanged in the space of six months, or sooner if possible. . . .

SELECTION

Achievement of Independence

Neither the defeat of Burgoyne at Saratoga nor the entry of the French into the war seemed, initially at least, to have brought the war any nearer to an end. In the north the Americans could claim some gains as Clinton, who replaced Howe as the head of British forces in May, 1778, withdrew British troops from Philadelphia to New York in June, 1778, in order to prepare for a rumored attack by the French, and evacuated British troops from Newport, Rhode Island, in October, 1779, for use in the south. In the south, however, the Americans suffered one loss after another. During the winter of 1778–1779 British troops occupied Savannah and most of Georgia, and in 1780 Clinton himself captured Charleston at a cost to the Americans of well over five thousand men. Although Clinton returned to his headquarters at New York, General Cornwallis and his subordinates, after crushing an American force at the Battle of Camden in August, proceeded to establish control over most of South Carolina. American victories at King's Mountain (October 7, 1780) and Cowpens (January 17, 1781) weakened Cornwallis, but did not prevent him from pursuing a smaller American Army under the command of General Nathanael Greene (1742–1786) across North Carolina during February and early March, 1781. On March 15, 1781, he finally engaged Greene at the Battle of Guilford Courthouse. Although this battle, which was described by Greene the next day in the letter to Thomas Jefferson reprinted below as Selection 45 A, was technically a British victory, American losses were slight while those of the British were so heavy that Cornwallis had to fall back to Wilmington, North Carolina, to obtain reinforcements and supplies by sea. While Greene took advantage of Cornwallis's withdrawal to push into South Carolina, Cornwallis decided to invade Virginia in an attempt to cut off Greene's sources of reinforcements and supplies.

That decision set in motion a chain of events that led to the defeat and capture of Cornwallis's entire army, the conclusion of the war, and the final achievement of

American independence. With only token opposition from a small American force under the Marquis de Lafayette (1757–1834) and General Anthony Wayne (1745–1796), Cornwallis penetrated far into Virginia during May and June before he retired to the coast to establish closer contacts with Clinton and the British Navy and set up camp at Yorktown in August. In a hastily improvised but effective maneuver that caught Cornwallis completely off guard, Washington and the Comte de Rochambeau (1725–1807), who had gathered their troops around New York for a joint attack on Clinton, moved quickly southward while a large French naval force under Admiral De Grasse drove British naval units in the area away and set up a blockade in early September. By late September a vastly superior allied army had laid Yorktown under siege, and Cornwallis, cut off from any sources of support, surrendered his entire army of 8,000 men on October 19, 1781. Cornwallis's letter reporting these events to Clinton is reprinted below as Selection 45 B.

Although Cornwallis's defeat at Yorktown did not immediately bring an end to hostilities, which dragged on for another year, it did, despite the opposition of George III, bring down the ministry of Lord North, which had been in power since 1770, and drive the British to the peace table. Peace talks began in April, 1782, and the American commissioners, John Jay (1745–1829), Benjamin Franklin, and John Adams, signed the preliminary articles of peace on November 30, 1782, by which the British government agreed to recognize the independence of the United States. Hostilities formally ceased as soon as Britain had negotiated a separate preliminary settlement with France early in 1783, and the final Treaty of Paris, reprinted here as Selection 45 C, was signed on September 3, 1783.

For further reading on the military events leading up to Yorktown see the references listed in the introduction to Selection 43. Samuel Flagg Bemis, The Diplomacy of the American Revolution *(1935), and Richard B. Morris,* The Peacemakers: The Great Powers and American Independence *(1965), provide full accounts of the peace negotiations.*

A. A COSTLY BRITISH VICTORY: GENERAL NATHANAEL GREENE REPORTS ON THE BATTLE OF GUILFORD COURT HOUSE IN A LETTER TO THOMAS JEFFERSON (MAR. 16, 1781)*

SIR

Having formed a junction on the 8th with Colonel Campbells detachment of 18 Months Men and a Body of Carolina Militia under the command of General Butler, I determined to advance towards the Enemy and give them Battle upon the first favorable opportunity. On the 14th, we marched to Guilford Court House and took a position within 8 Miles of the Enemies encampment, with a view to attack them the next Morning, but they anticipated our designs and moved down upon us. We were in perfect readiness to receive them. A severe conflict ensued and after a struggle of near two Hours the Enemy gained the advantage of the field and four pieces of Artillery which could not be brought of[f] for the want of Horses, most of them being killed on the field. Our Army retired in good order to this place,

* These excerpts are reprinted from Julian P. Boyd (ed.), *The Papers of Thomas Jefferson* (1950–   ), vol. V, p. 156.

and are now in the most perfect readiness to give the Enemy Action again. The Carolina Brigades of Militia neglected to take advantage of their position, but fled, (at least the greater part of them, without giving more than one fire) and let in the Enemy upon the second Line, which was composed of Virginians under the command of Generals Stevens and Lawson. Here they met with a warm reception and were very much gauled by an incessant fire which lasted for a considerable length of time. Superior discipline at length prevailed, and the Militia were drove back upon the Continental Troops which made the Action general, but the Enemy breaking through the 2d. Maryland Regiment terminated the fortune of the Day in their favor. However, except the honor of the field they have nothing to boast off. Our loss is very trifling, not more than 300 killed, wounded, and taken; that of the Enemys, from a variety of circumstances and the best intelligence I can get, to at least six hundred. Having encumbered them with a number of Wounded Men, I have nothing to lament but the loss of several valuable Officers, killed and wounded. Among the former is Major Anderson, and among the latter Genl. Stevens. . . .

NATH. GREENE.

B. AMERICAN VICTORY AT YORKTOWN: EARL CORNWALLIS TO SIR HENRY CLINTON (OCT. 20, 1781)*

Sir,

I have the mortification to inform your Excellency that I have been forced to give up the posts of York and Gloucester, and to surrender the troops under my command, by capitulation on the 19th inst. as prisoners of war to the combined forces of America and France.

I never saw this post in a very favourable light, but when I found I was to be attacked in it in so unprepared a state, by so powerful an army and artillery, nothing but the hopes of relief would have induced me to attempt its defence; for I would either have endeavoured to escape to New-York, by rapid marches from the Gloucester side, immediately on the arrival of General Washington's troops at Williamsburgh, or I would notwithstanding the disparity of numbers have attacked them in the open field, where it might have been just possible that fortune would have favoured the gallantry of the handful of troops under my command: but being assured by your Excellency's letters, that every possible means would be tried by the navy and army to relieve us, I could not think myself at liberty to venture upon either of those desperate attempts; therefore, after remaining for two days in a strong position in front of this place, in hopes of being attacked, upon observing that the enemy were taking measures, which could not fail of turning my left flank in a short time, and receiving on the second evening your letter of the 24th of September, informing that the relief would sail about the 5th of October, I withdrew within the works on the night of the 29th of September, hoping by the labour and firmness of the soldiers, to protract the defence until you could arrive. Every thing was to be expected

* These excerpts are reprinted from Earl Cornwallis, *An Answer to That Part of the Narrative of Lieutenant-General Sir .Henry Clinton* (1783), pp. 206–214.

from the spirit of the troops, but every disadvantage attended their labour, as the works were to be continued under the enemy's fire, and our stock of intrenching tools, which did not much exceed four hundred, when we began to work in the latter end of August, was now much diminished.

The enemy broke ground on the night of the 30th, and constructed on that night, and the two following days and nights, two redoubts, which, with some works that had belonged to our outward position, occupied a gorge between two creeks or ravines, which come from the river on each side of the town. On the night of the 6th of October they made their first parallel, extending from its right on the river to a deep ravine on the left, nearly opposite to the center of this place, and embracing our whole left at the distance of six hundred yards. Having perfected this parallel, their batteries opened on the evening of the 9th, against our left, and other batteries fired at the same time against a redoubt, advanced over the Creek upon our right, and defended by about one hundred and twenty men of the 23d regiment and marines, who maintained that post with uncommon gallantry. The fire continued incessant from heavy cannon and from mortars and howitzes, throwing shells from eight to sixteen inches, until all our guns on the left were silenced, our work much damaged, and our loss of men considerable. On the night of the 11th they began their second parallel, about three hundred yards nearer to us; the troops being much weakened by sickness as well as by the fire of the besiegers, and observing that the enemy had not only secured their flanks, but proceeded in every respect with the utmost regularity and caution, I could not venture so large sorties, as to hope from them any considerable effect; but otherwise, I did every thing in my power to interrupt this work, by opening new embrazures for guns, and keeping up a constant fire with all the howitzes and small mortars that we could man. On the evening of the 14th, they assaulted and carried two redoubts that had been advanced about three hundred yards for the purpose of delaying their approaches, and covering our left flank, and during the night included them in their second parallel, on which they continued to work with the utmost exertion. Being perfectly sensible that our works could not stand many hours after the opening of the batteries of that parallel, we not only continued a constant fire with all our mortars, and every gun that could be brought to bear upon it, but a little before day break on the morning of the 16th, I ordered a sortie of about three hundred and fifty men under the direction of Lieutenant-colonel Abercrombie to attack two batteries, which appeared to be in the greatest forwardness, and to spike the guns. A detachment of guards with the eightieth company of Grenadiers, under the command of Lieutenant-colonel Lake attacked the one, and one of Light Infantry under the command of Major Armstrong attacked the other, and both succeeded by forcing the redoubts that covered them, spiking eleven guns, and killing or wounding about one hundred of the French troops, who had the guard of that part of the trenches, and with little loss on our side. This action, though extremely honourable to the officers and soldiers who executed it, proved of little public advantage, for the cannon having been spiked in a hurry, were soon rendered fit for service again, and before dark the whole parallel and batteries appeared to be nearly complete. At this time we knew that there was no part of the whole front attacked, on which we could show a single gun, and our shells were nearly expended; I therefore had only to chuse between preparing to surrender next day, or endeavouring to get off with the greatest part of the troops, and I determined to attempt the latter, reflecting that though it should prove unsuccessful in its immediate object, it might at least delay the enemy in the prosecution of further enterprizes: sixteen large boats were prepared, and upon other pretexts were ordered to be in readiness to receive troops precisely at ten o'clock. With these I hoped to pass the infantry during the night, abandoning our baggage, and leaving a detachment to capitulate for the town's people, and the sick and wounded; on which subject a letter was ready to be delivered to General Washington. After making my arrangements with the utmost secrecy, the Light Infantry, greatest part of the Guards, and part of the twenty-third regiment landed at Gloucester; but at this critical moment, the weather from being moderate and calm, changed to a most violent storm of wind and rain, and drove all the boats, some of which had troops on board, down the river. It was soon evident that the intended passage was impracticable, and the absence of the boats rendered it equally impossible to bring back the troops that had passed; which I had ordered about two in the morning. In this situation, with my little force divided, the enemy's batteries opened at day break; the passage between this place and Gloucester was much exposed, but the boats having now returned, they were ordered to bring back the troops that had passed during the night, and they joined us in the forenoon without much loss. Our works in the mean time were going to ruin, and not having been able to strengthen them by abbatis, nor in any other manner but by a slight fraizing which the enemy's artillery were demolishing wherever they fired, my opinion entirely coincided with that of the engineer and principal officers of the army, that they were in many places assailable in the forenoon, and that by the continuence of the same fire for a few hours longer, they would be in such a state as to render it desperate with our numbers to attempt to maintain them. We at that time could not fire a single gun, only one eight-inch and little more than an hundred cohorn shells remained; a diversion by the French ships of war that lay at the mouth of York-river, was to be expected. Our numbers had been diminished by the enemy's fire, but particularly by sickness, and the strength and spirits of those in the works were much exhausted by the fatigue of constant watching and unremitting duty. Under all these circumstances, I thought it would have been wanton and inhuman to the last degree to sacrifice the lives of this small body of gallant soldiers, who had ever behaved with so much fidelity and courage, by exposing them to an assault, which from the numbers and precautions of the enemy could not fail to succeed. I therefore proposed to capitulate, and I have the honour to inclose to your Excellency the copy of the correspondence between General Washington and me on that subject, and the terms of capitulation agreed upon. I sincerely lament that better could not be obtained, but I have neglected nothing in my power to alleviate the misfortune and distress of both officers and soldiers. The men are well cloathed and provided with necessaries, and I trust will be regularly supplied by the means of the officers that are permitted to remain with them. The treatment, in general, that we have received from the enemy since our surrender, has been perfectly good and proper; but the kindness and attention that has been shewn to us by the French officers in particular, their delicate sensibility of our situation, their generous and pressing offer of money both public and private, to any amount, has really gone beyond what I can possibly describe, and will, I hope, make an impression on the breast of every British officer, whenever the fortune of war should put any of them into our power.

Although the event has been so unfortunate, the patience of the soldiers in bearing the greatest fatigues, and their firmness and intrepidity under a persevering fire of shot and shells, that I believe has not often been exceeded, deserved the highest admiration and praise. A successful defence, however, in our situation was perhaps impossible, for the place could only be reckoned an entrenched camp, subject in most places to enfilade, and the ground in general so disadvantageous, that nothing but the necessity of fortifying it as a post to protect the navy, could have induced any person to erect works upon it. Our force diminished daily by sickness and other losses, and was reduced when we offered to capitulate on this side to little more than three thousand two hundred rank and file fit for duty, including officers, servants, and artificers; and at Gloucester about six hundred, including cavalry. The enemy's army consisted of upwards of eight thousand French, nearly as many continentals, and five thousand militia. They brought an immense train of heavy artillery, most amply furnished with ammunition, and perfectly well manned.

The constant and universal chearfulness and spirit of the officers in all hardships and danger, deserve my warmest acknowledgments; and I have been particularly indebted to Brigadier-general O'Hara, and to Lieutenant-colonel Abercrombie, the former commanding on the right and the latter on the left, for their attention and exertion on every occasion. The detachment of the twenty-third regiment of Marines in the redoubt on the right, commanded by Captain Apthorpe, and the subsequent detachments commanded by Lieutenant-colonel Johnson, deserve particular commendation. Captain Rochfort who commanded the artillery, and indeed every officer and soldier of that distinguished corps; and Lieutenant Sutherland the commanding Engineer have merited in every respect my highest approbation; and I cannot sufficiently acknowledge my obligations to Captain Symonds, who commanded his Majesty's ships, and to the other officers and seamen of the navy for their active and zealous co-operation. . . .

CORNWALLIS.

C. PEACE: THE TREATY OF PARIS (SEPT. 3, 1783)*

In the name of the Most Holy and Undivided Trinity.

It having pleased the Divine Providence to dispose the hearts of the most serene and most potent Prince George the Third, by the Grace of God King of Great Britain, France, and Ireland, Defender of the Faith, Duke of Brunswick and Luneburg, Arch-Treasurer and Prince Elector of the Holy Roman Empire, &ca., and of the United States of America, to forget all past misunderstandings and differences that have unhappily interrupted the good correspondence and friendship which they mutually wish to restore; and to establish such a beneficial and satisfactory intercourse between the two countries, upon the ground of reciprocal advantages and mutual convenience,

* These excerpts are reprinted from William M. Malloy (ed.), *Treaties, Conventions, International Acts, Protocols, and Agreements between the United States and Other Powers, 1776–1909* (2 vols., 1910), vol. I, pp. 586–590.

as may promote and secure to both perpetual peace and harmony: And
having for this desirable end already laid the foundation of peace and
reconciliation, by the provisional articles, signed at Paris, on the 30th of
Nov'r, 1782, by the commissioners empowered on each part, which articles
were agreed to be inserted in and to constitute the treaty of peace proposed
to be concluded between the Crown of Great Britain and the said United
States, but which treaty was not to be concluded until terms of peace should
be agreed upon between Great Britain and France, and His Britannic Majesty should be ready to conclude such treaty accordingly; and the treaty
between Great Britain and France having since been concluded, His Britannic Majesty and the United States of America, in order to carry into full
effect the provisional articles above mentioned, according to the tenor
thereof, have constituted and appointed, that is to say, His Britannic Majesty on his part, David Hartley, esqr., member of the Parliament of Great
Britain; and the said United States on their part, John Adams, esqr., late a
commissioner of the United States of America at the Court of Versailles,
late Delegate in Congress from the State of Massachusetts, and chief justice
of the said State, and Minister Plenipotentiary of the said United States to
their High Mightinesses the States General of the United Netherlands;
Benjamin Franklin, esq're, late Delegate in Congress from the State of
Pennsylvania, president of the convention of the said State, and Minister
Plenipotentiary from the United States of America at the Court of Versailles;
John Jay, esq're, late president of Congress, and chief justice of the State
of New York, and Minister Plenipotentiary from the said United States at
the Court of Madrid, to be the Plenipotentiaries for the concluding and
signing the present definitive treaty; who, after having reciprocally communicated their respective full powers, have agreed upon and confirmed the
following articles:

Article I

His Britannic Majesty acknowledges the said United States, viz. New
Hampshire, Massachusetts Bay, Rhode Island, and Providence Plantations,
Connecticut, New York, New Jersey, Pennsylvania, Delaware, Maryland,
Virginia, North Carolina, South Carolina, and Georgia, to be free, sovereign
and independent States; that he treats with them as such, and for himself,
his heirs and successors, relinquishes all claims to the Government, propriety
and territorial rights of the same, and every part thereof.

Article II

And that all disputes which might arise in future, on the subject of the
boundaries of the said United States may be prevented, it is hereby agreed
and declared, that the following are, and shall be their boundaries, viz:
From the northwest angle of Nova Scotia, viz. that angle which is formed by
a line drawn due north from the source of Saint Croix River to the Highlands; along the said Highlands which divide those rivers that empty themselves into the river St. Lawrence, from those which fall into the Atlantic
Ocean, to the northwesternmost head of Connecticut River; thence down

along the middle of that river, to the forty-fifth degree of north latitude; from thence, by a line due west on said latitude, until it strikes the river Iroquois or Cataraquy; thence along the middle of said river into Lake Ontario, through the middle of said lake until it strikes the communication by water between that lake and Lake Erie; thence along the middle of said communication into Lake Erie, through the middle of said lake until it arrives at the water communication between that lake and Lake Huron; thence along the middle of said water communication into the Lake Huron; thence through the middle of said lake to the water communication between that lake and Lake Superior; thence through Lake Superior northward of the Isles Royal and Phelipeaux, to the Long Lake; thence through the middle of said Long Lake, and the water communication between it and the Lake of the Woods, to the said Lake of the Woods; thence through the said lake to the most northwestern point thereof, and from thence on a due west course to the river Mississippi; thence by a line to be drawn along the middle of the said river Mississippi until it shall intersect the northernmost part of the thirty-first degree of north latitude. South, by a line to be drawn due east from the determination of the line last mentioned, in the latitude of thirty-one degrees north of the Equator, to the middle of the river Apalachicola or Catahouche; thence along the middle thereof to its junction with the Flint River; thence strait to the head of St. Mary's River; and thence down along the middle of St. Mary's River to the Atlantic Ocean. East, by a line to be drawn along the middle of the river St. Croix, from its mouth in the Bay of Fundy to its source, and from its source directly north to the aforesaid Highlands, which divide the rivers that fall into the Atlantic Ocean from those which fall into the river St. Lawrence; comprehending all islands within twenty leagues of any part of the shores of the United States, and lying between lines to be drawn due east from the points where the aforesaid boundaries between Nova Scotia on the one part, and East Florida on the other, shall respectively touch the Bay of Fundy and the Atlantic Ocean; excepting such islands as now are, or heretofore have been, within the limits of the said province of Nova Scotia.

Article III

It is agreed that the people of the United States shall continue to enjoy unmolested the right to take fish of every kind on the Grand Bank, and on all the other banks of Newfoundland; also in the Gulph of Saint Lawrence, and at all other places in the sea where the inhabitants of both countries used at any time heretofore to fish. And also that the inhabitants of the United States shall have liberty to take fish of every kind on such part of the coast of Newfoundland as British fishermen shall use (but not to dry or cure the same on that island) and also on the coasts, bays and creeks of all other of His Britannic Majesty's dominions in America; and that the American fishermen shall have liberty to dry and cure fish in any of the unsettled bays, harbours and creeks of Nova Scotia, Magdalen Islands, and Labrador, so long as the same shall remain unsettled; but so soon as the same or either of them shall be settled, it shall not be lawful for the said fishermen to dry or cure fish at such settlements, without a previous agreement for that purpose with the inhabitants, proprietors or possessors of the ground.

Article IV

It is agreed that creditors on either side shall meet with no lawful impediment to the recovery of the full value in sterling money, of all bona fide debts heretofore contracted.

Article V

It is agreed that the Congress shall earnestly recommend it to the legislatures of the respective States, to provide for the restitution of all estates, rights and properties which have been confiscated, belonging to real British subjects, and also of the estates, rights and properties of persons resident in districts in the possession of His Majesty's arms, and who have not borne arms against the said United States. And that persons of any other description shall have free liberty to go to any part or parts of any of the thirteen United States, and therein to remain twelve months, unmolested in their endeavours to obtain the restitution of such of their estates, rights and properties as may have been confiscated; and that Congress shall also earnestly recommend to the several States a reconsideration and revision of all acts or laws regarding the premises, so as to render the said laws or acts perfectly consistent, not only with justice and equity, but with that spirit of conciliation which, on the return of the blessings of peace, should universally prevail. And that Congress shall also earnestly recommend to the several States, that the estates, rights and properties of such last mentioned persons, shall be restored to them, they refunding to any persons who may be now in possession, the *bona fide* price (where any has been given) which such persons may have paid on purchasing any of the said lands, rights or properties, since the confiscation. And it is agreed, that all persons who have any interest in confiscated lands, either by debts, marriage settlements or otherwise, shall meet with no lawful impediment in the prosecution of their just rights.

Article VI

That there shall be no future confiscations made, nor any prosecutions commenc'd against any person or persons for, or by reason of the part which he or they may have taken in the present war; and that no person shall, on that account, suffer any future loss or damage, either in his person, liberty or property; and that those who may be in confinement on such charges, at the time of the ratification of the treaty in America, shall be immediately set at liberty, and the prosecutions so commenced be discontinued.

Article VII

There shall be a firm and perpetual peace between His Britannic Majesty and the said States, and between the subjects of the one and the citizens of the other, wherefore all hostilities, both by sea and land, shall from henceforth cease: All prisoners on both sides shall be set at liberty, and His

Britannic Majesty shall, with all convenient speed, and without causing any destruction, or carrying away any negroes or other property of the American inhabitants, withdraw all his armies, garrisons and fleets from the said United States, and from every post, place and harbour within the same; leaving in all fortifications the American artillery that may be therein: And shall also order and cause all archives, records, deeds and papers, belonging to any of the said States, or their citizens, which, in the course of the war, may have fallen into the hands of his officers, to be forthwith restored and deliver'd to the proper States and persons to whom they belong.

Article VIII

The navigation of the river Mississippi, from its source to the ocean, shall for ever remain free and open to the subjects of Great Britain, and the citizens of the United States.

Article IX

In case it should so happen that any place or territory belonging to Great Britain or to the United States, should have been conquer'd by the arms of either from the other, before the arrival of the said provisional articles in America, it is agreed, that the same shall be restored without difficulty, and without requiring any compensation.

Article X

The solemn ratifications of the present treaty, expedited in good and due form, shall be exchanged between the contracting parties, in the space of six months, or sooner if possible, to be computed from the day of the signature of the present treaty. In witness whereof, we the undersigned, their Ministers, Plenipotentiary, have in their name and in virtue of our full powers, signed with our hands the present definitive treaty, and caused the seals of our arms to be affix'd thereto.

SELECTION

"A New Prospect in Human Affairs": Richard Price, "Observations on the Importance of the American Revolution" (1784)

Critics of the existing order and "warm advocates for liberty" in both Great Britain and continental Europe hailed the successful conclusion of the War for Independence as a great victory for humanity. Dr. Richard Price (1723–1791), the English radical thinker, elaborated upon this theme in March, 1784, in his Observations on the Importance of the American Revolution, *portions of which are reprinted here from the original London edition, pages 1–8, 84–85. Persuaded by "Reason, as well as tradition and revelation . . . that a more improved and happy state of human affairs will take place before the consummation of all things," Price hailed the Revolution for opening up "a new prospect in human affairs" and ushering in a "new æra in the history of mankind" and predicted that it might even "prove the most important step in the progressive course of human improvement." It promised to make the new United States the seat of "liberty, science, peace, and virtue," a "place of refuge for opprest men in every region of the world," and a providential base for extending the "sacred blessings" of "universal liberty" to the rest of the earth. Precisely because so much depended on them, however, the Americans, Price warned, had to take special care "that the fairest experiment ever tried in human affairs" did not miscarry and that the promises of the Revolution would be fulfilled.*

The reaction to the American Revolution in Great Britain and Europe is described by R. R. Palmer, The Age of the Democratic Revolution, *vol. I (1959).*

HAVING, from pure conviction, taken a warm part in favour of the *British* colonies (now the United States of America) during the late war; and been exposed, in consequence of this, to *much* abuse and *some* danger; it must be supposed that I have been waiting for the issue with anxiety——I am thankful that my anxiety is removed; and that I have been spared to be a witness to that very issue of the war which has been all along the object of my wishes. With heart-felt satisfaction, I see the revolution in favour of universal liberty which has taken place in *America;*—a revolution which opens a new prospect in human affairs, and begins a new æra in the history of mankind;——a revolution by which *Britons* themselves will be the greatest gainers, if wise enough to improve properly the check that has been given to the despotism of their ministers, and to catch the flame of virtuous liberty which has saved their American brethren.

The late war, in its *commencement and progress*, did great good by disseminating just sentiments of the rights of mankind, and the nature of legitimate government; by exciting a spirit of resistance to tyranny which has emancipated one *European* country, and is likely to emancipate others; and by occasioning the establishment in *America* of forms of government more equitable and more liberal than any that the world has yet known. But, in its *termination*, the war has done still greater good by preserving the new governments from that destruction in which they must have been involved, had Britain conquered; by providing, in a sequestered continent possessed of many singular advantages, a place of refuge for opprest men in every region of the world; and by laying the foundation there of an empire which may be the seat of liberty, science and virtue, and from whence there is reason to hope these sacred blessings will spread, till they become universal, and the time arrives when kings and priests shall have no more power to oppress, and that ignominious slavery which has hitherto debased the world is exterminated. I therefore, think I see the hand of Providence in the late war working for the general good.

Reason, as well as tradition and revelation, lead us to expect that a more improved and happy state of human affairs will take place before the consummation of all things. The world has hitherto been gradually improving. Light and knowledge have been gaining ground, and human life *at present* compared with what it *once* was, is much the same that a youth approaching to manhood is compared with an infant.

Such are the natures of things that this progress must continue. During particular intervals it may be interrupted, but it cannot be destroy'd. Every present advance prepares the way for farther advances; and a single experiment or discovery may some times give rise to so many more as suddenly to raise the species higher, and to resemble the effects of opening a new sense, or of the fall of a spark on a train that springs a mine. For this reason, mankind may at last arrive at degrees of improvement which we cannot now even suspect to be possible. A dark age may follow an enlightened age; but, in this case, the light, after being smothered for a time, will break out again with a brighter lustre. The present age of increased light, considered as succeeding the age of *Greece* and *Rome* and an intermediate period of thick darkness, furnishes a proof of the truth of this observation. There are certain kinds of improvement which, when once made, cannot be entirely lost. During the dark ages, the improvements made in the ages that preceded them remained so far as to be recovered immediately at the resurrection of letters, and to produce afterwards that more rapid progress in improvement which has distinguished modern times.

There can scarcely be a more pleasing and encouraging object of reflection than this. An accidental observation of the effects of gravity in a garden has been the means of discovering the laws that govern the solar system,* and of enabling us to look down with pity on the ignorance of the most enlightened times among the antients. What new dignity has been given to man, and what additions have been made to his powers, by the invention of optical glasses, printing, gun-powder, &c. and by the late discoveries in navigation, mathematics, natural philosophy, &c.?

But among the events in modern times tending to the elevation of mankind, there are none probably of so much consequence as the recent one which occasions these observations. Perhaps, I do not go too far when I say that, next to the introduction of Christianity among mankind, the American revolution may prove the most important step in the progressive course of human improvement. It is an event which may produce a general diffusion of the principles of humanity, and become the means of setting free mankind from the shackles of superstition and tyranny, by leading them to see and know "that nothing is *fundamental* but impartial enquiry, an honest mind, and virtuous practice——that state policy ought not to be applied to the support of speculative opinions and formularies of faith."——"That the members of a civil community are† *confederates,* not *subjects;* and their rulers, *servants,* not *masters.*——And that all legitimate government consists in the dominion of equal laws made with common consent; that is, in the dominion of men over *themselves;* and not in the dominion of communities over communities, or of any men over other men."

Happy will the world be when these truths shall be every where acknowledged and practiced upon. Religious bigotry, that cruel demon, will be then

---

* This refers to an account given of Sir Isaac Newton in the Preface to Dr. PEMBERTON'S View of his Philosophy.

† These are the words of MONTESQUIEU.

laid asleep. Slavish governments and slavish Hierarchies will then sink; and the old prophecies be verified, "that the last universal empire upon earth shall be the empire of reason and virtue, under which the gospel of peace (better understood) *shall have free course and be glorified, many will run to and fro and knowledge be increased, the wolf dwell with the lamb and the leopard with the kid, and nation no more lift up a sword against nation."*

It is a conviction I cannot resist, that the independence of the *English* colonies in America is one of the steps ordained by Providence to introduce these times; and I can scarcely be deceived in this conviction, if the United States should escape some dangers which threaten them, and will take proper care to throw themselves open to future improvements, and to make the most of the advantages of their present situation. Should this happen, it will be true of them as it was of the people of the Jews, that *in them all the families of the earth shall be blessed.* It is scarcely possible they should think too highly of their own consequence. Perhaps, there never existed a people on whose wisdom and virtue more depended; or to whom a station of more importance in the plan of Providence has been assigned. They have begun nobly. They have fought with success for themselves and for the world; and, in the midst of invasion and carnage, established forms of government favourable in the highest degree to the rights of mankind. . . .

The united States of *America.* . . . may become the seats of liberty, science, peace, and virtue; happy within themselves, and a refuge to the world. . . .

The present moment, however auspicious to the united States if wisely improved, is critical; and, though apparently the end of all their dangers, may prove the time of their greatest danger. I have, indeed, since finishing this Address, been mortified more than I can express by accounts which have led me to fear that I have carried my ideas of them too high, and deceived myself with visionary expectations.——And should this be true— Should the return of peace and the pride of independence lead them to security and dissipation—Should they lose those virtuous and simple manners by which alone Republics can long subsist—Should false refinement, luxury, and irreligion spread among them; excessive jealousy district their governments; and clashing interests, subject to no strong controul, break the federal union——The consequence will be, that the fairest experiment ever tried in human affairs will miscarry; and that a REVOLUTION which had revived the hopes of good men and promised an opening to better times, will become a discouragement to all future efforts in favour of liberty, and prove only an opening to a new scene of human degeneracy and misery.

PART ELEVEN

The Confederation Period

The First National Constitution:
The Articles of Confederation (Mar. 1, 1781)

In mid-1776 there was virtually unanimous agreement among American leaders and the authors of the many proposals for reconstituting the polity that the new states should form some kind of permanent national government. The exigencies of war required concerted action, and in the face of a common enemy the variations in economic orientation, social values, religious beliefs, and political traditions from section to section and state to state seemed to be far less significant than the interests and traditions that bound them together and made it possible for them to think of themselves as one people, as Americans as well as Carolinians, Rhode Islanders, Pennsylvanians, or Virginians. Thus on June 12, 1776, just five days after Richard Henry Lee had introduced the resolutions for independence, Congress, acting on Lee's motion, appointed a committee under the chairmanship of John Dickinson to prepare a plan of confederation. The Dickinson committee brought in a series of proposals on July 12, 1776, that formed the basis for the Articles of Confederation adopted by the Congress some sixteen months later on November 15, 1777, and transmitted to the states two days later for ratification. By March, 1779, all of the states had ratified the Articles except Maryland, which refused to ratify until the larger states with extensive claims in the West had ceded their Western lands to the national government. Virginians charged, and not without some justice, that Maryland's position derived from the Western land schemes of some of its foremost political leaders who hoped to be able to manipulate Congress to their own advantage. After considerable delay, however, Virginia agreed on January 2, 1781, to cede all of its lands north of the Ohio River. Maryland thereupon ratified the Articles, and they went into effect on March 1, 1781, just a little less than eight months before Yorktown. The first constitution of the United States, the Articles of Confederation is reprinted here from Francis Newton Thorpe (ed.), The Federal and State Constitutions, and Other Organic Laws *(seven volumes, 1909), volume I, pages 9–17.*

The most detailed and authoritative account of the long conflict over the adoption of the Articles is in Merrill Jensen, The Articles of Confederation: An Interpretation of the Social-Constitutional History of the American Revolution, 1774–1781 *(1940). A detailed analysis of the Articles will be found in Andrew C. McLaughlin,* A Constitutional History of the United States *(1935).*

Whereas the Delegates of the United States of America in Congress assembled did on the fifteenth day of November in the Year of our Lord One Thousand Seven Hundred and Seventyseven, and in the Second Year of the Independence of America agree to certain articles of Confederation and perpetual Union between the States of New-hampshire, Massachusetts-bay, Rhodeisland and Providence Plantations, Connecticut, New York, New Jersey, Pennsylvania, Delaware, Maryland, Virginia, North-Carolina, South-Carolina and Georgia in the Words following, viz.

Articles of Confederation and perpetual Union between the States of New-hampshire, Massachusetts-bay, Rhodeisland and Providence Plantations, Connecticut, New-York, New-Jersey, Pennsylvania, Delaware, Maryland, Virginia, North-Carolina, South-Carolina and Georgia.

Article I

The stile of this confederacy shall be "The United States of America."

Article II

Each State retains its sovereignty, freedom and independence, and every power, jurisdiction and right, which is not by this confederation expressly delegated to the United States, in Congress assembled.

Article III

The said States hereby severally enter into a firm league of friendship with each other, for their common defence, the security of their liberties, and their mutual and general welfare, binding themselves to assist each other, against all force offered to, or attacks made upon them, or any of them, on account of religion, sovereignty, trade, or any other pretence whatever.

Article IV

The better to secure and perpetuate mutual friendship and intercourse among the people of the different States in this Union, the free inhabitants of each of these States, paupers, vagabonds and fugitives from justice excepted, shall be entitled to all privileges and immunities of free citizens in the several States; and the people of each State shall have free ingress and regress to and from any other State, and shall enjoy therein all the privileges of trade and commerce, subject to the same duties, impositions and restrictions as the inhabitants thereof respectively, provided that such restrictions shall not extend so far as to prevent the removal of property imported into any State, to any other State of which the owner is an inhabitant; provided also that no imposition, duties or restriction shall be laid by any State, on the property of the United States, or either of them.

If any person guilty of, or charged with treason, felony, or other high misdemeanor in any State, shall flee from justice, and be found in any of the United States, he shall upon demand of the Governor or Executive power, of the State from which he fled, be delivered up and removed to the State having jurisdiction of his offence.

Full faith and credit shall be given in each of these States to the records, acts and judicial proceedings of the courts and magistrates of every other State.

Article V

For the more convenient management of the general interests of the United States, delegates shall be annually appointed in such manner as the legislature of each State shall direct, to meet in Congress on the first Monday in November, in every year, with a power reserved to each State, to recall its delegates, or any of them, at any time within the year, and to send others in their stead, for the remainder of the year.

No State shall be represented in Congress by less than two, nor by more than seven members; and no person shall be capable of being a delegate for more than three years in any term of six years; nor shall any person, being a delegate, be capable of holding any office under the United States, for which he, or another for his benefit receives any salary, fees or emolument of any kind.

Each State shall maintain its own delegates in a meeting of the States, and while they act as members of the committee of the States.

In determining questions in the United States, in Congress assembled, each State shall have one vote.

Freedom of Speech and debate in Congress shall not be impeached or questioned in any court, or place out of Congress, and the members of Congress shall be protected in their persons from arrests and imprisonments, during the time of their going to and from, and attendance on Congress, except for treason, felony, or breach of the peace.

Article VI

No State without the consent of the United States in Congress assembled, shall send any embassy to, or receive any embassy from, or enter into any conferrence, agreement, alliance or treaty with any king prince or state; nor shall any person holding any office of profit or trust under the United States, or any of them, accept of any present, emolument, office or title of any kind whatever from any king, prince or foreign state; nor shall the United States in Congress assembled, or any of them, grant any title of nobility.

No two or more States shall enter into any treaty, confederation or alliance whatever between them, without the consent of the United States in Congress assembled, specifying accurately the purposes for which the same is to be entered into, and how long it shall continue.

No State shall lay any imposts or duties, which may interfere with any stipulations in treaties, entered into by the United States in Congress assembled, with any king, prince or state, in pursuance of any treaties already proposed by Congress, to the courts of France and Spain.

No vessels of war shall be kept up in time of peace by any State, except such number only, as shall be deemed necessary by the United States in Congress assembled, for the defence of such State, or its trade; nor shall any body of forces be kept up by any State, in time of peace, except such number only, as in the judgment of the United States, in Congress assembled, shall be deemed requisite to garrison the forts necessary for the defence of such State; but every State shall always keep up a well regulated and disciplined militia, sufficiently armed and accoutred, and shall provide and constantly have ready for use, in public stores, a due number of field pieces and tents, and a proper quantity of arms, ammunition and camp equipage.

No State shall engage in any war without the consent of the United States in Congress assembled, unless such State be actually invaded by enemies, or shall have received certain advice of a resolution being formed by some nation of Indians to invade such State, and the danger is so imminent as not to admit of a delay, till the United States in Congress assembled can be consulted: nor shall any State grant commissions to any ships or vessels of war, nor letters of marque or reprisal, except it be after a declaration of war by the United States in Congress assembled, and then only against the kingdom or state and the subjects thereof, against which war has been so declared, and under such regulations as shall be established by the United States in Congress assembled, unless such State be infested by pirates, in which case vessels of war may be fitted out for that occasion, and kept so long as the danger shall continue, or until the United States in Congress assembled shall determine otherwise.

Article VII

When land-forces are raised by any State for the common defence, all officers of or under the rank of colonel, shall be appointed by the Legislature of each State respectively by whom such forces shall be raised, or in such manner as such State shall direct, and all vacancies shall be filled up by the State which first made the appointment.

Article VIII

All charges of war, and all other expenses that shall be incurred for the common defence or general welfare, and allowed by the United States in Congress assembled, shall be defrayed out a common treasury, which shall be supplied by the several States, in proportion to the value of all land within each State, granted to or surveyed for any person, as such land and the buildings and improvements thereon shall be estimated according to such mode as the United States in Congress assembled, shall from time to time direct and appoint.

The taxes for paying that proportion shall be laid and levied by the authority and direction of the Legislatures of the several States within the time agreed upon by the United States in Congress assembled.

Article IX

The United States in Congress assembled, shall have the sole and exclusive right and power of determining on peace and war, except in the cases mentioned in the sixth article—of sending and receiving ambassadors—entering into treaties and alliances, provided that no treaty of commerce shall be made whereby the legislative power of the respective States shall be restrained from imposing such imposts and duties on foreigners, as their own people are subjected to, or from prohibiting the exportation or importation of any species of goods or commodities whatsoever—of establishing rules for deciding in all cases, what captures on land or water shall be legal, and in what manner prizes taken by land or naval forces in the service of the United States shall be divided or appropriated—of granting letters of marque and reprisal in times of peace—appointing courts for the trial of piracies and felonies committed on the high seas and establishing courts for receiving and determining finally appeals in all cases of captures, provided that no member of Congress shall be appointed a judge of any of the said courts.

The United States in Congress assembled shall also be the last resort on appeal in all disputes and differences now subsisting or that hereafter may arise between two or more States concerning boundary, jurisdiction or any other cause whatever; which authority shall always be exercised in the manner following. Whenever the legislative or executive authority or lawful agent of any State in controversy with another shall present a petition to Congress, stating the matter in question and praying for a hearing, notice thereof shall be given by order of Congress to the legislative or executive authority of the other State in controversy, and a day assigned for the appearance of the parties by their lawful agents, who shall then be directed to appoint by joint consent, commissioners or judges to constitute a court for hearing and determining the matter in question: but if they cannot agree, Congress shall name three persons out of each of the United States, and from the list of such persons each party shall alternately strike out one, the petitioners beginning, until the number shall be reduced to thirteen; and from that number not less than seven, nor more than nine names as Congress shall direct, shall in the presence of Congress be drawn out by lot, and the persons whose names shall be so drawn or any five of them, shall be commissioners or judges, to hear and finally determine the controversy, so always as a major part of the judges who shall hear the cause shall agree in the determination: and if either party shall neglect to attend at the day appointed, without showing reasons, which Congress shall judge sufficient, or being present shall refuse to strike, the Congress shall proceed to nominate three persons out of each State, and the Secretary of Congress shall strike in behalf of such party absent or refusing; and the judgment and sentence of the court is to be appointed in the manner before prescribed, shall be final and conclusive; and if any of the parties shall refuse to submit to the authority of such court, or to appear or defend their claim or cause, the court shall nevertheless proceed to pronounce sentence, or judgment, which shall in like manner be final and decisive, the judgment or sentence and other proceedings being in either case transmitted to Congress, and lodged among the acts of Congress for the security of the parties concerned: provided that every commissioner, before he sits in judgment, shall take an oath to be administered by one of the judges of the supreme or superior court of the State where the cause shall be tried, "well and truly to hear and determine the matter in question, according to the best of his judgment, without favour, affection or hope of reward:" provided also that no State shall be deprived of territory for the benefit of the United States.

All controversies concerning the private right of soil claimed under different grants of two or more States, whose jurisdiction as they may respect such lands, and the States which passed such grants are adjusted, the said grants or either of them being at the same time claimed to have originated antecedent to such settlement of jurisdiction, shall on the petition of either party to the Congress of the United States, be finally determined as near as may be in the same manner as is before prescribed for deciding disputes respecting territorial jurisdiction between different States.

The United States in Congress assembled shall also have the sole and exclusive right and power of regulating the alloy and value of coin struck by their own authority, or by that of the respective States.—fixing the standard of weights and measures throughout the United States.—regulating the trade and managing all affairs with the Indians, not members of any of the States, provided that the legislative right of any State within its own limits be not infringed or violated—establishing and regulating post-offices from one State to another, throughout all the United States, and exacting such postage on the papers passing thro' the same as may be requisite to defray the expenses of the said office—appointing all officers of the land forces, in the service of the United States, excepting regimental officers—appointing all the officers of the naval forces, and commissioning all officers whatever in the service of the United States—making rules for the government and regulation of the said land and naval forces, and directing their operations.

The United States in Congress assembled shall have authority to appoint a committee, to sit in the recess of Congress, to be denominated "a Committee of the States," and to consist of one delegate from each State; and to appoint such other committees and civil officers as may be necessary for managing the general affairs of the United States under their direction—to appoint one of their number to preside, provided that no person be allowed to serve in the office of president more than one year in any term of three years; to ascertain the necessary sums of money to be raised for the service of the United States, and to appropriate and apply the same for defraying the public expenses—to borrow money, or emit bills on the credit of the United States, transmitting every half year to the respective States an account of the sums of money so borrowed or emitted,—to build and equip a navy—to agree upon the number of land forces, and to make requisitions from each State for its quota, in proportion to the number of white inhabitants in such State; which requisition shall be binding, and thereupon the Legislature of each State shall appoint the regimental officers, raise the men and cloath, arm and equip them in a soldier like manner, at the expense of the United States; and the officers and men so cloathed, armed and equipped shall march to the place appointed, and within the time agreed on by the United States in Congress assembled: but if the United States in Congress assembled shall, on consideration of circumstances judge proper that any State should not raise men, or should raise a smaller number of men than the quota thereof, such extra number shall be raised, officered, cloathed, armed and equipped in the same manner as the quota of such State, unless the legislature of such State shall judge that such extra number cannot be safely spared out of the same, in which case they shall raise officer, cloath, arm and equip as many of such extra number as they judge can be safely spared. And the officers and men so cloathed, armed and equipped, shall march to the place appointed, and within the time agreed on by the United States in Congress assembled.

The United States in Congress assembled shall never engage in a war, nor grant letters of marque and reprisal in time of peace, nor enter into any treaties or alliances, nor coin money, nor regulate the value thereof, nor ascertain the sums and expenses necessary for the defence and welfare of the United States, or any of them, nor emit bills, nor borrow money on the credit of the United States, nor appropriate money, nor agree upon the number of vessels of war, to be built or purchased, or the number of land or sea forces to be raised, nor appoint a commander in chief of the army or navy, unless nine States assent to the same: nor shall a question on any other point, except for adjourning from day to day be determined, unless by the votes of a majority of the United States in Congress assembled.

The Congress of the United States shall have power to adjourn to any time within the year, and to any place within the United States, so that no period of adjournment be for a longer duration than the space of six months, and shall publish the journal of their proceedings monthly, except such parts thereof relating to treaties, alliances or military operations, as in their judgment require secrecy; and the delegates of a State, or any of them, at his or their request shall be furnished with a transcript of the said journal, except such parts as are above expected, to lay before the Legislatures of the several States.

Article X

The committee of the States, or any nine of them, shall be authorized to execute, in the recess of Congress, such of the powers of Congress as the United States in Congress assembled, by the consent of nine States, shall from time to time think expedient to vest them with; provided that no power be delegated to the said committee, for the exercise of which, by the articles of confederation, the voice of nine States in the Congress of the United States assembled is requisite.

Article XI

Canada acceding to this confederation, and joining in the measures of the United States, shall be admitted into, and entitled to all the advantages of this Union: but no other colony shall be admitted into the same, unless such admission be agreed to by nine States.

Article XII

All bills of credit emitted, monies borrowed and debts contracted by, or under the authority of Congress, before the assembling of the United States, in pursuance of the present confederation, shall be deemed and considered as a charge against the United States, for payment and satisfaction whereof the said United States, and the public faith are hereby solemnly pledged.

Article XIII

Every State shall abide by the determinations of the United States in Congress assembled, on all questions which by this confederation are submitted to them. And the articles of this confederation shall be inviolably observed by every State, and the Union shall be perpetual; nor shall any alteration at any time hereafter be made in any of them; unless such alteration be agreed to in a Congress of the United States, and be afterwards confirmed by the Legislatures of every State.

And whereas it has pleased the Great Governor of the world to incline the hearts of the Legislatures we respectively represent in Congress, to approve of, and to authorize us to ratify the said articles of confederation and perpetual union. Know ye that we the undersigned delegates, by virtue of the power and authority to us given for that purpose, do by these presents, in the name and in behalf of our respective constituents, fully and entirely ratify and confirm each and every of the said articles of confederation and perpetual union, and all and singular the matters and things therein contained: and we do further solemnly plight and engage the faith of our respective constituents, that they shall abide by the determinations of the United States in Congress assembled, on all questions, which by the said confederation are submitted to them. And that the articles thereof shall be inviolably observed by the States we re[s]pectively represent, and that the Union shall be perpetual.

In witness whereof we have hereunto set our hands in Congress. Done at Philadelphia in the State of Pennsylvania the ninth day of July in the year of our Lord one thousand seven hundred and seventy-eight, and in the third year of the independence of America.

On the part & behalf of the State of New Hampshire

JOSIAH BARTLETT,	JOHN WENTWORTH, JUNR.,
	August 8th, 1778.

On the part and behalf of the State of Massachusetts Bay

JOHN HANCOCK,	FRANCIS DANA,
SAMUEL ADAMS,	JAMES LOVELL,
ELBRIDGE GERRY,	SAMUEL HOLTEN.

On the part and behalf of the State of Rhode Island and Providence Plantations

WILLIAM ELLERY,	JOHN COLLINS.
HENRY MARCHANT,	

On the part and behalf of the State of Connecticut

ROGER SHERMAN,	TITUS HOSMER,
SAMUEL HUNTINGTON,	ANDREW ADAMS.
OLIVER WOLCOTT,	

On the part and behalf of the State of New York

JAS. DUANE,	WM. DUER,
FRA. LEWIS,	GOUV. MORRIS.

On the part and behalf of the State of New Jersey, Nov. 26, 1778

JNO. WITHERSPOON,	NATHL. SCUDDER.

On the part and behalf of the State of Pennsylvania

ROBT. MORRIS,	WILLIAM CLINGAN,
DANIEL ROBERDEAU,	JOSEPH REED, 22d July, 1778.
JONA. BAYARD SMITH,	

On the part & behalf of the State of Delaware

THO. M'KEAN,	NICHOLAS VAN DYKE.
Feby. 12, 1779.	
JOHN DICKINSON,	
May 5th, 1779.	

On the part and behalf of the State of Maryland
    JOHN HANSON,   DANIEL CARROLL,
       March 1, 1781.   Mar. 1, 1781.
On the part and behalf of the State of Virginia
    RICHARD HENRY LEE,   JNO. HARVIE,
    JOHN BANISTER,   FRANCIS LIGHTFOOT LEE.
    THOMAS ADAMS,
On the part and behalf of the State of No. Carolina
    JOHN PENN, July 21st, 1778.   JNO. WILLIAMS.
    CORNS. HARNETT,
On the part & behalf of the State of South Carolina
    HENRY LAURENS,   RICHD. HUTSON,
    WILLIAM HENRY DRAYTON,   THOS. HEYWARD, JUNR.
    JNO. MATHEWS,
On the part & behalf of the State of Georgia
    JNO. WALTON,   EDWD. TELFAIR,
      24th July, 1778.   EDWD. LANGWORTHY.

SELECTION 48

"The Time of . . . Political Probation": George Washington's Circular Letter to the States (June 8, 1783)

The government established under the Articles of Confederation was too weak to carry out its assigned tasks. Charged with responsibility for making war, conducting diplomacy, and handling other matters of common concern to the states, the Confederation Congress had no power to levy taxes and no authority to force the states to comply with its measures. The repeated failure of the states to respond promptly and fully with congressional requisitions for men and money during the war had resulted in delays and uncertainties that frequently hampered military operations and drove congressmen and military officers to despair. Even before the Articles of Confederation had gone into effect in March, 1781, many men associated with the national government had come to believe that if it were to survive something had to be done to strengthen it and counteract the particularistic and centrifugal tendencies manifest in the state governments. Most prominent among these was General George Washington, who understood better than anyone else the ill effects of the "distresses and disappointments" that had "resulted . . . from a want of energy in the Continental government" during the war. On June 8, 1783, he took advantage of the opportunity offered by the disbanding of the army and his approaching retirement to send a circular letter to the states (reprinted below from Worthington Chauncey Ford [ed.], The Writings of George Washington [fourteen volumes, 1889–1893], volume X, pages 254–265) in which he pointed out the defects of the Articles and urged the creation of "a supreme power to regulate and govern the general concerns of the confederated republic." That very moment, he argued, was "the time of their political probation," and upon the willingness of the states to give Congress sufficient power to coerce the states into complying with its requisitions and to preserve its honor and credit by paying its debts and fulfilling its promises depended whether the United States would "be respectable and prosperous, or contemptible and miserable, as a nation, . . . whether the revolution must ultimately be considered as a blessing or a curse . . . not to the present age alone" but to those "unborn millions" whose destiny would be determined by the fate of the American experiment.

For detailed discussions of the dissatisfaction with the Articles and the demand for a more powerful central government see Andrew C. McLaughlin, The Confederation and the Constitution, 1783–1789 *(1905), and Merrill Jensen,* The New Nation: A History of the United States during the Confederation, 1781–1789 *(1950).*

IR,

The great object, for which I had the honor to hold an appointment in the service of my country, being accomplished, I am now preparing to resign it into the hands of Congress, and to return to that domestic retirement, which it is well known, I left with the greatest reluctance; a retirement for which I have never ceased to sigh, through a long and painful absence, and in which (remote from the noise and trouble of the world) I meditate to pass the remainder of life, in a state of undisturbed repose. But before I carry this resolution into effect, I think it a duty incumbent on me to make this my last official communication; to congratulate you on the glorious events which Heaven has been pleased to produce in our favor, to offer my sentiments respecting some important subjects, which appear to me to be intimately connected with the tranquillity of the United States; to take my leave of your Excellency as a public character; and to give my final blessing to that country, in whose service I have spent the prime of my life, for whose sake I have consumed so many anxious days and watchful nights, and whose happiness, being extremely dear to me, will always constitute no inconsiderable part of my own.

Impressed with the liveliest sensibility on this pleasing occasion, I will claim the indulgence of dilating the more copiously on the subjects of our mutual felicitation. When we consider the magnitude of the prize we contended for, the doubtful nature of the contest, and the favorable manner in which it has terminated, we shall find the greatest possible reason for gratitude and rejoicing. This is a theme that will afford infinite delight to every benevolent and liberal mind, whether the event in contemplation be considered as the source of present enjoyment, or the parent of future happiness; and we shall have equal occasion to felicitate ourselves on the lot which Providence has assigned us, whether we view it in a natural, a political, or moral point of light.

The citizens of America, placed in the most enviable condition, as the sole lords and proprietors of a vast tract of continent, comprehending all the various soils and climates of the world, and abounding with all the necessaries and conveniences of life, are now, by the late satisfactory pacification, acknowledged to be possessed of absolute freedom and independency. They are, from this period, to be considered as the actors on a most conspicuous theatre, which seems to be peculiarly designated by Providence for the display of human greatness and felicity. Here they are not only surrounded with every thing, which can contribute to the completion of private and domestic enjoyment; but Heaven has crowned all its other blessings, by giving a fairer opportunity for political happiness, than any other nation has ever been favored with. Nothing can illustrate these observations more forcibly, than a recollection of the happy conjuncture of times and circumstances, under which our republic assumed its rank among the nations. The foundation of our empire was not laid in the gloomy age of ignorance and superstition; but at an epocha when the rights of mankind were better understood and more clearly defined, than at any former period. The researches of the human mind after social happiness have been carried to a great extent; the treasures of knowledge, acquired by the labors of philosophers, sages, and legislators, through a long succession of years, are laid open for our use, and their collected wisdom may be happily applied in the establishment of our forms of government. The free cultivation of letters, the unbounded extension of commerce, the progressive refinement of manners, the growing liberality of sentiment, and, above all, the pure and benign light of Revelation, have had a meliorating influence on mankind and increased the blessings of society. At this auspicious period, the United States came into existence as a nation; and, if their citizens should not be completely free and happy, the fault will be entirely their own.

Such is our situation, and such are our prospects; but notwithstanding the cup of blessing is thus reached out to us; nothwithstanding happiness is ours, if we have a disposition to seize the occasion and make it our own; yet it appears to me there is an option still left to the United States of America, that it is in their choice, and depends upon their conduct, whether they will be respectable and prosperous, or contemptible and miserable, as a nation. This is the time of their political probation; this is the moment when the eyes of the whole world are turned upon them; this is the moment to establish or ruin their national character for ever; this is the favorable moment to give such a tone to our federal government, as will enable it to answer the ends of its institution, or this may be the ill-fated moment for relaxing the powers of the Union, annihilating the cement of the confederation, and exposing us to become the sport of European politics, which may play one State against another, to prevent their growing importance, and to serve their own interested purposes. For, according to the system of policy the States shall adopt at this moment, they will stand or fall; and by their confirmation or lapse it is yet to be decided, whether the revolution must ultimately be considered as a blessing or a curse; a blessing or a curse, not to the present age alone, for with our fate will the destiny of unborn millions be involved.

With this conviction of the importance of the present crisis, silence in me would be a crime. I will therefore speak to your Excellency the language of freedom and of sincerity without disguise. I am aware, however, that those who differ from me in political sentiment, may perhaps remark, I am stepping out of the proper line of my duty, and may possibly ascribe to arrogance or ostentation, what I know is alone the result of the purest intention. But the rectitude of my own heart, which disdains such unworthy motives; the part I have hitherto acted in life; the determination I have formed, of not taking any share in public business hereafter; the ardent desire I feel, and shall continue to manifest, of quietly enjoying, in private life, after all the toils of war, the benefits of a wise and liberal government, will, I flatter myself, sooner or later convince my countrymen, that I could have no sinister views in delivering, with so little reserve, the opinions contained in this address.

There are four things, which, I humbly conceive, are essential to the well-being, I may even venture to say, to the existence of the United States, as an independent power.

First.   An indissoluble union of the States under one federal head.
Secondly.   A sacred regard to public justice.
Thirdly.   The adoption of a proper peace establishment; and,
Fourthly.   The prevalence of that pacific and friendly disposition among the people of the United States, which will induce them to forget their local prejudices and policies; to make those mutual concessions, which are requisite to the general prosperity; and, in some instances, to sacrifice their individual advantages to the interest of the community.

These are the pillars on which the glorious fabric of our independency and national character must be supported. Liberty is the basis; and whoever would dare to sap the foundation, or overturn the structure, under whatever specious pretext he may attempt it, will merit the bitterest execration, and the severest punishment, which can be inflicted by his injured country.

On the three first articles I will make a few observations, leaving the last to the good sense and serious consideration of those immediately concerned.

Under the first head, although it may not be necessary or proper for me, in this place, to enter into a particular disquisition on the principles of the Union, and to take up the great question which has been frequently agitated, whether it be expedient and requisite for the States to delegate a larger proportion of power to Congress, or not; yet it will be a part of my duty, and that of every true patriot, to assert without reserve, and to insist upon, the following positions. That, unless the States will suffer Congress to exercise those prerogatives they are undoubtedly invested with by the constitution, every thing must very rapidly tend to anarchy and confusion. That it is indispensable to the happiness of the individual States, that there should be lodged somewhere a supreme power to regulate and govern the general concerns of the confederated republic, without which the Union cannot be of long duration. That there must be a faithful and pointed compliance, on the part of every State, with the late proposals and demands of Congress, or the most fatal consequences will ensue. That whatever measures have a tendency to dissolve the Union, or contribute to violate or lessen the sovereign authority, ought to be considered as hostile to the liberty and independency of America, and the authors of them treated accordingly. And lastly, that unless we can be enabled, by the concurrence of the States, to participate of the fruits of the revolution, and enjoy the essential benefits of civil society, under a form of government so free and uncorrupted, so happily guarded against the danger of oppression, as has been devised and adopted by the articles of confederation, it will be a subject of regret, that so much blood and treasure have been lavished for no purpose, that so many sufferings have been encountered without a compensation, and that so many sacrifices have been made in vain.

Many other considerations might here be adduced to prove, that, without an entire conformity to the spirit of the Union, we cannot exist as an independent power. It will be sufficient for my purpose to mention but one or two, which seem to me of the greatest importance. It is only in our united character, as an empire, that our independence is acknowledged, that our power can be regarded, or our credit supported, among foreign nations. The treaties of the European powers with the United States of America will have no validity on a dissolution of the Union. We shall be left nearly in a state of nature; or we may find, by our own unhappy experience, that there is a natural and necessary progression from the extreme of anarchy to the extreme of tyranny, and that arbitrary power is most easily established on the ruins of liberty, abused to licentiousness.

As to the second article, which respects the performance of public justice, Congress have, in their late address to the United States, almost exhausted the subject; they have explained their ideas so fully, and have enforced the obligations the States are under, to render complete justice to all the public creditors, with so much dignity and energy, that, in my opinion, no real friend to the honor of independency of America can hesitate a single moment, respecting the propriety of complying with the just and honorable measures proposed. If their arguments do not produce conviction, I know of nothing that will have greater influence: especially when we recollect, that the system referred to, being the result of the collected wisdom of the continent, must be esteemed, if not perfect, certainly the least objectionable of any that could be devised; and that, if it shall not be carried into immediate execution, a national bankruptcy, with all its deplorable consequences, will take place, before any different plan can possibly be proposed and adopted. So pressing are the present circumstances, and such is the alternative now offered to the States.

The ability of the country to discharge the debts, which have been incurred in its defence, is not to be doubted; an inclination, I flatter myself, will not be wanting. The path of our duty is plain before us; honesty will be found, on every experiment, to be the best and only true policy. Let us then, as a nation, be just; let us fulfil the public contracts, which Congress had undoubtedly a right to make for the purpose of carrying on the war, with the same good faith we suppose ourselves bound to perform our private engagements. In the mean time, let an attention to the cheerful performance of their proper business, as individuals and as members of society, be earnestly inculcated on the citizens of America; then will they strengthen the hands of government, and be happy under its protection; every one will reap the fruit of his labors, every one will enjoy his own acquisitions, without molestation and without danger.

In this state of absolute freedom and perfect security, who will grudge to yield a very little of his property to support the common interest of society, and insure the protection of government? Who does not remember the frequent declarations, at the commencement of the war, that we should be completely satisfied, if, at the expense of one half, we could defend the remainder of our possessions? Where is the man to be found, who wishes to remain indebted for the defence of his own person and property to the exertions, the bravery, and the blood of others, without making one generous effort to repay the debt of honor and gratitude? In what part of the continent shall we find any man, or body of men, who would not blush to stand up and propose measures purposely calculated to rob the soldier of his stipend, and the public creditor of his due? And were it possible, that such a flagrant instance of injustice could ever happen, would it not excite the general indignation, and tend to bring down upon the authors of such measures the aggravated vengeance of Heaven? If, after all, a spirit of disunion, or a temper of obstinacy and perverseness should manifest itself in any of the States; if such an ungracious disposition should attempt to frustrate all the happy effects that might be expected to flow from the Union; if there should be a refusal to comply with the requisition for funds to discharge the annual interest of the public debts; and if that refusal should revive again all those jealousies, and produce all those evils, which are now happily removed, Congress, who have, in all their transactions, shown a great degree of magnanimity and justice, will stand justified in the sight of God and man; and the State alone, which puts itself in opposition to the aggregate wisdom of the continent, and follows such mistaken and pernicious counsels, will be responsible for all the consequences.

For my own part, conscious of having acted, while a servant of the public, in the manner I conceived best suited to promote the real interests of my country; having, in consequence of my fixed belief, in some measure pledged myself to the army, that their country would finally do them complete and ample justice; and not wishing to conceal any instance of my official conduct from the eyes of the world, I have thought proper to transmit to your Excellency the enclosed collection of papers, relative to the half-pay and commutation granted by Congress to the officers of the army. From these communications, my decided sentiments will be clearly comprehended, together with the conclusive reasons which induced me, at an early period, to recommend the adoption of this measure, in the most earnest and serious manner. As the proceedings of Congress, the army, and myself, are open to all, and contain, in my opinion, sufficient information to remove the prejudices and errors, which may have been entertained by any, I think it unnecessary to say any thing more than just to observe, that the resolutions of Congress, now alluded to, are undoubtedly as absolutely binding upon the United States, as the most solemn acts of confederation or legislation.

As to the idea, which, I am informed, has in some instances prevailed, that the half-pay and commutation are to be regarded merely in the odious light of a pension, it ought to be exploded for ever. That provision should be viewed, as it really was, a reasonable compensation offered by Congress, at a time when they had nothing else to give to the officers of the army for services then to be performed. It was the only means to prevent a total dereliction of the service. It was a part of their hire. I may be allowed to say, it was the price of their blood, and of your independency; it is therefore more than a common debt, it is a debt of honor; it can never be considered as a pension or gratuity, nor be cancelled until it is fairly discharged.

With regard to a distinction between officers and soldiers, it is sufficient that the uniform experience of every nation of the world, combined with our own, proves the utility and propriety of the discrimination. Rewards, in proportion to the aids the public derives from them, are unquestionably due to all its servants. In some lines, the soldiers have perhaps generally had as ample a compensation for their services, by the large bounties which have been paid to them, as their officers will receive in the proposed commutation; in others, if, besides the donation of lands, the payment of arrearages of clothing and wages (in which articles all the component parts of the army must be put upon the same footing), we take into the estimate the douceurs many of the soldiers have received, and the gratuity of one year's full pay, which is promised to all, possibly their situation (every circumstance being duly considered) will not be deemed less eligible than that of the officers. Should a further reward, however, be judged equitable, I will venture to assert, no one will enjoy greater satisfaction than myself, on seeing an exemption from taxes for a limited time, (which has been petitioned for in some instances,) or any other adequate immunity or compensation granted to the brave defenders of their country's cause; but neither the adoption or rejection of this proposition will in any manner affect, much less militate against, the act of Congress, by which they have offered five years' full pay, in lieu of the half-pay for life, which had been before promised to the officers of the army.

Before I conclude the subject of public justice, I cannot omit to mention the obligations this country is under to that meritorious class of veteran non-commissioned officers and privates, who have been discharged for inability, in consequence of the resolution of Congress of the 23d of April, 1782, on an annual pension for life. Their peculiar sufferings, their singular merits, and claims to that provision, need only be known, to interest all the feelings of humanity in their behalf. Nothing but a punctual payment of their annual allowance can rescue them from the most complicated misery; and nothing could be a more melancholy and distressing sight, than to behold those, who have shed their blood or lost their limbs in the service of their country, without a shelter, without a friend, and without the means of obtaining any of the necessaries or comforts of life, compelled to beg their daily bread from door to door. Suffer me to recommend those of this description, belonging to your State, to the warmest patronage of your Excellency and your legislature.

It is necessary to say but a few words on the third topic which was proposed, and which regards particularly the defence of the republic; as there can be little doubt but Congress will recommend a proper peace establishment for the United States, in which a due attention will be paid to the importance of placing the militia of the Union upon a regular and respectable footing. If this should be the case, I would beg leave to urge the great advantage of it in the strongest terms. The militia of this country must be considered as the palladium of our security, and the first effectual resort in case of hostility. It is essential, therefore, that the same system should pervade the whole; that the formation and discipline of the militia of the continent should be absolutely uniform, and that the same species of arms, accoutrements, and military apparatus, should be introduced in every part of the United States. No one, who has not learned it from experience, can conceive the difficulty, expense, and confusion, which result from a contrary system, or the vague arrangements which have hitherto prevailed.

If, in treating of political points, a greater latitude than usual has been taken in the course of this address, the importance of the crisis, and the magnitude of the objects in discussion, must be my apology. It is, however, neither my wish or expectation, that the preceding observations should claim any regard, except so far as they shall appear to be dictated by a good intention, consonant to the immutable rules of justice, calculated to produce a liberal system of policy, and founded on whatever experience may have been acquired by a long and close attention to public business. Here I might speak with the more confidence, from my actual observations; and, if it would not swell this letter (already too prolix) beyond the bounds I had prescribed to myself, I could demonstrate to every mind open to conviction, that in less time, and with much less expense, than has been incurred, the war might have been brought to the same happy conclusion, if the resources of the continent could have been properly drawn forth; that the distresses and disappointments, which have very often occurred, have, in too many instances, resulted more from a want of energy in the Continental government, than a deficiency of means in the particular States; that the inefficacy of measures arising from the want of an adequate authority in the supreme power, from a partial compliance with the requisitions of Congress in some of the States, and from a failure of punctuality in others, while it tended to damp the zeal of those, which were more willing to exert themselves, served also to accumulate the expenses of the war, and to frustrate the best concerted plans; and that the discouragement occasioned by the complicated difficulties and embarrassments, in which our affairs were by this means involved, would have long ago produced the dissolution of any army, less patient, less virtuous, and less persevering, than that which I have had the honor to command. But, while I mention these things, which are notorious facts, as the defects of our federal constitution, particularly in the prosecution of a war, I beg it may be understood, that, as I have ever taken a pleasure in gratefully acknowledging the assistance and support I have derived from every class of citizens, so shall I always be happy to do justice to the unparalleled exertions of the individual States on many interesting occasions.

I have thus freely disclosed what I wished to make known, before I surrendered up my public trust to those who committed it to me. The task is now accomplished. I now bid adieu to your Excellency as the chief magistrate of your State, at the same time I bid a last farewell to the cares of office, and all the employments of public life.

It remains, then, to be my final and only request, that your Excellency will communicate these sentiments to your legislature at their next meeting, and that they may be considered as the legacy of one, who has ardently wished, on all occasions, to be useful to his country, and who, even in the shade of retirement, will not fail to implore the Divine benediction upon it.

I now make it my earnest prayer, that God would have you, and the State over which you preside, in his holy protection; that he would incline the hearts of the citizens to cultivate a spirit of subordination and obedience to government; to entertain a brotherly affection and love for one another, for their fellow citizens of the United States at large, and particularly for their brethren who have served in the field; and finally, that he would most graciously be pleased to dispose us all to do justice, to love mercy, and to demean ourselves with that charity, humility, and pacific temper of mind, which were the characteristics of the Divine Author of our blessed religion, and without an humble imitation of whose example in these things, we can never hope to be a happy nation. . . .

Enforcement of the Treaty of Paris

If, as Washington believed, the fulfillment of the promises of the Revolution de-
pended upon the willingness of the state governments to "suffer" Congress to exercise
the powers assigned it by the Articles of Confederation, then, it quickly became
clear in 1783, those promises had little chance of ever being realized. The Articles
gave the power to make treaties with foreign countries exclusively to the Congress,
and any treaty ratified by Congress was legally binding upon the states. That there
was no effective way for Congress to force the states to adhere to its treaty commit-
ments, however, was indicated by its failure in 1783 and after to persuade the
state governments to accept the unpopular provisions in the Treaty of Paris relating
to the treatment of loyalists and payment of British debts.

The provisions regarding loyalists had little chance of immediate acceptance.
Everywhere there was bitter popular resentment against loyalists—the residue of
eight long years of war and, in places like the Carolinas and New York, bloody
internecine conflict. During the war every state legislature had taken steps to con-
fiscate the property of proven loyalists, several states had also disfranchised and
banished them, and widespread sentiment, manifest in a spate of riots against return-
ing loyalists in several towns in 1783, favored further punitive measures at the end
of the war. By prohibiting any further prosecutions or confiscations and by requir-
ing that Congress recommend that the states permit all loyalists who had suffered
losses through confiscation to attempt for one year to secure restitution of their
property, the Treaty of Paris ran directly counter to the drift of public feeling.
Congress's recommendation of January 14, 1784, that these provisions be complied
with set off a vigorous debate between those who wanted to defy and those who
wanted to accept the recommendation. In New York, where the number of loyalists
had been particularly large and where the legislature had passed a Trespass Act in
March, 1783, that had led to a rash of new legal actions against loyalists, the debate
was especially fierce. The most effective spokesman for compliance with the treaty
provisions was Alexander Hamilton (1755–1804), only twenty-nine years old and
destined to play a major role in the politics of the 1790s. Against the contentions
of the predominant antiloyalists, who argued that any losses sustained by the
loyalists had been more than matched by damages upon American property in-
flicted by the British and that their crimes were so heinous as to justify much
harsher measures, Hamilton wrote two anonymous pamphlets, A Letter from
Phocion and A Second Letter from Phocion, portions of each of which are reprinted
here as Selection 49 A. In these he argued that the New York State legislature was
bound by the treaty not to take any further action against loyalists, that the con-
stitution of New York made any blanket punitive measures of the kind then under
consideration illegal by specifying that no man could be condemned unheard, and
that "justice, moderation, liberality, and a scrupulous regard to the constitution"
were the "surest supports of every government." But Hamilton's arguments, which
were especially interesting for their assertion that the people and the people's rep-
resentatives were alike bound by both the national and state constitutions, had
little impact on the New York legislature, which passed new and more drastic
antiloyalist statutes in early 1784 in direct defiance of the treaty and of the Con-
federation Congress. The legislatures of several other states behaved similarly, and

Congress was impotent to do anything in retaliation. More moderate measures toward the loyalists waited until wartime passions had subsided in the later 1780s.

Congress was similarly unable to secure state compliance with the stipulation in the treaty prohibiting any lawful impediment to the collection of British debts in full sterling value. Because of an unfavorable balance of trade all of the southern staple-producing states owed substantial debts to British merchants at the outbreak of the War for Independence. By far the largest debt—over £2 million—was owed by Virginians, and, not surprisingly, it was in Virginia that opposition to the treaty stipulation was strongest. With George Mason, whose opinions on the subject were set down in the letter to Patrick Henry of May 6, 1783, which is reprinted below as Selection 49 B, a large and powerful group of Virginia politicians insisted that justice and honesty as well as the necessity of abiding by the treaty required that the British be allowed to take steps to secure their debts. Under the leadership of Henry, however, the Virginia legislature in violation of the treaty adopted a variety of expedients to hinder legal action by British creditors in Virginia courts on the grounds that debt collection should depend on prior British compensation for slaves stolen and damages done by the British Army during the war and the evacuation of British troops from the forts in the Old Northwest that the British continued to hold contrary to provisions in the treaty. Not until after the establishment under the Constitution of 1787 of national courts which could overrule the Virginia courts were British merchants able to institute successful proceedings to collect their debts.

Discussions of the inability of Congress to coerce the states into abiding by the Treaty of Paris and of the actions by the various states on the loyalist and debt questions will be found in Allan Nevins, American States during and after the Revolution, 1775–1789 *(1924), and Merrill Jensen,* The New Nation: A History of the United States during the Confederation, 1781–1789 *(1950).*

A. TREATMENT OF LOYALISTS: [ALEXANDER HAMILTON], ''A LETTER FROM PHOCION'' AND ''A SECOND LETTER FROM PHOCION'' (1784)*

First Letter

WHILE not only every personal artifice is employed by a few heated and inconsiderate spirits, to practise upon the passions of the people, but the public papers are made the channel of the most inflammatory and pernicious doctrines, tending to the subversion of all private security and genuine liberty; it would be culpable in those who understand and value the true interests of the community to be silent spectators. It is, however, a common observation, that men, bent upon mischief, are more active in the pursuit of their object, than those who aim at doing good. Hence it is in the present moment, we see the most industrious efforts to violate, the constitution of this state, to trample upon the rights of the subject, and to chicane or infringe the most solemn obligations of treaty . . .

* These excerpts are reprinted from the third edition of *A Letter from Phocion* (1784), pp. 3–12, 21, and the original edition of *A Second Letter from Phocion* (1784), pp. 6, 29–34, 36–38, 41–43.

The persons alluded to, pretend to appeal to the spirit of Whiggism, while they endeavour to put in motion all the furious and dark passions of the human mind. The spirit of Whiggism is generous, humane, beneficent and just. These men inculcate revenge, cruelty, persecution, and perfidy. The spirit of Whiggism cherishes legal liberty, holds the rights of every individual sacred, condemns or punishes no man without regular trial and conviction of some crime declared by antecedent laws, reprobates equally the punishment of the citizen by arbitrary acts of legislature, as by the lawless combinations of unauthorized individuals:----While these men are advocates for expelling a large number of their fellow-citizens unheard, untried; or if they cannot effect this, are for disfranchising them, in the face of the constitution, without the judgment of their peers, and contrary to the law of the land.

The 13th article of the constitution declares, "that no member of this state shall be *disfranchised* or *defrauded of any of the rights or privileges* sacred to the subjects of this state by the constitution, unless *by the law of the land or the judgment of his peers."* If we enquire what is meant by the law of the land, the best commentators will tell us, that it means *due process of law, that is, by indictment or presentment of good and lawful men,* and trial and conviction in consequence. . . .

If there had been no treaty in the way, the legislature might, by *name,* have attainted particular persons of high treason for crimes committed during the war, but independent of the treaty it could not, and cannot, without tyranny, disfranchise or punish whole classes of citizens by general discriptions, without trial and conviction of offences known by laws previously established declaring the offence and prescribing the penalty.

This is a dictate of natural justice, and a fundamental principle of law and liberty.

Nothing is more common than for a free people, in times of heat and violence, to gratify momentary passions, by letting into the government, principles and precedents which afterwards prove fatal to themselves. Of this kind is the doctrine of disqualification, disfranchisement and banishment by acts of legislature. The dangerous consequences of this power are manifest. If the legislature can disfranchise any number of citizens at pleasure by general descriptions, it may soon confine all the votes to a small number of partizans, and establish an aristocracy or an oligarchy; if it may banish at discretion all those whom particular circumstances render obnoxious, without hearing or trial, no man can be safe, nor know when he may be the innocent victim of a prevailing faction. The name of liberty applied to such a government would be a mockery of common sense.

The English Whigs, after the revolution, from an overweening dread of popery and the Pretender, from triennial, voted the parliament septennial.---They have been trying ever since to undo this false step in vain, and are repenting the effects of their folly in the over-grown power of the new family. Some imprudent Whigs among us, from resentment to those who have taken the opposite side, (and many of them from worse motives) would corrupt the principles of our government, and furnish precedents for future usurpations on the rights of the community.

Let the people beware of such Counsellors.---However, a few designing men may rise in consequence, and advance their private interests by such expedients, the people, at large, are sure to be the losers in the event whenever they suffer a departure from the rules of general and equal justice, or from the true principles of universal liberty.

These men, not only overleap the barriers of the constitution without remorse, but they advise us to become the scorn of nations, by violating the solemn engagements of the United States. They endeavour to mould the Treaty with Great-Britain, into such form as pleases them, and to make it mean any thing or nothing as suits their views.----They tell us, that all the stipulations, with respect to the Tories, are merely that Congress will recommend, and the States may comply or not as they please.

But let any man of sense and candour read the Treaty, and it will speak for itself. The fifth article is indeed recommendatory; but the sixth is as positive as words can make it. *"There shall be* no future confiscations made, nor prosecutions commenced against any person or persons, for, or by reason of the part which he or they may have taken in the present war, and no person shall, on that account, suffer any future loss or damage, either in his person, liberty, or property."

As to the restoration of confiscated property which is the subject of the fifth article, the states may restore or not as they think proper, because Congress engage only to recommend; but there is not a word about recommendation in the 6th article. . . .

The sound and ingenuous construction of the two articles taken collectively, is this---that where the property of any persons, other than those who have been in arms against the United States, had been actually confiscated and themselves proscribed, there Congress are to recommend a restoration of estates, rights and properties; and with respect to those who had been in arms, they are to recommend permission for them to remain a twelvemonth in the country to solicit a like restoration: But with respect to all those who were not in this situation, and who had not already been the objects of confiscation and banishment, they were to be absolutely secured from all future injury to person, liberty or property.

To say that this exemption from positive injury, does not imply a right to live among us as citizens, is a pitiful sophistry; it is to say that the banishment of a person from his country, connexions and resources (one of the greatest punishments that can befal a man) is no punishment at all.

The meaning of the word *liberty* has been contested. Its true sense must be the enjoyment of the common privileges of subjects under the same government. There is no middle line of just construction between this sense and a mere exemption from personal imprisonment! If the last were adopted, the stipulation would become nugatory; and by depriving those who are the subjects of it, of the protection of government, it would amount to a virtual confiscation and banishment; for they could not have the benefit of the laws against those who should be aggressors.

Should it be said that they may receive protection without being admitted to a full enjoyment of the privileges of citizens, this must be either matter of right under the treaty, or matter of grace in the government. If the latter, the government may refuse it, and then the objection presents itself, that the treaty would by this construction be virtually defeated; if matter of right, then it follows that more is intended by the word liberty, than a mere exemption from imprisonment, and where shall the line be drawn---not a capricious and arbitrary line, but one warranted by rational and legal construction?

To say that by espousing the cause of Great-Britain they became aliens, and that it will satisfy the treaty to allow them the same protection to which aliens are entitled---is to admit that subjects may at pleasure renounce their allegiance to the state of which they are members, and devote themselves to a foreign jurisdiction; a principle contrary to law and subversive of government. But even this will not satisfy the treaty; for aliens cannot hold real property under our government; and if they are aliens, all their real estates belong to the public. This will be to all intents and purposes, a confiscation of property. But this is not all, how does it appear that the persons who are thus to be stripped of their citizenship, have been guilty of such an adherence to the enemy, as in legal contemplation amounts to a crime. Their merely remaining in their possessions under the power of the conqueror does not imply this; but is executed by the laws and customs of all civilized nations. To adjudge them culpable, they must be first tried and convicted; and this the treaty forbids. These are the difficulties involved, by recurring to subtle and evasive instead of simple and candid construction, which will teach us that the stipulations in the treaty, amount to an amnesty and act of oblivion.

There is a very simple and conclusive point of view in which this subject may be placed. No citizen can be deprived of any right which the citizens in general are entitled to, unless forfeited by some offence. It has been seen that the regular and constitutional mode of ascertaining whether this forfeiture has been incurred, is by legal process, trial and conviction. This *ex vi termini,* supposes prosecution. Now consistent with the treaty there can be no future prosecution for any thing done on account of the war. Can we then do by act of legislature, what the treaty disables us from doing by due course of law? This would be to imitate the Roman General, who having promised Antiochus to restore half his vessels, caused them to be sawed in two before their delivery; or the Platææ, who having promised the Thebans to restore their prisoners, had them first put to death and returned them dead.

Such fraudulent subterfuges are justly considered more odious than an open and avowed violation of treaty.

When these posture-masters in logic are driven from this first ground of the meaning of the treaty; they are forced to that of attacking the right of Congress to make such a stipulation, and arraigning the impudence of Great-Britain in attempting to make terms for our own subjects. But here as every where else, they are only successful in betraying their narrowness and ignorance.

Does not the act of confederation place the exclusive right of war and peace in the United States in Congress? Have they not the sole power of making treaties with foreign nations? Are not these among the first rights of sovereignty, and does not the delegation of them to the general confederacy, so far abridge the sovereignty of each particular state? Would not a different doctrine involve the contradiction of *imperium in imperio?* What reasonable limits can be assigned to these prerogatives of the union, other than the general safety and the *fundamentals* of the constitution? Can it be said that a treaty for arresting the future operation of positive acts of legislature, and which has indeed no other effect than that of a pardon for past offences, committed against these acts, is an attack upon the fundamentals of the state constitutions? Can it be denied that the peace which was made, taken collectively, was manifestly for the general good; that it was even favourable to the solid interests of this country, beyond the expectation of the most sanguine? If this cannot be denied; and none can deny it who know either the value of the objects gained by the treaty, or the necessity these states were under at the time of making peace?----It follows that Congress and their Ministers acted wisely in making the treaty which has been made; and it follows from this, that these states are bound by it, and ought religiously to observe it. . . .

Viewing the subject in every possible light, there is not a single interest of the community but dictates moderation rather than violence. That honesty is still the best policy; that justice and moderation are the surest supports of every government, are maxims, which however they may be called trite, at all times true, though too seldom regarded, but rarely neglected with impunity. Were the people of America, with one voice, to ask, What shall we do to perpetuate our liberties and secure our happiness? The answer would be, "govern well" and you have nothing to fear either from internal disaffection or external hostility. Abuse not the power you possess, and you need never apprehend its diminution or loss. But if you make a wanton use of it, if you furnish another example, that despotism may debase the government of the many as well as the few, you like all others that have acted the same part, will experience that licentiousness is the fore runner to slavery.

How wise was that policy of Augustus, who after conquering his enemies, when the papers of Brutus were brought to him, which would have disclosed all his secret associates, immediately ordered them to be burnt. He would not even know his enemies, that they might cease to hate when they had nothing to fear. . . .

Second Letter

THE principles of all the arguments I have used or shall use, lie within the compass of a few simple propositions, which, to be assented to, need only to be stated.

FIRST, That no man can forfeit or be justly deprived, without his consent, of any right, to which as a member of the community he is entitled, but for some crime incurring the forfeiture.

SECONDLY, That no man ought to be condemned unheard, or punished for supposed offences, without having an opportunity of making his defence.

THIRDLY, That a crime is an *act* committed or omitted, in violation of a public law, either forbidding or commanding it.

FOURTHLY, That a prosecution is in its most precise signification, an *inquiry* or *mode of ascertaining,* whether a particular person has committed, or omitted such *act.*

FIFTHLY, That *duties* and *rights* as applied to subjects are reciprocal; or in other words, that a man cannot be a *citizen* for the purpose of punishment, and not a *citizen* for the purpose of privilege. . . .

IT has been urged, in support of the doctrines under consideration, that every government has a right to take precautions for its own security, and to prescribe the terms on which its rights shall be enjoyed.

ALL this is true when understood with proper limitations; but when rightly understood will not be found to justify the conclusions, which have been drawn from the premises.

In the first formation of a government the society may multiply its precautions as much, and annex as many conditions to the enjoyment of its rights, as it shall judge expedient; but when it has once adopted a constitution, that constitution must be the measure of its discretion, in providing for its own safety, and in prescribing the conditions upon which its privileges are to be enjoyed. If the constitution declares that persons possessing certain qualifications shall be entitled to certain rights, while that constitution remains in force, the government which is the mere creature of the constitution, can divest no citizen, who has the requisite qualifications, of his corresponding rights. It may indeed enact laws and annex to the breach of them the penalty of forfeiture; but before that penalty can operate, the existence of the fact, upon which it is to take place, must be ascertained in that mode which the constitution and the fundamental laws have provided. If trial by jury is the mode known and established by that constitution and those laws, the persons who administer the government, in deviating from that course, will be guilty of usurpation. If the constitution declares that the legislative power of the state shall be vested in one set of men and the judiciary power in another; and those who are appointed to act in a legislative capacity undertake the office of judges, if, instead of confining themselves to passing laws, with proper sanctions to enforce their observance, they go out of their province to decide who are the violators of those laws, they subvert the constitution and erect a tyranny. If the constitution were even silent on particular points, those, who are entrusted with its power, would be bound in exercising their discretion to consult and pursue its spirit, and to conform to the dictates of reason and equity; if, instead of this, they should undertake to declare whole classes of citizens disfranchised and excluded from the common rights of the society, without hearing, trial, examination or proof; if, instead of waiting to take away the rights of citizenship from individuals, till the state has convicted them of crimes, by which they are to lose them, before the ordinary and regular tribunal, they institute an inquisition into mens consciences, and oblige them to give up their privileges, or undertake to interpret the law at the hazard of perjury; they expose themselves to the imputation of injustice and oppression.

THE right of a government to prescribe the conditions, on which its privileges shall be enjoyed, is bounded with respect to those who are already included in the compact, by its original conditions; in admitting strangers it may add new ones; but it cannot without a breach of the social compact deprive those, who have been once admitted, of their rights, unless for some declared cause of forfeiture authenticated with the solemnities required by the subsisting compact.

THE rights too of a republican government are to be modified and regulated by the principles of such a government. These principles dictate, that no man shall lose his rights without a hearing and conviction, before the proper tribunal; that previous to his disfranchisement, he shall have the full benefit of the laws to make his defence; and that his innocence shall be presumed till his guilt has been proved. These with many other maxims, never to be forgotten in any but tyrannical governments, oppose the aims of those, who quarrel with the principles of Phocion.

CASES indeed of extreme necessity are exceptions to all general rules; but these only exist, when it is manifest the safety of the community is in imminent danger. Speculations of possible danger never can be justifying causes of departures from principles on which in the ordinary course of things all private security depends---from principles which constitute the essential distinction between free and arbitrary governments.

WHEN the advocates for legislative discriminations are driven from one subterfuge to another, their last resting place is---that this is a new case, the case of a revolution. Your principles are all right say they, in the ordinary course of society, but they do not apply to a situation like ours. This is opening a wilderness, through all the labyrinths of which, it is impossible to pursue them: The answer to this must be, that there are principles eternally true and which apply to all situations; such as those that have been already enumerated---that we are not now in the midst of a revolution but have happily brought it to a successful issue---that we have a constitution formed as a rule of conduct---that the frame of our government is determined and the general principles of it settled---that we have taken our station among nations, have claimed the benefit of the laws which regulate them, and must in our turn be bound by the same laws---that those eternal principles of social justice forbid the inflicting punishment upon citizens, by an abridgement of rights, or in any other manner, without conviction of some specific offence by regular trial and condemnation---that the constitution we have formed makes the trial by jury the only proper mode of ascertaining the delinquences of individuals---that legislative discriminations, to supersede the necessity of inquiry and proof, would be an usurpation on the judiciary powers of the government, and a renunciation of all the maxims of civil liberty---that by the laws of nations and the rules of justice, we are bound to observe the engagements entered into on our behalf, by that power which is invested with the constitutional prerogative of treaty---and that the treaty we have made in its genuine sense, ties up the hands of government from any species of future prosecution or punishment, on account of the part taken by individuals in the war.

AMONG the extravagancies with which these prolific times abound, we hear it often said, that the constitution being the creature of the people, their sense with respect to any measure, if it even stand in opposition to the constitution, will sanctify and make it right.

HAPPILY, for us, in this country, the position is not to be controverted; that the constitution is the creature of the people; but it does not follow that they are not bound by it, while they suffer it to continue in force; nor does it follow, that the legislature, which is, on the other hand, a creature of the constitution, can depart from it, on any presumption of the contrary sense of the people.

THE constitution is the compact made between the society at large and each individual. The society therefore cannot, without breach of faith and injustice, refuse to any individual, a single advantage which he derives under that compact, no more than one man can refuse to perform his agreement with another. If the community have good reasons for abrogating the old compact and establishing a new one, it undoubtedly has a right to do it; but until the compact is dissolved with the same solemnity and certainty with which it was made, the society, as well as individuals, are bound by it.

ALL the authority of the legislature is delegated to them under the constitution; their rights and powers are there defined; if they exceed them, 'tis a treasonable usurpation upon the power and majesty of the people; and by the same rule that they may take away from a single individual the rights he claims under the constitution, they may erect themselves into perpetual dictators. The sense of the people, if urged in justification of the measure, must be considered as a mere pretext; for that sense cannot appear to them in a form so explicit and authoritative, as the constitution under which they act; and if it could appear with equal authenticity, it could only bind, when it had been preceded by a declared change in the form of government.

THE contrary doctrine serves to undermine all those rules, by which individuals can know their duties and their rights, and to convert the government into a government of *will* not of *laws*. . . .

The great majority of those, who took part against us, did it from accident, from the dread of the British power, and from the influence of others to whom they had been accustomed to look up. Most of the men, who had that kind of influence are already gone: The residue and their adherents must be carried along by the torrent; and with very few exceptions, if the government is mild and just, will soon come to view it with approbation and attachment. . . .

THERE is a bigotry in politics, as well as in religions, equally pernicious in both---The zealots, of either description, are ignorant of the advantage of a spirit of toleration: It was a long time before the kingdoms of Europe were convinced of the folly of persecution, with respect to those, who were schismatics from the established church. The cry was, these men will be equally the disturbers of the hierarchy and of the state. While some kingdoms were impoverishing and depopulating themselves, by their severities to the nonconformists, their wiser neighbours were reaping the fruits of their folly, and augmenting their own numbers, industry and wealth, by receiving with open arms the persecuted fugitives. Time and experience have taught a different lesson; and there is not an enlightened nation, which does not now acknowledge the force of this truth, that whatever speculative notions of religion may be entertained, men will not on that account, be enemies to a government, that affords them protection and security. The same spirit of toleration in politics, and for the same reasons, has made great progress among mankind, of which the history of most modern revolutions is a proof. Unhappily for this state, there are some among us, who possess too much influence, that have motives of personal ambition and interest to shut their minds against the entrance of that moderation, which the real welfare of the community teaches. . . .

I SHALL now with a few general reflections conclude.

THOSE, who are at present entrusted with power, in all these infant republics, hold the most sacred deposit that ever was confided to human hands. 'Tis with governments as with individuals, first impressions and early habits give a lasting bias to the temper and character. Our governments hitherto have no habits. How important to the happiness not of America alone, but of mankind, that they should acquire good ones.

IF we set out with justice, moderation, liberality, and a scrupulous regard to the constitution, the government will acquire a spirit and tone, productive of permanent blessings to the community. If on the contrary, the public councils are guided by humour, passion, and prejudice; if from resentment to individuals, or a dread of partial inconveniences, the constitution is slighted or explained away, upon every frivolous pretext, the future spirit of government will be feeble, distracted and arbitrary. The rights of the subject will be the sport of every party vicissitude. There will be no settled rule of conduct, but every thing will fluctuate with the alternate prevalency of contending factions.

THE world has its eye upon America. The noble struggle we have made in the cause of liberty, has occasioned a kind of revolution in human sentiment. The influence of our example has penetrated the gloomy regions of despotism, and has pointed the way to enquiries, which may shake it to its deepest foundations. Men begin to ask every where, who is this tyrant, that dares to build his greatness on our misery and degradation? What commission has he to sacrifice millions to the wanton appetites of himself, and the few minions that surround his throne?

To ripen inquiry into action, it remains for us to justify the revolution by its fruits.

IF the consequences prove, that we really have asserted the cause of human happiness, what may not be expected from so illustrious an example?-----In a greater or less degree, the world will bless and imitate!

BUT if experience, in this instance, verifies the lesson long taught by the enemies of liberty;----that the bulk of mankind are not fit to govern themselves, that they must have a master, and were only made for the rein and the spur: We shall then see the final triumph of despotism over liberty---The advocates of the latter must acknowledge it to be an *ignis fatuus,* and abandon the pursuit. With the greatest advantages for promoting it, that ever a people had, we shall have betrayed the cause of human nature.

LET those in whose hands it is placed, pause for a moment, and contemplate with an eye of reverence, the vast trust committed to them. Let them retire into their own bosoms and examine the motives which there prevail. Let them ask themselves this solemn question----Is the sacrifice of a few mistaken, or criminal individuals, an object worthy of the shifts to which we are reduced to evade the constitution and the national engagements? Then let them review the arguments that have been offered with dispassionate candour; and if they even doubt the propriety of the measures, they may be about to adopt, let them remember, that in a doubtful case, the constitution ought never to be hazarded, without extreme necessity.

B. PAYMENT OF BRITISH DEBTS: GEORGE MASON TO GOVERNOR PATRICK HENRY (MAY 6, 1783)*

Dear Sir:

. . . I congratulate you most sincerely on the accomplishment of what I know was the warmest wish of your heart, the establishment of American independence and the liberty of our country. We are now to rank among the nations of the world, but whether our independence shall prove a blessing or a curse, must depend on our own wisdom or folly, virtue or wickedness; judging of the future by the past, the prospect is not promising. Justice and virtue are the vital principles of republican government; but among us a depravity of manners and morals prevails to the destruction of all confidence

* These excerpts are reprinted from Kate Mason Rowland, *The Life of George Mason, 1725–1792* (2 vols., 1892), vol. II, pp. 44–46.

between man and man. It greatly behooves the Assembly to revise several
of our laws; to abolish all such as are contrary to the fundamental principles
of justice, and by a strict adherence to the distinctions between right and
wrong for the future to restore that confidence and reverence in the people
for the legislature which has been so greatly impaired by a contrary conduct,
and without which our laws can never be much more than a dead letter. It
is in your power, my dear sir, to do more good and prevent more mischief
than any man in this State; and I doubt not that you will exert the great
talents with which God has blessed you in promoting the public happiness
and prosperity. . . .

The people in this part of the country are made very uneasy by the reports we have from below, that the Assembly will make some laws or resolutions respecting British debts which may infringe the articles of the peace,
under the mistaken idea that Great Britain will not risk a renewal of the war
on account of such an infraction of the treaty. We see by the late public
papers that the terms of peace with America are so strongly censured in
both houses of Parliament, that it has occasioned or will occasion a total
change in the ministry. A new ministry averse to the treaty, or even the
ministry who concluded it, might resent or avenge any infraction of its
provisions in any particular State, by reprisals upon the ships or coasts of
such State, or by sending two or three frigates to intercept their trade,
without danger of involving themselves in a new war; for the power of war
and peace and of making treaties being in Congress and not in the separate
States, any such act would be considered as an unwarrantable assumption
of power in the State adopting it; and we have no reason to expect that
either the late belligerent powers in Europe, or even the American States in
general, would make a common cause of it. It is easy to foresee that, in such
an event, our situation would be neither safe nor honorable. Had it been in
the power of the American commissioners (which it certainly was not) to
have abolished the British debts here, it would have been but short-sighted
policy to have done so. The far-fetched arguments which have been used to
show the distinction between this and other wars, would not have been
approved or comprehended, by the bulk of mankind; and with what degree
of confidence would foreign merchants have ventured their effects here, if
upon any national quarrel they were liable to confiscation? I could have
wished, indeed, that some reasonable time had been allowed for the payment
of the British debts, and that the interest on them had been relinquished.
As to the first, the desire of the British merchants to reinstate themselves in
their trade here will probably prevent their pressing their debtors, and as to
the last, their bond-debts only will carry interest. It is notorious, that the
custom of giving interest upon common accounts was introduced by the
partiality of the merchants of whom the jurors at the general court were
chiefly composed for several years before the late Revolution. Under our
present circumstances, I think the accounts of the British creditors may be
safely trusted to the Virginia juries without any interposition of the legislature. In conversation upon this subject we hear sometimes a very absurd
question: "If we are now to pay the debts due to British merchants, what
have we been fighting for all this while?" Surely not to avoid our just debts
or to cheat our creditors; but to rescue our country from the oppression and
tyranny of the British government, and to secure the rights and liberties of
ourselves and of our posterity, which we have happily accomplished. The

ministry in Great Britain and the Tories here have indeed constantly accused us of engaging in the war to avoid the payment of our just debts; but every honest man has denied so injurious a charge with indignation. Upon the whole we have certainly obtained better terms of peace than America had cause to expect; all the great points are ceded to us, and I cannot but think it would be highly dangerous and imprudent to risk a breach of it.

The people here too are greatly alarmed at a prevailing notion, that those men who have paid the British debts into the Treasury in depreciated paper money, instead of making up the real value to their creditors, will now attempt to throw the difference upon the shoulders of the public and raise it by taxes upon the people. I should hope that such an iniquitous scheme will be rejected with the contempt it deserves. If it is adopted it will probably cause some violent convulsion; the people being determined, in many parts of the country, to form associations against it, and to resist the payment of any taxes imposed on them for discharging the private debts of individuals. . . .

SELECTION

The Specter of Aristocracy: Ædanus Burke, "Considerations on the Society or Order of Cincinnati" (Oct. 10, 1783)

Even among the wealthy, the group an earlier generation of historians customarily referred to as aristocrats, there was a marked aversion to and a strong fear of aristocracy among the Revolutionary generation. A term of opprobrium used by men of all political hues to describe the baneful tendencies of the actions and policies of their opponents, "aristocracy" in its most common contemporary usage meant not just or even necessarily the wealthy but a legally privileged and hereditary group. That no such group did or should exist in the United States was agreed upon by all parties. At the same time, however, it was widely believed that the thirst for power was so strong in men that small combinations of men would be perpetually trying to play upon the passions of the people to win popular support for their schemes to corrupt the constitution, make themselves omnipotent, and establish an aristocratic power that would ultimately sweep all liberty before it. During the Confederation period this fear of aristocracy was most clearly revealed in the controversy over the Society of the Cincinnati in 1783–1784.

This society, which was organized by a group of officers from the Continental Army on May 13, 1783, and named after the Roman farmer who took up his sword to defend the Republic, was to be composed of all officers who had served three years, their "eldest male posterity," and such other men "eminent for their abilities and patriotism" as the society might elect honorary members for their lives only. To a large extent, the society was lodgelike in its orientation, intended to perpetuate the camaraderie and esprit that had developed among the officers during the war. Established at the very time the officers were trying to obtain arrears in pay and a pension of six years' full pay from Congress and were even contemplating direct

*measures to coerce Congress into complying with their demands, the society was
also conceived as a political pressure group that would help to insure that the
officers would eventually obtain satisfaction. Whatever its intentions, however, the
society bore a sinister appearance for men who were not members and who were
haunted by the specter of aristocracy. Such a man was Ædanus Burke (1743–
1802), a South Carolina judge who had emigrated from Ireland just before the
Revolution. Assuming the role of Cassius, the classical foe of military despotism,
Burke furiously attacked the society in his pamphlet* Considerations on the Society
or Order of Concinnati *on the grounds that it would create, as he said in his sub-
title, "A RACE OF HEREDITARY PATRICIANS, or NOBILITY." Charging
that the order was "planted in a fiery, hot ambition, and thirst for power," he
pointed out that aristocracies had frequently had military origins and argued that,
however benign the intentions of many of its original founders, the society would
"soon be corrupted, and the spirit of the people depressed." The result would
inevitably be tyranny and the institution of "such an inequality in the condition of
our inhabitants, that the country will be composed only of two ranks of men; the
patricians or nobles, and the rabble." Enough people agreed with Burke to create
widespread popular opposition to the society, and at the insistence of Washington
it voted to drop the hereditary provision for membership at its first annual meeting
in May, 1784. This concession was sufficient to allay popular fears, although membership continued to be hereditary because all of the state societies did not ratify
the change.*

*There is no adequate study of either the reaction to the Society of the Cincinnati
or American concepts of aristocracy, though Merrill Jensen,* The New Nation: A
History of the United States during the Confederation, 1781–1789 *(1950), contains
a brief analysis of the former. The portions of Burke's pamphlet reprinted here are
taken from the edition published in Newport in 1783, pages 3–12, 14–15.*

THE following publication is intended to convey a few observations to
my fellow-citizens, on a new SOCIETY OR INSTITUTION lately established
throughout the continent, composed of the Major-Generals, Brigadiers, and
other Officers of our army. It is instituted by the name of "THE SOCIETY
OF THE CINCINNATI; "and it has arrived to considerable strength and
maturity already. For besides the Grand or GENERAL SOCIETY of this order,
a subordinate or STATE SOCIETY is established in each state, and these again
subdivided "into such districts as shall be directed by the State Societies.
The General Society is to be held on the first Monday in May annually, so
long as they shall deem necessary; and afterwards at least once in every
three years. The state Societies are to meet the fourth of July annually, or
oftener, if they shall find it expedient."

Major-General Baron Stuben is appointed GRAND MASTER OF THE ORDER,
under the more humble title of PRESIDENT; and each State Society as well
as the Grand one has also its President, Vice-President, Secretary, Treasurer
and Vice-Treasurer. Annual communications of the States with each other,
by circular letters are enjoined: "And a General Meeting of the Society,
shall consist of its officers, and a representation from each state in number
not exceeding five: whose expences shall be borne by the respective State
Societies." So that here are delegates to be sent to form a general convention
or congress of the order. They have also instituted a badge of honour, or

what they call "an Order by which its members shall be known and distinguished. It is a medal of gold in the figure of an eagle, with an inscription on the face and reverse, alluding to the time of establishing the order, and to their having saved the republic. And this badge of distinction, is to be suspended by a deep blue ribbon two inches wide, edged with white, descriptive of the Union between America and France;" and to be worn by each member, as the French and British nobility wear their stars and ribbons, the insignia of their peerage. They have already conferred the honour and freedom of their Order on his excellency the French Ambassador, his excellency the Sieur Gerard, late minister plenipotentiary, the count d'Estaing, count de Grasse, count de Barras, the chevalier de Touches, count Rochambeau, and the generals and colonels of his army. And it is reported that several crowned heads and princes in Europe, are to dignify it by becoming honorary members of it. Congress, for political reasons, no doubt, winks at it; and no one state, nor body of men in any one of them, have given it the least opposition. The discretion of the commander in chief, which I take to be his distinguishing characteristic, is signal on this occasion; for he has appeared quite neutral in this business, if we except his becoming an honorary member of it. I believe the officers do not declare themselves to each other; and that on this occasion, there is too much truth in the remark of an able philosopher, "that there is no man who lets his nearest friend see the bottom of his heart."

The more I reflect on this institution, and the political consequences it will involve, the more am I filled with astonishment, that self created as it is, and coming upon us in so bold and questionable an appearance, so deeply planned, and closely executed, yet that it should have been so little attended to, that it is not even the subject of private conversation. Could I for a moment view this Order with indifference, it would be impossible not to smile, to behold the populace of America, in their town committees and town meetings, so keenly bent on petty mischiefs, in full chase and cry after a few insignificant tories, and running on regardless of an establishment, which ere long must strip the posterity of the middling and lower classes of every influence or authority, and leave them nothing but insignificance, contempt, and the wretched privilege of murmuring when it is too late. So thoughtless are the multitude!

My design at present is to shew, first, What this Order or Society seems to be; in the next place, To demonstrate what it really is, and will turn out to be; and lastly, To prove there is an absolute necessity of extirpating it altogether.

From the outside appearance of their ASSOCIATION, or instrument of writing which combines this Order, and which has been sent thro' the states by circular letters, it is nothing more than an "Association, Constitution, and Combination of the Generals, and other Officers of the Army, who have served three years, or were deranged by Congress, into a Society of Friends, to perpetuate the memory of the Revolution, and their own mutual friendship; to endure as long as they shall endure, OR ANY OF THEIR ELDEST MALE POSTERITY: and in failure thereof, THE COLLATERAL BRANCHES WHO MAY BE JUDGED WORTHY OF BECOMING ITS SUPPORTERS AND MEMBERS; To attend incessantly to preserve in violate the exalted rights and liberties of human nature; for which they fought and bled. To promote and cherish between the respective states, Union and National Honor, To render permanent, cordial affection, and the spirit of brotherly kindness among the Officers: To extend acts of beneficence towards those officers and their families who may unfortunately be under the necessity of receiving it." They advance each a month's pay, and open a door for donations from others not of the society, and for the charitable purpose of raising a fund, as well as for the POLITICAL one, of engaging the leading men of each state in the interests of the Order, they have the following rule: "And as there will at all times be men in the respective states, eminent for their abilities and patriotism, whose views may be directed to the same laudable objects with those of the Cincinnati; it shall be a rule to admit such characters, as honorary members of the society for their own lives only: Provided that the number of the honorary members does not exceed a ratio of one to four of the officers and their descendents."

The quotations I have made are the words of the General ASSOCIATION; so that it seems to be the offspring of patriotism, friendship, and humanity. And that many of the officers who have not closely viewed the subject, favour it from those principles, I have no doubt. But as several of them are equal in knowledge and abilities to any men in America, it is hardly possible but that some of them must see into the nature and consequences of the institution. For, to come to the second part of my argument, it is in reality, and will turn out to be, AN HEREDITARY PEERAGE; a nobility to them and their MALE ISSUE, and in default thereof, to the COLLATERAL BRANCHES: what the lawyers would call—A title of peerage of Cincinnati to them and their heirs male, remainder to their heirs general.

The sixth article of our confederation says, "Nor shall the United States in Congress assembled, nor any of them grant any title of nobility." But the order of Cincinnati usurp a nobility without gift or grant, in defiance of Congress and the states, as I shall shew presently. And though the order cannot, at present be sanctified by legal authority, yet that makes nothing against the consequences which will ensue. Though the Order is self-created, and an infringement of a general law of the Union; yet if the courage of the officers does not fail them; if they but keep up with firmness and perseverance against opposition, for this will be but trifling, so unthinking are the people; if they have but patience, subtilty, and address to cloke their design under a pious name of raising a charitable fund; so as to make it go down only for a few years; even if they are obliged from policy to lay aside the BADGE AND BLUE RIBBON: My life for it, they will have leisure to laugh at, and master their opponents. And the next generation will drink as deep of noble blood, and a hereditary peerage be as firmly settled in each potent family, and rivetted in our government, as any order of nobility is in the monarchies of Europe. This Order is planted in a fiery, hot ambition, and thirst for power; and its branches will end in tyranny. The Cincinnati will soon be corrupted, and the spirit of the people depressed; for in less than a century it will occasion such an inequality in the condition of our inhabitants, that the county will be composed only of two ranks of men; the patricians or nobles, and the rabble. This is the natural result of an establishment, whose departure is so sudden from our open professions of republicanism, that it must give a thinking mind most melancholy forebodings. This treating of a nobility, and breaking through our constitution, just as we were setting out in the world, is making that liberty which the Almighty has given us a means for feeding our pride; and turning the blessings of Providence into a curse upon us.

Had this order been created by Congress or our own legislature, even in violation of the confederation and of our laws, I should not think it a matter of such moment; dukes, earls, or peers of the Cincinnati, sanctified by an act of Assembly or of Congress, would be understood by all of us. Their pretensions and exclusive privileges, the mode of their trial for life and death, &c. ascertained. But the self-created Cincinnati, like a proud imperious man, would set no bounds to its claims. Jealous that it held not any thing on its own ambitious terms, as they had cut and carved titles for themselves and their posterity, they would be still grasping for everything; and rising from one usurpation to another, as they succeeded,

Let us examine the ostensible reasons for instituting the Cincinnati. First, "to perpetuate the remembrance of the revolution." But will not the historian more effectually transmit to posterity, the memory of the revolution, and the illustrious actions achieved in bringing it about? And as to "preserving inviolate the exalted rights of human nature; these rights will in my opinion be much better preserved inviolate by having no DISTINCT ORDER of patricians or nobility among us: which, however thought necessary to support the throne of a prince, or form a barrier between him and his people, is a bane and a curse to a republic; for unless you destroy the one, you cannot have the other.

Again. They will "attend incessantly to preserve inviolate the exalted rights of human nature." Are there then, most illustrious Cincinnati, two sorts of rights belonging to human nature? Is there one kind, subordinate and on a level with the humble condition of Plebeians? and others MORE EXALTED, which the citizens are incapable of preserving inviolate, without the INCESSANT WATCHING of a dignified order of patricians? They must mean this or nothing. The people of America, it seems, are not fit to be trusted with their own NATIONAL HONOR, or their own affairs, unless the Order takes the superintendence and direction of them. Can contradiction be more strong and glaring? In one moment they institute an order, and raise a DISTINCTION, which looks down, as from an high mountain, on all beneath them: They have laid in ruins that fine, plain, level state of civil equality, over which the sight of the beholder passed with pleasure; which God laid out for our use and happiness, and which our Laws and the nature of a Republican government promised us: They have violated all, yet in the same breath, by way of a mask thrown over their doings, they spread before us the fine words last quoted. But the disguise is too thin: for in the name of Heaven, can any man in his senses believe that the remaining rights of the people which are yet left untouched, will not be invaded and violated, by men, who disdaining the condition of private citizens, as below them, left it, and mounted up to the elevated and exclusive dignity of hereditary title?

But say they, "an order of nobility will give strength, duration, and reverance to our government." Has not the war of America, I say, convinced mankind that society in the most trying conjunctures, and fiercest dangers, can do better without them? When we first set out we had scarcely a distinction among us; for the body of our people was chiefly composed of Yeomanry. But though they had no titles nor badges, they soon produced excellent officers, soldiers and statesmen; and every corner of America, at this moment, abounds with men, as well militia as continentals, as capable of command in calvalry or infantry, as any regular officers Europe can boast of.

This military virtue of our citizens; their sense of dignity and contempt of danger; the gallant efforts they made; was not this, I say, the offspring of the equality and independent temper of men, who fought for themselves, and not for masters; and whose spirit was not trammeled or broken down by the oppression of an insolent nobility? This was that warm animating pride which disdained to look up to any human creature as a superior, which raised us armies, and fought campaigns without pay or covering; efforts so glorious, as never were, nor can possibly be made by any nation where a nobility have got a considerable footing.

But if this order prevails in our country, the generous, gallant virtues of the present day will soon be extinguished, never to appear again. What Salust calls THE COMMON DISEASE OF A NOBILITY, . . . PRIDE AND INSOLENCE on the one hand, and oppression and cringing habits on the other, will break the spirit of our children to such a degree of debasement, they would shortly be impressed in good earnest with the idea, that the independence of America was from the beginning ordained: that such an effusion of human life and human blood: so great a variety of glorious atchievements and honorable sufferings through the war: that all this I say was effected, not for the good of the people, but for a few families to aggrandize themselves, and monopolize the power of the continent, and to enjoy the fruits of it.

The other pretext is, "to promote and cherish between the respective states, Union and National Honor." But I have the honour to tell Baron Steuben, that though an order of peerage may do very well under the petty princes of Germany, yet in America it is incompatible with our freedom; and instead of being a bond of POLITICAL UNION, it would on a future day, prove a source of CIVIL DISSENSION AND MISERY: by establishing two DISTINCT orders; one whose foundation is the ARMY; the other composed of the COMMONALTY. Thus it opens a theatre for ignominious distinctions, for jealousy and hatred, and ends in civil war, between these patricians and the people, if the latter had any spirit left. And as the Order would be firmly established by time, the world in less than an hundred years, would find its descendants a race of men distinct from the rest of society, with the eyes of all fixed upon them, as objects of such worship, that it is not at all improbable, but our children should find the Order foisting the divinity of their institution into our pulpits, under a JURE DIVINO title. In a few generations hence, such are the extravagancies which enter into the heart of man, the peers of Cincinnati might consider themselves as deriving their lineage from heaven. Let us examine the story of those heroes celebrated in the two immortal poems of Homer and Virgil: strip it of the bewitching charms of poetry; and you shall find they afford not a better foundation for idolatry and the Yahoo-like worship of men, than the peers of our Order. The courage of Hector, engaged in defence of his country against a foreign invasion: The valour of Achilles in avenging an insult to his nation: The piety of Æneas in saving his father and a few images of the Trojan Gods out of the ruins of his native city: I speak agreeable to truth and common sense, when I say that all these exploits have been equalled by the Cincinnati. And it is equally probable that they would produce in some future generation of American plebeians, such an admiration and idolatry, that would in the fervor of its operation, as in Rome of old, enable some leading man of the Order to set up a tyranny. Some sycophant poet would not be wanting to prostitute the talents which God gave him, for the vile purpose of dubbing with divinity, as Virgil did Augustus, a tyrant who had swallowed up the liberties of his country.

The Cincinnati at any rate would soon HAVE AND HOLD an exclusive right to offices, honors, and authorities, civil and military. And the whole country besides themselves a mere mob of plebeians, without weight or estimation; degraded in the eyes of our patricians, as the Roman people were by their republican nobility. These held the others as Livy says, . . . AS IF THEY WERE ODIOUS TO THE VERY GODS; and as the Cincinnati soon would, held it an abomination to intermarry with them. This degradation of the people on one hand, and the insolence of the nobles on the other, was in Rome, as it would be with us, a political disease, which never ceased to distract that republic, until at last it occasioned its overthrow. Arising solely from the ignominious DISTINCTION between the Commons, and the Patricians, as an hereditary order: who from the expulsion of the Tarquins, to the time of the Gracchi, about 300 years, produced such perpetual discord and tumults in that republic, that nothing but its good fortune and military virtue preserved it so long from destruction. At last when the people became corrupted, their dissentions swelled to open rupture, or civil war; Sylla heading the nobility, and Marius the commons. The latter being completely vanquished, the conqueror, as perpetual dictator, set up a tyranny; and exercised confiscation, banishment, and every other species of cruelty which marks a disorderly people. Still civil discord admitted of no cessation; for in a short time afterwards, the fire broke out with multiplied fury, under Cæsar, the leader of the commons, and Pompey, at the head of the nobility. The event is well known; Cæsar triumphed over his adversary, and over the liberty of his fellow-citizens; and the whole ended in a cruel despotism. And thus so many wars carried on—so many illustrious actions performed by that gallant people, only to gratify the ambition of an order, similar to the Cincinnati, but in its origin by no means so respectable, as I shall presently shew; and finally to become the slaves of barbarous masters, the Roman Emperors.

I mention these few plain, notorious facts, to prove, that the institution of this nobility is not the way to promote and cherish UNION and NATIONAL HONOUR. Out of it will arise DISCORD and not UNION. And that the people should, without so much as saying a word about the matter, behold this poisonous EXOTIC plant taking root throughout the land. That they should commit such a vile abuse of their liberty as to allow it, is a reproach upon human nature; and would, in the eyes of posterity, be a national dishonour to us. I have often thought that the revolution in America would reduce it to a certainty, whether mankind was destined by nature for liberty or slavery; for a republican government never before has had what we call fair play, in any part of the globe. But the Order of Cincinnati would give a fatal wound to civil liberty thro' the world, and prove that all that Plato, Sidney, Lock and others have bequeathed to posterity on the subject of political happiness, though appearing well on paper; yet was no more than ideal pictures of a fine imagination. Our example too would serve to strengthen tyranny in Europe, by evincing that a people brought up under a monarchy, and accustomed to be governed by others, are too degenerate to govern themselves in a state of liberty; and that after all we have done, we still keep a hankering after the orders, titles and trumpery we have been used to under the royal government, where the people are so bewitched, that abilities, virtue or wealth itself, are not such objects of reverence as a star or ribbon.

The following clause of the ASSOCIATION, I think an extraordinary one. "The officers of the American army having generally been taken from the citizens of America, possess high veneration for the character of that illustrious Roman, Lucius Quintus Cincinnatus; and being resolved to follow his example, by returning to their citizenship, they think they may with propriety denominate themselves the society of the Cincinnati."

Then as they were taken from the citizens, why in the name of God not be contented "to return to citizenship," without usurping an hereditary order? Or with what "propriety can they denominate" themselves from Cincinnatus, with an ambition so rank, as to aim at nothing less, than . . . "RETIREMENT AND A PEERAGE?" Did that virtuous Roman, having subdued the enemies of his country, and returned home to tend his vineyard and plant his cabbages; did he confer an hereditary order of peerage on himself and his fellow soldiers? I answer No; it was more than he dared to do. For a less crime, that republic, in the days of its liberty put to death, banished or disgraced some of her citizens, as illustrious and renowned as any we have, without exception.

The Romans had learned from sad experience, a lesson which seems to be brought home to ourselves in the example before me; that military commanders acquiring fame, and accustomed to receive the obedience of armies, are generally in their hearts aristocratics, and enemies to the popular equality of a republic. That becoming illustrious by their services, they are ever ready, under plausible appearances of JUSTICE AND MERIT, to assume usurpations of the most pernicious tendency. The people first adore them with a stupid veneration, which swells their pride; enables them to form factions; procure followers; create distinctions; aggrandize their families; split the state into divisions, and like Cæsar, Cromwell, and others, under the smoke they had created, raise themselves to despotism. This is the reason that in wise republics, such citizens were so often and so justly put out of the way; banished their country, or excluded from dignities or influence. And their fame and eclat was thought an ample reward to console them under it. It is probable therefore that it was as much through fear, as republican virtue, that Cincinnatus and his officers were restrained from instituting a new order; for I do not suppose they were either better or worse than our own. Only that republic had wise laws to bridle the ambition and controul the factions of potent citizens, and we have as yet no such laws.

I know it will be denied, that the order is what I do boldly assert it to be, an HEREDITARY PEERAGE. Some of its members assume the cloak of political modesty, and under it talk, that they are no more dangerous than a city-corporation of "shop-keepers, taylors, or other mechanics; or like the Free Masons and other clubs who wear badges or medals." Here we see how ambition can assume all shapes and colour, and humble itself to the very dust to accomplish its purpose! This moment take upon them the superintendence of empire, the HONOUR, UNION AND HAPPINESS OF NATIONS, and the EXALTED RIGHTS OF HUMAN NATURE; and the very next, prostrate themselves to the level of men, with whom to be compared on any other occasion, the Order would deem an insult. I say, that a body of military commanders, distinguished from the rest of society under an institution founded on the illustrious actions of so singular a revolution as that of America: invested with the exclusive privilege of wearing a badge of their order, honourable to themselves, as it is ignominious to the people; elevated above others, and in parity among themselves: These, I say, are peers of the realm, PARES REGNI, and nothing more or less. And that this order, being entailed on the MALE ISSUE, and in default thereof, on the COLLATERAL LINE, makes it HEREDITARY. And whether it be instituted by the legislature, who alone have the legal power to do it, or be usurped by the officers, it makes no difference in its consequences. For as I observed before, in one generation the order of Cincinnati will be established immoveably. The rank, number and influence of the members; the remembrance of their glorious actions, still heightened by the propensity of mankind to the marvellous: all this, I say will raise the order to grandeur, antiquity, veneration and arbitrary power; acquisitions which will become hereditary with the peerage, and once obtained, not one family of them will ever think of renouncing.

But in support of the order, it will be alledged, that the states cannot pay the army: the officers will be contented with this BAUBLE, and they will not abuse it. " 'Tis like throwing a tub to a whale," say they. Should the states commit such a national iniquity, as not to pay their army, they merit eternal infamy, and to be PEER-RIDDEN into the bargain. And as to the officers resting satisfied with the BLUE RIBBON, it is the nature of man never to be contented with any thing, nor secure of what he has, unless he be perpetually adding. And as this order would still be apprehensive of losing the exclusive honour and influence they had, they would eternally be caballing and working for more, to the disquiet of the government. And admitting the present members would not abuse it, is any one certain, that their children will make no ill use of it? The officers can transmit to their posterity, their fortunes, their reputation, and the peerage of Cincinnati: but can they leave to them, as a legacy, that virtue which lately led them to encounter the hardships of a perilous war? Or when the present generation is off the stage, will the sons of our self-created patricians, who will not experience the adversity their fathers bore in defending their liberties; will they, finding themselves raised above their neighbours, agree to defend, and live on a footing of equality with them? Or will they not rather, relying on the rank and power of an aristocratic nobility, disdaining private men, nor standing in fear of public laws, engross the offices, powers and influence of the republic, which should belong to the body of the people? Or in case any ambitious leader, of a few, should threaten the liberties of the commons; or Congress on a future day, invested with a revenue, a fleet and army, attempt a point of consequence: will they not support the one or the other, as it will be most likely to support their order? In such a dispute their weight would turn the scale, for the number of the peers of the order, reckoning honorary members (which their good policy would lead them to choose out of the first-rate men) cannot be far short of ten thousand; and as they will be the principal men in America, to suppose that each can, by his influence, procure two or three followers, who will adhere to his interest and service, is a reasonable calculation. Here is a body of 20 or 30,000 men immediately; and every generation will be adding to the number.

Had our officers less merit and claim to the applause of their countrymen at home, and to fame abroad, I should not be so alarmed at this bold usurpation of theirs. For a class of men of little worth, could never have

influence to render an institution of this nature detrimental to the freedom
of their country. It would rather meet with ridicule, and dwindle into
nothing. But it must be remembered, that a series of hardy, gallant, splendid
actions, through a fierce and desperate conflict; their toils and sufferings:
and their patience under them; and above all, the glorious success which
crowned the whole; have rendered the officers of the American army, the
most renowned band of men, that this day walk on the face of the globe.
And was it as well acquainted as I am, with the temper of goodness and
humanity which runs through the whole of them; they would be as much
beloved as they are admired. Their bravery the world knows: . . .

My observations here go to prove, that the order of Cincinnati, composed
of our Major Generals, Brigadiers, and field officers, reinforced and firmly
supported by all the potent families and leading first-rate men, in and out
of the different legislatures and public bodies throughout America, whose
influence and interest the deep policy of the Order has already determined
to pre-engage as honorary members: that this body, I say, in consequence
of their merit, services, and lustre of character, forms a very broad and
respectable foundation for raising an hereditary nobility in America; and
are much more likely to produce it, than were the heads and first founders
of ancient or modern nobility in the old world.

Let us go up to the source of nobility among the Romans, and see whether
it will bear a comparison with the Cincinnati, the fountain of American
peerage. In the first age of that republic, they had no idea of instituting
such an order. We have only to imagine a society of men, living in a state
of simplicity, with fortunes on a level, each possessing no more than two
acres of ground. A few old men were chosen for the legislature: distinguished
for nothing but the experience of years, and an affection they were supposed
to have for the people; hence they were called PATRES or FATHERS. But the
descendents of these plain homespun families, in a few years by considering
themselves as distinct from their fellow-citizens; assuming pretensions; "forming family unions; and cementing them by intermarriages": This policy
alone, without title or badge of honor, laid in Rome the foundation of a
nobility, with such pride and thirst of domineering, that even AFTER MON-
ARCHY WAS ABOLISHED, by the deposition of the TARQUIN FAMILY, the people,
by whose assistance it was brought about, gained but little by the bargain.
For the great families having once got the government into their hands, and
united all the powers of the monarchy and nobility in their own order: then
I say, EVERY PATRICIAN TURNED OUT A TARQUIN, with this difference, that the
whole body was worse, by as much as a thousand tyrants are a greater curse
than a single one.

So simple and contracted was the origin of peerage in that republic; as
much inferior to the Cincinnati, the foundation of nobles in America, as the
disorderly, plundering banditti, who first built their cabins on the foundation
of Rome, were beneath a corps of illustrious leaders, such as Washington,
Greene, St. Clair, Moultrie, Wayne, and the rest of them. The beginning
of Roman nobility may be compared to a small spring which forms the head
of a great river: it made at first but a feeble stream; but running in a long
tract of time it acquired strength from other rivulets. But the Cincinnati
and its honorary members, is THAT RIVER pretty nearly formed already:
broad, deep and forcible, and swoln to such a height, that rolling on in
DIRECT LINES, and COLLATERAL MEANDERS, it would in a short time rise into

such a FRESH, as to overrun its banks, and lay the country round it in one dismal scene of ruin.

As to the modern nobility of Europe, it was formed out of the rude, barbarian Generals and field officers of the Goth and Vandal army. And . . . many of those titles were, like the Cincinnati, self-created. The British nobles or barons sprung from the like origin: and their orders of knighthood particularly, had the most silly, trifling beginning. The knighthood of the garter took its rise, it is said, from the countess of Salisbury, in the reign of Edward III, dropping her garter while she was dancing. That of the Bath, from another idle story. The order of St. Andrew, very dignified formerly, from a dream of a superstitious prince of Scotland. That of St. Patrick, lately instituted among the Irish (who, though it is only a link in the chain which ties them down, are it seems, very fond of it) from a legendary tale of a fanatic preacher; who, if he ever existed at all, had not half the learning or merit of Whitefield or Wesley. At least nobody will insist that the men or circumstances which gave existence to those orders, were so likely to produce an HEREDITARY DISTINCTION, as the American Revolution and the Cincinnati, the fame of whose exploits resounds through the world.

If we trace nobility up to the head in Venice and other parts of Europe we shall find it in every nation small and contemptible, but that the very creating a PUBLIC DISTINCT ORDER, uniformly terminated in every country, in servitude to the people. For the consequences of nobility all over Europe, as it would soon turn out in America, are deplorable. There, instead of being pillars for supporting the crown, as judge Blackstone is pleased to call them, peers are actually tools and rivets for driving and clenching poverty, meanness and abasement on the people who are chilled and stunted by the noble families, as the brush and under wood in the forest, is overshadowed and starved by the towering oaks above.

But although the force of those remarks is well known to men of sense of the army, yet they cannot be contented with the reputation which their services have secured to them, unless they appropriate an hereditary peerage. EXCEPT THEIR PAY, I cannot see any thing they want to satisfy them, unless that their eclat being so universal, popularity has, like a mistress after possession, lost her charms in their eyes; they consider her too common, and seek some other beauty out of the ordinary way. Are not their fellow-citizens already as far below many of them, as the earth is below the Heavens? Or can the glory of a human creature go higher, than it has carried some of them? Is it not enough that every muse will raise trophies over their urns, which neither the revolution of ages, nor power of fortune can demolish? But all this, it seems is nothing to the all-grasping, infatuating ambition of our Generals and field officers; unless they have A QUAINT TITLE stuck upon their family, and a badge or bauble dangling at their button hole; which answers no other purpose in the world but to introduce the misfortunes I have been pointing out, and to draw upon them the well-merited suspicion and jealousy of every man of any thought on the continent. Did these officers but consider what reputation and satisfaction they fly from, they would dissolve their institution at once, and sit down contented with the love and veneration of their fellow-citizens. . . .

I have proved I hope to the reader's satisfaction, that the Cincinnati creates two distinct orders amongst us. 1st. A race of hereditary Nobles; founded on the military, together with the powerful families, and first-rate, leading men in the state, whose view it will ever be, TO RULE: and 2d. The people or plebeians, whose only view is not to be oppressed, but whose certain fate it will be to suffer oppression under the institution; I have shewed that it is a deep laid contrivance to beget and perpetuate family grandeur in an aristocratic Nobility, to terminate at last in monarchical tyranny. And I shall now pass on to point out the constitutional means of opposing it.

I feel sensibly that the few remarks I have to make, are too bold and decisive to meet the approbation of some men. But if there be among my readers one, who merits the name of a republican, I have the confidence to believe his opinion will go along with mine.

To crush this Order, then, without embroiling the state, there is but one way. Let the legislature immediately enter into spirited resolutions against it; let them tell the Order, and the world, that however pious or patriotic the pretence, yet any political combination of military commanders, is, in a republican government, extremely hazardous, and highly censurable. But that instituting exclusive honours and privileges of an Hereditary Order, is a daring usurpation on the sovereignty of the republic; a dangerous insult to the rights and liberties of the people, and a fatal stab to that principle of equality, which forms the basis of our government; to establish which the people fought and bled as well as the Cincinnati; though the latter are now taking every measure to rob them of the credit, and of the fruits of it. If this would not do, and the Order still go on; yet such a resolve would have a good effect. It would, like Ithruriel's spear in Milton, touch the Order; and however plausible the external appearance, under which it now fits transformed, the resolution would oblige it, as the fallen angel in paradise, to start up in its own true hideous shape and likeness; and then we should know how to grapple with it. And afterwards, though I am willing to consider our officers as the plank, which bore us through the storm safe to land, yet I am one that would not let it be the means of drowning us in a calm, within the harbour. The examples of the wisest, and most renowned republics of which history furnishes any account, and the opinion of the ablest political writers, will support me in a doctrine, which I should discuss on the present occasion, if I were certain that our citizens, for whose information I am writing, were good stuff for republicans. . . .

CASSIUS

SELECTION

Achievement in the West

By far the most important achievement of the Articles of Confederation was in devising a policy for the settlement of the West, the only area in which it could act independently of the states. No sooner had Virginia's cession of its lands north of the Ohio River become final on March 1, 1784, than Congress appointed a com-

mittee headed by Thomas Jefferson to work out a plan for the administration and occupation of the area. The committee report, which called for the division of the region into seven territories, establishment of temporary governments, and the eventual admission of each territory into the Union on an equal basis with the original states, was accepted by Congress with some amendments on April 23, 1784. A second ordinance, passed the following year on May 20, 1785, and reprinted here in part as Selection 51 A, specified that each territory should be divided into townships six miles square and containing thirty-six sections of 640 acres each with one section in each township set aside for educational purposes.

The second ordinance was put into operation immediately and served as the basis for the public-land system until the passage of the Homestead Act during the Civil War, but before the first ordinance had even gone into effect Congress replaced it with the more elaborate Northwest Ordinance of July 13, 1787. The Northwest Ordinance, reprinted in full below as Selection 51 B, was passed at the urging of a group of New England land speculators known as the Ohio Company of Associates, who purchased 1½ million acres of land in the Northwest from Congress for a bargain price of less than ten cents an acre in specie and who wanted to make the region attractive for prospective New England settlers. Similar in spirit to Jefferson's original ordinance of 1784, the Northwest Ordinance reduced the number of territories to be created from seven to between three and five; provided for the establishment of a temporary government under the supervision of Congress to administer each territory; specified the procedures to be followed for transforming each territory into a state when it attained a population of 60,000; guaranteed trial by jury, representation apportioned according to population, freedom of religion, and public support of education; and prohibited slavery. With this ordinance the Confederation Congress thus provided for the extension of republican institutions and the main features of the libertarian inheritance of the Revolution to the Western territories.

Brief discussions of the development of a western policy in the 1780s will be found in Merrill Jensen, The Articles of Confederation: An Interpretation of the Social-Constitutional History of the American Revolution, 1774–1781 *(1940), and* The New Nation: A History of the United States during the Confederation, 1781– 1789 *(1950), and Edmund S. Morgan,* The Birth of the Republic, 1763–1789 *(1956). A more detailed treatment of the ordinance of 1785 is Payson Jackson Treat,* The National Land System, 1785–1820 *(1910).*

A. A WESTERN LAND POLICY: THE LAND ORDINANCE OF 1785 (MAY 20, 1785)*

Be it ordained by the United States in Congress assembled, that the territory ceded by individual States to the United States, which has been purchased of the Indian inhabitants, shall be disposed of in the following manner:

A surveyor from each state shall be appointed by Congress, or a committee of the States, who shall take an Oath for the faithful discharge of his duty, before the Geographer of the United States. . . .

* These excerpts are reprinted from *Journals of the Continental Congress,* vol. XXVIII, pp. 375–380.

The Surveyors, as they are respectively qualified, shall proceed to divide the said territory into townships of six miles square, by lines running due north and south, and others crossing these at right angles, as near as may be, unless where the boundaries of the late Indian purchases may render the same impracticable, and then they shall depart from this rule no farther than such particular circumstances may require . . .

The first line, running north and south as aforesaid, shall begin on the river Ohio, at a point that shall be found to be due north from the western termination of a line, which has been run as the southern boundary of the state of Pennsylvania; and the first line, running east and west, shall begin at the same point, and shall extend throughout the whole territory. Provided, that nothing herein shall be construed, as fixing the western boundary of the state of Pennsylvania. The geographer shall designate the townships, or fractional parts of townships, by numbers progressively from south to north; always beginning each range with number one; and the ranges shall be distinguished by their progressive numbers to the westward. The first range, extending from the Ohio to the lake Erie, being marked number one. The Geographer shall personally attend to the running of the first east and west line; and shall take the latitude of the extremes of the first north and south line, and of the mouths of the principal rivers.

The lines shall be measured with a chain; shall be plainly marked by chaps on the trees, and exactly described on a plat; whereon shall be noted by the surveyor, at their proper distances, all mines, salt springs, salt licks and mill seats, that shall come to his knowledge, and all water courses, mountains and other remarkable and permanent things, over and near which such lines shall pass, and also the quality of the lands.

The plats of the townships respectively, shall be marked by subdivisions into lots of one mile square, or 640 acres, in the same direction as the external lines, and numbered from 1 to 36; always beginning the succeeding range of the lots with the number next to that with which the preceding one concluded. . . .

As soon as seven ranges of townships, and fractional parts of townships, in the direction from south to north, shall have been surveyed, the geographer shall transmit plats thereof to the board of treasury, who shall record the same, with the report, in well bound books to be kept for that purpose. And the geographer shall make similar returns, from time to time, of every seven ranges as they may be surveyed. The Secretary at War shall have recourse thereto, and shall take by lot therefrom, a number of townships, and fractional parts of townships, as well from those to be sold entire as from those to be sold in lots, as will be equal to one seventh part of the whole of such seven ranges, as nearly as may be, for the use of the late continental army . . .

The board of treasury shall transmit a copy of the original plats, previously noting thereon, the townships, and fractional parts of townships, which shall have fallen to the several states, by the distribution aforesaid, to the Commissioners of the loan office of the several states, who, after giving notice of not less than two nor more than six months, by causing advertisements to be posted up at the court houses, or other noted places in every county, and to be inserted in one newspaper, published in the states of their residence respectively, shall proceed to sell the townships, or fractional parts of townships, at public vendue . . . provided, that none of the lands, within the said territory, be sold under the price of one dollar the acre, to be paid in specie, or loan office certificates, reduced to specie value, by the scale of depreciation, or certificates of liquidated debts of the United States, including interest, besides the expense of the survey and other charges thereon, which are hereby rated at thirty six dollars the township, in specie, or certificates as aforesaid, and so in the same proportion for a fractional part of a township, or of a lot, to be paid at the time of sales; on failure of which payment, the said lands shall again be offered for sale.

There shall be reserved for the United States out of every township, the four lots, being numbered 8, 11, 26, 29, and out of every fractional part of a township, so many lots of the same numbers as shall be found thereon, for future sale. There shall be reserved the lot N 16, of every township, for the maintenance of public schools, within the said township; also one third part of all gold, silver, lead and copper mines, to be sold, or otherwise disposed of as Congress shall hereafter direct. . . .

And whereas Congress, by their resolutions of September 16 and 18 in the year 1776, and the 12th of August, 1780, stipulated grants of land to certain officers and soldiers of the late continental army, and by the resolution of the 22d September, 1780, stipulated grants of land to certain officers in the hospital department of the late continental army; for complying therefore with such engagements, Be it ordained, That the secretary at war, from the returns in his office, or such other sufficient evidence as the nature of the case may admit, determine who are the objects of the above resolutions and engagements, and the quantity of land to which such persons or their representatives are respectively entitled, and cause the townships, or fractional parts of townships, hereinbefore reserved for the use of the late continental army, to be drawn for in such manner as he shall deem expedient, to answer the purpose of an impartial distribution. . . .

B. TOWARD THE CREATION OF NEW STATES: THE NORTHWEST ORDINANCE (JULY 13, 1787)*

Be it ordained by the United States in Congress assembled, That the said territory, for the purposes of temporary government, be one district, subject, however, to be divided into two districts, as future circumstances may, in the opinion of Congress, make it expedient.

Be it ordained by the authority aforesaid, That the estates both of resident and non-resident proprietors in the said territory, dying intestate, shall descend to, and be distributed among, their children and the descendants of a deceased child in equal parts, the descendants of a deceased child or grandchild to take the share of their deceased parent in equal parts among them; and where there shall be no children or descendants, then in equal parts to the next of kin, in equal degree; and among collaterals, the children of a deceased brother or sister of the intestate shall have, in equal parts among them, their deceased parent's share; and there shall, in no case, be a distinction between kindred of the whole and half blood; saving in all cases

* Reprinted in full from Francis Newton Thorpe (ed.), *The Federal and State Constitutions, and Other Organic Laws* (7 vols., 1909), vol. II, pp. 957–962.

to the widow of the intestate, her third part of the real estate for life, and one-third part of the personal estate; and this law relative to descents and dower, shall remain in full force until altered by the legislature of the district. And until the governor and judges shall adopt laws as hereinafter mentioned, estates in the said territory may be devised or bequeathed by wills in writing, signed and sealed by him or her in whom the estate may be (being of full age) and attested by three witnesses;—and real estates may be conveyed by lease and release, or bargain and sale, signed, sealed, and delivered by the person, being of full age, in whom the estate may be, and attested by two witnesses, provided such wills be duly proved, and such conveyances be acknowledged, or the execution thereof duly proved, and be recorded within one year after proper magistrates, courts, and registers, shall be appointed for that purpose; and personal property may be transferred by delivery, saving, however, to the French and Canadian inhabitants, and other settlers of the Kaskaskies, Saint Vincents, and the neighboring villages, who have heretofore professed themselves citizens of Virginia, their laws and customs now in force among them, relative to the descent and conveyance of property.

Be it ordained by the authority aforesaid, That there shall be appointed, from time to time, by Congress, a governor, whose commission shall continue in force for the term of three years, unless sooner revoked by Congress; he shall reside in the district, and have a freehold estate therein, in one thousand acres of land, while in the exercise of his office.

There shall be appointed from time to time, by Congress, a secretary, whose commission shall continue in force for four years, unless sooner revoked; he shall reside in the district, and have a freehold estate therein, in five hundred acres of land, while in the exercise of his office. It shall be his duty to keep and preserve the acts and laws passed by the legislature, and the public records of the district, and the proceedings of the governor in his executive department, and transmit authentic copies of such acts and proceedings every six months to the secretary of Congress. There shall also be appointed a court, to consist of three judges, any two of whom to form a court, who shall have a common-law jurisdiction, and reside in the district, and have each therein a freehold estate, in five hundred acres of land, while in the exercise of their offices; and their commissions shall continue in force during good behavior.

The governor and judges, or a majority of them, shall adopt and publish in the district such laws of the original States, criminal and civil, as may be necessary, and best suited to the circumstances of the district, and report them to Congress from time to time, which laws shall be in force in the district until the organization of the general assembly therein, unless disapproved of by Congress; but afterwards the legislature shall have authority to alter them as they shall think fit.

The governor, for the time being, shall be commander-in-chief of the militia, appoint and commission all officers in the same below the rank of general officers; all general officers shall be appointed and commissioned by Congress.

Previous to the organization of the general assembly the governor shall appoint such magistrates, and other civil officers, in each county or township, as he shall find necessary for the preservation of the peace and good order in the same. After the general assembly shall be organized the powers and duties of magistrates and other civil officers shall be regulated and defined by the said assembly; but all magistrates and other civil officers, not herein otherwise directed, shall, during the continuance of this temporary government, be appointed by the governor.

For the prevention of crimes and injuries, the laws to be adopted or made shall have force in all parts of the district, and for the execution of process, criminal and civil, the governor shall make proper divisions thereof; and he shall proceed, from time to time, as circumstances may require, to lay out the parts of the district in which the Indian titles shall have been extinguished, into counties and townships, subject, however, to such alterations as may thereafter be made by the legislature.

So soon as there shall be five thousand free male inhabitants, of full age, in the district, upon giving proof thereof to the governor, they shall receive authority, with time and place, to elect representatives from their counties or townships, to represent them in the general assembly; *Provided*, That for every five hundred free male inhabitants there shall be one representative, and so on, progressively, with the number of free male inhabitants, shall the right of representation increase, until the number of representatives shall amount to twenty-five; after which the number and proportion of representatives shall be regulated by the legislature: *Provided*, That no person be eligible or qualified to act as a representative, unless he shall have been a citizen of one of the United States three years, and be a resident in the district, or unless he shall have resided in the district three years; and, in either case, shall likewise hold in his own right, in fee-simple, two hundred acres of land within the same: *Provided also*, That a freehold in fifty acres of land in the district, having been a citizen of one of the States, and being resident in the district, or the like freehold and two years' residence in the district, shall be necessary to qualify a man as an elector of a representative.

The representatives thus elected shall serve for the term of two years; and in case of the death of a representative, or removal from office, the governor shall issue a writ to the county or township, for which he was a member, to elect another in his stead, to serve for the residue of the term.

The general assembly, or legislature, shall consist of the governor, legislative council, and a house of representative. The legislative council shall consist of five members, to continue in office five years, unless sooner removed by Congress; any three of whom to be a quorum: and the members of the council shall be nominated and appointed in the following manner, to wit: As soon as representatives shall be elected the governor shall appoint a time and place for them to meet together, and when met they shall nominate ten persons, residents in the district, and each possessed of a freehold in five hundred acres of land, and return their names to Congress, five of whom Congress shall appoint and commission to serve as aforesaid; and whenever a vacancy shall happen in the council, by death or removal from office, the house of representatives shall nominate two persons, qualified as aforesaid, for each vacancy, and return their names to Congress, one of whom Congress shall appoint and commission for the residue of the term; and every five years, four months at least before the expiration of the time of service of the members of the council, the said house shall nominate ten persons, qualified as aforesaid, and return their names to Congress, five of whom Congress shall appoint and commission to serve as members of the council five years, unless sooner removed. And the governor, legislative council, and house of representatives shall have authority to make laws in all cases for the good government of the district, not repugnant to the principles and articles in this ordinance established and declared. And all bills, having passed by a majority in the house, and by a majority in the council, shall be referred to the governor for his assent; but no bill, or legislative act whatever, shall be of any force without his assent. The governor shall have power to convene, prorogue, and dissolve the general assembly when, in his opinion, it shall be expedient.

The governor, judges, legislative council, secretary, and such other officers as Congress shall appoint in the district, shall take an oath or affirmation of fidelity, and of office; the governor before the president of Congress, and all other officers before the governor. As soon as a legislature shall be formed in the district, the council and house assembled, in one room, shall have authority, by joint ballot, to elect a delegate to Congress, who shall have a seat in Congress, with a right of debating, but not of voting, during this temporary government.

And for extending the fundamental principles of civil and religious liberty, which form the basis whereon these republics, their laws and constitutions, are erected; to fix and establish those principles as the basis of all laws, constitutions, and governments, which forever hereafter shall be formed in the said territory; to provide, also, for the establishment of States, and permanent government therein, and for their admission to a share in the Federal councils on an equal footing with the original States, at as early periods as may be consistent with the general interest:

It is hereby ordained and declared, by the authority aforesaid, that the following articles shall be considered as articles of compact, between the original States and the people and States in the said territory, and forever remain unalterable, unless by common consent, to wit:

Article I

No person, demeaning himself in a peaceable and orderly manner, shall ever be molested on account of his mode of worship, or religious sentiments, in the said territory.

Article II

The inhabitants of the said territory shall always be entitled to the benefits of the writs of *habeas corpus*, and of the trial by jury; of a proportionate representation of the people in the legislature, and of judicial proceedings according to the course of the common law. All persons shall be bailable, unless for capital offences, where the proof shall be evident, or the presumption great. All fines shall be moderate; and no cruel or unusual punishments shall be inflicted. No man shall be deprived of his liberty or property, but by the judgment of his peers, or the law of the land, and should the public exigencies make it necessary, for the common preservation, to take any person's property, or to demand his particular services, full compensation shall be made for the same. And, in the just preservation of rights and property, it is understood and declared, that no law ought ever to be made or have force in the said territory, that shall, in any manner whatever, interfere with or affect private contracts, or engagements, *bona fide*, and without fraud previously formed.

Article III

Religion, morality, and knowledge being necessary to good government and the happiness of mankind, schools and the means of education shall forever be encouraged. The utmost good faith shall always be observed towards the Indians; their lands and property shall never be taken from them without their consent; and in their property, rights and liberty they never shall be invaded or disturbed, unless in just and lawful wars authorized by Congress; but laws founded in justice and humanity shall, from time to time, be made, for preventing wrongs being done to them, and for preserving peace and friendship with them.

Article IV

The said territory, and the States which may be formed therein shall forever remain a part of this confederacy of the United States of America, subject to the Articles of Confederation, and to such alterations therein as shall be constitutionally made; and to all the acts and ordinances of the United States in Congress assembled, conformable thereto. The inhabitants and settlers in the said territory shall be subject to pay a part of the Federal debts, contracted, or to be contracted, and a proportional part of the expenses of government to be apportioned on them by Congress, according to the same common rule and measure by which apportionments thereof shall be made on the other States; and the taxes for paying their proportion shall be laid and levied by the authority and direction of the legislatures of the district, or districts, or new States, as in the original States, within the time agreed upon by the United States in Congress assembled. The legislatures of those districts, or new States, shall never interfere with the primary disposal of the soil by the United States in Congress assembled, nor with any regulations Congress may find necessary for securing the title in such soil to the *bona-fide* purchasers. No tax shall be imposed on land the property of the United States; and in no case shall non-resident proprietors be taxed higher than residents. The navigable waters leading into the Mississippi and Saint Lawrence, and the carrying places between the same, shall be common highways, and forever free, as well to the inhabitants of the said territory as to the citizens of the United States, and those of any other States that may be admitted into the confederacy, without any tax, impost, or duty therefor.

Article V

There shall be formed in the said territory not less than three nor more than five States; and the boundaries of the States, as soon as Virginia shall alter her act of cession and consent to the same, shall become fixed and established as follows, to wit: The western State, in the said territory, shall be bounded by the Mississippi, the Ohio, and the Wabash Rivers; a direct line drawn from the Wabash and Post Vincents, due north, to the territorial line between the United States and Canada; and by the said territorial line to the Lake of the Woods and Mississippi. The middle State shall be bounded by the said direct line, the Wabash from Post Vincents to the Ohio, by the Ohio, by a direct line drawn due north from the mouth of the Great Miami to the said territorial line, and by the said territorial line. The eastern State shall be bounded by the last-mentioned direct line, the Ohio, Pennsylvania, and the said territorial line: *Provided, however,* And it is further understood and declared, that the boundaries of these three States shall be subject so far to be altered, that, if Congress shall hereafter find it expedient, they shall have authority to form one or two States in that part of the said territory which lies north of an east and west line drawn through the southerly bend or extreme of Lake Michigan. And whenever any of the said States shall have sixty thousand free inhabitants therein, such State shall be admitted, by its delegates, into the Congress of the United States, on an equal footing with the original States, in all respects whatever; and shall be at liberty to form a permanent constitution and State government: *Provided,* The constitution and government, so to be formed, shall be republican, and in conformity to the principles contained in these articles, and, so far as it can be consistent with the general interest of the confederacy, such admission shall be allowed at an earlier period, and when there may be a less number of free inhabitants in the State than sixty thousand.

Article VI

There shall be neither slavery nor involuntary servitude in the said territory, otherwise than in punishment of crimes, whereof the party shall have been duly convicted: *Provided always,* That any person escaping from the same, from whom labor or service is lawfully claimed in any one of the original States, such fugitive may be lawfully reclaimed, and conveyed to the person claiming his or her labor or service as aforesaid. . . .

Diplomatic Weakness and Sectional Rivalry: "Charles Pinckney's Speech . . . on the Question of a Treaty with Spain" (Aug. 16, 1786)

In sharp contrast to its accomplishments in the West, the diplomatic record of the Confederation government was dismal in the years after 1783 as representatives of the infant Republic found it almost impossible to command respect among the ancient powers in Europe. Despite repeated American protests, the British refused to withdraw their troops from several forts in the Old Northwest in contravention of the Treaty of Paris, and the Spanish, who had entered the war against Britain in 1779 and had obtained Florida and control of the mouth of the Mississippi River by the peace settlement of 1783, closed the lower Mississippi to American shipping in 1784 and hoped ultimately to gain possession of the entire Mississippi Valley. In May, 1785, John Jay, who had become Secretary for Foreign Affairs in May, 1784, began negotiations with the Spanish minister to the United States, Don Diego de Gardoqui, in an attempt to obtain commercial concessions from Spain. But de Gardoqui would agree to concessions only if the United States would give up its claim to navigate the Mississippi for twenty-five or thirty years. Although he had been specifically instructed by Congress not to enter into any agreements that would abridge American rights on the Mississippi, Jay asked Congress in the summer of 1786 for power to negotiate a treaty on the terms proposed by de Gardoqui. A bitter debate followed in which the alignment was clearly sectional. Delegates from the northern states hoped that their citizens would profit from the commercial concessions, while those from the southern states, which had much more immediate interests in and closer contacts with the West, insisted that the American claim to free navigation of the Mississippi should not be given up even for a moment. On August 16, 1786, Charles Pinckney (1757–1824), lawyer and delegate from South Carolina, spoke for the southern delegates, arguing that the commercial concessions offered by de Gardoqui were trivial and that, in any case, Congress should never adopt any policy that was "calculated to acquire benefits for one part of the confederacy at the expense of the other." The final vote, which was along strict sectional lines, was seven states to five in favor of empowering Jay to negotiate the treaty, but because the approval of nine states was required for the ratification of any treaty Jay let the matter drop. Outstanding difficulties with Spain, as well as with Britain, remained unsettled for another decade.

Pinckney's speech, which was printed as a broadside, is reprinted in part here from the original New York edition. It contains an excellent analysis of the diplomatic problems confronting the United States in the mid-1780s and reveals the nature of the sectional split over the issue—the first in a recurring pattern of north-south divisions in American national political life.

Samuel Flagg Bemis, Pinckney's Treaty: A Study of America's Advantage from Europe's Distress, 1783–1800 *(1926) and* Jay's Treaty: A Study in Commerce and Diplomacy *(1923), and A. L. Burt,* The United States, Great Britain and British North America from the Revolution to the Establishment of Peace after the War of 1812 *(1940), are the standard works on Confederation diplomacy, while John Richard Alden,* The First South *(1961), traces the beginnings of sectional rivalry in the national government.*

R. PRESIDENT,

THE Secretary for Foreign Affairs has reported, that, in consequence of the commission and instructions he had received from Congress for the purpose of negotiating with Mr. Gardoqui, he has had several conferences with him upon this subject.

That he had received an offer from Mr. Gardoqui to enter into a commercial treaty upon certain principles, but that he insisted as a part of the treaty, that Spain and the United States should fix the boundaries of their respective territories; and that the latter should relinquish all claim to the right of navigating the river Missisippi.

The Secretary adds, as his opinion, that a treaty may be formed with

Spain, upon principles which he then stated, upon the United States for-
bearing to assert their right to navigate the river for twenty-five or thirty
years; and used some arguments to prove the policy of our acceding to this
arrangement with her. . . .

In order to bring the objects of the proposed treaty more clearly before the
view of the house, permit me to examine them, as they may affect the different states in their operation.

The New-England states (in which can be scarcely included New-
Hampshire and Connecticut, their European commerce being inconsiderable,
and Rhode-Island not extensive) enjoy at present a beneficial trade with
Spain, in the export of their fish, lumber, and other articles, for which they
receive valuable returns. Their peltry trade is of no consequence, nor except
in the articles mentioned have they any considerable export that will suit
the Spanish European markets. The Spaniards have no fisheries of their
own;---they consume a great quantity of fish, and are always in want of timber; they will therefore find it their policy to keep their ports open to all the
nations that will bring them. Spain does not offer to give us exclusive privileges or preferences, but leaves herself at liberty to form treaties with whom
she pleases. The French, in virtue of the family compact, are entitled to the
privileges of the most favored nation; and if we examine the treaties of commerce that have formerly existed between Great-Britain and Spain, particularly that of 1667, which is the ground work of all their future treaties, and
those of 1713 and 1715, we shall find these nations have been in the habits
of a commercial intercourse for a great number of years.---The policy of
Europe at present, seems to be peace and commerce. The English and French
are pushing their fisheries with astonishing exertions, and endeavouring to
depress ours--while therefore Spain in her treaty proposes no advantages
that we do not now enjoy, and which it can never be her interest to curtail,
and while she leaves herself open to trade with other nations who may
attempt to rival them; I cannot see any particular benefit that will result
even to the New-England States, under the present project.

New-York and Pennsylvania have the power of exporting wheat and
staves, and some other articles; their wheat is valuable in proportion to the
scarcity, and failure of crops, and depends upon the contingencies I have
already stated---under the treaty nothing more is proposed to them. New-
Jersey not being an importing State, cannot be materially interested. Maryland and Virginia may export as they do at present, some wheat and lumber;
their great staple tobacco is expressly prohibited, and to remain under its
present regulations, so that while the latter must be more injured than any
State in the union, by the cession, she will be the least benefitted under the
treaty. The tobacco of North and South-Carolina, and Georgia, is in the
same situation, nor will the sale of their other productions be promoted.
Indigo, one of their staple commodities, is the product of the Spanish
American Island and Colonies in much greater quantities than they can
consume, and of a superior quality to that made in the Southern States, so
that there does not remain a probability of this ever becoming an article of
commerce.

Rice is always in such demand in Europe, that it wants not the aid of a
treaty, nor if it did, would those States which produce it, wish an advantage
at the expence of the rights and possessions of any part of the Confederacy.

I trust that upon a candid and disinterested view of the proposed arrangement--the partial, not to say ungenerous, manner in which it is offered, and the few advantages to be derived from its operation, which we do not at present enjoy, that Congress will be induced to suppose it is not an offer of that liberal and extensive kind, which promises a lasting or mutually beneficial intercourse, nor does it hold out such privileges as we might have expected from a power who wishes to tempt us to even the temporary surrender of an important national right. In my judgment she proposes nothing more than she will always be willing to grant you without a treaty, and nothing which can be termed an equivalent for the forbearance she demands.

The true mode to determine this, is to examine the nature and consequences of the demand she makes, on our compliance with which alone a treaty may be formed with her.

It is to forbear the assertion of the right of the United States to navigate the river Missisippi, for the terms of 25 or 30 years. It is said the treaty will not be concluded without this stipulation--that the navigation is unimportant, and that a forbearance will be no sacrifice, as Spain excludes us by force, and will continue to do so---that it would be disgraceful to continue the claim without asserting it--that war is inexpedient, and that the best way would be to enter into a treaty with them, and consent to suspend the claim for a certain time.

The right of the United States to navigate the Missisippi has been so often asserted, and so fully stated by Congress, that it is unnecessary to say any thing upon this subject, particularly as the Secretary in his Report appears to be in sentiment with Congress. But if the treaty proposed was of the most advantageous nature in other respects, while it insisted upon the forbearance, I should think the impolicy of consenting to it, must be obvious for the following reasons:

Because the sale and disposal of the lands ceded in the western territory, has ever been considered by Congress as a sufficient fund, under proper management, for the discharge of the domestic debt. Large sums of efficient money have already been expended in quieting the Indians--purchasing their rights of soil, and in sending out persons to survey it. The offers which are to be made the purchasers, and already established by your resolutions, are the protection and support of the Union---the establishment of republican governments, and the equal enjoyment of all the privileges of citizens of the United States. To those in the least acquainted with that country, it is known that the value of their lands must altogether depend upon the right to navigate the Missisippi. This is the great out-let with which, and with the rivers running into it, nature washes their shores,--points to them the mode of exporting their productions, and of establishing a commercial intercourse with the rest of the world. Inform them you have consented to relinquish it even for a time, you check, perhaps destroy, the spirit of emigration, and prevent the accomplishment of the object proposed by the sale. But, it is said, the Spaniards already oppose us in the navigation, and that this will as effectually prevent emigration, as our consenting to suspend it. To this it may be shortly replied, that while the purchasers know that the United States claim and insist upon the right, and are negotiating for it, that if the Spaniards refuse to admit us to a participation, the occlusion will be founded in injury, must be supported by force, and will be resisted whenever circumstances shall authorise; a reliance on the support and protection of their parent state, will operate as a spur to emigration.

To me it appears most extraordinary that a doctrine should be attempted to prove, that because we have not at present a government sufficiently energetic to assert a national right, it would be more honorable to relinquish it.

The British government, in violation of the late treaty, hold by force and garrison posts within the territory of the United States. These posts give them the entire command of the valuable fur trade. If they were in our possession, as they ought to be, this important commerce would pursue its usual route, and become an article of considerable export to these states: but we are unable to recover them by force at present, war being inexpedient, and are obliged to submit to the injury and disgrace of their being forcibly withheld. We are now attempting to negociate with Britain:---suppose she was to offer certain commercial privileges, advantageous to the whole, but operating more particularly in favor of those exports which suit her market, and to which she more anxiously applies her attention than to any other part of your commerce; for to Britain, tobacco and rice are at least as important, as fish and timber to Spain. Suppose I say she was to offer to form a treaty, granting these privileges in lieu of your stipulating that she should hold these posts, and enjoy the fur trade for a given number of years, I ask, whether Congress would conceive themselves warranted in assenting to it, or think the honor of the nation was not wounded by the attempt? Would gentlemen representing the states, particularly interested, suppose themselves at liberty to consent to it without consulting their constituents? I should apprehend not---and yet the posts are held in defiance of the authority and remonstrances of this country. The claim to the Mississippi has been as strongly insisted upon as the claim to the posts, and the cases appear to me so similar, that I should think the same policy that would dictate the yielding the one, might with great propriety consent to the surrender of the other.

Another object more important than the sale and disposal of the Western territory, presents itself in objection to the suspension of the right.

Nature has so placed this country, that they must either be the future friends or enemies of the Atlantic states, and this will altogether depend upon the policy they shall observe towards them.

If they assist them in rearing their infant governments to maturity, and by extending the gentle influence of their laws gradually, cement their union with us upon equal principles, it is fair to suppose they may be an acquisition, rather than a disadvantage.

In their first settlement, exports cannot be much attended to, but if these states increase in the same proportion the United States did, and we are to presume they will exceed them, in the course of a few years, they will turn their views to the best mode of exporting and disposing of their productions. The large navigable rivers which all terminate in the Mississippi, point to them, as has been mentioned, this mode of export;---should the right remain unceded by Congress, the consideration of the future force of the inhabitants, and a number of eventual circumstances in our favor, which it is impossible at present to foresee, but which are probable, may induce, perhaps compel, Spain to yield us a share in the navigation.

But should it be surrendered, you at once deprive the citizens of the Atlantic states from navigating it, or from having intercourse with the settlements on its banks, and within your territory. You immediately destroy all connection between them and the inhabitants of the western country: for, after you have rendered them thus dependant on Spain, by using the first opportunity in your power to sacrifice their interests to those of the Atlantic States, can they be blamed for immediately throwing themselves into her arms for that protection and support which you have denied them--for the enjoyment of that right which you have placed it out of your power to grant. Is it not to be clearly seen by those who will see, that the policy of Spain, in thus inducing us to consent to a surrender of the navigation for a time, is, that by having a clear and unincumbered right, she may use it for the purpose of separating the interests of the inhabitants of the western country entirely from us, and making it subservient to her own purposes?---Will it not produce this? It will.--Will it not give her influence the entire command of the numerous and extensive Indian tribes within this country? It will certainly have this effect. When once this right is ceded, no longer can the United States be viewed as the friend or parent of the new States, nor ought they to be considered in any other light, than in that of their oppressors.

There is one consideration, and of some consequence, which ought to be recollected; that is, the impropriety of the United States ever acting under the influence of that kind of policy which is calculated to acquire benefits for one part of the confederacy at the expence of the other.

It is confessed our government is so feeble and unoperative, that unless a new portion of strength is infused, it must in all probability soon dissolve. Congress have it in contemplation to apply to the States on this subject. The concurrence of the whole will be necessary to effect it. Is it to be supposed, that if it is discovered a treaty is formed upon principles calculated to promote the interests of one part of the union at the expence of the other, that the part conceiving itself injured will ever consent to invest additional powers? Will they not urge, and with great reason, the impropriety of vesting that body with farther powers, which has so recently abused those they already possess? I have no doubt they will.

If therefore the entering into this treaty, which really does not in my opinion, hold out any important benefits, and if any, only to a part of the union, should interfere and prevent the States from assenting to invest Congress with proper powers, throwing justice and an equal attention to all the members of the confederacy out of view, ought not policy to induce us to make the lesser yield to the more important consideration?--If we are prudent it ought.

It may be said it is extremely oppressive, that the Northern and Eastern States should be deprived of a treaty which they conceive an advantageous one, merely to gratify the Southern in adhering to a claim to navigation, unimportant if in our possession, which we have not power to assert, and must therefore submit to be deprived of---but it should be remembered that the cession is the price of the treaty;--if you had not this right to grant, why should Spain treat with you? Will she derive any other benefits from the treaty? No. All she can expect, except the exclusive navigation, she now enjoys, unfettered by stipulations--it would therefore be extremely unwise and impolitic in her unnecessarily to restrict herself. I have stated the reasons which render her particularly anxious to treat with you, and those who are to pay the price, have at least a right to an opinion upon the subject: Besides, the delegates of the different States stand here upon different grounds. The delegates of some of the States, whose territories, or whose claims to territory extend to the Missisippi, or to the waters leading into it, and who consider these states as deriving a claim under the general title of the United States, to navigate the river, view this as an important national right, secured by treaty, upon which they doubt their power to decide without a reference to their constituents; for if, in time of war, under the exclusive rights of Congress, and justifiable only by the law of necessity, their right to divest their constituents of a national claim would be doubtful; how much more so is it in time of profound peace, and when this necessity cannot justify it?

Unless Spain would consent to treat with us upon terms which did not respect the Missisippi, and which afforded us many more advantages than those proposed, I should very much doubt the policy of treating with her at all at this time.

It does not appear to me honorable or politic, that the United States should at present form any treaties of commerce, except upon such principles as would insure to us very considerable benefits, and such as would execute themselves.

It is not honorable, because, though Congress have nominally a right to enter into treaties, they do not possess the power of taking such measures as will ensure an attention to them. The right retained to the States under the confederation; will create a dependence of Congress upon their conduct: this will be as different in the several States as their views and policy, they will each interfere with the other in their regulations, and be incapable of carrying the stipulations into effect. Sensible of this defect, Congress have already applied to the States for additional power. I would rather wait the issue of this application, which may place us more upon an equality with Spain, than treat under our present disadvantages. I have always been of opinion, that the true policy of the United States consisted in the endeavouring to obtain from their constituents powers sufficient to enable them to establish such regulations as were suited to our situation, and would render our commerce more lucrative to our own citizens than to any others. All our policy should consist in the establishment of these regulations---in the determination never to derogate from them in favour of foreigners; and, except in very particular cases, in not attempting to form commercial treaties, until we were in a situation to demand and expect privileges without purchasing them even with equivalents. This is the situation of Spain, as it respects you; and, therefore, it is wise in her to push her negociations, as she expects an important cession, without purchasing it with an equivalent; but I trust we shall have sufficient prudence not to precipitate ourselves into a measure which we may hereafter repent, without first very maturely considering it.

Upon the whole, as the present treaty proposes no real advantage that we do not at present enjoy, and it will always be the interest and policy of Spain to allow; as our situation by no means presses us to the formation of new connections; and as the suspension demanded, may involve us in uneasinesses with each other at a time when harmony is so essential to our true interests---as it may be the means of souring the states, and indispose them to grant us those additional powers of government, without which we cannot exist as a nation, and without which all the treaties you may form must be ineffectual; let me hope that upon this occasion the general welfare of the United States will be suffered to prevail, and that the house will on no account consent to alter Mr. Jay's instructions, or permit him to treat upon any other terms than those he has already proposed.

Divergent Responses to Economic Crisis

The demands of the armies during the War for Independence and the flood of paper money issued by Congress and the state legislatures to meet military obligations had together produced an economic boom of considerable proportions. Prices rose sharply, credit was easily obtained, and, except for those who had suffered direct personal losses at the hands of the British Army in the southern states, farmers and merchants alike were prosperous at the conclusion of the war. This general prosperity plus a widespread popular demand for foreign luxury goods that had been largely cut off during the war and the willingness of foreign merchants to extend credit on generous terms to American importers enabled British, French, Dutch, and other foreign merchants to dispose of a vast quantity of goods on the American market in 1783 and 1784. Such wholesale importations created an unfavorable balance of trade, and the difference between the amount expended for imports and that received for exports had to be made up in hard money. The result was that most of the gold and silver poured into the American economy by the French and British armies during the war quickly returned to Europe until by the spring of 1784 there was little hard money to be found anywhere in the United States. Along with high taxes levied by the state legislatures in an attempt both to pay off accumulated debts and to retire paper money emitted during the war, this specie drain created a severe currency contraction. The limitation of currency, in combination with a sharp drop in prices caused by the glutting of the market with foreign goods and a banking crisis in Britain, led to a major economic depression that lasted from the middle of 1784 until late 1788. Forced to sell their commodities at depressed prices and with little cash available, debtors of all kinds— large American importers as well as the planters, farmers, manufacturers, artisans, and others to whom they had sold foreign goods—found it almost impossible either to pay their debts or to obtain the further credit necessary for them to maintain the high rate of vertical economic mobility that they seem to have enjoyed during the war years. As creditors began to call in their loans in order to meet their obligations, debtors everywhere began to clamor for laws to postpone the collection of debts and for new issues of paper money.

The clamor for paper money touched off an acrimonious debate in the press and in legislative chambers up and down the Atlantic seaboard. The nature of that debate is illustrated by the two anonymous newspaper essays by "Curtius" and "Willing to Learn" published in New Jersey early in 1786 and reprinted below as Selection 53 A. Like "Curtius," opponents of paper money looked upon it as a dishonest, selfish, and unnecessary expedient to enable debtors to defraud their creditors by paying off their debts with depreciated paper at face value. Such a flagrant attack upon the property rights of creditors, they argued, would deal a staggering blow to the public credit of the states, would completely undermine the confidence in the state governments of an important segment of the public, and, because virtue, which was the necessary foundation for republics, consisted in part in meeting one's obligations punctually and in full, would perhaps even sound the death knell for the republican experiment in America. With William Paterson (1745–1806), another New Jersey foe of paper currency, they argued that "all the Citizens of a State ought to be viewed with equal Eyes; that one Order of them ought not to be preferred to another"; and, more specifically, that the interests of debtors ought not to be served at the expense of those of their creditors. It followed, therefore, as "Curtius" was at pains to make clear, that the legislature was obliged to reject any scheme, however popular, that discriminated against one segment of the community in favor of another. In answer, the advocates of paper money, denied, like "Willing to Learn," that they had any intention of enabling debtors to defraud their creditors and argued both that paper money was the only possible means debtors could get enough negotiable currency to pay their debts and that making the paper legal tender would effectively prevent its depreciation. As "Willing to Learn" also makes clear, the advocates of paper money saw it not simply as a means to permit them to pay current debts but also as a way to put more money into circulation so that borrowing would be easier and they could again have access to the capital necessary for their own economic advancement; and, in countering the suggestion of their opponents that legislators should resist popular pressures for legislation they thought unwise, they laid down the doctrines that in a republic the wishes of the people were the ultimate authority and that legislators could not violate the instructions of their constituents.

In a majority of the states—Pennsylvania, South Carolina, North Carolina, New York, Rhode Island, New Jersey, and Georgia—the advocates of paper money won out, and over £800,000 of paper was emitted in 1785–1786.

There was a pronounced tendency among the advocates of paper money to regard their opponents as conspirators intent upon persecuting their debtors and reserving available riches in America to themselves and as somehow responsible for the depressed state of the economy and the lack of money. In Pennsylvania the conspiracy was widely believed to have been connected with the Bank of North America. This bank had been founded by Robert Morris (1734–1806), a Philadelphia merchant, in 1781 after Congress had appointed him first superintendent of finance and had been of considerable help in bringing order into the country's chaotic finances and the war to a successful conclusion. Operating on the basis of charters issued in 1781 by both Congress and the government of Pennsylvania, the bank turned out to be enormously profitable for its investors and sufficiently powerful to prevent the attempted establishment of a rival bank in Philadelphia in 1784. Because the Bank of North America was one of the largest creditors in Pennsylvania and because it had sufficient resources to enable it to manipulate the economy and, as an institution, was a center for the opposition to paper money, it was easy for the proponents of paper money to blame it for most of the economic ills of the state, and the same legislature that voted to issue paper currency in March, 1785, revoked Pennsylvania's charter to the bank the following September. The attempt by the supporters of the bank and other opponents of paper money to persuade the next legislature to restore the charter in March, 1786, provoked a vigorous debate which was a harbinger of the debate over rechartering the Second United States Bank in the 1830s. Both sides accused each other of selfish interests, the opponents of the bank charging that its proponents were motivated only by avarice and their lust for power and the proponents insisting that the opponents only wanted the bank out of the way so they could more easily pursue their schemes to emit more paper money and thereby defraud their creditors. One of the most notable exchanges in the debate was between William Findley (1741–1821), farmer and obviously articulate representative from Westmoreland County in western Pennsylvania, and Robert Morris and is reprinted in large part below as Selection 53 B. Arguing that the Bank of North America was a monopoly, Findley insisted that the legislature of 1785 had behaved properly in revoking its charter because monopolies, by assigning special privileges to the few at the expense of the

*many, were contrary to the spirit of republican government. To counter the argu-
ment of the spokesmen for the bank that the legislature had no power to revoke
charters, Findley declared that the "supreme legislative power of every community
necessarily possesses a power of repealing every law inimical to the public safety"
by virtue of its function of being responsible for promoting the "good of society."
He also charged that a monopoly of the kind enjoyed by the bank made it possible
for the bank investors to acquire a preponderant amount of the wealth of the state,
created a powerful monolithic financial interest in opposition to the welfare of the
broad body of citizens, and thereby paved the way for the establishment of an
aristocracy. In answer to Findley, Morris pointed out that stock was available to
all citizens and not just to a few, denied that the bank's stockholders constituted a
unitary economic interest, and argued that the bank by extending credit, providing
money, and in general facilitating economic expansion and financial stability performed services useful to everyone in the state. Moreover, he reiterated the contention of other advocates of rechartering that only the courts and not the legislature
could revoke charters, and then only by due process of law, and hinted that the
courts would be justified in countermanding the revocation of the charter. This
debate between, as the opponents of the bank saw it, equality and privilege, or, as
the proponents argued, financial responsibility and the protection of property or
financial chaos and property repudiation, ended in an easy victory for the foes of
the bank. But the friends of the bank made a major effort in the election of the
following year and secured enough seats to recharter the bank.*

*The paper-money agitation of 1785–1786 and the conditions that created it are
discussed at length and from differing points of view in Merrill Jensen,* The New
Nation: A History of the United States during the Confederation, 1781–1789
(1950); Curtis P. Nettels, The Emergence of a National Economy, 1775–1815 *(1962);
and* Bray Hammond, Banks and Politics in America, from the Revolution to the
Civil War *(1957).* Richard P. McCormick, *Experiment in Independence: New
Jersey in the Critical Period, 1781–1789 (1950), describes the paper-money debate
in New Jersey, and* Janet Wilson, "The Bank of North America and Pennsylvania
Politics: 1781–1787," *The Pennsylvania Magazine of History and Biography, volume 66 (January, 1942), pages 3–28, the agitation over the Bank of North America.*

A. CLAMOR FOR PAPER MONEY, 1785–1786: THE DEBATE IN NEW JERSEY (JANUARY, 1786)*

The Case against Paper Money, January 4, 1786

"Honesty is the best policy."

IT having become a subject of great political magnitude, as well as, much
heated controversy, whether a new emission of paper currency, is not, under
present circumstances, an eligible measure, and would not redound to the
benefit of the community; one who declares himself uninfluenced by *sordid
self*, and purely disinterested in the issue of this great question (otherwise
than as a member of the republic feels himself concerned in an event, that

* These excerpts are reprinted from *The Political Intelligencer, And New-Jersey
Advertiser* (New Brunswick and Elizabeth Town), Jan. 4, 25, 1786.

must involve its happiness, reputation and prosperity,) begs leave to offer his sentiments on this momentous topic.—He is well aware of the unpopularity of the cause he espouses, and that *interest,* temporizing, predominant, *self interest* is against him—But regardful of the verity of his MOTTO, and looking beyond the present moment, he ventures to make a few observations on the proposed expedient.—These he hopes will not be the worse received, from having their source in common sense, and not the same lustre to recommend them as the refined speculations of subtle politicians—Such he means as imitate the dexterity of a certain fish recorded by naturalists, which when pursued by an enemy, thickens and obscures the water, the more easily to elude his discovery.

Without controverting the extent, or omnipotency of legislative authority, in the general scale of power, it may be worth while before we proceed farther, to consider the political necessity or expediency of legal sanction to any measure merely on account of its popularity. Laws in general we admit are to correspond with the wishes of the major part of the community; this indeed is the basis of all free government—but this as every other political axiom has its *ne plus ultra,* and these limits, we presume, (since even the mass of the people may err) are chaulked out by the propriety of the requisitions, and character and views of those who make them. Now if it appears that the morals of a people are corrupted—If it appears, that from too frequent temptation, the source of all seduction, their political integrity has been but too successfully tampered with—If it appears that they have lost in any degree, that purity of principle which alone could entitle them to implicit confidences—In these cases, their wishes, however plausible in appearance, however pre-emptory in pursuit, are by their representatives to be received with great caution and circumspection—numbers in their cases give no weight to the demand—But what intrepid, what hardy spirit, will pronounce this to be the state of society at present? The sheer popularity, or in other words, the numbers in favor of any measure where *abstracted interest* is intimately blended, is never a positive criterion of its fitness; tho' oftentimes the reverse—There are those of the most pernicious consequence in a moral view, as well as destructive of all political ideas of right and wrong, that need only to be seriously agitated to gain the suffrage of the *many* in their favor. *An equality of property,* for instance, has charms irresistable, and there is no man, that lacks honesty as much as he wants money, but would embrace the delusive idea with rapture, and would petition too, with all his soul, to procure so ravishing a distribution—But will any one say, that a virtuous legislature would give a more serious attention to so chimerical a proposal, than if such petitioner had prayed to have all *noses* reduced to the same standard, or all *understandings* to the same level? No, they would tell this humble supplicant, that they were the guardians of the people— that they were not set over them to sport with, but to protect their rights—that they were not assembled to give one man's property to another—that the right to property, whether acquired by industry purchase or descent, was as sacred and indisputable as the right to *noses* or *intellects.* Nor would this be the language of a virtuous legislature, only, where the wishes and views of their constituents had arisen at this summit of exorbitancy; wakeful to the true interest of society, they would check this extravagance of temper, this frenzy of the mind in its germe, they would behold with a gelous attention, the first feeble expressions of depravity, destroy them in their embryo, nor suffer them to gain strength by indulgence—In this would be their honor. In this the safety of the people. We have dwelt longer perhaps on this particular than would have been necessary. Were it not, that this *vox populi*, has given these paper money champions, too great confidence in their schemes, which must vanish, and leave them no room for triumph, when they have learned, that notwithstanding their numbers "marshal'd in dread array" a virtuous legislature will not, cannot listen to any propositions, however popular, that come within the description of being, *unjust, impolitic* or *unnecessary*—How far the object in view falls under those descriptions, we come now to consider.

1st. The injustice or iniquity of the proposed emission, appears in every point of light in which it is viewed. It must in a most unqualified sense be a legal tender if it is to gain circulation at all; this being the case, it must be taken in payment for all debts whether contracted before, or after its emission—Now is this consonant to the plainest principles of justice and equity? Does not justice require, and equity demand, that no law passed subsequent to a contract shall operate upon, or in any ways effect a bona fide agreement prior to it? *Ex post facto* laws, those engines of oppression, are only admissible in cases of apparent fraud; where combinations are formed against the general good, through some defect or oversight in a law, evidently intended indeed, but not adequate to prevent the mischief—this interference of legislature was necessary, and therefore exercised upon proper principles during the late war, where fraudulent conveyances had been made to prevent forfeiture of estates, by those who had become obnoxious to them. But does any one see the iniquity of an agreement, not made repugnant to any law existing at the time, but on the contrary made upon the flattering protection of law? The contractor in this case could not foresee, nor could he imagine, that an implicit confidence in his own rectitude and the justice of his country must terminate in his ruin—It is in vain to tell him, that altho' he has lent his hard money, under the presumption of receiving it again, and is now reduced to take paper in exchange, that he shall be no loser, for that the money he receives in lieu, is a valuable compensation—he knows, he feels the contrary—confined to a narrow circulation even admitting its credit to be good, within that compass, it is no equivalent for an unconfined, universal medium. The advocates for this doctrine, would think it peculiarly oppressive, were they, in a foreign land, to be reimbursed a sum due to them, and which had become so, from the loan of specie, or any specific article, that would command specie in any quarter of the globe, with a *sign* that answered the *thing signified* in that particular country and no where else—Would not this imprison, the supply of his wants, if not his person to that country?—And may not a New-Jersey-man draw his supplies if he pleases from abroad, and will *paper* do this? Again a man owes a sum of money in France, which he reasonably hoped (at the time he contracted the debt) to discharge with such money due to him here, as in that country would be acceptable in payment—Will *paper* be received in France? No, but he can (says some wiseacre) purchase produce, export it, and thus answer his creditors abroad—this is indeed an admirable device, not totally impracticable, but laughable in the extreme—Every man that owes money abroad must turn hugster—go to market—buy pigs and poultry—send them to Europe—establish a factor there; who when he had made sale of these hopeful commodities, is to place the proceeds in the hands of his creditors—

Yet this same *paper* which is to give its possessor all this trouble is called a *medium of trade,* a medium that requires the aid of pigs and poultry, to give it efficiency. Would it not save an immensity of roundabout and be infinitely more honest, to pay the credulous lender, in *coin* what in *coin* upon faith and honor he had advanced, and then leave him to shift for himself.—Once more, if the intended money is equal to specie, it will require no law to enforce its reception, for why enforce what no one would reject, but if from any circumstances it is not, it would be the sublimation of iniquity to use compulsion.—The legislature cannot we presume by any *ipse dixit* of theirs, *hocus pocus* it into precious metal—and so long as they cannot do this, it will be *paper* still, and as such will depreciate, and as depreciated paper will be good for nothing, and so being, it would be iniquitous, unjust, and rascally to force it upon any one, and therefore a virtuous legislature will not emit it. The first point being established we proceed to the second.

2d. The impolicy of the measure—This indeed is a natural inference from its dishonesty and injustice, since we have the experience of ages in favor of the adage prefixed to this paper, and would need no further illustration to convince those who have well weighed that important truth—but as there are some whose temporary triumph in fraud and unrighteousness, have led them to reverse the proverb; we will give this part of our subject a farther elucidation—It will be admitted by all, that every thing that tends to diminish that faith which is the cement of society public or private, must, however crowned with fugitive success, in the end be pernicious to both, and consequently impolitic, as the consummation and improvement of both, is the object most desirable.—Now public credit is attachable and supported in the same way, as faith between man and man, and in the same manner is destroyed—punctuality in the payment of debts—an ever ready responsibility to all lawful demands, and the invariable execution of all engagements are essential to the establishment of both—Suppose an individual who was an exception to all these—who had broken all engagements—who had neglected all stipulated payments—and who, in fact, had become unable to answer any pecuniary demand—Why, the man (you say) is to all intents a bankrupt. Now imagine this same man, with fair promises and rueful countenance in the act of borrowing again from the very person whom he `had injured by his former delinquency—Would his fine speeches and dire aspect gain him credit? No he would be told by his thus insulted benefactor, that he had injured him already—that he had no farther confidence in him; —and would in fine advise him as the only way to retrieve his lost credit, to discharge all old scores, and make good all fractured engagements—the same treatment would he receive from all who had heard his pristine conduct—a reader of a tolerable imagination will require no assistance to make the application. Confidence destroyed is not to be regained, by soliciting the further exercise of faith, but by its gradual renewal, through means diametrical to those, through which it was lost.—It is horrid to reflect on the consequences of decayed credit when applied to the public, and it by no means sweetens our reflections, when instead of pursuing the way to restore it, we behold a powerful confederacy forming to banish the little, that is left all the dreadful effects therefore, resulting from this distracting contemplation, must flow from the emission of money, substituted for the payment of debts—Let confidence be restored;—it is the best of all funds, and then let money be struck.—But what is all this to the man who wants money—his end is accomplished, and what is the public to him—it will procure him the opportunity of playing the scoundrel once more, and when this is over, he may possibly have grace enough to hope he may never be under the same temptation again; But should this happen, which would inevitably be the case, as the same means is ever productive of the same end. She must e'en trust to luck for a future supply.—This is the language of every reprobate in New Jersey, where this most serious consideration, the *extinction of public faith* comes into competition with his own contracted views, but the impolicy of the measure appears farther if we consider its obvious effect upon commerce —the merchants, an useful body of men to the community, must be totally ruined; this without entering here, into the merits of the trade itself, is a deplorable idea.—It was the people who encouraged them to open their stores, by consuming their commodities, and willing to administer to their farther convenience, they have from time to time replenished their shelves. "Ay, says some shrewd politician, in this consists the policy of the thing, we have allured them by our extravagance to bring their goods among us and now they are here *paper money* must command them." You may congratulate yourselves if you please upon the apparent craft of this stratagem, and when you have done, it remains to be told, that it is but a fraudulent dream at best—you may oblige the merchant by this redoutable exertion of cunning which you term policy, to shut up his store, but you cannot, oblige him to dispose of his goods for your *paper* it would not serve his purpose so to do—his debts are *hard money*, debts and *paper money*, remittances would not answer them, thus distressed and embarrassed, he would either return his goods at a discount to his creditors, or vend them where he could obtain a more *solid* payment.—Further—the merchant, we presume, does not sell his goods purely for his amusement—he has his profits upon his merchandise there must be a balance in his favour, this by remaining with him adds to his wealth and eventually to the opulence of the state. But all the money expended in the purchase of those goods would rest here, says one of your *paper mongers*, if this same trade was obstructed. Not so fast if those goods were not brought to your doors, you would, to the great consumption of time, run after them to some distant market—for, declaim against luxury as much as you will, our farmers would not confine themselves to *black broth*, nor their daughters to the modest attire of *spartan women;* thus we see that this visionary scheme falls to the ground, and what in a fit of self-applauding knavery was thought to be well weighed policy, proves the reverse. But suppose this to be really the case, would it be just, would it be honorable, to call in the aid of legislature to assist in the ruin of any set of men, and that without giving them time to say their prayers? The best policied states, have, in all their institutions where trade has been concerned, and which would remotely be affected, given the merchant time to cast about him, since the general failure of the mercantile body of a state, and that thro' an ill-considered act of that government, must ultimately affect the honor and reputation of the state itself—true policy would not hazard the consequence —What is all this to the *soft money man?* What cares he who sinks, so long as he swims?—the honor of his country—its reputation or prosperity, are but as dust in the ballance when compared to his own *invaluable self.*

The further impolicy of the measure in question, results from the effectual bar it will raise against any man's letting out his money among us in future;

people will not always be bubbled out of their property—like the boy in the fable having given repeated instances of infidelity, we shall not be credited, even when in earnest—the little specie left among us, kept close by its possessors, where are we to procure the necessary supply for the first demands of those manufactures we would wish and it is our interest to promote? Nations as well as individuals require an outset, and altho' necessity with both have, in some rare instances, proved the mother of invention, yet it will be found on enquiry, that on the general scale of prosperity, the major part of both, have owed their life to circumstances very foreign to *bare necessity.* An individual aided by reputation, friends, connections and other accidental advantages *ceteras puribus* has FORTUNE more in his power, than one destitute of all these. A nation too in the same eligible situation, is more likely to egrandize itself, than when surrounded with powerful rivals, without tools for its artizans to begin with, or credit or money to procure them—those who are for decrying specie as the preventive cause of arts, industry and manufactures, would do well to consider this, and before they give the fatal stab to the introduction of the necessary circulating quality, be certain they can do without it; otherwise they resemble the inconsiderate man, who hewed down the limb of the tree upon which he stood. Situate as we are between two powerful rivals, without a commerce of our own, it would be our policy to invite monied men from all quarters to reside among us; and this can only be effected by giving the most ample security to that species of property—But as the case now stands, and which will be rendered still worse by the *projected plan;* where shall we find one so purblind, as to risk his fortune on such precarious grounds? On the contrary is it not to be seated that the few among us, would rather look for security in foreign funds, than deposit it, where it must depend upon popular caprice, whether they ever get sight of it again? Nay, more, and dreadful in idea! May it not be expected, that many will look for stability of dependance even in *British funds,* and thus furnish our very enemy with the sinews of war? Thus it appears from these, as well as many other instances which might be adduced, that the measure in agitation is highly impolitic and therefore a wise and virtuous legislature will never accede to it. We pass on to the last point.

3d. The inutility of the measure—It may be advanced, without scruple, in support of this position, that there is as much money already, as is requisite to our circumstances, and if there was not *paper currency* might encrease the nominal quantity indeed, but not add an atom, to the bettering ourselves as a people. There is in fact, in every nation as much money (and sometimes more) as that country ought to have—that is, there is a quantity proportionate to the means of getting it, or as much as the trade, manufactures and industry of it commands—and what flows into it otherwise, than thro' these channels, is accidental and may leave it again, or is brought into it by credit, and must one day be refunded, and consequently does not increase its real and intrinsic wealth, for a man may as well expect to grow fat upon the food eaten by another, as a nation wealthy upon foreign property. —'Tis true indeed that a nation may sometimes be driven on the score of necessity to a *paper emission,* but this ought always to be for the supply of national and not *individual* wants, and this only when it cannot command its natural resources—Here we are arrested by some clamorous debtor, "how if you confine *paper emissions* to public necessities are our debts to get paid?" Softly good friend—How came you in debt? "Why we have purchased farms when we had not a shilling in our pockets, these we have secured to the persons from whom we had them, and now the unconscionable mortgagee would take them from us, and we shall be ruined" If you have not paid for those farms you have not bought them, and it is as equitable that you should be ruined, as the mortgagee compelled to take what is not *a quid pro quo*—But what is this to the state? Did the state of New Jersey tell you to involve yourselves? What business had you to buy the land, (or rather steal it, for buy it you did not, since there has been no payment made) when you did not foresee the least probability of clearing yourselves from the incumbrance! But suppose the real owner should take possession of the soil—It is a matter of indifference to the government surely, whether A or B holds the premises, the land won't run away and the taxes must be paid.—You were ready enough, when we pointed to you, *decayed faith* and *declining credit*, to demand what the state was to you? And you will not be affronted that we have retorted the question; although self embarrassed we would not insult your distresses, but point out the impropriety of such wishers, as must still more diminish that credit, which you now feel the want of, and which, even if complied with, would not, in the end, relieve you.—For, suppose the state was to advance you a sum equal to your demands; would this cancel the debt? No, it would at best be but a transfer, that would put off the evil day a little farther, and when it had first ruined your creditors by obliging them to take this *sham money*, would terminate in your own—The state must be repaid, and that in a summary way, not liable to any suspension arising from the procrastinating maneuvers of the law— The amount of the whole, therefore, is this—You are in debt, and there are ways and means to get out of it, without demolishing public credit for your rescue; and if there were not, it would be too much to seek it. There are some, however, who, from inevitable misfortune, deserve more compassion; that these should be subject to the distrust, occasioned by the destruction of credit, threatened by the *voluntarily involved* is a lamentable case—It is the fate sometimes of the best men to be punished through the roguery of the worst;—We trust, however, that such men will find relief, but they seek it where it is not to be found, if they league themselves with those of the other description, in pursuing a phantom, which however captivating in appearance, will soon burst like bubbles into air. The better way would be, by discountenancing every thing that is dishonest, and uniting with those who feel for the real interest of their country, join in every measure that will tend to restore confidence, and confidence once restored their remedy is at hand, the HONEST AND INDUSTRIOUS will never suffer. Deducing, therefore, from the foregoing premises, the inutility of the proposed expedient, a wise and virtuous legislature, cannot conceive themselves authorized, however popular the plan, to enforce the measure; but will receive with demonstrations evincive of the indignity offered them, every proposal for its establishment. We shall now close these reflections with a short address.

MY COUNTRYMEN,

YOU have emancipated yourselves from foreign domination, and laid the foundation of a fabric the admiration of the world. VIRTUE is the grand corner stone. For it is not to be supposed that Heaven would have favored you thus far, had not your views been honest, your intentions pure, and your principles uncorrupted. Are you not ambitious that the superstructure shall answer those splendid beginnings? VIRTUE must complete what VIRTUE began; what has been *attained* by VIRTUE must be *maintained*. Altho' this may be resolved into a variety of particulars in an ethical view, there is one in a political light in which it more immediately consists—that love of country and sacred regard to everything which constitutes its true credit and real interest—an interest detached from, and sometimes repugnant to, *individual advantage*—and here public and private *faith* present themselves as the first objects of your attention—Objects I had almost said of idolatry, for without these all is confusion, distrust and desolation—It was a love of country in this sense, added to a divine enthusiasm that lighted the torch, which gilded your way to the temple of LIBERTY—But RE-MEMBER you are still on the threshold—you are not fully in possession of that delightful FANE, nor will you be admitted as inmates, if you forget the principles that conducted you there.—CONSIDER you have an enemy jealous and vindictive, watching all your motions—The *British* are in possession of CANADA—the frontier forts have not been relinquished—the time may come when hostilities will be renewed—the low ebb of PUBLIC CREDIT will be the signal for attack—cherish therefore this grand pillar of your Empire—suffer her not, now reeking from recent wounds, to expire in your view.—In case of a war what substitute will answer her place? Want of confidence, mutual distrust, and ruined credit are infinitely worse than want of arms, ammunition and discipline.—The late war found you destitute of the latter—let not a future one find you without the former.—There are some among you, dreadful the tale now leading the sacred victim to the altar; but while bound and prostrate at your feet, repent—arisen the hand now raised to strike—give her *freedom,* and she will retaliate the favor.

CURTIUS

The Case for Paper Money, January 25, 1786

"Honesty is the best Policy."

HAD "CURTIUS" been influenced by his motto instead of declaring himself "uninfluenced by *sordid self*" perhaps he would have informed us that he was an attorney at law, and never had nor expected to obtain a livelihood by what is commonly called, labour; but that he expects to live by the death of others; and that a scarcity of money and great distress for want thereof, would give him an opportunity to live with doing but little business, until by another's death he may become a moneyed man, if that man may continue to enjoy his present emoluments, and by the scarcity of money, may lay up by grinding the face of the needy.

He calls himself "a member of the republic," and he gives us a sketch of his sentiments with respect to "the extent and omnipotency of legislative authority." He says, "laws in general we admit, are to correspond with the wishes of the major part of the community: This indeed is the basis of all free governments." But he informs us that it is self evident, the legislature may put their *"ne plus ultra"* on it, and by their almighty power, deny the request of their constituents, "however plausible in appearance, however peremptory in pursuit," and "numbers give no weight to the demand."

And after a tedious harangue, to establish premises which, if granted, would make nothing to his purpose, (but it being an essential of his function, thus to evade the truth, we could expect no better of him now), he says, "We have dwelt longer perhaps on this particular than would have been necessary, were it not that this *vox populi* has given these paper money champions too great confidence in their schemes which must vanish, and leave them no room for triumph, when they have learned that notwithstanding their numbers *marshal'd in dread array*, a virtuous legislature will not, cannot listen to any propositions, however popular, that come within the description of being *unjust, impolitic*, or *unnecessary*."

Then we are not a republican government, for the evident signification thereof is that the people [the majority of the people] bear rule, and it is for them to determine whether a proposition is *unjust, impolitic,* and *unnecessary* or not; and they have a right to enact what law they judge proper; the plain definition of republican government is that every elector has a voice in every law which is made to govern him the same as if he personally sat in council, and gave his voice in passing the laws which all have a right to do if the majority of the people should think proper: But it would be too expensive; therefore we choose representatives and pay them for doing our business, and have as good a right to instruct them how it shall be done, as a merchant has his agent; and they have no better right to act contrary to our instructions; and should they refuse or neglect to do what we request them, we know that we employ them but for one year at a time, and we will dismiss from our service at the end thereof, and appoint men who will do for us as we should do if personally present, and thus by each member's speaking what appears to him to be the voice of the county which he represents, the sentiments of the whole state is collected together, and the majority bears rule—and have a right to enact laws according to the voice of the people, and no representative can act contrary thereto, without being guilty of a breach of trust, and playing the tyrant, notwithstanding the ascription of omnipotence with which Curtius is pleased to worship them;—what has led him so far astray is uncertain, but perhaps he has been so long allied to government as to think it omniscient and not liable to err, if taken out of the hands of the people.—But I would inform him that the design of republican government is to prevent such despots from bearing rule, and that "in a multitude of counsellors there is safety;" therefore, when the people at large bear rule, they are not so likely to err as one man or a few neither are they so liable to be ruled by a tyrant—For when one man bears rule, and thinks himself established in authority by his natural propensity for domination, he is apt to think himself omnipotent, and that the people must be subservient to him, and not he to the people.

And in his next sentence I will join issue with him again, viz. "How far the object now in view [the emission of paper money] falls under those descriptions [unjust, impolitic and unnecessary,] we come now to consider."

1st. The justice and equity "of the proposed emission appears in every point of light in which it is viewed, it must in" every "sense be a legal tender," and it will "gain circulation—it must be taken in payment for all debts whether contracted before or after its emission;" and this is "consonant to the plainest principles of justice and equity.—Does not justice require, and equity demand that" although in common cases "no law passed subsequent to a contract shall operate upon, or in any wise effect a bona fide agreement prior to it;" yet "in cases of apparent fraud, or a combination is formed against the general good;" and "through some defect or oversight in the laws," there are none extant which are "adequate to prevent the mischief, then the interference of legislative power" is necessary, as it was necessary, "and therefore exercised upon proper principles during the late war."

If then it was necessary, it is now much more necessary and proper; for the combination is much greater now than that which did then exist within the power of our legislature,—and without the interference of legislative authority to prevent the evil, it will be much more detrimental to the state.

To make the combination against the general good, appear I need only appeal to every person's knowledge.

1st. Every one who has observed must know that it has been the custom for many years past, for industrious husbandmen and mechanics to take money on loan to purchase land and build with, and furnish themselves with materials to work with at their occupation, and thereby they commonly became useful members of the community, and if a creditor called for his money before the debtor could gain it by industry, he could generally procure it on loan of some other person which has given encouragement to those who are now in debt, to become debtors.

2d. It is also known that it has ever been countenanced by our legislature, and by all those men who now hold obligations in their hands, by which they are destroying so many honest industrious members of the community, else how came those obligations in their hands?

3d. It is also well known that the moneyed-men have agreed jointly and severally in a great combination not to let their money on loan, but confine it within their own coffers.

4th. And likewise it is known that the moneyed-men are generally demanding the payment of their debts at this time when they themselves have put it out of the power of the debtor to pay it by the aforesaid combination of hording the money, which shews them to be much more cruel than Pharoah, for he only with held straw from the people, and yet required the full sale of brick, but the moneyed men with hold the clay, and add to their demands long bills of cost;—so that, generally speaking, the man who was possessed of a farm in fee simple, which would have sold for eight hundred pounds, hard money, four or five years ago; and if he, then being clear of debt, did purchase land to the amount of three hundred pounds, and has by his industry paid the interest and one hundred pounds of the principal, he is now likely to be made a bankrupt, before he can pay the two hundred pounds yet behind—And the moneyed-men, not yet satisfied, are pressing the matter farther, and wishing for a greater advantage to grind the face of the needy, perhaps thinking that they are honestly providing for their own families; that they may set their nest on high and not be under the necessity of getting their bread by industry, but live by the labour of the honest farmer and mechanic, without being any service to church or state, but that of holding the purse in unrighteous hands—rioting in luxury by means of oppression, and living in idleness by other men's toils.

And seeing this is the true state of the case between the creditor and debtor, it is in vain to tell him "Softly, good friend, how came you in debt; what business had you to buy the land or rather steal it, for buy it you did not? He knows, he feels the contrary;" for "the contractor in this case could not forsee nor could he imagine that an implicit confidence in his own rectitude, and the justice of his country must terminate in his ruin."

It is objected that to make bills of credit, a legal tender is unjust, because it is confined to a narrow circulation; and is not an universal medium, and a New-Jersey man ought to be at liberty, if he pleases, to draw his supplies from abroad, which perhaps he could not do without the aid of pigs or poultry or some other produce.

It ever has been the practice of legislatures, when they judged it advantageous to their state, to lay an embargo on any commodity that was in their dominion, notwithstanding the capricious desire or firm agreements of some of their subjects to export them, and Briton has forbid the embarkation of specie for many years past, that it may not be exported; and if Curtius should send his money to their land for safety he could not bring cash from thence for interest not principal; therefore it is that Briton yet supports under an enormous debt; (I would be far from wishing to imitate Briton in general) but let us adopt that measure and we may soon be clear of debt, and I believe that no one (but Curtius in his wisdom) can evince that it is unjust or iniquitous.

And once more he objects that, if the money is equal to specie, it will require no law to inforce its reception; but if it is not, it would be the sublimation of iniquity to use compulsion.

If it was not a legal tender, it would not be equal to specie; for then I could not pay you with it; therefore it would not be as specie to me, and if you had it, it would not be as specie to you; for you could not let it as such at interest, nor buy pigs and poultry with it, because the owners would want to pay some other hard money man.

But let it be a legal tender, and it will be as good as gold; for I can pay it to you, and you can get it at interest or buy pigs and poultry with it; for he who has them to sell, can pay his debts, cost and lawyers with it: Hence you see that making it a legal tender, establishes its credit, and makes it equal to specie, therefore it is no iniquity, for no injury is done—for (when it is in the power of the legislature) it can be no crime to make a thing good that is not so, even if it was the hard money horder himself.

I will also say once more, suppose ten gentlemen from Europe or some other part shou'd come and settle in different counties of New Jersey, and each one of them had twenty thousand pounds in hard cash, which they let out on loan to the inhabitants of this state at the reasonable interest of six percent, and they eat and drank the produce of our land and traded with our merchants, and so spent the interest among us; would that not be greatly to our advantage. For then Curtius need not have the trouble of going the roundabouts of buying pigs and poultry etc. to trade abroad with, and our debtors would be relieved, our merchants, and tradesmen would receive ready money. But it would be far from being as beneficial to us, as the same quantity of paper money let on loan would be.

For, first, the industrious farmer and mechanic must labour many days to earn and procure the interest which they must pay them while those leade or take their ease in idleness, and eat, drink, and wear it out, without its being any real service to the state any more than if so much was consumed by him.

But if the money was borrowed from the state, the public would receive the interest, and every man's tax would be the lighter, and those things which those moneyed-men would consume, we might export, and in return for them receive hard cash, or such foreign goods as would be serviceable to us. And 2d if by its being a universal medium we traded abroad with the money, it would soon be chiefly gone out of the state, and our land must necessarily pay the principal, and we or our children must become tenants— and if we did not thus trade abroad with it—it would answer no better purpose to us than the same sum in bills of credit, for that would answer every occasion within this state, and by issuing paper money, we might save the whole interest which is twelve thousand pounds per annum to the benefit of the inhabitants of this state.

But Curtius tells us that "it is a matter of indifference to the government surely whether A or B" [*a native or a foreigner] "holds the premises, the land won't run away and the taxes must be paid."

Then surely when the inhabitants of New Jersey have elected representatives, and pay them for consulting upon and effecting their greatest benefits, those representatives have nothing to do but to take care that the land does not run away, and that the taxes are paid, they are not to seek the benefit and prosperity of their constituents more than that of foreigners, nay they should use means to bring their constituents to poverty, that they may be obliged to sell their lands to foreigners and become tenants to those moneyed-men, and thus invite them from all quarters, me thinks to do this, our legislature must be worse than lawyers, for they are true to their clients for their money.

If it is a matter of indifference to our legislature whether one twentieth part of their constituents become bankrupts and sell their lands to foreigners and so become their tenants or not; for the same reasons it is of a tenth part do thus become tenants and by the same parity of reasoning, it is a matter of indifference to the legislature if one fifth, one half or the whole of their constituents should become bankrupts, and be tenants to foreigners if the land did not run away, and the taxes were paid, so that our Governor, Council and Assembly might receive their pay.

I hope this error did not procede from the ruler; if it did, it is high time to find a better.

From hence we may infer that it is highly impolitic to admit those pests and traitors to New-Jersey, the Tories to dwell among us because they have money; should we not rather spurn them from us as filth, and not take those adders in our bosom merely for the love of money, which if we covet after, we shall pierce ourselves through with many sorrows.

And if the Tories were expelled and we had a large sum of money due to the state—our paper money in good credit—agriculture and manufactures flourishing, how much better situation should we be in to repulse an enemy than with a heavy debt on our backs which we could not pay the interest of—dependant on foreign manufactures and out of credit, so that we could not make a paper circulating medium, for it would be in vain to try a paper currency in war if it had not been established in peace, and our gold and silver would be chiefly exported except what little was horded which we could not command.

* *I think we may fairly understand a native or a foreigner by* A *or* B *when he has before informed us that "it would be our policy to invite moneyed-men from all quarters to reside among us."*

Curtius says, "let confidence be restored, it is the best of all funds and then let money be struck."

It is impossible to restore confidence without first striking money, for money is not to be had and many of the honestest men by frequent disappointment, are under the necessity of breaking their engagements, and failing in payment and in fact are become unable to pay money according to their promise; why the man you say is dishonest, he promises and does not perform, you say, no favor ought to be shewn him, you prosecute him and confiscate his estate.

But let money be struck, and he will receive his debts, and manifest an ever ready responsibility to all lawful demands, and the greatest punctuality in the payment of his debts, and by money being circulated, there will be a ready money market, so that the poorest mechanic, if industrious, may be a punctual pay master, and not being obliged to trust he will be rid of paying cost and the trouble of spending one third of his time in writing accompts, cunning for his pay and suing to recover it, consequently he can work cheaper and support his family better.

But "what is all this to the hard money-man? What cares he who sinks so long as he swims? the honor of his country—its reputation or propensity are but as dust in the balance when compared to his own invaluable self."

Thus much for his principal arguments with which I think his others must fall, but any thing but selfishness remains unanswered what it is,

WILLING TO LEARN.

B. WHETHER BANKS BE "INCONSISTENT WITH OUR LAWS": DEBATE OVER THE BANK OF NORTH AMERICA IN PENNSYLVANIA (MAR. 29–APR. 1, 1786)*

March 31, 1786

Mr. [William] Finlay [Findley]. This question, which has so long engaged the attention of the house, and on the merits of which, gentlemen eminent for discernment, have exercised so much ability, is of such importance in itself, and involves in it such extensive consequences, as to justify my requesting the attention of the house to a few observations which I propose to offer respecting it.

Much has been said respecting the extraordinary reasoning in the preamble of the report under debate, which bears evident marks of the manner in which disappointed avarice chagrins an interested mind. I shall observe, that though the reasoning in the report of the committee of the late house, recommending the passing a law to repeal the charter of the bank, were insufficient or mistaken, yet if sufficient reasons do now exist in the nature of the case, to support the principles thereof, it ought not to be repealed. This proposition is supported by legislative and judicial examples. In appeals

* These excerpts are reprinted from Matthew Carey (ed.), *Debates and Proceedings of the General Assembly of Pennsylvania on the Memorials Praying a Repeal or Suspension of the Law Annulling the Charter of the Bank* (1786), pp. 64–67, 69, 72–75, 86–88, 90–93, 96–99.

from the lower to the higher courts, the question is not—"what were the reasons the lower courts assigned for their decision?" but "whether was the decision just or not?"—Many examples might be produced, of reports of committees, and preambles of laws, not expressing the true and proper reasons of the respective resolutions or laws. To try all laws by the reason assigned in their preambles, would be an endless task. Therefore, not to dwell on this, I shall endeavour to prove, that the legislature had a power to repeal the charter of the bank; and that sufficient reasons did exist, to justify the expediency of their doing it.

All governments being instituted for the good of the society to which they belong, the supreme legislative power of every community necessarily possesses a power of repealing every law inimical to the public safety. But the government of Pennsylvania being a democracy, the bank is inconsistent with the bill of rights thereof, which says, that government is not instituted for the emolument of any man, family, or set of men. Therefore, this institution being a monopoly, and having a natural tendency, by affording the means, to promote the spirit of monopolizing, is inconsistent with not only the frame but the spirit of our government. If the legislature may mortgage, or, in other words, charter away portions of either the privileges or powers of the state—if they may incorporate bodies for the sole purposes of gain, with the power of making bye-laws, and of enjoying an emolument of privilege, profit, influence, or power,—and cannot disannul their own deed, and restore to the citizens their right of equal protection, power, privilege, and influence,—the consequence is, that some foolish and wanton assembly may parcel out the commonwealth into little aristocracies, and so overturn the nature of our government without remedy.

This institution is inconsistent with our laws—our habits—our manners. ——Our laws and habits countenance long credits, and afford slow methods for recovering debts. They subject our real estates to alienation, and to be sold for debts. They divide our estates, both real and personal, more equally among our heirs, than the laws or habits of any other country I know of. We are too unequal in wealth to render a perfect democracy suitable to our circumstances: yet we are so equal in wealth, power, &c. that we have no counterpoise sufficient to check or control an institution of such vast influence and magnitude. We have no kingly prerogative—no wealthy companies of merchants incorporated—no hereditary nobles, with vastly great estates and numerous dependents—no feudal laws to support family dignity, by keeping landed estates undivided. What security, then, can we purpose to ourselves against the eventual influence of such wealth, conducted under the direction of such a boundless charter?

This charter was for a perpetuity—not subject to change:—In this it was contrary to our constitution, which is liable to change every seven years.

But let us take a more distinct view of the nature of this institution, and of human nature itself. Enormous wealth, possessed by individuals, has always had its influence and danger in free states. Thus, even in Rome, where patriotism seems to have pervaded every mind, and all her measures to have been conducted with republican vigour, yet even there, the patricians always had their clients—their dependents—by the assistance of whom they often convulsed the counsels, and distracted the operations of the state, and finally overturned the government itself. But the Romans had no chartered institutions for the sole purposes of gain. They chartered no banks.

Wealth in many hands operates as many checks: for in numberless instances, one wealthy man has a control over another. Every man in the disposal of his own wealth, will act upon his own principles. His virtue, his honour, his sympathy, and generosity, will influence his disposals and designs; and he is in a state of personal responsibility. But when such an unlimited institution is erected with such a capital, for the sole purpose of increasing wealth, it must operate according to its principle; and being in the hands of many, having only one point in view, and being put in trust, the personal responsibility arising from the principles of honour, generosity, &c. can have no place. The special temper of the institution pervades all its operations: and thus, like a snow ball perpetually rolled, it must continually increase its dimensions and influence.

This institution having no principle but that of avarice, which dries and shrivels up all the manly—all the generous feelings of the human soul, will never be varied in its object: and, if continued, will accomplish its end, viz. to engross all the wealth, power, and influence of the state.

The human soul is affected by wealth, in almost all its faculties. It is affected by its present interest, by its expectations, and by its fears. And must not, therefore, every thinking man see what advantage this institution has on the human feelings, above that of wealth held by many individuals? If our wealth is less equal than our kind of government seems to require— and if agrarian laws are unjust in our present situation, how absurd must it be for government to lend its special aid in so partial a manner, to wealth, to give it that additional force and spring, which it must derive from an almost unlimited charter? Can any gentleman avoid seeing this to be eventually and effectually overturning our government? Democracy must fall before it. Wealth is its foundation, and gain its object and design.

Thus it appears that this institution is inconsistent with our general laws, customs, and circumstances, and even with the nature of our government. The proofs are not founded on facts of doubtful credibility. They are drawn from the nature of things: and the principles of nature being justly stated, this kind of arguments are conclusive. They carry their evidence with them, with a certainty like that of the sparks flying upwards, or the waters running to the sea.

The way for individuals or nations to get rich, is not to have artificial difficulties laid in the way of paying their debts; but to contract few of them. The debts must be paid: and the bank collects the money to a point, where it can be easier found in large sums for exportation, than in any other manner: and those little shifts, which depend on personal sagacity or integrity, are fit only for a plausible colouring for refusing to supply those who are not favourites; and the more effectually discover how well it is calculated to promote the monopolizing of trade. What security have we that its assistance will not be partially exerted for this purpose?

This institution is itself a monopoly—being incorporated a great trading company—and having a right to turn ten millions of dollars into trade, if the president and directors please—or to lay out that amount upon land. So, by taking advantage of a scarcity of money, which they have it so much in their power to occasion, they may become sole lords of the soil. If they may monopolize trade—if they may monopolize the soil—why not the government too? Doubtless they may.

I do not say whether or no the bank is a monopoly in the strict legal sense of the word. This is not to my purpose. But I say that it is, in its nature and principles, in the common popular sense, a monopoly: and being so in its nature, it must be so in its effects. This is a certain conclusion. I do not charge the directors or stock-holders personally with such designs: but this being the nature of the institution, it becomes the indispensible duty of the directors to conduct it according to its natural principles.

Great wealth seems, even with individuals, to have a tendency to monopolizing. It was the saying of a wise writer, when riches increase, they are increased that have them—increased in their appetite for riches, and in their endeavours to procure them. . . .

A worthy gentleman from the city [mr. (Thomas) Fitzsimons] informs us, that he is a stockholder in, and director of, the bank; and that there are several stockholders members of this house.—He justly observes, that this does not debar them from the constitutional right of canvassing for offices at elections—and advocating their own cause on the floor of this house. Doubtless the gentleman is right. For though the constitution excludes executive officers from seats in the legislature, lest they should influence it to make their salaries more lucrative, or their duties more easy: yet the convention neglected to guard against men, who have procured peculiar privileges by obtaining partial laws in their own favour, for the sole purpose of gain, advocating their own cause by the advantage of a seat in this house. This reminds me of the famous laws of Solon, which, though an excellent system, neglected to provide any punishment for a person who should murder his father or mother—doubtless not expecting such a crime would ever be committed. And indeed I think the convention guarded so well against the legislature of this state granting any kind of monopolies, or partial prerogatives, as cut off the probability of any such thing happening in this state: yet such is the course of affairs, that advantage has been taken of the embarrassments and inexperience of the state, and this very thing has happened.

As to canvassing at elections, I apprehend it is not common nor honourable to canvass for a seat in the legislature, where the candidate has only in view to serve the public. But where he has a cause of his own to advocate, interest will dictate the propriety of canvassing for a seat. Indeed the emolument arising from it, would induce but few wise men to canvass for a seat in this house purely to serve the public: for few who know the importance of the service, will think themselves fit for it. We also allow to the gentlemen that they have a right to advocate their own cause, on the floor of this house. But they will allow us to consider, that it is their own cause they are advocating; and to give credit to their opinions, and to think of their votes accordingly. And here I call the attention of the house for a moment, to consider the situation of the parties engaged in this argument: If the bank is a common good—diffusing beneficial influences through the whole state—increasing the price of lands and produce—if we saw it to be useful to the commonwealth—would it not be our own interest to encourage it? Can this house suppose us wicked enough to destroy our own interest or the public's from mere envy? On the other hand, this house must observe, that however hurtful and dangerous it is to the general good, the gentlemen on the other side are interested in supporting it: and if it were safe and beneficial, it would also be our interest to support it. . . .

Another worthy gentleman [mr. (Robert) Morris] has told us, that it is his opinion, if the question is to come before a court of justice, the judges, though their opinions might be otherwise, yet on account of their characters as law officers, would condemn the repealing law, as a nullity. What! would the judges complement the bank by deciding contrary, not only to their own sentiments, but to law itself? If this be the case, it must be a very influencing institution, and a very dangerous one indeed. . . .

There is now no chartered bank existing: therefore the case is before us on original ground. The question is not whether or no we will repeal a charter; but whether or no we will give one. Whether or no the last house assigned proper reasons for what they did, is not our business: for we know they did no injustice to the bank. They took away none of the property. The holders have their money; therefore it was not like an agrarian law, as the gentleman alleged—They may still keep a private bank. And here I beg leave to remark, that as a private bank is all the constitution admits of, so it would have the same advantages in trade, and more security to the people than a chartered bank. For, under the charter, the incorporated property was the only security to the public: therefore the stockholders, who have the property of it, and draw the dividends from it, might be rolling in wealth, and the bank break and ruin thousands. The bank might be robbed, or thrown into the Delaware, and the owners who profit by it, be safe as to their estates. None but men of wealth have money to spare to be bankers: and shall this house give a special law to enable monied people to increase their gain, without having either their persons or estates upon the same level of responsibility as the other citizens? By no means: this house will not do it. If the legislature did so, it would give a legal sanction to a snare of the greatest danger.

This is the only state in the union saddled with a bank. Our sister states, sensible of the magnitude and danger of such an institution, have, as far as I am informed, refused to sanction it. Maryland and New York, I know, have done so. They have seen the danger, and learned by our example. Let us for some time learn by theirs. Such an institution might in time be formidable to the whole united states.

I chearfully acknowledge, however, the great merit of the worthy gentleman who has informed us that he laid the plan of the bank, and led it into operations. I acknowledge that the bank has been of great service to the united states—not in our darkest times—for these were in some measure over, when Cornwallis was taken—which was before the bank existed. But the service was reciprocal. It was part of the French money, to the value of which the united states became stockholders, that enabled the bank to open its operations: and if that institution was, for a part of the next season, of essential service, it was but a suitable return: and the financier for making so proper a use of it, deserves and enjoys great credit. But the public are not indebted to this institution—or, if they are, they will doubtless give that debt a preference to debts even much earlier contracted. Congress money did us essential service in our darkest hours: shall it, therefore, be continued? No: it became dangerous; and consequently ceased. The army were no longer necessary, and would have been dangerous; and were therefore discontinued. General Washington, with all the virtue and glory of his persevering services, resigned his honours and authority, when he ceased to be necessary—though he did not cease to be either useful or safe. If we must be saddled with this dangerous institution for ever, because of its former usefulness and conveniency, surely Oliver Cromwell should have been re-warded in England by the continuing his heirs to occupy the government, instead of being branded as a usurper, and "damned to everlasting fame." By the same rule, despotic government, which is the most convenient, ought always to be preferred and continued.

One other observation occurs to me, which I have often thought of, and to which I yet request the attention of the house. If a bank is supported in Philadelphia, it will give another kind of credit, and another kind of circulating medium to the city and its vicinity, than to the more remote parts of this extended state: and the bank may increase the circulating medium to any quantity it pleases, which will occasion an artificial increase in the prices of things, and the manner of living. It will gradually affect the interests, manners, and habits, with such distinguishing peculiarities, as will occasion sooner or later a dissolution or separation of this state. This would be a very undesirable event: and yet the instituting a bank can scarcely fail producing it. Perhaps, when this event takes place, this city and a small territory around it, may, like Hamburgh and Dantzick, not only promote monopolies, but have its foundation placed in the principles of monopoly and aristocracy. For the common interest of Pennsylvania, for the honour and advantage of human nature, I wish such events may be at a great distance. . . .

[Robert Morris.] He [Mr. Findley] says the present house is not to enquire into what has been done by the late one—but whether sufficient reasons now exist, to warrant a renewal of the charter; and adds, that in all governments there must be a power lodged somewhere, which has a right to give and a right to take away.

I agree that in all governments, supreme power must be lodged some-where. In ours, the assembly has the sole right of granting charters—but no right to take them away. The power there goes on a different principle: and so it does in all except arbitrary governments. In Great Britain, the sovereign grants charters, but he cannot take them away: the laws of the land have pointed out another mode of annulling them. As well may it be said that the assembly of this state, having exercised their sovereign authority in the establishment of a land office, from whence grants of lands are made to individuals, have a right to exercise the same sovereign authority by destroying that office, and resuming the lands again. This would be exercising the power to give, and the power to take away: but the assembly has no right to such power: if it has, God help us! There are certain forms by which an individual may lose his lands; but never, I hope, by a wanton act of legislative power. A considerable part of its time has been spent by this house in granting charters of incorporation to religious societies, which are asked for the purpose of enabling them to receive donations and legacies, for the support of ministers and payment of contingent charges, &c. If those charters may be revoked at will, I should not be surprised to see it done a few years hence, on some pretence or other. What then is to become of the capital they may have respectively accumulated by means of the donations and legacies received in the mean time? Probably a certain gentleman, who is fond of escheats, may, if then in power, urge that the state should be heir to the corporations which suffer political death. What a hopeful situation must the country be in, under such systems as these! This gentleman says, let us examine our government—It is a democracy, and gives to all men equal rights: and agrarian laws may not be incompatible with the spirit of it: but we are not yet arrived at the period when such laws would be proper. I trust this member has better principles than to advocate so wicked a measure as a general division of property.

Mr. Finlay: I beg leave to explain. What I said, was, that agrarian laws would be unjust in our present situation.

Mr. R. Morris: They are unjust in all cases. The gentleman has remarked, "that wealth has a tendency to counteract our manners and the principles of our government. Why then should we give sanction, says he, to an institution founded on wealth? The stockholders must be men of wealth," &c.

If wealth be so obnoxious, I ask this gentleman why is he so eager in the pursuit of it? I frequently see him visiting the land office: Those visits, I presume, are not for pastime; although I do not doubt but they are for very proper purposes.——

Mr. Finlay: I never took up a foot of land in my life. What business I have transacted at that office, has been to serve others.

Mr. R. Morris: I have heard that some of the country gentlemen, whilst they are here attending in assembly, take up lands for their neighbours— and receive so much per cent. for transacting the business in the office.

Mr. Finlay: I must again set the gentleman right. I never received a farthing for such business in my life.

Mr. R. Morris: The gentleman has told us they had no banks in Rome, during the days of the republic. The Romans were a very different sort of people from the Pennsylvanians. They did in their days what they thought right and proper for them to do: but their conduct in this respect can never serve as a rule for ours.

"The object of the bank, he says, is gain—It is managed by themselves, that is, by the stockholders—and they have it always in view to *lift* their gain—Equality is the darling of our government—and the constitution says government is instituted to preserve equal privileges, &c.—the bank, he says, cannot be common amongst the citizens, and is therefore contrary to the constitution—and being perpetual, it is contrary to our laws, habits, manners," &c.

The charter of the bank being perpetual, is made use of as a strong argument against it: but really I do not know why we are told that the constitution is liable to change every seven years; and therefore it is inferred that the bank should not have longer duration: although the charter is perpetual, the stockholders are and will be constantly changing. It has been said that the charter is only a piece of paper, which the house may throw in the fire at pleasure. I say it did not derive its value from its being written on paper, but from having received the sanction of the legislature, which the house cannot so easily get rid of, as of the paper.

How does it appear that the bank is not common to our citizens? All of them who have money and inclination, may buy shares, or deposit there, at pleasure. How does it appear that the bank is contrary to our laws, habits, manners and customs? While the law incorporating the bank had existence, it certainly was consistent with our laws: and continues so now, while conducted as a private bank, against which there is no law. It consists well with our habits and customs—for we find the people in the daily habit and custom of lodging their money in the bank, and taking it away again at pleasure. . . .

The influence of the bank is again brought up. I have already observed, that such influence, if it exists at all, can never extend beyond the city: and even there, the necessity of sometimes refusing discounts, creates more enemies, than granting them makes friends. Probably, the gentleman may think that I stand indebted to this kind of influence for my seat in this house; but I promise him, that if I had thought so, I would not have accepted it. I am of too independent a spirit to accept any station or office that can be offered to me, unless I were convinced that the offer was made from public confidence in my being able to render the service expected of me. This influence has never existed: neither my colleagues nor myself owe any thing to it. . . .

The opposers of the bank, we are told, have no private interest to serve by their opposition. But so long as they regard the bank and its supporters as one party, and themselves as another, they are as much interested in the question as their opponents. In fact, we have all one common interest in the welfare of our country: and although the defenders of the bank may have a small and separate interest in that institution, I am confident there is not one of us that would urge the restoring of the charter, if we regarded it as incompatible with the public welfare. The member from Westmoreland asks, can it be supposed that the gentlemen on his side of the question would oppose the bank from mere motives of envy? I believe that if they had been left fairly to themselves, they would not have opposed it at all—or at least that they would not now oppose it: but there are others at the bottom of this opposition—people who feel a political interest in the matter, whose suspicions have been roused, by the dread of phantoms presented to their imagination through the medium of envy and jealousy. I could speak plainer —but it is unnecessary.

This same gentleman draws a curious conclusion, from my having, as he states it, formed an expectation that the judges, however opposed individually to the bank, would in the courts decide in its favour. His conclusion is, that I depend on bank influence to obtain such a decision. But the question to be decided in the courts, is not whether the bank is useful or injurious? It is, whether a charter once granted, can be annulled without proof or even pretence of forfeiture? This is a general question, affecting all corporations: and however some of the judges might be inclined to oppose the bank, I still rest satisfied in my opinion of the integrity of their decision, and in my belief that they will be too regardful of their law characters, which become an object for history, ever to subject the judgment seat to reproach.

In reply to my observations respecting the difficulty of selling inward and purchasing outward cargoes for shipping, he asks, how were our ships loaded before the revolution? I answer, and the fact is well known, that delays frequently, I may say constantly occurred for want of facilities in raising money, and the merchant had it not always in his power to purchase the produce brought to market by the farmer. The bank has remedied this inconvenience to both: destroy the bank, and I have no doubt the case will again become familiar to the most respectable traders.

He has observed that this is the only state *saddled* with a bank, altho' attempts to establish them have not been wanting at Boston, New York and Baltimore. But this observation will not serve the gentleman. At Boston they have an established bank, countenanced and incorporated by the government. At New-York they have a bank: a charter has not been obtained —but I have been informed that it was withheld, when applied for, only because the persons applying for it, were obnoxious to government. The attempt to establish a bank at Baltimore, failed for want of subscriptions to a sufficient amount of capital, and not for want of a charter. However, if the bank in this city be destroyed, I venture to pronounce, that banks will soon be established both in New-York and Baltimore: and our measures will give great advantage to those places, which are usually considered as our dangerous rivals. . . .

In effect, the utility of the bank is experienced by every man in the state, at some period or other. I have shewn clearly it is useful to the farmer and miller. The mechanic derives also his share of benefit and convenience from this institution. Punctuality in paying his workmen is of great advantage to the master, and absolutely necessary to the comfortable subsistence of the journeymen. The employer must have it in his power to make regular payments to the master mechanic,—or he, in his turn, cannot be punctual. It has heretofore happened, that those who built houses, or gave employment to various trades, have not had it in their power to pay punctually, according to their engagements. The like may be expected again. But in all such cases, on future occasions, relief may be found at the bank. The employer giving his note to the master, their joint credit, if they are entitled to credit, will procure the sum wanted, by discount at the bank. This observation must strike every mechanic at the first glance; and, if he turns his attention to the subject, his own thoughts will point out various modes by which he may draw resources and conveniences from this institution. In short, the same reasoning will apply to every description of men that have any thing to do with money.

Is it possible, then, that we shall pursue measures for the destruction of an institution so useful? One would think that the first thing which offers itself to our consideration, on the nature of a bank, would be sufficient to prevent the pursuit of such a measure. It is, that a number of persons have placed in the care of the president and directors of the bank a sum of money for the express purpose of lending to those that want to borrow; and this sum those persons (stockholders) cannot draw out again; but it must remain for that use. Besides this, there is also a further sum constantly in the power of the directors, which enables them to extend their loans beyond the capital or stock; and on which part of the profits of the bank arise. The integrity, punctuality and prudence of the president and directors have obtained such credit with the citizens of Philadelphia, that numbers of them deposit their money in bank for safety and convenience. It is received and paid at their pleasure, without expence or risque to the depositor. And the sums so collected to a point, being considerable, the bank is enabled always to lend a part of the money so placed: as it is not in the nature of things that the depositors should all call for their money at one and the same time—consequently, a part of the sum will answer the demands of the whole; and by this means, it must be seen, that sums of money are constantly brought into circulation and use, that would otherwise lie mouldering in the chests of those who would neither lend nor use them; and that the bank, by this credit, is enabled to extend its utility amongst those whose necessities, disappointments, interest, or convenience, incline them to borrow.

I have been frequently told, out of doors, although it has not been mentioned here—indeed it could not with propriety be mentioned here—that the opposition to the bank is in part levelled at me personally. If any oppose it in that view, and suppose that my interest would suffer by the annihilation of the bank, they are grossly mistaken. I am not stimulated by the consideration of private interest, to stand forth in defence of the bank: for be assured, sir, that if this be destroyed, another shall arise out of its ashes—one that will be of great advantage to my interest, and to the interest of those who may join me in the establishing it: nay, should I be disappointed in procuring such associates as I would choose in the undertaking, I will establish a bank on my own capital, credit, and resources; and so far from doubting its success, I do not hesitate to pronounce that even my enemies (and God knows I seem to have enough of them—at least political enemies—for I know of no other cause for their being so)—will deal with and trust me; not that I expect they may like me better then than now; but they have confidence in me; and, for the sake of their own interest and convenience, they will deal with me.

The gentleman from Westmoreland has acknowledged the utility of the bank during the war; and has drawn a comparison between it and the continental army. The continental army, says he, were useful during the war: and yet we disbanded them. But surely they were not disbanded because they had been useful—but because, when peace was established, they were no longer necessary. He acknowledges that this institution was useful; and yet endeavours to abolish it—because it has been said that it was injurious.

He also made a comparison between the bank and general Washington. I have ever acknowledged the services and merits of that great man. His utility during the war will never be denied: and in his resignation, he acted consistently with that noble and disinterested spirit by which he had been actuated during his command. He did what was expected of him: and it will ever be a part of my pride to join in paying him every tribute of praise. But this comparison ought not to have been made; the general's acceptance of command, and the establishment of the bank, are very different things; and took place on very different principles. The first was the patriotic act of a noble mind, which had not only the service of his country, but also honour and glory in view. The last arose from necessity, having also the service of the country for one part of its object, and the interest and emolument of those who should engage in it, for the other. The country has received the service: and now endeavours are used to requite it with ingratitude. But further services and benefits may be expected by America from this bank. We are now at war with the Algerines. Every one knows that peace must be purchased of them with arms or with money. In either case, money is necessary: and we know that the most pressing requisitions of congress, do not prevail with the states to raise it as fast as they ought: nay, whilst the several states are deliberating whether or how they shall raise money, one part of the citizens of the united states are plundered of their property by the seizure of their ships and cargoes; and another part of them are condemned to slavery. Let us suppose that the commissioners employed for the purpose, had so far succeeded, that the Algerines had agreed to make peace, on the receipt of a sum of money—where shall congress get the money? We have not so well enabled them to acquit their engagements in Europe, as to afford any reasonable prospect that they can borrow more. But upon such an occasion, this institution—the bank—might again be of essential service to the united states. In this state, we are now threatened with internal troubles at Wioming: no person can tell what may happen in that quarter: if things go on as they have done, we may be in want of every aid. Where are we to find sudden resources, or the sums that may become necessary to put an end to those troubles, and extend the protection of government over the boundaries of the state? Various circumstances tend to shew, that upon this and every proper occasion, the government of Pennsylvania might be sure to command every aid and assistance which the bank can give: And shall we then, from a mere pretended opinion that this institution has been injurious, "rip up the goose that lays the golden eggs?" . . .

SELECTION

Harbinger of Social Chaos: Shays's Rebellion

One state legislature that did not respond favorably to the cry for paper money was that of Massachusetts. To the great distress of many inhabitants of the western towns that body, which was dominated largely by eastern commercial interests, had pursued a conservative financial policy aimed at paying off the state's wartime debt throughout the early 1780s and had consistently refused to entertain western petitions for debtor relief and paper money. As the depression grew worse, westerners became more desperate, and, when the legislature of 1785–1786 broke up in July, 1786, without granting any of their requests, the discontented met in town meetings and county conventions, just as they had done earlier to protest British policy and the provisional Massachusetts government between 1774 and 1780, and denounced the legislature, the courts (through which their creditors were bringing suits for collection of debts and mortgage foreclosures), the legal system, and high taxes and called for the emission of paper money and revision of the constitution of 1780. These protests, the most important of which issued from the Hampshire County Convention on August 22, 1786, and is reprinted below as Selection 54 A, were followed, beginning on August 29, by armed uprisings and the forceable closing of courts in Worcester, Hampshire, Bristol, and Berkshire Counties and even as far east as Concord. The insurgents, who came under the leadership of Captain Daniel Shays (1747–1825), an impoverished farmer, reigned supreme in the west until they were defeated in a series of minor actions in late January and early February, 1787, by an army hastily raised by Governor James Bowdoin and placed under the command of General Benjamin Lincoln (1733–1810). After the rebellion had been crushed, the legislature in 1787 met some of the insurgents' demands and provided some measure of tax and debtor relief, though it steadfastly refused to issue paper money or call a convention to revise the constitution.

Shays's Rebellion, which took place in the one state that had a constitution written by a specially elected convention and ratified by the people, threw a chill into many leaders all over the United States. The reaction of George Washington set down in the letter of December 26, 1786, to Henry Knox and reprinted here as

Selection 54 B, was typical. Such mob defiance of duly constituted authority seemed to herald the arrival of social anarchy, the total collapse of government, and the failure of the American Revolution. To save the republic and to provide adequate protection for the liberty and property for which the Revolution had been fought, many were more than ever persuaded, required strong medicine in the form of an energetic central government that could check the popular excesses of the states.

Among several satisfactory analyses of the causes and meaning of Shays's Rebellion, Robert J. Taylor, Western Massachusetts in the Revolution *(1954); Lee Nathaniel Newcomer,* The Embattled Farmers: A Massachusetts Countryside in the American Revolution *(1953); and J. R. Pole,* Political Representation in England and the Origins of the American Republic *(1966), merit special attention.*

A. "GREAT UNEASINESS, SUBSISTING AMONG THE PEOPLE": THE VOTES OF THE HAMPSHIRE COUNTY CONVENTION (AUG. 22, 1786)*

AT a meeting of delegates from fifty towns in the county of *Hampshire,* in convention held at *Hatfield,* in said county, on Tuesday the 22d day of *August* instant, and continued by adjournments until the twenty fifth, &c. Voted, that this meeting is constitutional.

THE convention from a thorough conviction of great uneasiness, subsisting among the people of this county and Commonwealth, then went into an inquiry for the cause; and, upon mature consideration, deliberation and debate, were of opinion, that many grievances and unnecessary burdens now lying upon the people, are the sources of that discontent so evidently discoverable throughout this Commonwealth. Among which the following articles were voted as such, viz.

1st. The existence of the Senate.

2d. The present mode of representation.

3d. The officers of government not being annually dependent on the representatives of the people, in General Court assembled, for their salaries.

4th. All the civil officers of government, not being annually elected by the Representatives of the people, in General Court assembled.

5th. The existence of the Courts of Common Pleas, and General Sessions of the Peace.

6th. The Fee Table as it now stands.

7th. The present mode of appropriating the impost and excise.

8th. The unreasonable grants made to some of the officers of government.

9th. The supplementary aid.

10th. The present mode of paying the governmental securities.

11th. The present mode adopted for the payment and speedy collection of the last tax.

12th. The present mode of taxation as it operates unequally between the polls and estates, and between landed and mercantile interests.

* These excerpts are reprinted from George Richards Minot, *The History of the Insurrections in Massachusetts* (1788), pp. 34–37.

13th. The present method of practice of the attornies at law.

14th. The want of a sufficient medium of trade, to remedy the mischiefs arising from the scarcity of money.

15th. The General Court sitting in the town of *Boston*.

16th. The present embarrassments on the press.

17th. The neglect of the settlement of important matters depending between the Commonwealth and Congress, relating to monies and averages.

18th. Voted, This convention recommend to the several towns in this county, that they instruct their Representatives, to use their influence in the next General Court, to have emitted a bank of paper money, subject to a depreciation; making it a tender in all payments, equal to silver and gold, to be issued in order to call in the Commonwealth's securities.

19th. Voted, That whereas several of the above articles of grievances, arise from defects in the constitution; therefore a revision of the same ought to take place.

20th. Voted, That it be recommended by this convention to the several towns in this county, that they petition the Governour to call the General Court immediately together, in order that the other grievances complained of, may by the legislature, be redressed.

21st. Voted, That this convention recommend it to the inhabitants of this county, that they abstain from all mobs and unlawful assemblies, until a constitutional method of redress can be obtained.

22d. Voted, That Mr. *Caleb West* be desired to transmit a copy of the proceedings of this convention to the convention of the county of *Worcester*.

23d. Voted, That the chairman of this convention be desired to transmit a copy of the proceedings of this convention to the county of *Berkshire*.

24th. Voted, That the chairman of this convention be directed to notify a county convention, upon any motion made to him for that purpose, if he judge the reasons offered be sufficient, giving such notice, together with the reasons therefor, in the publick papers of this county.

25th. Voted, That a copy of the proceedings of this convention be sent to the press in *Springfield* for publication.

B. THE REACTION OF GEORGE WASHINGTON: LETTER TO HENRY KNOX (DEC. 26, 1786)*

MY DEAR SIR,

* * * I feel, my dear General Knox, infinitely more than I can express to you, for the disorders, which have arisen in these States. Good God! Who, besides a Tory, could have foreseen, or a Briton predicted them? Were these people wiser than others, or did they judge of us from the corruption and depravity of their own hearts? The latter I am persuaded was the case and that notwithstanding the boasted virtue of America we are very little if anything behind them in dispositions to every thing that is bad.

I do assure you, that even at this moment, when I reflect upon the present prospect of our affairs, it seems to me to be like the vision of a dream. My mind can scarcely realize it as a thing in actual existence; so strange, so wonderful does it appear to me. In this, as in most other matters, we are too slow. When this spirit first dawned, probably it might have been easily

* These excerpts are reprinted from Worthington Chauncey Ford (ed.), *The Writings of George Washington* (14 vols., 1889–1893), vol. XI, pp. 103–107.

checked; but it is scarcely within the reach of human ken, at this moment, to say when, where, or how it will terminate. There are combustibles in every State, which a spark might set fire to. In this a perfect calm prevails at present; and a prompt disposition to support and give energy to the federal system is discovered, if the unlucky stirring of the dispute respecting the navigation of the Mississippi does not become a leaven that will ferment and sour the mind of it.

The resolutions of the present session respecting a paper emission, military certificates, &c., have stamped justice and liberality on the proceedings of the Assembly. By a late act, it seems very desirous of a general convention to revise and amend the federal constitution. *Apropos;* what prevented the eastern States from attending the September meeting at Annapolis? Of all the States in the Union it should have seemed to me, that a measure of this sort, (distracted as they were with internal commotions and experiencing the want of energy in the government,) would have been most pleasing to them. What are the prevailing sentiments of the one now proposed to be held in Philadelphia in May next? and how will it be attended? You are at the fountain of intelligence, where the wisdom of the nation, it is to be presumed, is concentred; consequently better able, (as I have had sufficient experience of your intelligence, confidence, and candor,) to solve these questions. . . .

In both your letters you intimate, that the men of reflection, principle, and property in New England, feeling the inefficacy of their present government, are contemplating a change; but you are not explicit with respect to its nature. It has been supposed, that the constitution of the State of Massachusetts was amongst the most energetic in the Union. May not these disorders then be ascribed to an indulgent exercise of the powers of administration? If your laws authorized, and your powers are equal to the suppression of these tumults in the first instance, delay and unnecessary expedients were improper. These are rarely well applied; and the same causes would produce similar effects in any form of government, if the powers of it are not exercised. I ask this question for information. I know nothing of the facts.

That Great Britain will be an unconcerned spectator of the present insurrections, if they continue, is not to be expected. That she is at this moment sowing the seeds of jealousy and discontent among the various tribes of Indians on our frontiers, admits of no doubt in my mind; and that she will improve every opportunity to foment the spirit of turbulence within the bowels of the United States, with a view of distracting our governments and promoting divisions, is with me not less certain. Her first manœuvres in this will no doubt be covert, and may remain so till the period shall arrive when a decided line of conduct may avail her. Charges of violating the treaty, and other pretexts, will then not be wanting to color overt acts, tending to effect the great objects of which she has long been in labor. A man is now at the head of their American affairs, well calculated to conduct measures of this kind, and more than probably was selected for the purpose. We ought not therefore to sleep nor to slumber. Vigilance in watching and vigor in acting is become in my opinion indispensably necessary. If the powers are inadequate, amend or alter them; but do not let us sink into the lowest state of humiliation and contempt, and become a by-word in all the earth. I think with you, that the spring will unfold important and distressing scenes, unless much wisdom and good management is displayed in the interim. . . .

Call for a Constitutional Convention: Address of the Annapolis Convention (Sept. 14, 1786)

Attempts to strengthen the Articles of Confederation by giving Congress power to levy a 5 per cent duty on foreign imports in 1781, 1782, and 1783 failed to secure the necessary approval of all thirteen states required for amendments to the Articles. Through the mid-1780s the states virtually ignored Congress, the prestige of Congress steadily declined, and the cause of the men who thought that national salvation depended upon the reinvigoration of Congress appeared to be virtually dead. Only the popular excesses and the seeming dangers to property rights associated with the paper-money agitation of 1785–1786 and Shays's Rebellion succeeded in reviving their cause and creating a climate of opinion among politically powerful groups favorable to the kind of constitutional revolution inaugurated by the Federal Convention that met in Philadelphia in the summer of 1787.

This convention was traceable directly to two earlier intercolonial meetings. The first, a two-state conference which met at Mount Vernon in March, 1785, to negotiate outstanding differences between Maryland and Virginia concerning the navigation of the Potomac and Pocomoke Rivers and Chesapeake Bay, was so successful that the commissioners were emboldened to recommend to their respective states a series of annual conferences on commercial problems of mutual concern. One of the delegates, James Madison (1751–1836), an ardent advocate of strengthening the national government, persuaded the Virginia legislature to translate the commissioners' recommendation into a call for a general convention on commercial problems to meet at Annapolis in September, 1786. Only nine states responded favorably to the call, and delegates from only five were present when the Annapolis Convention met on September 11. In an attempt to salvage something from an obviously unpromising gathering, the delegates on September 14 adopted an address prepared by Alexander Hamilton, who was there as a delegate from New York, and printed below in full from Charles C. Tansill (comp.), Documents Illustrative of the Formation of the Union of the American States *(1927), pages 40–43, asking the states to send delegates to a new convention to meet at Philadelphia in May, 1787, to discuss ways and means of strengthening the Articles of Confederation. The Convention thereupon adjourned, and, after Congress had endorsed the proposed convention by issuing a resolution urging the states to elect delegates, all of the states except Rhode Island appointed delegates.*

The movement to strengthen the Articles of Confederation may be traced in Andrew C. McLaughlin, The Confederation and the Constitution, 1783–1789 *(1905), and Merrill Jensen,* The New Nation: A History of the United States during the Confederation, 1781–1789 *(1950). The hard economic and social forces behind and opposed to the movement for the Constitution are discussed by E. James Ferguson,* The Power of the Purse: A History of American Public Finance, 1776–1790 *(1961); Jackson Turner Main,* The Antifederalists: Critics of the Constitution, 1781–1788 *(1961); and Forrest McDonald,* E Pluribus Unum: The Formation of the American Republic, 1776–1790 *(1965). Some of the psychological forces are analyzed briefly by Stanley Elkins and Eric McKitrick, "The Founding Fathers: Young Men of the Revolution,"* Political Science Quarterly, *volume 76 (June, 1961), pages 181–216.*

To the Honorable, the Legislatures of Virginia, Delaware, Pennsylvania, New Jersey, and New York—

The Commissioners from the said States, respectively assembled at Annapolis, humbly beg leave to report.

That, pursuant to their several appointments, they met, at Annapolis in the State of Maryland, on the eleventh day of September Instant, and having proceeded to a Communication of their powers; they found that the States of New York, Pennsylvania, and Virginia, had, in substance, and nearly in the same terms, authorised their respective Commissioners "to meet such Commissioners as were, or might be, appointed by the other States in the Union, at such time and place, as should be agreed upon by the said Commissioners to take into consideration the trade and Commerce of the United States, to consider how far an uniform system in their commercial intercourse and regulations might be necessary to their common interest and permanent harmony, and to report to the several States such an Act, relative to this great object, as when unanimously ratified by them would enable the United States in Congress assembled effectually to provide for the same."

That the State of Delaware, had given similar powers to their Commissioners, with this difference only, that the Act to be framed in virtue of those powers, is required to be reported "to the United States in Congress assembled, to be agreed to by them, and confirmed by the Legislatures of every State."

That the State of New Jersey had enlarged the object of their appointment, empowering their Commissioners, "to consider how far an uniform system in their commercial regulations and *other important matters,* might be necessary to the common interest and permanent harmony of the several States," and to report such an Act on the subject, as when ratified by them "would enable the United States in Congress assembled, effectually to provide for the exigencies of the Union."

That appointments of Commissioners have also been made by the States of New Hampshire, Massachusetts, Rhode Island, and North Carolina, none of whom however have attended; but that no information has been received by your Commissioners, of any appointment having been made by the States of Connecticut, Maryland, South Carolina or Georgia.

That the express terms of the powers to your Commissioners supposing a deputation from all the States, and having for object the Trade and Commerce of the United States, Your Commissioners did not conceive it advisable to proceed on the business of their mission, under the Circumstance of so partial and defective a representation.

Deeply impressed however with the magnitude and importance of the object confided to them on this occasion, your Commissioners cannot forbear to indulge an expression of their earnest and unanimous wish, that speedy measures may be taken, to effect a general meeting, of the States, in a future Convention, for the same, and such other purposes, as the situation of public affairs, may be found to require.

If in expressing this wish, or in intimating any other sentiment, your Commissioners should seem to exceed the strict bounds of their appointment, they entertain a full confidence, that a conduct, dictated by an anxiety for the welfare, of the United States, will not fail to receive an indulgent construction.

In this persuasion, your Commissioners submit an opinion, that the Idea of extending the powers of their Deputies, to other objects, than those of Commerce, which has been adopted by the State of New Jersey, was an improvement on the original plan, and will deserve to be incorporated into that of a future Convention; they are the more naturally led to this conclusion, as in the course of their reflections on the subject, they have been induced to think, that the power of regulating trade is of such comprehensive extent, and will enter so far into the general System of the fœderal government, that to give it efficacy, and to obviate questions and doubts concerning its precise nature and limits, may require a correspondent adjustment of other parts of the Fœderal System.

That there are important defects in the system of the Fœderal Government is acknowledged by the Acts of all those States, which have concurred in the present Meeting; That the defects, upon a closer examination, may be found greater and more numerous, than even these acts imply, is at least so far probable, from the embarrassments which characterise the present State of our national affairs, foreign and domestic, as may reasonably be supposed to merit a deliberate and candid discussion, in some mode, which will unite the Sentiments and Councils of all the States. In the choice of the mode, your Commissioners are of opinion, that a Convention of Deputies from the different States, for the special and sole purpose of entering into this investigation, and digesting a plan for supplying such defects as may be discovered to exist, will be entitled to a preference from considerations, which will occur, without being particularised.

Your Commissioners decline an enumeration of those national circumstances on which their opinion respecting the propriety of a future Convention, with more enlarged powers, is founded; as it would be an useless intrusion of facts and observations, most of which have been frequently the subject of public discussion, and none of which can have escaped the penetration of those to whom they would in this instance be addressed. They are however of a nature so serious, as, in the view of your Commissioners to render the situation of the United States delicate and critical, calling for an exertion of the united virtue and wisdom of all the members of the Confederacy.

Under this impression, Your Commissioners, with the most respectful deference, beg leave to suggest their unanimous conviction, that it may essentially tend to advance the interests of the union, if the States, by whom they have been respectively delegated, would themselves concur, and use their endeavours to procure the concurrence of the other States, in the appointment of Commissioners, to meet at Philadelphia on the second Monday in May next, to take into consideration the situation of the United States, to devise such further provisions as shall appear to them necessary to render the constitution of the Fœderal Government adequate to the exigencies of the Union; and to report such an Act for that purpose to the United States in Congress assembled, as when agreed to, by them, and afterwards confirmed by the Legislatures of every State, will effectually provide for the same.

Though your Commissioners could not with propriety address these observations and sentiments to any but the States they have the honor to Represent, they have nevertheless concluded from motives of respect, to transmit Copies of this Report to the United States in Congress assembled, and to the executives of the other States.

PART TWELVE

Constitutional Revolution

The Case against the Articles of Confederation: James Madison, "Vices of the Political System of the United States" (April, 1787)

For the hard core of nationalists who had been working ever since the conclusion of the War for Independence for a stronger central government, the Federal Convention promised to be an extraordinary event. Whatever was decided there, they were convinced, would determine for some time to come, and perhaps even forever, the fate of the American Revolution, republicanism, and free government; and they prepared themselves to take advantage of the situation. James Madison, one of the most devoted nationalists, who was destined to be remembered primarily as the "Father of the Constitution" for his extraordinarily large role in the writing and adoption of that document, spent the months immediately prior to the Convention reviewing and jotting notes on the history, the problems and failures, of earlier confederacies for use in debate. He also prepared for his own use at the Convention an elaborate analysis of what he understood to be the principal defects of the Articles of Confederation, the causes of those defects, and some general remedies. This document, which he called "Vices of the Political System of the United States," stands as the most comprehensive statement of the reasons for the extreme dissatisfaction with the Articles leading to the Philadelphia Convention and of the problems the more dedicated and reflective delegates thought they were confronting on the eve of their gathering. It is reprinted here from Gaillard Hunt (ed.), The Writings of James Madison (nine volumes, 1900–1910), volume II, pages 361–369.

The high seriousness with which Madison and, for that matter, other delegates approached their task and the preparations they made are described in Douglass Adair, " 'That Politics May Be Reduced to a Science': David Hume, James Madison, and the Tenth Federalist," Huntington Library Quarterly, volume 20 (August, 1957), pages 343–360.

1. *Failure of the States to Comply with the Constitutional Requisitions.* This evil has been so fully experienced both during the war and since the peace, results so naturally from the number and independent authority of the States and has been so uniformly exemplified in every similar Confederacy, that it may be considered as not less radically and permanently inherent in than it is fatal to the object of the present system.

2. *Encroachments by the States on the Federal Authority.* Examples of this are numerous and repetitions may be foreseen in almost every case where any favorite object of a State shall present a temptation. Among these examples are the wars and treaties of Georgia with the Indians. The unlicensed compacts between Virginia and Maryland, and between Pena. & N. Jersey—the troops raised and to be kept up by Massts.

3. *Violations of the Law of Nations and of Treaties.* From the number of Legislatures, the sphere of life from which most of their members are taken, and the circumstances under which their legislative business is carried on, irregularities of this kind must frequently happen. Accordingly not a year has passed without instances of them in some one or other of the

States. The Treaty of Peace—the treaty with France—the treaty with Holland have each been violated. [See the complaints to Congress on these subjects.] The causes of these irregularities must necessarily produce frequent violations of the law of nations in other respects.

As yet foreign powers have not been rigorous in animadverting on us. This moderation, however cannot be mistaken for a permanent partiality to our faults, or a permanent security agst. those disputes with other nations, which being among the greatest of public calamities, it ought to be least in the power of any part of the community to bring on the whole.

4. *Trespasses of the States on the Rights of Each Other.* These are alarming symptoms, and may be daily apprehended as we are admonished by daily experience. See the law of Virginia restricting foreign vessels to certain ports—of Maryland in favor of vessels belonging to her *own citizens* —of N. York in favor of the same—

Paper money, instalments of debts, occlusion of Courts, making property a legal tender, may likewise be deemed aggressions on the rights of other States. As the Citizens of every State aggregately taken stand more or less in the relation of Creditors or debtors, to the Citizens of every other State, Acts of the debtor State in favor of debtors, affect the Creditor State, in the same manner as they do its own citizens who are relatively creditors towards other citizens. This remark may be extended to foreign nations. If the exclusive regulation of the value and alloy of coin was properly delegated to the federal authority, the policy of it equally requires a controul on the States in the cases above mentioned. It must have been meant 1. to preserve uniformity in the circulating medium throughout the nation. 2. to prevent those frauds on the citizens of other States, and the subjects of foreign powers, which might disturb the tranquillity at home, or involve the Union in foreign contests.

The practice of many States in restricting the commercial intercourse with other States, and putting their productions and manufactures on the same footing with those of foreign nations, though not contrary to the federal articles, is certainly adverse to the spirit of the Union, and tends to beget retaliating regulations, not less expensive and vexatious in themselves than they are destructve of the general harmony.

5. *Want of Concert in Matters Where Common Interest Requires It.* This defect is strongly illustrated in the state of our commercial affairs. How much has the national dignity, interest, and revenue, suffered from this cause? Instances of inferior moment are the want of uniformity in the laws concerning naturalization & literary property; of provision for national seminaries, for grants of incorporation for national purposes, for canals and other works of general utility, wch may at present be defeated by the perverseness of particular States whose concurrence is necessary.

6. *Want of Guaranty to the States of their Constitutions & Laws against Internal Violence.* The confederation is silent on this point and therefore by the second article the hands of the federal authority are tied. According to Republican Theory, Right and power being both vested in the majority, are held to be synonimous. According to fact and experience a minority may in an appeal to force, be an overmatch for the majority. 1. if the minority happen to include all such as possess the skill and habits of military life, & such as possess the great pecuniary resources, one-third only may conquer the remaining two-thirds. 2. one-third of those who participate in the choice

of the rulers, may be rendered a majority by the accession of those whose poverty excludes them from a right of suffrage, and who for obvious reasons will be more likely to join the standard of sedition than that of the established Government. 3. where slavery exists the republican Theory becomes still more fallacious.

7. *Want of Sanction to the Laws and of Coercion in the Government of the Confederacy.* A sanction is essential to the idea of law, as coercion is to that of Government. The federal system being destitute of both, wants the great vital principles of a Political Constitution. Under the form of such a constitution, it is in fact nothing more than a treaty of amity of commerce and of alliance, between independent and Sovereign States. From what cause could so fatal an omission have happened in the articles of Confederation? from a mistaken confidence that the justice, the good faith, the honor, the sound policy, of the several legislative assemblies would render superfluous any appeal to the ordinary motives by which the laws secure the obedience of individuals: a confidence which does honor to the enthusiastic virtue of the compilers, as much as the inexperience of the crisis apologizes for their errors. The time which has since elapsed has had the double effect, of increasing the light and tempering the warmth, with which the arduous work may be revised. It is no longer doubted that a unanimous and punctual obedience of 13 independent bodies, to the acts of the federal Government ought not to be calculated on. Even during the war, when external danger supplied in some degree the defect of legal & coercive sanctions, how imperfectly did the States fulfil their obligations to the Union? In time of peace, we see already what is to be expected. How indeed could it be otherwise? In the first place, Every general act of the Union must necessarily bear unequally hard on some particular member or members of it, secondly the partiality of the members to their own interests and rights, a partiality which will be fostered by the courtiers of popularity, will naturally exaggerate the inequality where it exists, and even suspect it where it has no existence, thirdly a distrust of the voluntary compliance of each other may prevent the compliance of any, although it should be the latent disposition of all. Here are causes & pretexts which will never fail to render federal measures abortive. If the laws of the States were merely recommendatory to their citizens, or if they were to be rejudged by County authorities, what security, what probability would exist, that they would be carried into execution? Is the security or probability greater in favor of the acts of Congs. which depending for their execution on the will of the State legislatures, wch. are tho' nominally authoritative, in fact recommendatory only?

8. *Want of Ratification by the People of the Articles of Confederation.* In some of the States the Confederation is recognized by, and forms a part of the Constitution. In others however it has received no other sanction than that of the legislative authority. From this defect two evils result:

1. Whenever a law of a State happens to be repugnant to an act of Congress, particularly when the latter [former] is of posterior date to the former, [latter] it will be at least questionable whether the latter [former] must not prevail; and as the question must be decided by the Tribunals of the State, they will be most likely to lean on the side of the State.
2. As far as the union of the States is to be regarded as a league of sovereign powers, and not as a political Constitution by virtue of which they are become one sovereign power, so far it seems to follow from the doctrine of compacts,

that a breach of any of the articles of the Confederation by any of the parties to it, absolves the other parties from their respective Obligations, and gives them a right if they chuse to exert it, of dissolving the Union altogether.

9. *Multiplicity of Laws in the Several States.*   In developing the evils which viciate the political system of the U S., it is proper to include those which are found within the States individually, as well as those which directly affect the States collectively, since the former class have an indirect influence on the general malady and must not be overlooked in forming a compleat remedy. Among the evils then of our situation may well be ranked the multiplicity of laws from which no State is exempt. As far as laws are necessary to mark with precision the duties of those who are to obey them, and to take from those who are to administer them a discretion which might be abused, their number is the price of liberty. As far as laws exceed this limit, they are a nuisance; a nuisance of the most pestilent kind. Try the Codes of the several States by this test, and what a luxuriancy of legislation do they present. The short period of independency has filled as many pages as the century which preceded it. Every year, almost every session, adds a new volume. This may be the effect in part, but it can only be in part, of the situation in which the revolution has placed us. A review of the several Codes will shew that every necessary and useful part of the least voluminous of them might be compressed into one tenth of the compass, and at the same time be rendered ten fold as perspicuous.

10. *Mutability of the Laws of the States.*   This evil is intimately connected with the former yet deserves a distinct notice, as it emphatically denotes a vicious legislation. We daily see laws repealed or superseded, before any trial can have been made of their merits, and even before a knowledge of them can have reached the remoter districts within which they were to operate. In the regulations of trade this instability becomes a snare not only to our citizens, but to foreigners also.

11. *Injustice of the Laws of the States.*   If the multiplicity and mutability of laws prove a want of wisdom, their injustice betrays a defect still more alarming: more alarming not merely because it is a greater evil in itself; but because it brings more into question the fundamental principle of republican Government, that the majority who rule in such governments are the safest Guardians both of public Good and private rights. To what causes is this evil to be ascribed?

These causes lie 1. in the Representative bodies. 2. in the people themselves.

1. Representative appointments are sought from 3 motives. 1. ambition. 2. personal interest. 3. public good. Unhappily the two first are proved by experience to be most prevalent. Hence the candidates who feel them, particularly, the second, are most industrious, and most successful in pursuing their object: and forming often a majority in the legislative Councils, with interested views, contrary to the interest and views of their constituents, join in a perfidious sacrifice of the latter to the former. A succeeding election it might be supposed, would displace the offenders, and repair the mischief. But how easily are base and selfish measures, masked by pretexts of public good and apparent expediency? How frequently will a repetition of the same arts and industry which succeeded in the first instance, again prevail on the unwary to misplace their confidence?

How frequently too will the honest but unenlightened representative be the dupe of a favorite leader, veiling his selfish views under the professions of public good, and varnishing his sophistical arguments with the glowing colours of popular eloquence?

2. A still more fatal if not more frequent cause, lies among the people themselves. All civilized societies are divided into different interests and factions, as they happen to be creditors or debtors—rich or poor—husbandmen, merchants or manufacturers —members of different religious sects—followers of different political leaders— inhabitants of different districts—owners of different kinds of property &c &c. In republican Government the majority however composed, ultimately give the law. Whenever therefore an apparent interest or common passion unites a majority what is to restrain them from unjust violations of the rights and interests of the minority, or of individuals? Three motives only 1. a prudent regard to their own good as involved in the general and permanent good of the community. This consideration although of decisive weight in itself, is found by experience to be too often unheeded. It is too often forgotten, by nations as well as by individuals, that honesty is the best policy. 2dly. respect for character. However strong this motive may be in individuals, it is considered as very insufficient to restrain them from injustice. In a multitude its efficacy is diminished in proportion to the number which is to share the praise or the blame. Besides, as it has reference to public opinion, which within a particular Society, is the opinion of the majority, the standard is fixed by those whose conduct is to be measured by it. The public opinion without the Society will be little respected by the people at large of any Country. Individuals of extended views, and of national pride, may bring the public proceedings to this standard, but the example will never be followed by the multitude. Is it to be imagined that an ordinary citizen or even Assemblyman of R. Island in estimating the policy of paper money, ever considered or cared, in what light the measure would be viewed in France or Holland; or even in Massts or Connect? It was a sufficient temptation to both that it was for their interest; it was a sufficient sanction to the latter that it was popular in the State; to the former, that it was so in the neighbourhood. 3dly. will Religion the only remaining motive be a sufficient restraint? It is not pretended to be such on men individually considered. Will its effect be greater on them considered in an aggregate view? quite the reverse. The conduct of every popular assembly acting on oath, the strongest of religious ties, proves that individuals join without remorse in acts, against which their consciences would revolt if proposed to them under the like sanction, separately in their closets. When indeed Religion is kindled into enthusiasm, its force like that of other passions, is increased by the sympathy of a multitude. But enthusiasm is only a temporary state of religion, and while it lasts will hardly be seen with pleasure at the helm of Government. Besides as religion in its coolest state is not infallible, it may become a motive to oppression as well as a restraint from injustice. Place three individuals in a situation wherein the interest of each depends on the voice of the others; and give to two of them an interest opposed to the rights of the third? Will the latter be secure? The prudence of every man would shun the danger. The rules & forms of justice suppose & guard against it. Will two thousand in a like situation be less likely to encroach on the rights of one thousand? The contrary is witnessed by the notorious factions & oppressions which take place in corporate towns limited as the opportunities are, and in little republics when uncontrouled by apprehensions of external danger. If an enlargement of the sphere is found to lessen the insecurity of private rights, it is not because the impulse of a common interest or passion is less predominant in this case with the majority; but because a common interest or passion is less apt to be felt and the requisite combinations less easy to be formed by a great than by a small number. The Society becomes broken into a greater variety of interests, of pursuits of passions, which check each other, whilst those who may feel a common sentiment have less opportunity of communication and concert. It may be inferred that the inconveniences of popular States contrary to the prevailing Theory, are in proportion not to the extent, but to the narrowness of their limits.

The great desideratum in Government is such a modification of the sovereignty as will render it sufficiently neutral between the different interests and factions, to controul one part of the society from invading the rights of another, and at the same time sufficiently controuled itself, from setting up an interest adverse to that of the whole Society. In absolute Monarchies the prince is sufficiently, neutral towards his subjects, but frequently sacrifices their happiness to his ambition or his avarice. In small Republics, the sovereign will is sufficiently controuled from such a sacrifice of the entire Society, but is not sufficiently neutral towards the parts composing it. As a limited monarchy tempers the evils of an absolute one; so an extensive Republic meliorates the administration of a small Republic.

An auxiliary desideratum for the melioration of the Republican form is such a process of elections as will most certainly extract from the mass of the society the purest and noblest characters which it contains; such as will at once feel most strongly the proper motives to pursue the end of their appointment, and be most capable to devise the proper means of attaining it.

SELECTION

Deciding "Forever the Fate of Republican Govt.": Debates in the Federal Convention at Philadelphia (May–September, 1787)

The Federal Convention was scheduled to meet on May 14, 1787, but a quorum of seven states was not secured or the first meeting held until May 25. The delegates, eventually numbering fifty-five, represented as formidable an array of political talent as perhaps has ever been assembled in American history. After selecting George Washington by unanimous vote to preside over their deliberations, they voted both to keep their proceedings secret so they would not be fettered by pressures from outside the Convention and, after surprisingly little debate, to abandon completely the Articles of Confederation in favor of a new plan. The broad outlines of this plan, subsequently known as the Virginia Resolutions (Selection 57 A), were submitted to the Convention by Edmund Randolph (1753–1813), one of the delegates from Virginia, on May 29. Calling for a bicameral legislature in which each state would be represented in both houses according to the size of its population, a national executive, and a national judiciary, Randolph's resolutions with various modifications worked out by the delegates in a committee of the whole between May 30 and June 13 served as the central focus of debate. The alternative New Jersey plan (Selection 57 B)—offered by William Paterson of New Jersey on June 16 with strong backing from delegates from the small states—called for among other things equal representation of the states in both houses. But it failed to secure enough support to supplant the Randolph plan as the basis of discussion, though several of Paterson's proposals found their way into the finished Constitution and, to pacify the small states, the Convention did provide on July 16 in the so-called great compromise for equal representation of the states in the Senate.

Although the framers were strongly opposed to unrestrained democracy and frightened by what they considered the popular excesses of the states in the 1780s, they quickly revealed their commitment to popular government by voting on May 31, 1787, that the people should elect the lower house of the legislature directly. The strength of that commitment along with the framers' reservations about democracy was revealed in the debates over the nature of the lower house. Selections from those debates including speeches by Roger Sherman (Connecticut), Elbridge Gerry (Massachusetts), George Mason (Virginia), James Wilson (Pennsylvania), and James Madison (Virginia) are reprinted below as Selection 57 C.

The framers' belief in popular government was accompanied by a conviction that a second house of the legislature was necessary to provide a check on the first. How and by whom that second house was to be elected, the term and qualifications of its members, and its function and role were among the knottiest and most challenging problems taken up by the Convention and were debated at length on June 7 and again on June 25–26. Perhaps better than the discussions on any other single subject, these debates disclosed the framers' ideas about such basic problems as the nature of man, the relationship of man to society, and the function of government. They show as well the framers' deep commitment to the idea that it was possible, by employing the principle of counterpoise and balancing the several potentially competing elements in the polity against one another in such a way as to prevent any of them from gaining ascendency and setting up an unlimited tyranny over the rest, to construct a good government out of human materials that, they were persuaded, were essentially bad. The more important portions of these debates are reprinted here as Selection 57 D and contain remarks by John Dickinson (Delaware), Sherman, Wilson, Robert Morris (Pennsylvania), George Read (Delaware), Madison, Gerry, Charles Pinckney (South Carolina), Mason, Oliver Ellsworth (Connecticut), Nathaniel Gorham (Massachusetts), C. C. Pinckney (South Carolina), and Alexander Hamilton (New York).

The split between the small states and the large states over the question of representation was matched in intensity by a division between the southern and "eastern" states over two questions: first, how slaves were to be counted in apportioning representation and taxes, and, second, whether Congress should have the power to prohibit the slave trade and pass navigation acts. Both questions were settled by compromise. After a long debate on July 11, the delegates finally agreed to count each slave as three-fifths of a citizen for purposes of both taxation and representation. Even sharper exchanges on August 22 and August 29 preceded the decision, on the latter date, by which the southern delegates, who had wanted to make it impossible for Congress to impose any restrictions upon the staple trade of their states, agreed to give Congress the power to pass navigation acts and the eastern representatives consented to restrict Congress from acting to put an end to the slave trade until 1808. Selections from the discussions over these questions, which foreshadowed the bitter sectional quarrels of the next century, are reprinted here as Selection 57 E. They include statements by Randolph, Mason, Hugh Williamson (North Carolina), Pierce Butler (South Carolina), C. C. Pinckney, Gerry, Gorham, Rufus King (Massachusetts), Sherman, Wilson, Gouverneur Morris (Pennsylvania), Ellsworth, Charles Pinckney, Dickinson, John Langdon (New Hampshire), John Rutledge (South Carolina), Luther Martin (Maryland), George Clymer (Pennsylvania), and Richard Dobbs Spaight (North Carolina).

The long, and at times heated, debates on these and other questions such as the process of selection and powers of both the executive and judiciary finally came to an end in early September. On September 8, the Convention selected a committee to put the Constitution in final form. This work, performed largely by Gouverneur Morris, was completed by September 12, and, after a clause by clause examination on the Convention floor, the Constitution was signed on September 17 by thirty-nine of the forty-two delegates still remaining at the Convention, Gerry, Mason, and Randolph, each for different reasons, refusing to sign. In a moving speech, printed below as Selection 57 F, Benjamin Franklin, at eighty-one the oldest of the delegates, offered the motion for signing and called upon the delegates to forget the animosities and disagreements that had divided them during the Convention and to present a united front to the states in seeking ratification of the Constitution.

All of the selections reprinted in Selection 57 are taken from the notes of the debates kept by James Madison or Robert Yates.

The literature on the Constitutional Convention is enormous. A very recent study, Clinton Rossiter, 1787: The Grand Convention (1966), is probably the most satisfactory. It should, however, be supplemented by reading in the following specialized works: Martin Diamond, "Democracy and The Federalist: *A Reconsideration of the Framers' Intent," American Political Science Review, volume 53 (March, 1959), pages 52–68, and A. O. Lovejoy, Reflections on Human Nature (1961), on the basic ideas of the framers and John Richard Alden, The South in the Revolution, 1763–1789 (1957) and The First South (1961) and Staughton Lynd, "The Compromise of 1787," Political Science Quarterly, volume 81 (June, 1966), pages 225–250, on the north-south split in the convention.*

A. THE LARGE STATE PLAN: THE EDMUND RANDOLPH OR VIRGINIA RESOLUTIONS (MAY 29, 1787)*

1. Resolved that the articles of Confederation ought to be so corrected & enlarged as to accomplish the objects proposed by their institution; namely. "common defence, security of liberty and general welfare."

2. Resd. therefore that the rights of suffrage in the National Legislature ought to be proportioned to the Quotas of contribution, or to the number of free inhabitants, as the one or the other rule may seem best in different cases.

3. Resd. that the National Legislature ought to consist of two branches.

4. Resd. that the members of the first branch of the National Legislature ought to be elected by the people of the several States every   for the term of   ; to be of the age of   years at least, to receive liberal stipends by which they may be compensated for the devotion of their time to public service; to be ineligible to any office established by a particular State, or under the authority of the United States, except those peculiarly belonging to the functions of the first branch, during the term of service, and for the space of   after its expiration; to be incapable of re-election for the space of   after the expiration of their term of service, and to be subject to recall.

5. Resold. that the members of the second branch of the National Legislature ought to be elected by those of the first, out of a proper number of persons nominated by the individual Legislatures, to be of the age of

* These excerpts are reprinted from Max Farrand (ed.), *The Records of the Federal Convention of 1787* (4 vols., 1911–1937), vol. I, pp. 20–23.

years at least; to hold their offices for a term sufficient to ensure their independency, to receive liberal stipends, by which they may be compensated for the devotion of their time to public service; and to be ineligible to any office established by a particular State, or under the authority of the United States, except those peculiarly belonging to the functions of the second branch, during the terms of service, and for the space of after the expiration thereof.

6. Resolved that each branch ought to possess the right of originating Acts; that the National Legislature ought to be impowered to enjoy the Legislative Rights vested in Congress by the Confederation & moreover to legislate in all cases to which the separate States are incompetent, or in which the harmony of the United States may be interrupted by the exercise of individual Legislation; to negative all laws passed by the several States, contravening in the opinion of the National Legislature the articles of Union; and to call forth the force of the Union agst. any member of the Union failing to fulfill its duty under the articles thereof.

7. Resd. that a National Executive be instituted; to be chosen by the National Legislature for the term of   years, to receive punctually at stated times, a fixed compensation for the services rendered, in which no increase or diminution shall be made so as to affect the Magistracy, existing at the time of increase or diminution, and to be ineligible a second time; and that besides a general authority to execute the National laws, it ought to enjoy the Executive rights vested in Congress by the Confederation.

8. Resd. that the Executive and a convenient number of the National Judiciary, ought to compose a council of revision with authority to examine every act of the National Legislature before it shall operate, & every act of a particular Legislature before a Negative thereon shall be final; and that the dissent of the said Council shall amount to a rejection, unless the Act of the National Legislature be again passed, or that of a particular Legislature be again negatived by   of the members of each branch.

9. Resd. that a National Judiciary be established to consist of one or more supreme tribunals, and of inferior tribunals to be chosen by the National Legislature, to hold their offices during good behaviour; and to receive punctually at stated times fixed compensation for their services, in which no increase or diminution shall be made so as to affect the persons actually in office at the time of such increase or diminution. that the jurisdiction of the inferior tribunals shall be to hear & determine in the first instance, and of the supreme tribunal to hear and determine in the dernier resort, all piracies & felonies on the high seas, captures from an enemy; cases in which foreigners or citizens of other States applying to such jurisdictions may be interested, or which respect the collection of the National revenue; impeachments of any National officers, and questions which may involve the national peace and harmony.

10. Resolvd. that provision ought to be made for the admission of States lawfully arising within the limits of the United States, whether from a voluntary junction of Government & Territory or otherwise, with the consent of a number of voices in the National legislature less than the whole.

11. Resd. that a Republican Government & the territory of each State, except in the instance of a voluntary junction of Government & territory, ought to be guaranteed by the United States to each State.

12. Resd. that provision ought to be made for the continuance of Con-

gress and their authorities and privileges, until a given day after the reform of the articles of Union shall be adopted, and for the completion of all their engagements.

13. Resd. that provision ought to be made for the amendment of the Articles of Union whensoever it shall seem necessary, and that the assent of the National Legislature ought not to be required thereto.

14. Resd. that the Legislative Executive & Judiciary powers within the several States ought to be bound by oath to support the articles of Union.

15. Resd. that the amendments which shall be offered to the Confederation, by the Convention ought at a proper time, or times, after the approbation of Congress to be submitted to an assembly or assemblies of Representatives, recommended by the several Legislatures to be expressly chosen by the people, to consider & decide thereon.

He concluded with an exhortation, not to suffer the present opportunity of establishing general peace, harmony, happiness and liberty in the U. S. to pass away unimproved.

B. THE SMALL STATE PLAN: THE PATERSON OR NEW JERSEY PROPOSALS (JUNE 16, 1787)*

Mr. [William] Paterson. said (as) he had on a former occasion given his sentiments on the plan proposed by Mr. R. he would now avoiding repetition as much as possible give his reasons in favor of that proposed by himself. He preferred it because it accorded 1. with the powers of the Convention. 2 with the sentiments of the people. If the confederacy was radically wrong, let us return to our States, and obtain larger powers, not assume them of ourselves. I came here not to speak my own sentiments, but (the sentiments of) those who sent me. Our object is not such a Governmt. as may be best in itself, but such a one as our Constituents have authorized us to prepare, and as they will approve. If we argue the matter on the supposition that no Confederacy at present exists, it can not be denied that all the States stand on the footing of equal sovereignty. All therefore must concur before any can be bound. If a proportional representation be right, why do we not vote so here? If we argue on the fact that a federal compact actually exists, and consult the articles of it we still find an equal Sovereignty to be the basis of it. He reads the 5th. art: of Confederation giving each State a vote—& the 13th. declaring that no alteration shall be made without unanimous consent. This is the nature of all treaties. What is unanimously done, must be unanimously undone. It was observed (by Mr. [James] Wilson) that the larger State gave up the point, not because it was right, but because the circumstances of the moment urged the concession. Be it so. Are they for that reason at liberty to take it back. Can the donor resume his gift Without the consent of the donee. This doctrine may be convenient, but it is a doctrine that will sacrifice the lesser States. The large States acceded readily to the confederacy. It was the small ones that came in reluctantly and slowly. N. Jersey & Maryland were the two last, the

* These selections are reprinted from Farrand (ed.), *The Records of the Federal Convention of 1787*, vol. I, pp. 250–252.

former objecting to the want of power in Congress over trade: both of them to the want of power to appropriate the vacant territory to the benefit of the whole. If the sovereignty of the States is to be maintained, the Representatives must be drawn immediately from the States, not from the people: and we have no power to vary the idea of equal sovereignty. The only expedient that will cure the difficulty, is that of throwing the States into Hotchpot. To say that this is impracticable, will not make it so. Let it be tried, and we shall see whether the Citizens of Massts. Pena. & Va. accede to it. It will be objected that Coercion will be impracticable. But will it be more so in one plan than the other? Its efficacy will depend on the quantum of power collected, not on its being drawn from the States, or from the individuals; and according to his plan it may be exerted on individuals as well as according that of Mr. R. a distinct executive & Judiciary also were equally provided by this plan. It is urged that two branches in the Legislature are necessary. Why? for the purpose of a check. But the reason of the precaution is not applicable to this case. Within a particular State, when party heats prevail, such a check may be necessary. In such a body as Congress it is less necessary, and besides, the delegations of the different States are checks on each other. Do the people at large complain of Congs.? No: what they wish is that Congs. may have more power. If the power now proposed be not eno'. the people hereafter will make additions to it. With proper powers Congs. will act with more energy & wisdom than the proposed Natl. Legislature; being fewer in number, and more secreted & refined by the mode of election. The plan of Mr. R. will also be enormously expensive. Allowing Georgia & Del. two representatives each in the popular branch the aggregate number of that branch will be 180. Add to it half as many for the other branch and you have 270. members coming once at least a year from the most distant parts as well as the most central parts of the republic. In the present deranged State of our finances can so expensive a system be seriously thought of? By enlarging the powers of Congs. the greatest part of this expense will be saved, and all purposes will be answered. At least a trial ought to be made.

C. THE COMMITMENT TO POPULAR GOVERNMENT: DEBATE OVER THE NATURE OF THE LOWER HOUSE (MAY 31, 1787)*

⟨Resol: 4. first clause⟩ "that the ⟨members of the first branch of the National Legislature⟩ ought to be elected by the people of ⟨the several⟩ States" ⟨being taken up,⟩

Mr. [Roger] Sherman opposed the election by the people, insisting that it ought to be by the ⟨State⟩ Legislatures. The people he said, ⟨immediately⟩ should have as little to do as may be about the Government. They want information and are constantly liable to be misled.

Mr. [Elbridge] Gerry. The evils we experience flow from the excess of democracy. The people do not want virtue; but are the dupes of pretended

* These excerpts are reprinted from Farrand (ed.), *The Records of the Federal Convention of 1787,* vol. I, pp. 48–50.

patriots. In Massts. it has been fully confirmed by experience that they are daily misled into the most baneful measures and opinions by the false reports circulated by designing men, and which no one on the spot can refute. One principal evil arises from the want of due provision for those employed in the administration of Governnt. It would seem to be a maxim of democracy to starve the public servants. He mentioned the popular clamour in Massts. for the reduction of salaries and the attack made on that of the Govr. though secured by the spirit of the Constitution itself. He had he said been too republican heretofore: he was still however republican, but had been taught by experience the danger of the levilling spirit.

Mr. [George] Mason. argued strongly for an election of the larger branch by the people. It was to be the grand depository of the democratic principle of the Govt. It was, so to speak, to be our House of Commons—It ought to know & sympathise with every part of the community; and ought therefore to be taken not only from different parts of the whole republic, but also from different districts of the larger members of it, which had in several instances particularly in Virga., different interests and views arising from difference of produce, of habits &c &. He admitted that we had been too democratic but was afraid we sd. incautiously run into the opposite extreme. We ought to attend to the rights of every class of the people. He had often wondered at the indifference of the superior classes of society to this dictate of humanity & policy, considering that however affluent their circumstances, or elevated their situations, might be, the course of a few years, not only might but certainly would, distribute their posterity throughout the lowest classes of Society. Every selfish motive therefore, every family attachment, ought to recommend such a system of policy as would provide no less carefully for the rights—and happiness of the lowest than of the highest orders of Citizens.

Mr. [James] Wilson contended strenuously for drawing the most numerous branch of the Legislature immediately from the people. He was for raising the federal pyramid to a considerable altitude, and for that reason wished to give it as broad a basis as possible. No government could long subsist without the confidence of the people. In a republican Government this confidence was peculiarly essential. He also thought it wrong to increase the weight of the State Legislatures by making them the electors of the national Legislature. All interference between the general and local Governmts. should be obviated as much as possible. On examination it would be found that the opposition of States to federal measures had proceded much more from the Officers of the States, than from the people at large.

Mr. [James] Madison considered the popular election of one branch of the national Legislature as essential to every plan of free Government. He observed that in some of the States one branch of the Legislature was composed of men already removed from the people by an intervening body of electors. That if the first branch of the general legislature should be elected by the State Legislatures, the second branch elected by the first—the Executive by the second together with the first; and other appointments again made for subordinate purposes by the Executive, the people would be lost sight of altogether; and the necessary sympathy between them and their rulers and officers, too little felt. He was an advocate for the policy of refining the popular appointments by successive filtrations, but thought it might be pushed too far. He wished the expedient to be resorted to only in the appointment of the second branch of the Legislature, and in the Executive & judiciary branches of the Government. He thought too that the great fabric to be raised would be more stable and durable if it should rest on the solid foundation of the people themselves, than if it should stand merely on the pillars of the Legislatures.

Mr. Gerry did not like the election by the people. The maxims taken from the British constitution were often fallacious when applied to our situation which was extremely different. Experience he said had shewn that the State Legislatures drawn immediately from the people did not always possess their confidence. He had no objection however to an election by the people if it were so qualified that men of honor & character might not be unwilling to be joined in the appointments. He seemed to think the people might nominate a certain number out of which the State legislatures should be bound to choose. . . .

D. THE COMMITMENT TO BICAMERALISM: DEBATES OVER THE FUNCTION AND ROLE OF THE SENATE (JUNE 7, 25–26, 1787)*

June 7

The Clause providing for ye appointment of the 2d branch of the national Legislature, having lain blank since the last vote on the mode of electing it, to wit, by the 1st. branch, Mr. [John] Dickenson now moved "that the members ⟨of the 2d. branch ought to be chosen⟩ by the individual Legislatures."

Mr. [Roger] Sherman seconded the motion; observing that the particular States would thus become interested in supporting the National Governmt. and that a due harmony between the two Governments would be maintained. He admitted that the two ought to have separate and distinct jurisdictions, but that they ought to have a mutual interest in supporting each other. . . .

Mr. Dickenson had two reasons for his motion. 1. because the sense of the States would be better collected through their Governments; than immediately from the people at large. 2. because he wished the Senate to consist of the most distinguished characters, distinguished for their rank in life and the weight of property, and bearing as strong a likeness to the British House of Lords as possible; and he thought such characters more likely to be selected by the State Legislatures, than in any other mode. . . .

Mr. [James] Wilson. If we are to establish a national Government, that Government ought to flow from the people at large. If one branch of it should be chosen by the Legislatures, and the other by the people, the two branches will rest on different foundations, and dissentions will naturally arise between them. He wished the Senate to be elected by the people as well as the other branch, and the people might be divided into proper districts for the purpose & moved to postpone the motion of Mr. Dickenson, in order to take up one of that import.

* These excerpts are reprinted from Farrand (ed.), *The Records of the Federal Convention of 1787*, vol. I, pp. 150–156, 397–407, 411–412, 421–426.

Mr. [Robert] Morris 2ded. him.

Mr. [George] Read proposed "that the Senate should be appointed by the Executive Magistrate out of a proper number of persons to be nominated by the individual legislatures." He said he thought it his duty, to speak his mind frankly. Gentlemen he hoped would not be alarmed at the idea. Nothing short of this approach towards a proper model of Government would answer the purpose, and he thought it best to come directly to the point at once.—His proposition was not seconded nor supported.

Mr. [James] Madison, if the notion (of Mr. Dickenson) should be agreed to, we must either depart from the doctrine of proportional representation; or admit into the Senate a very large number of members. The first is inadmissable, being evidently unjust. The second is inexpedient. The use of the Senate is to consist in its proceeding with more coolness, with more system, & with more wisdom, than the popular branch. Enlarge their number and you communicate to them the vices which they are meant to correct. He differed from Mr. D. who thought that the additional number would give additional weight to the body. On the contrary it appeared to him that their weight would be in an inverse ratio to their number. The example of the Roman Tribunes was applicable. They lost their influence and power, in proportion as their number was augmented. The reason seemed to be obvious: They were appointed to take care of the popular interests & pretensions at Rome, because the people by reason of their numbers could not act in concert; were liable to fall into factions among themselves, and to become a prey to their aristocratic adversaries. The more the representatives of the people therefore were multiplied, the more they partook of the infirmaties of their constituents, the more liable they became to be divided among themselves either from their own indiscretions or the artifices of the opposite factions, and of course the less capable of fulfilling their trust. When the weight of a set of men depends merely on their personal characters; the greater the number the greater the weight. When it depends on the degree of political authority lodged in them the smaller the number the greater the weight. These considerations might perhaps be combined in the intended Senate; but the latter was the material one.

Mr. [Elbridge] Gerry. 4 modes of appointing the Senate have been mentioned. 1. by the 1st. branch of the National Legislature. This would create a dependence contrary to the end proposed. 2. by the National Executive. This is a stride towards monarchy that few will think of. 3. by the people. the people have two great interests, the landed interest, and the commercial including the stockholders. To draw both branches from the people will leave no security to the latter interest; the people being chiefly composed of the landed interest, and erroneously, supposing, that the other interests are adverse to it. 4. by the Individual Legislatures. The elections being carried thro' this refinement, will be most likely to provide some check in favor of the commercial interest agst. the landed; without which oppression will take place, and no free Govt. can last long when that is the case. He was therefore in favor of this last.

Mr. Dickenson. The preservation of the States in a certain degree of agency is indispensible. It will produce that collision between the different authorities which should be wished for in order to check each other. To attempt to abolish the States altogether, would degrade the Councils of our Country, would be impracticable, would be ruinous. He compared the proposed National System to the Solar System, in which the States were the planets, and ought to be left to move freely in their proper orbits. The Gentleman from Pa. (Mr. Wilson) wished he said to extinguish these planets. If the State Governments were excluded from all agency in the national one, and all power drawn from the people at large, the consequence would be that the national Govt. would move in the same direction as the State Govts. now do, and would run into all the same mischiefs. The reform would only unite the 13 small streams into one great current pursuing the same course without any opposition whatever. He adhered to the opinion that the Senate ought to be composed of a large number, and that their influence ⟨from family weight & other causes⟩ would be increased thereby. He did not admit that the Tribunes lost their ⟨weight⟩ in proportion as their no. was augmented and gave a historical sketch of this institution. If the reasoning of (Mr. ⟨Madison⟩) was good it would prove that the number of the Senate ought to be reduced below ten, the highest no. of the Tribunitial corps.

Mr. Wilson. The subject it must be owned is surrounded with doubts and difficulties. But we must surmount them. The British Governmt. cannot be our model. We have no materials for a similar one. Our manners, our laws, the abolition of entails and of primogeniture, the whole genius of the people, are opposed to it. He did not see the danger of the States being devoured by the Nationl. Govt. On the contrary, he wished to keep them from devouring the national Govt. He was not however for extinguishing these planets as was supposed by Mr. D.—neither did he on the other hand, believe that they would warm or enlighten the Sun. Within their proper orbits they must still be suffered to act for subordinate purposes ⟨for which their existence is made essential by the great extent of our Country.⟩ He could not comprehend in what manner the landed interest wd. be rendered less predominant in the Senate, by an election through the medium of the Legislatures than by the people themselves. If the Legislatures, as was now complained, sacrificed the commercial to the landed interest, what reason was there to expect such a choice from them as would defeat their own views. He was for an election by the people in large districts which wd. be most likely to obtain men of intelligence & uprightness; subdividing the districts only for the accommodation of voters.

Mr. Madison could as little comprehend in what manner family weight, as desired by Mr. D. would be more certainly conveyed into the Senate through elections by the State Legislatures, than in some other modes. The true question was in what mode the best choice wd. be made? If an election by the people, or thro' any other channel than the State Legislatures promised as uncorrupt & impartial a preference of merit, there could surely be no necessity for an appointment by those Legislatures. Nor was it apparent that a more useful check would be derived thro' that channel than from the people thro' some other. The great evils complained of were that the State legislatures run into schemes of paper money &c, whenever solicited by the people, & sometimes without even the sanction of the people. Their influence then, instead of checking a like propensity in the National Legislature, may be expected to promote it. Nothing can be more contradictory than to say that the Natl. Legislature witht. a proper check will follow the example of the State legislatures, & in the same breath, that the State Legislatures are the only proper check.

Mr. Sharman opposed elections by the people in districts, as not likely to produce such fit men as elections by the State Legislatures.

Mr. Gerry insisted that the commercial & monied interest wd. be more secure in the hands of the State Legislatures, than of the people at large. The former have more sense of character, and will be restrained by that from injustice. The people are for paper money when the Legislatures are agst. it. In Massts. the County Conventions had declared a wish for a *depreciating* paper that wd. sink itself. Besides, in some States there are two Branches in the Legislature, one of which is somewhat aristocratic. There wd. therefore be so far a better chance of refinement in the choice. There seemed, he thought to be three powerful objections agst. elections by districts 1. It is impracticable; the people can not be brought to one place for the purpose; and whether brought to the same place or not, numberless frauds wd. be unavoidable. 2. small States forming part of the same district with a large one, or large part of a large one, wd. have no chance of gaining an appointment for its citizens of merit. 3. a new source of discord wd. be opened between different parts of the same district.

Mr. [Charles] Pinkney thought the 2d. branch ought to be permanent & independent, & that the members of it wd. be rendered more so by receiving their appointment from the State Legislatures. This mode wd. avoid the rivalships & discontents incident to the election by districts. He was for dividing the States into three classes according to their respective sizes, & for allowing to the 1st. class three members—to the 2d. two. & to the 3d. one.

On the question for postponing Mr. Dickinson's motion referring the appointment of the Senate to the State Legislatures, in order to consider Mr. Wilson's for referring it to the people.

Mass. no. Cont. no. N. Y. no. N. J. no. Pa. ay Del. no. Md. no. Va. no. N. C. no. S. C. no. Geo. no. [Ayes—1; noes—10.]

Col. [George] Mason. whatever power may be necesary for the Natl. Govt. a certain portion must necessarily be left in the States. It is impossible for one power to pervade the extreme parts of the U. S. so as to carry equal justice to them. The State Legislatures also ought to have some means of defending themselves agst. encroachments of the Natl. Govt. In every other department we have studiously endeavored to provide for its self-defence. Shall we leave the States alone unprovided with the means for this purpose? And what better means can we provide than the giving them some share in, or rather to make them a constituent part of, the Natl. Establishment. There is danger on both sides no doubt; but we have only seen the evils arising on the side of the State Govts. Those on the other side remain to be displayed. The example of Cong: does not apply. Congs. had no power to carry their acts into execution as the Natl. Govt. will have.

On Mr. Dickinson's motion for an appointment of the Senate by the State-Legislatures.

Mass. ay. Ct. ay. N. Y. ay. Pa. ay. Del. ay. Md. ay. Va. ay. N. C. ay. S. C. ay. Geo. ay. [Ayes—10; noes—0.]

June 25

Resolution 4 [relating to the composition of upper house]. (being taken up.)

Mr. [Charles] Pinkney (spoke as follows).—The efficacy of the System will depend on this article. In order to form a right judgmt. in the case it will be proper to examine the situation of this Country more accurately than it has yet been done. The people of the U. States are perhaps the most singular of any we are acquainted with. Among them there are fewer distinctions of fortune & less of rank, than among the inhabitants of any other nation. Every freeman has a right to the same protection & security; and a very moderate share of property entitles them to the possession of all the honors and privileges the public can bestow: hence arises a greater equality, than is to be found among the people of any other country, and an equality which is more likely to continue—I say this equality is likely to continue, because in a new Country, possessing immense tracts of uncultivated lands, where every temptation is offered to emigration & where industry must be rewarded with competency, there will be few poor, and few dependent— Every member of the Society almost, will enjoy an equal power of arriving at the supreme offices & consequently of directing the strength & sentiments of the whole Community. None will be excluded by birth, & few by fortune, from voting for proper persons to fill the offices of Government—the whole community will enjoy in the fullest sense that kind of political liberty which consists in the power the members of the State reserve to themselves, of arriving at the public offices, or at least, of having votes in the nomination of those who fill them.

If this State of things is true & the prospect of its continuing probable, it is perhaps not politic to endeavour too close an imitation of a Government calculated for a people whose situation is, & whose views ought to be extremely different.

Much has been said of the Constitution of G. Britain. I will confess that I believe it to be the best constitution in existence; but at the same time I am confident it is one that will not or can not be introduced into this Country, for many centuries.—If it were proper to go here into a historical dissertation on the British Constitution, it might easily be shewn that the peculiar excellence, the distinguishing feature of that Governmt. can not possibly be introduced into our System—that its balance between the Crown & the people can not be made a part of our Constitution.—that we neither have or can have the members to compose it, nor the rights, privileges & properties of so distinct a class of Citizens to guard.—that the materials for forming this balance or check do not exist, nor is there a necessity for having so permanent a part of our Legislative, until the Executive power is so constituted as to have something fixed & dangerous in its principle—By this I mean a sole, hereditary, though limited Executive.

That we cannot have a proper body for forming a Legislative balance between the inordinate power of the Executive and the people, is evident from a review of the accidents and circumstances which give rise to the peerage of Great. Britain—I believe it is well ascertained that the parts which compose the British Constitution arose immediately from the forests of Germany; but the antiquity of the establishment of nobility is by no means clearly defined. Some authors are of opinion that the dignity denoted by the titles of dux et comes, was derived from the old Roman to the German Empire; while others are of opinion that they existed among the Germans long before the Romans were acquainted with them. The institution however of nobility is immemorial among the nations who may probably be termed the ancestors of Britain—At the time they were summoned in England to become a part of the National Council, and the circumstances which have contributed to make them a constituent part of that constitution, must be well known to all gentlemen who have had industry & curiosity enough to investigate the subject—The nobles with their possessions & dependents composed a body permanent in their nature and formidable in point of power. They had a distinct interest both from the King and the people; an interest which could only be represented by themselves, and the guardianship could not be safely intrusted to others.—At the time they were originally called to form a part of the National Council, necessity perhaps as much as other cause, induced the Monarch to look up to them. It was necessary to demand the aid of his subjects in personal & pecuniary services. The power and possessions of the Nobility would not permit taxation from any assembly of which they were not a part: & the blending the deputies of the Commons with them, & thus forming what they called their parler-ment was perhaps as much the effect of chance as of any thing else. The Commons were at that time completely subordinate to the nobles, whose consequence & influence seem to have been the only reasons for their superiority; a superiority so degrading to the Commons that in the first Summons we find the peers are called upon to consult, the commons to consent. From this time the peers have composed a part of the British Legislature, and notwithstanding their power and influence have diminished & those of the Commons have increased, yet still they have always formed an excellent balance agst. either the encroachments of the crown or the people.

I have said that such a body cannot exist in this Country for ages, and that untill the situation of our people is exceedingly changed no necessity will exist for so permanent a part of the Legislature. To illustrate this I have remarked that the people of the United States are more equal in their circumstances than the people of any other Country—that they have very few rich men among them,—by rich men I mean those whose riches may have a dangerous influence, or such as are esteemed rich in Europe—perhaps there are not one hundred such on the Continent: that it is not probable this number will be greatly increased: that the genius of the people, their mediocrity of situation & the prospects which are afforded their industry in a country which must be a new one for centuries are unfavorable to the rapid distinction of ranks. The destruction of the right of primogeniture & the equal division of the property of Intestates will also have an effect to preserve this mediocrity: for laws invariably affect the manners of a people. On the other hand that vast extent of unpeopled territory which opens to the frugal & industrious a sure road to competency & independence will effectually prevent for a considerable time the increase of the poor or discontented, and be the means of preserving that equality of condition which so eminently distinguishes us.

If equality is as I contend the leading feature of the U. States, where then are the riches & wealth whose representation & protection is the peculiar province of this permanent body. Are they in the hands of the few who may be called rich; in the possession of less than a hundred citizens? certainly not. They are in the great body of the people, among whom there are no men of wealth, and very few of real poverty.—Is it probable that a change will be created, and that a new order of men will arise? If under the British Government, for a century no such change was probable, I think it may be fairly concluded it will not take place while even the semblance of Republicanism remains. How is this change to be effected? Where are the sources from whence it is to flow? From the landed interest? No. That is too unproductive & too much divided in most of the States. From the Monied interest? If such exists at present, little is to be apprehended from that source. Is it to spring from commerce? I believe it would be the first instance in which a nobility sprang from merchants. Besides, Sir, I apprehend that on this point the policy of the U. States has been much mistaken. We have unwisely considered ourselves as the inhabitants of an old instead of a new country. We have adopted the maxims of a State full of people & manufactures & established in credit. We have deserted our true interest, and instead of applying closely to those improvements in domestic policy which would have ensured the future importance of our commerce, we have rashly & prematurely engaged in schemes as extensive as they are imprudent. This however is an error which daily corrects itself & I have no doubt that a few more severe trials will convince us, that very different commercial principles ought to govern the conduct of these States.

The people of this country are not only very different from the inhabitants of any State we are acquainted with in the modern world; but I assert that their situation is distinct from either the people of Greece or Rome, or of any State we are acquainted with among the antients.—Can the orders introduced by the institution of Solon, can they be found in the United States? Can the military habits & manners of Sparta be resembled to our habits & manners? Are the distinctions of Patrician & Plebeian known among us? Can the Helvetic or Belgic confederacies, or can the unwieldly, unmeaning body called the Germanic Empire, can they be said to possess either the same or a situation like ours? I apprehend not.—They are perfectly different, in their distinctions of rank, their Constitutions, their manners & their policy.

Our true situation appears to me to be this.—a new extensive Country containing within itself the materials for forming a Government capable of extending to its citizens all the blessings of civil & religious liberty—capable of making them happy at home. This is the great end of Republican Establishments. We mistake the object of our government, if we hope or wish that it is to make us respectable abroad. Conquest or superiority among other powers is not or ought not ever to be the object of republican systems. If they are sufficiently active & energetic to rescue us from contempt & preserve our domestic happiness & security, it is all we can expect from them,— it is more than almost any other Government ensures to its citizens.

I believe this observation will be found generally true: that no two people are so exactly alike in their situation or circumstances as to admit the exercise of the same Government with equal benefit: that a system must be suited to the habits & genius of the People it is to govern, and must grow out of them.

The people of the U. S. may be divided into three classes—*Professional men* who must from their particular pursuits always have a considerable weight in the Government while it remains popular—*Commercial men,* who may or may not have weight as a wise or injudicious commercial policy is pursued.—If that commercial policy is pursued which I conceive to be the true one, the merchants of this Country will not or ought not for a considerable time to have much weight in the political scale.—The third is the *landed interest,* the owners and cultivators of the soil, who are and ought ever to be the governing spring in the system.—These three classes, how-ever distinct in their pursuits are individually equal in the political scale, and may be easily proved to have but one interest. The dependence of each on the other is mutual. The merchant depends on the planter. Both must in private as well as public affairs be connected with the professional men; who in their turn must in some measure depend on them. Hence it is clear from this manifest connection, & the equality which I before stated exists, & must for the reasons then assigned, continue, that after all there is one, but one great & equal body of citizens composing the inhabitants of this Country among whom there are no distinctions of rank, and very few or none of fortune.

For a people thus circumstanced are we then to form a Government & the question is what kind of Government is best suited to them.

Will it be the British Govt.? No. Why? Because G. Britain contains three orders of people distinct in their situation, their possessions & their princi-ples.—These orders combined form the great body of the Nation, And as in national expences the wealth of the whole community must contribute, so ought each component part to be properly & duly represented.—No other combination of power could form this due representation, but the one that exists.—Neither the peers or the people could represent the royalty, nor could the Royalty & the people form a proper representation for the Peers. —Each therefore must of necessity be represented by itself, or the sign of itself; and this accidental mixture has certainly formed a Government admirably well balanced.

But the U. States contain but one order that can be assimilated to the British Nation.—this is the order of Commons. They will not surely then attempt to form a Government consisting of three branches, two of which shall have nothing to represent. They will not have an Executive & Senate (hereditary) because the King & Lords of England are so. The same reasons do not exist and therefore the same provisions are not necessary.

We must as has been observed suit our Governmt. to the people it is to direct. These are I believe as active, intelligent & susceptible of good Governmt. as any people in the world. The Confusion which has produced the present relaxed State is not owing to them. It is owing to the weakness & (defects) of a Govt. incapable of combining the various interests it is intended to unite, and destitute of energy.—All that we have to do then is to distribute the powers of Govt. in such a manner, and for such limited periods, as while it gives a proper degree of permanency to the Magistrate, will reserve to the people, the right of election they will not or ought not frequently to part with.—I am of opinion that this may be easily done; and that with some amendments the propositions before the Committee will fully answer this end.

No position appears to me more true than this; that the General Govt. can not effectually exist without reserving to the States the possession of their local rights.—They are the instruments upon which the Union must frequently depend for the support & execution of their powers, however immediately operating upon the people, and not upon the States. . . .

The United States include a territory of about 1500 miles in length, and in breadth about 400; the whole of which is divided into states and districts. While we were dependent on the crown of Great Britain, it was in contem-plation to have formed the whole into one—but it was found impracticable.

No legislature could make good laws for the whole, nor can it now be done. It would necessarily place the power in the hands of the few, nearest the seat of government. State governments must therefore remain, if you mean to prevent confusion. The general negative powers will support the general government. Upon these considerations I am led to form the second branch differently from the report. Their powers are important and the number not too large, upon the principle of proportion. I have considered the subject with great attention; and I propose this plan (reads it) and if no better plan is proposed, I will then move its adoption. . . .

Mr. [James] Wilson. the question is shall the members of the 2d. branch be chosen by the Legislatures of the States? When he considered the amazing extent of country—the immense population which is to fill it, the influence which the Govt. we are to form will have, not only on the present generation of our people & their multiplied posterity, but on the whole Globe, he was lost in the magnitude of the object. The project of Henry the 4th. & ⟨his Statesmen⟩ was but the picture in miniature of the great portrait to be exhibited. He was opposed to an election by the State Legislatures. In explaining his reasons it was necessary to observe the twofold relation in which the people would stand. 1. as Citizens of the Gen'l Gov't. 2. as Citizens of their particular State. The Genl. Govt. was meant for them in the first capacity; the State Govts. in the second. Both Govts. were derived from the people—both meant for the people—both therefore ought to be regulated on the same principles. The same train of ideas which belonged to the relation of the Citizens to their State Govts. were applicable to their relations to the Genl. Govt. and in forming the latter, we ought to proceed, by abstracting as much as possible from the idea of State Govts. With respect to the province & objects of the Gen'l Govt. they should be considered as having no existence. The election of the 2d. branch by the Legislatures, will introduce & cherish local interests & local prejudices. The Genl. Govt. is not an assemblage of States, but of individuals for certain political purposes—it is not meant for the States, but for the individuals composing them: the *individuals* therefore not the *States*, ought to be represented in it: A proportion in this representation can be preserved in the 2d. as well as in the 1st. branch; and the election can be made by electors chosen by the people for that purpose. He moved an amendment to that effect, which was not seconded.

Mr. [Oliver] Elseworth saw no reason for departing from the mode contained in the Report. Whoever chooses the member, he will be a citizen of the State he is to represent & will feel the same spirit and act the same part whether he be appointed by the people or the Legislature. Every State has its particular views & prejudices, which will find their way into the general councils, through whatever channel they may flow. Wisdom was one of the characteristics which it was in contemplation to give the second branch. Would not more of it issue from the Legislatures; than from an immediate election by the people. He urged the necessity of maintaining the existence & agency of the States. Without their co-operation it would be impossible to support a Republican Govt. over so great an extent of Country. An army could scarcely render it practicable. The largest States are the Worst Governed. Virga. is obliged to acknowledge her incapacity to extend her Govt. to Kentucky. Masts can not keep the peace one hundred miles from her capitol and is now forming an army for its support. How long Pena. may be free from a like situation can not be foreseen. If the principles & materials of our Govt. are not adequate to the extent of these single States; how can it be imagined that they can support a single Govt. throughout the U. States. The only chance of supporting a Genl. Govt. lies in engrafting it on that of the individual States. . . .

Mr. [George] Mason. It has been agreed on all hands that an efficient Govt. is necessary that to render it such it ought to have the faculty of self-defence, that to render its different branches effectual each of them ought to have the same power of self defence. He did not wonder that such an agreement should have prevailed in these points. He only wondered that there should be any disagreement about the necessity of allowing the State Govts. the same self-defence. If they are to be preserved as he conceived to be essential, they certainly ought to have this power, and the only mode left of giving it to them, was by allowing them to appoint the 2d. branch of the Natl. Legislature. . . .

June 26

The duration of the 2d. branch under consideration.

Mr. [Nathaniel] Ghorum moved to fill the blank with "six years". ⟨one third of the members to go out every second year.⟩

Mr. [James] Wilson 2ded. the motion.

Genl. [C. C.] Pinkney opposed six years in favor of four years. The States he said had different interests. Those of the Southern, and of S. Carolina in particular were different from the Northern. If the Senators should be appointed for a long term, they wd. settle in the State where they exercised their functions; and would in a little time be rather the representatives of that than of the State appoint'g them. . . .

Mr. [James] Madison. In order to judge of the form to be given to this institution, it will be proper to take a view of the ends to be served by it. These were first to protect the people agst. their rulers: secondly to protect ⟨the people⟩ agst. the transient impressions into which they themselves might be led. A people deliberating in a temperate moment, and with the experience of other nations before them, on the plan of Govt. most likely to secure their happiness, would first be aware, that those chargd. with the public happiness, might betray their trust. An obvious precaution agst. this danger wd. be to divide the trust between different bodies of men, who might watch & check each other. In this they wd. be governed by the same prudence which has prevailed in organizing the subordinate departments of Govt. where all business liable to abuses is made to pass thro' separate hands, the one being a check on the other. It wd. next occur to such a people, that they themselves were liable to temporary errors, thro' want of information as to their true interest, and that men chosen for a short term, & employed but a small portion of that in public affairs, might err from the same cause. This reflection wd. naturally suggest that the Govt. be so constituted, as that one of its branches might have an oppy. of acquiring a competent knowledge of the public interests. Another reflection equally becoming a people on such an occasion, wd. be that they themselves, as well as a numerous body of Representatives, were liable to err also, from fickleness and passion. A necessary fence agst. this danger would be to select a portion of enlightened citizens, whose limited number, and firmness might seasonably interpose agst. impetuous counsels. It ought finally to occur to a people deliberating on a Govt. for themselves, that as different interests necessarily result from the liberty meant to be secured, the major interest might under sudden impulses be tempted to commit injustice on the minority. In all civilized Countries the people fall into different classes havg. a real or supposed difference of interests. There will be creditors & debtors, farmers, merchts. & manufacturers. There will be particularly the distinction of rich & poor. It was true as had been observd. (by Mr. Pinkney) we had not among us those hereditary distinctions, of rank which were a great source of the contests in the ancient Govts. as well as the modern States of Europe, nor those extremes of wealth or poverty which characterize the latter. We cannot however be regarded even at this time, as one homogeneous mass, in which every thing that affects a part will affect in the same manner the whole. In framing a system which we wish to last for ages, we shd. not lose sight of the changes which ages will produce. An increase of population will of necessity increase the proportion of those who will labour under all the hardships of life, & secretly sigh for a more equal distribution of its blessings. These may in time outnumber those who are placed above the feelings of indigence. According to the equal laws of suffrage, the power will slide into the hands of the former. No agrarian attempts have yet been made in this Country, but symptoms of a leveling spirit, as we have understood, have sufficiently appeared in a certain quarters to give notice of the future danger. How is this danger to be guarded agst. on republican principles? How is the danger in all cases of interested co-alitions to oppress the minority to be guarded agst.? Among other means by the establishment of a body in the Govt. sufficiently respectable for its wisdom & virtue, to aid on such emergencies, the preponderance of justice by throwing its weight into that scale. Such being the objects of the second branch in the proposed Govt. he thought a considerable duration ought to be given to it. He did not conceive that the term of nine years could threaten any real danger; but in pursuing his particular ideas on the subject, he should require that the long term allowed to the 2d. branch should not commence till such a period of life as would render a perpetual disqualification to be re-elected little inconvenient either in a public or private view. He observed that as it was more than probable we were now digesting a plan which in its operation wd. decide forever the fate of Republican Govt. we ought not only to provide every guard to liberty that its preservation cd. require, but be equally careful to supply the defects which our own experience had particularly pointed out. . . .

Mr. [Alexander] Hamilton. He did not mean to enter particularly into the subject. He concurred with Mr. Madison in thinking we were now to decide for ever the fate of Republican Government; and that if we did not give to that form due stability and wisdom, it would be disgraced & lost among ourselves, disgraced & lost to mankind for ever. He acknowledged himself not to think favorably of Republican Government; but addressed his remarks to those who did think favorably of it, in order to prevail on them to tone their Government as high as possible. He professed himself to be as zealous an advocate for liberty as any man whatever, and trusted he should be as willing a martyr to it though he differed as to the form in which it was most eligible.—He concurred also in the general observations of (Mr. Madison) on the subject, which might be supported by others if it were necessary.

It was certainly true that nothing like an equality of property existed: that an inequality would exist as long as liberty existed, and that it would unavoidably result from that very liberty itself. This inequality of property constituted the great & fundamental distinction in Society. When the Tribunitial power had levelled the boundary between the *patricians* & *plebeians* what followed? The distinction between rich & poor was substituted. . . .

Mr. [James] Wilson did not mean to repeat what had fallen from others, but wd. add an observation or two which he believed had not yet been suggested. Every nation may be regarded in two relations 1 to its own citizens. 2 to foreign nations. It is therefore not only liable to anarchy & tyranny within but has wars to avoid & treaties to obtain from abroad. The Senate will probably be the depository of the powers concerning the latter objects. It ought therefore to be made respectable in the eyes of foreign nations. The true reason why G. Britain has not yet listened to a commercial treaty with us has been, because she had no confidence in the stability or efficacy of our Government. 9 years with a rotation, will provide these desirable qualities; and give our Govt. an advantage in this respect over Monarchy itself. In a monarchy much must alway depend on the temper of the man. In such a body, the personal character will be lost in the political. He wd. add another observation. The popular objection agst. appointing any public body for a long term was that it might by gradual encroachments prolong itself first into a body for life, and finally become a hereditary one. It would be a satisfactory answer to this objection that as ⅓ would go out triennially, there would be always three divisions holding their places for unequal terms, and consequently acting under the influence of different views, and different impulses—On the question for 9 years. ⅓ to go out triennially

Massts no. Cont. no. N. Y. no. N. J. no. Pa. ay. Del. ay. Md. no. Va. ay. N. C. no. S. C. no. Geo. no. [Ayes—3; noes—8.]

On the question for 6 years ⅓ to go out biennially

Massts. ay. Cont. ay. N. Y. no. N. J. no. Pa. ay. Del. ay. Md. ay. Va. ay. N. C. ay. S. C. no. Geo. no. [Ayes—7; noes—4.] . . .

E. SECTIONAL CLASH: DEBATES OVER HOW TO COUNT SLAVES IN APPORTIONING REPRESENTATIVES AND TAXES AND GIVING CONGRESS THE RIGHT TO PROHIBIT THE SLAVE TRADE AND PASS NAVIGATION ACTS (JULY 11, AUG. 22, 29, 1787)*

July 11 [Counting the Slaves]

Mr. [Edmund] Randolph's motion requiring the Legislre. to take a periodical census for the purpose of redressing inequalities in the Representation was resumed. . . .

Mr. [George] Mason. The greater the difficulty we find in fixing a proper rule of Representation, the more unwilling ought we to be, to throw the task from ourselves, on the Genl. Legislre. He did not object to the conjectural ratio which was to prevail in the outset; but considered a Revision

* These excerpts are reprinted from Farrand (ed.), *The Records of the Federal Convention of 1787*, vol. I, pp. 578–581, 586–588, vol. II, pp. 369–375, 449–453.

from time to time according to some permanent & precise standard as essential to ye. fair representation required in the 1st. branch. According to the present population of America, the Northn. part of it had a right to preponderate, and he could not deny it. But he wished it not to preponderate hereafter when the reason no longer continued. From the nature of man we may be sure, that those who have power in their hands will not give it up while they can retain it. On the Contrary we know they will always when they can rather increase it. If the S. States therefore should have ¾ of the people of America within their limits, the Northern will hold fast the majority of Representatives. ¼ will govern the ¾. The S. States will complain: but they may complain from generation to generation without redress. Unless some principle therefore which will do justice to them hereafter shall be inserted in the Constitution, disagreable as the declaration was to him, he must declare he could neither vote for the system here nor support it, in his State. Strong objections had been drawn from the danger to the Atlantic interests from new Western States. Ought we to sacrifice what we know to be right in itself, lest it should prove favorable to States which are not yet in existence. If the Western States are to be admitted into the Union as they arise, they must, he wd. repeat, be treated as equals, and subjected to no degrading discriminations. They will have the same pride & other passions which we have, and will either not unite with or will speedily revolt from the Union, if they are not in all respects placed on an equal footing with their brethren. It has been said they will be poor, and unable to make equal contributions to the general Treasury. He did not know but that in time they would be both more numerous & more wealthy than their Atlantic brethren. The extent & fertility of their soil, made this probable; and though Spain might for a time deprive them of the natural outlet for their productions, yet she will, because she must, finally yield to their demands. He urged that numbers of inhabitants; though not always a precise standard of wealth was sufficiently so for every substantial purpose.

Mr. [Hugh] Williamson was for making it the duty of the Legislature to do what was right & not leaving it at liberty to do or not do it. He moved that Mr. Randolph's proposition be postpond. in order to consider the following "that in order to ascertain the alterations that may happen in the population & wealth of the several States, a census shall be taken of the free white inhabitants and ⅗ths of those of other descriptions on the 1st year ⟨after this Government shall have been adopted⟩ and every   year thereafter; and that the Representation be regulated accordingly."

Mr. Randolph agreed that Mr. Williamson's proposition should stand in the place of his. He observed that the ratio fixt for the 1st. meeting was a mere conjecture, that it placed the power in the hands of that part of America, which could not always be entitled to it, that this power would not be voluntarily renounced; and that it was consequently the duty of the Convention to secure its renunciation when justice might so require; by some constitutional provisions. If equality between great & small States be inadmissible, because in that case unequal numbers of Constituents wd. be represented by equal number of votes; was it not equally inadmissible that a larger & more populous district of America should hereafter have less representation, than a smaller & less populous district. If a fair representation of the people be not secured, the injustice of the Govt. will shake it to its foundations.

Mr. [Pierce] Butler & Genl. [C. C.] Pinkney insisted that blacks be included in the rule of Representation, *equally* with the Whites: ⟨and for that purpose moved that the words "three fifths" be struck out.⟩

Mr. [Elbridge] Gerry thought that ⅗ of them was to say the least the full proportion that could be admitted.

Mr. [Nathaniel] Ghorum. This ratio was fixed by Congs. as a rule of taxation. Then it was urged by the Delegates representing the States having slaves that the blacks were still more inferior to freemen. At present when the ratio of representation is to be established, we are assured that they are equal to freemen. The arguments on ye. former occasion had convinced him that ⅗ was pretty near the just proportion and he should vote according to the same opinion now.

Mr. Butler insisted that the labour of a slave in S. Carola. was as productive & valuable as that of a freeman in Massts., that as wealth was the great means of defence and utility to the Nation they are equally valuable to it with freemen; and that consequently an equal representation ought to be allowed for them in a Government which was instituted principally for the protection of property, and was itself to be supported by property.

Mr. Mason. could not agree to the motion, notwithstanding it was favorable to Virga. because he thought it unjust. It was certain that the slaves were valuable, as they raised the value of land, increased the exports & imports, and of course the revenue, would supply the means of feeding & supporting an army, and might in cases of emergency become themselves soldiers. As in these important respects they were useful to the community at large, they ought not to be excluded from the estimate of Representation. He could not however regard them as equal to freemen and could not vote for them as such. He added as worthy of remark, that the Southern States have this peculiar species of property, over & above the other species of property common to all the States.

Mr. Williamson reminded Mr. Ghorum that if the Southn. States contended for the inferiority of blacks to whites when taxation was in view, the Eastern States on the same occasion contended for their equality. He did ⟨not⟩ however either then or now, concur in either extreme, but approved of the ratio of ⅗.

On Mr. Butlers motion for considering blacks as equal to Whites in the apportionmt. of Representation

Massts. no. Cont. no. (N. Y. not on floor.) N. J. no. Pa. no. Del. ay. Md. no. ⟨Va no⟩ N. C. no. S. C. ay. Geo. ay. [Ayes—3; noes—7.]

On the question . . . as to ⅗ of the negroes considered

Mr. [Rufus] King. being much opposed to fixing numbers as the rule of representation, was particularly so on account of the blacks. He thought the admission of them along with Whites at all, would excite great discontents among the States having no slaves. He had never said as to any particular point that he would in no event acquiesce in & support it; but he wd. say that if in any case such a declaration was to be made by him, it would be in this. He remarked that in the ⟨temporary⟩ allotment of Representatives made by the Committee, the Southern States had received more than the number of their white & three fifths of their black inhabitants entitled them to.

Mr. [Roger] Sherman. S. Carola. had not more beyond her proportion than N. York & N. Hampshire, nor either of them more than was necessary in order to avoid fractions or reducing them below their proportion. Georgia had more; but the rapid growth of that State seemed to justify it. In general the allotment might not be just, but considering all circumstances, he was satisfied with it. . . .

Mr. [James] Wilson did not well see on what principle the admission of blacks in the proportion of three fifths could be explained. Are they admitted as Citizens? Then why are they not admitted on an equality with White Citizens? Are they admitted as property? then why is not other property admitted into the computation? These were difficulties however which he thought must be overruled by the necessity of compromise. He had some apprehensions also from the tendency of the blending of the blacks with the whites, to give disgust to the people of Pena. as had been intimated by his colleague (Mr Govr. Morris). . . .

Mr. Gov[erneu]r Morris was compelled to declare himself reduced to the dilemma of doing injustice to the Southern States or to human nature, and he must therefore do it to the former. For he could never agree to give such encouragement to the slave trade as would be given by allowing them a representation for their negroes, and he did not believe those States would ever confederate on terms that would deprive them of that trade.

On Question for agreeing to include ⅗ of the blacks

Masts. no. Cont. ay N. J. no. Pa. no. Del. no. Mard. no. Va. ay. N. C. ay. S. C. no. Geo. ay [Ayes—6; noes—4.] . . .

August 22 [Slave Trade]

Art. VII sect 4. resumed. Mr. [Roger] Sherman was for leaving the clause as it stands. He disapproved of the slave trade: yet as the States were now possessed of the right to import slaves, as the public good did not require it to be taken from them, & as it was expedient to have as few objections as possible to the proposed scheme of Government, he thought it best to leave the matter as we find it. He observed that the abolition of slavery seemed to be going on in the U. S. & that the good sense of the several States would probably by degrees compleat it. He urged on the Convention the necessity of despatch⟨ing its business.⟩

Col. [George] Mason. This infernal traffic originated in the avarice of British Merchants. The British Govt. constantly checked the attempts of Virginia to put a stop to it. The present question concerns not the importing States alone but the whole Union. The evil of having slaves was experienced during the late war. Had slaves been treated as they might have been by the Enemy, they would have proved dangerous instruments in their hands. But their folly dealt by the slaves, as it did by the Tories. He mentioned the dangerous insurrections of the slaves in Greece and Sicily; and the instructions given by Cromwell to the Commissioners sent to Virginia, to arm the servants & slaves, in case other means of obtaining its submission should fail. Maryland & Virginia he said had already prohibited the importation of slaves expressly. N. Carolina had done the same in substance. All this would be in vain if S. Carolina & Georgia be at liberty to import. The Western people are already calling out for slaves for their new lands; and will fill that Country with slaves if they can be got thro' S. Carolina & Georgia. Slavery discourages arts & manufactures. The poor despise labor when performed by slaves. They prevent the immigration of Whites, who really enrich & strengthen a Country. They produce the most pernicious effect on manners. Every master of slaves is born a petty tyrant. They bring the judgment of heaven on a Country. As nations can not be rewarded or punished in the next world they must be in this. By an inevitable chain of causes & effects providence punishes national sins, by national calamities. He lamented that some of our Eastern brethren had from a lust of gain embarked in this nefarious traffic. As to the States being in possession of the Right to import, this was the case with many other rights, now to be properly given up. He held it essential in every point of view, that the Genl. Govt. should have power to prevent the increase of slavery.

Mr. [Oliver] Elsworth. As he had never owned a slave could not judge of the effects of slavery on character. He said however that if it was to be considered in a moral light we ought to go farther and free those already in the Country.—As slaves also multiply so fast in Virginia & Maryland that it is cheaper to raise than import them, whilst in the sickly rice swamps foreign supplies are necessary, if we go no farther than is urged, we shall be unjust towards S. Carolina & Georgia—Let us not intermeddle. As population increases; poor laborers will be so plenty as to render slaves useless. Slavery in time will not be a speck in our Country. Provision is already made in Connecticut for abolishing it. And the abolition has already taken place in Massachusetts. As to the danger of insurrections from foreign influence, that will become a motive to kind treatment of the slaves.

Mr. [Charles] Pinkney— If slavery be wrong, it is justified by the example of all the world. He cited the case of Greece Rome & other antient States; the sanction given by France England, Holland & other modern States. In all ages one half of mankind have been slaves. If the S. States were let alone they will probably of themselves stop importations. He wd. himself as a Citizen of S. Carolina vote for it. An attempt to take away the right as proposed will produce serious objections to the Constitution which he wished to see adopted.

General [C. C.] Pinkney declared it to be his firm opinion that if himself & all his colleagues were to sign the Constitution & use their personal influence, it would be of no avail towards obtaining the assent of their Constituents. S. Carolina & Georgia cannot do without slaves. As to Virginia she will gain by stopping the importations. Her slaves will rise in value, & she has more than she wants. It would be unequal to require S. C. & Georgia to confederate on such unequal terms. He said the Royal assent before the Revolution had never been refused to S. Carolina as to Virginia. He contended that the importation of slaves would be for the interest of the whole Union. The more slaves, the more produce to employ the carrying trade; The more consumption also, and the more of this, the more of revenue for the common treasury. He admitted it to be reasonable that slaves should be dutied like other imports, but should consider a rejection of the clause as an exclusion of S. Carola from the Union. . . .

Mr. [John] Dickenson considered it as inadmissible on every principle of honor & safety that the importation of slaves should be authorized to the States by the Constitution. The true question was whether the national happiness would be promoted or impeded by the importation, and this question ought to be left to the National Govt. not to the States particularly interested. If Engd. & France permit slavery, slaves are at the same time excluded from both those Kingdoms. Greece and Rome were made unhappy by their slaves. He could not believe that the Southn. States would refuse to confederate on the account apprehended; especially as the power was not likely to be immediately exercised by the Genl. Government.

Mr. [Hugh] Williamson stated the law of N. Carolina on the subject, to wit that it did not directly prohibit the importation of slaves. It imposed a duty of £5. on each slave imported from Africa £10. on each from elsewhere, & £50 on each from a State licensing manumission. He thought the S. States could not be members of the Union if the clause should be rejected, and that it was wrong to force any thing down, not absolutely necessary, and which any State must disagree to.

Mr. [Rufus] King thought the subject should be considered in a political light only. If two States will not agree to the Constitution as stated on one side, he could affirm with equal belief on the other, that great & equal opposition would be experienced from the other States. He remarked on the exemption of slaves from duty whilst every other import was subjected to it, as an inequality that could not fail to strike the commercial sagacity of the Northn. & middle States.

Mr. [John] Langdon was strenuous for giving the power to the Genl. Govt. He cd. not with a good conscience leave it with the States who could then go on with the traffic, without being restrained by the opinions here given that they will themselves cease to import slaves.

Genl. Pinkney thought himself bound to declare candidly that he did not think S. Carolina would stop her importations of slaves in any short time, but only stop them occasionally as she now does. He moved to commit the clause that slaves might be made liable to an equal tax with other imports which he thought right & wch. wd. remove one difficulty that had been started.

Mr. [John] Rutlidge. If the Convention thinks that N.C; S. C. & Georgia will ever agree to the plan, unless their right to import slaves be untouched, the expectation is vain. The people of those States will never be such fools as to give up so important an interest. He was strenuous agst. striking out the Section, and seconded the motion of Genl. Pinkney for a commitment.

Mr Govr. Morris wished the whole subject to be committed including the clauses relating to taxes on exports & to a navigation act. These things may form a bargain among the Northern & Southern States.

Mr. [Pierce] Butler declared that he never would agree to the power of taxing exports. . . .

Mr. [Edmund] Randolph was for committing in order that some middle ground might, if possible, be found. He could never agree to the clause as it stands. He wd. sooner risk the constitution—He dwelt on the dilemma to which the Convention was exposed. By agreeing to the clause, it would revolt the Quakers, the Methodists, and many others in the States having no slaves. On the other hand, two States might be lost to the Union. Let us then, he said, try the chance of a commitment.

On the question for committing the remaining part of Sect 4 & 5. of art: 7. N. H. no. Mas. abst. Cont. ay N. J. ay Pa. no. Del. no Maryd ay. Va. ay. N. C. ay S. C. ay. Geo. ay. [Ayes—7; noes—3; absent—1.]

Mr. Pinkney & Mr. Langdon moved to commit sect. 6. as to navigation act ⟨by two thirds of each House.⟩

Mr. [Nathaniel] Gorham did not see the propriety of it. Is it meant to require a greater proportion of votes? He desired it to be remembered that the Eastern States had no motive to Union but a commercial one. They were able to protect themselves. They were not afraid of external danger, and did not need the aid of the Southn. States.

Mr. [James] Wilson wished for a commitment in order to reduce the proportion of votes required.

Mr. Elsworth was for taking the plan as it is. This widening of opinions has a threatening aspect. If we do not agree on this middle & moderate ground he was afraid we should lose two States, with such others as may be disposed to stand aloof, should fly into a variety of shapes & directions, and most probably into several confederations and not without bloodshed.

On Question for committing 6 sect. as to navigation Act to a member from each State—N. H. ay—Mas. ay. Ct no. N. J. no. Pa. ay. Del. ay. Md. ay. Va. ay. N. C. ay. S. C. ay. Geo. ay. [Ayes—9; noes—2.]

The Committee appointed were Mr. Langdon, King, [William Samuel] Johnson, [William] Livingston, [George] Clymer, Dickenson, L[uther] Martin, [James] Madison, Williamson, C. C. Pinkney, & [Abraham] Baldwin. . . .

August 29 [Navigation Acts]

Art. VII Sect. 6 by ye. Committee ⟨of eleven⟩ reported to be struck out (see the 24 instant) being now taken up,

Mr. [Charles] Pinkney moved to postpone the Report in favor of the following proposition—"That no act of the Legislature for the purpose of regulating the commerce of the U— S. with foreign powers, or among the several States, shall be passed without the assent of two thirds of the members of each House—" —He remarked that there were five distinct commercial interests— 1. the fisheries & W. India trade, which belonged to the N. England States. 2. the interest of N. York lay in a free trade. 3. Wheat & flour the Staples of the two Middle States, (N. J. & Penna.)— 4 Tobo. the staple of Maryd. & Virginia ⟨& partly of N. Carolina.⟩ 5. Rice & Indigo, the staples of S. Carolina & Georgia. These different interests would be a source of oppressive regulations if no check to a bare majority should be provided. States pursue their interests with less scruple than individuals. The power of regulating commerce was a pure concession on the part of the S. States. They did not need. the protection of the N. States at present.

Mr. [Luther] Martin 2ded. the motion

Genl. [C. C.] Pinkney said it was the true interest of the S. States to have no regulation of commerce; but considering the loss brought on the commerce of the Eastern States by the revolution, their liberal conduct towards the views* of South Carolina, and the interest the weak Southn. States had in being united with the strong Eastern States, he thought it proper that no fetters should be imposed on the power of making commercial regulations; and that his constituents though prejudiced against the Eastern States, would be reconciled to this liberality— He had himself, he

* He meant the permission to import slaves. An understanding on the two subjects of *navigation* and *slavery,* had taken place between those parts of the Union, which explains the vote on the Motion depending, as well as the language of Genl. Pinkney & others.

said, prejudices agst the Eastern States before he came here, but would acknowledge that he had found them as liberal and candid as any men whatever.

Mr. [George] Clymer. The diversity of commercial interests, of necessity creates difficulties, which ought not to be increased by unnecessary restrictions. The Northern & middle States will be ruined, if not enabled to defend themselves against foreign regulations.

Mr. [Roger] Sherman, alluding to Mr. Pinkney's enumeration of particular interests, as requiring a security agst. abuse of the power; observed that, the diversity was of itself a security. adding that to require more than a majority to decide a question was always embarrassing as had been experienced in cases requiring the votes of nine States in Congress.

Mr. Pinkney replied that his enumeration meant the five minute interests— It still left the two great divisions of Northern & Southern Interests.

Mr. Govr. Morris. opposed the object of the motion as highly injurious— Preferences to american ships will multiply them, till they can carry the Southern produce cheaper than it is now carried——A navy was essential to security, particularly of the S. States, and can only be had by a navigation act encouraging american bottoms & seamen— In those points of view then alone, it is the interest of the S. States that navigation acts should be facilitated. Shipping he said was the worst & most precarious kind of property. and stood in need of public patronage.

Mr. [Hugh] Williamson was in favor of making two thirds instead of a majority requisite, as more satisfactory to the Southern people. No useful measure he believed had been lost in Congress for want of nine votes As to the weakness of the Southern States, he was not alarmed on that account. The sickliness of their climate for invaders would prevent their being made an object. He acknowledged that he did not think the motion requiring ⅔ necessary in itself, because if a majority of Northern States should push their regulations too far, the S. States would build ships for themselves: but he knew the Southern people were apprehensive on this subject and would be pleased with the precaution.

Mr. [Richard Dobbs] Spaight was against the motion. The Southern States could at any time save themselves from oppression, by building ships for their own use.

Mr. [Pierce] Butler differed from those who considered the rejection of the motion as no concession on the part of the S. States. He considered the interests of these and of the Eastern States, to be as different as the interests of Russia and Turkey. Being notwitstanding desirous of conciliating the affections of the East: States, he should vote agst. requiring ⅔ instead of a majority.

Col: [George] Mason. If the Govt. is to be lasting, it must be founded in the confidence & affections of the people, and must be so constructed as to obtain these. The *Majority* will be governed by their interests. The Southern States are the *minority* in both Houses. Is it to be expected that they will deliver themselves bound hand & foot to the Eastern States, and enable them to exclaim, in the words of Cromwell on a certain occasion—"the lord hath delivered them into our hands."

Mr. [James] Wilson took notice of the several objections and remarked that if every peculiar interest was to be secured, *unanimity* ought to be required. The majority he said would be no more governed by interest than the minority— It was surely better to let the latter be bound hand and foot than the former. Great inconveniences had, he contended, been experienced in Congress from the article of confederation requiring nine votes in certain cases.

Mr. [James] Madison. went into a pretty full view of the subject. He observed that the disadvantage to the S. States from a navigation act, lay chiefly in a temporary rise of freight, attended however with an increase of Southn. as well as Northern Shipping—with the emigration of Northern seamen & merchants to the Southern States—& with a removal of the existing & injurious retaliations among the States (on each other). The power of foreign nations to obstruct our retaliating measures on them by a corrupt influence would also be less if a majority shd be made competent than if ⅔ of each House shd. be required to legislative acts in this case. An abuse of the power would be qualified with all these good effects. But he thought an abuse was rendered improbable by the provision of 2 branches—by the independence of the Senate, by the negative of the Executive, by the interest of Connecticut & N. Jersey which were agricultural, not commercial States; by the interior interest which was also agricultural in the most commercial States— by the accession of Western States which wd. be altogether agricultural. He added that the Southern States would derive an essential advantage in the general security afforded by the increase of our maritime strength. He stated the vulnerable situation of them all, and of Virginia in particular. The increase of the Coasting trade, and of seamen, would also be favorable to the S. States, by increasing, the consumption of their produce. If the Wealth of the Eastern should in a still greater proportion be augmented, that wealth wd. contribute the more to the public wants, and be otherwise a national benefit.

Mr. [John] Rutledge was agst. the motion of his colleague. It did not follow from a grant of the power to regulate trade, that it would be abused. At the worst a navigation act could bear hard a little while only on the S. States. As we are laying the foundation for a great empire, we ought to take a permanent view of the subject and not look at the present moment only. He reminded the House of the necessity of securing the West India to this country. That was the great object, and a navigation Act was necessary for obtaining it. . . .

The Report of the Committee for striking out sect: 6. requiring two thirds of each House to pass a navigation act was then agreed to, nem: con:

F. "A RISING AND NOT A SETTING SUN": THE SPEECH OF BENJAMIN FRANKLIN (SEPT. 17, 1787)*

Mr. President

I confess that there are several parts of this constitution which I do not at present approve, but I am not sure I shall never approve them: For having lived long, I have experienced many instances of being obliged by better information or fuller consideration, to change opinions even on impor-

* These excerpts are reprinted from Farrand (ed.), *The Records of the Federal Convention of 1787*, vol. II, pp. 641–643, 648.

tant subjects, which I once thought right, but found to be otherwise. It is therefore that the older I grow, the more apt I am to doubt my own judgment, and to pay more respect to the judgment of others. Most men indeed as well as most sects in Religion, think themselves in possession of all truth, and that whereever others differ from them it is so far error. Steele, a Protestant in a Dedication tells the Pope, that the only difference between our Churches in their opinions of the certainty of their doctrines is, the Church of Rome is infallible and the Church of England is never in the wrong. But though many private persons think almost as highly of their own infallibility as of that of their sect, few express it so naturally as a certain french lady, who in a dispute with her sister, said "I don't know how it happens, Sister but I meet with no body but myself, that's always in the right"—*Il n'y a que moi qui a toujours raison.*

In these sentiments, Sir, I agree to this Constitution with all its faults, if they are such; because I think a general Government necessary for us, and there is no form of Government but what may be a blessing to the people if well administered, and believe farther that this is likely to be well administered for a course of years, and can only end in Despotism, as other forms have done before it, when the people shall become so corrupted as to need despotic Government, being incapable of any other. I doubt too whether any other Convention we can obtain may be able to make a better Constitution. For when you assemble a number of men to have the advantage of their joint wisdom, you inevitably assemble with those men, all their prejudices, their passions, their errors of opinion, their local interests, and their selfish views. From such an Assembly can a perfect production be expected? It therefore astonishes me, Sir, to find this system approaching so near to perfection as it does; and I think it will astonish our enemies, who are waiting with confidence to hear that our councils are confounded like those of the Builders of Babel; and that our States are on the point of separation, only to meet hereafter for the purpose of cutting one another's throats. Thus I consent, Sir, to this Constitution because I expect no better, and because I am not sure, that it is not the best. The opinions I have had of its errors, I sacrifice to the public good— I have never whispered a syllable of them abroad— Within these walls they were born, and here they shall die— If every one of us in returning to our Constituents were to report the objections he has had to it, and endeavor to gain partizans in support of them, we might prevent its being generally received, and thereby lose all the salutary effects & great advantages resulting naturally in our favor among foreign Nations as well as among ourselves, from our real or apparent unanimity. Much of the strength & efficiency of any Government in procuring and securing happiness to the people, depends. on opinion, on the general opinion of the goodness of the Government, as well as of the wisdom and integrity of its Governors. I hope therefore that for our own sakes as a part of the people, and for the sake of posterity, we shall act heartily and unanimously in recommending this Constitution (if approved by Congress & confirmed by the Conventions) wherever our influence may extend, and turn our future thoughts & endeavors to the means of having it well administered.

On the whole, Sir, I cannot help expressing a wish that every member of the Convention who may still have objections to it, would with me, on this occasion doubt a little of his own infallibility—and to make manifest our unanimity, put his name to this instrument." . . .

Whilst the last members were signing it Doctr. Franklin looking towards the Presidents Chair, at the back of which a rising sun happened to be painted, observed to a few members near him, that Painters had found it difficult to distinguish in their art a rising from a setting sun. I have, said he, often and often in the course of the Session, and the vicissitudes of my hopes and fears as to its issue, looked at that behind the President without being able to tell whether it was rising or setting: But now at length I have the happiness to know that it is a rising and not a setting Sun.

SELECTION

"We the People": The Constitution of the United States (Sept. 17, 1787)

To the extent that the Constitution represented an attempt to check the popular "frenzies" that, the framers felt, seemed to have seized many of the state governments in the mid-1780s, it was clearly a counterrevolutionary instrument. To the degree that it was designed to secure liberty and property against unrestrained power from any source, from the many as well as the few, it was as well the embodiment of the goals for which the Revolution had originally been fought and therefore the logical culmination of the Revolution.

The final version of the Constitution as it was accepted and signed by the Convention on September 17, 1787, and submitted by Congress on September 28 to the states for ratification or rejection by special ratifying conventions is reprinted in full below from Francis Newton Thorpe (ed.), The Federal and State Constitutions and Other Organic Laws (seven volumes, 1909), volume I, pages 19–28. Clinton Rossiter, 1787: The Grand Convention (1966), contains a clause-by-clause analysis of it.

WE THE PEOPLE of the United States, in Order to form a more perfect Union, establish Justice, insure domestic Tranquility, provide for the common defence, promote the general Welfare, and secure the Blessings of Liberty to ourselves and our Posterity, do ordain and establish this CONSTITUTION for the United States of America.

Article I

Section 1.   All legislative Powers herein granted shall be vested in a Congress of the United States, which shall consist of a Senate and House of Representatives.

Section 2.   The House of Representatives shall be composed of Members chosen every second Year by the People of the several States, and the Electors in each State shall have the Qualifications requisite for Electors of the most numerous Branch of the State Legislature.

No Person shall be a Representative who shall not have attained to the Age of twenty five Years, and been seven Years a Citizen of the United States, and who shall not, when elected, be an Inhabitant of that State in which he shall be chosen.

Representatives and direct Taxes shall be apportioned among the several States which may be included within this Union, according to their respective Numbers, which shall be determined by adding to the whole Number of Free persons, including those bound to Service for a Term of Years, and excluding Indians not taxed, three fifths of all other Persons. The actual Enumeration shall be made within three Years after the first Meeting of the Congress of the United States, and within every subsequent Term of ten Years, in such Manner as they shall by Law direct. The Number of Representatives shall not exceed one for every thirty Thousand, but each State shall have at Least one Representative; and until such enumeration shall be made, the State of New Hampshire shall be entitled to chuse three, Massachusetts eight, Rhode Island and Providence Plantations one, Connecticut five, New York six, New Jersey four, Pennsylvania eight, Delaware one, Maryland six, Virginia ten, North Carolina five, South Carolina five, and Georgia three.

When vacancies happen in the Representation from any State, the Executive Authority thereof shall issue Writs of Election to fill such Vacancies.

The House of Representatives shall chuse their Speaker and other Officers; and shall have the sole Power of Impeachment.

Section 3.   The Senate of the United States shall be composed of two Senators from each State, chosen by the Legislature thereof, for six Years; and each Senator shall have one Vote.

Immediately after they shall be assembled in Consequence of the first Election, they shall be divided as equally as may be into three Classes. The seats of the Senators of the first Class shall be vacated at the Expiration of the second year, of the second Class at the Expiration of the fourth Year, and of the third Class at the Expiration of the sixth Year, so that one-third may be chosen every second Year; and if Vacancies happen by Resignation, or otherwise, during the Recess of the Legislature of any State, the Executive thereof may make temporary Appointments until the next Meeting of the Legislature, which shall then fill such Vacancies.

No Person shall be a Senator who shall not have attained to the Age of thirty Years, and been nine Years a Citizen of the United States, and who shall not, when elected, be an Inhabitant of that State for which he shall be chosen.

The Vice President of the United States shall be President of the Senate, but shall have no Vote, unless they be equally divided.

The Senate shall chuse their other Officers, and also a President pro tempore, in the Absence of the Vice President, or when he shall exercise the Office of President of the United States.

The Senate shall have the sole Power to try all Impeachments. When sitting for that Purpose, they shall be on Oath or Affirmation. When the

President of the United States is tried, the Chief Justice shall preside: and no Person shall be convicted without the Concurrence of two thirds of the Members present.

Judgment in Cases of Impeachment shall not extend further than to removal from Office, and disqualification to hold and enjoy any Office of honor, Trust or Profit under the United States: but the Party convicted shall nevertheless be liable and subject to Indictment, Trial, Judgment and Punishment, according to Law.

Section 4. The Times, Places and manner of holding Elections for Senators and Representatives, shall be prescribed in each State by the Legislature thereof; but the Congress may at any time by Law make or alter such Regulations, except as to the Places of chusing Senators.

The Congress shall assemble at least once in every Year, and such Meeting shall be on the first Monday in December, unless they shall by Law appoint a different Day.

Section 5. Each House shall be the Judge of the Elections, Returns and Qualifications of its own Members, and a Majority of each shall constitute a Quorum to do Business; but a smaller Number may adjourn from day to day, and may be authorized to compel the Attendance of absent Members, in such Manner, and under such Penalties as each House may provide.

Each House may determine the Rules of its Proceedings, punish its Members for disorderly Behaviour, and, with the Concurrence of two thirds, expel a Member.

Each House shall keep a Journal of its Proceedings, and from time to time publish the same, excepting such Parts as may in their Judgment require Secrecy; and the Yeas and Nays of the Members of either House on any question shall, at the desire of one fifth of those Present, be entered on the Journal.

Neither House, during the Session of Congress, shall, without the Consent of the other, adjourn for more than three days, nor to any other Place than that in which the two Houses shall be sitting.

Section 6. The Senators and Representatives shall receive a Compensation for their Services, to be ascertained by Law, and paid out of the Treasury of the United States. They shall in all Cases, except Treason, Felony and Breach of the Peace, be privileged from Arrest during their Attendance at the Session of their respective Houses, and in going to and returning from the same; and for any Speech or Debate in either House, they shall not be questioned in any other Place.

No Senator or Representative shall, during the Time for which he was elected, be appointed to any civil Office under the Authority of the United States, which shall have been created, or the Emoluments whereof shall have been encreased during such time; and no Person holding any Office under the United States, shall be a Member of either House during his Continuance in Office.

Section 7. All Bills for raising Revenue shall originate in the House of Representatives; but the Senate may propose or concur with Amendments as on other Bills.

Every Bill which shall have passed the House of Representatives and the Senate, shall, before it become a Law, be presented to the President of the United States; If he approve he shall sign it, but if not he shall return it, with his Objections to that House in which it shall have originated, who shall enter the Objections at large on their Journal, and proceed to reconsider it. If after such Reconsideration two thirds of that House shall agree to pass the Bill, it shall be sent, together with the Objections, to the other House, by which it shall likewise be reconsidered, and if approved by two thirds of that House, it shall become a Law. But in all such Cases the Votes of both Houses shall be determined by yeas and Nays, and the Names of the Persons voting for and against the Bill shall be entered on the Journal of each House respectively. If any Bill shall not be returned by the President within ten Days (Sundays excepted) after it shall have been presented to him, the Same shall be a Law, in like Manner as if he had signed it, unless the Congress by their Adjournment prevent its Return, in which Case it shall not be a Law.

Every Order, Resolution, or Vote to which the Concurrence of the Senate and House of Representatives may be necessary (except on a question of Adjournment) shall be presented to the President of the United States; and before the Same shall take Effect, shall be approved by him, or being disapproved by him, shall be repassed by two thirds of the Senate and House of Representatives, according to the Rules and Limitations prescribed in the Case of a Bill.

Section 8.   The Congress shall have Power to lay and collect Taxes, Duties, Imposts and Excises, to pay the Debts and provide for the common Defence and general Welfare of the United States; but all Duties, Imposts and Excises shall be uniform throughout the United States;

To borrow Money on the credit of the United States;

To regulate Commerce with foreign Nations, and among the several States, and with the Indian Tribes;

To establish an uniform Rule of Naturalization, and uniform Laws on the subject of Bankruptcies throughout the United States;

To coin Money, regulate the Value thereof, and of foreign Coin, and fix the Standard of Weights and Measures;

To provide for the Punishment of counterfeiting the Securities and current Coin of the United States;

To establish Post Offices and post Roads;

To promote the Progress of Science and useful Arts, by securing for limited Times to Authors and Inventors the exclusive Right to their respective Writings and Discoveries;

To constitute Tribunals inferior to the supreme Court;

To define and punish Piracies and Felonies committed on the high Seas, and Offences against the Law of Nations;

To declare War, grant Letters of Marque and Reprisal, and make Rules concerning Captures on Land and Water;

To raise and support Armies, but no Appropriation of Money to that Use shall be for a longer Term than two Years;

To provide and maintain a Navy;

To make Rules for the Government and Regulation of the land and naval Forces;

To provide for calling forth the Militia to execute the Laws of the Union, suppress Insurrections and repel Invasions;

To provide for organizing, arming, and disciplining, the Militia, and for governing such Part of them as may be employed in the Service of the United States, reserving to the States respectively, the Appointment of the

Officers, and the Authority of training the Militia according to the discipline prescribed by Congress;

To exercise exclusive Legislation in all Cases whatsoever, over such District (not exceeding ten Miles square) as may, by Cession of particular States, and the Acceptance of Congress, become the Seat of the Government of the United States, and to exercise like Authority over all Places purchased by the Consent of the Legislature of the State in which the Same shall be, for the Erection of Forts, Magazines, Arsenals, dock-Yards, and other needful Buildings;—And

To make all Laws which shall be necessary and proper for carrying into Execution the foregoing Powers, and all other Powers vested by this Constitution in the Government of the United States, or in any Department or Officer thereof.

Section 9. The Migration or Importation of such Persons as any of the States now existing shall think proper to admit, shall not be prohibited by the Congress prior to the Year one thousand eight hundred and eight, but a Tax or duty may be imposed on such Importation, not exceeding ten dollars for each Person.

The Privilege of the Writ of Habeas Corpus shall not be suspended, unless when in Cases of Rebellion or Invasion the public Safety may require it.

No Bill of Attainder or ex post facto Law shall be passed.

No Capitation, or other direct, tax shall be laid, unless in Proportion to the Census or Enumeration herein before directed to be taken.

No Tax or Duty shall be laid on Articles exported from any State.

No Preference shall be given by any Regulation of Commerce or Revenue to the Ports of one State over those of another: nor shall Vessels bound to, or from, one State, be obliged to enter, clear, or pay Duties in another.

No Money shall be drawn from the Treasury, but in Consequence of Appropriations made by Law; and a regular Statement and Account of the Receipts and Expenditures of all public Money shall be published from time to time.

No Title of Nobility shall be granted by the United States: And no Person holding any Office of Profit or Trust under them, shall, without the Consent of the Congress, accept of any present, Emolument, Office, or Title, of any kind whatever, from any King, Prince, or foreign State.

Section 10. No State shall enter into any Treaty, Alliance, or Confederation; grant Letters of Marque and Reprisal; coin Money; emit Bills of Credit; make any Thing but gold and silver Coin a Tender in Payment of Debts; pass any Bill of Attainder, ex post facto Law, or Law impairing the Obligation of Contracts, or grant any Title of Nobility.

No State shall, without the Consent of the Congress, lay any Imposts or Duties on Imports or Exports, except what may be absolutely necessary for executing it's inspection Laws: and the net Produce of all Duties and Imposts, laid by any State on Imports or Exports, shall be for the Use of the Treasury of the United States; and all such Laws shall be subject to the Revision and Controul of the Congress.

No State shall, without the Consent of Congress, lay any Duty of Tonnage, keep Troops, or Ships of War in time of Peace, enter into any Agreement or Compact with another State, or with a foreign Power, or engage in War, unless actually invaded, or in such imminent Danger as will not admit of delay.

Article II

Section 1. The executive Power shall be vested in a President of the United States of America. He shall hold his Office during the Term of four Years, and, together with the Vice President, chosen for the same Term, be elected, as follows

Each State shall appoint, in such Manner as the Legislature thereof may direct, a Number of Electors, equal to the whole Number of Senators and Representatives to which the State may be entitled in the Congress: but no Senator or Representative, or Person holding an Office of Trust or Profit under the United States, shall be appointed an Elector.

The Electors shall meet in their respective States, and vote by Ballot for two Persons, of whom one at least shall not be an Inhabitant of the same State with themselves. And they shall make a List of all the Persons voted for, and of the Number of Votes for each; which List they shall sign and certify, and transmit sealed to the Seat of the Government of the United States, directed to the President of the Senate. The President of the Senate shall, in the Presence of the Senate and House of Representatives, open all the Certificates, and the Votes shall then be counted. The Person having the greatest Number of Votes shall be the President, if such Number be a Majority of the whole Number of Electors appointed; and if there be more than one who have such Majority, and have an equal Number of Votes, then the House of Representatives shall immediately chuse, by Ballot one of them for President; and if no Person have a Majority, then from the five highest on the List, the said House shall in like manner chuse the President. But in chusing the President, the Votes shall be taken by States, the Representation from each State having one vote; A quorum for this Purpose shall consist of a Member or Members from two thirds of the States, and a Majority of all the States shall be necessary to a Choice. In every Case, after the Choice of the President, the Person having the greatest Number of Votes of the Electors shall be the Vice President. But if there should remain two or more who have equal Votes, the Senate shall chuse from them by Ballot the Vice-President.

The Congress may determine the Time of chusing the Electors, and the Day on which they shall give their Votes; which Day shall be the same throughout the United States.

No person except a natural born Citizen, or a Citizen of the United States, at the time of the Adoption of this Constitution, shall be eligible to the Office of President; neither shall any Person be eligible to that office who shall not have attained to the Age of thirty five Years, and been fourteen Years a Resident within the United States.

In Case of the Removal of the President from Office, or of his Death, Resignation or Inability to discharge the Powers and Duties of the said Office, the Same shall devolve on the Vice President, and the Congress may by Law provide for the Case of Removal, Death, Resignation or Inability, both of the President and Vice President, declaring what Officer shall then act as President, and such Officer shall act accordingly, until the Disability be removed, or a President shall be elected.

The President shall, at stated Times, receive for his Services, a Compensation, which shall neither be encreased nor diminished during the Period for which he shall have been elected, and he shall not receive within that Period any other Emolument from the United States, or any of them.

Before he enter on the Execution of his Office, he shall take the following Oath or Affirmation:—"I do solemnly swear (or affirm) that I will faithfully execute the Office of President of the United States, and will to the best of my Ability, preserve, protect and defend the Constitution of the United States."

Section 2.   The President shall be Commander in Chief of the Army and Navy of the United States, and of the Militia of the several States, when called into the actual Service of the United States; he may require the Opinion, in writing, of the principal Officer in each of the executive Departments, upon any Subject relating to the Duties of their respective Offices, and he shall have Power to grant Reprieves and Pardons for Offences against the United States, except in Cases of Impeachment.

He shall have Power, by and with the Advice and Consent of the Senate, to make Treaties, provided two thirds of the Senators present concur; and he shall nominate, and by and with the Advice and Consent of the Senate, shall appoint Ambassadors, other public Ministers and Consuls, Judges of the supreme Court, and all other Officers of the United States, whose Appointments are not herein otherwise provided for, and which shall be established by Law: but the Congress may by Law vest the Appointment of such inferior Officers, as they think proper, in the President alone, in the Courts of Law, or in the Heads of Departments.

The President shall have Power to fill up all Vacancies that may happen during the Recess of the Senate, by granting Commissions which shall expire at the End of their next session.

Section 3.   He shall from time to time give to the Congress Information of the State of the Union, and recommend to their Consideration such Measures as he shall judge necessary and expedient; he may, on extraordinary Occasions, convene both Houses, or either of them, and in Case of Disagreement between them, with Respect to the time of Adjournment, he may adjourn them to such Time as he shall think proper; he shall receive Ambassadors and other public Ministers; he shall take Care that the Laws be faithfully executed, and shall commission all the Officers of the United States.

Section 4.   The President, Vice President, and all civil Officers of the United States, shall be removed from Office on Impeachment for, and Conviction of, Treason, Bribery, or other high Crimes and Misdemeanors.

Article III

Section 1.   The judicial Power of the United States, shall be vested in one supreme Court, and in such inferior Courts as the Congress may from time to time ordain and establish. The Judges, both of the supreme and inferior Courts, shall hold their Offices during good Behaviour, and shall, at stated Times, receive for their Services, a Compensation, which shall not be diminished during their Continuance in Office.

Section 2.   The judicial Power shall extend to all Cases, in Law and Equity, arising under this Constitution, the Laws of the United States, and Treaties made, or which shall be made, under their Authority;—to all Cases affecting Ambassadors, other public Ministers and Consuls;—to all Cases of admiralty and maritime Jurisdiction;—to Controversies to which the United States shall be a Party;—to Controversies between two or more States;—between a State and Citizens of another State;—between Citizens of different States,—between Citizens of the same State claiming Lands under Grants of different States, and between a State, or the Citizens thereof, and foreign States, Citizens or Subjects.

In all Cases affecting Ambassadors, other public Ministers and Consuls, and those in which a State shall be Party, the supreme Court shall have original Jurisdiction. In all the other Cases before mentioned, the supreme Court shall have appellate Jurisdiction, both as to Law and Fact, with such Exceptions, and under such Regulations as the Congress shall make.

The Trial of all Crimes, except in Cases of Impeachment, shall be by Jury; and such Trial shall be held in the State where the said Crimes shall have been committed; but when not committed within any State, the Trial shall be at such Place or Places as the Congress may by Law have directed.

Section 3. Treason against the United States, shall consist only in levying War against them, or in adhering to their Enemies, giving them Aid and Comfort. No Person shall be convicted of Treason unless on the Testimony of two Witnesses to the same overt Act, or on Confession in open Court.

The Congress shall have Power to declare the Punishment of Treason, but no Attainder of Treason shall work Corruption of Blood, or Forfeiture except during the Life of the Person attained.

Article IV

Section 1. Full Faith and Credit shall be given in each State to the public Acts, Records, and judicial Proceedings of every other State. And the Congress may by general Laws prescribe the Manner in which such Acts, Records and Proceedings shall be proved, and the Effect thereof.

Section 2. The Citizens of each State shall be entitled to all Privileges and Immunities of Citizens in the several States.

A person charged in any State with Treason, Felony, or other Crime, who shall flee from Justice, and be found in another State, shall on Demand of the executive Authority of the State from which he fled, be delivered up to be removed to the State having Jurisdiction of the Crime.

No person held to Service or Labour in one State, under the Laws thereof, escaping into another, shall, in Consequence of any Law or Regulation therein, be discharged from such Service or Labour, but shall be delivered up on Claim of the Party to whom such Service or Labour may be due.

Section 3. New States may be admitted by the Congress into this Union; but no new State shall be formed or erected within the Jurisdiction of any other State; nor any State be formed by the Junction of two or more States, or Parts of States, without the Consent of the Legislatures of the States concerned as well as of the Congress.

The Congress shall have Power to dispose of and make all needful Rules and Regulations respecting the Territory or other Property belonging to the United States; and nothing in this Constitution shall be so construed as to Prejudice any Claims of the United States, or of any particular State.

Section 4. The United States shall guarantee to every State in this

Union a Republican Form of Government, and shall protect each of them against Invasion; and on Application of the Legislature, or of the Executive (when the Legislature cannot be convened) against domestic Violence.

Article V

The Congress, whenever two thirds of both Houses shall deem it necessary, shall propose amendments to this Constitution, or, on the Application of the Legislatures of two thirds of the several States, shall call a Convention for proposing Amendments, which, in either Case, shall be valid to all Intents and Purposes, as Part of this Constitution, when ratified by the Legislatures of three fourths of the several States, or by Conventions in three fourths thereof, as the one or the other Mode of Ratification may be proposed by the Congress; Provided that no Amendment which may be made prior to the Year One thousand eight hundred and eight shall in any Manner affect the first and fourth Clauses in the Ninth Section of the first Article; and that no State, without its Consent, shall be deprived of its equal Suffrage in the Senate.

Article VI

All Debts contracted and Engagements entered into, before the Adoption of this Constitution, shall be as valid against the United States under this Constitution, as under the Confederation.

This Constitution, and the Laws of the United States which shall be made in Pursuance thereof; and all Treaties made, or which shall be made, under the Authority of the United States, shall be the supreme Law of the Land; and the Judges in every State shall be bound thereby, any Thing in the Constitution or Laws of any State to the Contrary notwithstanding.

The Senators and Representatives before mentioned, and the Members of the several State Legislatures, and all executive and judicial Officers, both of the United States and of the several States, shall be bound by Oath or Affirmation, to support this Constitution; but no religious Test shall ever be required as a Qualification to any Office or public Trust under the United States.

Article VII

The Ratification of the Conventions of nine States, shall be sufficient for the Establishment of this Constitution between the States so ratifying the Same.

DONE in Convention by the Unanimous Consent of the States present the Seventeenth Day of September in the Year of our Lord one thousand seven hundred and Eighty seven and of the Independance of the United States of America the Twelfth *In Witness* whereof We have hereunto subscribed our Names,

Attest WILLIAM JACKSON *Secretary*   GO. WASHINGTON—*Presidt.*
and deputy from Virginia

New Hampshire	JOHN LANGDON NICHOLAS GILMAN
Massachusetts	NATHANIEL GORHAM RUFUS KING
Connecticut	WM: SAML. JOHNSON ROGER SHERMAN
New York	ALEXANDER HAMILTON
New Jersey	WIL: LIVINGSTON DAVID BREARLEY, WM. PATERSON, JONA: DAYTON
Pennsylvania	B FRANKLIN THOMAS MIFFLIN ROBT. MORRIS GEO. CLYMER THOS. FITZ SIMONS JARED INGERSOLL JAMES WILSON GOUV MORRIS
Delaware	GEO: READ GUNNING BEDFORD jun JOHN DICKINSON RICHARD BASSETT JACO: BROOM
Maryland	JAMES McHENRY DAN OF ST THOS. JENIFER DANL CARROLL
Virginia	JOHN BLAIR— JAMES MADISON Jr.
North Carolina	WM: BLOUNT RICHD. DOBBS SPAIGHT. HU WILLIAMSON
South Carolina	J. RUTLEDGE, CHARLES PINCKNEY, CHARLES COTESWORTH PINCKNEY, PIERCE BUTLER.
Georgia	WILLIAM FEW, ABR. BALDWIN.

Attest: WILLIAM JACKSON, *Secretary.*

SELECTION **59**

Opposition to the Constitution

The refusals of George Mason, Edmund Randolph, and Elbridge Gerry to sign the finished Constitution marked the beginnings of an intensive, if quite disorganized, campaign against the Constitution by a disparate group—dubbed "Anti-Federalists" by their opponents—largely united only by their fear of the Constitution. This group wrote pamphlets, letters, and essays, bitterly contested with the "Federalists" in the elections to the state ratifying conventions, and made speeches and voted against the Constitution in those conventions. What they found most distressing was what seemed to them to be the overwhelming amount of power given to the central government and the failure of the framers to incorporate a Bill of Rights. They feared that the states would be swallowed up, that the interests of their respective localities would be sacrificed to those of others, and that the people would lose control over the distant national government which would eventually transmute itself into an irresponsible aristocracy which would then violate the liberties of the people with impunity and establish an onerous despotism. But their most effective argument, an argument they could buttress with manifold historical precedents, was that republican governments could be successful only in small polities where the government could be an exact miniature of the people.

The views of the Anti-Federalists are here represented by three selections. Selection 59 A is a portion of the first of seventeen Letters from the Federal Farmer *published by Richard Henry Lee—who had been selected as a delegate to the Convention but had not served—between October 8, 1787, and January 23, 1788. The* Letters *presented in broad outline many of the main points in the Anti-Federal case against the Constitution. In the selection reprinted here Lee warned against the Federalist desire for hasty ratification and, voicing his conviction that the new government would be a consolidated rather than a federal one, expressed his opinion that a consolidated government was incompatible with republicanism. In Selection 59 B, which consists of brief excerpts from three of* The Agrippa Letters, *published in the* Massachusetts Gazette *(Boston) between November, 1787, and February, 1788, and usually attributed to James Winthrop (1752–1821), scion of an old Massachusetts family, the author argued that it was absurd to try to extend republican government over so large and diverse a territory and that local interests could be secured only in a decentralized state in which the central government had a minimum of power. Selection 59 C is a speech delivered on June 21, 1788 in the New York ratifying convention by Melancton Smith (1744–1798), merchant, lawyer, and delegate to Congress since 1785. In this speech Smith elaborated upon the Anti-Federal arguments that the number of Representatives in the lower house provided for by the Constitution was too small to reflect accurately the sentiments and interests of the people and that unless the number was increased the government would "fall into the hands of the few and the great" and become a "government of oppression."*

Discussions of the Anti-Federalists may be found in Jackson Turner Main, The Antifederalists: Critics of the Constitution, 1781–1788 *(1961); Forrest McDonald, "The Anti-Federalists, 1781–1789,"* Wisconsin Magazine of History, *volume 46 (Spring, 1963), pages 206–214, and* E Pluribus Unum: The Formation of the American Republic, 1776–1790 *(1965); and, most importantly, Cecelia M. Kenyon, "Men of Little Faith: The Anti-Federalists on the Nature of Representative*

Government," William and Mary Quarterly, *third series, volume 12 (January, 1955), pages 3–43, and* The Antifederalists *(1966), the latter of which contains a large selection of Anti-Federalist writings.*

A. THE DANGERS OF HASTE AND A CONSOLIDATED GOVERNMENT: RICHARD HENRY LEE, ''LETTERS FROM THE FEDERAL FARMER'' (OCTOBER, 1787)*

Letter One

The first principal question that occurs, is, Whether, considering our situation, we ought to precipitate the adoption of the proposed constitution? If we remain cool and temperate, we are in no immediate danger of any commotions; we are in a state of perfect peace, and in no danger of invasions; the state governments are in the full exercise of their powers; and our governments answer all present exigencies, except the regulation of trade, securing credit, in some cases, and providing for the interest, in some instances, of the public debts; and whether we adopt a change three or nine months hence, can make but little odds with the private circumstances of individuals; their happiness and prosperity, after all, depend principally upon their own exertions. We are hardly recovered from a long and distressing war: The farmers, fishmen, &c. have not fully repaired the waste made by it. Industry and frugality are again assuming their proper station. Private debts are lessened, and public debts incurred by the war have been, by various ways, diminished; and the public lands have now become a productive source for diminishing them much more. I know uneasy men, who with very much to precipitate, do not admit all these facts; but they are facts well known to all men who are thoroughly informed in the affairs of this country. It must, however, be admitted, that our federal system is defective, and that some of the state governments are not well administered; but, then, we impute to the defects in our governments many evils and embarrassments which are most clearly the result of the late war. . . .

It is natural for men, who wish to hasten the adoption of a measure, to tell us, now is the crisis—now is the critical moment which must be seized or all will be lost; and to shut the door against free enquiry, whenever conscious the thing presented has defects in it, which time and investigation will probably discover. This has been the custom of tyrants, and their dependants in all ages. If it is true, what has been so often said, that the people of this country cannot change their condition for the worse, I presume it still behoves them to endeavour deliberately to change it for the better. The fickle and ardent, in any community are the proper tools for establishing despotic government. But it is deliberate and thinking men, who must establish and secure governments on free principles. Before they decide on the plan proposed, they will enquire whether it will probably be a blessing or a curse to this people.

* These excerpts are reprinted from Paul Leicester Ford (ed.), *Pamphlets on the Constitution of the United States* (1888), pp. 280–282, 286–288.

The present moment discovers a new face in our affairs. Our object has been all along, to reform our federal system, and to strengthen our governments—to establish peace, order and justice in the community—but a new object now presents. The plan of government now proposed is evidently calculated totally to change, in time, our condition as a people. Instead of being thirteen republics, under a federal head, it is clearly designed to make us one consolidated government. . . . The plan proposed appears to be partly federal, but principally however, calculated ultimately to make the states one consolidated government.

The first interesting question, therefore suggested, is, how far the states can be consolidated into one entire government on free principles. In considering this question extensive objects are to be taken into view, and important changes in the forms of government to be carefully attended to in all their consequences. The happiness of the people at large must be the great object with every honest statesman, and he will direct every movement to this point. If we are so situated as a people, as not to be able to enjoy equal happiness and advantages under one government, the consolidation of the states cannot be admitted.

There are three different forms of free government under which the United States may exist as one nation; and now is, perhaps, the time to determine to which we will direct our views. 1. Distinct republics connected under a federal head. In this case the respective state governments must be the principal guardians of the peoples rights, and exclusively regulate their internal police; in them must rest the balance of government. The congress of the states, or federal head, must consist of delegates amenable to, and removable by the respective states: This congress must have general directing powers; powers to require men and monies of the states; to make treaties; peace and war; to direct the operations of armies, &c. Under this federal modification of government, the powers of congress would be rather advisary or recommendatory than coercive. 2. We may do away the federal state governments, and form or consolidate all the states into one entire government, with one executive, one judiciary, and one legislature, consisting of senators and representatives collected from all parts of the union: In this case there would be a compleat consolidation of the states. 3. We may consoldate the states as to certain national objects, and leave them severally distinct independent republics, as to internal police generally. Let the general government consist of an executive, a judiciary, and balanced legislature, and its powers extend exclusively to all foreign concerns, causes arising on the seas to commerce, imports, armies, navies, Indian affairs, peace and war, and to a few internal concerns of the community; to the coin, post-offices, weights and measures, a general plan for the militia, to naturalization, *and, perhaps to bankruptcies,* leaving the internal police of the community, in other respects, exclusively to the state governments; as the administration of justice in all causes arising internally, the laying and collecting of internal taxes, and the forming of the militia according to a general plan prescribed. In this case there would be a compleat consolidation, *quoad* certain objects only.

Touching the first, or federal plan, I do not think much can be said in its favor: The sovereignty of the nation, without coercive and efficient powers to collect the strength of it, cannot always be depended on to answer the purposes of government; and in a congress of representatives of foreign states, there must necessarily be an unreasonable mixture of powers in the same hands.

As to the second, or compleat consolidating plan, it deserves to be carefully considered at this time by every American: If it be impracticable, it is a fatal error to model our governments, directing our views ultimately to it.

The third plan, or partial consolidation, is, in my opinion, the only one that can secure the freedom and happiness of this people. I once had some general ideas that the second plan was practicable, but from long attention, and the proceedings of the convention, I am fully satisfied, that this third plan is the only one we can with safety and propriety proceed upon. Making this the standard to point out, with candor and fairness, the parts of the new constitution which appear to be improper, is my object. The convention appears to have proposed the partial consolidation evidently with a view to collect all powers ultimately, in the United States into one entire government; and from its views in this respect, and from the tenacity of the small states to have an equal vote in the senate, probably originated the greatest defects in the proposed plan.

Independent of the opinions of many great authors, that a free elective government cannot be extended over large territories, a few reflections must evince, that one government and general legislation alone never can extend equal benefits to all parts of the United States: Different laws, customs, and opinions exist in the different states, which by a uniform system of laws would be unreasonably invaded. The United States contain about a million of square miles, and in half a century will, probably, contain ten millions of people; and from the center to the extremes is about 800 miles. . . .

B. THE CASE AGAINST CENTRALIZATION: [JAMES WINTHROP], "THE AGRIPPA LETTERS" (1787–1788)*

Letter IV Dec. 3, 1787

. . . It is the opinion of the ablest writers on the subject, that no extensive empire can be governed upon republican principles, and that such a government will degenerate to a despotism, unless it be made up of a confederacy of smaller states, each having the full powers of internal regulation. This is precisely the principle which has hitherto preserved our freedom. No instance can be found of any free government of considerable extent which has been supported upon any other plan. Large and consolidated empires may indeed dazzle the eyes of a distant spectator with their splendor, but if examined more nearly are always found to be full of misery. The reason is obvious. In large states the same principles of legislation will not apply to all the parts. The inhabitants of warmer climates are more dissolute in their manners, and less industrious, than in colder countries. A degree of severity is, therefore, necessary with one which would cramp the spirit of the other. We accordingly find that the very great empires have always been despotick.

---

* These excerpts are reprinted from E. H. Scott (ed.), *The Federalist and Other Constitutional Papers* (2 vols., 1894), vol. II, pp. 515–516, 521–522, 554–555.

They have indeed tried to remedy the inconveniences to which the people were exposed by local regulations; but these contrivances have never answered the end. The laws not being made by the people, who felt the inconveniences, did not suit their circumstances. It is under such tyranny that the Spanish provinces languish, and such would be our misfortune and degradation, if we should submit to have the concerns of the whole empire managed by one legislature. To promote the happiness of the people it is necessary that there should be local laws; and it is necessary that those laws should be made by the representatives of those who are immediately subject to the want of them. By endeavoring to suit both extremes, both are injured.

It is impossible for one code of laws to suit Georgia and Massachusetts. They must, therefore, legislate for themselves. Yet there is, I believe, not one point of legislation that is not surrendered in the proposed plan. Questions of every kind respecting property are determinable in a continental court, and so are all kinds of criminal causes. The continental legislature has, therefore, a right to make rules in all cases by which their judicial courts shall proceed and decide causes. No rights are reserved to the citizens. The laws of Congress are in all cases to be the supreme law of the land, and paramount to the constitutions of the individual states. The Congress may institute what modes of trial they please, and no plea drawn from the constitution of any state can avail. This new system is, therefore, a consolidation of all the states into one large mass, however diverse the parts may be of which it is to be composed. The idea of an uncompounded republick, on an average one thousand miles in length, and eight hundred in breadth, and containing six millions of white inhabitants all reduced to the same standard of morals, of habits, and of laws, is in itself an absurdity, and contrary to the whole experience of mankind. The attempt made by Great Britain to introduce such a system, struck us with horrour, and when it was proposed by some theorist that we should be represented in parliament, we uniformly declared that one legislature could not represent so many different interests for the purposes of legislation and taxation. This was the leading principle of the revolution, and makes an essential article in our creed. All that part, therefore, of the system, which relates to the internal government of the states, ought at once to be rejected. . . .

Letter VII Dec. 18, 1787

. . . We ought . . . to be particularly attentive to securing so great an interest. It is vain to tell us that we ought to overlook local interests. It is only by protecting local concerns that the interest of the whole is preserved. No man when he enters into society does it from a view to promote the good of others, but he does it for his own good. All men having the same view are bound equally to promote the welfare of the whole. To recur then to such a principle as that local interests must be disregarded, is requiring of one man to do more than another, and is subverting the foundation of a free government. The Philadelphians would be shocked with a proposition to place the seat of general government and the unlimited right to regulate trade in the Massachusetts. There can be no greater reason for our surrendering the preference to them. Such sacrifices, however we may delude ourselves with the form of words, always originate in folly, and not in generosity. . . .

Letter XVIII Feb. 5, 1788

. . . It is now generally understood that it is for the security of the people that the powers of the government should be lodged in different branches. By this means publick business will go on when they all agree, and stop when they disagree. The advantage of checks in government is thus manifested where the concurrence of different branches is necessary to the same act, but the advantage of a division of business is advantageous in other respects. As in every extensive empire, local laws are necessary to suit the different interests, no single legislature is adequate to the business. All human capacities are limited to a narrow space, and as no individual is capable of practising a great variety of trades, no single legislature is capable of managing all the variety of national and state concerns. Even if a legislature was capable of it, the business of the judicial department must, from the same cause, be slovenly done. Hence arises the necessity of a division of the business into national and local. Each department ought to have all the powers necessary for executing its own business, under such limitations as tend to secure us from any inequality in the operations of government. I know it is often asked against whom in a government by representation is a bill of rights to secure us? I answer, that such a government is indeed a government by ourselves; but as a just government protects all alike, it is necessary that the sober and industrious part of the community should be defended from the rapacity and violence of the vicious and idle. A bill of rights, therefore, ought to set forth the purposes for which the compact is made, and serves to secure the minority against the usurpation and tyranny of the majority. It is a just observation of his excellency, Doctor Adams, in his learned defence of the American constitutions that unbridled passions produce the same effect, whether in a king, nobility, or a mob. The experience of all mankind has proved the prevalence of a disposition to use power wantonly. It is therefore as necessary to defend an individual against the majority in a republick as against the king in a monarchy. Our state constitution has wisely guarded this point. The present confederation has also done it. . . .

C. THE ARGUMENT FOR LARGER REPRESENTATION: MELANCTON SMITH, SPEECH BEFORE THE NEW YORK RATIFYING CONVENTION (JUNE 21, 1788)*

I had the honor, yesterday, of submitting an amendment to the clause under consideration, with some observations in support of it. I hope I shall be indulged in making some additional remarks in reply to what has been offered by the honorable gentleman [Alexander Hamilton] from New York.

He has taken up much time in endeavoring to prove that the great defect in the old Confederation was, that it operated upon states instead of individuals. It is needless to dispute concerning points on which we do not disagree. It is admitted that the powers of the general government ought to

* Reprinted in full from Jonathan Elliot (comp.), *The Debates in the Several State Conventions on the Adoption of the Federal Constitution,* 2d ed. (5 vols., 1876), vol. II, pp. 243–251.

operate upon individuals to a certain degree. How far the powers should extend, and in what cases to individuals, is the question.

As the different parts of the system will come into view in the course of our investigation, an opportunity will be afforded to consider this question. I wish, at present, to confine myself to the subject immediately under the consideration of the committee. I shall make no reply to the arguments offered by the honorable gentleman to justify the rule of apportionment fixed by this clause; for, though I am confident they might be easily refuted, yet I am persuaded we must yield this point, in accommodation to the Southern States. The amendment therefore proposes no alteration to the clause in this respect.

The honorable gentleman says, that the clause, by obvious construction, fixes the representation. I wish not to torture words or sentences. I perceive no such obvious construction.

I see clearly that, on one hand, the representatives cannot exceed one for thirty thousand inhabitants; and, on the other, that whatever larger number of inhabitants may be taken for the rule of apportionment, each state shall be entitled to send one representative. Every thing else appears to me in the discretion of the legislature. If there be any other limitation, it is certainly implied. Matters of moment should not be left to doubtful construction. It is urged that the number of representatives will be fixed at one for thirty thousand, because it will be the interest of the larger states to do it. I cannot discern the force of this argument. To me it appears clear, that the relative weight of influence of the different states will be the same, with the number of representatives at sixty-five as at six hundred, and that of the individual members greater; for each member's share of power will decrease as the number of the House of Representatives increases. If, therefore, this maxim be true, that men are unwilling to relinquish powers which they once possess, we are not to expect the House of Representatives will be inclined to enlarge the numbers. The same motive will operate to influence the President and Senate to oppose the increase of the number of representatives; for, in proportion as the House of Representatives is augmented, they will feel their own power diminished. It is, therefore, of the highest importance that a suitable number of representatives should be established by the Constitution.

It has been observed, by an honorable member, that the Eastern States insisted upon a small representation, on the principles of economy. This argument must have no weight in the mind of a considerate person. The difference of expense, between supporting a House of Representatives sufficiently numerous, and the present proposed one, would be twenty or thirty thousand dollars per annum. The man who would seriously object to this expense, to secure his liberties, does not deserve to enjoy them. Besides, by increasing the number of representatives, we open a door for the admission of the substantial yeomanry of our country, who, being possessed of the habits of economy, will be cautious of imprudent expenditures, by which means a greater saving will be made of public money than is sufficient to support them. A reduction of the numbers of the state legislatures might also be made, by which means there might be a saving of expense much more than sufficient for the purpose of supporting the general legislature; for as, under this system, all the powers of legislation, relating to our general concerns, are vested in the general government, the powers of the state legislatures will be so curtailed as to render it less necessary to have them so numerous as they now are.

But an honorable gentleman has observed, that it is a problem that cannot be solved, what the proper number is which ought to compose the House of Representatives, and calls upon me to fix the number. I admit that this is a question that will not admit of a solution with mathematical certainty; few political questions will; yet we may determine with certainty that certain numbers are too small or too large. We may be sure that ten is too small, and a thousand too large a number. Every one will allow that the first number is too small to possess the sentiments, be influenced by the interests of the people, or secure against corruption; a thousand would be too numerous to be capable of deliberating.

To determine whether the number of representatives proposed by this Constitution is sufficient, it is proper to examine the qualifications which this house ought to possess, in order to exercise their power discreetly for the happiness of the people. The idea that naturally suggests itself to our minds, when we speak of representatives, is, that they resemble those they represent. They should be a true picture of the people, possess a knowledge of their circumstances and their wants, sympathize in all their distresses, and be disposed to seek their true interests. The knowledge necessary for the representative of a free people not only comprehends extensive political and commercial information, such as is acquired by men of refined education, who have leisure to attain to high degrees of improvement, but it should also comprehend that kind of acquaintance with the common concerns and occupations of the people, which men of the middling class of life are, in general, more competent to than those of a superior class. To understand the true commercial interests of a country, not only requires just ideas of the general commerce of the world, but also, and principally, a knowledge of the productions of your own country, and their value, what your soil is capable of producing, the nature of your manufactures, and the capacity of the country to increase both. To increase the power of laying taxes, duties, and excises, with discretion, requires something more than an acquaintance with the abstruse parts of the system of finance. It calls for a knowledge of the circumstances and ability of the people in general—a discernment how the burdens imposed will bear upon the different classes.

From these observations results this conclusion—that the number of representatives should be so large, as that, while it embraces the men of the first class, it should admit those of the middling class of life. I am convinced that this government is so constituted that the representatives will generally be composed of the first class in the community, which I shall distinguish by the name of the *natural aristocracy* of the country. I do not mean to give offence by using this term. I am sensible this idea is treated by many gentlemen as chimerical. I shall be asked what is meant by the *natural aristocracy*, and told that no such distinction of classes of men exists among us. It is true, it is our singular felicity that we have no legal or hereditary distinctions of this kind; but still there are real differences. Every society naturally divides itself into classes. The Author of nature has bestowed on some greater capacities than others; birth, education, talents, and wealth, create distinctions among men as visible, and of as much influence, as titles, stars, and garters. In every society, men of this class will command a superior degree of respect; and if the government is so constituted as to admit but few to exercise the powers of it, it will, according to the natural course of things, be in their hands. Men in the middling class, who are qualified as representatives, will not be so anxious to be chosen as those of the first. When the number is so small, the office will be highly elevated and distinguished; the style in which the members live will probably be high; circumstances of this kind will render the place of a representative not a desirable one to sensible, substantial men, who have been used to walk in the plain and frugal paths of life.

Besides, the influence of the great will generally enable them to succeed in elections. It will be difficult to combine a district of country containing thirty or forty thousand inhabitants,—frame your election laws as you please, —in any other character, unless it be in one of conspicuous military, popular, civil, or legal talents. The great easily form associations; the poor and middling class form them with difficulty. If the elections be by plurality,— as probably will be the case in this state,—it is almost certain none but the great will be chosen, for they easily unite their interests: the common people will divide, and their divisions will be promoted by the others. There will be scarcely a chance of their uniting in any other but some great man, unless in some popular demagogue, who will probably be destitute of principle. A substantial yeoman, of sense and discernment, will hardly ever be chosen. From these remarks, it appears that the government will fall into the hands of the few and the great. This will be a government of oppression. I do not mean to declaim against the great, and charge them indiscriminately with want of principle and honesty. The same passions and prejudices govern all men. The circumstances in which men are placed in a great measure give a cast to the human character. Those in middling circumstances have less temptation; they are inclined by habit, and the company with whom they associate, to set bounds to their passions and appetites. If this is not sufficient, the want of means to gratify them will be a restraint: they are obliged to employ their time in their respective callings; hence the substantial yeomanry of the country are more temperate, of better morals, and less ambition, than the great. The latter do not feel for the poor and middling class; the reasons are obvious—they are not obliged to use the same pains and labor to procure property as the other. They feel not the inconveniences arising from the payment of small sums. The great consider themselves above the common people, entitled to more respect, do not associate with them; they fancy themselves to have a right of preëminence in every thing. In short, they possess the same feelings, and are under the influence of the same motives, as an hereditary nobility. I know the idea that such a distinction exists in this country is ridiculed by some; but I am not the less apprehensive of danger from their influence on this account. Such distinctions exist all the world over, have been taken notice of by all writers on free government, and are founded in the nature of things. It has been the principal care of free governments to guard against the encroachments of the great. Common observation and experience prove the existence of such distinctions. Will any one say that there does not exist in this country the pride of family, of wealth, of talents, and that they do not command influence and respect among the common people? Congress, in their address to the inhabitants of the province of Quebec, in 1775, state this distinction in the following forcible words, quoted from the Marquis Beccaria: "In every human society there is an essay continually tending to confer on one part the height of power and happiness, and to reduce the other to the extreme of weakness and misery. The intent of good laws is to oppose this effort, and to diffuse their influence universally and equally." We ought to guard against the government being placed in the hands of this class. They cannot have that sympathy with their constituents which is necessary to connect them closely to their interests. Being in the habit of profuse living, they will be profuse in the public expenses. They find no difficulty in paying their taxes, and therefore do not feel public burdens. Besides, if they govern, they will enjoy the emoluments of the government. The middling class, from their frugal habits, and feeling themselves the public burdens, will be careful how they increase them.

But I may be asked, Would you exclude the first class in the community from any share in legislation? I answer, By no means. They would be factious, discontented, and constantly disturbing the government. It would also be unjust. They have their liberties to protect, as well as others, and the largest share of property. But my idea is, that the Constitution should be so framed as to admit this class, together with a sufficient number of the middling class to control them. You will then combine the abilities and honesty of the community, a proper degree of information, and a disposition to pursue the public good. A representative body, composed principally of respectable yeomanry, is the best possible security to liberty. When the interest of this part of the community is pursued, the public good is pursued, because the body of every nation consists of this class, and because the interest of both the rich and the poor are involved in that of the middling class. No burden can be laid on the poor but what will sensibly affect the middling class. Any law rendering property insecure would be injurious to them. When, therefore, this class in society pursue their own interest, they promote that of the public, for it is involved in it.

In so small a number of representatives, there is great danger from corruption and combination. A great politician has said that every man has his price. I hope this is not true in all its extent; but I ask the gentleman to inform me what government there is in which it has not been practised. Notwithstanding all that has been said of the defects in the constitution of the ancient confederacies in the Grecian republics, their destruction is to be imputed more to this cause than to any imperfection in their forms of government. This was the deadly poison that effected their dissolution. This is an extensive country, increasing in population and growing in consequence. Very many lucrative offices will be in the grant of the government, which will be objects of avarice and ambition. How easy will it be to gain over a sufficient number, in the bestowment of offices, to promote the views and the purposes of those who grant them! Foreign corruption is also to be guarded against. A system of corruption is known to be the system of government in Europe. It is practised without blushing; and we may lay it to our account, it will be attempted amongst us. The most effectual as well as natural security against this is a strong democratic branch in the legislature, frequently chosen, including in it a number of the substantial, sensible yeomanry of the country. Does the House of Representatives answer this description? I confess, to me they hardly wear the complexion of a democratic branch; they appear the mere shadow of representation. The whole number, in both houses, amounts to ninety-one; of these forty-six make a quorum; and twenty-four of those, being secured, may carry any point. Can the liberties of three millions of people be securely trusted in the hands of twenty-four men? Is it prudent to commit to so small a number the decision of the great questions which will come before them? Reason revolts at the idea.

The honorable gentleman from New York has said, that sixty-five members in the House of Representatives are sufficient for the present situation of the country; and, taking it for granted that they will increase as one for thirty thousand, in twenty-five years they will amount to two hundred. It is admitted, by this observation, that the number fixed in the Constitution is not sufficient without it is augmented. It is not declared that an increase shall be made, but is left at the discretion of the legislature, by the gentleman's own concession; therefore the Constitution is imperfect. We certainly ought to fix, in the Constitution, those things which are essential to liberty. If any thing falls under this description, it is the number of the legislature. To say, as this gentleman does, that our security is to depend upon the spirit of the people, who will be watchful of their liberties, and not suffer them to be infringed, is absurd. It would equally prove that we might adopt any form of government. I believe, were we to create a despot, he would not immediately dare to act the tyrant; but it would not be long before he would destroy the spirit of the people, or the people would destroy him. If our people have a high sense of liberty, the government should be congenial to this spirit, calculated to cherish the love of liberty, while yet it had sufficient force to restrain licentiousness. Government operates upon the spirit of the people, as well as the spirit of the people operates upon it; and if they are not conformable to each other, the one or the other will prevail. In a less time than twenty-five years, the government will receive its tone. What the spirit of the country may be at the end of that period, it is impossible to foretell. Our duty is to frame a government friendly to liberty and the rights of mankind, which will tend to cherish and cultivate a love of liberty among our citizens. If this government becomes oppressive, it will be by degrees: it will aim at its end by disseminating sentiments of government opposite to republicanism, and proceed from step to step in depriving the people of a share in the government. A recollection of the change that has taken place in the minds of many in this country in the course of a few years, ought to put us on our guard. Many, who are ardent advocates for the new system, reprobate republican principles as chimerical, and such as ought to be expelled from society. Who would have thought, ten years ago, that the very men, who risked their lives and fortunes in support of republican principles, would now treat them as the fictions of fancy? A few years ago, we fought for liberty; we framed a general government on free principles; we placed the state legislatures, in whom the people have a full and a fair representation, between Congress and the people. We were then, it is true, too cautious, and too much restricted the powers of the general government. But now it is proposed to go into the contrary, and a more dangerous extreme—to remove all barriers, to give the new government free access to our pockets, and ample command of our persons, and that without providing for a genuine and fair representation of the people. No one can say what the progress of the change of sentiment may be in twenty-five years. The same men who now cry up the necessity of an energetic government, to induce a compliance with this system, may, in much less time, reprobate this in as severe terms as they now do the Confederation, and may as strongly urge the necessity of going as far beyond this as this is beyond the Confederation. Men of this class are increasing: they have influence, talents, and industry. It is time to form a barrier against them. And while we are willing to establish a government adequate to the purposes of the Union, let us be careful to establish it on the broad basis of equal liberty.

SELECTION

The Case for the Constitution: "The Federalist" (1787–1788)

The case for the Constitution was presented best by Publius in eighty-five essays— most of which first appeared in New York newspapers between October 27, 1787, and April 2, 1788—entitled The Federalist *and published together first in New York in the spring of 1788 and republished elsewhere. Publius was three men: Alexander Hamilton, who wrote fifty-one numbers; James Madison, who wrote twenty-nine; and John Jay, who wrote five. The brief selections below, all written by Madison, consist of the whole of Number 10 and portions of Numbers 51, 55, 62, and 63 and are reprinted here from E. H. Scott (ed.),* The Federalist and Other Constitutional Papers *(two volumes, 1894), volume I, pages 53–60, 286–288, 309– 310, 341–342, and 347.*

In Number 10, by far the most famous of The Federalist *papers, Madison sought to answer the charges by Anti-Federalists that republican government would not work in a large area. All other republican experiments had failed, Madison argued, precisely because they had been made in small territories in which a majority faction had been able to gain control of all political machinery and manipulate the people for its own selfish ends. What would save the United States from a similar fate under the proposed Constitution, Madison argued in a remarkable insight that he had gained from his reading of Scottish philosopher David Hume, was its enormous size and the multitude of interests and factions that would necessarily result from that size. With so many diverse and competing interests, Madison contended, there would be no possibility of enough of them submerging their differences to form a majority faction. In a large republic, then, the struggle of manifold interests, according to Madison, would perforce operate in such a way as to insure the continuance and success of republican government.*

In the selections from the other numbers printed here, Madison tried to spell out the assumptions about human nature and the function of government that underlay the various checks and balances included in the Constitution and to explain the role and argue for the necessity of the Senate.

Among the most enlightening discussions of The Federalist *are Martin Diamond, "Democracy and* The Federalist: *A Reconsideration of the Framer's Intent," *American Political Science Review, volume 53 (March, 1959), pages 52–68, and the introduction to Benjamin F. Wright (ed.),* The Federalist *(1961). Douglass Adair, "The Authorship of the Disputed* Federalist *Papers," William and Mary*

Quarterly, *third series, volume I (April, July, 1944), pages 97–122, 235–264, and Frederick Mosteller and David L. Wallace,* Inference and Disputed Authorship: The Federalist *(1964), effectively argue for Madison's authorship of the numbers published here.*

Number 10

AMONG the numerous advantages promised by a well constructed Union, none deserves to be more accurately developed, than its tendency to break and control the violence of faction. The friend of popular governments, never finds himself so much alarmed for their character and fate, as when he contemplates their propensity to this dangerous vice. He will not fail, therefore, to set a due value on any plan which, without violating the principles to which he is attached, provides a proper cure for it. The instability, injustice, and confusion introduced into the public councils, have, in truth, been the mortal diseases under which popular governments have everywhere perished; as they continue to be the favorite and fruitful topics from which the adversaries to liberty derive their most precious declamations. The valuable improvements made by the American Constitutions on the popular models, both ancient and modern, cannot certainly be too much admired; but it would be an unwarrantable partiality, to contend that they have as effectually obviated the danger on this side, as was wished and expected. Complaints are everywhere heard from our most considerate and virtuous citizens, equally the friends of public and private faith, and of public and personal liberty, that our governments are too unstable; that the public good is disregarded in the conflicts of rival parties; and that measures are too often decided, not according to the rules of justice, and the rights of the minor party, but by the superior force of an interested and overbearing majority. However anxiously we may wish that these complaints had no foundation, the evidence of known facts will not permit us to deny that they are in some degree true. It will be found, indeed, on a candid review of our situation, that some of the distresses under which we labor, have been erroneously charged on the operations of our governments: but it will be found, at the same time, that other causes will not alone account for many of our heaviest misfortunes; and, particularly, for that prevailing and increasing distrust of public engagements, and alarm for private rights, which were echoed from one end of the continent to the other. These must be chiefly, if not wholly, effects of the unsteadiness and injustice, with which a factious spirit has tainted our public administration;

By a faction, I understand a number of citizens, whether amounting to a majority or minority of the whole, who are united and actuated by some common impulse of passion, or of interest, adverse to the rights of other citizens, or to the permanent and aggregate interests of the community.

There are two methods of curing the mischiefs of faction: The one by removing its causes; the other by controlling its effects.

There are again two methods of removing the causes of faction: The one by destroying the liberty which is essential to its existence; the other, by giving to every citizen the same opinions, the same passions, and the same interests.

It could never be more truly said, than of the first remedy, that it is worse than the disease. Liberty is to faction, what air is to fire, an aliment, without which it instantly expires. But it could not be a less folly to abolish liberty, which is essential to political life, because it nourishes faction, than it would be to wish the annihilation of air, which is essential to animal life, because it imparts to fire its destructive agency.

The second expedient is as impracticable, as the first would be unwise. As long as the reason of man continues fallible, and he is at liberty to exercise it, different opinions will be formed. As long as the connection subsists between his reason and his self-love, his opinions and his passions will have a reciprocal influence on each other; and the former will be the objects to which the latter will attach themselves. The diversity in the faculties of men, from which the rights of property originate, is not less an insuperable obstacle to an uniformity of interests. The protection of these faculties, is the first object of government. From the protection of different and unequal faculties of acquiring property, the possession of different degrees and kinds of property immediately results: and from the influence of these on the sentiments and views of the respective proprietors, ensues a division of the society into different interests and parties.

The latent causes of faction are thus sown in the nature of man; and we see them everywhere brought into different degrees of activity, according to the different circumstances of civil society. A zeal for different opinions concerning religion, concerning government, and many other points, as well of speculation as of practice; an attachment to different leaders, ambitiously contending for pre-eminence and power; or to persons of other descriptions, whose fortunes have been interesting to the human passions, have, in turn, divided mankind into parties, inflamed them with mutual animosity, and rendered them much more disposed to vex and oppress each other, than to co-operate for their common good. So strong is this propensity of mankind, to fall into mutual animosities, that where no substantial occasion presents itself, the most frivolous and fanciful distinctions have been sufficient to kindle their unfriendly passions, and excite their most violent conflicts. But the most common and durable source of factions, has been the various and unequal distribution of property.—Those who hold and those who are without property, have ever formed distinct interests in society. Those who are creditors, and those who are debtors, fall under a like discrimination. A landed interest, a manufacturing interest, a mercantile interest, a monied interest, with many lesser interests, grow up of necessity in civilized nations, and divide them into different classes, actuated by different sentiments and views. The regulation of these various and interfering interests, forms the principal task of modern legislation, and involves the spirit of party and faction in the necessary and ordinary operations of government.

No man is allowed to be a judge in his own cause; because his interest would certainly bias his judgment, and, not improbably, corrupt his integrity. With equal, nay, with greater reason, a body of men are unfit to be both judges and parties, at the same time; yet, what are many of the most important acts of legislation but so many judicial determinations, not indeed concerning the rights of single persons, but concerning the rights of large bodies of citizens? And what are the different classes of legislators, but advocates and parties to the causes which they determine? Is a law proposed concerning private debts? It is a question to which the creditors are parties on the one side, and the debtors on the other. Justice ought to hold the balance between them. Yet the parties are, and must be, themselves the judges; and the most numerous party, or, in other words, the most powerful faction, must be expected to prevail. Shall domestic manufactures be encouraged, and in what degree, by restrictions on foreign manufactures? are questions which would be differently decided by the landed and the manufacturing classes; and probably by neither with a sole regard to justice and the public good. The apportionment of taxes, on the various descriptions of property, is an act which seems to require the most exact impartiality; yet there is, perhaps, no legislative act in which greater opportunity and temptation are given to a predominant party, to trample on the rules of justice. Every shilling with which they overburden the inferior number, is a shilling saved to their own pockets.

It is in vain to say, that enlightened statesmen will be able to adjust these clashing interests, and render them all subservient to the public good. Enlightened statesmen will not always be at the helm: nor, in many cases, can such an adjustment be made at all, without taking into view indirect and remote considerations, which will rarely prevail over the immediate interest which one party may find in disregarding the rights of another, or the good of the whole.

The inference to which we are brought is, that the *causes* of faction cannot be removed; and that relief is only to be sought in the means of controlling its *effects*.

If a faction consists of less than a majority, relief is supplied by the republican principle, which enables the majority to defeat its sinister views, by regular vote. It may clog the administration, it may convulse the society; but it will be unable to execute and mask its violence under the forms of the Constitution. When a majority is included in a faction, the form of popular government, on the other hand, enables it to sacrifice to its ruling passion or interest, both the public good and the rights of other citizens. To secure the public good and private rights against the danger of such a faction, and at the same time to preserve the spirit and the form of popular government, is then the great object to which our inquiries are directed. Let me add, that it is the great desideratum, by which alone this form of government can be rescued from the opprobrium under which it has so long labored, and be recommended to the esteem and adoption of mankind.

By what means is this object attainable? Evidently by one of two only. Either the existence of the same passion or interest in a majority, at the same time, must be prevented; or the majority, having such co-existent passion or interest, must be rendered, by their number and local situation, unable to concert and carry into effect schemes of oppression. If the impulse and the opportunity be suffered to coincide, we well know, that neither moral nor religious motives can be relied on as an adequate control. They are not found to be such on the injustice and violence of individuals, and lose their efficacy in proportion to the number combined together; that is, in proportion as their efficacy becomes needful.

From this view of the subject, it may be concluded that a pure democracy, by which I mean a society consisting of a small number of citizens, who assemble and administer the government in person, can admit of no cure for the mischiefs of faction. A common passion or interest will, in almost every case, be felt by a majority of the whole; a communication and concert, results from the form of government itself; and there is nothing to check the inducements to sacrifice the weaker party, or an obnoxious individual. Hence it is, that such democracies have ever been spectacles of turbulence and contention; have ever been found incompatible with personal security, or the rights of property; and have, in general, been as short in their lives, as they have been violent in their deaths. Theoretic politicians, who have patronized this species of government, have erroneously supposed, that by reducing mankind to a perfect equality in their political rights, they would, at the same time, be perfectly equalized and assimilated in their possessions, their opinions, and their passions.

A republic, by which I mean a government in which the scheme of representation takes place, opens a different prospect, and promises the cure for which we are seeking. Let us examine the points in which it varies from pure democracy, and we shall comprehend both the nature of the cure, and the efficacy which it must derive from the union.

The two great points of difference, between a democracy and a republic, are, first, the delegation of the government, in the latter, to a small number of citizens elected by the rest; secondly, the greater number of citizens, and greater sphere of country, over which the latter may be extended.

The effect of the first difference is, on the one hand, to refine and enlarge the public views, by passing them through the medium of a chosen body of citizens, whose wisdom may best discern the true interest of their country, and whose patriotism and love of justice will be least likely to sacrifice it to temporary or partial considerations. Under such a regulation, it may well happen, that the public voice, pronounced by the representatives of the people, will be more consonant to the public good, than if pronounced by the people themselves, convened for the purpose. On the other hand, the effect may be inverted. Men of factious tempers, of local prejudices, or of sinister designs, may by intrigue, by corruption, or by other means, first obtain the suffrages and then betray the interest of the people. The question repeating is whether small or extensive republics are most favorable for the election of proper guardians of the public weal; and it is clearly decided in favor of the latter by two obvious considerations.

In the first place, it is to be remarked, that however small the republic may be, the representatives must be raised to a certain number, in order to guard against the cabals of a few; and that however large it may be, they must be limited to a certain number, in order to guard against the confusion of a multitude. Hence the number of representatives in the two cases not being in proportion to that of the constituents, and being proportionably greatest in the small republic, it follows, that if the proportion of fit characters be not less in the large than in the small republic, the former will present a greater option, and consequently a greater probability of a fit choice.

In the next place, as each representative will be chosen by a greater number of citizens in the large than in the small republic, it will be more difficult for unworthy candidates to practice with success the vicious arts, by which elections are too often carried; and the suffrages of the people being more free, will be more likely to centre in men who possess the most attractive merit, and the most diffusive and established characters.

It must be confessed, that in this, as in most other cases, there is a mean, on both sides of which inconveniences will be found to lie. By enlarging too much the number of electors, you render the representative too little acquainted with all their local circumstances and lesser interests; as by reducing it too much, you render him unduly attached to these, and too little fit to comprehend and pursue great and national objects. The Federal Constitution forms, in this respect, a happy combination; the great and aggregate interest being referred to the National—the local and particular, to the State Legislatures.

The other point of difference is, the greater number of citizens and extent of territory, which may be brought within the compass of republican, than of democratic government; and it is this circumstance principally which renders factious combinations less to be dreaded in the former, than in the latter. The smaller the society, the fewer probably will be the distinct parties and interests composing it; the fewer the distinct parties and interests, the more frequently will a majority be found of the same party; and the smaller the number of individuals composing a majority, and the smaller the compass within which they are placed, the more easily will they concert and execute their plans of oppression. Extend the sphere, and you take in a greater variety of parties and interest; you make it less probable that a majority of the whole will have a common motive to invade the rights of other citizens; or if such a common motive exists, it will be more difficult for all who feel it to discover their own strength, and to act in unison with each other. Besides other impediments, it may be remarked, that where there is a consciousness of unjust or dishonorable purpose, communication is always checked by distrust, in proportion to the number whose concurrence is necessary.

Hence it clearly appears, that the same advantage, which a republic has over a democracy, in controlling the effects of faction, is enjoyed by a large over a small republic—is enjoyed by the Union over the States composing it. Does this advantage consist in the substitution of representatives, whose enlightened views and virtuous sentiments render them superior to local prejudices, and to schemes of injustice? It will not be denied, that the representation of the Union will be most likely to possess these requisite endowments. Does it consist in the greater security afforded by a greater variety of parties, against the event of any one party being able to outnumber and oppress the rest? In an equal degree does the increased variety of parties, comprised within the Union, increase this security. Does it, in fine, consist in the greater obstacles opposed to the concert and accomplishment of the secret wishes of an unjust and interested majority? Here, again, the extent of the Union gives it the most palpable advantage.

The influence of factious leaders may kindle a flame within their particular States, but will be unable to spread a general conflagration through the other States. A religious sect may degenerate into a political faction in a part of the Confederacy; but the variety of sects dispersed over the entire face of it must secure the national councils against any danger from that source. A rage for paper money, for an abolition of debts, for an equal division of property, or for any other improper or wicked project, will be less apt to pervade the whole body of the Union, than a particular member of it; in the same proportion as such a malady is more likely to taint a particular county or district, than an entire State.

In the extent and proper structure of the Union, therefore, we behold a republican remedy for the diseases most incident to a republican government. And according to the degree of pleasure and pride we feel in being republicans, ought to be our zeal in cherishing the spirit, and supporting the character, of Federalists. . . .

Number 51

. . . the great security against a gradual concentration of the several powers in the same department, consists in giving to those who administer each department, the necessary constitutional means, and personal motives, to resist encroachments of the others. The provision for defence must in this, as in all other cases be made commensurate to the danger of attack.— Ambition must be made to counteract ambition. The interest of the man, must be connected with the constitutional rights of the place. It may be a reflection on human nature, that such devices should be necessary to control the abuses of government. But what is government itself, but the greatest of all reflections on human nature? If men were angels, no government would be necessary. If angels were to govern men, neither external nor internal controls on government would be necessary. In framing a government, which is to be administered by men over men, the great difficulty lies in this: You must first enable the Government to control the governed; and in the next place, oblige it to control itself. A dependence on the people is, no doubt, the primary control on the Government; but experience has taught mankind the necessity of auxiliary precautions.

This policy of supplying, by opposite and rival interests, the defect of better motives, might be traced through the whole system of human affairs, private as well as public. We see it particularly displayed in all the subordinate distributions of power; where the constant aim is, to divide and arrange the several officers in such a manner, as that each may be a check on the other; that the private interest of every individual may be a sentinel over the public rights. These inventions of prudence cannot be less requisite in the distributions of the supreme power of the State. . . .

There are, moreover, two considerations particularly applicable to the Federal system of America, which place it in a very interesting point of view.

First. In a single republic, all the power surrendered by the people, is submitted to the administration of a single government; and the usurpations are guarded against, by a division of the Government into distinct and separate departments. In the compound republic of America, the power surrendered by the people, is first divided between two distinct governments, and then the portion allotted to each subdivided among distinct and separate departments. Hence a double security arises to the rights of the people. The different governments will control each other; at the same time that each will be controlled by itself.

Second. It is of great importance in a republic, not only to guard the society against the oppression of its rulers; but to guard one part of the society against the injustice of the other part. Different interests necessarily exist in different classes of citizens. If a majority be united by a common interest, the rights of the minority will be insecure. There are but two methods of providing against this evil: The one by creating a will in the community independent of the majority, that is, of the society itself; the other, by comprehending in the society so many separate descriptions of citizens, as will render an unjust combination of a majority of the whole very improbable, if not impracticable. The first method prevails in all governments possessing an hereditary, or self-appointed authority. This, at best, is but a precarious security; because a power independent of the society may as well espouse the unjust views of the major, as the rightful interests of the minor party, and may possibly be turned against both parties. The second method will be exemplified in the Federal Republic of the United States. Whilst all authority in it will be derived from, and dependent on the society, the society itself will be broken into so many parts, interests, and classes of citizens, that the rights of individuals, or of the minority, will be in little danger from interested combinations of the majority. In a free government, the security for civil rights must be the same as that for religious rights. It consists in the one case in the multiplicity of interests, and in the other, in the multiplicity of sects. The degree of security in both cases will depend on the number of interests and sects; and this may be presumed to depend on the extent of country and number of people comprehended under the same government. . . .

Number 55

. . . The sincere friends of liberty, who give themselves up to the extravagancies of this passion, are not aware of the injury they do their own cause. As there is a degree of depravity in mankind, which requires a certain degree of circumspection and distrust: so there are other qualities in human nature, which justify a certain portion of esteem and confidence. Republican government presupposes the existence of these qualities in a higher degree, than any other form. Were the pictures which have been drawn by the political jealousy of some among us, faithful likenesses of the human character, the inference would be, that there is not sufficient virtue among men for self-government; and that nothing less than the chains of despotism, can restrain them from destroying and devouring one another. . . .

Number 62

. . . a Senate, as a second branch of the Legislative Assembly, distinct from, and dividing the power with a first, must be in all cases a salutary check on the Government. It doubles the security to the people, by requiring the concurrence of two distinct bodies in schemes of usurpation or perfidy, where the ambition or corruption of one would otherwise be sufficient. This is a precaution founded on such clear principles, and now so well understood in the United States, that it would be more than superfluous to enlarge on it. I will barely remark, that, as the improbability of sinister combinations will be in proportion to the dissimilarity in the genius of the two bodies, it must be politic to distinguish them from each other by every circumstance which will consist with a due harmony in all proper measures, and with the genuine principles of republican government.

Second. The necessity of a Senate is not less indicated by the propensity of all single and numerous assemblies, to yield to the impulse of sudden and violent passions, and to be seduced by factious leaders into intemperate and pernicious resolutions. Examples on this subject might be cited without number: and from proceedings within the United States, as well as from the history of other nations. But a position that will not be contradicted, need not be proved. All that need be remarked is, that a body which is to correct this infirmity ought itself to be free from it, and consequently ought to be less numerous. It ought moreover to possess great firmness, and consequently ought to hold its authority by a tenure of considerable duration.

Third. Another defect to be supplied by a Senate, lies in a want of due acquaintance with the objects and principles of legislation. It is not possible that an assembly of men, called for the most part from pursuits of a private nature, continued in appointment for a short time, and led by no permanent motive to devote the intervals of public occupation to a study of the laws, the affairs, and the comprehensive interests of their country, should, if left wholly to themselves, escape a variety of important errors in the exercise of their Legislative trust. It may be affirmed on the best grounds, that no small share of the present embarrassments of America is to be charged on the blunders of our governments; and that these have proceeded from the heads, rather than the hearts of most of the authors of them. What indeed are all the repealing, explaining, and amending laws, which fill and disgrace our voluminous codes, but so many monuments of deficient wisdom; so many impeachments exhibited by each succeeding against each preceding session; so many admonitions to the people, of the value of those aids, which may be expected from a well constituted Senate. . . .

Number 63

. . . Thus far I have considered the circumstances which point out the necessity of a well-constructed Senate, only as they relate to the representatives of the people. To a people as little blinded by prejudice, or corrupted by flattery, as those whom I address, I shall not scruple to add, that such an institution may be sometimes necessary, as a defence to the people against their own temporary errors and delusions. As the cool and deliberate sense of the community ought, in all governments, and actually will in all free governments, ultimately prevail over the views of its rulers; so there are particular moments in public affairs, when the people, stimulated by some irregular passion, or some illicit advantage, or misled by the artful misrepresentations of interested men, may call for measures which they themselves will afterwards be the most ready to lament and condemn. In these critical moments, how salutary will be the interference of some temperate and respectable body of citizens, in order to check the misguided career and to suspend the blow meditated by the people against themselves, until reason, justice, and truth, can regain their authority over the public mind? What bitter anguish would not the people of Athens have often avoided, if their government had contained so provident a safeguard against the tyranny of their own passions? Popular liberty might then have escaped the indelible reproach of decreeing, to the same citizens, the hemlock on one day, and statues on the next. . . .

SELECTION

Conditions of Acceptance: The Virginia Amendments (June 27, 1788)

As the opposition in the press early indicated, ratification was by no means a foregone conclusion. Favorable action by the conventions of Delaware, Pennsylvania, and New Jersey in December, 1787, Georgia and Connecticut in January, 1788, Massachusetts in February, Maryland in April, and South Carolina in May gave the Constitution eight of the necessary nine votes. But the contests had been close and bitter in both Pennsylvania and Massachusetts, and the Rhode Island legislature had rejected the Constitution by refusing even to call a ratifying convention. New Hampshire was uncertain, and Virginia and New York, two states whose participation was considered essential for the success of the Constitution, had strong Anti-Federal groups headed by Governors Patrick Henry and George Clinton. After a long and dramatic debate in the Virginia convention the Federalists finally secured approval by agreeing to an arrangement earlier successfully employed by their counterparts in Massachusetts to parry Anti-Federalist opposition: ratification with suggestions for amendment. The Virginia amendments, reprinted below from Jonathan Elliot (comp.), Debates in the Several State Conventions, *(five volumes, 1876) volume III, pages 657–661, consisted of a bill of rights and twenty suggested changes. New Hampshire having already acted favorably on June 21, Virginia became the tenth state to ratify, and New York followed suit on July 26. North Carolina's emphatic rejection of the Constitution in August, largely because of its lack of a bill of rights, was only a hollow victory for the Anti-Federalists. Congress announced on July 2 that the Constitution had been ratified and on September 13 called for elections under the new Constitution. At last, the men who regarded a strong central government as necessary to fulfill the promise of the American Revolution could regard the Revolution as complete.*

Robert Allen Rutland, The Ordeal of the Constitution: The Antifederalists and the Ratification Struggle of 1787–1788 *(1966), is a recent detailed narrative of the struggle over ratification. Jackson Turner Main,* The Antifederalists: Critics of the Constitution, 1781–1788 *(1961), and Forrest McDonald,* E Pluribus Unum: The Formation of the American Republic, 1776–1790 *(1965), should also be consulted.*

Mr. WYTHE reported, from the committee appointed, such *amendments* to the proposed Constitution of government for the United States as were by them deemed necessary to be recommended to the consideration of the Congress which shall first assemble under the said Constitution, to be acted upon according to the mode prescribed in the 5th article thereof; and he read the same in his place, and afterwards delivered them in at the clerk's table, where the same were again read, and are as follows:—

"That there be a declaration or bill of rights asserting, and securing from encroachment, the essential and unalienable rights of the people, in some such manner as the following:—

"1st. That there are certain natural rights, of which men, when they form a social compact, cannot deprive or divest their posterity; among which are the enjoyment of life and liberty, with the means of acquiring, possessing, and protecting property, and pursuing and obtaining happiness and safety.

"2d. That all power is naturally invested in, and consequently derived from, the people; that magistrates therefore are their *trustees* and *agents*, at all times amenable to them.

"3d. That government ought to be instituted for the common benefit, protection, and security of the people; and that the doctrine of non-resistance against arbitrary power and oppression is absurd, slavish, and destructive to the good and happiness of mankind.

"4th. That no man or set of men are entitled to separate or exclusive public emoluments or privileges from the community, but in consideration of public services, which not being descendible, neither ought the offices of magistrate, legislator, or judge, or any other public office, to be hereditary.

"5th. That the legislative, executive, and judicial powers of government should be separate and distinct; and, that the members of the two first may be restrained from oppression by feeling and participating the public burdens, they should, at fixed periods, be reduced to a private station, return into the mass of the people, and the vacancies be supplied by certain and regular elections, in which all or any part of the former members to be eligible or ineligible, as the rules of the Constitution of government, and the laws, shall direct.

"6th. That the elections of representatives in the legislature ought to be free and frequent, and all men having sufficient evidence of permanent common interest with, and attachment to, the community, ought to have the right of suffrage; and no aid, charge, tax, or fee, can be set, rated, or levied, upon the people without their own consent, or that of their representatives, so elected; nor can they be bound by any law to which they have not, in like manner, assented, for the public good.

"7th. That all power of suspending laws, or the execution of laws, by any authority, without the consent of the representatives of the people in the legislature, is injurious to their rights, and ought not to be exercised.

"8th. That, in all criminal and capital prosecutions, a man hath a right to demand the cause and nature of his accusation, to be confronted with the accusers and witnesses, to call for evidence, and be allowed counsel in his favor, and to a fair and speedy trial by an impartial jury of his vicinage, without whose unanimous consent he cannot be found guilty, (except in the government of the land and naval forces;) nor can he be compelled to give evidence against himself.

"9th. That no freeman ought to be taken, imprisoned, or disseized of his freehold, liberties, privileges, or franchises, or outlawed, or exiled, or in any manner destroyed, or deprived of his life, liberty, or property, but by the law of the land.

"10th. That every freeman restrained of his liberty is entitled to a remedy, to inquire into the lawfulness thereof, and to remove the same, if unlawful, and that such remedy ought not to be denied nor delayed.

"11th. That, in controversies respecting property, and in suits between man and man, the ancient trial by jury is one of the greatest securities to the rights of the people, and to remain sacred and inviolable.

"12th. That every freeman ought to find a certain remedy, by recourse to the laws, for all injuries and wrongs he may receive in his person, property, or character. He ought to obtain right and justice freely, without sale, completely and without denial, promptly and without delay; and that all establishments or regulations contravening these rights are oppressive and unjust.

"13th. That excessive bail ought not to be required, nor excessive fines imposed, nor cruel and unusual punishments inflicted.

"14th. That every freeman has a right to be secure from all unreasonable searches and seizures of his person, his papers, and property; all warrants, therefore, to search suspected places, or seize any freeman, his papers, or property, without information on oath (or affirmation of a person religiously scrupulous of taking an oath) of legal and sufficient cause, are grievous and oppressive; and all general warrants to search suspected places, or to apprehend any suspected person, without specially naming or describing the place or person, are dangerous, and ought not to be granted.

"15th. That the people have a right peaceably to assemble together to consult for the common good, or to instruct their representatives; and that every freeman has a right to petition or apply to the legislature for redress of grievances.

"16th. That the people have a right to freedom of speech, and of writing and publishing their sentiments; that the freedom of the press is one of the greatest bulwarks of liberty, and ought not to be violated.

"17th. That the people have a right to keep and bear arms; that a well-regulated militia, composed of the body of the people trained to arms, is the proper, natural, and safe defence of a free state; that standing armies, in time of peace, are dangerous to liberty, and therefore ought to be avoided, as far as the circumstances and protection of the community will admit; and that, in all cases, the military should be under strict subordination to, and governed by, the civil power.

"18th. That no soldier in time of peace ought to be quartered in any house without the consent of the owner, and in time of war in such manner only as the law directs.

"19th. That any person religiously scrupulous of bearing arms ought to be exempted, upon payment of an equivalent to employ another to bear arms in his stead.

"20th. That religion, or the duty which we owe to our Creator, and the manner of discharging it, can be directed only by reason and conviction, not by force or violence; and therefore all men have an equal, natural, and unalienable right to the free exercise of religion, according to the dictates of conscience, and that no particular religious sect or society ought to be favored or established, by law, in preference to others."

Amendments to the Constitution

"1st. That each state in the Union shall respectively retain every power, jurisdiction, and right, which is not by this Constitution delegated to the Congress of the United States, or to the departments of the federal government.

"2d. That there shall be one representative for every thirty thousand, according to the enumeration or census mentioned in the Constitution, until the whole number of representatives amounts to two hundred; after which, that number shall be continued or increased, as Congress shall direct, upon the principles fixed in the Constitution, by apportioning the representatives of each state to some greater number of people, from time to time, as population increases.

"3d. When the Congress shall lay direct taxes or excises, they shall immediately inform the executive power of each state, of the quota of such state, according to the census herein directed, which is proposed to be thereby raised; and if the legislature of any state shall pass a law which shall be effectual for raising such quota at the time required by Congress, the taxes and excises laid by Congress shall not be collected in such state.

"4th. That the members of the Senate and House of Representatives shall be ineligible to, and incapable of holding, any civil office under the authority of the United States, during the time for which they shall respectively be elected.

"5th. That the journals of the proceedings of the Senate and House of Representatives shall be published at least once in every year, except such parts thereof, relating to treaties, alliances, or military operations, as in their judgment, require secrecy.

"6th. That a regular statement and account of the receipts and expenditures of public money shall be published at least once a year.

"7th. That no commercial treaty shall be ratified without the concurrence of two thirds of the whole number of the members of the Senate; and no treaty ceding, contracting, restraining, or suspending, the territorial rights or claims of the United States, or any of them, or their, or any of their rights or claims to fishing in the American seas, or navigating the American rivers, shall be made, but in cases of the most urgent and extreme necessity; nor shall any such treaty be ratified without the concurrence of three fourths of the whole number of the members of both houses respectively.

"8th. That no navigation law, or law regulating commerce, shall be passed without the consent of two thirds of the members present, in both houses.

"9th. That no standing army, or regular troops, shall be raised, or kept up, in time of peace, without the consent of two thirds of the members present, in both houses.

"10th. That no soldier shall be enlisted for any longer term than four years, except in time of war, and then for no longer term than the continuance of the war.

"11th. That each state respectively shall have the power to provide for organizing, arming, and disciplining its own militia, whensoever Congress shall omit or neglect to provide for the same. That the militia shall not be subject to martial law, except when in actual service, in time of war, invasion, or rebellion; and when not in the actual service of the United States, shall be subject only to such fines, penalties, and punishments, as shall be directed or inflicted by the laws of its own state.

"12th. That the exclusive power of legislation given to Congress over the federal town and its adjacent district, and other places, purchased or to be purchased by Congress of any of the states, shall extend only to such regulations as respect the police and good government thereof.

"13th. That no person shall be capable of being President of the United States for more than eight years in any term of sixteen years.

"14th. That the judicial power of the United States shall be vested in one Supreme Court, and in such courts of admiralty as Congress may from time to time ordain and establish in any of the different states. The judicial power shall extend to all cases in law and equity arising under treaties made, or which shall be made, under the authority of the United States; to all cases affecting ambassadors, other foreign ministers, and consuls; to all cases of admiralty and maritime jurisdiction; to controversies to which the United States shall be a party; to controversies between two or more states, and between parties claiming lands under the grants of different states. In all cases affecting ambassadors, other foreign ministers, and consuls, and those in which a state shall be a party, the Supreme Court shall have original jurisdiction; in all other cases before mentioned, the Supreme Court shall have appellate jurisdiction, as to matters of law only, except in cases of equity, and of admiralty, and maritime jurisdiction, in which the Supreme Court shall have appellate jurisdiction both as to law and fact, with such exceptions and under such regulations as the Congress shall make: but the judicial power of the United States shall extend to no case where the cause of action shall have originated before the ratification of the Constitution, except in disputes between states about their territory, disputes between persons claiming lands under the grants of different states, and suits for debts due to the United States.

"15th. That, in criminal prosecutions no man shall be restrained in the exercise of the usual and accustomed right of challenging or excepting to the jury.

"16th. That Congress shall not alter, modify, or interfere in the times, places, or manner of holding elections for senators and representatives, or either of them, except when the legislature of any state shall neglect, refuse, or be disabled, by invasion or rebellion, to prescribe the same.

"17th. That those clauses which declare that Congress shall not exercise certain powers, be not interpreted, in any manner whatsoever, to extend the powers of Congress; but that they be construed either as making exceptions to the specified powers where this shall be the case, or otherwise, as inserted merely for greater caution.

"18th. That the laws ascertaining the compensation of senators and representatives for their services, be postponed, in their operation, until after the election of representatives immediately succeeding the passing thereof; that excepted which shall first be passed on the subject.

"19th. That some tribunal other than the Senate be provided for trying impeachments of senators.

"20th. That the salary of a judge shall not be increased or diminished during his continuance in office, otherwise than by general regulations of salary, which may take place on a revision of the subject at stated periods of not less than seven years, to commence from the time such salaries shall be first ascertained by Congress."

SELECTION

Removing Anti-Federal Discontent: The Bill of Rights (Dec. 15, 1791)

The first Congress under the new Constitution met in March, 1789, and James Madison, one of the representatives from Virginia, quickly moved to fulfill Federalist promises to add a bill of rights. From a large number of suggested articles Congress selected twelve which it submitted on September 9 to the states for ratification as amendments to the Constitution. The ten amendments ratified by the necessary three-fourths of the states formally became part of the Constitution on Decem-

ber 15, 1791, and are reprinted here from Francis Newton Thorpe (ed.), The Federal and State Constitutions, and Other Organic Laws *(seven volumes, 1909), volume I, pages 29–30. As soon as it became clear that the Federalists intended to add a bill of rights, opposition to the Constitution disappeared almost completely. North Carolina ratified the Constitution in November, 1789, and Rhode Island in May, 1790.*

For further reading, see Robert Allen Rutland, The Birth of the Bill of Rights, 1776–1791 *(1955).*

[Article I]

Congress shall make no law respecting an establishment of religion, or prohibiting the free exercise thereof; or abridging the freedom of speech, or of the press; or the right of the people peaceably to assemble, and to petition the Government for a redress of grievances.

[Article II]

A well regulated Militia, being necessary to the security of a free State, the right of the people to keep and bear Arms, shall not be infringed.

[Article III]

No Soldier shall, in time of peace, be quartered in any house, without the consent of the Owner, nor in time of war, but in a manner to be prescribed by law.

[Article IV]

The right of the people to be secure in their persons, houses, papers, and effects, against unreasonable searches and seizures, shall not be violated, and no Warrants shall issue, but upon probable cause, supported by Oath or affirmation, and particularly describing the place to be searched, and the persons or things to be seized.

[Article V]

No person shall be held to answer for a capital, or otherwise infamous crime, unless on a presentment or indictment of a Grand Jury, except in cases arising in the land or naval forces, or in the Militia, when in actual service in time of War or public danger; nor shall any person be subject for the same offence to be twice put in jeopardy of life or limb; nor shall be compelled in any Criminal Case to be a witness against himself, nor be deprived of life, liberty, or property, without due process of law; nor shall private property be taken for public use, without just compensation.

[Article VI]

In all criminal prosecutions, the accused shall enjoy the right to a speedy and public trial, by an impartial jury of the State and district wherein the crime shall have been committed, which district shall have been previously ascertained by law, and to be informed of the nature and cause of the accusation; to be confronted with the witnesses against him; to have compulsory process for obtaining witnesses in his favor, and to have the Assistance of Counsel for his defence.

[Article VII]

In suits at common law, where the value in controversy shall exceed twenty dollars, the right of trial by jury shall be preserved, and no fact tried by a jury shall be otherwise re-examined in any Court of the United States, than according to the rules of the common law.

[Article VIII]

Excessive bail shall not be required, nor excessive fines imposed, nor cruel and unusual punishments inflicted.

[Article IX]

The enumeration in the Constitution, of certain rights, shall not be construed to deny or disparage others retained by the people.

[Article X]

The powers not delegated to the United States by the Constitution, nor prohibited by it to the States, are reserved to the States respectively, or to the people.